THE DYNASTS

THE NEW WESSEX EDITIONS

The Novels of Thomas Hardy
General Editor P. N. Furbank

The Stories of Thomas Hardy
edited by F. B. Pinion

The Complete Poems of Thomas Hardy
edited by James Gibson

The Dynasts
edited by Harold Orel

THE DYNASTS

AN EPIC-DRAMA

OF THE WAR WITH NAPOLEON, IN
THREE PARTS, NINETEEN ACTS, AND
ONE HUNDRED AND THIRTY SCENES

THE TIME COVERED BY THE ACTION
BEING ABOUT TEN YEARS

BY

THOMAS HARDY

And I heard sounds of insult, shame, and wrong,
And trumpets blown for wars.

Thomas Hardy

M

ISBN 0 333 21321 1

The New Wessex Edition
first published in Great Britain 1978 by
MACMILLAN LONDON LTD

CONTENTS

INTRODUCTION

The Dynasts is an extraordinary work in so many ways that the occasion of its being reprinted in the New Wessex Edition provides a welcome opportunity to review what it meant to Hardy, and what it has since come to mean to generations of readers. It took more time to prepare for, and to write, than any other work in Hardy's career. It was undoubtedly his most ambitious undertaking. Its thirty separate rhyme-schemes illustrate his command of prosody on a very generous scale. It contains the most explicit statement of his philosophical views about man's relationship to the universe. At the time of its appearance, in the first decade of this century, it was immediately recognised as the greatest imaginative treatment by an English author of the Napoleonic Wars, and no poem, play or novel has since superseded it. During two world wars, both conducted as if the dividing-line between civilian and military targets had been obliterated by high explosives, Hardy's characterisations of Pitt, Nelson, Wellington and ordinary Englishmen served as inspiration for a very large number of readers.

Hardy felt some chagrin at the puzzled reviews that greeted the publication of Part First as a separate volume (1903), and he regretted that he had not waited until the work was complete. (Part Second was completed in 1905 and published the following year; Part Third, completed in 1907, appeared in print in 1908.) Like any author, he treasured the praise of those who liked it. Max Beerbohm, Ford Madox Ford, Siegfried Sassoon, Walter de la Mare and A. M. Broadley, among others, told him of their admiration.

Years later Hardy confided to Ellen Glasgow that he considered it 'his greatest work (he may have said "best")'.[1] *The Dynasts*, more than any other single work, earned Hardy his Order of Merit. At the time of the conferral of the honorary degree of Doctor of Letters at Oxford in 1920, a special, and flattering, mention of *The Dynasts* was part of the ceremony. And St John Ervine, sending him, in 1921, an address that had been signed by 106 younger writers, concluded:

From your first book to your last you have written in the 'high style, as when that men to kinges write', and you have crowned a great prose with a noble poetry.

We thank you, Sir, for all that you have written . . . but most of all, perhaps, for *The Dynasts*.[2]

A masterwork, *The Dynasts* is perhaps the greatest long poem in English published during this century (the claim has been made more than once). Yet, oddly enough, many lovers of Hardy have not read it, and many books about Hardy dismiss it in a footnote or a dèsultory paragraph. Some critics are still bemused by 'its experimental mixture of epic and drama, prose and poetry, narrative, theatrical, and even cinematic technique';[3] by the attraction that it exerts on 'writers interested only in philosophy';[4] and by the somewhat patronising judgement, 'As a whole it is flawed . . . the ambition and the form were not quite manageable.'[5]

These views, current more than a half-century after publication of *The Dynasts*, should warn us that Hardy's

[1] Ellen Glasgow, *The Woman Within* (New York: Harcourt, Brace, 1954), p. 197.

[2] Florence Emily Hardy, *The Life of Thomas Hardy 1840–1928* (London: Macmillan, 1962), p. 413.

[3] Paul Zietlow, *Moments of Vision: The Poetry of Thomas Hardy* (Cambridge, Mass.: Harvard University Press, 1974), p. ix.

[4] Kenneth Marsden, *The Poems of Thomas Hardy: A Critical Introduction* (University of London: Athlone Press, 1969), p. viii.

[5] Bert G. Hornback, *The Metaphor of Chance: Vision and Technique in the Works of Thomas Hardy* (Athens, Ohio: Ohio University Press, 1971), pp. 165–6.

epic-drama does not clearly resemble his earlier and more readily understandable productions. Hardy's determination to write a new kind of fiction grew from a number of reasons, not all clearly sorted out in the memoirs that he dictated to Florence Emily Hardy many years later. Moreover, the doctrine of the Immanent Will has never been congenial to all readers, and Hardy, in *The Dynasts*, made his concept of Its nature inescapable, something not to be rushed over. And it is understandable that he did not, perhaps could not, achieve complete success in handling a full decade of European history in three parts, nineteen acts, and 131 scenes.[6] Still, the degree of success that Hardy achieved is astonishing, and will be best appreciated if we take a closer look at what he thought he was up to. That, in turn, requires our looking at some biographical considerations.

Hardy's renunciation of the novel after the publication of *Jude the Obscure* (1895) is usually attributed to the hostility of the reviews. Jeannette Gilder's two notorious attacks in the *New York World* (Hardy's mind 'seems to run to pigs – animal and human'; when she finished the story, she opened the windows 'and let in the fresh air'; Hardy's realism was 'disgusting') appeared almost simultaneously with a review entitled 'Jude the Obscene' in the *Pall Mall Gazette*, a denunciation of Hardy's 'morbid animality' in the *New York Critic*, a sneer at the 'prevailing gloom' of the novel in the *Daily Telegraph*, and a slating in the *Manchester Guardian*, which accused Hardy of having insulted 'marriage, religion and all the obligations and relations of life which most people hold sacred'. Other angry notices, all assuming that realism had its limits and that Hardy had overstepped them, sternly notified Hardy that still another effort to depict the 'night-cart' side of nature would not be tolerated.

---

[6] Hardy always listed the number of scenes as 130, but, as Purdy points out, there are 131, plus the Fore Scene and the After Scene. Richard Little Purdy, *Thomas Hardy: A Bibliographical Study* (London: Oxford University Press, 1954), p. 134.

Hardy's reaction – 'A man must be a fool to deliberately stand up to be shot at' – followed immediately. He did not relish being described, by Mrs Oliphant, as a member of 'The Anti-Marriage League', one who seemed to suggest that hanging a child was the best way to remove the principal obstruction to the abolition of marriage. He had always been sensitive to unfriendly reviews (and had ample reason to be); but not even the reception of *Tess* had prepared him for what seemed to be an orchestrated outcry.

In addition, he knew well the hostility of his wife to the dangerous direction that his career as a novelist was following.[7] More novels along the lines of *Jude* might well destroy his marriage for all the world to see.

Yet these facts do not justify the speculation that Hardy, in 1895, thought he had accomplished all he wanted to in the world of prose fiction, and that *Jude* had been sent to the press as a self-conscious final statement. Even riskier is the claim that Hardy had no more stories to tell that warranted novelistic treatment; that his blaming the reviewers proved a convenient method of ending a long dry spell of failed creativity. The point is important for two reasons: first, Hardy never admitted, either in the mid-1890s or later, that such a spell existed, and such speculation cannot be confirmed by anything that Hardy himself wrote down or said; and, second, Hardy had always regarded the novel as a form of literature inferior to poetry, and the decision to renounce novel-writing was an inevitable event once Hardy had assured himself of financial independence.

Hardy's resolve to turn away from novels meant that he could now devote time to a vast, still awkwardly defined

[7] The story of the special trip made by Emma to the British Museum, where she wept as she begged Dr Richard Garnett for aid 'in inducing her husband to burn his vicious manuscript', apparently originated with Ford Madox Ford, and was repeated several times by Carl Weber without supporting documentation. Neither Robert Gittings nor Richard Garnett's descendants have found any evidence that Emma made this particular trip.

project about the Napoleonic Wars that he had been considering, on and off, for more than two decades *before* he started on *Jude*. After all, he had been born in 1840, and grown up among adults who remembered and reminisced about alarums when it seemed that Boney's troops might invade Dorset; about the Peninsular Campaign, and foot-slogging across the Continent. He had read with fascination several numbers of *A History of the Wars*, a periodical that he discovered in a cupboard at home. His grandfather, a volunteer, had subscribed to it, and, as Hardy wrote in the *Life*, 'The torn pages of these contemporary numbers with their melodramatic prints of serried ranks, crossed bayonets, huge knapsacks, and dead bodies, were the first to set him on the train of ideas that led to *The Trumpet-Major* and *The Dynasts*.' He read, and often quoted, Carlyle's *The History of the French Revolution*. From the age of fifteen, when he first began to study the French language, his studies led him to Thiers, and to Hugo's view that the Bourbons were dynasts no less subject than Napoleon to the workings of destiny. By 1868 Hardy was toying with the notion of a narrative poem on the battle of the Nile; he completed an outline, now lost, of the poem. (What would Hardy have made of Napoleon's first direct confrontation with Nelson?) Within two years he paid the first of several visits to Chelsea Hospital, conducting interviews that tested the vividness of veterans' memories of Waterloo. The reading in primary and secondary sources that he conducted during 1878 and 1879 for *The Trumpet-Major* included C. H. Gifford's two-volume *History of the Wars Occasioned by the French Revolution, 1792–1816*, a work that he would return to some two decades later.

'Let Europe be the stage,' Hardy wrote on 13 March 1874, 'and have scenes continually shifting.' Perhaps, as Hardy thought when he discovered his note after more than a quarter-century, it was then that he first thought of 'a conception of *The Dynasts*'. His puzzlement indicated that he had forgotten the exact moment of genesis. Far more likely, indeed, that there was no one moment; that the

associations and leisure readings of a lifetime were preparing
him for a major dramatisation of the most significant
European wars of the century; and that his visit of 1874
(with Emma) to locales in France associated with Napoleon,
and again in 1876, to Waterloo, provided him with the
continuing inspiration he needed. By June 1875 he was
considering the possibility of 'A Ballad of the Hundred
Days', another ballad on Moscow, and a series of ballads
about earlier campaigns, 'forming altogether an Iliad of
Europe from 1789 to 1815'.[8] These interlinked ballads
would have constituted 'an epic on the war with Napoleon'.
In June 1877, Hardy recorded his intention of creating 'a
grand drama, based on the wars with Napoleon, or some one
campaign (but not as Shakespeare's historical dramas).' He
was uncertain whether to call it 'Napoleon' or 'Josephine',
or some other person's name. Josephine as heroine would
have feminised his subject-matter in ways that are difficult
to imagine today, and Hardy still had not made up his mind
about the span of years he intended to cover; but this
jotting of 1877 was indicative of Hardy's interest in the
form of his new work. By November 1880, when he called it
a 'Great Modern Drama', his use of the word 'modern'
signified the resonances of the theme to Englishmen three-
quarters of a century after Trafalgar. On 27 March 1881 he
conceived of Napoleon as 'a sort of Achilles' who would
serve as the protagonist of 'a Homeric Ballad', yet a few
days later he returned to the thought that drama was more
suitable as a genre: 'Mode for a historical Drama. Action
mostly automatic; reflex movement, etc. Not the result of
what is called *motive*, though always ostensibly so, even to
the actors' own consciousness. Apply an enlargement of
these theories to, say, "The Hundred Days"!'[9] Here, for the
first time, Hardy was relating the Napoleonic era to a
'philosophic scheme or framework', something larger in
import, 'enclosing the historic scenes'.

During the 1880s, in brief, *The Dynasts* became a lingering, obsessive concern to which he could not devote as much

8 *Life*, p. 106.   9 Ibid., p. 148.

time as he would have liked. In 1886 he was reading system-
atically in the British Museum Library 'and elsewhere',
preparing himself for what he was later to call 'the question
of *The Dynasts*'. In the spring of 1887 he visited the roof of
Milan Cathedral, and there probably imagined the scene in
The Dynasts which uses the Cathedral as a means of
character revelation. In November he worked on another
outline scheme: Napoleon would be 'haunted by an Evil
Genius or Familiar, whose existence he has to confess to his
wives'. Perhaps unsurprisingly, this concept proved
deficient; and similarly to be abandoned was the scheme
of Napoleon's use of necromancy to 'see the thoughts of
opposing generals'. Yet, within a month, he knew that
Coleridge's rule ('a long poem should not attempt to be
poetical all through') would guide him as he concentrated
the 'ornaments of diction' in particular passages of the epic
he was yet to write.

Most biographers and critics underestimate the length of
the gestation-period. By 1895 Hardy had clearly identified
the historical period he wished to treat (1805–15), regarded
Napoleon as his major figure (one hesitates to use the word
'hero'), thought of this unwritten work as differing in scope
from and presenting a greater challenge than anything he
had written before, and intended to present a recension of
his opinions on the nature and significance of the Immanent
Will. Moreover, he planned to cast it in the form of a drama
or of an epic; possibly, he had begun to speculate, as a
hybridised genre. An illuminating note was recorded on
21 September 1889: 'For carrying out that idea of Napoleon,
the Empress, Pitt, Fox, etc., I feel continually that I
require a larger canvas. . . . A spectral tone must be
adopted. . . . Royal ghosts. . . . Title: "A Drama of Kings".'
It is true that the striking similarity of this projected title
to that of Robert Buchanan's closet drama (1871) has
caught the eye of scholars;[10] but Buchanan's fustian,

---

[10] Hoxie N. Fairchild, 'The Immediate Source of *The Dynasts*',
PMLA, LXVII (March 1952), pp. 43–64.

historical digressions, and failure to consider adequately the English role in defeating Napoleon could have presented Hardy with only the feeblest type of inspiration for his own *magnum opus*. Moreover, Hardy needed a tighter time-frame than Buchanan had used (two of the three parts of Buchanan's play dealt with 1870–1), and he soon dropped plans to review the stormy events of the French Revolution as a luxury of chronology that he could not afford. Then followed a note dated 1891, when Hardy was completing *Tess*: 'A Bird's-Eye View of Europe at the beginning of the Nineteenth Century. . . . It may be called "A Drama of the Times of the First Napoleon".' The 'Napoleon drama' was to obsess him for the next fifteen years.

At one level, then, Hardy was writing about a French general whose character and actions had affected the lives of millions. If he focused on the time-period between the day when Napoleon put the crown of Lombardy on his own head in the Cathedral of Milan and the day when he was 'stung by spectral questionings' in the wood of Bossu after the battle of Waterloo, he had ready-made a reasonably well-shaped drama of the meteor-like fall of a dynast. For almost any other writer of his generation, that would have been enough of a creative problem.

But *The Dynasts*, as the Fore Scene informs us, takes place partly in the Overworld, where choral observers named Spirits talk continually about the Immanent Will and Its designs. Hardy's epic-drama is (among other things) an eloquent, detailed and by-and-large consistent statement about the relationship of human beings to the forces that shape the universe. The Preface maintains with prudent modesty that the doctrines of the Spirits are 'but tentative', and should be taken 'as contrivances of the fancy merely'. Hardy argues that these doctrines might, at best, secure, 'in the words of Coleridge, "that willing suspension of disbelief for the moment which constitutes poetic faith".'

Nevertheless, Hardy knew, even better than most of his critics, how radically his epic-drama differed from previous literary models. Since the gods of the old dispensation were no longer believed in, the 'celestial machinery' of the *Iliad*, the *Eddas* and *Paradise Lost* was irrelevant to a modern Poet. God was no longer creditable as an 'anthropomorphic conception'. Napoleon's defeat, if it were ever to become important to the twentieth century, must be rendered in the language of an artist, certainly not that of a biographer or historian. He would invent – as he put it – a 'modern expression of a modern outlook'.

The notion that a participant in battle does not perceive the larger outlines of strategy had been dramatised by Stendhal; the doctrine that war moves at its own lumbering, inevitable pace, unaffected by anything Napoleon did, or could do, had been argued by Tolstoy (a writer whom Hardy greatly admired, though Hardy had not as yet read his *War and Peace*). Still, the 'supernatural spectators of the terrestrial action' had a great deal more to say about the follies of mankind at war, and much of it was bound to disturb those readers and reviewers who had already been upset by authorial comments made in *Tess* and *Jude*. The Immanent Will had already been discussed seriously, and at length, by Eduard von Hartmann (*Philosophy of the Unconscious*, translated into English in 1884) and Arthur Schopenhauer (*The World as Will and Idea*, read by Hardy in its 1890 translation), but Hardy knew even as Part First moved through the press that his treatment would stir up the British Philistines. If we keep in mind that Hardy's renunciation of the novel as an art-form was not meant to be taken as a renunciation of literature itself or of his personal religious views, and the fact that Hardy had formulated most of the over-all plan for *The Dynasts* well before the turn of the century, the famous note of 17 October 1896, may be seen as doubly artful:

Poetry. Perhaps I can express more fully in verse ideas and emotions which run counter to the inert crystallized opinion – hard as a rock – which the vast body of men have vested interests in supporting. To cry out in a passionate poem that (for instance) the Supreme Mover or Movers, the Prime Force or Forces, must be either limited in power, unknowing, or cruel – which is obvious enough, and has been for centuries – will cause them merely a shake of the head; but to put it in argumentative prose will make them sneer, or foam, and set all the literary contortionists jumping upon me, a harmless agnostic, as if I were a clamorous atheist, which in their crass illiteracy they seem to think is the same thing. . . . If Galileo had said in verse that the world moved, the Inquisition might have let him alone.[11]

Hardy's opinion – that the Immanent Will is indifferent to man's aspirations – is lucidly argued by the Spirits (and *The Dynasts* is 'a passionate poem', as we shall see). The Immanent Will does not speak directly for Itself; it is 'viewless' and 'voiceless'; most of what we learn about It comes from the speeches of the Spirits. It works unconsciously. We may cherish only the faintest hope that some day, after the passing of aeons, It may become self-aware, and thus help to improve the lot of the human race. At the present time, It controls human destiny. Whether history is to be regarded as terrestrial tragedy (according to the Spirit of the Pities) or comedy (Spirit Ironic), 'these flesh-hinged mannikins' do not operate independently, and can not. They move as one organism. Wars have long been ordained:

> Ere systemed suns were globed and lit
> The slaughters of the race were writ. . . .
> [Part I, Act ii, scene v]

Thus, Napoleon's schemes for the continuation of dynastic power are foredoomed, and at the end of the epic-drama the dynasts who succeed him have no clearer sense of their own limitations, of their vulnerability to 'the Immanent Unrecking'. Men do not learn from one generation to the next. After Waterloo, when – presumably – the forces of humanity have defeated the discredited, exhausted army of the Emperor, the Spirit of the Years can say, in melancholy

11 *Life*, pp. 284–5.

tones no less intense because its message has been pre-figured:

> So hath the Urging Immanence used to-day
> Its inadvertent might to field this fray;
> And Europe's wormy dynasties rerobe
> Themselves in their old gilt, to dazzle anew the globe!
> [III, vii, viii]

The Spirits are as much subject to the Will as 'the frail ones' who 'gyrate like animalcula/In tepid pools'. Hardy differentiates them, nevertheless. Most important is the Spirit of the Years, to whom the deterministic shape of this grim decade is clear from the very beginning. Years rationalises whenever he speaks:

> The Will has woven with an absent heed
> Since life first was; and ever will so weave. [Fore Scene]

Years sees no point in moaning about 'the World-Soul's way'. He insists that the Semichoruses of the Pities pay attention again to 'the ordered potencies,/Nerves, sinews, trajects, eddies, ducts' of the Will (I, vi, iii) – as if by grim repetition the refractory student will learn his lesson.

More attractive for many readers is the Spirit of the Pities, who came into the world late, during the Tertiary Age of human beings, and hence must defer to the older Years. Remembering Christianity from 'its early, lovingkindly days', before it became ceremonial and institutionalised, Pities recognises the illogicality of emotion:

> I feel, Sire, as I must! This tale of Will
> And Life's impulsion by Incognizance
> I cannot take. [I, i, vi]

Unable to accept the grimness of Years's teaching, Pities cannot delay the passing of men 'to dark corruption, at the best' (II, iv, viii), and change its inevitability. The importance of this Figure lies in the advocacy of compassion; the suggestion, however faint, that men may choose between alternatives.

The names of the other Spirits are suggestive: Ironic, Sinister, Rumours, Recording Angels. Shade of the Earth must be thought of as feminine, even Shelleyan: she regards herself as the 'ineffectual Shade' of the earth, and looks forward to a time when those 'who love the true, the excellent' will inherit her bounties. She is on the side of Pities, who, after all the campaigns have ended, speaks last.

Hardy refracted through the speeches of his Spirits the significance of a grand cavalcade of events that no mere human participant could appreciate. He solved the problem of perspective by viewing Europe as the Spirits might, from an awesome height above the earth. For some readers, this has always been Hardy's most original contribution, the angles of vision that relate 'the mindless minions' wheeling 'in mechanised enchantment' to huger vistas, to the curvature of the earth itself. The Fore Scene begins with one such spectacle, as the nether sky opens to disclose Europe: 'a prone and emaciated figure, the Alps shaping like a backbone, and the branching mountain-chains like ribs, the peninsular plateau of Spain forming a head. Broad and lengthy lowlands stretch from the north of France across Russia like a grey-green garment hemmed by the Ural mountains and the glistening Arctic Ocean.' Hardy moves closer: 'The point of view then sinks downwards through space, and draws near to the surface of the perturbed countries, where the peoples, distressed by events which they did not cause, are seen writhing, crawling, heaving, and vibrating in their various cities and nationalities.' At times Hardy imagines himself 'on high over the Straits of Dover, and stretching from city to city' ('The Route between London and Paris', II, i, ii), or above the open sea between the English coasts and the Spanish Peninsula ('Four groups of moth-like transport and war ships are discovered silently skimming this wide liquid plain', II, ii, v), or over the spacious field later to be commemorated by the name of the village Borodino (III, i, v), or so high that Leipzig may be seen as 'somewhat in the shape of the letter D, the straight part of which is the river

Pleisse' (III, III, ii). Some of Hardy's finest descriptive writing may be found in these openings to scenes of momentous import, of sanguinary excess, whether at Cape Trafalgar or Torrès Védras or Vimiero, and as representative as any, and as splendidly imagined, is the field of Waterloo itself, to which an impatient reader may be referred (III, VII, i).

This mode of seeing may be termed Burkean. Hardy found ample warrant for it in a book he knew well, *A Philosophical Enquiry into the Origin of Our Ideas of the Sublime and Beautiful* (first published in 1757, enlarged in 1759). There, he found defined several causes of the Sublime, among them vastness, also called 'greatness of dimension'. Burke mused that looking down from a precipice was probably more striking 'than . . . looking up at an object of equal height' (II, vii), and Hardy took the thought as a guide to the writing of dozens of descriptions throughout the poem.

In addition to his desire to impose order upon a jumble of childhood impressions, to confer significance upon history by the devising of a philosophical and theological argument, and to exploit a novel way of treating European vistas (one that still defies the technical resources of the cinema), Hardy had still another reason for wanting to write *The Dynasts*. In his Preface, he admitted that completing *The Trumpet-Major* and seeing it into print had brought him only to 'the fringe of a vast international tragedy', and he had been unable to do more artistically with its 'events'. 'But', he added, 'the slight regard paid to English influence and action throughout the struggle by so many Continental writers who had dealt with Napoléon's career, seemed always to leave room for a new handling of the theme which should re-embody the features of this influence in their true proportion; and accordingly. . . .' What Hardy was saying, in brief, was that the Napoleonic Wars had failed to attract writers willing to give proper credit to the younger Pitt, Nelson, Wellington, and the thousands of English soldiers and sailors who had fought, and finally defeated, the French

Emperor. The failure of imaginative writers – of Romantic and Victorian poets and novelists – to exploit the riches of these materials has puzzled not only Hardy, but also historians and literary critics. William R. Rutland, for example, has dismissed as relatively minor efforts the celebrated Waterloo passage in the third canto of Byron's *Childe Harold*, and the Odes in Contribution to the Song of French History written by Meredith (less than a thousand lines survive). When Tennyson memorialised the Great Duke, he predicted that in some later age ('Far on in summers that we shall not see') another poet would celebrate Wellington's triumph over Napoleon; he did not attempt the task himself. Rutland went on to say, in a judgement that has not been challenged: '*The Dynasts* is to-day the greatest imaginative representation of the Napoleonic epoch in the literature of Western Europe. As far as English is concerned, it is likely to remain without successors, as it was without forerunners. No major English poet before Hardy had cared to dedicate himself to that theme; and after Hardy none will either dare or desire to sing again the lay he sang once for all.'[12]

At this point we come to the baffling problem for which no critic has yet proposed a satisfactory solution: the discrepancy between Hardy's grim, unrelenting vision of a helpless humanity, 'atoms', entangled by the weavings of an unthinking Will, and the heroism of a few individuals (mostly English, though Hardy admired Marshal Ney, and always depicted him favourably). *The Dynasts*, without descending to the level of crude caricature of 'Boney' save in a few Wessex scenes, and without flinching from the unflattering record of English war-profiteering, cowardice and a strong desire to act as if Napoleon were an ephemeral phenomenon, is essentially a patriotic work. It is true that the first long movement of *The Dynasts* describes Trafalgar, a naval battle that pitted Villeneuve of the *Bucentaure*

---

[12] William R. Rutland, *Thomas Hardy, A Study of His Writings and Their Background* (Oxford: Blackwell, 1938; reprinted New York: Russell & Russell, 1962), p. 271.

against Nelson of the *Victory* (I, v), with Napoleon only a
name; that Napoleon is not directly involved as a character
in any of the scenes depicting Spanish battlefields (II,
II–IV and VI); and that Wellington is not in direct confrontation with Napoleon during the Russian campaign (III, I–II).
But England is throughout and everywhere the Nemesis of
the French Emperor's dynastic schemes. It is certainly
more real to him than the Immanent Will, the workings of
which he only faintly apprehends. For Napoleon, the
English are 'licentious', like all 'canting peoples' (III, II, ii),
insolent, able and willing to stir up dissension on the
Continent, using their wealth to frustrate him, a nation
skilled in a 'tough, enisled, self-centred, kindless craft'. If
Nelson had not blocked him at sea and, at the cost of his
own life, crippled his great armada, he would have invaded
England. If England had not heartened and supported the
guerilla forces on the Iberian Peninsula, he could have
secured a minimal army there while he turned his attention
to Russia. He blamed England for turning the Tsar's head
from his resolve to destroy that nation, a pledge made at
Tilsit and the River Niemen (II, I, vii). The English
resolutely refused to recognise the government of Joseph,
King of Spain. Later, if he succeeded in his Russian invasion, he would march on to the Ganges, and then

> Once ripped by a French sword, the scaffolding
> Of English merchant-mastership in Ind
> Will fall a wreck. . . . [III, I, i]

All that he did in Russia (Napoleon told himself) was done
to revenge himself upon England.

Hardy's emphasis on Napoleon's monomaniacal hatred of
his enemy across the Channel distorts the historical record,
for England was out of Napoleon's mind for long periods of
time. But these iterations do redress the balance for
generations of neglect by previous historians, and do give
the English their due for the first time in imaginative
literature. Moreover, Hardy's heroes are astonishingly
god-like. When the candle-snuffers do their duty (I, I, iii),

Pitt rises to speak, and 'During the momentary pause . . .
the House assumes an attentive stillness, in which can be
heard the rustling of the trees without, a horn from an early
coach, and the voice of the watch crying the hour.' To Pitt
a 'strange fatality' now 'haunts the times' wherein the lot
of Englishmen is cast, but he is determined to face the perils
created by Napoleon. The King may reject his counsel
(Pitt wants to form a coalition government with Fox and
Lord Grenville), but he will not despair. After Nelson's
astonishing victory – England is not to be threatened at sea
for the remainder of the century – he proffers a toast at the
Guildhall:

> . . . no man has saved England, let me say:
> England has saved herself, by her exertions:
> She will, I trust, save Europe by her example! [I, v, v]

Years calls this speech 'his last large words'; but dying, Pitt
is to call, 'My country! How I leave my country! . . .'
(I, vi, viii) and we are reminded of Nelson's valedictory,
after the great sailor has ordered Beatty to 'Go to the others
who lie bleeding there', and Hardy to kiss him. (Hardy
framed and kept the portrait of Sir Thomas Masterman
Hardy, his kinsman and Nelson's flag-captain, framed
opposite a portrait of himself in the drawing-room of Max
Gate.) 'I'm satisfied,' Nelson murmurs. 'Thank God, I have
done my duty!'

Wellington is less quotable, and Hardy indicated, by
printing his name in italics among the list of characters at
the beginning of Part Second, that he would remain mute
throughout the Peninsular Campaign. But Wellington is
no less devoted to King and country than Pitt or Nelson: he
speaks often of 'poor devils' and 'brave men'; he never
loses faith in the ultimate victory; and every speech at
Waterloo – during the most perilous and undecided
moments of that see-saw engagement – is a rallying-cry:

> At Talavera, Salamanca, boys,
> And at Vitoria, we saw smoke together;

And though the day seems wearing doubtfully,
Beaten we must not be! [III, vii, vii]

The royal blood of courage runs freely among the common people, in the scenes of Wessex ('Rainbarrows' Beacon, Egdon Heath, I, ii, v; and Durnover Green, Casterbridge, III, v, vi), the streets of London, the reception-room of the Marchioness of Salisbury's ('At last, then, England will take her place in the forefront of this mortal struggle, and in pure disinterestedness fight with all her strength for the European deliverance. God defend the right!' – II, ii, iii), in a Viennese café in the Stephans-Platz, at the Ford of Santa Marta, Salamanca, on the plain of Vitoria, and at the famous ball in the now-legendary ballroom of the Duke and Duchess of Richmond's, Brussels, the night before Waterloo. These men and women – and Hardy, too – regarded Napoleon as someone to take seriously. He is, of course, the most important character in the epic-drama. Hardy's characterisation of the nineteenth-century Alexander depended heavily on 'oral tradition, accessible scenery, and existing relics', as well as 'the abundant pages of the historian, the biographer, and the journalist, English and Foreign', as he wrote in the Preface. The historians were by far the most useful. Among the most important were Sir Archibald Alison's *History of Europe* (ten volumes, useful as background for III, i); William Hazlitt's *Life of Napoleon Buonaparte* (four volumes); Adolphe Thiers' *Histoire du Consulat et de l'Empire* (twenty volumes, and perhaps Hardy's most important single source, available to the poet in both the Paris edition of 1857 and the D. Forbes Campbell translation); W. F. P. Napier's *The History of the War in the Peninsula* (six volumes); and le Comte de Ségur, William Beatty and the Baron Claude-François de Meneval.[13] If

---

[13] See R. J. White, *Thomas Hardy and History* (London: Macmillan, 1974), ch. 8, 'The Historians', *passim*; Rutland, *Thomas Hardy*, chapter vii, 'The Poems and *The Dynasts*'; and Walter Wright, *The Shaping of The Dynasts: A Study in Thomas Hardy* (Lincoln, Nebr.: University of Nebraska Press, 1967), ch. 4, 'The Substance'.

occasionally the inconsistencies of Hardy's characterisation puzzle us, if the Napoleon who acts as master of his destiny seems oddly incongruous with the Napoleon who cowers before premonitions, ghostly warnings and dreams, the roots of the problem lie in the baffled studies of the Emperor's life that Hardy consulted. The historians, despite the passage of more than seven decades, had not formed a consensus. The legend of Napoleon as legitimate heir of the French Revolution and as Lawgiver still seemed attractive. Part of Hardy's originality must be accounted his willingness to endorse the historian Pierre Lanfrey's harsh verdict on Napoleon's character. In his structuring of scenes that dramatise the impossible and thankless assignment to Villeneuve, the hypocritical negotiations with representatives of rival nations, the ruthless treatment of Josephine, Marie Louise, and Louisa of Prussia, and the delight in war's carnage, Hardy presents us with a loveless and unlovable hero.

Nevertheless, a *hero*; and Hardy's portrait, despite its sombre colouration, is more subtle, human and credible than any other fictionalised version. Napoleon unifies the work; he is present more often, and has more to say, than any other of the 297 human beings with speaking roles. His vision of himself as Emperor, and of the King of Rome as his legitimate successor, is at least as appealing as the mean and corroded ambitions of the other dynasts of Europe. If such a vision is to be bought at excessive cost, Hardy makes sure that we know how much the royal houses have earned their destruction. (Hardy reserves his pity for the soldiers who die for causes they do not understand, and for the civilians who suffer for no cause at all.) Napoleon's interest in moral and ethical questions, his sincere belief that he works 'for France', and his obvious zest in holding centre-stage, make him more than two-dimensional. As his character deteriorates, the images of his physical debilitation multiply, particularly after Borodino; yet for most of the epic-drama, as in life, he exerts a genuine, almost sexual attraction over worldly-wise men and women who share with him his conviction that he follows a personal star. The speech to Queen Louisa, delivered at a moment when he is determined to deny her Magdeburg, or what she prizes most, impresses us as what Napoleon must, in fact, have believed about himself:

> Know you, my Fair,
> That I – ay, I – in this deserve your pity. –
> Some force within me, baffling mine intent,
> Harries me onward, whether I will or no.
> My star, my star is what's to blame – not I.
> It is unswervable! [II, i, viii]

The reviewers of Part First carped at its 'hard Pyrrhonism', its 'quasi-dramatic form', and its occasionally crabbed and unpoetical language. The Dynasts, as they saw immediately, did not resemble anything that Hardy had written earlier. But, as the years have passed, it has become more clear that The Dynasts is the most authentic continuator of epic tradition in the twentieth century. It fulfils every requirement listed by E. M. W. Tillyard in The English Epic and Its Background (1954): high quality and high seriousness, amplitude and variety, rigorous control, and choric appropriateness.

The term 'epic-drama' was adopted rather late by Hardy, after he had dallied with such coinages as 'a mental drama, a vision drama . . . or a chronicle poem of the Napoleonic Wars under the similitude of a drama'. Hardy freely acknowledged the unplayability of The Dynasts in a conventional theatre. Still, as he suggested in his Preface, the speeches of such a play 'of poesy and dream' might well be recited in 'a monotonic delivery . . . with dreamy conventional gestures, something in the manner traditionally maintained by the old Christmas mummers'. He was understandably irritated when Arthur Bingham Walkley (1855–1926), in an unsigned article printed in The Times Literary Supplement on 29 January 1904, suggested that since The Dynasts treated Pitt, Nelson and Napoleon as 'puppets', the epic-drama might well be staged as a puppet-show. The exchange of letters that followed (Hardy on 5 February, Walkley on 12 February and Hardy once again, and for the last time, on 19 February) made clear two things: Hardy saw quite clearly that considerations of form were distracting readers from an appreciation of what, in fact, he had accomplished, and the degree to which he had achieved his multiple intentions; and Hardy early formed the notion – unchangeable to his dying day – that adverse reactions to *The Dynasts* had developed from a dislike of his 'argument', with its reliance on the idea of Immanent Will, and of its fundamental principle, Predestination.

In recent years, and particularly since the Second World War, Hardy's work has been praised more generously, and seen for what it is: the central event of his life, and not an aberration from a developing career as a poet of love lyrics and dramatic sketches and satires. *The Dynasts* treats issues of great magnitude, challenges the imagination, and achieves something very close to sublimity in the Burkean sense. It triumphs over its faults, the mixed materials, the lengthy passages of ill-disguised prose and only partially versified transcription, the tedious repetitions of the querulous Spirits, the inconsistent treatments of heroism in a predetermined universe. These faults are inseparable from a splendour of vision unique to Hardy.

Disillusioned by the Great War and by the Treaty of Versailles, Hardy wrote, years later, that Napoleon had thrown back 'human altruism scores, perhaps hundreds of years'. If he could have foreseen the Great War, he might not have written *The Dynasts* at all, or at least might not have concluded it with a carefully worded promise of a developing self-awareness on the part of the Immanent Will. Two months before his death he brooded that 'he had done all that he meant to do, but he did not know whether it had been worth doing'. The starkness of these final views, recorded in the poignant section of the *Life* entitled 'Life's Decline', should not obscure the fact that, long before the revulsion caused by trench warfare, Hardy had recorded the strongest possible indictment of the bloodiness and impersonality of modern warfare. No reader of Hardy's descriptions of the débâcle of the Satschan lake (Austerlitz), the 'ghastly climax' of Albuera, the slaughter at the bridge of the Beresina, or of what takes place during the snowstorm on the road from Smolensko into Lithuania, can mistake Hardy's moral indignation as being that of a cynical or neutral perspective. Anger at the futility of war, compassion for the defenceless and the defeated, admiration for the inspired leadership of Nelson, Pitt and Wellington, and love of country – the epic-drama surges with emotion. Thomas Hardy never spoke more directly than through the Chorus of the Years in that great lyric timed just before the fighting begins at Waterloo (III, vi, viii). One may not read it unmoved; nor, once having read the whole, remember it without affection.

HAROLD OREL

THE DYNASTS

PREFACE

THE Spectacle here presented to the mind's eye in the likeness of a Drama is concerned with the Great Historical Calamity, or Clash of Peoples, artificially brought about some hundred years ago. The choice of such a subject was mainly due to three accidents of locality. It chanced that the writer was familiar with a part of England that lay within hail of the watering - place in which King George the Third had his favourite summer residence during the war with the first Napoléon, and where he was visited by ministers and others who bore the weight of English affairs on their more or less competent shoulders at that stressful time. Secondly, this district, being also near the coast which had echoed with rumours of invasion in their intensest form while the descent threatened, was formerly animated by memories and traditions of the desperate military preparations for that contingency. Thirdly, the same countryside happened to include the village which was the birthplace of Nelson's flag-captain at Trafalgar.

When, as the first published result of these accidents, *The Trumpet-Major* was printed, more than twenty years ago, I found myself in the tantalizing position of having touched the fringe of a vast international tragedy without being able, through limits of plan, knowledge, and opportunity, to enter further into its events ; a restriction that prevailed for many years. But the slight regard paid to English influence and action throughout the struggle by so many Continental writers who had dealt with Napoléon's career, seemed always to leave room for a new handling of the theme which should re - embody the features of this influence in their true proportion ; and accordingly, on a belated day about six years back, the following drama was outlined, to be taken up now and then at wide intervals ever since.

It may, I think, claim at least a tolerable fidelity to the facts of its date as they are given in ordinary records. Whenever any evidence of the words really spoken or written by the characters in their various situations was attainable, as close a paraphrase has been aimed at as was compatible with the form chosen. And in all cases outside oral tradition, accessible scenery, and existing relics, my indebtedness for detail to the abundant pages of the historian, the biographer, and the journalist, English and Foreign, has been, of course, continuous.

It was thought proper to introduce, as supernatural spectators of the terrestrial action, certain impersonated abstractions, or Intelligences, called Spirits. They are intended to be taken by the reader for what they may be worth as contrivances of the fancy merely. Their doctrines are but tentative, and are advanced with little eye to a clear metaphysic, or systematized philosophy warranted to lift " the burthen of the mystery " of this unintelligible world. The chief thing hoped for them is that they and their utterances may have dramatic plausibility enough to procure for them, in the words of Coleridge, " that willing suspension of disbelief for the moment which constitutes poetic faith." The wide acceptance of the Monistic theory of the Universe forbade, in this twentieth century, the importation of Divine personages from any antique Mythology as ready-made sources or channels of Causation, even in verse, and excluded the celestial machinery of, say, *Paradise Lost*, as peremptorily as that of the *Iliad* or the *Eddas*. And the abandonment of the masculine pronoun in allusions to the First or Fundamental Energy seemed a necessary and logical consequence of the long abandonment by thinkers of the anthropomorphic conception of the same.

These phantasmal Intelligences are divided into groups, of which one only, that of the Pities, approximates to " the Universal Sympathy of human nature—the spectator idealized " [1] of the Greek Chorus; it is impressionable and inconsistent in its views, which sway hither and thither as wrought on by events. Another group approximates to the passionless Insight of the Ages. The remainder are eclectically chosen auxiliaries whose signification may be readily discerned. In point of literary form, the scheme of contrasted Choruses and other conventions of this external feature was shaped with a single view to the modern expression of a modern outlook, and in frank divergence from classical and other dramatic precedent which ruled the ancient voicings of ancient themes.

[1] Schlegel.

It may hardly be necessary to inform readers
that in devising this chronicle-piece no attempt
has been made to create that completely organic
structure of action, and closely-webbed develop-
ment of character and motive, which are demanded
in a drama strictly self-contained. A panoramic
show like the present is a series of historical
" ordinates " (to use a term in geometry) : the
subject is familiar to all ; and foreknowledge is
assumed to fill in the junctions required to combine the scenes into an artistic unity. Should
the mental spectator be unwilling or unable to
do this, a historical presentment on an intermittent
plan, in which the *dramatis personæ* number some
hundreds, exclusive of crowds and armies, becomes
in his individual case unsuitable.

In this assumption of a completion of the action
by those to whom the drama is addressed, it is
interesting, if unnecessary, to name an exemplar
as old as Aeschylus, whose plays are, as Dr. Verrall
reminds us,[1] scenes from stories taken as known,
and would be unintelligible without supplementary
scenes of the imagination.

Readers will readily discern, too, that *The
Dynasts* is intended simply for mental performance,
and not for the stage. Some critics have averred
that to declare a drama [2] as being not for the stage
is an announcement whose subject and predicate
cancel each other. The question seems to be an
unimportant matter of terminology. Composi-
tions cast in this shape were, without doubt,
originally written for the stage only, and as a
consequence their nomenclature of " Act," " Scene,"

---

[1] Introduction to the *Choephori*.
[2] It is now called an Epic-drama (1909).

and the like, was drawn directly from the vehicle of representation. But in the course of time such a shape would reveal itself to be an eminently readable one ; moreover, by dispensing with the theatre altogether, a freedom of treatment was attainable in this form that was denied where the material possibilities of stagery had to be rigorously remembered. With the careless mechanicism of human speech, the technicalities of practical mumming were retained in these productions when they had ceased to be concerned with the stage at all.

To say, then, in the present case, that a writing in play-shape is not to be played, is merely another way of stating that such writing has been done in a form for which there chances to be no brief definition save one already in use for works that it superficially but not entirely resembles.

Whether mental performance alone may not eventually be the fate of all drama other than that of contemporary or frivolous life, is a kindred question not without interest. The mind naturally flies to the triumphs of the Hellenic and Elizabethan theatre in exhibiting scenes laid " far in the Unapparent," and asks why they should not be repeated. But the meditative world is older, more invidious, more nervous, more quizzical, than it once was, and being unhappily perplexed by—

<blockquote>Riddles of Death Thebes never knew,</blockquote>

may be less ready and less able than Hellas and old England were to look through the insistent, and often grotesque, substance at the thing signified.

In respect of such plays of poesy and dream

a practicable compromise may conceivably result, taking the shape of a monotonic delivery of speeches, with dreamy conventional gestures, something in the manner traditionally maintained by the old Christmas mummers, the curiously hypnotizing impressiveness of whose automatic style—that of persons who spoke by no will of their own—may be remembered by all who ever experienced it. Gauzes or screens to blur outlines might still further shut off the actual, as has, indeed, already been done in exceptional cases. But with this branch of the subject we are not concerned here.

T. H.

September 1903.

CONTENTS

PART FIRST

PART SECOND

CONTENTS   13

PART FIRST

PART FIRST

CHARACTERS

I. Phantom Intelligences

The Ancient Spirit of the Years.
Chorus of the Years.

The Spirit of the Pities.
Chorus of the Pities.

Spirits Sinister and Ironic.
Choruses of Sinister and Ironic Spirits.

The Spirit of Rumour.
Chorus of Rumours.

The Shade of the Earth.

Spirit-Messengers.

Recording Angels.

II. Persons

The names printed in italics are those of mute figures.

MEN

George the Third.
The Duke of Cumberland.
Pitt.
Fox.
Sheridan.
Windham.
Whitbread.
Tierney.
Bathurst and Fuller.
Lord Chancellor Eldon.
Earl of Malmesbury.
Lord Mulgrave.
Another Cabinet Minister.
Lord Grenville.
Viscount Castlereagh.
Viscount Sidmouth.
Another Noble Lord.
Rose.
Canning.
Perceval.

Grey.
Speaker Abbot.
Tomline, Bishop of Lincoln
Sir Walter Farquhar.
Count Münster.
Other Peers, Ministers, ex-Ministers, Members of Parliament, and Persons of Quality.

———

Nelson.
Collingwood.
Hardy.
Secretary Scott.
Dr. Beatty.
Dr. Magrath.
Dr. Alexander Scott.
Burke, Purser.
Lieutenant Pasco.
Another Lieutenant.

17

POLLARD, A MIDSHIPMAN.
ANOTHER MIDSHIPMAN.
Captain Adair.
Lieutenants Ram and Whipple.
Other English Naval Officers.
Sergeant - Major Secker and Marines.
Staff and other Officers of the English Army.
A COMPANY OF SOLDIERS.
Regiments of the English Army and Hanoverian.
SAILORS AND BOATMEN.
A MILITIAMAN.
Naval crews.

The Lord Mayor and Corporation of London.
A GENTLEMAN OF FASHION.
WILTSHIRE, A COUNTRY GENTLE-
MAN.
A HORSEMAN.
TWO BEACON-WATCHERS.
ENGLISH CITIZENS AND BUR-
GESSES.
COACH AND OTHER HIGHWAY
PASSENGERS.
MESSENGERS, SERVANTS, AND
RUSTICS.

NAPOLÉON BONAPARTE.
DARU, NAPOLÉON'S WAR SECRE-
TARY.
LAURISTON, AIDE-DE-CAMP.
MONGE, A PHILOSOPHER.
BERTHIER.
MURAT, BROTHER - IN - LAW OF
NAPOLÉON.
SOULT.
NEY.
LANNES.
Bernadotte.
Marmont.
Dupont.
Oudinot.
Davout.
Vandamme.
Other French Marshals.
A SUB-OFFICER.

VILLENEUVE, NAPOLÉON'S AD-
MIRAL.
DECRÈS, MINISTER OF MARINE.

FLAG-CAPTAIN MAGENDIE.
LIEUTENANT DAUDIGNON.
LIEUTENANT FOURNIER.
DE PRIGNY, HEAD OF STAFF.
Captain Lucas.
OTHER FRENCH NAVAL OFFI-
CERS AND PETTY OFFICERS.
Seamen of the French and Spanish Navies.
Regiments of the French Army.
COURIERS.
HERALDS.
Aides, Officials, Pages, etc.
ATTENDANTS.
French Citizens.

CARDINAL CAPRARA.
Priests, Acolyths, and Choristers.
Italian Doctors and Presidents of Institutions.
Milanese Citizens.

THE EMPEROR FRANCIS.
THE ARCHDUKE FERDINAND.
Prince John of Lichtenstein.
PRINCE SCHWARZENBERG.
MACK, AUSTRIAN GENERAL.
JELLACHICH.
RIESC.
WEIROTHER.
ANOTHER AUSTRIAN GENERAL.
TWO AUSTRIAN OFFICERS.

The Emperor Alexander.
PRINCE KUTÚZOF, RUSSIAN
FIELD-MARSHAL.
COUNT LANGERON.
COUNT BUXHÖVDEN.
COUNT MILORÁDOVICH.
DOKHTÓROF.

Giulay, Gottesheim, Klenau, and Prschebiszewsky.
Regiments of the Austrian Army.
Regiments of the Russian Army.

WOMEN

Queen Charlotte.
English Princesses.
Ladies of the English Court.
LADY HESTER STANHOPE.
A LADY.
Lady Caroline Lamb, Mrs.
Damer, and other English
Ladies.

———

THE EMPRESS JOSÉPHINE.

Princesses and Ladies of José-
phine's Court.
Seven Milanese Young Ladies.

———

City- and Towns-women.
Country-women.
A MILITIAMAN'S WIFE.
A STREET-WOMAN.
Ship-women.
Servants.

FORE SCENE

THE OVERWORLD

Enter the Ancient Spirit and Chorus of the Years, the Spirit
and Chorus of the Pities, the Shade of the Earth, the Spirits
Sinister and Ironic with their Choruses, Rumours, Spirit-
Messengers, and Recording Angels.

SHADE OF THE EARTH

What of the Immanent Will and Its designs?

SPIRIT OF THE YEARS

IT works unconsciously, as heretofore,
Eternal artistries in Circumstance,
Whose patterns, wrought by rapt æsthetic rote,
Seem in themselves Its single listless aim,
And not their consequence.

CHORUS OF THE PITIES (aerial music)

Still thus?   Still thus?
Ever unconscious!
An automatic sense
Unweeting why or whence?
Be, then, the inevitable, as of old,
Although that so it be we dare not hold!

SPIRIT OF THE YEARS

Hold what ye list, fond unbelieving Sprites,
You cannot swerve the pulsion of the Byss,

21

Which thinking on, yet weighing not Its thought,
Unchecks Its clock-like laws.

SPIRIT SINISTER (aside)

                 Good, as before.
My little engines, then, will still have play.

SPIRIT OF THE PITIES

Why doth It so and so, and ever so,
This viewless, voiceless Turner of the Wheel?

SPIRIT OF THE YEARS

As one sad story runs, It lends Its heed
To other worlds, being wearied out with this ;
Wherefore Its mindlessness of earthly woes.
Some, too, have told at whiles that rightfully
Its warefulness, Its care, this planet lost
When in her early growth and crudity
By bad mad acts of severance men contrived,
Working such nescience by their own device.—
Yea, so it stands in certain chronicles,
Though not in mine.

SPIRIT OF THE PITIES

            Meet is it, none the less,
To bear in thought that though Its consciousness
May be estranged, engrossed afar, or sealed,
Sublunar shocks may wake Its watch anon?

SPIRIT OF THE YEARS

Nay. In the Foretime, even to the germ of Being,
Nothing appears of shape to indicate
That cognizance has marshalled things terrene,
Or will (such is my thinking) in my span.
Rather they show that, like a knitter drowsed,
Whose fingers play in skilled unmindfulness,

The Will has woven with an absent heed
Since life first was ; and ever will so weave.

Spirit Sinister

Hence we've rare dramas going—more so since
It wove Its web in that Ajaccian womb !

Spirit of the Years

Well, no more thus on what no mind can mete.
Our scope is but to register and watch
By means of this great gift accorded us—
The free trajection of our entities.

Spirit of the Pities

On things terrene, then, I would say that though
The human news wherewith the Rumours stirred us
May please thy temper, Years, 'twere better far
Such deeds were nulled, and this strange man's career
Wound up, as making inharmonious jars
In her creation whose meek wraith we know.
The more that he, turned man of mere traditions,
Now profits naught.   For the large potencies
Instilled into his idiosyncrasy—
To throne fair Liberty in Privilege' room—
Are taking taint, and sink to common plots
For his own gain.

Shade of the Earth

And who, then, Cordial One,
Wouldst substitute for this Intractable ?

Chorus of the Pities (aerial music)

We would establish those of kindlier build,
In fair Compassions skilled,
Men of deep art in life-development ;
Watchers and warders of thy varied lands,

Men surfeited of laying heavy hands
Upon the innocent,
The mild, the fragile, the obscure content
Among the myriads of thy family.
Those, too, who love the true, the excellent,
And make their daily moves a melody.

SHADE OF THE EARTH

They may come, will they.   I am not averse.
Yet know I am but the ineffectual Shade
Of her the Travailler, herself a thrall
To It ; in all her labourings curbed and kinged !

SPIRIT OF THE YEARS

Shall such be mooted now ?   Already change
Hath played strange pranks since first I brooded here.
But old Laws operate yet ; and phase and phase
Of men's dynastic and imperial moils
Shape on accustomed lines.   Though, as for me,
I care not how they shape, or what they be.

SPIRIT OF THE PITIES

You seem to have small sense of mercy, Sire ?

SPIRIT OF THE YEARS

Mercy I view, not urge ;—nor more than mark
What designate your titles Good and Ill.
'Tis not in me to feel with, or against,
These flesh-hinged mannikins Its hand upwinds
To click-clack off Its preadjusted laws ;
But only through my centuries to behold
Their aspects, and their movements, and their mould.

SPIRIT OF THE PITIES

They are shapes that bleed, mere mannikins or no,
And each has parcel in the total Will.

SPIRIT OF THE YEARS

Which overrides them as a whole its parts
In other entities.

SPIRIT SINISTER (aside)

Limbs of Itself:
Each one a jot of It in quaint disguise?
I'll fear all men henceforward!

SPIRIT OF THE PITIES

Go to. Let this terrestrial tragedy—

SPIRIT IRONIC

Nay, comedy—

SPIRIT OF THE PITIES

Let this earth-tragedy
Whereof ye spake, afford a spectacle
Forthwith conned closelier than your custom is.—

SPIRIT OF THE YEARS

How does it stand? (To a Recording Angel)
Open and chant the page
Thou'st lately writ, that sums these happenings,
In brief reminder of their instant points
Slighted by us amid our converse here.

RECORDING ANGEL (from a book, in recitative)

Now mellow-eyed Peace is made captive,
And Vengeance is chartered
To deal forth its dooms on the Peoples
With sword and with spear.

Men's musings are busy with forecasts
Of musters and battle,

And visions of shock and disaster
   Rise red on the year.

The easternmost ruler sits wistful,
   And tense he to midward ;
The King to the west mans his borders
   In front and in rear.

While one they eye, flushed from his crowning,
   Ranks legions around him
To shake the enisled neighbour nation
   And close her career !

SEMICHORUS I OF RUMOURS (aerial music)

O woven-winged squadrons of Toulon
   And fellows of Rochefort,
Wait, wait for a wind, and draw westward
   Ere Nelson be near !

For he reads not your force, or your freightage
   Of warriors fell-handed,
Or when they will join for the onset,
   Or whither they steer !

SEMICHORUS II

O Nelson, so zealous a watcher
   Through months-long of cruizing,
Thy foes may elude thee a moment,
   Put forth, and get clear ;

And rendezvous westerly straightway
   With Spain's aiding navies,
And hasten to head violation
   Of Albion's frontier !

SPIRIT OF THE YEARS

Methinks too much assurance thrills your note
On secrets in my locker, gentle sprites ;

But it may serve.—Our thought being now reflexed
To forces operant on this English isle,
Behoves it us to enter scene by scene,
And watch the spectacle of Europe's moves
In her embroil, as they were self-ordained
According to the naïve and liberal creed
Of our great-hearted young Compassionates,
Forgetting the Prime Mover of the gear,
As puppet-watchers him who pulls the strings.—
You'll mark the twitchings of this Bonaparte
As he with other figures foots his reel,
Until he twitch him into his lonely grave :
Also regard the frail ones that his flings
Have made gyrate like animalcula
In tepid pools.—Hence to the precinct, then,
And count as framework to the stagery
Yon architraves of sunbeam-smitten cloud.—
So may ye judge Earth's jackaclocks to be
Not fugled by one Will, but function-free.

The nether sky opens, and Europe is disclosed as a prone
and emaciated figure, the Alps shaping like a backbone, and
the branching mountain-chains like ribs, the peninsular plateau
of Spain forming a head. Broad and lengthy lowlands stretch
from the north of France across Russia like a grey-green
garment hemmed by the Ural mountains and the glistening
Arctic Ocean.

The point of view then sinks downwards through space, and
draws near to the surface of the perturbed countries, where the
peoples, distressed by events which they did not cause, are seen
writhing, crawling, heaving, and vibrating in their various cities
and nationalities.

SPIRIT OF THE YEARS (to the Spirit of the Pities)

As key-scene to the whole, I first lay bare
The Will-webs of thy fearful questioning ;
For know that of my antique privileges
This gift to visualize the Mode is one
(Though by exhaustive strain and effort only).
See, then, and learn, ere my power pass again.

A new and penetrating light descends on the spectacle,
enduing men and things with a seeming transparency, and

exhibiting as one organism the anatomy of life and movement
in all humanity and vitalized matter included in the display.

SPIRIT OF THE PITIES (after a pause)

Amid this scene of bodies substantive
Strange waves I sight like winds grown visible,
Which bear men's forms on their innumerous coils,
Twining and serpentining round and through.
Also retracting threads like gossamers—
Except in being irresistible—
Which complicate with some, and balance all.

SPIRIT OF THE YEARS

These are the Prime Volitions,—fibrils, veins,
Will-tissues, nerves, and pulses of the Cause,
That heave throughout the Earth's compositure.
Their sum is like the lobule of a Brain
Evolving always that it wots not of ;
A Brain whose whole connotes the Everywhere,
And whose procedure may but be discerned
By phantom eyes like ours ; the while unguessed
Of those it stirs, who (even as ye do) dream
Their motions free, their orderings supreme ;
Each life apart from each, with power to mete
Its own day's measures ; balanced, self-complete;
Though they subsist but atoms of the One
Labouring through all, divisible from none ;
But this no further now. Deem yet man's deeds self-
done.

The anatomy of the Immanent Will disappears.

GENERAL CHORUS OF INTELLIGENCES (aerial music)

We'll close up Time, as a bird its van,
We'll traverse Space, as spirits can,
Link pulses severed by leagues and years,
Bring cradles into touch with biers ;
So that the far-off Consequence appears
Prompt at the heel of foregone Cause.—

The PRIME, *that willed ere wareness was,*
Whose Brain perchance is Space, whose Thought its
    laws,
Which we as threads and streams discern,
We may but muse on, never learn.

END OF THE FORE SCENE

ACT FIRST

SCENE I

ENGLAND. A RIDGE IN WESSEX

The time is a fine day in March 1805. A highway crosses the ridge, which is near the sea, and the south coast is seen bounding the landscape below, the open Channel extending beyond.

SPIRIT OF THE YEARS

Hark now, and gather how the martial mood
Stirs England's humblest hearts. Anon we'll trace
Its heavings in the upper coteries there.

SPIRIT SINISTER

Ay ; begin small, and so lead up to the greater.
It is a sound dramatic principle. I always aim to
follow it in my pestilences, fires, famines, and other
comedies. And though, to be sure, I did not in my
Lisbon earthquake, I did in my French Terror, and
my St. Domingo burlesque.

SPIRIT OF THE YEARS

THY Lisbon earthquake, THY French Terror. Wait.
Thinking thou will'st, thou dost but indicate.

A stage-coach enters, with passengers outside. Their voices after the foregoing sound small and commonplace, as from another medium.

30

First Passenger

There seems to be a deal of traffic over Ridgeway, even at this time o' year.

Second Passenger

Yes. It is because the King and Court are
coming down here later on. They wake up this
part rarely ! . . . See, now, how the Channel and
coast open out like a chart. That patch of mist
below us is the town we are bound for. There's the
Isle of Slingers beyond, like a floating snail. That
wide bay on the right is where the " Abergavenny,"
Captain John Wordsworth, was wrecked last month.
One can see half across to France up here.

First Passenger

Half across. And then another little half, and
then all that's behind—the Corsican mischief !

Second Passenger

Yes. People who live hereabout—I am a native
of these parts—feel the nearness of France more
than they do inland.

First Passenger

That's why we have seen so many of these
marching regiments on the road. This year his
grandest attempt upon us is to be made, I reckon.

Second Passenger

May we be ready !

First Passenger

Well, we ought to be. We've had alarms
enough, God knows.

Third Passenger

I much doubt his intention to come at all.

Some companies of infantry are seen ahead, and the coach presently overtakes them.

Soldiers (singing as they walk)

We be the King's men, hale and hearty,
Marching to meet one Buonaparty ;
If he won't sail, lest the wind should blow,
We shall have marched for nothing, O !
Right fol-lol !

We be the King's men, hale and hearty,
Marching to meet one Buonaparty ;
If he be sea-sick, says " No, no ! "
We shall have marched for nothing, O !
Right fol-lol !

The soldiers draw aside, and the coach passes on.

Second Passenger

Is there truth in it that Bonaparte wrote a letter to the King last month ?

First Passenger

Yes, sir. A letter in his own hand, in which he expected the King to reply to him in the same manner.

Soldiers (continuing, as they are left behind)

We be the King's men, hale and hearty,
Marching to meet one Buonaparty ;
Never mind, mates ; we'll be merry, though
We may have marched for nothing, O !
Right fol-lol !

THIRD PASSENGER

And was Boney's letter friendly ?

FIRST PASSENGER

Certainly, sir. He requested peace with the King.

THIRD PASSENGER

And why shouldn't the King reply in the same manner ?

FIRST PASSENGER

What ! Encourage this man in an act of shameless presumption, and give him the pleasure of considering himself the equal of the King of England —whom he actually calls his brother !

THIRD PASSENGER

He must be taken for what he is, not for what he was ; and if he calls King George his brother it doesn't speak badly for his friendliness.

FIRST PASSENGER

Whether or no, the King, rightly enough, did not reply in person, but through Lord Mulgrave our Foreign Minister, to the effect that his Britannic Majesty cannot give a specific answer till he has communicated with the Continental powers.

THIRD PASSENGER

Both the manner and the matter of the reply are British ; but a huge mistake.

FIRST PASSENGER

Sir, am I to deem you a friend of Bonaparte, a traitor to your country——

THIRD PASSENGER

Damn my wig, sir, if I'll be called a traitor by you or any Court sycophant at all at all!

[He unpacks a case of pistols.

SECOND PASSENGER

Gentlemen, forbear, forbear! Should such differences be suffered to arise on a spot where we may, in less than three months, be fighting for our very existence? This is foolish, I say. Heaven alone, who reads the secrets of this man's heart, can tell what his meaning and intent may be, and if his letter has been answered wisely or no.

The coach is stopped to skid the wheel for the descent of the hill, and before it starts again a dusty horseman overtakes it.

SEVERAL PASSENGERS

A London messenger! (To horseman) Any news, sir? We are from Bristol only.

HORSEMAN

Yes; much. We have declared war against Spain, an error giving vast delight to France. Bonaparte says he will date his next dispatches from London, and the landing of his army may be daily expected.

[Exit horseman.

THIRD PASSENGER (to First)

Sir, I apologize. He's not to be trusted! War is his name, and aggression is with him!

He repacks the pistols. A silence follows. The coach and passengers move downwards and disappear towards the coast.

SPIRIT OF THE PITIES

Ill chanced it that the English monarch George
Did not respond to the said Emperor!

Spirit Sinister

I saw good sport therein, and pœan'd the Will
For leaving lax so stultifying a move !
Which would have marred the European broil,
And sheathed all swords, and silenced every gun
That furrows human flesh.

Spirit of the Pities

                    O say no more ;
If aught could gratify the Absolute
'Twould verily be thy censure, not thy praise !

Spirit of the Years

The ruling was that we should witness things
And not dispute them.   To the drama, then.
Emprizes over-Channel are the key
To this land's stir and ferment.—Thither we.

Clouds gather over the scene, and slowly open elsewhere.

SCENE II

PARIS.   OFFICE OF THE MINISTER OF MARINE

Admiral Decrès seated at a table.   A knock without.

Decrès

Come in !   Good news, I hope !

[An attendant enters.

Attendant

                    A courier, sir.

Decrès

Show him in straightway.

[The attendant goes out.

From the Emperor
As I expected !

A courier is admitted, who delivers a dispatch.

COURIER

Sir, for your own hand
And yours alone.

DECRÈS

Thanks.   Be in waiting near.

[The courier withdraws.

DECRÈS *reads* :

" I am resolved that no wild dream of Ind,
And what we there might win ; or of the West,
And bold re-conquest there of Surinam
And other Dutch retreats along those coasts,
Or British islands nigh, shall draw me now
From piercing into England through Boulogne
As lined in my first plan.   If I do strike,
I strike effectively ; to forge which feat
There's but one way—planting a mortal wound
In England's heart—the very English land—
Whose insolent and cynical reply
To my well-pleaded plaint on breach of faith
Concerning Malta, as at Amiens pledged,
Has lighted up anew such brands of ire
As may bescorch the world.—Now to the case :
Our naval forces can be all amassed
Without the foe's foreknowledge or surmise,
By these rules following ; to whose text I ask
Your gravest application ; and, when conned,
That steadfastly you stand by word and word,
Making no question of one jot therein.

" First, then, let Villeneuve wait a favouring wind
For process westward swift to Martinique,

Coaxing the English after.   Join him there
Gravina, Missiessy, and Ganteaume ;
Which junction once effected all our keels—
Now nigh to sixty sail—regain the Manche,
While the pursuers linger in the West
At hopeless fault.—Having hoodwinked them thus,
Our boats skim over, disembark the army,
And in the twinkling of a patriot's eye
All London will be ours.

  " In strictest secrecy carve this to shape—
Let never an admiral or captain scent
Save Villeneuve and Ganteaume ; and pen each charge
With your own quill.   The surelier to outwit them
I start for Italy ; and there, as 'twere
Engrossed in fêtes and Coronation rites,
Abide till, at the need, I reach Boulogne,
And head the enterprize.—NAPOLÉON."

> DECRÈS reflects, and turns to write.

SPIRIT OF THE PITIES

More ills ?   How is Decrès ordained to move ?

SPIRIT OF THE YEARS

He buckles to the work.   First to Villeneuve,
His onetime comrade and his boyhood's friend,
Now lingering at Toulon, he jots swift lines,
Then duly to Ganteaume.—They are sealed forthwith,
And superscribed : " Break not till on the main."

> Boisterous singing is heard in the street.

SPIRIT OF THE PITIES

I hear confused and simmering sounds without,
Like those which thrill the hives at evenfall
When swarming pends.

Spirit of the Years

They but proclaim the crowd,
Which sings and shouts its hot enthusiasms
For this dead-ripe design on England's shore,
Till the persuasion of its own plump words,
Acting upon mercurial temperaments,
Makes hope as prophecy. " Our Emperor
Will show himself (say they) in this exploit
Unwavering, keen, and irresistible
As is the lightning-prong. Our vast flotillas
Have been embodied as by sorcery ;
Soldiers made seamen, and the ports transformed
To rocking cities casemented with guns.
Against these valiants balance England's means :
Raw merchant-fellows from the counting-house,
Raw labourers from the fields, who thumb for arms
Clumsy untempered pikes forged hurriedly,
And cry them full-equipt. Their batteries,
Their flying carriages, their catamarans,
Shall profit not, and in one summer night
We'll find us there ! "

Recording Angel

And is this prophecy true ?

Spirit of the Years

Occasion will reveal.

Shade of the Earth

What boots it, Sire,
To down this dynasty, set that one up,
Goad panting peoples to the throes thereof,
Make wither here my fruit, maintain it there,
And hold me travailling through fineless years
In vain and objectless monotony,

When all such tedious conjuring could be shunned
By uncreation?   Howsoever wise
The governance of these massed mortalities,
A juster wisdom his who should have ruled
They had not been.

SPIRIT OF THE YEARS

           Nay, something hidden urged
The giving matter motion ; and these coils
Are, maybe, good as any.

SPIRIT OF THE PITIES

           But why any ?

SPIRIT OF THE YEARS

Sprite of Compassions, ask the Immanent !
I am but an accessory of Its works,
Whom the Ages render conscious ; and at most
Figure as bounden witness of Its laws.

SPIRIT OF THE PITIES

How ask the aim of unrelaxing Will
Tranced in Its purpose to unknowingness ?
(If thy words, Ancient Phantom, token true).

SPIRIT OF THE YEARS

Thou answerest well.   But cease to ask of me.
Meanwhile the mime proceeds.—We turn herefrom,
Change our homuncules, and observe forthwith
How the High Influence sways the English realm,
And how the jacks lip out their reasonings there.

The Cloud-curtain draws.

SCENE III

LONDON.   THE OLD HOUSE OF COMMONS

A long chamber with a gallery on each side supported by thin columns having gilt Ionic capitals.   Three round-headed windows are at the further end, above the Speaker's chair, which is backed by a huge pedimented structure in white and gilt, surmounted by the lion and the unicorn.   The windows are uncurtained, one being open, through which some boughs are seen waving in the midnight gloom without.   Wax candles, burnt low, wave and gutter in a brass chandelier which hangs from the middle of the ceiling, and in branches projecting from the galleries.

The House is sitting, the benches, which extend round to the Speaker's elbows, being closely packed, and the galleries likewise full.   Among the members present on the Government side are PITT and other ministers with their supporters, including CANNING, CASTLEREAGH, LORD C. SOMERSET, ERSKINE, W. DUNDAS, HUSKISSON, ROSE, BEST, ELLIOT, DALLAS, and the general body of the party.   On the opposite side are noticeable FOX, SHERIDAN, WINDHAM, WHITBREAD, GREY, T. GRENVILLE, TIERNEY, EARL TEMPLE, PONSONBY, G. and H. WALPOLE, DUDLEY NORTH, and TIMOTHY SHELLEY.   Speaker ABBOT occupies the Chair.

SPIRIT OF THE YEARS (to two Recording Angels)

As prelude to the scene, as means to aid
Our younger comrades in its construing,
Pray spread your scripture, and rehearse in brief
The reasonings here of late—to whose effects
Words of to-night form sequence.

The Recording Angels chant from their books, antiphonally, in a minor recitative.

ANGEL I (aerial music)

Feeble-framed dull unresolve, unresourcefulness,
Sat in the halls of the Kingdom's high Councillors,

Whence the grey glooms of a ghost-eyed despondency
Wanned as with winter the national mind.

ANGEL II

England stands forth to the sword of Napoléon
Nakedly—not an ally in support of her ;
Men and munitions dispersed inexpediently ;
Projects of range and scope poorly defined.

ANGEL I

Once more doth Pitt deem the land crying loud to him.—
Frail though and spent, and an-hungered for restfulness
Once more responds he, dead fervours to energize,
Aims to concentre, slack efforts to bind.

ANGEL II

Ere the first fruit thereof voices grow audible,
Holding as hapless his dream of good guardianship,
Jestingly, earnestly, shouting it serviceless,
Tardy, inept, and uncouthly designed.

ANGELS I AND II

So now, to-night, in the slashing old sentences,
Hear them speak,—gravely these, those with gay-
    heartedness,—
Midst their admonishments little .conceiving how
Scarlet the scroll that the years will unwind !

SPIRIT OF THE PITIES (to the Spirit of the Years)

Let us put on and suffer for the nonce
The feverish fleshings of Humanity,
And join the pale debaters here convened.
So may thy soul be won to sympathy
By donning their poor mould.

Spirit of the Years

I'll humour thee,
Though my unpassioned essence could not change
Did I incarn in moulds of all mankind!

Spirit Ironic

'Tis enough to make every little dog in England run
to mixen to hear this Pitt sung so strenuously! I'll
be the third of the incarnate, on the chance of hearing
the tune played the other way.

Spirit Sinister

And I the fourth. There's sure to be something in
my line toward, where politicians are gathered together!

The four Phantoms enter the Gallery of the House in the
disguise of ordinary strangers.

Sheridan (rising)

The Bill I would have leave to introduce
Is framed, sir, to snuff out last Session's Act,
By party-scribes intituled a Provision
For England's Proper Guard; but elsewhere known
As Mr. Pitt's new Patent Parish Pill.   (Laughter.)
    The ministerial countenances, I mark,
Congeal to dazed surprise at my straight motion—
Why, passes sane conjecture. It may be
That, with a haughty and unwavering faith
In their own battering-rams of argument,
They deemed our buoyance whelmed, and sapped,
        and sunk
To hope's sheer bottom, whence a miracle
Was all could friend and float us; or, maybe,
They are amazed at our damned disrespect
In making mockery of an English Law
Sprung sacred from the King's own Premier's brain!
—I hear them snort; but let them wince at will,

My duty must be done ; shall be done quickly
By citing some few facts.

An Act for our defence !

It weakens, not defends ; and oversea
Swoln France's despot and his myrmidons
This moment know it, and can scoff thereat.
Our people know it too—those who can peer
Behind the scenes of this poor painted show
Called soldiering !—The Act has failed, must fail,
As my right honourable friend well proved
When speaking t'other night, whose silencing
By his right honourable *vis-à-vis*
Was of the genuine Governmental sort,
And like the catamarans their sapience shaped
All fizzle and no harm.   (Laughter.)   The Act, in brief,
Effects this much : that the whole force of England
Is strengthened by—eleven thousand men !
So sorted that the British infantry
Are now eight hundred less than heretofore !
In Ireland, where the glamouring influence
Of the right honourable gentleman
Prevails with magic might, *eleven* men
Have been amassed.   And in the Cinque-Port towns,
Where he is held in absolute veneration,
His method has so quickened martial fire
As to bring in—one man.   O would that man
Might meet my sight !   (Laughter.)   A Hercules, no
      doubt,
A god-like emanation from this Act,
Who with his single arm will overthrow
All Buonaparté's legions ere their keels
Have scraped one pebble of our fortless shores ! . . .
Such is my motion, sir, and such my mind.

[He sits down amid cheers.

The candle-snuffers go round, and PITT rises. During the
momentary pause before he speaks the House assumes an
attentive stillness, in which can be heard the rustling of the
trees without, a horn from an early coach, and the voice of
the watch crying the hour.

PITT

Not one on this side but appreciates
Those mental gems and airy pleasantries
Flashed by the honourable gentleman,
Who shines in them by birthright.   Each device
Of drollery he has laboured to outshape,
(Or treasured up from others who have shaped it,)
Displays that are the conjurings of the moment,
(Or mellowed and matured by sleeping on)—
Dry hoardings in his book of commonplace,
Stored without stint of toil through days and
     months—
He heaps into one mass, and lights and fans
As fuel for his flaming eloquence,
Mouthed and maintained without a thought or care
If germane to the theme, or not at all.
    Now vain indeed it were should I assay
To match him in such sort.   For, sir, alas,
To use imagination as the ground
Of chronicle, take myth and merry tale
As texts for prophecy, is not my gift,
Being but a person primed with simple fact,
Unprinked by jewelled art.—But to the thing.
    The preparations of the enemy,
Doggedly bent to desolate our land,
Advance with a sustained activity.
They are seen, they are known, by you and by us all.
But they evince no clear-eyed tentative
In furtherance of the threat, whose coming off,
Ay, years may yet postpone ; whereby the Act
Will far outstrip him, and the thousands called
Duly to join the ranks by its provisions,
In process sure, if slow, will ratch the lines
Of English regiments—seasoned, cool, resolved—
To glorious length and firm prepotency.
And why, then, should we dream of its repeal
Ere profiting by its advantages ?
Must the House listen to such wilding words

As this proposal, at the very hour
When the Act's gearing finds its ordered grooves
And circles into full utility ?
The motion of the honourable gentleman
Reminds me aptly of a publican
Who should, when malting, mixing, mashing's past,
Fermenting, barrelling, and spigoting,
Quick taste the brew, and shake his sapient head,
And cry in acid voice : The ale is new !
Brew old, you varlets; cast this slop away ! (Cheers.)
　But gravely, sir, I would conclude to-night,
And, as a serious man on serious things,
I now speak here. . . . I pledge myself to this :
Unprecedented and magnificent
As were our strivings in the previous war,
Our efforts in the present shall transcend them,
As men will learn.　Such efforts are not sized
By this light measuring-rule my critic here
Whips from his pocket like a clerk-o'-works ! . . .
Tasking and toilsome war's details must be,
And toilsome, too, must be their criticism,—
Not in a moment's stroke extemporized.
　The strange fatality that haunts the times
Wherein our lot is cast, has no example.
Times are they fraught with peril, trouble, gloom ;
We have to mark their lourings, and to face them.
Sir, reading thus the full significance
Of these big days, large though my lackings be,
Can any hold of those who know my past
That I, of all men, slight our safeguarding ?
No : by all honour no !—Were I convinced
That such could be the mind of members here,
My sorrowing thereat would doubly shade
The shade on England now !　So I do trust
All in the House will take my tendered word,
And credit my deliverance here to-night,
That in this vital point of watch and ward
Against the threatenings from yonder coast
We stand prepared ; and under Providence

Shall fend whatever hid or open stroke
A foe may deal.

*He sits down amid loud ministerial cheers, with symptoms
of exhaustion.*

WINDHAM

The question that compels the House to-night
Is not of differences in wit and wit,
But if for England it be well or no
To null the new-fledged Act, as one inept
For setting up with speed and hot effect
The red machinery of desperate war.—
Whatever it may do, or not, it stands,
A statesman's raw experiment.   If ill,
Shall yet more raw assays and more be tried
In stress of jeopardy that stirs demand
For sureness of proceeding ?   Must this House
Exchange safe action based on practised lines
For yet more ventures into risks unknown
To gratify a quaint projector's whim,
While enemies hang grinning round our gates
To profit by mistake ?
                              My friend who spoke
Found comedy in the matter.   Comical
As it may be in parentage and feature,
Most grave and tragic in its consequence
This Act may prove.   We are moving thoughtlessly,
We squander precious, brief, life-saving time
On idle guess-games.   Fail the measure must,
Nay, failed it has already ; and should rouse
Resolve in its progenitor himself
To move for its repeal !   (Cheers.)

WHITBREAD

I rise but to subjoin a phrase or two
To those of my right honourable friend.
I, too, am one who reads the present pinch
As passing all our risks of heretofore.

For why ?   Our bold and reckless enemy,
Relaxing not his plans, has treasured time
To mass his monstrous force on all the coigns
From which our coast is close assailable.
Ay, even afloat his concentrations work :
Two vast united squadrons of his sail
Move at this moment viewless on the seas.—
Their whereabouts, untraced, unguessable,
Will not be known to us till some black blow
Be dealt by them in some undreamt-of quarter
To knell our rule.
That we are reasonably enfenced therefrom
By such an Act is but a madman's dream. . . .
A commonwealth so situate cries aloud
For more, far mightier, measures !   End an Act
In Heaven's name, then, which only can obstruct
The fabrication of more trusty tackle
For building up an army !   (Cheers.)

BATHURST

                    Sir, the point
To any sober mind is bright as noon ;
Whether the Act should have befitting trial
Or be blasphemed at sight.   I firmly hold
The latter loud iniquity.—One task
Is theirs who would inter this corpse-cold Act
(So said)—to bring to birth a substitute !
Sir, they have none ; they have given no thought to
      one,
And thus their deeds incautiously disclose
Their cloaked intention and most secret aim !
With them the question is not how to frame
A finer trick to trounce intrusive foes,
But who shall be the future ministers
To whom such trick against intrusive foes,
Whatever it may prove, shall be entrusted !
They even ask the country gentlemen
To join them in this job.   But, God be praised,

Those gentlemen are sound, and of repute ;
Their names, their property, their character,
Their numbers, their attainments, and their blood,

                          (Ironical Opposition cheers.)

Safeguard them from an onslaught on an Act
For ends so sinister and palpable !

                             (Cheers and jeerings.)

FULLER

I disapprove of censures of this Act.—
All who can entertain such hostile thought
Would swear that black is white, that night is day.
No honest man will join a reckless crew
Who'd overthrow their country for their gain !

                               (Laughter.)

TIERNEY

It is incumbent on me to declare
In the last speaker's face my censure, based
On grounds most clear and constitutional.—
An Act it is that studies to create
A standing army, large and permanent ;
Which kind of force has ever been beheld
With jealous-eyed disfavour in this House.
It makes for sure oppression, binding men
To serve for less than service proves it worth
Conditioned by no hampering penalty.
For these and late-spoke reasons, then, I say,
Let not the Act deface the statute-book,
But blot it out forthwith !　(Hear, hear.)

Fox (rising amid cheers)

                     At this late hour,
After the riddling fire the Act has drawn on't,
My words shall hold the House the briefest while.
Too obvious to the most unwilling mind
It grows that the existence of this law
Experience and reflection have condemned.

Professing to do much, it makes for nothing ;
Vouched as assuring all, it comforts none.
Not only so ; while feeble in effect
It shows it vicious in its principle.
Engaging to raise men for the common weal,
It sets a harmful and unequal tax
Capriciously on our communities.—
The annals of a century fail to show
More flagrant cases of oppressiveness
Than those this statute works to perpetrate,
Which (like all Bills this favoured statesman frames,
And clothes with tapestries of rhetoric
Disguising their real web of commonplace)
Though held as shaped for English bulwarking,
Breathes in its heart perversities of party,
And instincts toward oligarchic power,
Galling the many to relieve the few !   (Cheers.)
    Whatever breadth and sense of equity
Inform the methods of this minister,
Those mitigants near always trace their root
To measures that his predecessors wrought.
And ere his Government can dare assert
Superior claims to England's confidence,
They owe it to their honour and good name
To furnish better proof of such a claim
Than is revealed by the abortiveness
Of this thing called an Act for our Defence.
    To the great gifts of its artificer
No member of this House is more disposed
To yield full recognition than am I.
No man has found more reason so to do
Through the long roll of disputatious years
Wherein we have stood opposed. . . .
But if one single fact could counsel me
To entertain a doubt of those great gifts,
And cancel faith in his capacity,
That fact would be the vast imprudence shown
In staking recklessly repute like his
On such an Act as he has offered us—

So false in principle, so poor in fruit.
Sir, the achievements and effects thereof
Have furnished not one fragile argument
Which all the partiality of friendship
Can kindle to consider as the mark
Of a clear, vigorous, freedom-fostering mind !

He sits down amid lengthy cheering from the Opposition.

SHERIDAN

My summary shall be brief, and to the point.—
The said right honourable Prime Minister
Has thought it proper to declare my speech
The jesting of an irresponsible ;—
Words from a person who has never read
The Act he claims him urgent to repeal.
Such quips and quizzings (as he reckons them)
He implicates as gathered from long hoards
Stored up with cruel care, to be discharged
With sudden blaze of pyrotechnic art
On the devoted, gentle, shrinking head
O' the right incomparable gentleman !   (Laughter.)
But were my humble, solemn, sad oration   (Laughter.)
Indeed such rattle as he rated it,
Is it not strange, and passing precedent,
That the illustrious chief of Government
Should have uprisen with such indecent speed
And strenuously replied ?   He, sir, knows well
That vast and luminous talents like his own
Could not have been demanded to choke off
A witcraft marked by nothing more of weight
Than ignorant irregularity !
Nec Deus intersit—and so-and-so—
Is a well-worn citation whose close fit
None will perceive more clearly in this Fane
Than its presiding Deity opposite.   (Laughter.)
His thunderous answer thus perforce condemns
    him !

Moreover, to top all, the while replying,
He still thought best to leave intact the reasons
On which my blame was founded !
                            Thus, then, stands
My motion unimpaired, convicting clearly
Of dire perversion that capacity
We formerly admired.—   (Cries of " Oh, oh.")
                           This minister
Whose circumventions never circumvent,
Whose coalitions fail to coalesce ;
This dab at secret treaties known to all,
This darling of the aristocracy—
   (Laughter, " Oh, oh," cheers, and cries of " Divide.")
Has brought the millions to the verge of ruin,
By pledging them to Continental quarrels
Of which we see no end !   (Cheers.)

          The members rise to divide.

SPIRIT OF THE PITIES

It irks me that they thus should Yea and Nay
As though a power lay in their oraclings,
If each decision work unconsciously,
And would be operant though unloosened were
A single lip !

SPIRIT OF RUMOUR

        There may react on things
Some influence from these, indefinitely,
And even on That, whose outcome we all are.

SPIRIT OF THE YEARS

Hypotheses !—More boots it to remind
The younger here of our ethereal band
And hierarchy of Intelligences,
That this thwart Parliament whose moods we watch—
So insular, empiric, un-ideal—

May figure forth in sharp and salient lines
To retrospective eyes of afterdays,
And print its legend large on History.
For one cause—if I read the signs aright—
To-night's appearance of its Minister
In the assembly of his long-time sway
Is near his last, and themes to-night launched forth
Will take a tincture from that memory,
When men recall the scene and circumstance
That hung about his pleadings.—But no more ;
The ritual of each party is rehearsed,
Dislodging not one vote or prejudice ;
The ministers their ministries retain,
And Ins as Ins, and Outs as Outs, remain.

Spirit of the Pities

Meanwhile what of the Foeman's vast array
That wakes these tones ?

Spirit of the Years

Abide the event, young Shade :
Soon stars will shut and show a spring-eyed dawn,
And sunbeams fountain forth, that will arouse
Those forming bands to full activity.

A member reports strangers.

A quaint curt token that we dally here !
We now cast off these mortal manacles,
And speed us seaward.

The Phantoms vanish from the Gallery. The members file
out to the lobbies. The House and Westminster recede into
the films of night, and the point of observation shifts rapidly
across the Channel.

SCENE IV

THE HARBOUR OF BOULOGNE

The morning breaks, radiant with early sunlight. The French Army of Invasion is disclosed. On the hills on either side of the town and behind appear large military camps formed of timber huts. Lower down are other camps of more or less permanent kind, the whole affording accommodation for one hundred and fifty thousand men.

South of the town is an extensive basin surrounded by quays, the heaps of fresh soil around showing it to be a recent excavation from the banks of the Liane. The basin is crowded with the flotilla, consisting of hundreds of vessels of sundry kinds : flat-bottomed brigs with guns and two masts ; boats of one mast, carrying each an artillery waggon, two guns, and a two-stalled horse-box ; transports with three low masts ; and long narrow pinnaces arranged for many oars.

Timber, saw-mills, and new-cut planks spread in profusion around, and many of the town residences are seen to be adapted for warehouses and infirmaries.

DUMB SHOW

Moving in this scene are countless companies of soldiery, engaged in a drill-practice of embarking and disembarking, and of hoisting horses into the vessels and landing them again. Vehicles bearing provisions of many sorts load and unload before the temporary warehouses. Further off, on the open land, bodies of troops are at field-drill. Other bodies of soldiers, half stripped and encrusted with mud, are labouring as navvies in repairing the excavations.

An English squadron of about twenty sail, comprising a ship or two of the line, frigates, brigs, and luggers, confronts the busy spectacle from the sea.

The Show presently dims and becomes broken, till only its flashes and gleams are visible. Anon a curtain of cloud closes over it.

SCENE V

LONDON.   THE HOUSE OF A LADY OF QUALITY

A fashionable crowd is present at an evening party, which includes the DUKES of BEAUFORT and RUTLAND, LORDS MALMESBURY, HARROWBY, ELDON, GRENVILLE, CASTLEREAGH, SIDMOUTH, and MULGRAVE, with their ladies; also CANNING, PERCEVAL, TOWNSHEND, LADY ANNE HAMILTON, MRS. DAMER, LADY CAROLINE LAMB, and many other notables.

A GENTLEMAN (offering his snuff-box)

So, then, the Treaty anxiously concerted
Between ourselves and frosty Muscovy
Is duly signed ?

A CABINET MINISTER

        Was signed a few days back,
And is in force.   And we do firmly hope
The loud pretensions and the stunning dins
From new aggressiveness by France's chief,
Now daily heard, these laudable exertions
May keep in curb ; that ere our greening land
Darken its leaves beneath the Dogday suns,
The independence of the Continent
May be assured, and all the rumpled flags
Of famous dynasties so foully mauled,
Extend their honoured hues as heretofore.

GENTLEMAN

So be it.   Yet this man is a volcano ;
And proven 'tis, by God, volcanoes choked
Have ere now turned to earthquakes !

      A lady comes up and playfully taps his arm.

LADY

                What's the news ?—
The chequerboard of diplomatic moves
Is London, all the world knows : here are born
All inspirations of the Continent—
So tell !

GENTLEMAN

    Ay.   Inspirations now abound !

LADY

Nay, but your looks are grave !   That measured
    speech
Betokened matter that will waken us.—
Is it some piquant cruelty of his ?
Or other tickling horror from abroad
The packet has brought in ?

GENTLEMAN

              The treaty's signed !

MINISTER

Whereby the parties mutually agree
To knit in union and in general league
All outraged Europe.

LADY

          So to knit sounds well ;
But how ensure its not unravelling ?

MINISTER

Well ; by the terms.   There are among them these :
Five hundred thousand active men in arms
Shall strike (supported by Britannic aid
In vessels, men, and money subsidies)

To free North Germany and Hanover
From trampling foes ; deliver Switzerland,
Unbind the galled republic of the Dutch,
Rethrone in Piedmont the Sardinian King,
Make Naples sword-proof, un-French Italy
From shore to shore ; and thoroughly guarantee
A settled order to the divers states ;
Thus rearing breachless barriers in each realm
Against the thrust of his usurping hand.

SPIRIT OF THE YEARS

They trow not what is shaping otherwhere
The while they talk thus stoutly !

SPIRIT OF RUMOUR

Bid me go
And join them, and all blandly kindle them
By bringing, ere material transit can,
A new surprise !

SPIRIT OF THE YEARS

Yea, for a moment, wouldst.

The Spirit of Rumour enters the apartment in the form
of a personage of fashion, newly arrived. He advances and
addresses the group.

SPIRIT

The Treaty moves all tongues to-night.—Ha, well—
So much on paper !

GENTLEMAN

What on land and sea ?
You look, old friend, full primed with latest thence.

Spirit

Yea, this.   The Italy our mighty pact
Delivers from the French and Bonaparte
Makes haste to crown him !—Turning from Boulogne
He speeds toward Milan, there to glory him
In second coronation by the Pope,
And set upon his irrepressible brow
Lombardy's iron crown.

The Spirit of Rumour mingles with the throng, moves away, and disappears.

Lady

                 Fair Italy,
Alas, alas !

Lord

            Yet thereby English folk
Are freed him.—Faith, as ancient people say,
It's an ill wind that blows good luck to none !

Minister

Who is your friend that drops so airily
This precious pinch of salt on our raw skin ?

Gentleman

Why, Norton.   You know Norton well enough ?

Minister

Nay, 'twas not he.   Norton of course I know.
I thought him Stewart for a moment, but——

Lady

But I well scanned him—'twas Lord Abercorn ;
For, said I to myself, " O quaint old beau,

To sleep in black silk sheets so funnily "—
That is, if the town rumour on't be true.

LORD

My wig, ma'am, no ! 'Twas a much younger man.

GENTLEMAN

But let me call him ! Monstrous silly this,
That I don't know my friends !

They look around. The gentleman goes among the surging and babbling guests, makes inquiries, and returns with a perplexed look.

GENTLEMAN

                They tell me, sure,
That he's not here to-night !

MINISTER

                 I can well swear
It was not Norton.—'Twas some lively buck,
Who chose to put himself in masquerade
And enter for a whim. I'll tell our host.
—Meantime the absurdity of his report
Is more than manifested. How knows he
The plans of Bonaparte by lightning-flight,
Before another man in England knows ?

LADY

Something uncanny's in it all, if true.
Good Lord, the thought gives me a sudden sweat,
That fairly makes my linen stick to me !

MINISTER

Ha-ha ! It's excellent. But we'll find out
Who this impostor was.

They disperse, look furtively for the stranger, and speak of the incident to others of the crowded company.

SPIRIT OF THE YEARS

Now let us vision onward, till we sight
Famed Milan's aisles of marble, sun-alight,
And there behold, unbid, the Coronation-rite.

The confused tongues of the assembly waste away into distance, till they are heard but as the babblings of the sea from a high cliff, the scene becoming small and indistinct therewith. This passes into silence, and the whole disappears.

SCENE VI

MILAN. THE CATHEDRAL

The interior of the building on a sunny May day.
The walls, arches, and columns are draped in silk fringed with gold. A gilded throne stands in front of the High Altar. A closely packed assemblage, attired in every variety of rich fabric and fashion, waits in breathless expectation.

DUMB SHOW

From a private corridor leading to a door in the aisle the EMPRESS JOSÉPHINE enters, in a shining costume, and diamonds that collect rainbow-colours from the sunlight piercing the clerestory windows. She is preceded by PRINCESS ELIZA, and surrounded by her ladies. A pause follows, and then comes the procession of the EMPEROR, consisting of hussars, heralds, pages, aides-de-camp, presidents of institutions, officers of state bearing the insignia of the Empire and of Italy, and seven ladies with offerings. The EMPEROR himself is in royal robes, wearing the Imperial crown, and carrying the sceptre. He is followed by ministers and officials of the household. His gait is rather defiant than dignified, and a bluish pallor overspreads his face.

He is met by the Cardinal Archbishop CAPRARA and the clergy, who burn incense before him as he proceeds towards the throne. Rolling notes of music burst forth, and loud applause from the congregation.

Spirit of the Pities

What is the creed that these rich rites disclose ?

Spirit of the Years

A local cult called Christianity,
Which the wild dramas of the wheeling spheres
Include, with divers other such, in dim
Pathetical and brief parentheses,
Beyond whose span, uninfluenced, unconcerned,
The systems of the suns go sweeping on
With all their many-mortaled planet train
In mathematic roll unceasingly.

Spirit of the Pities

I did not recognize it here, forsooth ;
Though in its early, lovingkindly days
Of gracious purpose it was much to me.

Archbishop (addressing Bonaparte)

Sire, with that clemency and right goodwill
Which beautify Imperial Majesty,
You deigned acceptance of the homages
That we the clergy and the Milanese
Were proud to offer when your entrance here
Streamed radiance on our ancient capital.
Please, then, to consummate the boon to-day
Beneath this holy roof, so soon to thrill
With solemn strains and lifting harmonies
Befitting such a coronation hour ;
And bend a tender fatherly regard
On this assembly, now at one with me
To supplicate the Author of All Good
That He endow your most Imperial person
With every Heavenly gift.

The procession advances, and the Emperor seats himself on
the throne, with the banners and regalia of the Empire on his

right, and those of Italy on his left hand. Shouts and triumphal music accompany the proceedings, after which Divine service commences.

SPIRIT OF THE PITIES

Thus are the self-styled servants of the Highest
Constrained by earthly duress to embrace
Mighty imperiousness as it were choice,
And hand the Italian sceptre unto one
Who, with a saturnine, sour-humoured grin,
Professed at first to flout antiquity,
Scorn limp conventions, smile at mouldy thrones,
And level dynasts down to journeymen !—
Yet he, advancing swiftly on that track
Whereby his active soul, fair Freedom's child,
Makes strange decline, now labours to achieve
The thing it overthrew.

SPIRIT OF THE YEARS

Thou reasonest ever thuswise—even as if
A self-formed force had urged his loud career.

SPIRIT SINISTER

Do not the prelate's accents falter thin,
His lips with inheld laughter grow deformed,
While blessing one whose aim is but to win
The golden seats that other b——s have warmed ?

SPIRIT OF THE YEARS

Soft, jester ; scorn not puppetry so skilled,
Even made to feel by one men call the Dame.

SHADE OF THE EARTH

Yea ; that they feel, and puppetry remain,
Is an owned flaw in her consistency

Men love to dub Dame Nature—that lay-shape
They use to hang phenomena upon—
Whose deftest mothering in fairest spheres
Is girt about by terms inexorable !

Spirit Sinister

The lady's remark is apposite, and reminds me that
I may as well hold my tongue as desired.   For if my
casual scorn, Father Years, should set thee trying to
prove that there is any right or reason in the Universe,
thou wilt not accomplish it by Doomsday !   Small
blame to her, however ; she must cut her coat according
to her cloth, as they would say below there.

Spirit of the Years

O would that I could move It to enchain thee,
And shut thee up a thousand years !—(to cite
A grim terrestrial tale of one thy like)
Thou Dragon of the Incorporeal World,
"As they would say below there."

Spirit of the Pities

                          Would thou couldst !
But move That Which is scoped above percipience,
It cannot be !

Shade of the Earth

The spectacle proceeds.

Spirit Sinister

And we may as well give all attention thereto, for
the evils at work in other continents are not worth
eyesight by comparison.

The ceremonial in the Cathedral continues.   Napoléon
goes to the front of the altar, ascends the steps, and, taking
up the crown of Lombardy, places it on his head.

NAPOLÉON

'Tis God has given it to me.   So be it.
Let any who shall touch it now beware !

(Reverberations of applause.)

The Sacrament of the Mass.   NAPOLÉON reads the Coronation Oath in a loud voice.

HERALDS

Give ear !   Napoléon, Emperor of the French
And King of Italy, is crowned and throned !

CONGREGATION

Long live the Emperor and King.   Huzza !

Music.   The Te Deum.

SPIRIT OF THE PITIES

*That vulgar stroke of vauntery he displayed
In planting on his brow the Lombard crown,
Means sheer erasure of the Luneville pacts,
And lets confusion loose on Europe's peace
For many an undawned year !   From this rash hour
Austria but waits her opportunity
By secret swellings of her armaments
To link her to his foes.—I'll speak to him.*

He throws a whisper into NAPOLÉON's ear.

*Lieutenant Bonaparte,
Would it not seemlier be to shut thy heart
To these unhealthy splendours ?—helmet thee
For her thou swar'st-to first, fair Liberty ?*

NAPOLÉON

Who spoke to me ?

ARCHBISHOP

Not I, Sire.   Not a soul.

NAPOLÉON

Dear Joséphine, my queen, didst call my name ?

JOSÉPHINE

I spoke not, Sire.

NAPOLÉON

Thou didst not, tender spouse ;
I know it.   Such harsh utterance was not thine.
It was aggressive Fancy, working spells
Upon a mind o'erwrought !

The service closes. The clergy advance with the canopy to the foot of the throne, and the procession forms to return to the Palace.

SPIRIT OF THE YEARS

Officious sprite,
Thou art young, and dost not heed the Cause of things
Which some of us have inkled to thee here ;
Else wouldst thou not have hailed the Emperor,
Whose acts do but outshape Its governing.

SPIRIT OF THE PITIES

I feel, Sire, as I must !   This tale of Will
And Life's impulsion by Incognizance
I cannot take.

SPIRIT OF THE YEARS

Let me then once again
Show to thy sceptic eye the very streams
And currents of this all-inhering Power,
And bring conclusion to thy unbelief.

The scene assumes the preternatural transparency before mentioned, and there is again beheld as it were the interior

of a brain which seems to manifest the volitions of a Universal
Will, of whose tissues the personages of the action form portion.

SPIRIT OF THE PITIES

Enough.   And yet for very sorriness
I cannot own the weird phantasma real !

SPIRIT OF THE YEARS

Affection ever was illogical.

SPIRIT IRONIC (aside)

How should the Sprite own to such logic—a mere
juvenile—who only came into being in what the
earthlings call their Tertiary Age !

The scene changes. The exterior of the Cathedral takes the
place of the interior, and the point of view recedes, the whole
fabric smalling into distance and becoming like a rare, deli-
cately carved alabaster ornament. The city itself sinks to miniature, the Alps show afar as a white corrugation, the Adriatic
and the Gulf of Genoa appear on this and on that hand, with
Italy between them, till clouds cover the panorama.

ACT SECOND

SCENE I

THE DOCKYARD, GIBRALTAR

The Rock is seen rising behind the town and the Alameda Gardens, and the English fleet rides at anchor in the Bay, across which the Spanish shore from Algeciras to Carnero Point shuts in the West. Southward over the Strait is the African coast.

SPIRIT OF THE YEARS

Our migratory Proskenion now presents
An outlook on the storied Kalpe Rock,
As preface to the vision of the Fleets
Spanish and French, linked for fell purposings.

RECORDING ANGEL (reciting)

Their motions and manœuvres, since the fame
Of Bonaparte's enthronement at Milan
Swept swift through Europe's dumbed communities,
Have stretched the English mind to wide surmise.
Many well-based alarms (which strange report
Much aggravates) as to the pondered blow,
Flutter the public pulse ; all points in turn—
Malta, Brazil, Wales, Ireland, British Ind—
Being held as feasible for force like theirs,
Of lavish numbers and unrecking aim.

" *Where, where is Nelson?*" *questions every tongue;—*
" *How views he so unparalleled a scheme?*"
Their slow uncertain apprehensions ask.
" *When Villeneuve puts to sea with all his force,*
What may he not achieve, if swift his course?"

SPIRIT OF THE YEARS

I'll call in Nelson, who has stepped ashore
For the first time these thrice twelvemonths and more,
And with him one whose insight has alone
Pierced the real project of Napoléon.

Enter NELSON and COLLINGWOOD, who pace up and down.

SPIRIT OF THE PITIES

Note Nelson's worn-out features.   Much has he
Suffered from ghoulish ghast anxiety!

NELSON

In short, dear Coll, the letter which you wrote me
Had so much pith that I was fain to see you;
For I am sure that you indeed divine
The true intent and compass of a plot
Which I have spelled in vain.

COLLINGWOOD

              I weighed it thus :
Their flight to the Indies being to draw us off,
That and no more, and clear these coasts of us—
The standing obstacle to his device—
He cared not what was done at Martinique,
Or where, provided that the general end
Should not be jeopardized—that is to say,
The full-united squadron's quick return.—

Gravina and Vill'neuve, once back to Europe,
Can straight make Ferrol, raise there the blockade,
Then haste to Brest, there to relieve Ganteaume,
And next with four- or five-and-fifty sail
Bear down upon our coast as they see fit.—
I read they aim to strike at Ireland still,
As formerly, and as I wrote to you.

NELSON

So far your thoughtful and sagacious words
Have hit the facts.   But 'tis no Irish bay
The villains aim to drop their anchors in ;
My word for it : they make the Wessex shore,
And this vast squadron handled by Vill'neuve
Is meant to cloak the passage of their strength,
Massed in those transports—we being kept elsewhere
By feigning forces.—Good God, Collingwood,
I must be gone ! ᐧ Yet two more days remain
Ere I can get away.—I must be gone !

COLLINGWOOD

Wherever you may go to, my dear lord,
You carry victory with you.   Let them launch,
Your name will blow them back, as sou'-west gales
The gulls that beat against them from the shore.

NELSON

Good Collingwood, I know you trust in me ;
But ships are ships, and do not kindly come
Out of the slow docks of the Admiralty
Like wharfside pigeons when they are whistled for :—
And there's a damned disparity of force,
Which means tough work awhile for you and me !

The Spirit of the Years whispers to NELSON.

And I have warnings, warnings, Collingwood,
That my effective hours are shortening here ;
Strange warnings now and then, as 'twere within me,
Which, though I fear them not, I recognize ! . . .
However, by God's help, I'll live to meet
These foreign boasters ; yea, I'll finish them ;
And then—well, Gunner Death may finish me !

COLLINGWOOD

View not your life so gloomily, my lord :
One charmed, a needed purpose to fulfil !

NELSON

Ah, Coll.   Lead bullets are not all that wound. . . .
I have a feeling here of dying fires,
A sense of strong and deep unworded censure,
Which, compassing about my private life,
Makes all my public service lustreless
In my own eyes.—I fear I am much condemned
For those dear Naples and Palermo days,
And her who was the sunshine of them all ! . . .
He who is with himself dissatisfied,
Though all the world find satisfaction in him,
Is like a rainbow-coloured bird gone blind,
That gives delight it shares not.   Happiness ?
It's the philosopher's stone no alchemy
Shall light on in this world I am weary of.—
Smiling I'd pass to my long home to-morrow
Could I with honour, and my country's gain.
—But let's adjourn.   I waste your hours ashore
By such ill-timed confessions !

> They pass out of sight, and the scene closes.

SCENE II

OFF FERROL

The French and Spanish combined squadrons. On board the French admiral's flag-ship. VILLENEUVE is discovered in his cabin, writing a letter.

SPIRIT OF THE PITIES

He pens in fits, with pallid restlessness,
Like one who sees Misfortune walk the wave,
And can nor face nor flee it.

SPIRIT OF THE YEARS

> *He indites*
To his long friend the minister Decrès
Words that go heavily ! . . .

VILLENEUVE (writing)

" I am made the arbiter in vast designs
Whereof I see black outcomes. Do I this
Or do I that, success, that loves to jilt
Her anxious wooer for some careless blade,
Will not reward me. For, if I must pen it,
Demoralized past prayer is the marine—
Bad masts, bad sails, bad officers, bad men ;
We cling to naval technics long outworn,
And time and opportunity do not avail me
To take up new. I have long suspected such,
But till I saw my helps, the Spanish ships,
I hoped somewhat.—Brest is my nominal port ;
Yet if so, Calder will again attack—
Now reinforced by Nelson or Cornwallis—

And shatter my whole fleet. . . . Shall I admit
That my true inclination and desire
Is to make Cadiz straightway, and not Brest ?
Alas ! thereby I fail the Emperor ;
But shame the navy less.—
           Your friend, VILLENEUVE."

GENERAL LAURISTON enters.

LAURISTON

Admiral, my missive to the Emperor,
Which I shall speed by special courier
From Ferrol this near eve, runs thus and thus :—
" Gravina's ships, in Ferrol here at hand,
Embayed but by a temporary wind,
Are all we now await.   Combined with these
We sail herefrom to Brest ; there promptly give
Cornwallis battle, and release Ganteaume ;
Thence, all united, bearing Channelwards :—
A step that sets in motion the first wheel
In the proud project of your Majesty
Now to be engined to the very close,
To wit : that a French fleet shall enter in
And hold the Channel four-and-twenty hours."—
Such clear assurance to the Emperor
That our intent is modelled on his will
I hasten to dispatch to him forthwith.[1]

VILLENEUVE

Yes, Lauriston.   I sign to every word.

LAURISTON goes out.   VILLENEUVE remains at his table in reverie.

SPIRIT OF THE YEARS

*We may impress him under visible shapes
That seem to shed a silent circling doom ;*

---

[1] Through this tangle of intentions the writer has in the main followed Thiers, whose access to documents would seem to authenticate his details of the famous scheme for England's ruin.

He's such an one as can be so impressed,
And this much is among our privileges,
Well bounded as they be.

The Spirits of the Years and of the Pities take the form of white sea-birds, which alight on the stern-balcony of VILLE-NEUVE'S ship, immediately outside his cabin window. VILLE-NEUVE after a while looks up and sees the birds watching him with large piercing eyes.

VILLENEUVE

My apprehensions even outstep their cause,
As though some influence smote through yonder
　　pane.

He gazes listlessly at the birds, and resumes his broodings.

——Why dared I not disclose to him my thought,
As nightly worded by the whistling shrouds,
That Brest will never see our battled hulls
Helming to north in pomp of cannonry
To take the front in this red pilgrimage !
——If so it were, now, that I'd screen my skin
From risks of bloody business in the brunt,
My acts could scarcely wear a difference.
Yet I would die to-morrow—not ungladly—
So far removed is carcase-care from me.
For no self do these apprehensions spring,
But for the cause.—Yes, rotten is our marine,
Which, while I know, the Emperor knows not,
And the pale secret chills ! Though some there be
Would beard contingencies and buffet all,
I'll not command a course so conscienceless.
Rather I'll stand, and face Napoléon's rage
When he shall learn what mean the ambiguous lines
That facts have forced from me.

SPIRIT OF THE PITIES (to the Spirit of the Years)

O Eldest-born of the Unconscious Cause—
If such thou beest, as I can fancy thee—

Why dost thou rack him thus ?   Consistency
Might be preserved, and yet his doom remain.
His olden courage is without reproach ;
Albeit his temper trends toward gaingiving !

SPIRIT OF THE YEARS

I say, as I have said long heretofore,
I know but narrow freedom.   Feel'st thou not
We are in Its hand, as he ?—Here, as elsewhere,
We do but as we may ; no further dare.

The birds disappear, and the scene is lost behind sea-mist.

SCENE III

THE CAMP AND HARBOUR OF BOULOGNE

The English coast in the distance.   Near the Tour d'Ordre
stands a hut, with sentinels and aides outside ; it is NAPOLÉON'S
temporary lodging when not at his headquarters at the Château
of Pont-de-Briques, two miles inland.

DUMB SHOW

A courier arrives with dispatches, and enters the Emperor's
quarters, whence he emerges and goes on with other dispatches
to the hut of DECRÈS, lower down.   Immediately after
NAPOLÉON comes out from his hut with a paper in his hand,
and musingly proceeds towards an eminence commanding the
Channel.

Along the shore below are forming in a far-reaching line
more than a hundred thousand infantry.   On the downs in the
rear of the camps fifteen thousand cavalry are manœuvring,
their accoutrements flashing in the sun like a school of mackerel.
The flotilla lies in and around the port, alive with moving
figures.

With his head forward and his hands behind him the
Emperor surveys these animated proceedings in detail, but
more frequently turns his face towards the telegraph on the

cliff to the south-west, erected to signal when VILLENEUVE and the combined squadrons shall be visible on the west horizon.

He summons one of the aides, who descends to the hut of DECRÈS. DECRÈS comes out from his hut, and hastens to join the Emperor. Dumb show ends.

NAPOLÉON and DECRÈS advance to the foreground of the scene.

NAPOLÉON

Decrès, this wrestle with Sir Robert Calder
Three weeks aback, whereof we dimly heard,
And clear details of which I have just unsealed,
Is on the whole auspicious for our plan.
It seems that twenty of our ships and Spain's—
None over eighty-gunned, and some far less—
Leapt at the English off Cape Finisterre
With fifteen vessels of a hundred each.
We coolly fought and orderly as they,
And, but for mist, we had closed with victory.
Two English were much mauled, some Spanish scarred,
And Calder then drew off with his two wrecks
And Spain's in tow, we giving chase forthwith.
Not overtaking him, our admiral,
Having the coast clear for his purposes,
Entered Coruña, and found orders there
To open the port of Brest and come on hither.
Thus hastes the moment when the double fleet
Of Villeneuve and of Ganteaume should appear.

He looks again towards the telegraph.

DECRÈS (with hesitation)

And should they not appear, your Majesty ?

NAPOLÉON

Not ? But they will ; and do it early, too !
There's nothing hinders them. My God, they must,

For I have much before me when this stroke
At England's dealt.   I learn from Talleyrand
That Austrian preparations threaten hot,
While Russia's hostile schemes are ripening,
And shortly must be met.—My plan is fixed :
I am in trim for each alternative.
If Villeneuve come, I brave the British coast,
Convulse the land with fear ('tis even now
So far distraught, that generals cast about
To find new modes of warfare ; yea, design
Carriages to transport their infantry !).—
Once on the English soil I hold it firm,
Descend on London, and the while my men
Salute the dome of Paul's I cut the knot
Of all Pitt's coalitions ; setting free
From bondage to a cold manorial caste
A people who await it.

>   They stand and regard the chalky cliffs of England, till
> NAPOLÉON resumes :

                              Should it be
Even that my admirals fail to keep the tryst—
A thing scarce thinkable, when all's reviewed—
I strike this seaside camp, cross Germany,
With these two hundred thousand seasoned men,
And pause not till within Vienna's walls
I cry checkmate.   Next, Venice, too, being taken,
And Austria's other holdings down that way,
The Bourbons also driven from Italy,
I strike at Russia—each in turn, you note,
Ere they can act conjoined.

                    Report to me
What has been scanned to-day upon the main,
And on your passage down request them there
To send Daru this way.

DECRÈS (as he withdraws)

The Emperor can be sanguine.   Scarce can I.
His letters are more promising than mine.

Alas, alas, Villeneuve, my dear old friend,
Why do you pen me this at such a time !

[He retires reading VILLENEUVE's letter.

The Emperor walks up and down till DARU, his private
secretary, joins him.

NAPOLÉON

Come quick, Daru ; sit down upon the grass,
And write whilst I am in mind.
                              First to Villeneuve :—
" I trust, Vice-Admiral, that before this date
Your fleet has opened Brest, and gone.   If not,
These lines will greet you there.   But pause not,
        pray :
Waste not a moment dallying.   Sail away :
Once bring my coupled squadrons Channelwards
And England's soil is ours.   All's ready here,
The troops alert, and every store embarked.
Hold the nigh sea but four-and-twenty hours
And our vast end is gained."
                              Now to Ganteaume :—
" My telegraphs will have made known to you
My object and desire to be but this,
That you forbid Villeneuve to lose an hour
In getting fit and putting forth to sea,
To profit by the fifty first-rate craft
Wherewith I now am bettered.   Quickly weigh,
And steer you for the Channel with all your strength.
I count upon your well-known character,
Your enterprize, your vigour, to do this.
Sail hither, then ; and we will be avenged
For centuries of despite and contumely."

DARU

Shall a fair transcript, Sire, be made forthwith ?

NAPOLÉON

This moment.　And the courier will depart
And travel without pause.

DARU goes to his office a little lower down, and the Emperor
lingers on the cliffs looking through his glass.

The point of view shifts across the Channel, the Boulogne
cliffs sinking behind the water-line.

SCENE IV

SOUTH WESSEX.　A RIDGE-LIKE DOWN
NEAR THE COAST

The down commands a wide view over the English Channel
in front of it, including the popular Royal watering-place,
with the Isle of Slingers and its roadstead, where men-of-war
and frigates are anchored.　The hour is ten in the morning,
and the July sun glows upon a large military encampment
round about the foreground, and warms the stone field-walls
that take the place of hedges here.

Artillery, cavalry, and infantry, English and Hanoverian,
are drawn up for review under the DUKE OF CUMBERLAND
and officers of the staff, forming a vast military array, which
extends three miles, and as far as the downs are visible.

In the centre by the Royal Standard appears KING GEORGE
on horseback, and his suite.　In a coach drawn by six cream-
coloured Hanoverian horses QUEEN CHARLOTTE sits with three
Princesses ; in another carriage with four horses are two more
Princesses.　There are also present with the Royal Party the
LORD CHANCELLOR, LORD MULGRAVE, COUNT MÜNSTER, and
many other luminaries of fashion and influence.

The Review proceeds in dumb show; and the din of many
bands mingles with the cheers.　The turf behind the saluting-
point is crowded with carriages and spectators on foot.

A SPECTATOR

And you've come to see the sight, like the King
and myself ?　Well, one fool makes many.　What a

mampus o' folk it is here to-day ! And what a time
we do live in, between wars and wassailings, the
goblin o' Boney, and King George in flesh and
blood !

SECOND SPECTATOR

Yes. I wonder King George is let venture down
on this coast, where he might be snapped up in a
moment, like a minney by a her'n, so near as we be
to the field of Boney's vagaries ! Begad, he's as
like to land here as anywhere. Gloucester Lodge
could be surrounded, and George and Charlotte
carried off before he could put on his hat, or she her
red cloak and pattens !

THIRD SPECTATOR

'Twould be no such joke to kidnap 'em as you
think. Look at the frigates down there. Every
night they are drawn up in a line across the mouth of
the Bay, almost touching each other ; and ashore
a double line of sentinels, well primed with beer and
ammunition, one at the water's edge, and the other
on the Esplanade, stretch along the whole front.
Then close to the Lodge a guard is mounted after
eight o'clock ; there be pickets on all the hills ; at
the Harbour mouth is a battery of twenty four-
pounders ; and over-right 'em a dozen six-pounders,
and several howitzers. And next look at the size
of the camp of horse and foot up here.

FIRST SPECTATOR

Everybody however was fairly gallied this week
when the King went out yachting, meaning to be
back for the theatre ; and the time passed, and it
got dark, and the play couldn't begin, and eight or
nine o'clock came, and never a sign of him. I don't

know when 'a did land ; but 'twas said by all that
it was a foolhardy pleasure to take.

Fourth Spectator

He's a very obstinate and comical old gentleman ;
and by all account 'a wouldn't make port when
asked to.

Second Spectator

Lard, Lard, if 'a were nabbed, it wouldn't make
a deal of difference ! We should have nobody to
zing to, and play singlestick to, and grin at through
horse-collars, that's true. And nobody to sign our
few documents. But we should rub along some
way, goodnow.

First Spectator

Step up on this barrow ; you can see better. The
troopers now passing are the York Hussars—
foreigners to a man, except the officers—the same
regiment the two young Germans belonged to who
were shot here four years ago. Now come the Light
Dragoons ; what a time they take to get all past !
See, the King turns to speak to one of his notables.
Well, well ! this day will be recorded in history.

Second Spectator

Or another soon to follow it ! (He gazes over the
Channel.) There's not a speck of an enemy upon
that shiny water yet ; but the Brest fleet is zaid to
have put to sea, to act in concert with the army
crossing from Boulogne ; and if so the French will
soon be here ; when God save us all ! I've took to
drinking neat, for, says I, one may as well have his
innerds burnt out as shot out, and 'tis a good deal
pleasanter for the man that owns 'em. They say
that a cannon-ball knocked poor Jim Popple's maw

right up into the futtock-shrouds at the Nile, where
'a hung like a nightcap out to dry. Much good to
him his obeying his old mother's wish and refusing
his allowance o' rum !

The bands play and the Review continues till past eleven
o'clock. Then follows a sham fight. At noon precisely the
royal carriages draw off the ground into the highway that leads
down to the town and Gloucester Lodge, followed by other
equipages in such numbers that the road is blocked. A multitude comes after on foot. Presently the vehicles manage to
proceed to the watering-place, and the troops march away to
the various camps as a sea-mist cloaks the perspective.

SCENE V

THE SAME.   RAINBARROWS' BEACON, EGDON HEATH

Night in mid-August of the same summer. A lofty ridge of
heathland reveals itself dimly, terminating in an abrupt slope,
at the summit of which are three tumuli. On the sheltered
side of the most prominent of these stands a hut of turves
with a brick chimney. In front are two ricks of fuel, one of
heather and furze for quick ignition, the other of wood, for
slow burning. Something in the feel of the darkness and in
the personality of the spot imparts a sense of uninterrupted
space around, the view by day extending from the cliffs of the
Isle of Wight eastward to Blackdon Hill by Deadman's Bay
westward, and south across the Valley of the Froom to the
ridge that screens the Channel.

An old and a young man with pikes loom up, on duty as
beacon-keepers beside the ricks.

OLD MAN

Now, Jems Purchess, once more mark my words.
Black'on is the point we've to watch, and not
Kingsbere ; and I'll tell 'ee for why. If he do land
anywhere hereabout 'twill be inside Deadman's
Bay, and the signal will straightway come from

Black'on. But there thou'st stand, glowering and staring with all thy eyes at Kingsbere! I tell 'ee what 'tis, Jems Purchess, your brain is softening; and you be getting too daft for business of state like ours!

Young Man

You've let your tongue wrack your few rames of good breeding, John.

Old Man

The words of my Lord-Lieutenant was, whenever you see Kingsbere-Hill Beacon fired to the eastward, or Black'on to the westward, light up; and keep your second fire burning for two hours. Was that our documents or was it not?

Young Man

I don't gainsay it. And so I keep my eye on Kingsbere, because that's most likely o' the two, says I.

Old Man

That shows the curious depths of your ignorance. However, I'll have patience, and say on. Didst ever larn geography?

Young Man

No. Nor no other corrupt practices.

Old Man

Tcht-tcht!—Well, I'll have patience, and put it to him in another form. Dost know the world is round—eh? I warrant dostn't.

Young Man

I warrant I do !

Old Man

How d'ye make that out, when th'st never been to school ?

Young Man

I larned it at church, thank God.

Old Man

Church ? What have God A'mighty got to do with profane knowledge ? Beware that you baint blaspheming, Jems Purchess !

Young Man

I say I did, whether or no ! 'Twas the zingers up in gallery that I had it from. They busted out that strong with " the round world and they that dwell therein," that we common folks down under could do no less than believe 'em.

Old Man

Canst be sharp enough in the wrong place as usual—I warrant canst ! However, I'll have patience with 'en, and say on !—Suppose, now, my hat is the world ; and there, as might be, stands the Camp of Belong, where Boney is. The world goes round, so, and Belong goes round too. Twelve hours pass ; round goes the world still—so. Where's Belong now ?

A pause. Two other figures, a man's and a woman's, rise against the sky out of the gloom.

OLD MAN (shouldering his pike)

Who goes there ? Friend or foe, in the King's
name !

WOMAN

Piece o' trumpery ! " Who goes " yourself !
What d'ye talk o', John Whiting ! Can't your eyes
earn their living any longer, then, that you don't
know your own neighbours ? 'Tis Private Cantle
of the Locals and his wife Keziar, down at Bloom's-
End—who else should it be !

OLD MAN (lowering his pike)

A form o' words, Mis'ess Cantle, no more ;
ordained by his Majesty's Gover'ment to be spoke
by all we on sworn duty for the defence o' the
country. Strict rank-and-file rules is our only horn
of salvation in these times.—But, my dear woman,
why ever have ye come lumpering up to Rainbarrows
at this time o' night ?

WOMAN

We've been troubled with bad dreams, owing to
the firing out at sea yesterday ; and at last I could
sleep no more, feeling sure that sommat boded of
His coming. And I said to Cantle, I'll ray myself,
and go up to Beacon, and ask if anything have been
heard or seen to-night. And here we be.

OLD MAN

Not a sign or sound—all's as still as a churchyard. And how is your good man ?

PRIVATE (advancing)

Clk ! I be all right ! I was in the ranks, helping
to keep the ground at the review by the King this

week. We was a wonderful sight—wonderful!
The King said so again and again.—Yes, there was
he, and there was I, though not daring to move a'
eyebrow in the presence of Majesty. I have come
home on a night's leave—off there again to-morrow.
Boney's expected every day, the Lord be praised!
Yes, our hopes are to be fulfilled soon, as we say in
the army.

OLD MAN

There, there, Cantle; don't ye speak quite so
large, and stand so over-upright. Your back is as
holler as a fire-dog's. Do ye suppose that we on
active service here don't know war news? Mind
you don't go taking to your heels when the next
alarm comes, as you did at last year's.

PRIVATE

That had nothing to do with fighting, for I'm as
bold as a lion when I'm up, and " Shoulder Fawlocks! " sounds as common as my own name to me.
'Twas—— (Lowering his voice.) Have ye heard?

OLD MAN

To be sure we have.

PRIVATE

Ghastly, isn't it!

OLD MAN

Ghastly! Frightful!

YOUNG MAN (to Private)

He don't know what it is! That's his pride and
puffery. What is it that's so ghastly—hey?

PRIVATE

Well, there, I can't tell it. 'Twas that that made the whole eighty of our company run away—though we be the bravest of the brave in natural jeopardies, or the little boys wouldn't run after us and call us the " Bang-up-Locals."

WOMAN (in undertones)

I can tell you a word or two on't. It is about His victuals. They say that He lives upon human flesh, and has rashers o' baby every morning for breakfast—for all the world like the Cernel Giant in old ancient times !

YOUNG MAN

Ye can't believe all ye hear.

PRIVATE

I only believe half. And I only own—such is my challengeful character—that perhaps He do eat pagan infants when He's in the desert. But not Christian ones at home. O no—'tis too much.

WOMAN

Whether or no, I sometimes—-God forgie me !— laugh wi' horror at the queerness o't, till I am that weak I can hardly go round house. He should have the washing of 'em a few times ; I warrant 'a wouldn't want to eat babies any more !

A silence, during which they gaze around at the dark dome of starless sky.

YOUNG MAN

There'll be a change in the weather soon, by the look o't. I can hear the cows moo in Froom Valley

as if I were close to 'em, and the lantern at Max
Turnpike is shining quite plain.

Old Man

Well, come in and taste a drop o' sommat we've
got here, that will warm the cockles of your heart as
ye wamble homealong. We housed eighty tubs last
night for them that shan't be named—landed at
Lullwind Cove the night afore, though they had a
narrow shave with the riding-officers this run.

They make towards the hut, when a light on the west
horizon becomes visible, and quickly enlarges.

Young Man

He's come !

Old Man

Come he is, though 'tis you that say it ! This,
then, is the beginning of what England's waited for !

They stand and watch the light awhile.

Young Man

Just what you was praising the Lord for by-now,
Private Cantle.

Private

My meaning was——

Woman (simpering)

O that I hadn't married a fiery sojer, to make me
bring fatherless children into the world, all through
his dreadful calling ! Why didn't a man of no
sprawl content me !

OLD MAN (shouldering his pike)

We can't heed your innocent pratings any longer, good neighbours, being in the King's service, and a hot invasion on. Fall in, fall in, mate. Straight to the tinder-box. Quick march !

The two men hasten to the hut, and are heard striking a flint and steel. Returning with a lit lantern they ignite a wisp of furze, and with this set the first stack of fuel in a blaze. The private of the Locals and his wife hastily retreat by the light of the flaming beacon, under which the purple rotundities of the heath show like bronze, and the pits like the eye-sockets of a skull.

SPIRIT SINISTER

This is good, and spells blood. (To the Chorus of the Years.) *I assume that It means to let us carry out this invasion with pleasing slaughter, so as not to disappoint my hope ?*

SEMICHORUS I OF THE YEARS (aerial music)

We carry out ? Nay, but should we
Ordain what bloodshed is to be !

SEMICHORUS II

The Immanent, that urgeth all,
Rules what may or may not befall !

SEMICHORUS I

Ere systemed suns were globed and lit
The slaughters of the race were writ,

SEMICHORUS II

And wasting wars, by land and sea,
Fixed, like all else, immutably !

Spirit Sinister

Well ; be it so. My argument is that War makes rattling good history ; but Peace is poor reading. So I back Bonaparte for the reason that he will give pleasure to posterity.

Spirit of the Pities

Gross hypocrite !

Chorus of the Years

We comprehend him not.

The day breaks over the heathery upland, on which the beacon is still burning. The morning reveals the white surface of a highway which, coming from the royal watering-place beyond the hills, stretches towards the outskirts of the heath and passes away eastward.

DUMB SHOW

Moving figures and vehicles dot the surface of the road, all progressing in one direction, away from the coast. In the foreground the shapes appear as those of civilians, mostly on foot, but many in gigs and tradesmen's carts and on horseback. When they reach an intermediate hill some pause and look back ; others enter on the next decline landwards without turning their heads.

From the opposite horizon numerous companies of volunteers, in the local uniform of red with green facings,[1] are moving coastwards in companies ; as are also irregular bodies of pikemen without uniform ; while on the upper slopes of the downs towards the shore regiments of the line are visible, with cavalry and artillery ; all passing over to the coast.

At a signal from the Chief Intelligences two Phantoms of Rumour enter on the highway in the garb of country-men.

---

[1] These historic facings, which, I believe, won for the local (old 39th) regiment the nickname of " Green Linnets," have been changed for no apparent reason. (They are now restored.—1909.)

FIRST PHANTOM (to Pedestrians)

Whither so fast, good neighbours, and before break-
fast, too ?   Empty bellies be bad to vamp on.

FIRST PEDESTRIAN

(laden with a pack, and speaking breathlessly)

He's landed west'ard, out by Abbot's Beach.
And if you have property you'll save it and yourselves, as we are doing !

SECOND PEDESTRIAN

All yesterday the firing at Boulogne
Was like the seven thunders heard in Heaven
When the fierce angel spoke.   So did he draw
Men's eyes that way, the while his thousand boats
Full-manned, flat-bottomed for the shallowest shore,
Dropped down to west, and crossed our frontage
    here.
Seen from above they specked the water-shine
As will a flight of swallows towards dim eve,
Descending on a smooth and loitering stream
To seek some eyot's sedge.

SECOND PHANTOM

We are sent to enlighten you and ease your souls.
Even now a courier canters to the port
To check the baseless scare.

FIRST PEDESTRIAN (to Second Pedestrian)

These be inland men who, I warrant 'ee, don't
know a lerret from a lighter !   Let's take no heed of
such, comrade ; and hurry on !

First Phantom

Will you not hear
That what was seen behind the midnight mist,
Their oar-blades tossing twinkles to the moon,
Was but a fleet of fishing-craft belated
By reason of the vastness of their haul?

First Pedestrian

Hey? And d'ye know it?—Now I look back to
the top o' Rudgeway the folk do seem as come to a
pause there.—Be this true, never again do I stir my
stumps for any alarm short of the Day of Judgment!
Nine times has my rheumatical rest been broke in
these last three years by hues and cries of Boney
upon us. 'Od rot the feller; now he's made a fool
of me once more, till my inside is like a wash-tub,
what wi' being so gallied, and running so leery!—
But how if you be one of the enemy, sent to sow these
tares, so to speak it, these false tidings, and coax us
into a fancied safety? Hey, neighbours? I don't,
after all, care for this story!

Second Pedestrian

Onwards again!
If Boney's come, 'tis best to be away;
And if he's not, why, we've a holiday!

[Exeunt Pedestrians.

The Spirits of Rumour vanish, while the scene seems to
become involved in the smoke from the beacon, and slowly
disappears.[1]

---

[1] The remains of the lonely hut occupied by the beacon-keepers, consisting of some half-buried brickbats, and a little mound of peat over-
grown with moss, are still visible on the elevated spot referred to. The
two keepers themselves, and their eccentricities and sayings, are tradi-
tionary.

ACT THIRD

SCENE I

BOULOGNE. THE CHÂTEAU AT PONT-DE-BRIQUES

A room in the Château, which is used as the Imperial quarters. The EMPEROR NAPOLÉON, and M. GASPARD MONGE, the mathematician and philosopher, are seated at breakfast.

Enter the officer in attendance.

OFFICER

Monsieur the Admiral Decrès awaits
A moment's audience with your Majesty,
Or now, or later.

NAPOLÉON

       Bid him in at once—
At last Villeneuve has raised the Brest blockade !

Enter DECRÈS.

What of the squadrons' movements, good Decrès ?
Brest opened, and all sailing Channelwards,
Like swans into a creek at feeding-time ?

DECRÈS

Such news was what I'd hoped, your Majesty,
To send across this daybreak.   But events

91

Have proved intractable, it seems, of late ;
And hence I haste in person to report
The featless facts that just have dashed my——

NAPOLÉON (darkening)

Well ?

DECRÈS

Sire, at the very juncture when the fleets
Sailed out from Ferrol, fever raged aboard
" L'Achille " and " l'Algeciras " : later on,
Mischief assailed our Spanish comrades' ships ;
Several ran foul of neighbours ; whose new hurts,
Being added to their innate clumsiness,
Gave hap the upper hand ; and in quick course
Demoralized the whole ; until Villeneuve,
Judging that Calder now with Nelson rode,
And prescient of unparalleled disaster
If he pushed on in so disjoint a trim,
Bowed to the inevitable ; and thus, perforce,
Leaving to other opportunity
Brest and the Channel scheme, with vast regret
Steered southward into Cadiz.

NAPOLÉON (having risen from the table)

What !—Is, then,
My scheme of years to be disdained and dashed
By this man's like, a wretched moral coward,
Whom you must needs foist on me as one fit
For full command in pregnant enterprise !

MONGE (aside)

I'm one too many here ! Let me step out
Till this black squall blows over. Poor Decrès.
Would that this precious project, disinterred

From naval archives of King Louis' reign,
Had ever lingered fusting where 'twas found ! [1]

[Exit MONGE.

NAPOLÉON

To help a friend you foul a country's fame !—
Decrès, not only chose you this Villeneuve,
But you have nourished secret sour opinions
Akin to his, and thereby helped to scathe
As stably based a project as this age
Has sunned to ripeness.   Ever the French marine
Have you decried, ever contrived to bring
Despair into the fleet !   Why, this Villeneuve,
Your man, this rank incompetent, this traitor—
Of whom I asked no more than fight and lose,
Provided he detained the enemy—
A frigate is too great for his command !
What shall be said of one who, at a breath,
When a few casual sailors find them sick,
When falls a broken boom or slitten sail,
When rumour hints that Calder's tubs and Nelson's
May join, and bob about in company,
Is straightway paralyzed, and doubles back
On all his ripened plans !—
Bring him, ay, bodily ; hale him out from Cadiz,
Compel him up the Channel by main force,
And, having doffed him his supreme command,
Give the united squadrons to Ganteaume !

DECRÈS

Your Majesty, while umbraged, righteously,
By an event my tongue dragged dry to tell,
Makes my hard situation over-hard
By your ascription to the actors in't

---

[1] " Le projet existe encore aux archives de la marine que Napoléon
consultait incessamment : il sentait que cette marine depuis Louis **XIV.**
avait fait de grandes choses : le plan de l'Expédition d'Egypte et de la
descente en Angleterre se trouvaient au ministère de la marine."—CAPE-
FIGUE : *L'Europe pendant le Consulat et l'Empire.*

Of motives such and such.   'Tis not for me
To answer these reproaches, Sire, and ask
Why years-long mindfulness of France's fame
In things marine should win no confidence.
I speak ; but am unable to convince !
　　True is it that this man has been my friend
Since boyhood made us schoolmates ; and I say
That he would yield the heel-drops of his heart
With joyful readiness this day, this hour,
To do his country service.   Yet no less
Is it his drawback that he sees too far.
And there are times, Sire, when a shorter sight
Charms Fortune more.   A certain sort of bravery
Some people have—to wit, this same Lord Nelson—
Which is but fatuous faith in their own star,
Swoln to the very verge of childishness,
(Smugly disguised as putting trust in God,
A habit with these English folk) ; whereby
A headstrong blindness to contingencies
Carries the actor on, and serves him well
In some nice issues clearer sight would mar.
Such eyeless bravery Villeneuve has not ;
But, Sire, he is no coward.

NAPOLÉON

Well, have it so !—What are we going to do ?
My brain has only one wish—to succeed !

DECRÈS

My   voice   wanes   weaker   with   you,   Sire ;   is
　　nought !
Yet these few words, as Minister of Marine,
I'll venture now.—My process would be thus :—
Our projects for a junction of the fleets
Being well-discerned and read by every eye
Through long postponement, England is prepared.

I would recast them.   Later in the year
Form sundry squadrons of this massive one,
Harass the English till the winter time,
Then rendezvous at Cadiz ;   where leave half
To catch the enemy's eye and call their cruizers,
While, rounding Scotland with the other half,
You make the Channel by the eastern strait,
Cover the passage of our army-boats,
And plant the blow.

NAPOLÉON

        And what if they perceive
Our Scottish route, and meet us eastwardly ?

DECRÈS

I have thought of it, and planned a countermove ;
I'll write the scheme more clearly and at length,
And send it hither to your Majesty.

NAPOLÉON

Do so forthwith ;   and send me in Daru.

        Exit DECRÈS.   Re-enter MONGE.

Our breakfast, Monge, to-day has been cut short,
And those discussions on the ancient tongues
Wherein you shine, must yield to modern moils.
Nay, hasten not away ;   though feeble wills,
Incompetence, ay, imbecility,
In some who feign to serve the cause of France,
Do make me other than myself just now !—
Ah—here's Daru.

        DARU enters.   MONGE takes his leave.

Daru, sit down and write.   Yes, here, at once,
This room will serve me now.   What think you, eh ?
Villeneuve has just turned tail and run to Cadiz,
So quite postponed—perhaps even overthrown—

My long-conned project against yonder shore
As 'twere a juvenile's snow-built device
But made for melting ! Think of it, Daru,—
My God, my God, how can I talk thereon !
A plan well judged, well charted, well upreared,
To end in nothing ! . . . Sit you down and write.

NAPOLÉON walks up and down, and resumes after a silence :

Write this. — A volte-face 'tis, indeed ! — Write,
    write !

DARU (holding pen to paper)

I wait, your Majesty.

NAPOLÉON

          First Bernadotte—
Yes ; " Bernadotte moves out from Hanover
Through Hesse upon Würzburg and the Danube.—
Marmont from Holland bears along the Rhine,
And joins at Mainz and Würzburg Bernadotte . . .
    While these prepare their routes the army here
Will turn its rump on Britain's tedious shore,
And, closing up with Augereau at Brest,
Set out full force due eastward. . . .
By the Black Forest feign a straight attack,
The while our purpose is to skirt its left,
Meet in Franconia Bernadotte and Marmont ;
Traverse the Danube somewhat down from Ulm ;
Entrap the Austrian columns by their rear ;
Surround them, cleave them ; roll upon Vienna,
Where, Austria settled, I engage the Tsar,
While Masséna detains in Italy
The Archduke Charles.
             " Foreseeing such might shape,
Each high- and by-way to the Danube hence
I have of late had measured, mapped, and judged ;
Such spots as suit for depôts chosen and marked ;
Each regiment's daily pace and bivouac

Writ tablewise for ready reference ;
All which itineraries are sent herewith."
   So shall I crush the two gigantic sets
Upon the Empire, now grown imminent.
—Let me reflect.—First Bernadotte——But nay,
The courier to Marmont must go first.
Well, well.—The order of our march from hence
I will advise. . . . My knock at George's door
With bland inquiries why his royal hand
Withheld due answer to my friendly lines,
And tossed the irksome business to his clerks,
Is thus perforce delayed.   But not for long.
Instead of crossing, thitherward I tour
By roundabout contrivance not less sure !

                    DARU

I'll bring the writing to your Majesty.

           NAPOLÉON and DARU go out severally.

       CHORUS OF THE YEARS (aerial music)
          Recording Angel, trace
This bold campaign his thought has spun apace—
One that bids fair for immortality
Among the earthlings—if immortal deeds
May be ascribed to oafs so temporary—
          So transient a race !
It will be called, in rhetoric and rhyme,
          As son to sire succeeds,
A model for the tactics of all time ;
" The great Campaign of that so famed year Five,"
By millions of mankind not yet alive.

SCENE II

THE FRONTIERS OF UPPER AUSTRIA AND BAVARIA

A view of the country from mid-air, at a point south of the
River Inn, which is seen as a silver thread, winding northward
between its junction with the Salza and the Danube, and
forming the boundaries of the two countries. The Danube
shows itself as a crinkled satin riband, stretching from left to
right in the far background of the picture, the Inn discharging
its waters into the larger river.

DUMB SHOW

A vast Austrian army creeps dully along the mid-distance,
in the form of detached masses and columns of a whitish
cast. The columns insensibly draw nearer to each other, and
are seen to be converging from the east upon the banks of the
Inn aforesaid.

A RECORDING ANGEL (in recitative)

This movement as of molluscs on a leaf,
Which from our vantage here we scan afar,
Is one manœuvred by the famous Mack
To countercheck Napoléon, still believed
To be intent on England from Boulogne,
And heedless of such rallies in his rear.
Mack's enterprise is now to cross Bavaria—
Beneath us stretched in ripening summer peace
As field unwonted for these ugly jars—
And seize on Ulm, past Swabia leftward there.
  Outraged Bavaria, simmering in disquiet
At Munich down behind us, Isar-fringed,
And torn between his fair wife's hate of France
And his own itch to gird at Austrian bluff
For riding roughshod through his territory,

Wavers from this to that.   The while Time hastes
The eastward streaming of Napoléon's host,
As soon we see.

The silent insect-creep of the Austrian columns towards the banks of the Inn continues to be seen till the view fades to nebulousness and dissolves.

SCENE III

BOULOGNE.   THE ST. OMER ROAD

It is a morning at the end of August, and the pale road stretches out of the town eastward.

The divisions of the " Army-for-England " are making preparations to march.   Some portions are in marching order. Bands strike up, and the regiments start on their journey towards the Rhine and Danube.   Bonaparte and his officers watch the movements from an eminence.   The soldiers, as they pace along under their eagles with beaming eyes, sing " Le Chant du Départ," and other martial songs, shout " Vive l'Empereur ! " and babble of repeating the days of Italy, Egypt, Marengo, and Hohenlinden.

NAPOLÉON

Anon to England !

CHORUS OF INTELLIGENCES (aerial music)

If Time's weird threads so weave !

The scene as it lingers exhibits the gradual diminishing of the troops along the roads through the undulating August landscape, till each column is seen but as a train of dust; and the disappearance of each marching mass over the eastern horizon.

ACT FOURTH

SCENE I

KING GEORGE'S WATERING-PLACE, SOUTH WESSEX

A sunny day in autumn. A room in the red-brick royal residence known as Gloucester Lodge.[1]

At a front triple-lighted window stands a telescope on a tripod. Through the open middle sash is visible the crescent-curved expanse of the Bay as a sheet of brilliant translucent green, on which ride vessels of war at anchor. On the left hand white cliffs stretch away till they terminate in St. Aldhelm's Head, and form a background to the level water-line on that side. In the centre are the open sea and blue sky. A near headland rises on the right, surmounted by a battery, over which appears the remoter bald grey brow of the Isle of Slingers.

In the foreground yellow sands spread smoothly, whereon there are sundry temporary erections for athletic sports; and closer at hand runs an esplanade on which a fashionable crowd is promenading. Immediately outside the Lodge are companies of soldiers, groups of officers, and sentries.

Within the room the KING and PITT are discovered. The KING's eyes show traces of recent inflammation, and the Minister has a wasted look.

KING

Yes, yes; I grasp your reasons, Mr. Pitt,
And grant you audience gladly. More than that,
Your visit to this shore is apt and timely,
And if it do but yield you needful rest
From fierce debate, and other strains of office

---

[1] This weather-beaten old building, though now an hotel, is but little altered.

100

Which you and I in common have to bear,
'Twill be well earned.   The bathing is unmatched
Elsewhere in Europe,—see its mark on me !—
The air like liquid life.—But of this matter :
What argue these late movements seen abroad ?
What of the country now the session's past ;
What of the country, eh ? and of the war ?

PITT

The thoughts I have laid before your Majesty
Would make for this, in sum :—
That Mr. Fox, Lord Grenville, and their friends,
Be straightway asked to join.   With Melville gone,
With Sidmouth, and with Buckinghamshire too,
The steerage of affairs has stood of late
Somewhat provisional, as you, sir, know,
With stop-gap functions thrust on offices
Which common weal can tolerate but awhile.
So, for the weighty reasons I have urged,
I do repeat my most respectful hope
To win your Majesty's ungrudged assent
To what I have proposed.

KING

                      But nothing, sure,
Has been more plain to all, dear Mr. Pitt,
Than that your own proved energy and scope
Is ample, without aid, to carry on
Our just crusade against this Corsican.
Why, then, go calling Fox and Grenville in ?
Such helps we need not.   Pray you think upon't,
And speak to me again.—We'd lately news
Making us skip like crackers at our heels,
That Bonaparte had landed close hereby.

PITT

Such rumours come as regularly as harvest.

KING

And now he has left Boulogne with all his host ?
Was it his object to invade at all,
Or was his vast assemblage there a blind ?

PITT

Undoubtedly he meant invasion, sir,
Had fortune favoured.   He may try it yet.
And, as I said, could we but close with Fox——

KING

But, but ;—I ask, what is his object now ?
Lord Nelson's Captain—Hardy—whose old home
Stands in a peaceful vale hard by us here—
Who came two weeks ago to see his friends,
I talked to in this room a lengthy while.
He says our navy still is in thick night
As to the aims by sea of Bonaparte
Now the Boulogne attempt has fizzled out,
And what he schemes afloat with Spain combined.
The " Victory " lay that fortnight at Spithead,
And Nelson since has gone aboard and sailed ;
Yes, sailed again.   The " Royal Sovereign " follows,
And others her.   Nelson was hailed and cheered
To huskiness while leaving Southsea shore,
Gentle and simple wildly thronging round.

PITT

Ay, sir.   Young women hung upon his arm,
And old ones blessed, and stroked him with their
      hands.

KING

Ah—you have heard, of course.   God speed him,
      Pitt.

PITT

Amen, amen !

KING

I read it as a thing
Of signal augury, and one which bodes
Heaven's confidence in me and in my line,
That I should rule as King in such an age ! . . .
Well, well.—So this new march of Bonaparte's
Was unexpected, forced perchance on him ?

PITT

It may be so, your Majesty ; it may. . . .
Last noon the Austrian ambassador,
Whom I consulted ere I posted down,
Assured me that his latest papers word
How General Mack and eighty thousand men
Have made good speed across Bavaria
To wait the French and give them check at Ulm,
That fortress-frontier-town, entrenched and walled,
A place long chosen as a vantage-point
Whereon to encounter them as they outwind
From the blind shades and baffling green defiles
Of the Black Forest, worn with wayfaring.
Here Mack will intercept his agile foe
Hasting to meet the Russians in Bohemia,
And cripple him, if not annihilate.
    Thus now, sir, opens out this Great Alliance
Of Russia, Austria, England, whereto I
Have lent my earnest efforts through long months,
And the realm gives her money, ships, and men.—
It claps a muffler round this Cock's steel spurs,
And leaves me sanguine on his overthrow.
But then,—this coalition of resources
Demands a strong and active Cabinet
To aid your Majesty's directive hand ;
And thus I urge again the said additions—
These brilliant intellects of the other side
Who stand by Fox.   With us conjoined, they——

KING

What, what, again—in face of my sound reasons !
Believe me, Pitt, you underrate yourself ;
You do not need such aid.   The splendid feat
Of banding Europe in a righteous cause
That you have achieved, so soon to put to shame
This wicked bombardier of dynasties
That rule by right Divine, goes straight to prove
We had best continue as we have begun,
And call no partners to our management.
To fear dilemmas horning up ahead
Is not your wont.   Nay, nay, now, Mr. Pitt,
I must be firm.   And if you love your King
You'll goad him not so rashly to embrace
This Fox-and-Grenville faction and its friends.
Rather than Fox, why, give me civil war !
Hey, what ?   But what besides ?

PITT

I say besides, sir, . . . nothing !

A silence.

KING (cheerfully)

The Chancellor's here, and many friends of
mine : Lady Winchelsea, Lord and Lady Chester-
field, Lady Bulkeley, General Garth, and Mr.
Phipps the oculist — not the least important to
me.   He is a worthy and a skilful man.   My eyes,
he says, are as marvellously improved in durability
as I know them to be in power.   I have arranged
to go to-morrow with the Princesses, and the
Dukes of Cumberland, Sussex, and Cambridge
(who are also here) for a ride on the Ridgeway, and
through the Camp on the downs.   You'll accompany us there ?

PITT

I am honoured by your Majesty's commands.

PITT *looks resignedly out of the window.*

What curious structure do I see outside, sir ?

KING

It's but a stage, a type of all the world.   The
burgesses have arranged it in my honour.   At six
o'clock this evening there are to be combats at
single-stick to amuse the folk ;   four guineas the
prize for the man who breaks most heads.   Afterwards there is to be a grinning match through horse-
collars—a very humorous sport which I must stay
here and witness ;   for I am interested in whatever
entertains my subjects.

PITT

Not one in all the land but knows it, sir.

KING

Now, Mr. Pitt, you must require repose ;
Consult your own convenience then, I beg,
On when you leave.

PITT

I thank your Majesty.

*He departs as one whose purpose has failed ;   and the scene
shuts.*

SCENE II

BEFORE THE CITY OF ULM

A prospect of the city from the east, showing in the fore-ground a low-lying marshy country bounded in mid-distance by the banks of the Danube, which, bordered by poplars and willows, flows across the picture from the left to the Elchingen Bridge near the right of the scene, and is backed by irregular heights and terraces of espaliered vines. Between these and the river stands the city, crowded with old gabled houses and surrounded by walls, bastions, and a ditch, all the edifices being dominated by the nave and tower of the huge Gothic Münster.

On the most prominent of the heights at the back—the Michaelsberg—to the upper-right of the view, is encamped the mass of the Austrian army, amid half-finished entrenchments. Advanced posts of the same are seen south-east of the city, not far from the advanced corps of the French Grand-Army under SOULT, MARMONT, MURAT, LANNES, NEY, and DUPONT, which occupy in a semicircle the whole breadth of the flat landscape in front, and extend across the river to higher ground on the right hand of the panorama.

Heavy mixed drifts of rain and snow are descending im-partially on the French and on the Austrians, the downfall nearly blotting out the latter on the hills. A chill October wind wails across the country, and the poplars yield slantingly to the gusts.

DUMB SHOW

Drenched peasants are busily at work, fortifying the heights of the Austrian position in the face of the enemy. Vague companies of Austrians above, and of the French below, hazy and indistinct in the thick atmosphere, come and go without apparent purpose near their respective lines.

Closer to the spectator NAPOLÉON, in his familiar blue-grey overcoat, rides hither and thither with his marshals, haranguing familiarly the bodies of soldiery as he passes them, and observ-ing and pointing out the disposition of the Austrians to his companions.

Thicker sheets of rain fly across as the murk of evening increases, which at length entirely obscures the prospect, and cloaks its bleared lights and fires.

SCENE III

ULM. WITHIN THE CITY

The interior of the Austrian headquarters on the following morning. A tempest raging without.

GENERAL MACK, haggard and anxious, the ARCHDUKE FERDINAND, PRINCE SCHWARZENBERG, GENERAL JELLACHICH, GENERALS RIESC, BIBERACH, and other field officers discovered, seated at a table with a map spread out before them. A wood fire blazes between tall andirons in a yawning fireplace. At every more than usually boisterous gust of wind the smoke flaps into the room.

MACK

The accursèd cunning of our adversary
Confounds all codes of honourable war,
Which ever have held as granted that the track
Of armies bearing hither from the Rhine—
Whether in peace or strenuous invasion—
Should pierce the Schwarzwald, and through Mem-
    mingen,
And meet us in our front. But he must wind
And corkscrew meanly round, where foot of man
Can scarce find pathway, stealing up to us
Thiefwise, by our back door ! Nevertheless,
If English war-fleets be abreast Boulogne,
As these deserters tell, and ripe to land there,
It destines Bonaparte to pack him back
Across the Rhine again. We've but to wait,
And see him go.

ARCHDUKE

But who shall say if these bright tales be true ?

Mack

Even then, small matter, your Imperial Highness ;
The Russians near us daily, and must soon—
Ay, far within the eight days I have named—
Be operating to untie this knot,
If we hold on.

Archduke

　　　　　　Conjectures these—no more ;
I stomach not such waiting.　Neither hope
Has kernel in it.　I and my cavalry
With caution, when the shadows fall to-night,
Can bore some hole in this engirdlement ;
Outpass the gate north-east ; join General Werneck,
And somehow cut our way Bohemia-wards :
Well worth the hazard, in our straitened case !

Mack (firmly)

The body of our force stays here with me.
And I am much surprised, your Highness, much,
You mark not how destructive 'tis to part !
If we wait on, for certain we should wait
In our full strength, compacted, undispersed
By such partition as your Highness plans.

Schwarzenberg

There's truth in urging we should not divide,
But weld more closely.—Yet why stay at all ?
Methinks there's but one sure salvation left,
To wit, that we conjunctly march herefrom,
And with much circumspection, towards the Tyrol.
The subtle often rack their wits in vain—
Assay whole magazines of strategy—
To shun ill loomings deemed insuperable,
When simple souls by stumbling up to them
Find the grim shapes but air.　But let us grant

That the investing French so ring us in
As to leave not a span for such exploit ;
Then go we—throw ourselves upon their steel,
And batter through, or die !—
What say you, Generals ? Speak your minds, I
    pray.

JELLACHICH

I favour marching out—the Tyrol way.

RIESC

Bohemia best ! The route thereto is open.

ARCHDUKE

My course is chosen. O this black campaign,
Which Pitt's alarmed dispatches pricked us to,
All unforeseeing ! Any risk for me
Rather than court humiliation here !

    MACK has risen during the latter remarks, walked to the
window, and looked out at the rain. He returns with an air
of embarrassment.

MACK (to Archduke)

It is my privilege firmly to submit
That your Imperial Highness undertake
No venturous vaulting into risks unknown.—
Assume that you, Sire, as you have proposed,
With your light regiments and the cavalry,
Detach yourself from us, to scoop a way
By circuits northwards through the Rauhe Alps
And Herdenheim, into Bohemia :
Reports all point that you will be attacked,
Enveloped, borne on to capitulate.
What worse can happen here ?—
Remember, Sire, the Emperor deputes me,
Should such a clash arise as has arisen,
To exercise supreme authority.

The honour of our arms, our race, demands
That none of your Imperial Highness' line
Be pounded prisoner by this vulgar foe,
Who is not France, but an adventurer
Imposing on that country for his gain.

Archduke

I amply recognize the drear disgrace
Involving Austria if this upstart chief
Should of his cunning seize and hold in pawn
A royal-lineaged son, whose ancestors
Root on the primal rocks of history.

Spirit Ironic

Note that.   Five years, and legal brethren they—
This feudal treasure and the upstart man !

Archduke

But it seems clear to me that loitering here
Is full as like to compass our surrender
As moving hence.   And ill it therefore suits
The mood of one of my high temperature
To pause inactive while await me means
Of desperate cure for these so desperate ills !

> [The Archduke Ferdinand goes out.

A troubled silence follows, during which the gusts call
hollowly into the chimney, and raindrops spit on the fire.

Schwarzenberg

The Archduke bears him shrewdly in this course.—
We may as well look matters in the face,
And that we are cooped and cornered is most clear ;
Clear is it, too, that but a miracle
Can work to loose us !   I have stoutly held
That this man's three years' ostentatious scheme
To fling his army on the tempting shores

Of our allies the English was a—well—
Scarce other than a trick of thimble-rig
To still us into false security.

JELLACHICH

Well, I know nothing. None needs list to me,
But, on the whole, to southward seems the course
For plunging, all in force, immediately.

Another pause.

SPIRIT SINISTER

The Will throws Mack again in agitation :
Ho-ho—what he'll do now !

SPIRIT OF THE PITIES

                    Nay, hard one, nay ;
The clouds weep for him !

SPIRIT SINISTER

                 If he must he must ;
And it's good antic at a vacant time !

MACK goes restlessly to the door, and is heard pacing about
the vestibule, and questioning the aides and other officers
gathered there.

A GENERAL

He wavers like this smoke-wreath that inclines
Or north, or south, as the storm-currents rule !

MACK (returning)

Bring that deserter hither once again.

A French soldier is brought in, blindfolded and guarded.
The bandage is removed.

Well, tell us what he says.

AN OFFICER (after speaking to the prisoner in
            French)

                    He still repeats
That the whole body of the British strength
Is even now descending on Boulogne,
And that self-preservation must, of need,
Clear us from Bonaparte ere many days,
Who momently· is moving.

                    MACK

                    Still retain him.

    He walks to the fire, and stands looking into it. The soldier
is taken out.

                    JELLACHICH
        (bending over the map in argument with RIESC)

I much prefer our self-won information ;
And if we have Marshal Soult at Landsberg here,
(Which seems to be the truth, despite this man,)
And Dupont hard upon us at Albeck,
With Ney not far from Günzburg ; somewhere here,
Or further down the river, lurking Lannes,
Our game's to draw off southward—if we can !

                    MACK (turning)

I have it.   This we'll do.   You, Jellachich,
Unite with Spangen's troops at Memmingen,
To fend off mischief there.   And you, Riesc,
Will make your utmost haste to occupy
The bridge and upper ground at Elchingen,
And all along the left bank of the stream,
Till you observe whereon to concentrate
And sever their connections.   I couch here,
And hold the city till the Russians come.

A GENERAL (in a low voice)

Disjunction seems of all expedients worst :
If any stay, then stay should every man,
Gather, inlace, and close up hip to hip,
And perk and bristle hedgehog-like with spines !

MACK

The conference is ended, friends, I say,
And orders will be issued here forthwith.

Guns heard.

AN OFFICER

Surely that's from the Michaelsberg above us ?

MACK

Never care.   Here we stay.   In five more days
The Russians hail, and we regain our bays.

[Exeunt severally.

SCENE IV

BEFORE ULM.   THE SAME DAY

A high wind prevails, and rain falls in torrents.   An elevated
terrace near Elchingen forms the foreground.

DUMB SHOW

From the terrace BONAPARTE surveys and dictates operations against the entrenched heights of the Michaelsberg that
rise in the middle distance on the right above the city.   Through
the gauze of descending waters the French soldiery can be
discerned climbing to the attack under NEY.

They slowly advance, recede, re-advance, halt. A time of suspense follows. Then they are seen in a state of irregular movement, even confusion; but in the end they carry the heights with the bayonet.

Below the spot whereon NAPOLÉON and his staff are gathered, glistening wet and plastered with mud, obtrudes on the left the village of Elchingen, now in the hands of the French. Its white - walled monastery, its bridge over the Danube, recently broken by the irresistible NEY, wear a desolated look, and the stream, which is swollen by the rainfall and rasped by the storm, seems wanly to sympathize.

Anon shells are dropped by the French from the summits they have gained into the city below. A bomb from an Austrian battery falls near NAPOLÉON, and in bursting raises a fountain of mud. The Emperor retreats with his officers to a less conspicuous station.

Meanwhile LANNES advances from a position near NAPOLÉON till his columns reach the top of the Frauenberg hard by. The united corps of LANNES and NEY descend on the inner slope of the heights towards the city walls, in the rear of the retreating Austrians. One of the French columns scales a bastion, but NAPOLÉON orders the assault to be discontinued, and with the wane of day the spectacle disappears.

SCENE V

THE SAME.   THE MICHAELSBERG

A chilly but rainless noon three days later. On the right of the scene, northward, rise the Michaelsberg heights; below, on the left, stretches the panorama of the city and the Danube. On a secondary eminence near at hand, forming a spur of the upper hill, a fire of logs is burning, the foremost group beside it being NAPOLÉON and his staff, the latter in gorgeous uniform, the former in his shabby greatcoat and plain turned-up hat, walking to and fro with his hands behind him, and occasionally stopping to warm himself. The French infantry are drawn up in a dense array at the back of these.

The whole Austrian garrison of Ulm marches out of the city gate opposite NAPOLÉON. GENERAL MACK is at the head, followed by GIULAY, GOTTESHEIM, KLENAU, LICHTENSTEIN, and many other officers, who advance to BONAPARTE and deliver their swords.

MACK

Behold me, Sire.   Mack the unfortunate !

NAPOLÉON

War, General, ever has its ups and downs,
And you must take the better and the worse
As impish chance or destiny ordains.
Come near and warm you here.   A glowing fire
Is life on these depressing, mired, moist days
Of smitten leaves down-dropping clammily,
And toadstools like the putrid lungs of men.

(To his lieutenants)

Cause them to stand to right and left of me.

The Austrian officers arrange themselves as directed, and
the body of the Austrians now file past their Conqueror, laying
down their arms as they approach ; some with angry gestures
and words, others in moody silence.

Listen, I pray you, Generals gathered here.
I tell you frankly that I know not why
Your master wages this wild war with me.
I know not what he seeks by such injustice,
Unless to give me practice in my trade—
That of a soldier—whereto I was bred :
Deemed he my craft might slip from me, unplied ?
Let him now own me still a dab therein !

MACK

Permit me, your Imperial Majesty,
To speak one word in answer ; which is this,
No war was wished for by my Emperor :
Russia constrained him to it !

NAPOLÉON
                     If that be,
You are no more a European power.—

I would point out to him that my resources
Are not confined to these my musters here ;
My prisoners of war, in route for France,
Will see some marks of my resources there !
Two hundred thousand volunteers, right fit,
Will join my standards at a single nod,
And in six weeks prove soldiers to the bone,
Whilst your recruits, compulsion's scavengings,
Scarce weld to warriors after toilsome years.
    But I want nothing on this Continent :
The English only are my enemies.
Ships, colonies, and commerce I desire,
Yea, therewith to advantage you as me.
Let me then charge your Emperor, my brother,
To turn his feet the shortest way to peace.—
All states must have an end, the weak, the strong ;
Ay ; even may fall the dynasty of Lorraine !

    The filing past and laying down of arms by the Austrian
army continues with monotonous regularity, as if it would
never end.

NAPOLÉON (in a murmur, after a while)

Well, what cares England !   She has won her game ;
I have unlearnt to threaten her from Boulogne. . . .
    Her gold it is that forms the weft of this
Fair tapestry of armies marshalled here !
Likewise of Russia's, drawing steadily nigh.
But they may see what these see, by and by.

SPIRIT OF THE YEARS

So let him speak, the while we clearly sight him
Moved like a figure on a lantern-slide,
Which, much amazing uninitiate eyes,
The all-compelling crystal pane but drags
Whither the showman wills.

Spirit Ironic

And yet, my friend,
The Will Itself might smile at this collapse
Of Austria's men-at-arms, so drolly done ;
Even as, in your phantasmagoric show,
The deft manipulator of the slide
Might smile at his own art.

Chorus of the Years (aerial music)

Ah, no : ah, no !
It is impassible as glacial snow.—
Within the Great Unshaken
These painted shapes awaken
A lesser thrill than doth the gentle lave
Of yonder bank by Danube's wandering wave
Within the Schwarzwald heights that give it flow !

Spirit of the Pities

But see the intolerable antilogy
Of making figments feel.

Spirit Ironic

Logic's in that.
It does not, I must own, quite play the game.

Chorus of Ironic Spirits (aerial music)

And this day wins for Ulm a dingy fame,
Which centuries shall not bleach from her old name !

The procession of Austrians continues till the scene is hidden
by haze.

SCENE VI

LONDON. SPRING GARDENS

Before LORD MALMESBURY'S house, on a Sunday morning
in the same autumn. Idlers pause and gather in the background.
PITT enters, and meets LORD MULGRAVE.

MULGRAVE

Good day, Pitt. Ay, these leaves that skim the
    ground
With withered voices, hint that sunshine-time
Is well-nigh past.—And so the game's begun
Between him and the Austro-Russian force,
As second movement in the faceabout
From Boulogne shore, with which he has hocussed
    us ?—
What has been heard on't ? Have they clashed as
    yet ?

PITT

The Emperor Francis, partly at my instance,
Has thrown the chief command on General Mack,
A man most capable and far of sight.
He centres by the Danube-bank at Ulm,
A town well-walled, and firm for leaning on
To intercept the French in their advance
From the Black Forest towards the Russian troops
Approaching from the east. If Bonaparte
Sustain his marches at the break-neck speed
That all report, they must have met ere now.
—There is a rumour . . . quite impossible ! . . .

MULGRAVE

You still have faith in Mack as strategist ?
There have been doubts of his far-sightedness.

PITT (hastily)

I know, I know.—I am calling here at Malmesbury's
At somewhat an unceremonious time
To ask his help to translate this Dutch print
The post has brought. Malmesbury is great at
      Dutch,
Learning it long at Leyden, years ago.

He draws a newspaper from his pocket, unfolds it, and
glances it down.

There's news here unintelligible to me
Upon the very matter !   You'll come in ?

They call at LORD MALMESBURY'S. He meets them in the
hall, and welcomes them with an apprehensive look of foreknowledge.

PITT

Pardon this early call. The packet's in,
And wings me this unreadable Dutch paper,
So, as the offices are closed to-day,
I have brought it round to you.

(Handing the paper.)

                                    What does it say ?
For God's sake, read it out. You know the tongue.

MALMESBURY (with hesitation)

I have glanced it through already—more than
      once—
A copy having reached me, too, by now . . .
We are in the presence of a great disaster !

See here.   It says that Mack, enjailed in Ulm
By Bonaparte—from four sides shutting round—
Capitulated, and with all his force
Laid down his arms before his conqueror !

PITT's face changes.   A silence.

MULGRAVE

Outrageous !   Ignominy unparalleled !

PITT

By God, my lord, these statements must be false !
These foreign prints are trustless as Cheap Jack
Dumfounding yokels at a country fair.
I heed no word of it.—Impossible.
What !   Eighty thousand Austrians, nigh in touch
With Russia's levies that Kutúzof leads,
To lay down arms before the war's begun ?
'Tis too much !

MALMESBURY

But I fear it is too true !

Note the assevered source of the report—
One beyond thought of minters of mock tales.
The writer adds that military wits
Cry that the Little Corporal now makes war
In a new way, using his soldiers' legs
And not their arms, to bring him victory.
Ha-ha !   The quip must sting the Corporal's foes.

PITT (after a pause)

O vacillating Prussia !   Had she moved,
Had she but planted one foot firmly down,
All this had been averted.—I must go.
'Tis sure, 'tis sure, I labour but in vain !

MALMESBURY accompanies him to the door, and PITT walks
away disquietedly towards Whitehall, the other two regarding
him as he goes.

MULGRAVE

Too swiftly he declines to feebleness,
And these things well might shake a stouter frame !

MALMESBURY

Of late the burden of all Europe's cares,
Of hiring and maintaining half her troops,
His single pair of shoulders has upborne,
Thanks to the obstinacy of the King.—
His thin, strained face, his ready irritation,
Are ominous signs. He may not be for long.

MULGRAVE

He alters fast, indeed,—as do events.

MALMESBURY

His labour's lost ; and all our money gone !
It looks as if this doughty coalition
On which we have lavished so much pay and pains
Would end in wreck.

MULGRAVE

         All is not over yet ;
The gathering Russian forces are unbroke.

MALMESBURY

Well ; we shall see. Should Boney vanquish these,
And silence all resistance on that side,
His move will then be backward to Boulogne,
And so upon us.

MULGRAVE

Nelson to our defence !

Malmesbury

Ay ; where is Nelson ?   Faith, by this late time
He may be sodden ; churned in Biscay swirls ;
Or blown to polar bears by boreal gales ;
Or sleeping amorously in some calm cave
On the Canaries' or Atlantis' shore
Upon the bosom of his Dido dear,
For all that we know !   Never a sound of him
Since passing Portland one September day—
To make for Cadiz ; so 'twas then believed.

Mulgrave

He's staunch.   He's watching, or I am much
    deceived.

    Mulgrave departs. Malmesbury goes within. The scene
shuts.

ACT FIFTH

SCENE I

OFF CAPE TRAFALGAR

A bird's-eye view of the sea discloses itself. It is daybreak, and the broad face of the ocean is fringed on its eastern edge (right) by the Cape and the Spanish shore. On the rolling surface immediately beneath the eye, ranged more or less in two parallel lines running north and south, one group from the twain standing off somewhat, are the vessels of the combined French and Spanish navies, whose canvases, as the sun edges upward, shine in its rays like satin.

On the western (left) horizon two columns of ships appear in full sail, small as moths to the aerial vision. They are bearing down towards the combined squadrons.

RECORDING ANGEL I (intoning from his book)

At last Villeneuve accepts the sea and fate,
Despite the Cadiz council called of late,
Whereat his stoutest captains—men the first
          To do all mortals durst—
Willing to sail, and bleed, and bear the worst,
Short of cold suicide, did yet opine
That plunging mid those teeth of treble line
          In jaws of oaken wood,
Held open by the English navarchy
With suasive breadth and artful modesty,
Would smack of purposeless foolhardihood.

Recording Angel II

But word came, writ in mandatory mood,
To put from Cadiz, gain Toulon, and straight
At a said sign on Italy operate.
Moreover that Villeneuve, arrived as planned,
Would find Rosily in supreme command.—
Gloomy Villeneuve grows rash, and, darkly brave,
Leaps to meet war, storm, Nelson—even the grave.

Semichorus I of the Years (aerial music)

Ere the concussion hurtle, draw abreast
　　　Of the sea.

Semichorus II

Where Nelson's hulls are rising from the west,
　　　Silently.

Semichorus I

Each linen wing outspread, each man and lad
　　　Sworn to be

Semichorus II

Amid the vanmost, or for Death, or glad
　　　Victory !

The point of sight descends till it is near the deck of the
" Bucentaure," the flag-ship of Villeneuve. Present thereon
are the Admiral, his Flag-Captain Magendie, Lieutenant
Daudignon, other naval officers and seamen.

Magendie

All night we have read their signals in the air,
Whereby the peering frigates of their van
Have told them of our trend.

VILLENEUVE

The enemy
Makes threat as though to throw him on our stern :
Signal the fleet to wear ; bid Gravina
To come in from manœuvring with his twelve,
And range himself in line.

Officers murmur.

I say again
Bid Gravina draw hither with his twelve,
And signal all to wear !—and come upon
The larboard tack with every bow anorth !—
So we make Cadiz in the worst event,
And patch our rags up there.   As we head now
Our only practicable thoroughfare
Is through Gibraltar Strait—a fatal door !
   Signal to close the line and leave no gaps.
Remember, too, what I have already told :
Remind them of it now.   They must not pause
For signallings from me amid a strife
Whose chaos may prevent my clear discernment,
Or may forbid my signalling at all.
The voice of honour then becomes the chief's ;
Listen they thereto, and set every stitch
To heave them on into the fiercest fight.
Now I will sum up all : heed well the charge ;
EACH CAPTAIN, PETTY OFFICER, AND MAN
IS ONLY AT HIS POST WHEN UNDER FIRE.

The ships of the whole fleet turn their bows from south to
north as directed, and close up in two parallel curved columns,
the concave side of each column being towards the enemy,
and the interspaces of the first column being, in general,
opposite the hulls of the second.

AN OFFICER
(straining his eyes towards the English fleet)

How they skip on !   Their overcrowded sails
Bulge like blown bladders in a tripeman's shop
The market-morning after slaughterday !

PETTY OFFICER (aside)

It's morning before slaughterday with us,
I make so bold to bode !

The English Admiral is seen to be signalling to his fleet.
The signal is : "ENGLAND EXPECTS EVERY MAN WILL DO HIS
DUTY." A loud cheering from all the English ships comes
undulating on the wind when the signal is read.

VILLENEUVE

They are signalling too. — Well, business soon
    begins !
You will reserve your fire. And be it known
That we display no admirals' flags at all
Until the action's past. 'Twill puzzle them,
And work to our advantage when we close.—
Yes, they are double-ranked, I think, like us ;
But we shall see anon.

MAGENDIE

                    The foremost one
Makes for the " Santa Ana." In such case
The " Fougueux " might assist her.

VILLENEUVE

                            Be it so—
There's time enough.—Our ships will be in place,
And ready to speak back in iron words
When theirs cry Hail ! in the same sort of voice.

They prepare to receive the northernmost column of the
enemy's ships headed by the " Victory," trying the distance
by an occasional single shot. During their suspense a discharge is heard southward, and turning they behold COLLING-
WOOD at the head of his column in the " Royal Sovereign,"
just engaging with the Spanish " Santa Ana." Meanwhile the
" Victory " draws still nearer, preserving silence with brazen
sang-froid. At a concerted moment full broadsides are dis-

charged into her simultaneously from the " Bucentaure," the
" Santísima Trinidad," and the " Redoutable."

When the smoke clears the " Victory's " mizzen-topmast,
with spars and a quantity of rigging, is seen to have fallen,
her wheel to be shot away, and her deck encumbered with dead
and wounded men.

VILLENEUVE

'Tis well ! But see ; their course is undelayed,
And still they near in clenched audacity !

DAUDIGNON

This northmost column bears upon our beam.
Their prows will pierce us thwartwise. That's the
     aim.

MAGENDIE

Which aim deft Lucas o' the " Redoutable "
Most gallantly bestirs him to outscheme.—
See, how he strains, that on his timbers fall
Blows that were destined for his Admiral !

During this the French ship " Redoutable " is moving
forward to interpose itself between the approaching " Victory "
and the " Bucentaure."

VILLENEUVE

Now comes it ! The " Santísima Trinidad,"
The old " Redoutable's " hard sides, and ours,
Will take the touse of this bombastic blow.
Your grapnels and your boarding-hatchets—ready !
We'll dash our eagle on the English deck,
And swear to fetch it !

CREW

         Aye ! We swear. Huzza !
Long live the Emperor !

But the " Victory " suddenly swerves to the rear of the
" Bucentaure," and crossing her stern-waters, discharges a

broadside into her and the " Redoutable " endwise, wrapping
the scene in folds of smoke.
                    The point of view changes.

SCENE II

THE SAME.   THE QUARTER-DECK OF THE " VICTORY."

The van of each division of the English fleet has drawn to
the windward side of the combined fleets of the enemy, and
broken their order, the " Victory " being now parallel to and
alongside the " Redoutable," the " Téméraire " taking up a
station on the other side of that ship.   The " Bucentaure "
and the " Santísima Trinidad " become jammed together a
little way ahead.   A smoke and din of cannonading prevail,
amid which the studding-sail booms are shot away.
    NELSON, HARDY, BLACKWOOD, SECRETARY SCOTT, LIEU-
TENANT PASCO, BURKE the Purser, CAPTAIN ADAIR of the
Marines, and other officers are on or near the quarter-deck.

NELSON

See, there, that noble fellow Collingwood,
How straight he helms his ship into the fire !—
Now you'll haste back to yours (to Blackwood).
                              —We must henceforth
Trust to the Great Disposer of events,
And justice of our cause ! . . .
                              [BLACKWOOD leaves.
    The battle grows hotter.   A double-headed shot cuts down
seven or eight marines on the " Victory's " poop.

Captain Adair, part those marines of yours,
And hasten to disperse them round the ship.—
Your place is down below, Burke, not up here ;
Ah, yes ; like David you would see the battle !

    A heavy discharge of musket-shot comes from the tops of
the " Santísima Trinidad."   ADAIR and PASCO fall.   Another
swathe of marines is mowed down by chain-shot.

SCOTT

My lord, I use to you the utmost prayers
That I have privilege to shape in words :
Remove your stars and orders, I would beg ;
That shot was aimed at you.

NELSON

They were awarded to me as an honour,
And shall I do despite to those who prize me,
And slight their gifts ?   No, I will die with them,
If die I must.

> He walks up and down with HARDY.

HARDY

At least let's put you on
Your old greatcoat, my lord—(the air is keen).—
'Twill cover all.   So while you still retain
Your dignities, you baulk these deadly aims.

NELSON

Thank 'ee, good friend.   But no,—I haven't time,
I do assure you—not a trice to spare,
As you well see.

> A few minutes later SCOTT falls dead, a bullet having pierced his skull.   Immediately after a shot passes between the Admiral and the Captain, tearing the instep of HARDY's shoe, and striking away the buckle.   They shake off the dust and splinters it has scattered over them.   NELSON glances round, and perceives what has happened to his secretary.

NELSON

Poor Scott, too, carried off !   Warm work this,
    Hardy ;
Too warm to go on long.

HARDY

I think so, too ;
Their lower ports are blocked against our hull,
And our charge now is less.   Each knock so near
Sets their old wood on fire.

NELSON

Ay, rotten as peat.
What's that ?   I think she has struck, or pretty
  nigh !

A cracking of musketry.

HARDY

Not yet.—Those small-arm men there, in her tops,
Thin our crew fearfully.   Now, too, our guns
Have to be dipped full down, or they would rake
The "Téméraire" there on the other side.

NELSON

True.—While you deal good measure out to these,
Keep slapping at those giants over here—
The "Trinidad," I mean, and the "Bucentaure,"
To win'ard—swelling up so pompously.

HARDY

I'll see no slackness shall be shown that way.

They part and go in their respective directions.   Gunners,
naked to the waist and reeking with sweat, are now in swift
action on the several decks, and firemen carry buckets of water
hither and thither.   The killed and wounded thicken around,
and are being lifted and examined by the surgeons.   NELSON
and HARDY meet again.

NELSON

Bid still the firemen bring more bucketfuls,
And dash the water into each new hole
Our guns have gouged in the " Redoutable,"
Or we shall all be set ablaze together.

HARDY

Let me once more advise, entreat, my lord,
That you do not expose yourself so clearly.
Those fellows in the mizzen-top up there
Are peppering round you quite perceptibly.

NELSON

Now, Hardy, don't offend me.   They can't aim ;
They only set their own rent sails on fire.—
But if they could, I would not hide a button
To save ten lives like mine.   I have no cause
To prize it, I assure 'ee.—Ah, look there,
One of the women hit,—and badly, too.
Poor wench !   Let some one shift her quickly down.

HARDY

My lord, each humblest sojourner on the seas,
Dock-labourer, lame longshore-man, bowed bargee,
Sees it as policy to shield his life
For those dependent on him.   Much more, then,
Should one upon whose priceless presence here
Such issues hang, so many strivers lean,
Use average circumspection at an hour
So critical for us all.

NELSON

        Ay, ay.   Yes, yes ;
I know your meaning, Hardy ; and I know
That you disguise as frigid policy

What really is your honest love of me.
But, faith, I have had my day. My work's nigh
    done ;
I serve all interests best by chancing it
Here with the commonest.—Ah, their heavy guns
Are silenced every one ! Thank God for that.

HARDY

'Tis so. They only use their small arms now.

He goes to larboard to see what is progressing on that side
between his ship and the " Santísima Trinidad."

OFFICER (to a seaman)

Swab down these stairs. The mess of blood about
Makes 'em so slippery that one's like to fall
In carrying the wounded men below.

While CAPTAIN HARDY is still a little way off, LORD NELSON
turns to walk aft, when a ball from one of the muskets in the
mizzen-top of the " Redoutable " enters his left shoulder.
He falls upon his face on the deck. HARDY looks round, and
sees what has happened.

HARDY (hastily)

Ah—what I feared, and strove to hide I feared ! . . .

He goes towards NELSON, who in the meantime has been
lifted by SERGEANT-MAJOR SECKER and two seamen.

NELSON

Hardy, I think they've done for me at last !

HARDY

I hope not !

NELSON

Yes. My backbone is shot through.
I have not long to live.

> The men proceed to carry him below.

                 Those tiller ropes
They've torn away, get instantly repaired !

> At sight of him borne along wounded there is great agitation
> among the crew.

Cover my face.   There will no good be done
By drawing their attention off to me.
Bear me along, good fellows ; I am but one
Among the many darkened here to-day !

> He is carried on to the cockpit over the crowd of dead and
> wounded.
>   (To the Chaplain)

Doctor, I'm gone.   I am waste o' time to you.

HARDY (remaining behind)

Hills, go to Collingwood and let him know
That we've no Admiral here.

> He passes on.

A LIEUTENANT

Now quick and pick him off who did the deed—
That white-bloused man there in the mizzen-top.

POLLARD, a midshipman (shooting)

No sooner said than done.   A pretty aim !

> The Frenchman falls dead upon the poop.

> The spectacle seems now to become enveloped in smoke,
> and the point of view changes.

SCENE III

THE SAME. ON BOARD THE " BUCENTAURE "

The bowsprit of the French Admiral's ship is stuck fast in
the stern-gallery of the " Santísima Trinidad," the starboard
side of the " Bucentaure " being shattered by shots from two
English three-deckers which are pounding her on that hand.
The poop is also reduced to ruin by two other English ships that
are attacking her from behind.

On the quarter-deck are ADMIRAL VILLENEUVE, the FLAG-
CAPTAIN MAGENDIE, LIEUTENANTS DAUDIGNON, FOURNIER,
and others, anxiously occupied. The whole crew is in desperate
action of battle and stumbling among the dead and dying, who
have fallen too rapidly to be carried below.

VILLENEUVE

We shall be crushed if matters go on thus.—
Direct the " Trinidad " to let her drive,
That this foul tangle may be loosened clear !

DAUDIGNON

It has been tried, sir ; but she cannot move.

VILLENEUVE

Then signal to the " Hero " that she strive
Once more to drop this way.

MAGENDIE

                        We may make signs,
But in the thickened air what signal's marked ?—
'Tis done, however.

VILLENEUVE

The " Redoutable "
And " Victory " there,—they grip in dying throes !
Something's amiss on board the English ship.
Surely the Admiral's fallen ?

A PETTY OFFICER

Sir, they say
That he was shot some hour, or half, ago.—
With dandyism raised to godlike pitch
He stalked the deck in all his jewellery,
And so was hit.

MAGENDIE

Then Fortune shows her face !
We have scotched England in dispatching him.

(He watches.)

Yes ! He commands no more ; and Lucas, joying,
Has taken steps to board. Look, spars are laid,
And his best men are mounting at his heels.

A crash is heard.

VILLENEUVE

Ah, God—he is too late ! Whence came that hurl
Of heavy grape ? The smoke prevents my seeing
But at brief whiles.—The boarding band has fallen,
Fallen almost to a man.—'Twas well assayed !

MAGENDIE

That's from their " Téméraire," whose vicious broadside
Has cleared poor Lucas' decks.

VILLENEUVE

And Lucas, too.
I see him no more there.   His red planks show
Three hundred dead if one.   Now for ourselves !

Four of the English three-deckers have gradually closed
round the " Bucentaure," whose bowsprit still sticks fast in
the gallery of the " Santísima Trinidad." A broadside comes
from one of the English, resulting in worse havoc on the
" Bucentaure." The main and mizzen masts of the latter
fall, and the boats are beaten to pieces. A raking fire of
musketry follows from the attacking ships, to which the
" Bucentaure " heroically continues still to keep up a reply.

CAPTAIN MAGENDIE falls wounded. His place is taken by
LIEUTENANT DAUDIGNON.

VILLENEUVE

Now that the fume has lessened, code my biddance
Upon our only mast, and tell the van
At once to wear, and come into the fire.
(Aside) If it be true that, as *he* sneers, success
Demands of me but cool audacity,
To-day shall leave him nothing to desire !

Musketry continues. DAUDIGNON falls. He is removed,
his post being taken by LIEUTENANT FOURNIER. Another
crash comes, and the deck is suddenly encumbered with
rigging.

FOURNIER

There goes our foremast !   How for signalling now ?

VILLENEUVE

To try that longer, Fournier, is in vain
Upon this haggard, scorched, and ravaged hulk,
Her decks all reeking with such gory shows,
Her starboard side in rents, her stern nigh gone !
How does she keep afloat ?—

" Bucentaure," O unlucky good old ship !
My part in you is played.   Ay—I must go ;
I must tempt Fate elsewhere,—if but a boat
Can bear me through this wreckage to the van.

FOURNIER

Our boats are stove in, or as full of holes
As the cook's skimmer, from their cursèd balls !

    Musketry. VILLENEUVE's Head-of-Staff, DE PRIGNY, falls
wounded, and many additional men. VILLENEUVE glances
troublously from ship to ship of his fleet.

VILLENEUVE

How hideous are the waves, so pure this dawn !—
Red-frothed ;   and   friends   and   foes   all   mixed
     therein.—
Can we in some way hail the " Trinidad "
And get a boat from her ?

    They attempt to attract the attention of the " Santísima
Trinidad " by shouting.
                        Impossible ;
Amid the loud combustion of this strife
As well try holloing to the antipodes ! . . .
So here I am.   The bliss of Nelson's end
Will not be mine ; his full refulgent eve
Becomes my midnight !   Well ; the fleets shall see
That I can yield my cause with dignity.

       The " Bucentaure " strikes her flag.

    A boat then puts off from the English ship " Conqueror,"
and VILLENEUVE, having surrendered his sword, is taken out
from the " Bucentaure."   But being unable to regain her own
ship, the boat is picked up by the " Mars," and the French
Admiral is received aboard her.

       The point of view changes.

SCENE IV

THE SAME. THE COCKPIT OF THE " VICTORY "

A din of trampling and dragging overhead, which is accompanied by a continuous ground-bass roar from the guns of the warring fleets, culminates at times in loud concussions. The wounded are lying around in rows for treatment, some groaning, some silently dying, some dead. The gloomy atmosphere of the low-beamed deck is pervaded by a thick haze of smoke, powdered wood, and other dust, and is heavy with the fumes of gunpowder and candle-grease, the odour of drugs and cordials, and the smell from abdominal wounds.

NELSON, his face now pinched and wan with suffering, is lying undressed in a midshipman's berth, dimly lit by a lantern. Dr. BEATTY, Dr. MAGRATH, the Rev. Dr. SCOTT the Chaplain, BURKE the Purser, the Steward, and a few others stand around.

MAGRATH (in a low voice)

Poor Ram, and poor Tom Whipple, have just gone.

BEATTY

There was no hope for them.

NELSON (brokenly)

Who have just died ?

BEATTY

Two who were badly hit by now, my lord ;
Lieutenant Ram and Mr. Whipple.

NELSON

Ah !—
So many lives—in such a glorious cause. . . .
I join them soon, soon, soon !—O where is Hardy ?
Will nobody bring Hardy to me—none ?
He must be killed, too. Surely Hardy's dead ?

A MIDSHIPMAN

He's coming soon, my lord. The constant call
On his full heed of this most mortal fight
Keeps him from hastening hither as he would.

NELSON

I'll wait, I'll wait. I should have thought of it.

Presently HARDY *comes down.* NELSON *and he grasp hands.*

Hardy, how goes the day with us and England ?

HARDY

Well ; very well, thank God for't, my dear lord.
Villeneuve their Admiral has this moment struck,
And put himself aboard the " Conqueror."
Some fourteen of their first-rates, or about,
Thus far we've got. The said " Bucentaure " chief :
The " Santa Ana," the " Redoutable,"
The " Fougueux," the " Santísima Trinidad,"
" San Augustino," " San Francisco," " Aigle " ;
And our old " Swiftsure," too, we've grappled back,
To every seaman's joy. But now their van
Has tacked to bear round on the " Victory "
And crush her by sheer weight of wood and brass :
Three of our best I am therefore calling up,
And make no doubt of worsting theirs, and France.

NELSON

That's well.   I swore for twenty.—But it's well.

HARDY

We'll have 'em yet !   But without you, my lord,
We have to make slow plodding do the deeds
That sprung by inspiration ere you fell ;
And on this ship the more particularly.

NELSON

No, Hardy.—Ever 'twas your settled fault
So modestly to whittle down your worth.
But I saw stuff in you which admirals need
When, taking thought, I chose the " Victory's " keel
To do my business with these braggarts in.
A business finished now, for me !—Good friend,
Slow shades are creeping on me. . . . I scarce see
    you.

HARDY

The smoke from ships upon our win'ard side,
And the dust raised by their worm-eaten hulks,
When our balls touch 'em, blind the eyes, in truth.

NELSON

No ; it is not that dust ; 'tis dust of death
That darkens me.

    A shock overhead. HARDY goes up.   One or two other
officers go up, and by and by return.

                What was that extra noise ?

OFFICER

The " Formidable " passed us by, my lord,
And thumped a stunning broadside into us.—

But, on their side, the " Hero's " captain's fallen ;
The " Algeciras " has been boarded, too,
By Captain Tyler, and the captain shot :
Admiral Gravina desperately holds out ;
They say he's lost an arm.

NELSON

And we ourselves—
Who have we lost on board here ?   Nay, but tell me !

BEATTY

Besides poor Scott, my lord, and Charles Adair,
Lieutenant Ram, and Whipple, captain's clerk,
There's Smith, and Palmer, midshipmen, just killed,
And fifty odd of seamen and marines.

NELSON

Poor youngsters !   Scarred old Nelson joins you soon.

BEATTY

And wounded : Bligh, lieutenant ; Pasco, too,
And Reeves, and Peake, lieutenants of marines,
And Rivers, Westphall, Bulkeley, midshipmen,
With, of the crew, a hundred odd just now,
Unreckoning those late fallen not brought below.

BURKE

That fellow in the mizzen-top, my lord,
Who made it his affair to wing you thus,
We took good care to settle ; and he fell
Like an old rook, smack from his perch, stone dead.

Nelson

'Twas not worth while !—He was, no doubt, a man
Who in simplicity and sheer good faith
Strove but to serve his country.   Rest be to him !
And may his wife, his friends, his little ones,
If such he had, be tided through their loss,
And soothed amid the sorrow brought by me.

HARDY re-enters.

Who's that ?   Ah—here you come !   How, Hardy,
    now ?

Hardy

The Spanish Admiral's rumoured to be wounded,
We know not with what truth.   But, be as 'twill,
He sheers away with all he could call round,
And some few frigates, straight to Cadiz port.

A violent explosion is heard above the confused noises on
deck.   A midshipman goes above and returns.

Midshipman (in the background)

It is the enemy's first-rate, the " Achille,"
Blown to a thousand atoms !—While on fire,
Before she burst, the captain's woman there,
Desperate for life, climbed from the gunroom port
Upon the rudder-chains ; stripped herself stark,
And swam for the Pickle's boat.   Our men in charge,
Seeing her great breasts bulging on the brine,
Sang out, " A mermaid 'tis, by God ! "—then rowed
And hauled her in.—

Burke

             Such unbid sights obtrude
On death's dyed stage !

MIDSHIPMAN

Meantime the " Achille " fought on,
Even while the ship was blazing, knowing well
The fire must reach their powder ; which it did.
The spot is covered now with floating men,
Some whole, the main in parts ; arms, legs, trunks,
    heads,
Bobbing with tons of timber on the waves,
And splinters looped with entrails of the crew.

NELSON (arousing)

Our course will be to anchor.   Let them know.

HARDY

But let me ask, my lord, as needs I must,
Seeing your state, and that our work's not done,
Shall I, from you, bid Admiral Collingwood
Take full on him the conduct of affairs ?

NELSON (trying to raise himself)

Not while I live, I hope !   No, Hardy ; no.
Give Collingwood my order.   Anchor all !

HARDY (hesitating)

You mean the signal's to be made forthwith ?

NELSON

I do !—By God, if but our carpenter
Could rig me up a jury-backbone now,
To last one hour—until the battle's done,
I'd see to it !   But here I am—stove in—
Broken—all logged and done for !   Done, ay done !

BEATTY (returning from the other wounded)

My lord, I must implore you to lie calm !
You shorten what at best may not be long.

NELSON (exhausted)

I know, I know, good Beatty !   Thank you well.
Hardy, I was impatient.   Now I am still.
Sit here a moment, if you have time to spare ?

BEATTY and the others retire, and the two abide in silence,
except for the trampling overhead and the moans from adjoining berths. NELSON is apparently in less pain, seeming to
doze.

NELSON (suddenly)

What are you thinking, that you speak no word ?

HARDY (waking from a short reverie)

Thoughts all confused, my lord :—their needs on deck,
Your own sad state, and your unrivalled past ;
Mixed up with flashes of old things afar—
Old childish things at home, down Wessex way,
In the snug village under Blackdon Hill
Where I was born.   The tumbling stream, the garden,
The placid look of the grey dial there,
Marking unconsciously this bloody hour,
And the red apples on my father's trees,
Just now full ripe.

NELSON

            Ay, thus do little things
Steal into my mind, too.   But ah, my heart
Knows not your calm philosophy !—There's one—
Come nearer to me, Hardy.—One of all,
As you well guess, pervades my memory now ;
She, and my daughter—I speak freely to you.

'Twas good I made that codicil this morning
That you and Blackwood witnessed.   Now she rests
Safe on the nation's honour. . . . Let her have
My hair, and the small treasured things I owned,
And take care of her, as you care for me !

HARDY promises.

NELSON (resuming in a murmur)

Does love die with our frame's decease, I wonder,
Or does it live on ever ? . . .

A silence.   BEATTY reapproaches.

HARDY
Now I'll leave,
See if your order's gone, and then return.

NELSON
(symptoms of death beginning to change his face)

Yes, Hardy ; yes ; I know it.   You must go.—
Here we shall meet no more ; since Heaven forfend
That care for me should keep you idle now,
When all the ship demands you.   Beatty, too,
Go to the others who lie bleeding there ;
Them you can aid.   Me you can render none !
My time here is the briefest.—If I live
But long enough I'll anchor. . . . But—too late—
My anchoring's elsewhere ordered ! . . . Kiss me,
Hardy :
HARDY bends over him.

I'm satisfied.   Thank God, I have done my duty !

HARDY brushes his eyes with his hand, and withdraws to
go above, pausing to look back before he finally disappears.

BEATTY (watching Nelson)

Ah !—Hush around ! . . .
He's sinking. It is but a trifle now
Of minutes with him. Stand you, please, aside,
And give him air.

BEATTY, the Chaplain, MAGRATH, the Steward, and attendants continue to regard NELSON. BEATTY looks at his watch.

BEATTY

Two hours and fifty minutes since he fell,
And now he's going.

They wait. NELSON dies.

CHAPLAIN

Yes. . . . He has homed to where
There's no more sea.

BEATTY

We'll let the Captain know,
Who will confer with Collingwood at once.
I must now turn to these.

He goes to another part of the cockpit, a midshipman ascends to the deck, and the scene overclouds.

CHORUS OF THE PITIES (aerial music)

His thread was cut too slowly ! When he fell,
And bade his fame farewell,
He might have passed, and shunned his long-drawn
pain,
Endured in vain, in vain !

SPIRIT OF THE YEARS

Young Spirits, be not critical of That
Which was before, and shall be after you !

SPIRIT OF THE PITIES

But out of tune the Mode and meritless
That quickens sense in shapes whom, thou hast said,
Necessitation sways! A life there was
Among these self-same frail ones—Sophocles—
Who visioned it too clearly, even the while
He dubbed the Will " the gods." Truly said he,
" Such gross injustice to their own creation
Burdens the time with mournfulness for us,
And for themselves with shame." [1]*—Things mechanized*
By coils and pivots set to foreframed codes
Would, in a thorough-sphered melodic rule,
And governance of sweet consistency,
Be cessed no pain, whose burnings would abide
With That Which holds responsibility,
Or inexist.

CHORUS OF THE PITIES (aerial music)

Yea, yea, yea!
Thus would the Mover pay
The score each puppet owes,
The Reaper reap what his contrivance sows!
Why make Life debtor when it did not buy?
Why wound so keenly Right that it would die?

SPIRIT OF THE YEARS

Nay, blame not! For what judgment can ye blame?—
In that immense unweeting Mind is shown
One far above forethinking; prócessive,
Rapt, superconscious; a Clairvoyancy
That knows not what It knows, yet works therewith.—
The cognizance ye mourn, Life's doom to feel,
If I report it meetly, came unmeant,
Emerging with blind gropes from impercipience
By listless sequence—luckless, tragic Chance,
In your more human tongue.

[1] Soph. *Trach.* 1266-72.

SPIRIT OF THE PITIES

And hence unneeded
In the economy of Vitality,
Which might have ever kept a sealed cognition
As doth the Will Itself.

CHORUS OF THE YEARS (aerial music)

Nay, nay, nay ;
Your hasty judgments stay,
Until the topmost cyme
Have crowned the last entablature of Time.
O heap not blame on that in-brooding Will ;
O pause, till all things all their days fulfil !

SCENE V

LONDON.   THE GUILDHALL

A crowd of citizens has gathered outside to watch the carriages as they drive up and deposit guests invited to the Lord Mayor's banquet, for which event the Hall is brilliantly lit within.   A cheer rises when the equipage of any popular personage arrives at the door.

FIRST CITIZEN

Well, well !   Nelson is the man who ought to have been banqueted to-night.   But he is coming to Town in a coach different from these.

SECOND CITIZEN

Will they bring his poor splintered body home ?

FIRST CITIZEN

Yes. They say he's to be tombed in marble, at Paul's or Westminster. We shall see him if he lays in state. It will make a patriotic spectacle for a fine day.

BOY

How can you see a dead man, father, after so long ?

FIRST CITIZEN

They'll embalm him, my boy, as they did all the great Egyptian admirals.

BOY

His lady will be handy for that, won't she ?

FIRST CITIZEN

Don't ye ask awkward questions.

SECOND CITIZEN

Here's another coming !

FIRST CITIZEN

That's my Lord Chancellor Eldon. Wot he'll say, and wot he'll look !—Mr. Pitt will be here soon.

BOY

I don't like Billy. He killed Uncle John's parrot.

SECOND CITIZEN

How may ye make that out, youngster ?

Boy

Mr. Pitt made the war, and the war made us want sailors; and Uncle John went for a walk down Wapping High Street to talk to the pretty ladies one evening; and there was a press all along the river that night—a regular hot one—and Uncle John was carried on board a man-of-war to fight under Nelson; and nobody minded Uncle John's parrot, and it talked itself to death. So Mr. Pitt killed Uncle John's parrot; see it, sir?

Second Citizen

You had better have a care of this boy, friend. His brain is too precious for the common risks of Cheapside. Not but what he might as well have said Boney killed the parrot when he was about it. And as for Nelson—who's now sailing shinier seas than ours, if they've rubbed Her off his slate where he's gone to,—the French papers say that our loss in him is greater than our gain in ships; so that logically the victory is theirs. Gad, sir, it's almost true!

A hurrahing is heard from Cheapside, and the crowd in that direction begins to hustle and show excitement.

First Citizen

He's coming, he's coming! Here, let me lift you up, my boy.—Why, they have taken out the horses, as I am man alive!

Second Citizen

Pitt for ever!—Why, here's a blade opening and shutting his mouth like the rest, but never a sound does he raise!

THIRD CITIZEN

I've not too much breath to carry me through my day's work, so I can't afford to waste it in such luxuries as crying Hurrah to aristocrats. If ye was ten yards off y'd think I was shouting as loud as any.

SECOND CITIZEN

It's a very mean practice of ye to husband yourself at such a time, and gape in dumbshow like a frog in Plaistow Marshes.

THIRD CITIZEN

No, sir ; it's economy ; a very necessary instinct in these days of ghastly taxations to pay half the armies in Europe ! In short, in the words of the Ancients, it is scarcely compass-mentas to do otherwise ! Somebody must save something, or the country will be as bankrupt as Mr. Pitt himself is, by all account ; though he don't look it just now.

PITT's coach passes, drawn by a troop of running men and boys. The Prime Minister is seen within, a thin, erect, upnosed figure, with a flush of excitement on his usually pale face. The vehicle reaches the doorway to the Guildhall and halts with a jolt. PITT gets out shakily, and amid cheers enters the building.

FOURTH CITIZEN

Quite a triumphal entry. Such is power ;
Now worshipped, now accursed! The overthrow
Of all Pitt's European policy
When his hired army and his chosen general
Surrendered them at Ulm a month ago,
Is now forgotten ! Ay ; this Trafalgár
Will botch up many a ragged old repute,

Make Nelson figure as domestic saint
No less than country's saviour, Pitt exalt
As zenith-star of England's firmament,
And uncurse all the bogglers of her weal
At this adventurous time.

THIRD CITIZEN

Talk of Pitt being ill. He looks hearty as a buck.

FIRST CITIZEN

It's the news—no more. His spirits are up like a rocket for the moment.

BOY

Is it because Trafalgar is near Portingal that he loves Port wine ?

SECOND CITIZEN

Ah, as I said, friend ; this boy must go home and be carefully put to bed !

FIRST CITIZEN

Well, whatever William's faults, it is a triumph for his virtues to-night !

PITT having disappeared, the Guildhall doors are closed, and the crowd slowly disperses, till in the course of an hour the street shows itself empty and dark, only a few oil lamps burning.

The SCENE OPENS, revealing the interior of the Guildhall, and the brilliant assembly of City magnates, Lords, and Ministers seated there, Mr. PITT occupying a chair of honour by the Lord Mayor. His health has been proposed as that of the Saviour of England, and drunk with acclamations.

PITT (standing up after repeated calls)

My lords and gentlemen :—You have toasted me
As one who has saved England and her cause.
I thank you gentlemen, unfeignedly.
But—no man has saved England, let me say :
England has saved herself, by her exertions :
She will, I trust, save Europe by her example !

Loud applause, during which he sits down, rises, and sits
down again. The scene then shuts, and the night without
has place.

SPIRIT OF THE YEARS

Those words of this man Pitt—his last large words,
As I may prophesy—that ring to-night
In their first mintage to the feasters here,
Will spread with ageing, lodge, and crystallize,
And stand embedded in the English tongue
Till it grow thin, outworn, and cease to be.—
So is't ordained by That Which all ordains ;
For words were never winged with apter grace,
Or blent with happier choice of time and place,
To hold the imagination of this strenuous race.

SCENE VI[1]

AN INN AT RENNES

Night. A sleeping-chamber. Two candles are burning near
a bed in an alcove, and writing-materials are on the table.
The French admiral, VILLENEUVE, partly undressed, is
pacing up and down the room.

VILLENEUVE

These hauntings have at last nigh proved to me
That this thing must be done. Illustrious foe

---

[1] This scene is a little antedated, to include it in the Act to which it
essentially belongs.

And teacher, Nelson : blest and over blest
In thy outgoing at the noon of strife
When glory clasped thee round ; while wayward
    Death
Refused my coaxings for the like-timed call !
Yet I did press where thickest missiles fell,
And both by precept and example showed
Where lay the line of duty, patriotism,
And honour, in that combat of despair.

> He sees himself in the glass as he passes.

Unfortunate Villeneuve !—whom fate has marked
To suffer for too firm a faithfulness.—
An Emperor's chide is a command to die.—
By him accursed, forsaken by my friend,
Awhile stern England's prisoner, then unloosed
Like some poor dolt unworth captivity,
Time serves me now for ceasing. Why not
    cease ? . . .
When, as Shades whisper in the chasmal night,
" Better, far better, no percipience here."—
O happy lack, that I should have no child
To come into my hideous heritage,
And groan beneath the burden of my name ! [1]

Spirit of the Years

I'll speak.   His mood is ripe for such a parle.

> (Sending a voice into Villeneuve's ear.)

Thou dost divine the hour !

Villeneuve

                    But those stern Nays,
That heretofore were audible to me
At each unhappy time I strove to pass ?

---

[1] " Quel bonheur que je n'aie aucun enfant pour recueillir mon horrible
héritage et qui soit chargé du poids de mon nom ! "—(Extract from the
poignant letter to his wife written on this night.—See Lanfrey iii. 374.)

SPIRIT OF THE YEARS

Have been annulled.   The Will grants exit freely ;
Yea, It says "Now."   Therefore make now thy time.

SPIRIT OF THE PITIES

May his sad sunken soul merge into nought
Meekly and gently as a breeze at eve !

VILLENEUVE

From skies above me and the air around
Those callings which so long have circled me
At last do whisper " Now."   Now it shall be !

He seals a letter, and addresses it to his wife : then takes a
dagger from his accoutrements that are hanging alongside,
and, lying down upon his back on the bed, stabs himself deter-
minedly in many places, leaving the weapon in the last wound.

Ungrateful master ; generous foes ; Farewell !

VILLENEUVE dies ; and the scene darkens.

SCENE VII

KING GEORGE'S WATERING-PLACE, SOUTH WESSEX

The interior of the " Old Rooms " Inn.   Boatmen and
burghers are sitting on settles round the fire, smoking and
drinking.

FIRST BURGHER

So they've brought him home at last, hey ? And
he's to be solemnized with a roaring funeral ?

FIRST BOATMAN

Yes, thank God. . . . 'Tis better to lie dry than wet, if canst do it without stinking on the road gravewards. And they took care that he shouldn't.

SECOND BOATMAN

'Tis to be at Paul's; so they say that know. And the crew of the " Victory " have to walk in front, and Captain Hardy is to carry his stars and garters on a great velvet pincushion.

FIRST BURGHER

Where's the Captain now ?

SECOND BOATMAN (nodding in the direction of Captain Hardy's house)

Down at home here biding with his own folk a bit. I zid en walking with them on the Esplanade yesterday. He looks ten years older than he did when he went. Ay—he brought the galliant hero home !

SECOND BURGHER

Now how did they bring him home so that he could lie in state afterwards to the naked eye !

FIRST BOATMAN

Well, as they always do,—in a cask of sperrits.

SECOND BURGHER

Really, now !

FIRST BOATMAN (lowering his voice)

But what happened was this. They were a long
time coming, owing to contrary winds, and the
" Victory " being little more than a wreck. And
grog ran short, because they'd used near all they
had to peckle his body in. So—they broached
the Adm'l !

SECOND BURGHER

How ?

FIRST BOATMAN

Well ; the plain calendar of it is, that when he
came to be unhooped, it was found that the crew
had drunk him dry. What was the men to do ?
Broke down by the battle, and hardly able to keep
afloat, 'twas a most defendable thing, and it fairly
saved their lives. So he was their salvation after
death as he had been in the fight. If he could have
knowed it, 'twould have pleased him down to the
ground ! How 'a would have laughed through
the spigot-hole : " Draw on, my hearties ! Better
I shrivel than you famish." Ha-ha !

SECOND BURGHER

It may be defendable afloat ; but it seems queer
ashore.

FIRST BOATMAN

Well that's as I had it from one that knows—
Bob Loveday of Overcombe—one of the " Victory "
men that's going to walk in the funeral. However,
let's touch a livelier string. Peter Green, strike up
that new ballet that they've lately had prented here,
and were hawking about town last market-day.

Second Boatman

With all my heart.   Though my wyndpipe's a bit clogged since the wars have made beer so mortal small !

SONG

THE NIGHT OF TRAFALGÁR

I

In the wild October night-time, when the wind
    raved round the land,
And the Back-sea [1] met the Front-sea, and our doors
    were blocked with sand,
And we heard the drub of Dead-man's Bay, where
    bones of thousands are,
We knew not what the day had done for us at
    Trafalgár.
        (All)   Had done,
             Had done,
         For us at Trafalgár !

II

" Pull hard, and make the Nothe, or down we go ! "
    one says, says he.
We pulled ; and bedtime brought the storm ; but
    snug at home slept we.
Yet all the while our gallants after fighting through
    the day,
Were beating up and down the dark, sou'-west of
    Cadiz Bay.
         The dark,
         The dark,
     Sou'-west of Cadiz Bay !

---

[1] In those days the hind-part of the harbour adjoining this scene was so named, and at high tides the waves washed across the isthmus at a point called " The Narrows."

III

The victors and the vanquished then the storm it
    tossed and tore,
As hard they strove, those worn-out men, upon that
    surly shore ;
Dead Nelson and his half-dead crew, his foes from
    near and far,
Were rolled together on the deep that night at
    Trafalgár !

The deep,
The deep,
That night at Trafalgár !

The Cloud-curtain draws.

CHORUS OF THE YEARS (aerial music)

Meanwhile the month moves on to counter-deeds
    Vast as the vainest needs,
And fiercely the predestined plot proceeds.

ACT SIXTH

SCENE I

THE FIELD OF AUSTERLITZ. THE FRENCH POSITION

The night is the 1st of December following, and the eve of the battle. The view is from the elevated position of the Emperor's bivouac. The air cuts keen and the sky glistens with stars, but the lower levels are covered with a white fog stretching like a sea, from which the heights protrude as dusky rocks.

To the left are discernible high and wooded hills. In the front mid-distance the plateau of Pratzen outstands, declining suddenly on the right to a low flat country covered with marshes and pools now mostly obscured. On the plateau itself are seen innumerable and varying lights, marking the bivouac of the centre divisions of the Austro-Russian army. Close to the foreground the fires of the French are burning, surrounded by soldiery. The invisible presence of the countless thousands of massed humanity that compose the two armies makes itself felt indefinably.

The tent of NAPOLÉON rises nearest at hand, with sentinel and other military figures looming around, and saddled horses held by attendants. The accents of the Emperor are audible, through the canvas from inside, dictating a proclamation.

VOICE OF NAPOLÉON

" Soldiers, the hordes of Muscovy now face you,
To mend the Austrian overthrow at Ulm !
But how so ?   Are not these the self-same bands
You met and swept aside at Hollabrünn,
And whose retreating forms, dismayed to flight,
Your feet pursued along the trackways here ?

" Our own position, massed and menacing,
Is rich in chance for opportune attack ;
For, say they march to cross and turn our right—
A course almost their need—their stretching flank
Will offer us, from points now prearranged——"

VOICE OF A MARSHAL

Shows it, your Majesty, the wariness
That marks your usual far-eyed policy,
To openly announce your tactics thus
Some twelve hours ere their form can actualize ?

VOICE OF NAPOLÉON

The zest such knowledge will impart to all
Is worth the risk of leakages.   (To Secretary)
    Write on.
         (Dictation resumed)

" Soldiers, your sections I myself shall lead ;
But ease your minds who would expostulate
Against my undue rashness.   If your zeal
Sow hot confusion in the hostile files
As your old manner is, and in our rush
We mingle with our foes, I'll use fit care.
Nevertheless, should issues stand at pause
But for a wink-while, that time you will eye
Your Emperor the foremost in the shock,
Taking his risk with every ranksman here.
For victory, men, must be no thing surmised,
As that which may or may not beam on us,
Like noontide sunshine on a dubious morn ;
It must be sure !—The honour and the fame
Of France's gay and gallant infantry—
So dear, so cherished all the Empire through—
Binds us to compass it !
               " Maintain the ranks ;
Let none be thinned by impulse or excuse

Of bearing back the wounded : and, in fine,
Be every one in this conviction firm :—
That 'tis our sacred bond to overthrow
These hirelings of a country not their own :
Yea, England's hirelings, they ! — a realm stiff-
　　steeled
In deathless hatred of our land and lives.
　" The campaign closes with this victory ;
And we return to find our standards joined
By vast young armies forming now in France.
Forthwith resistless, Peace establish we,
Worthy of you, the nation, and of me !
　　　　　　　　　　　　　　" NAPOLÉON."
　　　　　　　(To his Marshals)

So shall we prostrate these paid slaves of hers—
England's, I mean—the root of all the war.

VOICE OF MURAT

The further details sent of Trafalgár
Are not assuring.

VOICE OF LANNES

　　　　　　　What may the details be ?

VOICE OF NAPOLÉON (moodily)

We learn that six-and-twenty ships of war,
During the fight and after, struck their flags,
And that the tigerish gale throughout the night
Gave fearful finish to the English rage.
By luck their Nelson's gone, but gone withal
Are twenty thousand prisoners, taken off
To gnaw their finger-nails in British hulks.
Of our vast squadrons of the summer-time
But rags and splintered remnants now remain.—
Thuswise Villeneuve, poor craven, quitted him !

Thus are my projects for the navy damned,
And England puffed to yet more bombastry.
—Well, well ; I can't be everywhere.   No matter ;
A victory's brewing here as counterpoise !
These water-rats may paddle in their slush,
And welcome.   'Tis not long they'll have the lead.
Ships can be wrecked by land !

ANOTHER VOICE

And how by land,
Your Majesty, if one may query such ?

VOICE OF NAPOLÉON (sardonically)

I'll bid all states of Europe shut their ports
To England's arrogant bottoms, slowly starve
Her bloated revenues and monstrous trade,
Till all her hulls lie sodden in their docks,
And her grey island eyes in vain shall seek
One jack of hers upon the ocean plains !

VOICE OF SOULT

A few more master-strokes, your Majesty,
Must be dealt hereabout to compass such !

VOICE OF NAPOLÉON

God, yes !—Even here Pitt's guineas are the foes :
'Tis all a duel 'twixt this Pitt and me ;
And, more than Russia's host, and Austria's flower,
I everywhere to-night around me feel
As from an unseen monster haunting nigh
His country's hostile breath ! — But come : to
    choke it
By our to-morrow's feats, which now, in brief,
I recapitulate.—First Soult will move
To forward the grand project of the day :

Namely : ascend in échelon, right to front,
With Vandamme's men, and those of Saint Hilaire :
Legrand's division somewhere further back—
Nearly whereat I place my finger here—
To be there reinforced by tirailleurs :
Lannes to the left here, on the Olmütz road,
Supported by Murat's whole cavalry.
While in reserve, here, are the grenadiers
Of Oudinot, the corps of Bernadotte,
Rivaud, Drouet, and the Imperial Guard.

MARSHALS' VOICES

Even as we understood, Sire, and have ordered.
Nought lags but day, to light our victory !

VOICE OF NAPOLÉON

Now let us up and ride the bivouacs round,
And note positions ere the soldiers sleep.
—Omit not from to-morrow's home dispatch
Direction that this blow of Trafalgár
Be hushed in all the news-sheets sold in France,
Or, if reported, let it be portrayed
As a rash fight whereout we came not worst,
But were so broken by the boisterous eve
That England claims to be the conqueror.

There emerge from the tent NAPOLÉON and the Marshals,
who all mount the horses that are led up, and proceed through
the frost and rime towards the bivouacs. At the Emperor's
approach to the nearest soldiery they spring up.

SOLDIERS

The Emperor ! He's here ! The Emperor's
here !

AN OLD GRENADIER
(approaching Napoléon familiarly)

We'll bring thee Russian guns and flags galore
To celebrate thy coronation-day !

They gather into wisps the straw, hay, and other litter on which they have been lying, and kindling these at the dying fires, wave them as torches. This is repeated as each fire is reached, till the whole French position is one wide illumination. The most enthusiastic of the soldiers follow the Emperor in a throng as he progresses, and his whereabouts in the vast field is denoted by their cries.

CHORUS OF THE PITIES (aerial music)

Strange suasive pull of personality !

CHORUS OF IRONIC SPIRITS

His projects they unknow, his grin unsee !

CHORUS OF THE PITIES

Their loyal luckless hearts say blindly—He !

The night-shades close over.

SCENE II

THE SAME. THE RUSSIAN POSITION

Midnight at the quarters of FIELD-MARSHAL PRINCE KUTÚ-ZOF at Kresnowitz. An inner apartment is discovered, roughly adapted as a council-room. On a table with candles is unfolded a large map of Austerlitz and its environs.

The Generals are assembled in consultation round the table, WEIROTHER pointing to the map, LANGERON, BUXHÖVDEN,

and MILORÁDOVICH standing by, DOKHTÓROF bending over
the map, PRSCHEBISZEWSKY [1] indifferently walking up and
down. KUTÚZOF, old and weary, with a scarred face and
only one eye, is seated in a chair at the head of the table,
nodding, waking, and nodding again. Some officers of lower
grade are in the background, and horses in waiting are heard
hoofing and champing outside.

WEIROTHER speaks, referring to memoranda, snuffing the
nearest candle, and moving it from place to place on the map
as he proceeds importantly :

WEIROTHER

Now here, our right, along the Olmütz Road
Will march and oust our counterfacers there,
Dislodge them from the Sainton Hill, and thence
Advance direct to Brünn.—You heed me, sirs ?—
The cavalry will occupy the plain :
Our centre and main strength,—you follow me ?—
Count Langeron, Dokhtórof, with Prschebiszewsky
And Kollowrath—now on the Pratzen heights—
Will down and cross the Goldbach rivulet,
Seize Tilnitz, Kobelnitz, and hamlets nigh,
Turn the French right, move onward in their rear,
Cross Schwarsa, hold the great Vienna road :—
So, with the nightfall, centre, right, and left,
Will rendezvous beneath the walls of Brünn.

LANGERON (taking a pinch of snuff)

Good, General ; very good !—if Bonaparte
Will kindly stand and let you have your way.
But what if he do not !—if he forestall
These sound slow movements, mount the Pratzen
    hills
When we descend, fall on *our* rear forthwith,
While we go crying for *his* rear in vain ?

---

[1] This General's name should, it is said, be pronounced in three syllables,
nearly PRESH-EV'-SKY.

KUTÚZOF (waking up)

Ay, ay, Weirother ; that's the question—eh ?

WEIROTHER (impatiently)

If Bonaparte had meant to climb up there,
Being one so spry and so determinate,
He would have set about it ere this eve !
He has not troops to do so, sirs, I say :
His utmost strength is forty thousand men.

LANGERON

Then if so weak, how can so wise a brain
Court ruin by abiding calmly here
The impact of a force so large as ours ?
He may be mounting up this very hour !
What think you, General Milorádovich ?

MILORÁDOVICH

I ? What's the use of thinking, when to-morrow
Will tell us, with no need to think at all !

WEIROTHER

Pah ! At this moment he retires apace.
His fires are dark ; all sounds have ceased that way
Save voice of owl or mongrel wintering there.
But, were he nigh, these movements I detail
Would knock the bottom from his enterprize.

KUTÚZOF (rising)

Well, well. Now this being ordered, set it going.
One here shall make fair copies of the notes,
And send them round. Colonel von Toll I ask
To translate part.—Generals, it grows full late,

And half-a-dozen hours of needed sleep
Will aid us more than maps.   We now disperse,
And luck attend us all.   Good-night.   Good-night.

The Generals and other officers go out severally.

Such plans are—paper !   Only to-morrow's light
Reveals the true manœuvre to my sight !

He flaps out with his hand all the candles but one or two,
slowly walks outside the house, and listens.   On the high
ground in the direction of the French lines are heard shouts,
and a wide illumination grows and strengthens ;   but the
hollows are still mantled in fog.

Are these the signs of regiments out of heart,
And beating backward from an enemy !

[*He remains pondering.*

On the Pratzen heights immediately in front there begins
a movement among the Russians, signifying that the plan
which involves desertion of that vantage-ground is about to
be put in force.   Noises of drunken singing arise from the
Russian lines at various points elsewhere.

KUTÚZOF re-enters his quarters with a face of misgiving.

The night shades involve the whole.[1]

SCENE III

THE SAME.   THE FRENCH POSITION

Shortly before dawn on the morning of the 2nd of December.
A white frost and fog still prevail in the low-lying areas ;   but
overhead the sky is clear.   A dead silence reigns.

NAPOLÉON, on a grey horse, closely attended by BERTHIER,
and surrounded by MARSHALS SOULT, LANNES, MURAT, and
their aides-de-camp all cloaked, is discernible in the gloom

---

[1] In depicting this scene, the writer, like others, has followed without
question the MS. of Count Langeron quoted by M. Thiers.   But the
singular soundness of the Count's own opinion in the consultation, as
recorded, suggests that it may have been somewhat strengthened on
paper at the expense of that of his companions.

riding down from the high ground before Bellowitz, on which they have bivouacked, to the village of Puntowitz on the Goldbach stream, quite near the front of the Russian position of the day before on the Pratzen crest. The Emperor and his companions come to a pause, look around and upward to the hills, and listen.

NAPOLÉON

Their bivouac fires, that lit the top last night,
Are all extinct.

LANNES

         And hark you, Sire ; I catch
A sound which, if I err not, means the thing
We have hoped, and hoping, feared fate would not
     yield !

NAPOLÉON

Faith, can it surely be the tramp of horse
And jolt of cannon downward from the hill
Towards our right here, by the swampy lakes
That face Davout ? Thus, as I sketched, they work !

MURAT

Yes ! They already move upon Tilnitz.

NAPOLÉON

Leave them alone ! Nor stick nor stone we'll stir
To interrupt them. Nought that we can scheme
Will help us like their own stark sightlessness !—
Let them get down to those white lowlands there,
And so far plunge in the level that no skill,
When sudden vision flashes on their fault,
Can help them, though despair-stung, to regain
The key to mastery held at yestereve !

Meantime move onward these divisions here
Under the fog's kind shroud ; descend the slope,
And cross the stream below the Russian lines :
There halt concealed, till I waft down the word.

NAPOLÉON and his staff retire to the hill south-east of Bellowitz as the day dawns pallidly.

'Tis good to get above that rimy cloak
And into cleaner air. It chilled me through.

When they reach the summit they are over the fog : and
suddenly the sun breaks forth radiantly to the left of the
Pratzen upland, illuminating the ash-hued face of NAPOLÉON
and the faces of those around him. All eyes are turned first
to the sun, and thence to look for the dense masses of men
that had occupied the upland the night before.

MURAT

I see them not. The plateau seems deserted !

NAPOLÉON (exultantly)

Gone ; verily !—Ah, how much will you bid,
An hour hence, for the coign abandoned now !
The battle's ours.—It was, then, their rash march
Downwards to Tilnitz and the Goldbach swamps
Before dawn, that we heard.—No hurry, Lannes !
Enjoy this sun, that rests its chubby jowl
Upon the plain, and thrusts its bristling beard
Across the lowlands' fleecy counterpane,
Peering beneath our broadest hat-brims' shade. . . .
Soult, how long hence to win the Pratzen top ?

SOULT

Some twenty minutes or less, your Majesty :
Our troops down there, still mantled by the mist,
Are half upon the way.

NAPOLÉON

        Good ! Set forthwith
Vandamme   and   Saint   Hilaire   to   mount   the
    slopes——

*Firing begins in the marsh to the right by Tilnitz and the
pools, though the thick air yet hides the operations.*

O, there you are, Buxhövden, boozy, blind !
Achieve your worst.   Davout will hold you firm.

*The head of an aide-de-camp rises through the fog on that
side, and he hastens up to* NAPOLÉON *and his companions,
to whom the officer announces what has happened.* DAVOUT
*rides off, disappearing legs first into the white stratum that
covers the attack.*

Lannes and Murat, you have concern enough
Here on the left, with Prince Bagration
And all the Austro-Russian cavalry.
Haste off.   The victory promising to-day
Will, like a thunder-clap, conclude the war !

*The Marshals with their aides gallop away towards their
respective divisions.   Soon the two divisions under* SOULT *are
seen ascending in close column the inclines of the Pratzen
height.   Thereupon the heads of the Russian centre columns
disclose themselves, breaking the sky-line of the summit
from the other side, in a desperate attempt to regain the
position vacated by the Russian left.   A fierce struggle develops
there between* SOULT'S *divisions and these, who, despite their
tardy attempt to recover the lost post of dominance, are pressed
by the French off the slopes into the lowland.*

SEMICHORUS I OF THE PITIES (aerial music)

O Great Necessitator, heed us now !
    If it indeed must be
That this day Austria smoke with slaughtery,
Quicken the issue as Thou knowest how ;
And dull to suffering those whom it befalls
To quit their lodgment in a flesh that galls !

Semichorus II

If it be in the future human story
To lift this man to yet intenser glory,
Let the exploit be done
With the least sting, or none,
To those, his kind, at whose expense such pitch is won !

Spirit of the Years

Again ye deprecate the World-Soul's way
That I so long have told ?   Then note anew
(Since ye forget) the ordered potencies,
Nerves, sinews, trajects, eddies, ducts of It
The Eternal Urger, pressing change on change.

At once, as earlier, a preternatural clearness possesses the atmosphere of the battle-field, in which the scene becomes anatomized and the living masses of humanity transparent. The controlling Immanent Will appears therein, as a brain-like network of currents and ejections, twitching, interpenetrating, entangling, and thrusting hither and thither the human forms.

Semichorus I of Ironic Spirits (aerial music)

O Innocents, can ye forget
That things to be were shaped and set
Ere mortals and this planet met ?

Semichorus II

Stand ye apostrophizing That
Which, working all, works but thereat
Like some sublime fermenting-vat

Semichorus I

Heaving throughout its vast content
With strenuously transmutive bent
Though of its aim unsentient ?—

SEMICHORUS II

Could ye have seen Its early deeds
Ye would not cry, as one who pleads
For quarter, when a Europe bleeds !

SEMICHORUS I

Ere ye, young Pities, had upgrown
From out the deeps where mortals moan
Against a ruling not their own,

SEMICHORUS II

He of the Years beheld, and we,
Creation's prentice artistry
Express in forms that now unbe

SEMICHORUS I

Tentative dreams from day to day ;
Mangle its types, re-knead the clay
In some more palpitating way ;

SEMICHORUS II

Beheld the rarest wrecked amain,
Whole nigh-perfected species slain
By those that scarce could boast a brain ;

SEMICHORUS I

Saw ravage, growth, diminish, add,
Here peoples sane, there peoples mad,
In choiceless throws of good and bad ;

SEMICHORUS II

Heard laughters at the ruthless dooms
Which tortured to the eternal glooms
Quick, quivering hearts in hecatombs.

CHORUS

Us Ancients, then, it ill befits
To quake when Slaughter's spectre flits
Athwart this field of Austerlitz !

SHADE OF THE EARTH

Pain not their young compassions by such lore,
But hold you mute, and read the battle yonder :
The moment marks the day's catastrophe.

SCENE IV

THE SAME. THE RUSSIAN POSITION

It is about noon, and the vital spectacle is now near the village of Tilnitz. The fog has dispersed, and the sun shines clearly, though without warmth, the ice on the pools gleaming under its radiance.

GENERAL BUXHÖVDEN and his aides-de-camp have reined up, and remain at pause on a hillock. The General watches through a glass his battalions, which are still disputing the village. Suddenly approach down the track from the upland of Pratzen large companies of Russian infantry helter-skelter. COUNT LANGERON is beheld to be retreating with them ; and soon, pale and agitated, he hastens up to GENERAL BUXHÖVDEN, whose face is flushed.

LANGERON

While they are upon us you stay idle here !
Prschebiszewsky's column is distraught and rent,
And more than half my own made captive ! Yea,
Kreznówitz carried, and Sokólnitz hemmed :
The enemy's whole strength will stound you soon !

BUXHÖVDEN

You seem to see the enemy everywhere.

LANGERON

You cannot see them, be they here or no !

BUXHÖVDEN

I only wait Prschebiszewsky's nearing corps
To join Dokhtórof's to them.   Here they come.

SOULT, supported by BERNADOTTE and OUDINOT, having
cleared and secured the Pratzen height, his battalions are
perceived descending from it on this side, behind DOKHTÓROF's
division, so placing the latter between themselves and the
pools.

LANGERON

You cannot tell the Frenchmen from ourselves !
These are the victors.—Ah—Dokhtórof—lost !

DOKHTÓROF's troops are seen to be retreating towards the
water.   The watchers stand in painful tenseness.

BUXHÖVDEN

Dokhtórof tell to save him as he may !
We, Count, must gather up our shaken flesh
And hurry them by the road through Austerlitz.

BUXHÖVDEN's regiments and the remains of LANGERON's
are rallied and collected, and they retreat by way of the hamlet
of Aujezd.   As they go over the summit of a hill BUXHÖVDEN
looks back.   LANGERON's columns, which were behind his
own, have been cut off by VANDAMME's division coming down
from the Pratzen plateau.   This and some detachments
from DOKHTÓROF's column rush towards the Satschan lake
and endeavour to cross it on the ice.   It cracks beneath their
weight.   At the same moment NAPOLÉON and his brilliant staff
appear on the top of the Pratzen.
   The Emperor watches the scene with a vulpine smile ; and
directs a battery near at hand to fire down upon the ice on

which the Russians are crossing. A ghastly crash and splashing
follows the discharge, the shining surface breaking into pieces
like a mirror, which fly in all directions. Two thousand fugitives
are engulfed, and their groans of despair reach the ears of the
watchers like ironical huzzas.

A general flight of the Russian army from wing to wing
is now disclosed, involving in its current the EMPEROR ALEX-
ANDER and the EMPEROR FRANCIS, with the reserve, who are
seen towards Austerlitz endeavouring to rally their troops
in vain. They are swept along by the disordered soldiery.

SCENE V

THE SAME.   NEAR THE WINDMILL OF PALENY

The mill is about seven miles to the southward, between the
French advanced posts and the Austrians.

A bivouac fire is burning. NAPOLÉON, in grey overcoat
and beaver hat turned up front and back, rides to the spot
with BERTHIER, SAVARY, and his aides, and alights. He
walks to and fro complacently, meditating or talking to
BERTHIER. Two groups of officers, one from each army, stand
in the background on their respective sides.

NAPOLÉON

What's this of Alexander ?   Weep, did he,
Like his old namesake, but for meaner cause ?
Ha, ha !

BERTHIER

Word goes, your Majesty, that Colonel Toll,
One of Field-Marshal Prince Kutúzof's staff,
In the retreating swirl of overthrow,
Found Alexander seated on a stone
Beneath a leafless roadside apple-tree,
Out here by Göding on the Holitsch way ;
His coal-black uniform and snowy plume
Unmarked, his face disconsolate, his grey eyes

Mourning in tears the fate of his brave array—
All flying southward, save the steadfast slain.

NAPOLÉON

Poor devil !—But he'll soon get over it—
Sooner than his employers oversea !—
Ha !—this will make friend Pitt and England writhe,
And cloud somewhat their lustrous Trafalgár.

An open carriage approaches from the direction of Holitsch,
accompanied by a small escort of Hungarian guards. NAPOLÉON
walks forward to meet it as it draws up, and welcomes the
Austrian Emperor, who alights. He is wearing a grey cloak
over a white uniform, carries a light walking-cane, and is
attended by PRINCE JOHN OF LICHTENSTEIN, SWARZENBERG,
and others. His fresh-coloured face contrasts strangely with
the bluish pallor of NAPOLÉON'S ; but it is now thin and
anxious.

They formally embrace. BERTHIER, PRINCE JOHN, and the
rest retire, and the two Emperors are left by themselves before
the fire.

NAPOLÉON

Here on the roofless ground do I receive you—
My only mansion for these two months past !

FRANCIS

Your tenancy thereof has brought such fame
That it must needs be one which charms you, Sire.

NAPOLÉON

Good ! Now this war. It has been forced on me
Just at a crisis most inopportune,
When all my energies and arms were bent
On teaching England that her watery walls
Are no defence against the wrath of France
Aroused by breach of solemn covenants.

FRANCIS

I had no zeal for violating peace
Till ominous events in Italy
Revealed the gloomy truth that France aspires
To conquest there, and undue sovereignty.
Since when mine eyes have seen no sign outheld
To signify a change of purposings.

NAPOLÉON

Yet there were terms distinctly specified
To General Giulay in November past,
Whereon I'd gladly fling the sword aside.
To wit : that hot armigerent jealousy
Stir us no further on transalpine rule,
I'd take the Isonzo River as our bounds.

FRANCIS

Roundly, that I cede all !—And how may stand
Your views as to the Russian forces here ?

NAPOLÉON

You have all to lose by that alliance, Sire.
Leave Russia.   Let the Emperor Alexander
Make his own terms ; whereof the first must be
That he retire from Austrian territory.
I'll grant an armistice therefor.   Anon
I'll treat with him to weld a lasting peace,
Based on some simple understandings ; chief,
That Russian armies keep to Russian soil,
And that, moreover, every English keel
Be locked from out the ports of his domain.
Meanwhile to you I'll tender this good word :
Keep Austria to herself.   To Russia bound,
You pay your own costs with your provinces,
And Alexander's likewise therewithal.

FRANCIS

I see as much, and long have seen it, Sire ;
And standing here the vanquished, let me own
What happier issues might have left unsaid :
Long, long I have lost the wish to bind myself
To Russia's purposings and Russia's risks ;
Full little do I count alliances
With Powers that have no substance seizable !

> As they converse they walk away.

AN AUSTRIAN OFFICER

O strangest scene of an eventful life,
This junction that I witness here to-day !
An Emperor—in whose majestic veins
Aeneas and the proud Caesarian line
Claim yet to live ; and those scarce less renowned,
The dauntless Hawks'-Hold Counts, of gallantry
So great in fame a thousand years ago—
To bend with deference and manners mild
In talk with this adventuring campaigner,
Raised but by pikes above the common herd !

ANOTHER AUSTRIAN OFFICER

Ay! There be Satschan swamps and Pratzen heights
In royal lines, as here at Austerlitz.

> The Emperors again draw near.

FRANCIS

Then, to this armistice, which shall be called
Immediately at all points, I agree ;
And pledge my word that my august ally
Accept it likewise, and withdraw his force
By daily measured march to his own realm.

NAPOLÉON

For him I take your word. And pray believe
That rank ambitions are your own, not mine ;
That though I have postured as your enemy,
And likewise Alexander's, we are one
In interests, have in all things common cause.
    One country sows these mischiefs Europe through
By her insidious chink of luring ore—
False-featured England, who, to aggrandize
Her name, her influence, and her revenues,
Schemes to impropriate the whole world's trade,
And starves and bleeds the folk of other lands.
Her rock-rimmed situation walls her off
Like a slim selfish mollusk in its shell
From the wide views and fair fraternities
Which on the mainland we reciprocate,
And quicks her quest for profit in our woes !

FRANCIS

I am not competent, your Majesty,
To estimate that country's conscience now,
Nor to engage on my ally's behalf
That English ships be shut from Russian trade.
But joyful am I that in all things else
My promise can be made ; and that this day
Our conference ends in friendship and esteem.

NAPOLÉON

I will send Savary at to-morrow's blink
And make all lucid to the Emperor.
For us, I wholly can avow as mine
The cordial spirit of your Majesty.

    They retire towards the carriage of FRANCIS. BERTHIER,
SAVARY, LICHTENSTEIN, and the suite of officers advance from
the background, and with mutual gestures of courtesy and
amicable leave-takings the two Emperors part company.

CHORUS OF THE PITIES (aerial music)

Each for himself, his family, his heirs ;
For the wan weltering nations who concerns, who cares?

CHORUS OF IRONIC SPIRITS

A pertinent query, in truth !—
But spoil not the sport by your ruth :
*   'Tis enough to make half*
*   Yonder zodiac laugh*
When rulers begin to allude
*   To their lack of ambition,*
*   And strong opposition*
To all but the general good !

SPIRIT OF THE YEARS

Hush levities.   Events press : turn to westward.

A nebulous curtain draws slowly across.

SCENE VI

SHOCKERWICK HOUSE, NEAR BATH

The interior of the Picture Gallery.   Enter WILTSHIRE the owner, and PITT, who looks emaciated and walks feebly.

WILTSHIRE (pointing to a portrait)

Now here you have the lady we discussed :
A fine example of his manner, sir ?

PITT

It is a fine example, sir, indeed,—
With that transparency amid the shades,

And those thin blue-green-greyish leafages
Behind the pillar in the background there,
Which seem the leaves themselves.—Ah, this is Quin.

(*Moving to another picture.*)

WILTSHIRE

Yes, Quin.   A man of varied parts, though rough
And choleric at times.   Yet, at his best,
As Falstaff, never matched, they say.   But I
Had not the fate to see him in the flesh.

PITT

Churchill well carves him in his " Characters " :—
" His eyes, in gloomy socket taught to roll,
Proclaimed the sullen habit of his soul.
In fancied scenes, as in Life's real plan,
He could not for a moment sink the man :
Nature, in spite of all his skill, crept in ;
Horatio, Dorax, Falstaff—still 'twas Quin."
—He was at Bath when Gainsborough settled there
In that house in the Circus which we know.—
I like the portrait much.—The brilliancy
Of Gainsborough lies in this his double sway :
Sovereign of landscape he ; of portraiture
Joint monarch with Sir Joshua. . . . Ah?—that's
        —hark !
Is that the patter of a horse's hoofs
Along the road ?

WILTSHIRE

I notice nothing, sir.

PITT

It is a gallop, growing quite distinct.
And—can it be a messenger for me !

WILTSHIRE

I hope no awkward European news
To stop the honour of this visit, sir !

They listen. The gallop of the horse grows louder, and is
checked at the door of the house. There is a hasty knocking,
and a courier, splashed with mud from hard riding, is shown
into the gallery. He presents a dispatch to PITT, who sits
down and hurriedly opens it.

PITT (to himself)

O heavy news indeed ! . . . Disastrous ; dire !

He appears overcome as he sits, and covers his forehead
with his hand.

WILTSHIRE

I trust you are not ill, sir ?

PITT (after some moments)

Could I have
A little brandy, sir, quick brought to me ?

WILTSHIRE

In one brief minute.

Brandy is brought in, and PITT takes it.

PITT

Now leave me, please, alone. I'll call anon.
Is there a map of Europe handy here ?

WILTSHIRE fetches a map from the library, and spreads it
before the minister. WILTSHIRE, courier, and servant go out.

O God that I should live to see this day !

He remains awhile in a profound reverie ; then resumes the
reading of the dispatch.

" Defeated—the Allies—quite overthrown
At Austerlitz—last week."—Where's Austerlitz ?
—But what avails it where the place is now ;
What corpse is curious on the longitude
And situation of his cemetery ! . . .
The Austrians and the Russians overcome,
That vast adventuring army is set free
To bend unhindered strength against our strand. . . .
So do my plans through all these plodding years
Announce them built in vain !
His heel on Europe, monarchies in chains
To France, I am as though I had never been !

*He gloomily ponders the dispatch and the map some minutes
longer. At last he rises with difficulty, and rings the bell.*

A servant enters.

Call up my carriage, please you, now at once ;
And tell your master I return to Bath
This moment—I may want a little help
In getting to the door here.

SERVANT

                    Sir, I will,
And summon you my master instantly.

He goes out and re-enters with WILTSHIRE. PITT *is assisted
from the room.*

PITT

Roll up that map.   'Twill not be needed now
These ten years!   Realms, laws, peoples, dynasties,
Are churning to a pulp within the maw
Of empire-making Lust and personal Gain !

[*Exeunt* PITT, WILTSHIRE, *and servant ; and in a few
minutes the carriage is heard driving off, and the
scene closes.*

SCENE VII

PARIS.   A STREET LEADING TO THE TUILERIES

It is night, and the dim oil lamps reveal a vast concourse of citizens of both sexes around the Palace gates and in the neighbouring thoroughfares.

SPIRIT OF THE YEARS (to the Spirit of Rumour)

Thou may'st descend and join this crowd awhile,
And speak what things shall come into thy mouth.

SPIRIT SINISTER

I'll harken ! I wouldn't miss it for the groans of
another Austerlitz !

The Spirit of Rumour enters on the scene in the disguise of a young foreigner.

SPIRIT (to a street-woman)

Lady, a late hour this to be afoot !

WOMAN

But such is meet in gallant dames like me,
For now He nears !—after a three months' whirl
Of victories won on fields whose homely names
Had never swept the ear of mortal man
Beyond the haunts of neighbour peasantry ;
But, cymballed now by deathless deeds, become
Familiar rhythms in remotest homes !

SPIRIT

Rare ! To it again. I could give heed all night.

WOMAN

Poor profit, then, to me from my true trade,
Wherein hot competition is so rife
Already, since these victories brought to town
So many foreign jobbers in my line,
That I'd best hold my tongue from praise of fame !
However, one is caught by popular zeal,
And though five midnights have not brought a sou,
I, too, chant *Jubilate* like the rest.—
   In courtesies have haughty monarchs vied
Towards the Conqueror ! who, with men-at-arms
One quarter theirs, has vanquished by his nerve
Vast musterings four-hundred-thousand strong,
And given new tactics to the art of war
Unparalleled in Europe's history !

SPIRIT

What man is this, whose might thou blazonest so—
Who makes the earth to tremble, shakes old thrones,
And turns the plains to wilderness ?

WOMAN

                                        Dost ask
As ignorant, yet asking can define ?
What mean you, traveller ?

SPIRIT

                         I am a stranger here,
A wandering wight, whose life has not been spent
This side the globe, though I can speak the tongue.

WOMAN

Your air has truth in't ; but your state is strange !
Had I a husband he should tackle thee.

SPIRIT

Dozens thou hast had—batches more than she
Samaria knew, if now thou hast not one !

WOMAN

Wilt take the situation from this hour ?

SPIRIT

Thou know'st not what thy frailty asks, good dame !

WOMAN

Well, learn in small the Emperor's chronicle,
As gleaned from what my soldier-husbands say :—
Some five-and-forty standards of his foes
Are brought to Paris, borne triumphantly
In proud procession through the surging streets,
Ever as brands of fame to shine aloft
In dim-lit senate-halls and city aisles.

SPIRIT

Fair Munich sparkled with festivity
As there awhile he tarried, and was met
By the gay Joséphine your Empress here.—
There, too, Eugène—

WOMAN

Napoléon's stepson he——

SPIRIT

Received for gift the hand of fair Princess
Augusta (daughter of Bavaria's crown,
Forced from her plighted troth to Baden's heir),

And, to complete his honouring, was hailed
Successor to the throne of Italy.

WOMAN

How know you, ere this news has got abroad ?

SPIRIT

Channels have I the common people lack.—
There, on the nonce, the forenamed Baden prince
Was joined to Stéphanie Beauharnais, her
Who stands as daughter to the man we wait,
Some say as more.

WOMAN

       They do ?   Then such not I.
Can revolution's dregs so soil thy soul
That thou shouldst doubt the eldest son thereof ?
'Tis dangerous to insinuate nowadays !

SPIRIT

Right !   Lady many-spoused, more charity
Upbrims in thee than in some loftier ones
Who would not name thee with their white-washed
    tongues.—
Enough.   I am one whom, didst thou know my name,
Thou would'st not grudge a claim to speak his mind.

WOMAN

A thousand pardons, sir.

SPIRIT

        Resume thy tale
If so thou wishest.

WOMAN

Nay, but you know best——

SPIRIT

How laurelled progress through applauding crowds
Have marked his journey home. How Strasburg town,
Stuttgart, Carlsruhe, acclaimed him like the rest :
How pageantry would here have welcomed him,
Had not his speed outstript intelligence.
—Now will a glimpse of him repay thee. Hark !

    Shouts arise and increase in the distance, announcing
BONAPARTE's approach.

Well, Buonaparté has revived by land,
But not by sea. On that thwart element
Never will he incorporate his dream,
And float as master !

WOMAN

What shall hinder him ?

SPIRIT

That which has hereto. England, so to say.

WOMAN

But she's in straits. She's lost her Nelson now,
(A worthy man : he loved a woman well !)
George drools and babbles in a darkened room ;
Her heaven-born Minister declines apace ;
All smooths the Emperor's sway.

SPIRIT

                    Tales have two sides,
Sweet lady. Vamped-up versions reach thee here.—

That Austerlitz was lustrous none ignores,
But would it shock thy garrulousness to know
That the true measure of this Trafalgár—
Utter defeat, ay, France's naval death—
Your Emperor bade be hid?

WOMAN

The seer's gift
Has never plenteously endowed me, sir,
As in appearance you.   But to plain sense
Things seem as stated.

SPIRIT

We'll let seemings be.—
But know, these English take to liquid life
Right patly—nursed therefor in infancy
By rimes and rains which creep into their blood,
Till like seeks like.   The sea is their dry land,
And, as on cobbles you, they wayfare there.

WOMAN

Heaven prosper, then, their watery wayfarings
If they'll leave us the land !—

(The Imperial carriage appears.)

The Emperor !—
Long live the Emperor !—He's the best by land.

BONAPARTE's carriage arrives, without an escort.   The street
lamps shine in, and reveal the EMPRESS JOSÉPHINE seated
beside him.   The plaudits of the people grow boisterous as
they hail him Victor of Austerlitz.   The more active run after
the carriage, which turns in from the Rue St. Honoré to the
Carrousel, and thence vanishes into the Court of the Tuileries.

WOMAN

May all success attend his next exploit !

Spirit

Namely : to put the knife in England's trade,
And teach her treaty-manners—if he can !

Woman

I like not your queer knowledge, creepy man.
There's weirdness in your air.   I'd call you ghost
Had not the Goddess Reason laid all such
Past Mother Church's cunning to restore.
—Adieu.   I'll not be yours to-night.   I'd starve first !

She withdraws.   The crowd wastes away, and the Spirit
vanishes.

SCENE VIII

PUTNEY.   BOWLING GREEN HOUSE

Pitt's bedchamber, from the landing without.   It is afternoon.   At the back of the room as seen through the doorway
is a curtained bed, beside which a woman sits, the Lady
Hester Stanhope.   Bending over a table at the front of the
room is Sir Walter Farquhar, the physician.   Parslow the
footman and another servant are near the door.

Tomline, Bishop of Lincoln, enters.

Farquhar (in a subdued voice)

I grieve to call your lordship up again,
But symptoms lately have disclosed themselves
That mean the knell to the frail life in him.
And whatsoever things of gravity
It may be needful to communicate,
Let them be spoken now.   Time may not serve
If they be much delayed.

TOMLINE

           Ah, stands it thus ? . . .
The name of his disease is—Austerlitz !
His brow's inscription has been Austerlitz
From that dire morning in the month just past
When tongues of rumour twanged the word across
From its hid nook on the Moravian plains.

FARQUHAR

And yet he might have borne it, had the weight
Of governmental shackles been unclasped,
Even partly, from his limbs last Lammastide,
When that despairing journey to the King
At Gloucester Lodge by Wessex shore was made
To beg such.   But relief the King refused.
" Why want you Fox ?   What—Grenville and his
    friends ? "
He harped.   " You are sufficient without these—
Rather than Fox, why, give me civil war ! "
And fibre that would rather snap than shrink
Held out no longer.   Now the upshot nears.

    LADY HESTER STANHOPE turns her head and comes forward.

LADY HESTER

I am grateful you are here again, good friend !
He's sleeping some light seconds ; but once more
Has asked for tidings of Lord Harrowby,
And murmured of his mission to Berlin
As Europe's haggard hope ; if, sure, it be
That any hope remain !

TOMLINE

           There's no news yet.—
These several days while I have been sitting by him

He has inquired the quarter of the wind,
And where that moment beaked the stable-cock.
When I said " East," he answered " That is well !
Those are the breezes that will speed him home ! "
So cling his heart-strings to his country's cause.

FARQUHAR

I fear that Wellesley's visit here by now
Strung him to tensest strain.   He quite broke down,
And has fast faded since.

LADY HESTER

        Ah ! now he wakes.
Please come and speak to him as you would wish.

                         (To TOMLINE.)

    LADY HESTER, TOMLINE, and FARQUHAR retire behind the
bed, where in a short time voices are heard in prayer. Afterwards the Bishop goes to a writing-table, and LADY HESTER
comes to the doorway. Steps are heard on the stairs, and
PITT's friend ROSE, the President of the Board of Trade,
appears on the landing and makes inquiries.

LADY HESTER (whispering)

He wills the wardenry of his affairs
To his old friend the Bishop.   But his words
Bespeak too much anxiety for me,
And underrate his services so far
That he has doubts if his high deeds deserve
Such size of recognition by the State
As would award slim pensions to his kin.
He had been fain to write down his intents,
But the quill dropped from his unmuscled hand.—
Now his friend Tomline pens what he dictates
And gleans the lippings of his last desires.

    ROSE and LADY HESTER turn. They see the Bishop bending
over the bed with a sheet of paper on which he has previously

been writing. A little later he dips a quill and holds it within the bed-curtain, spreading the paper beneath. A thin white hand emerges from behind the curtain and signs the paper. The Bishop beckons forward the two servants, who also sign.

FARQUHAR on one side of the bed, and TOMLINE on the other, are spoken to by the dying man. The Bishop afterwards withdraws from the bed and comes to the landing where the others are.

TOMLINE

A list of his directions has been drawn,
And feeling somewhat more at mental ease
He asks Sir Walter if he has long to live.
Farquhar just answered, in a soothing tone,
That hope still frailly breathed recovery.
At this my dear friend smiled and shook his head,
As if to say : " I can translate your words,
But I reproach not friendship's lullabies."

ROSE

Rest he required ; and rest was not for him.

FARQUHAR comes forward as they wait.

FARQUHAR

His spell of concentration on these things,
Determined now, that long have wasted him,
Have left him in a numbing lethargy,
From which I fear he may not rouse to strength
For speech with earth again.

ROSE

But hark. He does.

They listen.

PITT

My country ! How I leave my country ! . . .

TOMLINE

Ah,—
Immense the matter those poor words contain !

ROSE

Still does his soul stay wrestling with that theme,
And still it will, even semi-consciously,
Until the drama's done.

> They continue to converse by the doorway in whispers.
> PITT sinks slowly into a stupor, from which he never awakens.

SPIRIT OF THE PITIES (to the Spirit of the Years)

Do you intend to speak to him ere the close ?

SPIRIT OF THE YEARS

Nay, I have spoke too often ! Time and time,
When all Earth's light has lain on the nether side,
And yapping midnight winds have leapt on roofs,
And raised for him an evil harlequinade
Of national disasters in long train,
That tortured him with harrowing grimace,
Have I communed with that intelligence.
Now I would leave him to pass out in peace,
And seek the silence unperturbedly.

SPIRIT SINISTER

Even ITS official Spirit can show ruth
At man's fag end, when his destruction's sure !

SPIRIT OF THE YEARS

It suits us ill to cavil each with each.
I might retort. I only say to thee
ITS slaves we are : ITS slaves must ever be !

CHORUS (aerial music)

Yea, from the Void we fetch, like these,
*　　And tarry till That please*
To null us by Whose stress we emanate.—
*　　Our incorporeal sense,*
Our overseeings, our supernal state,
*　　Our readings Why and Whence,*
Are but the flower of Man's intelligence ;
And that but an unreckoned incident
Of the all-urging Will, raptly magnipotent.

A gauze of shadow overdraws.

PART SECOND

PART SECOND

CHARACTERS

I. Phantom Intelligences

{ The Ancient Spirit of the Years.
  Chorus of the Years.

{ The Spirit of the Pities.
  Chorus of the Pities.

{ Spirits Sinister and Ironic.
  Choruses of Sinister and Ironic Spirits.

{ The Spirit of Rumour.
  Chorus of Rumours.

The Shade of the Earth.

Spirit-Messengers.

Recording Angels.

II. Persons

The names printed in italics are those of mute figures.

MEN

George the Third.
The Prince of Wales, afterwards Prince Regent.
The Royal Dukes.
Fox.
Perceval.
Castlereagh.
An Under-Secretary of State.
Sheridan.
The Duke of Bedford.
Lord Yarmouth.
Two Young Lords.
Lords Moira and Keith.
Another Lord.
Other Peers, Ambassadors, Ministers, ex-Ministers, Members of Parliament, and Persons of Quality and Office.

———

Sir Arthur Wellesley, afterwards Lord Wellington.

Sir John Moore.
Sir John Hope.
Sir David Baird.
General Beresford.
Colonel Anderson.
Colonel Graham.
Major Colborne, principal Aide-de-Camp to Moore.
Captain Hardinge.
Paget, Fraser, Hill, Napier.
A Captain of Hussars and Others.
Other English Generals, Colonels, Aides, Couriers, and Military Officers.
Two Spies.
Two Army Surgeons.
An Army Chaplain.
A Sergeant of the Waggon-Train.
A Sergeant of the Forty-Third.

TWO SOLDIERS OF THE NINTH.
English Forces.
DESERTERS AND STRAGGLERS.

DR. WILLIS.
SIR HENRY HALFORD.
DR. HEBERDEN.
DR. BAILLIE.
THE KING'S APOTHECARY.
A GENTLEMAN.
TWO ATTENDANTS ON THE KING.

MEMBERS OF A LONDON CLUB.
AN ENGLISHMAN IN VIENNA.
TROTTER, SECRETARY TO FOX.
MR. BAGOT.
MR. FORTH, MASTER OF CERE-
      MONIES.
SERVANTS.
A Beau, A Constable, etc.

NAPOLÉON BONAPARTE.
Joseph Bonaparte.
*Louis and Jérôme Bonaparte, and
      other Members of Napoléon's
      Family.*
CAMBACÉRÈS, ARCH - CHAN-
      CELLOR.
TALLEYRAND.
PRESIDENT OF THE SENATE.
Caulaincourt.
*Lebrun, Duroc, Prince of Neuf-
      châtel, Grand-Duke of Berg.*
Eugène de Beauharnais.
CHAMPAGNY, FOREIGN MINISTER.
DE BAUSSET, CHAMBERLAIN.

MURAT.
SOULT.
MASSÉNA.
BERTHIER.
JUNOT.
FOY.
LOISON.
*Ney, Lannes, and other French
      Marshals, general and regi-
      mental Officers, Aides, and
      Couriers.*
TWO FRENCH SUBALTERNS.
ANOTHER FRENCH OFFICER.
French Forces.

*Grand Marshal, Grand Almoners,
      Heralds, and other Officials at
      Napoléon's marriage.*
ABBÉ DE PRADT, CHAPEL-
      MASTER.
Corvisart, First Physician ⎤ To
BOURDIER, SECOND ⎬ Marie
      PHYSICIAN. ⎥ Louise.
DUBOIS, ACCOUCHEUR. ⎦
Maskers at a Ball.
TWO SERVANTS AT THE TUI-
      LERIES.
A PARISIAN CROWD.
GUILLET DE GEVRILLIÈRE, A
      CONSPIRATOR.
Louis XVIII. of France.
French Princes in England.

THE KING OF PRUSSIA.
Prince Henry of Prussia.
Prince Royal of Bavaria.
PRINCE HOHENLOHE.
*Generals Ruchel, Tauenzien, and
      Attendant Officers.*
Prussian Forces.
PRUSSIAN STRAGGLERS.
BERLIN CITIZENS.

CARLOS IV., KING OF SPAIN.
FERNANDO, PRINCE OF ASTURIAS,
      Son to the King.
GODOY, "PRINCE OF PEACE,"
      Lover of the Queen.
COUNT OF MONTIJO.
VISCOUNT MATEROSA. ⎤ Spanish
DON DIEGO DE LA ⎬ Deputies.
      VEGA. ⎦
Godoy's Guards and other Soldiery.
SPANISH CITIZENS.
A LIFE-GUARDSMAN OF ARAN-
      JUEZ.
A SERVANT TO GODOY.
Spanish Forces.
Camp-Followers.
Muleteers.

FRANCIS, EMPEROR OF AUSTRIA.
METTERNICH.
ANOTHER AUSTRIAN MINISTER.
SCHWARZENBERG.
D'AUDENARDE, AN EQUERRY.
AUSTRIAN OFFICERS.
AIDES-DE-CAMP.

Austrian Forces.
Couriers and Secretaries.
VIENNESE CITIZENS.

———

THE EMPEROR ALEXANDER.

The Grand-Duke Constantine.
Prince Labanoff.
Count Lieven.
Generals Bennigsen, Ouwaroff, and others.
Officers in attendance on Alexander.

WOMEN

CAROLINE, PRINCESS OF WALES.
DUCHESS OF YORK.
DUCHESS OF RUTLAND.
MARCHIONESS OF SALISBURY.
MARCHIONESS OF HERTFORD.
Other Peeresses.
MRS. FITZHERBERT.
Ambassadors' Wives, Wives of Ministers and Members of Parliament, and other Ladies of Note.

———

THE EMPRESS JOSÉPHINE.
HORTENSE, QUEEN OF HOLLAND.
The Mother of Napoléon.
Princess Pauline, and others of Napoléon's Family.
DUCHESS OF MONTEBELLO.
MADAME DE MONTESQUIOU.
MADAME BLAISE, NURSE TO MARIE LOUISE.
Wives of French Ministers, and of other Officials.
Other Ladies of the French Court.
DUCHESS OF ANGOULÊME.

———

LOUISA, QUEEN OF PRUSSIA.
The Countess Voss, Lady-in-Waiting.
BERLIN LADIES.

———

MARÍA LUISA, QUEEN OF SPAIN.
THEREZA OF BOURBON, WIFE OF GODOY.
DOÑA JOSEFA TUDO, MISTRESS OF GODOY.
Lady-in-Waiting to the Queen.
A Servant.

———

M. LOUISA BEATRIX, EMPRESS OF AUSTRIA.
THE ARCHDUCHESS MARIA LOUISA, afterwards the EMPRESS MARIE LOUISE.
MADAME METTERNICH.
LADIES OF THE AUSTRIAN COURT.

———

THE EMPRESS - MOTHER OF RUSSIA.
GRAND - DUCHESS ANNE OF RUSSIA.

ACT FIRST

SCENE I

LONDON. FOX'S LODGINGS, ARLINGTON STREET

Fox, the Foreign Secretary in the new Ministry of All-the-Talents, sits at a table writing. He is a stout, swarthy man, with shaggy eyebrows, and his breathing is somewhat obstructed. His clothes look as though they had been slept in. TROTTER, his private secretary, is writing at another table near.

A servant enters.

SERVANT

Another stranger presses to see you, sir.

Fox (without raising his eyes)

Oh ; another. What's he like ?

SERVANT

A foreigner, sir ; though not so out-at-elbows as might be thought from the denomination. He says he's from Gravesend, having lately left Paris, and that you sent him a passport. He comes with a police-officer.

Fox

Ah, to be sure. I remember. Bring him in, and tell the officer to wait outside. (Servant goes out.)

Trotter, will you leave us for a few minutes ? But
be within hail.

*The secretary retires, and the servant shows in a man who
calls himself* GUILLET DE GEVRILLIÈRE—*a tall, thin figure of
thirty, with restless dark eyes. The door being shut behind
him, he is left alone with the minister. Fox points to a seat,
leans back, and surveys his visitor.*

GEVRILLIÈRE

Thanks to you, sir, for this high privilege
Of hailing England, and of entering here.
Without a fore-extended confidence
Like this of yours, my plans would not have sped.

(A pause.)

Europe, alas ! sir, has her waiting foot
Upon the sill of further slaughter-scenes !

Fox

I fear it is so !—In your lines you wrote,
I think, that you are a true Frenchman born ?

GEVRILLIÈRE

I did, sir.

Fox

How contrived you, then, to cross ?

GEVRILLIÈRE

It was from Embden that I shipped for Gravesend,
In a small sailer called the " Toby," sir,
Masked under Prussian colours. Embden I reached
On foot, on horseback, and by sundry shifts,
From Paris over Holland, secretly.

Fox

And you are stored with tidings of much pith,
Whose tenour would be priceless to the state ?

GEVRILLIÈRE

I am.   It is, in brief, no more nor less
Than means to mitigate and even end
These welfare-wasting wars ; ay, usher in
A painless spell of peace.

Fox

               Prithee speak on.
No statesman can desire it more than I.

GEVRILLIÈRE (looking to see that the door is shut)

No nation, sir, can live its natural life,
Or think its thoughts in these days unassailed,
No crown-capt head enjoy tranquillity.
The fount of such high spring-tide of disorder,
Fevered disquietude, and forceful death,
Is One,—a single man.   He—need I name ?—
The ruler is of France.

Fox

              Well, in the past
I fear that it has looked so.   But we see
Good reason still to hope that broadening views,
Politer wisdom, now is helping him
To saner guidance of his arrogant car.

GEVRILLIÈRE

The generous hope will never be fulfilled !
Ceasing to bluff, then ceases he to be.
None sees that written largelier than himself.

Fox

Then what may be the valued revelation
That you can unlock in such circumstance ?
Sir, I incline to spell you as a spy,
And not the honest help for honest men
You gave you out to be !

Gevrillière

            I beg you, sir,
To spare me that suspicion.   Never a thought
Could be more groundless.   Solemnly I vow
That notwithstanding what his signals show
The Emperor of France is as I say.—
Yet bring I good assurance, and declare
A medicine for all bruised Europe's sores !

Fox (impatiently)

Well, parley to the point, for I confess
No new negotiation do I note
That you can open up to work such cure.

Gevrillière

To speak then to the point permit me, sir :—
The sovereign remedy for an ill effect
Is the extinction of its evil cause.
Safely and surely how to compass this
I have the weighty honour to disclose,
Certain immunities being guaranteed
By those your power can influence, and yourself.

Fox (astonished)

Assassination ?

GEVRILLIÈRE

I care not for names !
A deed's true name is as its purpose is.
The lexicon of Liberty and Peace
Defines not this deed as assassination ;
Though maybe it is writ so in the tongue
Of courts and universal tyranny.

FOX

Why brought you this proposal here to me ?

GEVRILLIÈRE

My knowledge of your love of things humane,
Things free, things fair, of truth, of tolerance,
Right, justice, national felicity,
Prompted belief and hope in such a man !—
The matter is by now well forwarded,
A house at Plassy hired as pivot-point
From which the sanct intention can be worked,
And soon made certain.   To our good allies
No risk attaches ; merely to ourselves.

Fox (touching a private bell)

Sir, your unconscienced hardihood confounds me,
And your mind's measure of my character
Insults it sorely.   By your late-sent lines
Of specious import, by your bland address,
I have been led to prattle hopefully
With a cut-throat confessed !

   The head constable and the secretary enter at the same moment.

                          Ere worse befall,
Sir, up and get you gone most dexterously !
Conduct this man ; lose never sight of him

                                     (to the officer)

Till haled aboard some anchor-weighing craft
Bound to remotest coasts from us and France.

GEVRILLIÈRE (unmoved)

How you may handle me concerns me little.
The project will as roundly ripe itself
Without as with me.   Trusty souls remain,
Though my far bones bleach white on austral
      shores !—
I thank you for the audience.   Long ere this
I might have reft your life !   Ay, notice here—

(He produces a dagger ; which is snatched from him.)

They need not have done that !   Even had you
      risen
To wrestle with, insult, strike, pinion me,
It would have lain unused.   In hands like mine
And my allies', the man of peace is safe,
Treat as he may our corporal tenement
In his misreading of a moral code.

[Exeunt GEVRILLIÈRE and the constable.

Fox

Trotter, indeed you well may stare at me !
I look warm, eh ?—and I am windless, too ;
I have sufficient reason to be so.
That dignified and pensive gentleman
Was a bold bravo, waiting for his chance.
He sketched a scheme for murdering Bonaparte,
Either—as in my haste I understood—
By shooting from a window as he passed,
Or by some other wry and stealthy means
That haunt sad brains which brood on despotism,
But lack the tools to justly cope therewith ! . . .
On later thoughts I feel not fully sure
If, in my ferment, I did right in this.

No ; hail at once the man in charge of him,
And give the word that he is to be detained.

The secretary goes out. Fox walks to the window in deep
reflection till the secretary returns.

SECRETARY

I was in time, sir. He has been detained.

Fox

Now what does strict state-honour ask of me ?—
No less than that I bare this poppling plot
To the French ruler and our fiercest foe !—
Maybe 'twas but a hoax to pocket pay ;
And yet it can mean more . . .
The man's indifference to his own vague doom
Beamed out as one exalted trait in him,
And showed the altitude of his rash dream !—
Well, now I'll get me on to Downing Street,
There to draw up a note to Talleyrand
Retailing him the facts.—What signature
Subscribed this desperate fellow when he wrote ?

SECRETARY

" Guillet de la Gevrillière." Here it stands.

Fox

Doubtless it was a false one. Come along.

(Looking out of the window.)

Ah—here's Sir Francis Vincent : he'll go with us.
Ugh, what a twinge ! Time signals that he draws
Towards the twelfth stroke of my working-day !
I fear old England soon must voice her speech
With Europe through another mouth than mine !

SECRETARY

I trust not, sir. Though you should rest awhile.
The very servants half are invalid
From the unceasing labours of your post,
And these cloaked visitors of every clime
That market on your magnanimity
To gain an audience morning, night, and noon,
Leaving you no respite.

FOX

             'Tis true ; 'tis true.—
How I shall love my summer holiday
At pleasant Saint-Ann's Hill !

      He leans on the secretary's arm, and they go out.

SCENE II

THE ROUTE BETWEEN LONDON AND PARIS

A view now nocturnal, now diurnal, from on high over the
Straits of Dover, and stretching from city to city. By night
Paris and London seem each as a little swarm of lights surrounded by a halo ; by day as a confused glitter of white
and grey. The Channel between them is as a mirror reflecting
the sky, brightly or faintly, as the hour may be.

SPIRIT OF THE PITIES

What mean these couriers shooting shuttlewise
To Paris and to London, turn and turn?

RUMOURS (chanting in antiphons)

I

The aforesaid tidings from the minister, spokesman in
England's cause to states afar,

II

Traverse the waters borne by one of such ; and thereto
Bonaparte's responses are :

I

" The principles of honour and of truth which ever
actuate the sender's mind

II

" Herein are written largely ! Take our thanks : we
read that this conjuncture undesigned

I

" Unfolds felicitous means of showing you that still
our eyes are set, as yours, on peace,

II

" To which great end the Treaty of Amiens must be the
ground-work of our amities."

I

From London then : " The path to amity the King of
England studies to pursue ;

II

" With Russia hand in hand he is yours to close the
long convulsions thrilling Europe through."

I

Still fare the shadowy missioners across, by Dover-road
and Calais Channel-track,

II

From Thames-side towers to Paris palace-gates ; from
Paris leisurely to London back.

I

Till thus speaks France : " Much grief it gives us that,
being pledged to treat, one Emperor with one King,

II

" You yet have struck a jarring counternote and tone
that keys not with such promising.

I

" In these last words, then, of this pregnant parle ; I
trust I may persuade your Excellency

II

" That in no circumstance, on no pretence, a party to
our pact can Russia be."

SPIRIT SINISTER

Fortunately for the manufacture of corpses by
machinery Napoléon sticks to this veto, and so wards
off the awkward catastrophe of a general peace descend-
ing upon Europe. Now England.

RUMOURS (continuing)

I

Thereon speeds down through Kent and Picardy, evenly
as some southing sky-bird's shade :—

II

" We gather not from your Imperial lines a reason why
our words should be reweighed.

I

" We hold to Russia not as our ally that is to be : she
stands full-plighted so ;

II

" *Thus trembles peace upon this balance-point : will
you that Russia be let in or no ? "*

I

*Then France rolls out rough words across the strait :
" To treat with you confederate with the Tsar,*

II

" *Presumes us sunk in sloughs of shamefulness from
which we yet stand gloriously afar !*

I

" *The English army must be Flanders-flung, and
entering Picardy with pompous prance,*

II

" *To warrant such ! Enough. Our comfort is, the
crime of further strife lies not with France.*"

Spirit of the Pities

*Alas ! what prayer will save the struggling lands,
Whose lives are ninepins to these bowling hands ?*

Chorus of Rumours

*France secretly with—Russia plights her troth !
Britain, that lonely isle, is slurred by both.*

Spirit Sinister

*It is as neat as an uncovered check at chess ! You
may now mark Fox's blank countenance at finding
himself thus rewarded for the good turn done to
Bonaparte, and at the extraordinary conduct of his
chilly friend the Muscovite.*

Spirit of the Pities

His hand so trembles it can scarce retain
The quill wherewith he lets Lord Yarmouth know
Reserve is no more needed !

Spirit Ironic

Now enters another character of this remarkable
little piece — Lord Lauderdale — and again the
messengers fly !

Spirit of the Pities

But what strange figure, pale and noiseless, comes,
By us perceived, unrecognized by those,
Into the very closet and retreat
Of England's Minister ?

Spirit of the Years

        The Tipstaff he
Of the Will—the Many-masked, my good friend
Death.—
The statesman's feeble form you may perceive
Now hustled into the Invisible,
And the unfinished game of Dynasties
Left to proceed without him !

Spirit of the Pities

        Here, then, ends
My hope for Europe's reason-wrought repose !
He was the friend of peace—did his great best
To shed her balms upon humanity ;
And now he's gone ! No substitute remains.

Spirit Ironic

Ay ; the remainder of the episode is frankly farcical.
Negotiations are again affected ; but finally you discern

Lauderdale applying for passports ; and the English Parliament declares to the nation that peace with France cannot be made.

RUMOURS (concluding)

I

The smouldering dudgeon of the Prussian king, mean-
*   while, upon the horizon's rim afar*

II

Bursts into running flame, that all his signs of friendli-
*   ness were met by moves for war.*

I

Attend and hear, for hear ye faintly may, his manifesto
*   made at Erfurt town,*

II

That to arms only dares he now confide the safety and
*   the honour of his crown !*

SPIRIT OF THE YEARS

Draw down the curtain, then, and overscreen
This too-protracted verbal fencing-scene,
And let us turn to clanging foot and horse,
Ordnance, and all the enginry of Force !

Clouds close over the perspective.

SCENE III

THE STREETS OF BERLIN

It is afternoon, and the thoroughfares are crowded with citizens in an excited and anxious mood. A central path is left open for some expected arrival.

There enters on horseback a fair woman, whose rich brown curls stream flutteringly in the breeze, and whose long blue

habit flaps against the flank of her curvetting white mare.
She is the renowned Louisa, Queen of Prussia, riding at the
head of a regiment of hussars and wearing their uniform.
As she prances along the thronging citizens acclaim her
enthusiastically.

SPIRIT OF THE PITIES

Who is this fragile Fair, in fighting trim ?

SPIRIT OF THE YEARS

She is the pride of Prussia, whose resolve
Gives ballast to the purpose of her spouse,
And holds him to what men call governing.

SPIRIT OF THE PITIES

Queens have engaged in war ; but war's loud trade
Rings with a roar unnatural, fitful, forced,
Practised by woman's hands !

SPIRIT OF THE YEARS

                   Of her we view
The enterprise is that of scores of men,
The strength but half-a-one's.

SPIRIT OF THE PITIES

                   Would fate had ruled
The valour had been his, hers but the charm !

SPIRIT OF RUMOUR

But he has nothing on't, and she has all.
The shameless satires of the bulletins
Dispatched to Paris, thence the wide world through,
Disturb the dreams of her by those who love her,
And thus her brave adventures for the realm

Have blurred her picture, soiled her gentleness,
And wrought her credit harm.

FIRST CITIZEN (vociferously)

Yes, by God: send an ultimatum to Paris
forthwith ; that's what we'll do, by God. This
Confederation of the Rhine was the evil thought of
an evil man bent on ruining us !

SECOND CITIZEN

This country double-faced and double-tongued,
This France, or rather say, indeed, this Man—
(Peoples are honest dealers in the mass)—
This man, to sign a stealthy scroll with Russia
That shuts us off from all indemnities,
While swearing faithful friendship with our King,
And, still professing our safe wardenry,
To fatten other kingdoms at our cost,
Insults us grossly, and makes Europe clang
With echoes of our wrongs.   The little states
Of this antique and homely German land
Are severed from their blood-allies and kin—
Hereto of one tradition, interest, hope—
In calling lord this rank adventurer,
Who'll thrust them as a sword against ourselves.—
Surely Great Frederick sweats within his tomb !

THIRD CITIZEN

Well, we awake, though we have slumbered long,
And She is sent by Heaven to kindle us.

The QUEEN approaches to pass back again with her suite.
The vociferous applause is repeated. They regard her as she
nears.

To cry her Amazon, a blusterer,
A brazen comrade of the bold dragoons

Whose uniform she dons !   Her, whose each act
Shows but a mettled modest woman's zeal,
Without a hazard of her dignity
Or moment's sacrifice of seemliness,
To fend off ill from home !

FOURTH CITIZEN (entering)

The tidings fly that Russian Alexander
Declines with emphasis to ratify
The pact of his ambassador with France,
And that the offer made the English King
To compensate the latter at our cost
Has not been taken.

THIRD CITIZEN

                      And it never will be !
Thus evil does not always flourish, faith.
Throw down the gage while God is fair to us ;
He may be foul anon !   (A pause.)

FIFTH CITIZEN (entering)

Our ambassador Lucchesini is already leaving
Paris. He could stand the Emperor no longer, so
the Emperor said he could not stand Lucchesini.
Knobelsdorf, who takes his place, has decided to
order his snuff by the ounce and his candles by the
pound, lest he should not be there long enough to
use more.

The QUEEN goes by, and they gaze at her and at the escort
of soldiers.

Haven't we soldiers ?   Haven't we the Duke of
Brunswick to command 'em ? Haven't we provisions,
hey ?   Haven't we fortresses and an Elbe, to bar the
bounce of an invader ?

The cavalcade passes out of sight and the crowd draws off.

FIRST CITIZEN

Heaven, I must to beer and 'bacco, to soften my
rage !   [Exeunt citizens.

SPIRIT OF THE YEARS

So doth the Will objectify Itself
In likeness of a sturdy people's wrath,
Which takes no count of the new trends of time,
Trusting ebbed glory in a present need.—
What if their strength should equal not their fire,
And their devotion dull their vigilance ?—
Uncertainly, by fits, the Will doth work
In Brunswick's blood, their chief, as in themselves ;
It ramifies in streams that intermit
And make their movement vague, old-fashioned, slow
To foil the modern methods counterposed !

Evening descends on the city, and it grows dusk. The
soldiers being dismissed from duty, some young officers in a
frolic of defiance halt, draw their swords and whet them on
the steps of the FRENCH AMBASSADOR'S residence as they
pass. The noise of whetting is audible through the street.

CHORUS OF THE PITIES (aerial music)

The soul of a nation distrest
Is aflame,
And heaving with eager unrest
In its aim
To assert its old prowess, and stouten its chronicled fame!

SEMICHORUS I

It boils in a boisterous thrill
Through the mart,
Unconscious well-nigh as the Will
Of its part :
Would it wholly might be so, and feel not the forth-
coming smart !

Semichorus II

In conclaves no voice of reflection
Is heard,
King, Councillors, grudge circumspection
A word,
And victory is visioned, and seemings as facts are
averred.

Chorus

Yea, the soul of a nation distrest
Is aflame,
And heaving with eager unrest
In its aim
At supreme desperations to blazon the national name !

Midnight strikes, lights are extinguished one by one, and the scene disappears.

SCENE IV

THE FIELD OF JENA

Day has just dawned through a grey October haze. The French, with their backs to the nebulous light, loom out and show themselves to be already under arms ; Lannes holding the centre, Ney the right, Soult the extreme right, and Augereau the left. The Imperial Guard and Murat's cavalry are drawn up on the Landgrafenberg, behind the centre of the French position. In a valley stretching along to the rear of this height flows northward towards the Elbe the little river Saale, on which the town of Jena stands.

On the irregular plateaux in front of the French lines, and almost close to the latter, are the Prussians under Tauenzien ; and away on their right rear towards Weimar the bulk of the army under Prince Hohenlohe. The Duke of Brunswick (father of the Princess of Wales) is twelve miles off with his force at Auërstadt, in the valley of the Ilm.

Enter Napoléon, and men bearing torches who escort him. He moves along the front of his troops, and is lost to view

behind the mist and surrounding objects. But his voice is
audible.

NAPOLÉON

Keep you good guard against their cavalry,
In past repute the formidablest known,
And such it may be now ; so asks our heed.
Receive it, then, in square, unflinchingly.—
Remember, men, last year you captured Ulm,
So make no doubt that you will vanquish these !

SOLDIERS

Long live the Emperor !   Advance, advance !

NAPOLÉON

Nay, caution, men ! 'Tis mine to time your deeds
By light of long experience : yours to do them.

DUMB SHOW

Almost immediately glimpses reveal that LANNES' corps is
moving forward, and amid an unbroken clatter of firelocks
spreads out further and wider upon the stretch of country
in front of the Landgrafenberg. The Prussians, surprised at
discerning in the fog such masses of the enemy close at hand,
recede towards the Ilm.

From PRINCE HOHENLOHE, who is with the body of the
Prussians on the Weimar road to the south, comes perspiring
the bulk of the infantry to rally the retreating regiments of
TAUENZIEN, and he hastens up himself with the cavalry and
artillery. The action is renewed between him and NEY as the
clocks of Jena strike ten.

But AUGEREAU is seen coming to NEY's assistance on one
flank of the Prussians, SOULT bearing down on the other,
while NAPOLÉON on the Landgrafenberg orders the Imperial
Guard to advance. The doomed Prussians are driven back,
this time more decisively, falling in great numbers and losing
many as prisoners as they reel down the sloping land towards
the banks of the Ilm behind them. GENERAL RUCHEL, in a
last despairing effort to rally, faces the French onset in person
and alone. He receives a bullet through the chest and falls
dead.

The crisis of the struggle is reached, though the battle is not over. NAPOLÉON, discerning from the Landgrafenberg that the decisive moment has come, directs MURAT to sweep forward with all his cavalry. It engages the shattered Prussians, surrounds them, and cuts them down by thousands.

From behind the horizon, a dozen miles off, between the din of guns in the visible battle, there can be heard an ominous roar, as of a second invisible battle in progress there. Generals and other officers look at each other and hazard conjectures between whiles, the French with exultation, the Prussians gloomily.

HOHENLOHE

That means the Duke of Brunswick, I conceive,
Impacting on the enemy's further force
Led by, they say, Davout and Bernadotte. . . .
God grant his star less lurid rays than ours,
Or this too pregnant, hoarsely-groaning day
Shall, ere its loud delivery be done,
Have twinned disasters to the fatherland
That fifty years will fail to sepulchre!

Enter a straggler on horseback.

STRAGGLER

Prince, I have circuited by Auërstadt,
And bring ye dazzling tidings of the fight,
Which, if report by those who saw't be true,
Has raged thereat from clammy day-dawn on,
And left us victors!

HOHENLOHE

Thitherward go I,
And patch the mischief wrought upon us here!

Enter a second and then a third straggler.

Well, wet-faced men, whence come ye? What d'ye
bring?

STRAGGLER II

Your Highness, I rode straight from Hassenhausen,
Across the stream of battle as it boiled
Betwixt that village and the banks of Saale,
And such the turmoil that no man could speak
On what the issue was !

HOHENLOHE (to Straggler III)

                   Can you add aught ?

STRAGGLER III

Nothing that's clear, your Highness.

HOHENLOHE

                         Man, your mien
Is that of one who knows, but will not say.
Detain him here.

STRAGGLER III

               The blackness of my news,
Your Highness, darks my sense ! . . . I saw this
     much :
The Duke of Brunswick, spurring on to head
His charging grenadiers, received in the face
A grape-shot stroke that gouged out half of it,
Proclaiming then and there his life fordone.

HOHENLOHE

Fallen ? Brunswick ! Reed in council, rock in fire . . .
Ah, this he looked for.   Many a time of late
Has he, by some strange gift of foreknowing,
Declared his fate was hovering in such wise !

STRAGGLER III

His aged form being borne beyond the strife,
The gallant Moellendorf, in flushed despair,
Swore he would not survive ; and, pressing on,
He, too, was slaughtered. Patriotic rage
Brimmed marshals' breasts and men's. The King
 himself
Fought like the commonest. But nothing served.
His horse is slain ; his own doom yet unknown.
Prince William, too, is wounded. Brave Schmettau
Is broke ; himself disabled. All give way,
And regiments crash like trees at felling-time !

HOHENLOHE

No more. We match it here. The yielding lines
Still sweep us backward. Backward we must go !

   [Exeunt HOHENLOHE, Staff, stragglers, etc.

  The Prussian retreat from Jena quickens to a rout, many
thousands being taken prisoners by MURAT, who pursues them
to Weimar, where the inhabitants fly shrieking through the
streets.

  The October day closes in to evening. By this time the
troops retiring with the King of Prussia from the second
battlefield of Auërstadt have intersected RUCHEL's and HOHEN-
LOHE's flying battalions from Jena. The crossing streams of
fugitives strike panic into each other, and the tumult increases
with the thickening darkness till night renders the scene
invisible, and nothing remains but a confused diminishing
noise, and fitful lights here and there.

  The fog of the morning returns, and curtains all.

SCENE V

BERLIN.   A ROOM OVERLOOKING A PUBLIC PLACE

A fluttering group of ladies is gathered at the window, gazing out and conversing anxiously. The time draws towards noon, when the clatter of a galloping horse's hoofs is heard echoing up the long Potsdamer-Strasse, and presently turning into the Leipziger-Strasse reaches the open space commanded by the ladies' outlook. It ceases before a Government building opposite them, and the rider disappears into the courtyard.

First Lady

Yes : surely he is a courier from the field !

Second Lady

Shall we not hasten down, and take from him
The doom his tongue may deal us ?

Third Lady

                        We shall catch
As soon by watching here as hastening hence
The tenour of his news. (They wait.) Ah, yes : see—
    see
The bulletin is straightway to be nailed !
He was, then, from the field. . . .

        They wait on while the bulletin is affixed.

Second Lady

I cannot scan the words the scroll proclaims ;
Peer as I will, these too quick-thronging dreads
Bring water to the eyes.   Grant us, good Heaven,

That victory be where she is needed most
To prove Thy goodness! . . . What do you make
    of it ?

THIRD LADY (reading, through a glass)

" The battle strains us sorely ; but resolve
May save us even now.   Our last attack
Has failed, with fearful loss.   Once more we strive."

    A long silence in the room.   Another rider is heard approach-
ing, above the murmur of the gathering citizens.   The second
lady looks out.

SECOND LADY

A straggler merely he. . . . But they decide,
At last, to post his news, wild-winged or no.

THIRD LADY (reading again through her glass)

" The Duke of Brunswick, leading on a charge,
Has met his death-doom.   Schmettau, too, is slain ;
Prince William wounded.   But we stand as yet,
Engaging with the last of our reserves."

    The agitation in the street communicates itself to the room.
Some of the ladies weep silently as they wait, much longer
this time.   Another horseman is at length heard clattering
into the Platz, and they lean out again with painful eagerness.

SECOND LADY

An adjutant of Marshal Moellendorf's,
If I define him rightly.   Read—O read !—
Though reading draw them from their socket-holes
Use your eyes now !

THIRD LADY (glass up)

            As soon as 'tis affixed. . . .
Ah—this means much !   The people's air and gait
Too well betray disaster.   (Reading.)   " Berliners,
The King has lost the battle !   Bear it well.

The foremost duty of a citizen
Is to maintain a brave tranquillity.
This is what I, the Governor, demand
Of men and women now. . . . The King lives still."

They turn from the window and sit in a silence broken only by monosyllabic words, hearing abstractedly the dismay without that has followed the previous excitement and hope.

The stagnation is ended by a cheering outside, of subdued emotional quality, mixed with sounds of grief. They again look forth. QUEEN LOUISA is leaving the city with a very small escort, and the populace seem overcome. They strain their eyes after her as she disappears.

Enter fourth lady.

FIRST LADY

How does she bear it ?   Whither does she go ?

FOURTH LADY

She goes to join the King at Cüstrin, there
To abide events—as we.   Her heroism
So schools her sense of her calamities
As out of grief to carve new queenliness,
And turn a mobile mien to statuesque,
Save for a sliding tear.

The ladies leave the window severally.

SPIRIT IRONIC

So the Will plays at flux and reflux still.
This monarchy, one-half whose pedestal
Is built of Polish bones, has bones home-made !
Let the fair woman bear it.   Poland did.

SPIRIT OF THE YEARS

Meanwhile the mighty Emperor nears apace,
And soon will glitter at the city gates

With palpitating drums, and breathing brass,
And rampant proudly jingling retinue.

An evening mist cloaks the scene.

SCENE VI

THE SAME

It is a brilliant morning, with a fresh breeze, and not a cloud. The open Platz and the adjoining streets are filled with dense crowds of citizens, in whose upturned faces curiosity has mastered consternation and grief.

Martial music is heard, at first faint, then louder, followed by a trampling of innumerable horses and a clanking of arms and accoutrements. Through a street on the right hand of the view from the windows come troops of French dragoons heralding the arrival of BONAPARTE.

Re-enter the room hurriedly and cross to the windows several ladies as before, some in tears.

FIRST LADY

The kingdom late of Prussia, can it be
That thus it disappears ?—a patriot-cry,
A battle, bravery, ruin ; and no more ?

SECOND LADY

Thank God the Queen's gone !

THIRD LADY

                To what sanctuary ?
From earthquake shocks there is no sheltering cell !
—Is this what men call conquest ? Must it close
As historied conquests do, or be annulled
By modern reason and the urbaner sense ?—

Such issue none would venture to predict,
Yet folly 'twere to nourish foreshaped fears
And suffer in conjecture and in deed.—
If verily our country be dislimbed,
Then at the mercy of his domination
The face of earth will lie, and vassal kings
Stand waiting on himself the Overking,
Who ruling them rules all ; till desperateness
Sting and excite a bonded last resistance,
And work its own release.

SECOND LADY

                    He comes even now
From sacrilege.   I learn that, since the fight,
In marching here by Potsdam yesterday,
Sans-Souci Palace drew his curious feet,
Where even great Frederick's tomb was bared to him.

FOURTH LADY

All objects in the Palace—cared for, kept
Even as they were when our arch-monarch died—
The books, the chair, the inkhorn, and the pen
He quizzed with flippant curiosity ;
And entering where our hero's bones are urned
He seized the sword and standards treasured there,
And with a mixed effrontery and regard
Declared that Paris soon should see them all
As gifts to the Hôtel des Invalides.

THIRD LADY

Such rodomontade is cheap : what matters it !

   A galaxy of marshals, forming Napoléon's staff, now enters
the Platz immediately before the windows.   In the midst
rides the EMPEROR himself.   The ladies are silent.   The procession passes along the front until it reaches the entrance
to the Royal Palace.   At the door NAPOLÉON descends from his
horse and goes into the building amid the resonant trumpetings
of his soldiers and the silence of the crowd.

SECOND LADY (impressed)

O why does such a man debase himself
By countenancing loud scurrility
Against a queen who cannot make reprise !
A power so ponderous needs no littleness—
The last resort of feeble desperates !

Enter fifth lady.

FIFTH LADY (breathlessly)

Humiliation grows acuter still.
He placards rhetoric to his soldiery
On their distress of us and our allies,
Declaring he'll not stack away his arms
Till he has choked the remaining foes of France
In their own gainful glut.—Whom means he, think
    you ?

FIRST LADY

Us ?

THIRD LADY

   Russia ?   Austria ?

FIFTH LADY

             Neither : England.—Yea,
Her he still holds the master mischief-mind,
And marrer of the countries' quietude,
By exercising untold tyranny
Over all ports and seas.

SECOND LADY

         Then England's doomed !
When he has overturned the Russian rule,
England comes next for wrack. They say that
    know ! . . .

Look—he has entered by the Royal doors
And makes the Palace his.—Now let us go !—
Our course, alas ! is—whither ?

                        [Exeunt ladies.

       The curtain drops temporarily.

SEMICHORUS I OF IRONIC SPIRITS (aerial music)

Deeming himself omnipotent
With the Kings of the Christian continent,
To warden the waves was his further bent.

SEMICHORUS II

But the weaving Will from eternity,
(Hemming them in by a circling sea)
Evolved the fleet of the Englishry.

SEMICHORUS I

The wane of his armaments ill-advised,
At Trafalgár, to a force despised,
Was a wound which never has cicatrized.

SEMICHORUS II

This, O this is the cramp that grips !
And freezes the Emperor's finger-tips
From signing a peace with the Land of Ships.

CHORUS

The Universal-empire plot
Demands the rule of that wave-walled spot ;
And peace with England cometh not !

THE SCENE REOPENS

     A lurid gloom now envelops the Platz and city; and
Bonaparte is heard as from the Palace :

Voice of Napoléon

These monstrous violations being in train
Of law and national integrities
By English arrogance in things marine,
(Which dares to capture simple merchant-craft,
In honest quest of harmless merchandize,
For crime of kinship to a hostile power)
Our vast, effectual, and majestic strokes
In this unmatched campaign, enable me
To bar from commerce with the Continent
All keels of English frame.   Hence I decree :—

Spirit of Rumour

This outlines his august " Berlin Decree."
Maybe he meditates its scheme in sleep,
Or hints it to his suite, or syllables it
While shaping, to his scribes.

Voice of Napoléon (continuing)

All England's ports to suffer strict blockade ;
All traffic with that land to cease forthwith ;
All natives of her isles, wherever met,
To be detained as windfalls of the war.
All chattels of her make, material, mould,
To be good prize wherever pounced upon :
And never a bottom hailing from her shores
But shall be barred from every haven here.
This for her heavy harms to human rights,
And shameless sauciness to neighbour powers !

Spirit Sinister

I spell herein that our excellently high-coloured
drama is not played out yet !

SPIRIT OF THE YEARS

Nor will it be for many a month of moans,
And summer shocks, and winter-whitened bones.

The night gets darker, and the Palace outlines are lost.

SCENE VII

TILSIT AND THE RIVER NIEMEN

The scene is viewed from the windows of BONAPARTE'S
temporary quarters. Some sub-officers of his suite are looking
out upon it.

It is the day after midsummer, about one o'clock. A
multitude of soldiery and spectators lines each bank of the
broad river which, stealing slowly north-west, bears almost
exactly in its midst a moored raft of bonded timber. On this
as a floor stands a gorgeous pavilion of draped woodwork,
having at each side, facing the respective banks of the stream,
a round-headed doorway richly festooned. The cumbersome
erection acquires from the current a rhythmical movement,
as if it were breathing, and the breeze now and then produces
a shiver on the face of the stream.

DUMB SHOW

On the south-west or Prussian side rides the EMPEROR
NAPOLÉON in uniform, attended by the GRAND DUKE OF BERG,
the PRINCE OF NEUFCHÂTEL, MARSHAL BESSIÈRES, DUROC
Marshal of the Palace, and CAULAINCOURT Master of the Horse.
The EMPEROR looks well, but is growing fat. They embark
on an ornamental barge in front of them, which immediately
puts off. It is now apparent to the watchers that a precisely
similar enactment has simultaneously taken place on the
opposite or Russian bank, the chief figure being the EMPEROR
ALEXANDER—a graceful, flexible man of thirty, with a courteous
manner and good-natured face. He has come out from an inn
on that side, accompanied by the GRAND-DUKE CONSTANTINE,
GENERAL BENNIGSEN, GENERAL OUWAROFF, PRINCE LABANOFF,
and ADJUTANT-GENERAL COUNT LIEVEN.

The two barges draw towards the raft, reaching the opposite
sides of it about the same time, amidst discharges of cannon.

Each Emperor enters the door that faces him, and meeting in the centre of the pavilion they formally embrace each other. They retire together to the screened interior, the suite of each remaining in the outer half of the pavilion.

More than an hour passes while they are thus invisible. The French officers who have observed the scene from the lodging of NAPOLÉON walk about idly, and ever and anon go curiously to the windows, again to watch the raft.

CHORUS OF THE YEARS (aerial music)

The prelude to this smooth scene—mark well!—were
    the shocks whereof the times gave token
Vaguely to us ere last year's snows had greyed Lithuan
    pine and pool,
Which we told at the fall of the faded leaf, when the
    pride of Prussia was bruised and broken,
And the Man of Adventure sat in the seat of the Man
    of Method and rigid Rule.

SEMICHORUS I OF THE PITIES

Snows incarnadined were thine, O Eylau, field of the
    wide white spaces,
And frozen lakes, and frozen limbs, and blood iced hard
    as it left the veins :
Steel-cased squadrons swathed in cloud-drift, plunging
    to doom through pathless places,
And forty thousand dead and nigh dead, strewing the
    early-nighted plains.

SEMICHORUS II

Friedland to these adds its tale of victims, its midnight
    marches and hot collisions,
Its plunge, at his word, on the enemy hooped by the
    bended river and famed Mill stream,
As he shatters the moves of the loose-knit nations to
    curb his exploitful soul's ambitions,
And their great Confederacy dissolves like the diorama
    of a dream.

DUMB SHOW (continues)

NAPOLÉON and ALEXANDER emerge from their seclusion, and each is beheld talking to the suite of his companion apparently in flattering compliment. An effusive parting, which signifies itself to be but temporary, is followed by their return to the river shores amid the cheers of the spectators.

NAPOLÉON and his marshals arrive at the door of his quarters and enter, and pass out of sight to other rooms than that of the foreground in which the observers are loitering. Dumb show ends.

A murmured conversation grows audible, carried on by two persons in the crowd beneath the open windows where the French officers are gathered. Their dress being the native one, and their tongue unfamiliar, they seem to the officers to be merely inhabitants gossiping; and their voices continue unheeded.

FIRST ENGLISH SPY [1] (below)

Did you get much for me to send on ?

SECOND ENGLISH SPY [1]

I have got hold of the substance of their parley. Surely no truce in European annals ever led to so odd an interview. They were like a belle and her beau, by God ! But, queerly enough, one of Alexander's staff said to him as he reached the raft : " Sire, let me humbly ask you not to forget your father's fate ! " Grim—Eh ?

FIRST SPY

Anything about the little island which shall be nameless ?

SECOND SPY

Much; and startling, too. " Why are we at war ? " says Napoléon when they met.—" Ah—why ! " said t'other.—" Well," said Boney, " I am fighting

---

[1] It has been conjectured of late that these adventurous spirits were Sir Robert Wilson and, possibly, Lord Hutchinson, present there at imminent risk of their lives.

you only as an ally of the English, and you are
simply serving them, and not yourself, in fighting
me."—" In that case," says Alexander, " we shall
soon be friends, for I owe her as great a grudge as
you."

FIRST SPY

Dammy, go that length, did they !

SECOND SPY

Then they plunged into the old story about
English selfishness, and greed, and duplicity. But
the climax related to Spain, and it amounted to this :
they agreed that the Bourbons of the Spanish throne
should be made to abdicate, and Bonaparte's
relations set up as sovereigns instead of them.

FIRST SPY

Somebody must ride like hell to let our Cabinet
know !

SECOND SPY

I have written it down in cipher, not to trust to
memory, and to guard against accidents.—They also
agreed that France should have the Pope's dominions,
Malta, and Egypt ; that Napoléon's brother Joseph
should have Sicily as well as Naples, and that they
would partition the Ottoman Empire between them.

FIRST SPY

Cutting up Europe like a plum-pudding. Par
nobile fratrum !

SECOND SPY

Then the worthy pair came to poor Prussia, whom
Alexander, they say, was anxious about, as he is

under engagements to her. It seems that Napoléon agrees to restore to the King as many of his states as will cover Alexander's promise, so that the Tsar may feel free to strike out in this new line with his new friend.

FIRST SPY

Surely this is but surmise ?

SECOND SPY

Not at all. One of the suite overheard, and I got round him. There was much more, which I did not learn. But they are going to soothe and flatter the unfortunate King and Queen by asking them to a banquet here.

FIRST SPY

Such a spirited woman will never come !

SECOND SPY

We shall see. Whom necessity compels needs must : and she has gone through an Iliad of woes !

FIRST SPY

It is this Spanish business that will stagger England, by God ! And now to let her know it.

FRENCH SUBALTERN (looking out above)

What are those townspeople talking about so earnestly, I wonder ? The lingo of this place has an accent akin to English.

SECOND SUBALTERN

No doubt because the races are both Teutonic.

The spies observe that they are noticed, and disappear in the crowd.

The curtain drops.

SCENE VIII

THE SAME

The midsummer sun is low, and a long table in the afore-shown apartment is laid out for a dinner, among the decorations being bunches of the season's roses.

At the vacant end of the room (divided from the dining end by folding-doors, now open) there are discovered the EMPEROR NAPOLÉON, the GRAND-DUKE CONSTANTINE, PRINCE HENRY OF PRUSSIA, the PRINCE ROYAL OF BAVARIA, the GRAND DUKE OF BERG, and attendant officers.

Enter the TSAR ALEXANDER. NAPOLÉON welcomes him, and the twain move apart from the rest, BONAPARTE placing a chair for his visitor and flinging himself down on another.

NAPOLÉON

The comforts I can offer are not great,
Nor is the accommodation more than scant
That falls to me for hospitality ;
But, as it is, accept.

ALEXANDER

It serves me well.
And to unbrace the bandages of state
Is as clear air to incense-stifled souls.
What of the Queen ?

NAPOLÉON

She's coming with the King.
We have some quarter-hour to spare or more
Before their Majesties are timed for us.

ALEXANDER

Good. I would speak of them. That she should
    show here
After the late events, betokens much !
Abasement in so proud a woman's heart

(His voice grows tremulous.)

Is not without a dash of painfulness.
And I beseech you, sire, that you hold out
Some soothing hope to her ?

NAPOLÉON

I have, already !—
Now, sire, to those affairs we entered on :
Strong friendship, grown secure, bids me repeat
That you have been much duped by your allies.

ALEXANDER shows mortification.

Prussia's a shuffler, England a self-seeker,
Nobility has shone in you alone.
Your error grew of over-generous dreams,
And misbeliefs by dullard ministers.
By treating personally we speed affairs
More in an hour than they in blundering months.
Between us two, henceforth, must stand no third.
There's peril in it, while England's mean ambition
Still works to get us skewered by the ears ;
And in this view your chiefs-of-staff concur.

ALEXANDER

The judgment of my officers I share.

NAPOLÉON

To recapitulate. Nothing can greaten you
Like this alliance. Providence has flung

My good friend Sultan Selim from his throne,
Leaving me free in dealings with the Porte ;
And I discern the hour as one to end
A rule that Time no longer lets cohere.
If I abstain, its spoils will go to swell
The power of this same England, our annoy ;
That country which enchains the trade of towns
With such bold reach as to monopolize,
Among the rest, the whole of Petersburg's—
Ay ! — through her purse, friend, as the lender
    there !—
Shutting that purse, she may incite to—what ?
Muscovy's fall, its ruler's murdering.
Her fleet at any minute can encoop
Yours in the Baltic ; in the Black Sea, too ;
And keep you snug as minnows in a glass !
    Hence we, fast-fellowed by our mutual foes,
Seaward the British, Germany by land,
And having compassed, for our common good,
The Turkish Empire's due partitioning,
As comrades can conjunctly rule the world
To its own gain and our eternal fame !

ALEXANDER (stirred and flushed)

I see vast prospects opened !—yet, in truth,
Ere you, sire, broached these themes, their outlines
    loomed
Not seldom in my own imaginings ;
But with less clear a vision than endows
So clear a captain, statesman, philosoph,
As centre in yourself ; whom had I known
Sooner by some few years, months, even weeks,
I had been spared full many a fault of rule.
—Now as to Austria.   Should we call her in ?

NAPOLÉON

Two in a bed I have slept, but never three.

ALEXANDER

Ha-ha !   Delightful.   And, then nextly, Spain ?

NAPOLÉON

I lighted on some letters at Berlin,
Wherein King Carlos offered to attack me.
A Bourbon, minded thus, so near as Spain,
Is dangerous stuff.   He must be seen to soon ! . . .
A draft, then, of our treaty being penned,
We will peruse it later.   If King George
Will not, upon the terms there offered him,
Conclude a ready peace, he can be forced.
Trumpet yourself as France's firm ally,
And Austria will be fain to do the same :
England, left nude to such joint harassment,
Must shiver—fall.

ALEXANDER (with naïve enthusiasm)

It is a great alliance !

NAPOLÉON

Would it were one in blood as well as brain—
Of family hopes, and sweet domestic bliss !

ALEXANDER

Ah—is it to my sister you refer ?

NAPOLÉON

The launching of a lineal progeny
Has been much pressed upon me, much, of late,
For reasons which I will not dwell on now.
Staid counsellors, my brother Joseph, too,
Urge that I loose the Empress by divorce,
And re-wive promptly for the country's good.

Princesses even have been named for me !—
However this, to-day, is premature,
And 'twixt ourselves alone. . . .
    The Queen of Prussia must ere long be here :
Berthier escorts her.   And the King, too, comes.
She's one whom you admire ?

ALEXANDER (reddening ingenuously)

                    Yes. . . . Formerly
I had—did feel that some faint fascination
Vaguely adorned her form.   And, to be plain,
Certain reports have been calumnious,
And wronged an honest woman.

NAPOLÉON

               As I knew !
But she is wearing thready : why, her years
Must be full one-and-thirty, if she's one.

ALEXANDER (quickly)

No, sire.   She's twenty-nine.   If traits teach more
It means that cruel memory gnaws at her
As fair inciter to that fatal war
Which broke her to the dust ! . . . I do confess
(Since now we speak on't) that this sacrifice
Prussia is doomed to, still disquiets me.
Unhappy King !   When I recall the oaths
Sworn him upon great Frederick's sepulchre,
And—and my promises to his sad Queen,
It pricks me that his realm and revenues
Should be stript down to the mere half they were !

NAPOLÉON (coolly)

Believe me, 'tis but my regard for you
Which lets me leave him that !   Far easier 'twere
To leave him none at all.
                [He rises and goes to the window.

                      But here they are.
No ; it's the Queen alone, with Berthier
As I directed.   Then the King will follow.

ALEXANDER

Let me, sire, urge your courtesy to bestow
Some gentle words on her.

NAPOLÉON

                Ay, ay ; I will.

    Enter QUEEN LOUISA OF PRUSSIA on the arm of BERTHIER.
She appears in majestic garments and with a smile on her lips,
so that her still great beauty is impressive. But her eyes bear
traces of tears. She accepts NAPOLÉON's attentions with the
stormily sad air of a wounded beauty. Whilst she is being
received the KING arrives. He is a plain, shy, honest-faced,
awkward man, with a wrecked and solitary look. His manner
to NAPOLÉON is, nevertheless, dignified, and even stiff.
    The company move into the inner half of the room, where
the tables are, and the folding-doors being shut, they seat
themselves at dinner, the QUEEN taking a place between
NAPOLÉON and ALEXANDER.

NAPOLÉON

Madame, I love magnificent attire ;
But in the present instance can but note
That each bright knot and jewel less adorns
The brighter wearer than the wearer it !

QUEEN (with a sigh)

You praise one, sire, whom now the wanton world
Has learnt to cease from praising !   But such words
From such a quarter are of worth, no less.

NAPOLÉON

Of worth as candour, madame ; not as gauge.
Your reach in rarity outsoars my scope.

Yet, do you know, a troop of my hussars,
That last October day, nigh captured you ?

QUEEN

Nay !　Never a single Frenchman did I see.

NAPOLÉON

Not less it was that you exposed yourself,
And should have been protected.　But at Weimar,
Had you but sought me, 'twould have bettered you.

QUEEN

I had no zeal to meet you, sire, alas !

NAPOLÉON (after a silence)

And how at Memel do you sport with time ?

QUEEN

Sport ?　I !—I pore on musty chronicles,
And muse on usurpations long forgot,
And other historied dramas of high wrong !

NAPOLÉON

Why con not annals of your own rich age ?
They treasure acts well fit for pondering.

QUEEN

I am reminded too much of my age
By having had to live in it.　May Heaven
Defend me now, and my wan ghost anon,
From conning it again !

NAPOLÉON

Alas, alas !
Too grievous, this, for one who is yet a queen !

QUEEN

No ; I have cause for vials more of grief.—
Prussia was blind in blazoning her power
Against the Mage of Earth ! . . .
The embers of great Frederick's deeds inflamed
     her :
His glories swelled her to her ruining.
Too well has she been punished !

(Emotion stops her.)

ALEXANDER

(in a low voice, looking anxiously at her)

Say not so.

You speak as all were lost.   Things are not thus !
Such desperation has unreason in it,
And bleeds the hearts that crave to comfort you.

NAPOLÉON (to the King)

I trust the treaty, further pondered, sire,
Has consolations ?

KING (curtly)

I am a luckless man ;

And muster strength to bear my lucklessness
Without vain hope of consolations now.
One thing, at least, I trust I have shown you, sire,
That *I* provoked not this calamity !
At Anspach first my feud with you began—
Anspach, my Eden, violated and shamed
By blushless tramplings of your legions there !

NAPOLÉON

It's rather late, methinks, to talk thus now.

KING (with more choler)

Never too late for truth and plainspeaking !

NAPOLÉON (blandly)

To your ally, the Tsar, I must refer you.
He was it, and not I, who tempted you
To push for war, when Eylau must have shown
Your every profit to have lain in peace.—
He can indemn ; yes, much or small ; and may.

KING (with a head-shake)

I would make up, would well make up, my mind
To half my kingdom's loss, could in such limb
But Magdeburg not lie.   Dear Magdeburg,
Place of my heart-hold ; *that* I would retain !

NAPOLÉON

Our words take not such pattern as is wont
To grace occasions of festivity.

[He turns brusquely from the King.

The banquet proceeds with a more general conversation.
When finished a toast is proposed : " The Freedom of the
Seas," and drunk with enthusiasm.

SPIRIT SINISTER

Another hit at England and her tubs !
I hear harsh echoes from her chalky chines.

SPIRIT OF THE PITIES

O heed not England now ! Still read the Queen.
One grieves to see her spend her pretty spells
Upon the man who has so injured her.

They rise from table, and the folding-doors being opened
they pass into the adjoining part of the room.

Here are now assembled MURAT, TALLEYRAND, KOURAKIN,
KALKREUTH, BERTHIER, BESSIÈRES, CAULAINCOURT, LABANOFF,
BENNIGSEN, and others. NAPOLÉON having spoken a few words
here and there resumes his conversation with QUEEN LOUISA,
and parenthetically offers snuff to the COUNTESS VOSS, her
lady-in-waiting. TALLEYRAND, who has observed NAPOLÉON's
growing interest in the QUEEN, contrives to get near him.

TALLEYRAND (in a whisper)

Sire, is it possible that you can bend
To let one woman's fairness filch from you
All the resplendent fortune that attends
The grandest victory of your grand career ?

The QUEEN's quick eye observes and flashes at the whisper,
and she obtains a word with the minister.

QUEEN (sarcastically)

I should infer, dear Monsieur Talleyrand,
Only two persons in the world regret
My having come to Tilsit.

TALLEYRAND

                Madame, two ?
Can any !—who may such sad rascals be ?

QUEEN

You, and myself, Prince. (Gravely.) Yes! myself
    and you.

TALLEYRAND's face becomes impassive, and he does not reply.

Soon the QUEEN prepares to leave, and NAPOLÉON rejoins her.

NAPOLÉON (taking a rose from a vase)

Dear Queen, do pray accept this little token
As souvenir of me before you go ?

> He offers her the rose, with his hand on his heart. She
> hesitates, but accepts it.

QUEEN (impulsively, with waiting tears)

Let Magdeburg come with it, sire !   O yes !

NAPOLÉON (with sudden frigidity)

It is for you to take what I can give,
And I give this—no more.[1]

> She turns her head to hide her emotion, and withdraws.
> NAPOLÉON steps up to her, and offers his arm. She takes it
> silently, and he perceives the tears on her cheeks. They cross
> towards the ante-room, away from the other guests.

NAPOLÉON (softly)

Still weeping, dearest lady !   Why is this ?

QUEEN (seizing his hand and pressing it)

Your speeches darn the tearings of your sword !—
Between us two, as man and woman now,
Is't even possible you question why !
O why did not the Greatest of the Age—
Of future ages—of the ages past,
This one time win a woman's worship—yea,
For all her little life !

NAPOLÉON (gravely)

             Know you, my Fair,
That I—ay, I—in this deserve your pity.—

---

[1] The traditional present of the rose was probably on this occasion,
though it is not quite matter of certainty.

Some force within me, baffling mine intent,
Harries me onward, whether I will or no.
My star, my star is what's to blame—not I.
It is unswervable !

QUEEN

Then now, alas !
My duty's done as mother, wife, and queen.—
I'll say no more—but that my heart is broken !

[Exeunt NAPOLÉON, QUEEN, and LADY-IN-WAITING.

SPIRIT OF THE YEARS

He spoke thus at the Bridge of Lodi. Strange,
He's of the few in Europe who discern
The working of the Will.

SPIRIT OF THE PITIES

If that be so,
Better for Europe lacked he such discerning !

NAPOLÉON returns to the room and joins TALLEYRAND.

NAPOLÉON (aside to his minister)

My God, it was touch-and-go that time, Talleyrand ! She was within an ace of getting over me.
As she stepped into the carriage she said in her
pretty way, " O I have been cruelly deceived by
you ! " And when she sank down inside, not
knowing I heard, she burst into sobs fit to move a
statue. The Devil take me if I hadn't a good mind
to stop the horses, jump in, give her a good kissing,
and agree to all she wanted. Ha-ha, well ; a miss
is as good as a mile. Had she come sooner with
those sweet, beseeching blue eyes of hers, who knows
what might not have happened ! But she didn't
come sooner, and I have kept in my right mind.

The RUSSIAN EMPEROR, the KING OF PRUSSIA, and other
guests advance to bid adieu. They depart severally. When
they are gone NAPOLÉON turns to TALLEYRAND.

> Adhere, then, to the treaty as it stands :
> Change not therein a single article,
> But write it fair forthwith.

[Exeunt NAPOLÉON, TALLEYRAND, and other ministers and
officers in waiting.

SHADE OF THE EARTH

Some surly voice afar I heard by now
Of an enisled Britannic quality ;
Wots any of the cause ?

SPIRIT IRONIC

> *Perchance I do !*
Britain is roused, in her slow, stolid style,
By Bonaparte's pronouncement at Berlin
Against her cargoes, commerce, life itself ;
And now from out her watery citadel
Blows counterblasting "Orders." Rumourers, tell.

RUMOUR I

" *From havens of fierce France and her allies,*
With poor or precious freight of merchandize
Whoso adventures, England pounds as prize ! "

RUMOUR II

Thereat Napoléon names her, furiously,
Curst Oligarch, Arch-pirate of the sea,
Who shall lack room to live while liveth he !

CHORUS OF THE PITIES (aerial music)

And peoples are enmeshed in new calamity !

Curtain of Evening Shades.

ACT SECOND

SCENE I

THE PYRENEES AND VALLEYS ADJOINING

The view is southward from upper air, immediately over the region that lies between Bayonne on the north, Pampeluna on the south, and San Sebastian on the west, including a portion of the Cantabrian mountains. The month is February, and snow covers not only the peaks but the lower slopes. The roads over the passes are well beaten.

DUMB SHOW

At various elevations multitudes of NAPOLÉON's soldiery, to the number of about thirty thousand, are discerned in a creeping progress across the frontier from the French to the Spanish side. The thin long columns serpentine along the roads, but are sometimes broken, while at others they disappear altogether behind vertical rocks and overhanging woods. The heavy guns and the whitey-brown tilts of the baggage-waggons seem the largest objects in the procession, which are dragged laboriously up the incline to the watershed, their lumbering being audible as high as the clouds.

Simultaneously the river Bidassoa, in a valley to the west, is being crossed by a train of artillery and another thirty thousand men, all forming part of the same systematic advance.

Along the great highway through Biscay the wondering native carters draw their sheep-skinned ox-teams aside, to let the regiments pass, and stray groups of peaceable field-workers in Navarre look inquiringly at the marching and prancing progress.

Time passes, and the various northern strongholds are approached by these legions. Their governors emerge at a summons, and when seeming explanations have been given the unwelcome comers are doubtfully admitted.

The chief places to which entrance is thus obtained are Pampeluna and San Sebastian near the front of the scene, and far away towards the shining horizon of the Mediterranean, Figueras and Barcelona.

Dumb Show concludes as the mountain mists close over.

SCENE II

ARANJUEZ, NEAR MADRID. A ROOM IN THE PALACE OF GODOY, THE "PRINCE OF PEACE"

A private chamber is disclosed, richly furnished with paintings, vases, mirrors, silk hangings, gilded lounges, and several lutes of rare workmanship. The hour is midnight, the room being lit by screened candelabra. In the centre at the back of the scene is a large window heavily curtained.

GODOY and the QUEEN MARÍA LUISA are dallying on a sofa. THE PRINCE OF PEACE is a fine handsome man in middle life, with curled hair and a mien of easy good-nature. The QUEEN is older, but looks younger in the dim light, from the lavish use of beautifying arts. She has pronounced features, dark eyes, low brows, black hair bound by a jewelled bandeau, and brought forward in curls over her forehead and temples, long heavy ear-rings, an open bodice, and sleeves puffed at the shoulders. A cloak and other mufflers lie on a chair beside her.

GODOY (after a silence)

The life-guards still insist, Love, that the King
Shall not leave Aranjuez.

QUEEN

Let them insist.
Whether we stay, or whether we depart,
Napoléon soon draws hither with his host !

GODOY

He says he comes pacifically. . . . But no !

QUEEN

Dearest, we must away to Andalusia,
Thence to America when time shall serve.

GODOY

I hold seven thousand men to cover us,
And ships in Cadiz port.   But then—the Prince
Flatly declines to go.   He lauds the French
As true deliverers.

QUEEN

                    Go Fernando *must*! . . .
O my sweet friend, that we—our sole two selves—
Could but escape and leave the rest to fate,
And in a western bower dream out our days!—
For the King's glass can run but briefly now,
Shattered and shaken as his vigour is.—
But ah—your love burns not in singleness!
Why, dear, caress Josefa Tudo still?
She does not solve her soul in yours as I.
And why those others even more than her? . . .
How little own I in thee!

GODOY

                    Such must be.
I cannot quite forsake them.   Don't forget
The same scope has been yours in former years.

QUEEN

Yes, Love; I know.   I yield!   You cannot leave
     them;
But if you ever would bethink yourself
How long I have been yours, how truly all
Those other pleasures were my desperate shifts
To soften sorrow at your absences,
You would be faithful to me!

GODOY

True, my dear.—
Yet I do passably keep troth with you,
And fond you with a fair-shown frequency ;—
A week beside you, and a week away.
Such is not schemed without some risk and strain.—
And you agreed Josefa should be mine,
And, too, Thereza, without jealousy !

(A noise is heard without.)

Ah, what means that ?

He jumps up from her side and crosses the room to the window, where he lifts the curtain cautiously. The Queen follows him with a scared look.

QUEEN

A riot can it be ?

GODOY

Let me put these out ere they notice them ;
They think me at the Royal Palace yonder.

He hastily extinguishes the candles except one taper, which he places in a recess, so that the room is in shade. He then draws back the curtains, and she joins him at the window, where, enclosing her with his arm, he and she look out together.

In front of the house a guard of hussars is stationed, beyond them spreading the Pláza or Square. On the other side rises in the lamplight the white front of the Royal Palace. On the flank of the Palace is a wall enclosing gardens, bowered alleys, and orange groves, and in the wall a small door.

A mixed multitude of soldiery and populace fills the space in front of the King's Palace, and they shout and address each other vehemently. During a lull in their vociferations is heard the peaceful purl of the Tagus over a cascade in the Palace grounds.

QUEEN

Lingering, we've risked too long our chance of flight !
The Paris Terror will repeat it here.

Not for myself I fear.   No, no ; for thee !
(She clings to him.)

If they should hurt you, it would murder me
By heart-bleedings and stabs intolerable !

GODOY (kissing her)

The first thought now is how to get you back
Within the Palace walls.   Why would you risk
To come here on a night so critical ?

QUEEN (passionately)

I could not help it—nay, I *would* not help !
Rather than starve my soul I venture all.—
Our last love-night—last, maybe, of long years,
Why do you chide me now ?

GODOY

              Dear Queen, I do not :
I shape these sharp regrets but for your sake.
Hence you must go, somehow, and quickly too.
They think not yet of you in threatening thus,
But of me solely. . . . Where does your lady wait ?

QUEEN

Below.   One servant with her.   They are true,
And can be let know all.   But you—but you !
(Uproar continues.)

GODOY

I can escape.   Now call them.   All three cloak
And veil as when you came.

   They retreat into the room.   QUEEN MARIA LUISA's lady-in-waiting and servant are summoned.   Enter both.   All three then muffle themselves up, and GODOY prepares to conduct the QUEEN downstairs.

QUEEN

Nay, now !   I will not have it.   We are safe ;
Think of yourself.   Can you get out behind ?

GODOY

I judge so—when I have done what's needful here.—
The mob knows not the bye-door—slip across ;
Thence around sideways.—All's clear there as yet.

[The QUEEN, her lady-in-waiting, and the servant go out
hurriedly.

GODOY looks again from the window. The mob is some
way off, the immediate front being for the moment nearly
free of loiterers ; and the three muffled figures are visible,
crossing without hindrance towards the door in the wall of
the Palace Gardens. The instant they reach it a sentinel
springs up, challenging them.

GODOY

Ah—now they are doomed !   My God, why did she
    come !

A parley takes place. Something, apparently a bribe, is
handed to the sentinel, and the three are allowed to slip in,
the QUEEN having obviously been unrecognized. He breathes
his relief.

Now for the others.   Then—ah, then Heaven knows!

He sounds a bell and a servant enters.

Where is the Countess of Castillofiel ?

SERVANT

She's looking for you, Prince.

GODOY

                              Find her at once.
Ah—here she is.—That's well.—Go watch the Pláza.

(To servant.)

Godoy's mistress, the Doña Josefa Tudo, enters. She is a young and beautiful woman, the vivacity of whose large dark eyes is now clouded. She is wrapped up for flight. The servant goes out.

Josefa (breathlessly)

I should have joined you sooner, but I knew
The Queen was fondling with you. She must needs
Come hampering you this night of all the rest,
As if not gorged with you at other times !

Godoy

Don't, pretty one ! needless it is in you,
Being so well aware who holds my love.—
I could not check her coming, since she would.
You well know how the old thing is, and how
I am compelled to let her have her mind !

He kisses her repeatedly.

Josefa

But look, the mob is swelling ! Pouring in
By thousands from Madrid—and all afoot.
Will they not come on hither from the King's ?

Godoy

Not just yet, maybe. You should have sooner fled !
The coach is waiting and the baggage packed.

(He again peers out.)

Yes, there the coach is ; and the clamourers near,
Led by Montijo, if I see aright.
Yes, they cry " Uncle Peter ! "—that means him.
There will be time yet. Now I'll take you down
So far as I may venture.

[They leave the room.

In a few minutes Godoy, having taken her down, re-enters and again looks out. Josefa's coach is moving off with a

small escort of GODOY's guards of honour. A sudden yelling
begins, and the crowd rushes up and stops the vehicle. An
altercation ensues.

CROWD

Uncle Peter, it is the Favourite carrying off
Prince Fernando. Stop him !

JOSEFA (putting her head out of the coach)

Silence their uproar, please, Señor Count of
Montijo ! It is a lady only, the Countess of Castillofiel.

MONTIJO

Let her pass, let her pass, friends ! It is only
that pretty wench of his, Pepa Tudo, who calls
herself a Countess. Our titles are put to comical
uses in these days. We shall catch the cock-bird
presently !

CROWD (to each other)

The King and Queen and Fernando are at their
own Palace—not here !

The DOÑA JOSEFA's carriage is allowed to pass on, as a
shout from some who have remained before the Royal Palace
attracts the attention of the multitude, which surges back
thither.

CROWD (nearing the Palace)

Call out the King and the Prince. Long live the
King ! He shall not go. Hola ! He is gone ! Let
us see him ! He shall abandon Godoy !

The clamour before the Royal Palace still increasing, a
figure emerges upon a balcony, whom GODOY recognizes by
the lamplight to be FERNANDO, Prince of Asturias. He can be
seen waving his hand. The mob grows suddenly silent.

FERNANDO (in a shaken voice)

Citizens! the King my father is in the palace with the Queen. He has been much tried to-day.

CROWD

Promise, Prince, that he shall not leave us. Promise!

FERNANDO

I do. I promise in his name. He has mistaken you, thinking you wanted his head. He knows better now.

CROWD

The villain Godoy misrepresented us to him! Throw out the Prince of the Peace!

FERNANDO

He is not here, my friends.

CROWD

Then the King shall announce to us that he has dismissed him! Let us see him. The King; the King!

FERNANDO goes in. KING CARLOS comes out reluctantly, and bows to their cheering. He produces a paper with a trembling hand.

KING (reading)

" As it is the wish of the people——"

CROWD

Speak up, your Majesty!

KING (more loudly)

" As it is the wish of the people, I release Don Manuel Godoy, Prince of the Peace, from the posts of Generalissimo of the Army and Grand Admiral of the Fleet, and give him leave to withdraw whither he pleases."

CROWD

Huzza ! Though it's mildly put. Huzza !

KING

Citizens, to-morrow the decree is to be posted in Madrid.

CROWD

Huzza ! Long life to the King, and death to Godoy !

KING CARLOS disappears from the balcony, and the populace, still increasing in numbers, look towards GODOY's mansion, as if deliberating how to attack it. GODOY retreats from the window into the room, and gazing round him starts. A pale, worn, but placid lady, in a sombre though elegant robe, stands here in the gloom. She is THEREZA OF BOURBON, the Princess of Peace.

PRINCESS

It is only your unhappy wife, Manuel. She will not hurt you !

GODOY (shrugging his shoulders)

Nor will *they* hurt *you* ! Why did you not stay in the Royal Palace ? You would have been more comfortable there.

PRINCESS

I don't recognize why you should specially value my comfort. You have saved your real wives. How can it matter what happens to your titular one ?

GODOY

Much, dear. I always play fair. But it being your blest privilege not to need my saving I was left free to practise it on those who did. (Mob heard approaching.) Would that I were in no more danger than you !

PRINCESS

Puf !

He again peers out. His guard of hussars stands firmly in front of the mansion ; but the life-guards from the adjoining barracks, who have joined the people, endeavour to break the hussars of GODOY. A shot is fired, GODOY's guard yields, and the gate and door are battered in.

CROWD (without)

Murder him ! murder him ! Death to Manuel Godoy !

They are heard rushing into the court and house.

PRINCESS

Go, I beseech you ! You can do nothing for me, and I pray you to save yourself ! The heap of mats in the lumber-room will hide you !

GODOY hastes to a jib-door concealed by sham book-shelves, presses the spring of it, returns, kisses her, and then slips out.

His wife sits down with her back against the jib-door, and fans herself. She hears the crowd trampling up the stairs, but she does not move, and in a moment people burst in. The leaders are armed with stakes, daggers, and various improvised weapons, and some guards in undress appear with halberds.

FIRST CITIZEN (peering into the dim light)

Where is he? Murder him! (Noticing the Princess.)
Come, where is he?

PRINCESS

The Prince of Peace is gone. I know not whither.

SECOND CITIZEN

Who is this lady?

LIFE-GUARDSMAN

Manuel Godoy's Princess.

CITIZENS (uncovering)

Princess, a thousand pardons grant us!—you
An injured wife—an injured people we!
Common misfortune makes us more than kin.
No single hair of yours shall suffer harm.

The PRINCESS bows.

FIRST CITIZEN

But this, Señora, is no place for you,
For we mean mischief here! Yet first will cede
Safe conduct for you to the Palace gates,
Or elsewhere, as you wish.

PRINCESS

My wish is nought.
Do what you will with me. But he's not here.

Several of them form an escort, and accompany her from
the room and out of the house. Those remaining, now a great
throng, begin searching the room, and in bands invade other
parts of the mansion.

Some Citizens (returning)

It is no use searching.   She said he was not here,
and she's a woman of honour.

First Citizen (drily)

She's his wife.

They leave the room for another search, but return still baffled.

Several Citizens

He must have slipped out somehow !   Smash his
nicknacks, since we can't smash him.

They begin knocking the furniture to pieces, tearing down
the hangings, trampling on the musical instruments, and
kicking holes through the paintings they have unhung from
the walls.   These, with clocks, vases, carvings, and other
movables, they throw out of the window, till the chamber
is a scene of utter wreck and desolation.   In the rout a musical
box is swept off a table, and starts playing a serenade as it
falls on the floor.

Enter the Count of Montijo.

Montijo

Stop, friends ; stop this !   There is no sense in it—
It shows but useless spite !   I have much to say :
The French Ambassador, de Beauharnais,
Has come, and sought the King.   And next Murat,
With thirty thousand men, half cavalry,
Is closing in upon our doomed Madrid !
I know not what he means, this Bonaparte ;
He makes pretence to gain us Portugal,
But what want we with her ?   'Tis like as not
His aim's to noose us vassals all to him !
The King will abdicate, and shortly too,
As those will live to see who live not long.—

We have saved our nation from the Favourite,
But who is going to save us from our Friend ?

The mob desists dubiously and goes out; the musical box upon the floor plays on, the taper burns to its socket, and the room becomes wrapt in the shades of night.

SCENE III

LONDON: THE MARCHIONESS OF SALISBURY'S

A large reception-room is disclosed, arranged for a conversazione. It is an evening in the summer following, and at present the chamber is empty and in gloom. At one end is an elaborate device, representing Britannia offering her assistance to Spain, and at the other a figure of Time crowning the Spanish Patriots' flag with laurel.

SPIRIT OF THE YEARS

O clarionists of human welterings,
Relate how Europe's madding movement brings
This easeful haunt into the path of palpitating things !

RUMOURS (chanting)

I

The Spanish King has bowed unto the Fate
Which bade him abdicate :
The sensual Queen, whose passionate caprice
Has held her chambering with " the Prince of Peace,"
And wrought the Bourbons' fall,
Holds to her Love in all ;
And Bonaparte has ruled that his and he
Henceforth displace the Bourbon dynasty.

II

The Spanish people, handled in such sort,
    As chattels of a Court,
Dream dreams of England. Messengers are sent
In secret to the assembled Parliament,
    In faith that England's hand
    Will stouten them to stand,
And crown a cause which, hold they, bond and free
Must advocate enthusiastically.

Spirit of the Years

So the Will heaves through Space, and moulds the times,
With mortals for Its fingers! We shall see
Again men's passions, virtues, visions, crimes,
    Obey resistlessly
The mutative, unmotived, dominant Thing
Which sways in brooding dark their wayfaring!

The reception-room is lighted up, and the hostess comes in. There arrive Ambassadors and their wives, the Dukes and Duchesses of RUTLAND and SOMERSET, the Marquis and Marchioness of STAFFORD, the Earls of STAIR, WESTMORELAND, GOWER, ESSEX, Viscounts and Viscountesses CRANLEY and MORPETH, Viscount MELBOURNE, Lord and Lady KINNAIRD, Baron de ROLLE, Lady CHARLES GREVILLE, the Ladies CAVENDISH, Mr. and Mrs. THOMAS HOPE, Mr. GUNNING, Mrs. FITZHERBERT, and many other notable personages. Lastly, she goes to the door to welcome severally the PRINCE OF WALES, the PRINCES OF FRANCE, and the PRINCESS CASTELCICALA, and returns to the room with them.

Lady Salisbury (to the Prince of Wales)

I am sorry to say, sir, that the Spanish Patriots are not yet arrived. I doubt not but that they have been delayed by their ignorance of the town, and will soon be here.

Prince of Wales

No hurry whatever, my dear hostess. Gad, we've enough to talk about! I understand that the arrangement between our ministers and these noblemen will include the liberation of Spanish prisoners in this country, and the providing 'em with arms, to go back and fight for their independence.

LADY SALISBURY

It will be a blessed event if they do check the career of this infamous Corsican. I have just heard that that poor foreigner Guillet de la Gevrillière, who proposed to Mr. Fox to assassinate him, died a miserable death a few days ago in the Bicêtre— probably by torture, though nobody knows. Really one almost wishes Mr. Fox had——. O here they are !

Enter the Spanish Viscount de MATEROSA and DON DIEGO de la VEGA. They are introduced by CAPTAIN HILL and Mr. BAGOT, who escort them. LADY SALISBURY presents them to the PRINCE and others.

PRINCE OF WALES

By Gad, Viscount, we were just talking of 'ee. You have had some adventures in getting to this country ?

MATEROSA (assisted by Bagot as interpreter)

Sir, it has indeed been a trying experience for us. But here we are, impressed by a deep sense of gratitude for the signal marks of attachment your country shows us.

PRINCE OF WALES

You represent, practically, the Spanish people ?

MATEROSA

We are immediately deputed, sir,
By the Assembly of Asturias,

More sailing soon from other provinces.
We bring official writings, charging us
To clinch and solder Treaties with this realm
That may promote our cause against the foe.
Nextly a letter to your gracious King ;
Also a Proclamation, soon to sound
And swell the pulse of the Peninsula,
Declaring that the act by which King Carlos
And his son Prince Fernando cede the throne
To whomsoe'er Napoléon may appoint,
Being an act of cheatery, not of choice,
Unfetters us from our allegiant oath.

MRS. FITZHERBERT

The usurpation began, I suppose, with the
divisions in the Royal Family ?

MATEROSA

Yes, madam, and the protection they foolishly
requested from the Emperor ; and their timid intent
of flying secretly helped it on.   It was an opportunity
he had been awaiting for years.

MRS. FITZHERBERT

All brought about by this man Godoy, Prince of
Peace !

PRINCE OF WALES

Dash my wig, mighty much you know about it,
Maria!   Why, sure, Boney thought to himself, "This
Spain is a pretty place ; 'twill just suit me as an
extra acre or two ; so here goes."

DON DIEGO (aside to Bagot)

This lady is the Princess of Wales ?

BAGOT

Hsh ! no, Señor. The Princess lives at large at Kensington and other places, and has parties of her own, and doesn't keep house with her husband. This lady is—well, really his wife, you know, in the opinion of many ; but——

DON DIEGO

Ah ! Ladies a little mixed, as they were at our Court ! She's the Pepa Tudo to *this* Prince of Peace ?

BAGOT

O no—not exactly that, Señor.

DON DIEGO

Ya, ya. Good. I'll be careful, my friend. You are not saints in England more than we are in Spain !

BAGOT

We are not. Only you sin with naked faces, and we with masks on.

DON DIEGO

Virtuous country !

DUCHESS OF RUTLAND

It was understood that Ferdinand, Prince of Asturias, was to marry a French princess, and so unite the countries peacefully ?

MATEROSA

It was. And our credulous prince was tempted to meet Napoléon at Bayonne. Also the poor simple King, and the infatuated Queen, and Manuel Godoy.

DUCHESS OF RUTLAND

Then Godoy escaped from Aranjuez ?

MATEROSA

Yes, by hiding in the garret. Then they all threw themselves upon Napoléon's protection. In his presence the Queen swore that the King was not Fernando's father! Altogether they form a queer little menagerie. What will happen to them nobody knows.

PRINCE OF WALES

And do you wish us to send an army at once ?

MATEROSA

What we most want, sir, are arms and ammunition. But we leave the English Ministry to co-operate in its own wise way, anyhow, so as to sustain us in resenting these insults from the Tyrant of the Earth.

DUCHESS OF RUTLAND (to the Prince of Wales)

What sort of aid shall we send, sir ?

PRINCE OF WALES

We are going to vote fifty millions, I hear. We'll whack him, and preserve your noble country for 'ee, Señor Viscount. The debate thereon is to come off to-morrow. It will be the finest thing the Commons

have had since Pitt's time. Sheridan, who is to
open it, says he and Canning are to be absolutely
unanimous ; and, by God, like the parties in his
" Critic," when Government and Opposition do
agree, their unanimity is wonderful ! Viscount
Materosa, you and your friends must be in the
Gallery. O dammy, you must !

MATEROSA

Sir, we are already pledged to be there.

PRINCE OF WALES

And hark ye, Señor Viscount. You will then
learn what a mighty fine thing a debate in the
English Parliament is ! No Continental humbug
there. Not but that the Court has a trouble to keep
'em in their places sometimes ; and I would it had
been one in the Lords instead. However, Sheridan
says he has been learning his speech these two days,
and has hunted his father's dictionary through for
some stunning long words.—Now, Maria (to Mrs.
Fitzherbert), I am going home.

LADY SALISBURY

At last, then, England will take her place in the
forefront of this mortal struggle, and in pure disinterestedness fight with all her strength for the
European deliverance. God defend the right !

The Prince of Wales leaves, and the other guests begin to
depart.

SEMICHORUS I OF THE YEARS (aerial music)

Leave this glib throng to its conjecturing,
And let four burdened weeks uncover what they bring !

SEMICHORUS II

The said Debate, to wit ; its close in deeds ;
Till England stands enlisted for the Patriots' needs.

SEMICHORUS I

And transports in the docks gulp down their freight
Of buckled fighting-flesh, and, gale-bound, watch and
    wait.

SEMICHORUS II

Till gracious zephyrs shoulder on their sails
To where the brine of Biscay moans its tragic tales.

CHORUS

Bear we, too, south, as we were swallow-vanned,
And mark the game now played there by the Master-
    hand !

The reception-chamber is shut over by the night without, and the point of view rapidly recedes south, London and its streets and lights diminishing till they are lost in the distance, and its noises being succeeded by the babble of the Channel and Biscay waves.

SCENE IV

MADRID AND ITS ENVIRONS

The view is from the housetops of the city on a dusty evening in this July, following a day of suffocating heat. The sunburnt roofs, warm ochreous walls, and blue shadows of the capital, wear their usual aspect except for a few feeble attempts at decoration.

DUMB SHOW

Gazers gather in the central streets, and particularly in the Puerta del Sol. They show curiosity, but no enthusiasm. Patrols of French soldiery move up and down in front of the people, and seem to awe them into quietude.

There is a discharge of artillery in the outskirts, and the church bells begin ringing ; but the peals dwindle away to a melancholy jangle, and then to silence. Simultaneously, on the northern horizon of the arid, unenclosed, and treeless plain swept by the eye around the city, a cloud of dust arises, and a Royal procession is seen nearing. It means the new king, JOSEPH BONAPARTE.

He comes on, escorted by a clanking guard of four thousand Italian troops, and the brilliant royal carriage is followed by a hundred coaches bearing his suite. As the procession enters the city many houses reveal themselves to be closed, many citizens leave the route and walk elsewhere, while many of those who remain turn their backs upon the spectacle.

KING JOSEPH proceeds thus through the Pláza Oriente to the granite-walled Royal Palace, where he alights and is received by some of the nobility, the French generals who are in occupation there, and some clergy. Heralds emerge from the Palace, and hasten to divers points in the city, where trumpets are blown and the Proclamation of JOSEPH as KING OF SPAIN is read in a loud voice. It is received in silence.

The sun sets, and the curtain falls.

SCENE V

THE OPEN SEA BETWEEN THE ENGLISH COASTS AND THE SPANISH PENINSULA

From high aloft, in the same July weather, and facing east, the vision swoops over the ocean and its coast-lines, from Cork Harbour on the extreme left, to Mondego Bay, Portugal, on the extreme right. Land's End and the Scilly Isles, Ushant and Cape Finisterre, are projecting features along the middle distance of the picture, and the English Channel recedes endwise as a tapering avenue near the centre.

DUMB SHOW

Four groups of moth-like transport and war ships are dis-covered silently skimming this wide liquid plain. The first group, to the right, is just vanishing behind Cape Mondego to enter Mondego Bay ; the second, in the midst, has come out from Plymouth Sound, and is preparing to stand down Channel ; the third is clearing St. Helen's point for the same course ; and the fourth, much further up Channel, is obviously to follow

on considerably in the rear of the two preceding. A south-
east wind is blowing strong, and, according to the part of
their course reached, they either sail direct with the wind on
their larboard quarter, or labour forward by tacking in zigzags.

Spirit of the Pities

What are these fleets that cross the sea
From British ports and bays
To coasts that glister southwardly
Behind the dog-day haze ?

Rumours (chanting)

Semichorus I

They are the shipped battalions sent
To bar the bold Belligerent
Who stalks the Dancers' Land.
Within these hulls, like sheep a-pen,
Are packed in thousands fighting-men
And colonels in command.

Semichorus II

The fleet that leans each aëry fin
Far south, where Mondego mouths in,
Bears Wellesley and his aides therein,
And Hill, and Crauford too ;
With Torrens, Ferguson, and Fane,
And majors, captains, clerks, in train,
And those grim needs that appertain—
The surgeons—not a few !
To them add near twelve thousand souls
In linesmen that the list enrolls,
Borne onward by those sheeted poles
As war's red retinue !

Semichorus I

The fleet that clears St. Helen's shore
Holds Burrard, Hope, ill-omened Moore,
Clinton and Paget ; while
The transports that pertain to those
Count six-score sail, whose planks enclose
Ten thousand rank and file.

Semichorus II

The third-sent ships, from Plymouth Sound,
With Acland, Anstruther, impound
Souls to six thousand strong.
While those, the fourth fleet, that we see
Far back, are lined with cavalry,
And guns of girth, wheeled heavily
To roll their weight along.

Spirit of the Years

Enough, and more, of inventories and names !
Many will fail ; many earn doubtful fames.
Await the fruitage of their acts and aims.

DUMB SHOW (continuing)

In the spacious scene visible the far-separated groups of transports, convoyed by battleships, float on before the wind almost imperceptibly, like preened duck-feathers across a pond. The southernmost expedition, under Sir Arthur Wellesley, soon comes to anchor within the Bay of Mondego aforesaid, and the soldiery are indefinitely discernible landing upon the beach from boats. Simultaneously the division commanded by Moore, as yet in the Chops of the Channel, is seen to be beaten back by contrary winds. It gallantly puts to sea again, and being joined by the division under Anstruther that has set out from Plymouth, labours round Ushant, and stands to the south in the track of Wellesley. The rearward transports do the same.

A moving stratum of summer cloud beneath the point of view covers up the spectacle like an awning.

SCENE VI

ST. CLOUD.   THE BOUDOIR OF JOSÉPHINE

It is the dusk of an evening in the latter summer of this year, and from the windows at the back of the stage, which are still uncurtained, can be seen the EMPRESS with NAPOLÉON and some ladies and officers of the Court playing Catch-me-if-you-can by torchlight on the lawn. The moving torches throw bizarre lights and shadows into the apartment, where only a remote candle or two are burning.

Enter JOSÉPHINE and NAPOLÉON together, somewhat out of breath. With careless suppleness she slides down on a couch and fans herself. Now that the candle-rays reach her they show her mellow complexion, her velvety eyes with long lashes, mouth with pointed corners and excessive mobility beneath its *duvet,* and curls of dark hair pressed down upon the temples by a gold band.

The EMPEROR drops into a seat near her, and they remain in silence till he jumps up, knocks over some nicknacks with his elbow, and begins walking about the boudoir.

NAPOLÉON (with sudden gloom)

These mindless games are very well, my friend ;
But ours to-night marks, not improbably,
The last we play together.

JOSÉPHINE (starting)

       Can you say it !
Why raise that ghastly nightmare on me now,
When, for a moment, my poor brain had dreams
Denied it all the earlier anxious day ?

NAPOLÉON

Things that verge nigh, my simple Joséphine,
Are not shoved off by wilful winking at.

Better quiz evils with too strained an eye
Than have them leap from disregarded lairs.

JOSÉPHINE

Maybe 'tis true, and you shall have it so !—
Yet all joy is but sorrow waived awhile.

NAPOLÉON

Ha, ha ! That's like you. Well, each day by day
I get sour news.   Each hour since we returned
From this queer Spanish business at Bayonne,
I have had nothing else ; and hence my brooding.

JOSÉPHINE

But all went well throughout our touring time ?

NAPOLÉON

Not so—behind the scenes.   Our arms at Baylen
Have been smirched badly.   Twenty thousand
    shamed
All through Dupont's ill-luck !   The selfsame day
My brother Joseph's progress to Madrid
Was glorious as a sodden rocket's fizz !
Since when his letters creak with querulousness.
" Napoléon el chico " 'tis they call him—
" Napoléon the Little," so he says.
Then notice Austria.   Much looks louring there,
And her sly new regard for England grows.
The English, next, have shipped an army down
To Mondego, under one Wellesley,
A man from India, and his march is south
To Lisbon, by Vimiero.   On he'll go
And do the devil's mischief ere he is met
By unaware Junot, and chevyed back
To English fogs and fumes !

JOSÉPHINE

                    My dearest one,
You have mused on worse reports with better grace
Full many and many a time. Ah—there is
    more! . . .
I know ; I know !

NAPOLÉON (kicking away a stool)

                    There is, of course ; that worm
Time ever keeps in hand for gnawing me !—
The question of my dynasty—which bites
Closer and closer as the years wheel on.

JOSÉPHINE

Of course it's that !   For nothing else could hang
My lord on tenterhooks through nights and days ;—
Or rather, not the question, but the tongues
That keep the question stirring.   Nought recked you
Of throne-succession or dynastic lines
When gloriously engaged in Italy !
I was your fairy then : they labelled me
Your Lady of Victories ; and much I joyed,
Till dangerous ones drew near and daily sowed
These choking tares within your fecund brain,—
Making me tremble if a panel crack,
Or mouse but cheep, or silent leaf sail down,
And murdering my melodious hours with dreads
That my late happiness, and my late hope,
Will oversoon be knelled !

NAPOLÉON (genially nearing her)

But years have passed since first we talked of it ;
And now, with loss of dear Hortense's son
Who won me as my own, it looms forth more.

And selfish 'tis in my good Joséphine
To blind her vision to the weal of France,
And this great Empire's solidarity.
The grandeur of your sacrifice would gild
Your life's whole shape.

JOSÉPHINE

                    Were I as coarse a wife
As I am limned in English caricature—
(Those cruel effigies they draw of me !)—
You could not speak more aridly.

NAPOLÉON

                        Nay, nay !
You know, my comrade, how I love you still.
Were there a long-notorious dislike
Betwixt us, reason might be in your dreads.
But all earth knows our conjugality.
There's not a bourgeois couple in the land
Who, should dire duty rule their severance,
Could part with scanter scandal than could we.

JOSÉPHINE (pouting)

Nevertheless there's one.

NAPOLÉON

                    A scandal ?   What ?

JOSÉPHINE

Madame Walewska !   How could you pretend
When, after Jena, I'd have come to you,
" The weather was so wild, the roads so rough,
That no one of my sex and delicate nerve
Could hope to face the dangers and fatigues."
Yes—so you wrote me, dear.   They hurt not her !

NAPOLÉON (blandly)

She was a week's adventure—not worth words !
I say 'tis France.—I have held out for years
Against the constant pressure brought on me
To null this sterile marriage.

JOSÉPHINE (bursting into sobs)

                 Me you blame !
But how know you that you are not the culprit ?

NAPOLÈON

I have reason so to know—if I must say.
The Polish lady you have chosen to name
Has proved the fault not mine.
              (JOSÉPHINE sobs more violently.)
              Don't cry, my cherished ;
It is not really amiable of you,
Or prudent, my good little Joséphine,
With so much in the balance.

JOSÉPHINE

               How—know you—
What may not happen ! Wait a—little longer !

NAPOLÉON (playfully pinching her arm)

O come, now, my adored ! Haven't I already !
Nature's a dial whose shade no hand puts back,
Trick as we may ! My friend, you are forty-three
This very year in the world—
           (JOSÉPHINE breaks out sobbing again.)
             And vain it is
To think of waiting longer ; pitiful
To dream of coaxing shy fecundity

To an unlikely freak by physicking
With superstitious drugs and quackeries
That work you harm, not good.   The fact being so,
I have looked it squarely down—against my heart !
Solicitations voiced repeatedly
At length have shown the soundness of their shape,
And left me no denial.   You, at times,
My dear one, have been used to handle it.
My brother Joseph, years back, frankly gave
His honest view that something should be done ;
And he, you well may know, shows no ill tinct
In his regard of you.

JOSÉPHINE

And what princess ?

NAPOLÉON

For wiving with ?   No thought was given to that,
She shapes as vaguely as the Veiled—

JOSÉPHINE

No, no ;

It's Alexander's sister, I'm full sure !—
But why this craze for home-made manikins
And lineage mere of flesh ?   You have said yourself
It mattered not.   Great Caesar, you declared,
Sank sonless to his rest ; was greater deemed
Even for the isolation.   Frederick
Saw, too, no heir.   It is the fate of such,
Often, to be denied the common hope
As fine for fulness in the rarer gifts
That Nature yields them.   O my husband long,
Will you not purge your soul to value best
That high heredity from brain to brain
Which supersedes mere sequences of blood,
That often vary more from sire to son
Than between furthest strangers ! . . .

Napoléon's offspring in his like must lie ;
The second of his line be he who shows
Napoléon's soul in later bodiment,
The household father happening as he may !

NAPOLÉON (smilingly wiping her eyes)

Little guessed I my dear would prove her rammed
With such a charge of apt philosophy
When tutoring me gay arts in earlier times !
She who at home coquetted through the years
In which I vainly penned her wishful words
To come and comfort me in Italy,
Might, faith, have urged it then effectually !
But never would you stir from Paris joys,

(With some bitterness).

And so, when arguments like this could move me,
I heard them not ; and get them only now
When their weight dully falls.   But I have said
'Tis not for me, but France—Good-bye an hour.

(Kissing her.)

I must dictate some letters.   This new move
Of England on Madrid may mean some trouble.
Come, dwell not gloomily on this cold need
Of waiving private joy for policy.
We are but thistle-globes on Heaven's high gales,
And whither blown, or when, or how, or why,
Can choose us not at all ! . . .
I'll come to you anon, dear : staunch Roustan
Will light me in.

[Exit NAPOLÉON.

The scene shuts in shadow.

SCENE VII

VIMIERO

A village among the hills of Portugal, about fifty miles
north of Lisbon. Around it are disclosed, as ten on Sunday
morning strikes, a blue army of fourteen thousand men in
isolated columns, and a red army of eighteen thousand in line
formation, drawn up in order of battle. The blue army is a
French one under JUNOT; the other an English one under
SIR ARTHUR WELLESLEY—portion of that recently landed.

The August sun glares on the shaven faces, white gaiters,
and white cross-belts of the English, who are to fight for their
lives while sweating under a quarter-hundredweight in knapsack and pouches, and with firelocks heavy as putlogs. They
occupy a group of heights, but their position is one of great
danger, the land abruptly terminating two miles behind their
backs in lofty cliffs overhanging the Atlantic. The French
occupy the valleys in the English front, and this distinction
between the two forces strikes the eye—the red army is accompanied by scarce any cavalry, while the blue is strong in
that arm.

DUMB SHOW

The battle is begun with alternate moves that match each
other like those of a chess opening. JUNOT makes an oblique
attack by moving a division to his right; WELLESLEY moves
several brigades to his left to balance it.

A column of six thousand French then climbs the hill
against the English centre, and drives in those who are planted
there. The English artillery checks its adversaries, and the
infantry recover and charge the baffled French down the
slopes. Meanwhile the latter's cavalry and artillery are attacking the village itself, and, rushing on a few squadrons of English
dragoons stationed there, cut them to pieces. A dust is raised
by this ado, and moans of men and shrieks of horses are heard.
Close by the carnage the little Maceira stream continues to
trickle unconcernedly to the sea.

On the English left five thousand French infantry, having
ascended to the ridge and maintained a stinging musket-fire
as sharply returned, are driven down by the bayonets of six
English regiments. Thereafter a brigade of the French, the

northernmost, finding that the English have pursued to the bottom and are resting after the effort, surprise them and bayonet them back to their original summit. The see-saw is continued by the recovery of the English, who again drive their assailants down.

The French army pauses stultified, till, the columns uniting, they fall back towards the hills behind them. The English, seeing that their chance has come, are about to pursue and settle the fortunes of the day. But a messenger dispatched from a distant group is marked riding up to the large-nosed man with a telescope and an Indian sword who, his staff around him, has been directing the English movements. He seems astonished at the message, appears to resent it, and pauses with a gloomy look. But he sends countermands to his generals, and the pursuit ends abortively.

The French retreat without further molestation by a circuitous march into the great road to Torrès Védras by which they came, leaving nearly two thousand dead and wounded on the slopes they have quitted.

Dumb Show ends and the curtain draws.

ACT THIRD

SCENE I

SPAIN. A ROAD NEAR ASTORGA

The eye of the spectator rakes the road from the interior of a cellar which opens upon it, and forms the basement of a deserted house, the roof, doors, and shutters of which have been pulled down and burnt for bivouac fires. The season is the beginning of January, and the country is covered with a sticky snow. The road itself is intermittently encumbered with heavy traffic, the surface being churned to a yellow mud that lies half knee-deep, and at the numerous holes in the track forming still deeper quagmires.

In the gloom of the cellar are heaps of damp straw, in which ragged figures are lying half-buried, many of the men in the uniform of English line-regiments, and the women and children in clouts of all descriptions, some being nearly naked. At the back of the cellar is revealed, through a burst door, an inner vault, where are discernible some wooden-hooped wine-casks ; in one sticks a gimlet, and the broaching-cork of another has been driven in. The wine runs into pitchers, washing-basins, shards, chamber-vessels, and other extemporized receptacles. Most of the inmates are drunk ; some to insensibility.

So far as the characters are doing anything they are contemplating the almost incessant traffic outside, passing in one direction. It includes a medley of stragglers from the Marquis of ROMANA's Spanish forces and the retreating English army under SIR JOHN MOORE—to which the concealed deserters belong.

FIRST DESERTER

Now he's one of the Eighty-first, and I'd gladly let that poor blade know that we've all that man

can wish for here—good wine and buxom women.
But if I do, we shan't have room for ourselves—
hey ?

He signifies a man limping past with neither firelock nor
knapsack. Where the discarded knapsack has rubbed for
weeks against his shoulder-blades the jacket and shirt are
fretted away, leaving his skin exposed.

Second Deserter (drowsily)

He may be the Eighty-firsht, or th' Eighty-
second ; but what I say is, without fear of contra-
diction, I wish to the Lord I was back in old Bristol
again. I'd sooner have a nipperkin of our own
real " Bristol milk " than a mash-tub full of this
barbarian wine !

Third Deserter

'Tis like thee to be ungrateful, after putting
away such a skinful on't. I am as much Bristol
as thee, but would as soon be here as there. There
ain't near such willing women, that are strict
respectable too, there as hereabout, and no open
cellars.—As there's many a slip in this country
I'll have the rest of my allowance now.

He crawls on his elbows to one of the barrels, and turning
on his back lets the wine run down his throat.

Fourth Deserter (to a fifth, who is snoring)

Don't treat us to such a snoaching there, mate.
Here's some more coming, and they'll sight us if
we don't mind !

Enter without a straggling flock of military objects, some
with fragments of shoes on, others bare-footed, many of the
latter's feet bleeding. The arms and waists of some are clutched
by women as tattered and bare-footed as themselves. They
pass on.

The Retreat continues. More of ROMANA's Spanish limp along in disorder ; then enters a miscellaneous group of English cavalry soldiers, some on foot, some mounted, the rearmost of the latter bestriding a shoeless foundered creature whose neck is vertebræ and mane only. While passing it falls from exhaustion ; the trooper extricates himself and pistols the animal through the head. He and the rest pass on.

FIRST DESERTER
(a new plashing of feet being heard)

Here's something more in order, or I am much mistaken. (He cranes out.) Yes, a sergeant of the Forty-third, and what's left of their second battalion. And, by God, not far behind I see shining helmets. 'Tis a whole squadron of French dragoons !

Enter the sergeant. He has a racking cough, but endeavours, by stiffening himself up, to hide how it is wasting away his life. He halts, and looks back, till the remains of the Forty-third are abreast, to the number of some three hundred, about half of whom are crippled invalids, the other half being presentable and armed soldiery.

SERGEANT

Now show yer nerve, and be men. If you die to-day you won't have to die to-morrow. Fall in ! (The miscellany falls in.) All invalids and men without arms march ahead as well as they can. Quick— maw-w-w-ch ! (Exeunt invalids, etc.) Now ! Tention ! Shoulder-r-r-r—fawlocks ! (Order obeyed.)

The sergeant hastily forms these into platoons, who prime and load, and seem preternaturally changed from what they were into alert soldiers.

Enter French dragoons at the left-back of the scene. The rear platoon of the Forty-third turns, fires, and proceeds. The next platoon covering them does the same. This is repeated several times, staggering the pursuers. Exeunt French dragoons, giving up the pursuit. The coughing sergeant and the remnant of the Forty-third march on.

FOURTH DESERTER (to a woman lying beside him)

What d'ye think o' that, my honey? It fairly
makes me a man again. Come, wake up! We
must be getting along somehow. (He regards the woman
more closely.) Why—my little chick? Look here,
friends. (They look, and the woman is found to be dead.)
If I didn't think that her poor knees felt cold! . . .
And only an hour ago I swore I'd marry her!

They remain silent. The Retreat continues in the snow
without, now in the form of a file of ox-carts, followed by a
mixed rabble of English and Spanish, and mules and muleteers
hired by English officers to carry their baggage. The muleteers,
looking about and seeing that the French dragoons have been
there, cut the bands which hold on the heavy packs, and
scamper off with their mules.

A VOICE (behind)

The Commander-in-Chief is determined to maintain discipline, and they must suffer. No more
pillaging here. It is the worst case of brutality
and plunder that we have had in this wretched
time!

Enter an English captain of hussars, a lieutenant, a guard
of about a dozen, and three men as prisoners.

CAPTAIN

If they choose to draw lots, only one need be
made an example of. But they must be quick
about it. The advance-guard of the enemy is not
far behind.

The three prisoners appear to draw lots, and the one on
whom the lot falls is blindfolded. Exeunt the hussars behind
a wall, with carbines. A volley is heard and something falls.
The wretches in the cellar shudder.

Fourth Deserter

'Tis the same for us but for this heap of straw.
Ah—my doxy is the only one of us who is safe and
sound !   (He kisses the dead woman.)

Retreat continues. A train of six-horse baggage-waggons
lumbers past, a mounted sergeant alongside. Among the
baggage lie wounded soldiers and sick women.

Sergeant of the Waggon-Train

If so be they are dead, ye may as well drop 'em
over the tail-board. 'Tis no use straining the
horses unnecessary.

Waggons halt. Two of the wounded who have just died
are taken out, laid down by the roadside, and some muddy
snow scraped over them. Exeunt waggons and waggon-
sergeant.
An interval. More English troops pass, on horses mostly
shoeless and foundered.
Enter Sir John Moore and officers. Moore appears in
the pale evening light as a handsome man, far on in the forties,
the orbits of his dark eyes showing marks of deep anxiety.
He is talking to some of his staff with vehement emphasis
and gesture. They cross the scene and go on out of sight, and the
squashing of their horses' hoofs in the snowy mud dies away.

Fifth Deserter (incoherently in his sleep)

Poise fawlocks — open pans — right hands to
pouch—handle ca'tridge—bring it—quick motion
—bite top well off—prime—shut pans—cast about
—load——

First Deserter (throwing a shoe at the sleeper)

Shut up that ! D'ye think you are a 'cruity in
the awkward squad still ?

SECOND DESERTER

I don't know what he thinks, but I know what I feel! Would that I were at home in England again, where there's old-fashioned tipple, and a proper God A'mighty instead of this eternal 'Ooman and baby;—ay, at home a-leaning against old Bristol Bridge, and no questions asked, and the winter sun slanting friendly over Baldwin Street as 'a used to do! 'Tis my very belief, though I have lost all sure reckoning, that if I wer there, and in good health, 'twould be New Year's day about now. What it is over here I don't know. Ay, to-night we should be a-setting in the tap of the "Adam and Eve"—lifting up the tune of "The Light o' the Moon." 'Twer a romantical thing enough. 'A used to go som'at like this (he sings in a nasal tone) :—

"O I thought it had been day,
    And I stole from her away ;
    But it proved to be the light o' the moon!"

Retreat continues, with infantry in good order. Hearing the singing, one of the officers looks around, and detaching a patrol enters the ruined house with the file of men, the body of soldiers marching on. The inmates of the cellar bury themselves in the straw. The officer peers about, and seeing no one prods the straw with his sword.

VOICES (under the straw)

Oh! Hell! Stop it! We'll come out! Mercy! Quarter !   [The lurkers are uncovered.

OFFICER

If you are well enough to sing bawdy songs, you are well enough to march. So out of it—or you'll be shot, here and now!

SEVERAL

You may shoot us, captain, or the French may shoot us—or the devil may take us ; we don't care which ! Only we can't stir. Pity the women, captain, but do what you will with us !

The searchers pass over the wounded, and stir out those capable of marching, both men and women, so far as they discover them. They are pricked on by the patrol. Exeunt patrol and deserters in its charge.

Those who remain look stolidly at the highway. The English Rear-guard of cavalry crosses the scene and passes out. An interval. It grows dusk.

SPIRIT IRONIC

Quaint poesy, and real romance of war !

SPIRIT OF THE PITIES

Mock on, Shade, if thou wilt ! But others find Poesy ever lurk where pit-pats poor mankind !

The scene is cloaked in darkness.

SCENE II

THE SAME

It is nearly midnight. The fugitives who remain in the cellar having slept off the effects of the wine, are awakened by a new tramping of cavalry, which becomes more and more persistent. It is the French, who now fill the road. The advance-guard having passed by, DELABORDE's division, LORGE's division, MERLE's division, and others, successively cross the gloom.

Presently come the outlines of the Imperial Guard, and then, with a start, those in hiding realize their situation, and

are wide awake. NAPOLÉON enters with his staff. He has
just been overtaken by a courier, and orders those round him
to halt.

NAPOLÉON

Let there a fire be lit : ay, here and now.
The lines within these letters brook no pause
In mastering their purport.

Some of the French approach the ruined house and, appro-
priating what wood is still left there, heap it by the roadside
and set it alight. A mixed rain and snow falls, and the sputtering flames throw a glare all round.

SECOND DESERTER (under his voice)

We be shot corpses ! Ay, faith, we be ! Why
didn't I stick to England, and true doxology, and
leave foreign doxies and their wine alone ! . . .
Mate, can ye squeeze another shardful from the
cask there, for I feel my time is come ! . . . O
that I had but the barrel of that firelock I throwed
away, and that wasted powder to prime and load !
This bullet I chaw to squench my hunger would do
the rest ! . . . Yes, I could pick him off now !

FIRST DESERTER

You lie low with your picking off, or he may
pick off you ! Thank God the babies are gone.
Maybe we shan't be noticed, if we've but the
courage to do nothing, and keep hid.

NAPOLÉON dismounts, approaches the fire, and looks around.

NAPOLÉON

Another of their dead horses here, I see.

Officer

Yes, sire.   We have counted eighteen hundred odd
From Benavente hither, pistoled thus.
Some we'd to finish for them : headlong haste
Spared them no time for mercy to their brutes.
One-half their cavalry now tramps afoot.

Napoléon

And what's the tale of waggons we've picked up ?

Officer

Spanish and all abandoned, some four hundred ;
Of magazines and firelocks, full ten load ;
And stragglers and their girls a numerous crew.

Napoléon

Ay, devil—plenty those !   Licentious ones
These English, as all canting peoples are.—
And prisoners ?

Officer

                    Seven hundred English, sire ;
Spaniards five thousand more.

Napoléon

                    'Tis not amiss.
To keep the new year up they run away !

(He soliloquizes as he begins tearing open the dispatches.)

Nor Pitt nor Fox displayed such blundering
As glares in this campaign !   It is, indeed,
Enlarging Folly to Foolhardiness
To combat France by land !   But how expect

Aught that can claim the name of government
From Canning, Castlereagh, and Perceval,
Caballers all—poor sorry politicians—
To whom has fallen the luck of reaping in
The harvestings of Pitt's bold husbandry.

*He unfolds a dispatch, and looks for something to sit on.
A cloak is thrown over a log, and he settles to reading by the
firelight. The others stand round. The light, crossed by the
snow-flakes, flickers on his unhealthy face and stoutening
figure. He sinks into the rigidity of profound thought, till his
features lour.*

So this is their reply !   They have done with me !
Britain declines negotiating further—
Flouts France and Russia indiscriminately.
" Since one dethrones and keeps as prisoners
The most legitimate kings "—that means myself—
" The other suffers their unworthy treatment
For sordid interests "—that's for Alexander ! . . .
And what is Georgy made to say besides ?—
" Pacific overtures to us are wiles
Woven to unnerve the generous nations round
Lately escaped the galling yoke of France,
Or waiting so to do.   Such, then, being seen,
These tentatives must be regarded now
As finally forgone ; and crimson war
Be faced to its fell worst, unflinchingly."
—The devil take their lecture !   What am I,
That England should return such insolence ?

*He jumps up, furious, and walks to and fro beside the fire.
By and by cooling he sits down again.*

Now as to hostile signs in Austria. . . .

(He breaks another seal and reads)

Ah,—swords to cross with her some day in spring !
Thinking me cornered over here in Spain
She speaks without disguise, the covert pact
'Twixt her and England owning now quite frankly,
Careless how works its knowledge upon me.
She, England, Germany : well—I can front them !

That there is no sufficient force of French
Between the Elbe and Rhine to prostrate her,
Let new and terrible experience
Soon disillude her of !   Yea ; she may arm :
The opportunity she late let slip
Will not subserve her now !

SPIRIT OF THE PITIES

Has he no heart-hints that this Austrian court,
Whereon his mood takes mould so masterful,
Is rearing naïvely in its nursery-room
A future wife for him ?

SPIRIT OF THE YEARS

                  Thou dost but guess it,
And how should his heart know ?

NAPOLÉON (opening and reading another dispatch)

                  Now eastward.   Ohè !—
The Orient likewise looms full sombrely. . . .
The Turk declines pacifically to yield
What I have promised Alexander.   Ah ! . . .
As for Constantinople being his prize
I'll see him frozen first.   His flight's too high !
And showing that I think so makes him cool.

                                        (Rises.)

Is Soult, the Duke Dalmatia, yet at hand ?

OFFICER

He has arrived along the Leon road
Just now, your Majesty ; and only waits
The close of your perusals.

              Enter SOULT, who is greeted by NAPOLÉON.

First Deserter

Good Lord deliver us from all great men, and
take me back again to humble life ! That's Marshal
Soult the Duke of Dalmatia !

Second Deserter

The Duke of Damnation for our poor rear, by
the look on't !

First Deserter

Yes—he'll make 'em rub their poor rears before
he has done with 'em ! But we must overtake
'em to-morrow by a cross-cut, please God !

Napoléon (pointing to the dispatches)

Here's matter enough for me, Duke, and to spare.
The ominous contents are like the threats
The ancient prophets dealt rebellious Judah !
Austria we soon shall have upon our hands,
And England still is fierce for fighting on,—
Strange humour in a concord-loving land !
So now I must to Paris straight away—
At least, to Valladolid ; so as to stand
More apt for couriers than I do out here
In this far western corner, and to mark
The veerings of these new developments,
And blow a counter-breeze. . . .
    Then, too, there's Lannes, still sweating at the
        siege
Of sullen Zaragoza as 'twere hell.
Him I must further counsel how to close
His twice too tedious battery.—You, then, Soult—
Ney is not yet, I gather, quite come up ?

Soult

He's near, sire, on the Benavente road ;
But some hours to the rear I reckon, still.

Napoléon

Him I'll direct to come to your support
In this pursuit and harassment of Moore
Wherein you take my place.   You'll follow up
And chase the flying English to the sea.
Bear hard on them, the bayonet at their loins,
With Merle's and Mermet's corps just gone ahead,
And Delaborde's, and Heudelet's here at hand,
While Lorge's and Lahoussaye's picked dragoons
Will follow, and Franceschi's cavalry.
To Ney I am writing that, in case of need,
He will support, with Marchand and Mathieu.—
Your total thus of seventy thousand odd,
Ten thousand horse, and cannon to five score,
Should near annihilate this British force,
And carve a triumph large in history.

(He bends over the fire and makes some notes rapidly.)

I move into Astorga ;   then turn back,
(Though only in my person do I turn)
And leave to you the destinies of Spain.

Spirit of the Years

More turning may be here than he designs.
In this small, sudden, swift turn backward, he
Suggests one turning from his apogee !

The characters disperse, the fire sinks, and snowflakes and
darkness blot out all.

SCENE III

BEFORE CORUÑA

The town, harbour, and hills at the back are viewed from
an aerial point to the north, over the lighthouse known as the
Tower of Hercules, rising at the extremity of the tongue of
land on which La Coruña stands, the open ocean being in the
spectator's rear.

In the foreground the most prominent feature is the walled
old town, with its white towers and houses, shaping itself
aloft over the harbour. The new town, and its painted fronts,
show bright below, even on this cloudy winter afternoon.
Further off, behind the harbour—now crowded with British
transports of all sizes—is a series of low broken hills, intersected by hedges and stone walls.

A mile behind these low inner hills is beheld a rocky chain
of outer and loftier heights that completely command the
former. Nothing behind them is seen but grey sky.

DUMB SHOW

On the inner hills aforesaid the little English army—a
pathetic fourteen thousand of foot only—is just deploying
into line : HOPE's division on the left, BAIRD's to the right.
PAGET with the reserve is in the hollow to the left behind
them ; and FRASER's division still further back shapes out
on a slight rise to the right.

This harassed force now appears as if composed of quite
other than the men observed in the Retreat insubordinately
straggling along like vagabonds. Yet they are the same men,
suddenly stiffened and grown amenable to discipline by the
satisfaction of standing to the enemy at last. They resemble
a double palisade of red stakes, the only gaps being those that
the melancholy necessity of scant numbers entails here and
there.

Over the heads of these red men is beheld on the outer hills
the twenty thousand French that have been pushed along the
road at the heels of the English by SOULT. They have an
ominous superiority, both in position and in their abundance
of cavalry and artillery, over the slender lines of English foot.
The left of this background, facing HOPE, is made up of DELA-
BORDE's and MERLE's divisions, while in a deadly arc round

BAIRD, from whom they are divided only by the village of Elvina, are placed MERMET'S division, LAHOUSSAYE'S and LORGE'S dragoons, FRANCESCHI'S cavalry, and, highest up of all, a formidable battery of eleven great guns that rake the whole British line.

It is now getting on for two o'clock, and a stir of activity has lately been noticed along the French front. Three columns are discerned descending from their position, the first towards the division of SIR DAVID BAIRD, the weakest point in the English line, the next towards the centre, the third towards the left. A heavy cannonade from the battery supports this advance.

The clash ensues, the English being swept down in swathes by the enemy's artillery. The opponents meet face to face at the village in the valley between them, and the fight there grows furious.

SIR JOHN MOORE is seen galloping to the front under the gloomy sky.

SPIRIT OF THE PITIES

I seem to vision in San Carlos' garden,
That rises salient in the upper town,
His name, and date, and doing, set within
A filmy outline like a monument,
Which yet is but the insubstantial air.

SPIRIT OF THE YEARS

Read visions as conjectures; not as more.

When MOORE arrives at the front, FRASER and PAGET move to the right, where the English are most sorely pressed. A grape-shot strikes off BAIRD'S arm. There is a little confusion, and he is borne to the rear; while MAJOR NAPIER disappears, a prisoner.

Intelligence of these misfortunes is brought to SIR JOHN MOORE. He goes further forward, and precedes in person the Forty-second regiment and a battalion of the Guards who, with fixed bayonets, bear the enemy back, MOORE'S gestures in cheering them being notably energetic. Pursuers, pursued, and SIR JOHN himself pass out of sight behind the hill. Dumb Show ends.

The point of vision descends to the immediate rear of the English position. The early January evening has begun to spread its shades, and shouts of dismay are heard from behind

the hill over which MOORE and the advancing lines have
vanished.

Straggling soldiers cross in the gloom.

FIRST STRAGGLER

He's struck by a cannon-ball, that I know; but
he's not killed, that I pray God A'mighty.

SECOND STRAGGLER

Better he were. His shoulder is knocked to a
bag of splinters. As Sir David was wounded, Sir
John was anxious that the right should not give
way, and went forward to keep it firm.

FIRST STRAGGLER

He didn't keep *you* firm, howsomever.

SECOND STRAGGLER

Nor you, for that matter.

FIRST STRAGGLER

Well, 'twas a serious place for a man with no
priming-horn, and a character to lose, so I judged it
best to fall to the rear by lying down. A man can't
fight by the regulations without his priming-horn,
and I am none of your slovenly anyhow fighters.

SECOND STRAGGLER

'Nation, having dropped my flint-pouch, I was
the same. If you'd had your priming-horn, and I
my flints, mind ye, we should have been there
now? Then, forty-whory, that we are not is the
fault o' Government for not supplying new ones
from the reserve!

FIRST STRAGGLER

What did he say as he led us on ?

SECOND STRAGGLER

" Forty-second, remember Egypt ! " I heard it
with my own ears. Yes, that was his strict
testament.

FIRST STRAGGLER

" Remember Egypt." Ay, and I do, for I was
there ! . . . Upon my salvation, here's for back
again, whether or no !

SECOND STRAGGLER

But here. " Forty-second, remember Egypt,"
he said in the very eye of that French battery
playing through us. And the next omen was that
he was struck off his horse, and fell on his back
to the ground. I remembered Egypt, and what
had just happened too, so thorough well that I
remembered the way over this wall !—Captain
Hardinge, who was close to him, jumped off his
horse, and he and one in the ranks lifted him,
and are now bringing him along.

FIRST STRAGGLER

Nevertheless, here's for back again, come what
will. Remember Egypt ! Hurrah !

[Exit First Straggler.
Second Straggler ponders, then suddenly follows First.
Enter COLONEL ANDERSON and others hastily.

AN OFFICER

Now fetch a blanket. He must be carried in.

[Shouts heard.

COLONEL ANDERSON

That means we are gaining ground ! Had fate but
    left
This last blow undecreed, the hour had shone
A star amid these girdling days of gloom !

                                      [Exit.

    Enter in the obscurity six soldiers of the Forty-second
bearing SIR JOHN MOORE on their joined hands. CAPTAIN
HARDINGE walks beside and steadies him. He is temporarily
laid down in the shelter of a wall, his left shoulder being pounded
away, the arm dangling by a shred of flesh.

    Enter COLONEL GRAHAM and CAPTAIN WOODFORD.

GRAHAM

The wound is more than serious, Woodford, far.
Ride for a surgeon—one of those, perhaps,
Who tend Sir David Baird ?   (Exit Captain Woodford.)
His blood throbs forth so fast, that I've dark fears
He'll drain to death ere anything can be done !

HARDINGE

I'll try to staunch it—since no skill's in call.

    (He takes off his sash and endeavours to bind the wound
with it. MOORE smiles and shakes his head.)

There's not much checking it ! The rent's too
    gross.
A dozen lives could pass that thoroughfare !

    Enter a soldier with a blanket. They lift MOORE into it.
During the operation the pommel of his sword, which he still
wears, is accidentally thrust into the wound.

I'll loose the sword—it bruises you, Sir John.

                          [He begins to unbuckle it.

MOORE

No. Let it be ! One hurt more matters not.
I wish it to go off the field with me.

HARDINGE

I like the sound of that.   It augurs well
For your much-hoped recovery.

MOORE (looking sadly at his wound)

Hardinge, no :
Nature is nonplussed there !   My shoulder's gone,
And this left side laid open to my lungs.
There's but a brief breath now for me, at most. . . .
Could you—move me along—that I may glimpse
Still how the battle's going ?

HARDINGE

Ay, Sir John—
A few yards higher up, where we can see.

He is borne in the blanket a little way onward, and lifted so
that he can view the valley and the action.

MOORE (brightly)

They seem to be advancing.   Yes, it is so !

Enter SIR JOHN HOPE.

Ah, Hope !—I am doing badly here enough ;
But they are doing rarely well out there.

(Presses Hope's hand.)

Don't leave ! my speech may flag with this fierce
    pain,
But you can talk to me.—Are the French foiled ?

HOPE

My dear friend, they are borne back steadily.

MOORE (his voice weakening)

I hope that England—will be satisfied—
I hope my native land—will do me justice ! . . .

I shall be blamed for sending Craufurd off
Along the Orense road.   But had I not,
Bonaparte would have headed us that way. . . .

HOPE

O would that Soult had but accepted fight
By Lugo town !   We should have crushed him
  there.

MOORE

Yes . . . yes.—But it has never been my lot
To owe much to good luck ; nor was it then.
Good fortune has been mine, but, (bitterly) mostly so
By the exhaustion of all shapes of bad ! . . .
Well, this does not become a dying man ;
And others have been chastened more than I
By Him who holds us in His hollowed hand ! . . .
  I grieve for Zaragoza if, as said,
The siege goes sorely with her, which it must.
I heard when at Dahagun that late day
That she was holding out heroically.
But I must leave such now.—You'll see my friends
As early as you can ?   Tell them the whole ;
Say to my mother . . .   (His voice fails.)
Hope, Hope, I have so much to charge you with,
But weakness clams my tongue ! . . . If I must die
Without a word with Stanhope, ask him, Hope,
To—name me to his sister.   You may know
Of what there was between us ? . . .
Is Colonel Graham well, and all my aides ?
My will I have made—it is in Colborne's charge
With other papers.

HOPE

He's now coming up.

Enter MAJOR COLBORNE, principal aide-de-camp.

MOORE

Are the French beaten, Colborne, or repulsed ?
Alas ! you see what they have done to me !

COLBORNE

I do, Sir John : I am more than sad thereat !
In brief time now the surgeon will be here.
The French retreat—pushed from Elvina far.

MOORE

That's good ! Is Paget anywhere about ?

COLBORNE

He's at the front, Sir John.

MOORE

                    Remembrance to him !

Enter two surgeons.

Ah, doctors,—you can scarcely mend up me.—
And yet I feel so tough—I have feverish fears
My dying will waste a long and tedious while ;
But not too long, I hope !

SURGEONS (after a hasty examination)

                    You must be borne
In to your lodgings instantly, Sir John.
Please strive to stand the motion—if you can ;
They will keep step, and bear you steadily.

MOORE

Anything . . . Surely fainter ebbs that fire ?

COLBORNE

Yes : we must be advancing everywhere :
Colbert their General, too, they have lost, I learn.

They lift him by stretching their sashes under the blanket,
and begin moving off. A light waggon enters.

MOORE

Who's in that waggon ?

HARDINGE

                Colonel Wynch, Sir John.
He's wounded, but he urges you to take it.

MOORE

No. I will not. This suits. . . . Don't come with
    me :
There's more for you to do out here as yet.

                        (Cheerful shouts.)

A-ha ! 'Tis *this* way I have wished to die !

Exeunt slowly in the twilight MOORE, bearers, surgeons, etc.,
towards Coruña.
            The scene darkens.

SCENE IV

CORUÑA. NEAR THE RAMPARTS

It is just before dawn on the following morning, objects
being still indistinct. The features of the elevated enclosure
of San Carlos can be recognized in dim outline, and also those
of the Old Town of Coruña around, though scarcely a lamp is
shining. The numerous transports in the harbour beneath
have still their riding-lights burning.

In a nook of the town walls a lantern glimmers. Some English soldiers of the Ninth regiment are hastily digging a grave there with extemporized tools.

A Voice (from the gloom some distance off)

" I am the resurrection and the life, saith the Lord : he that believeth in me, though he were dead, yet shall he live."

The soldiers look up, and see entering at the further end of the patch of ground a slow procession. It advances by the light of lanterns in the hands of some members of it. At moments the fitful rays fall upon bearers carrying a coffinless body rolled in a blanket, with a military cloak roughly thrown over by way of pall. It is brought towards the incomplete grave, and followed by Hope, Graham, Anderson, Colborne, Hardinge, and several aides-de-camp, a chaplain preceding.

First Soldier

They are here, almost as hasteful as ourselves.
There is no time to dig much deeper now :
Level a bottom just as far's we've got.
He'll couch as calmly in this scrabbled hole
As in a royal vault !

Second Soldier

Would it had been a foot deeper, here among foreigners, with strange manures manufactured out of no one knows what ! Surely we can give him another six inches ?

First Soldier

There is no time. Just make the bottom true.

The meagre procession approaches the spot, and waits while the half-dug grave is roughly finished by the men of the Ninth. They step out of it, and another of them holds a lantern to the chaplain's book. The winter day slowly dawns.

CHAPLAIN

" Man that is born of a woman hath but a short time to live, and is full of misery. He cometh up, and is cut down, like a flower ; he fleeth as it were a shadow, and never continueth in one stay."

A gun is fired from the French battery not far off ; then another. The ships in the harbour take in their riding-lights.

COLBORNE (in a low voice)

I knew that dawn would see them open fire.

HOPE

We must perforce be swift to use our time.
Would we had closed our too sad office sooner !

As the body is lowered another discharge echoes. They glance gloomily at the heights where the French are ranged, and then into the grave.

CHAPLAIN

" We therefore commit his body to the ground.
Earth to earth, ashes to ashes, dust to dust."

(Another gun.)

A spent ball falls not far off. They put out their lanterns. Continued firing, some shot splashing into the harbour below them.

HOPE

In mercy to the living, who are thrust
Upon our care for their deliverance,
And run much hazard till they are embarked,
We must abridge these duties to the dead,
Who will not mind be they abridged or no.

HARDINGE

And could he mind, would be the man to bid it . . .

HOPE

We shall do well, then, curtly to conclude
These mutilated prayers—our hurried best !—
And what's left unsaid, feel.

CHAPLAIN (his words broken by the cannonade)

" . . . . We give Thee hearty thanks for that
it hath pleased Thee to deliver this our brother out
of the miseries of this sinful world. . . . Who also
hath taught us not to be sorry, as men without
hope, for them that sleep in Him. . . . Grant this,
through Jesus Christ our Mediator and Redeemer."

OFFICERS AND SOLDIERS

Amen !

The diggers of the Ninth hastily fill in the grave, and the
scene shuts as the mournful figures retire.

SCENE V

VIENNA.   A CAFÉ IN THE STEPHANS-PLATZ

An evening between light and dark is disclosed, some lamps
being lit. The huge body and tower of St. Stephen's rise into
the sky some way off, the western gleam still touching the upper
stonework. Groups of people are seated at the tables, drinking
and reading the newspapers. One very animated group, which
includes an Englishman, is talking loudly. A citizen near looks
up from his newspaper.

CITIZEN (to the Englishman)

I read, sir, here, the troubles you·discuss
Of your so gallant army under Moore.

His was a spirit baffled but not quelled,
And in his death there shone a stoicism
That lent retreat the rays of victory.

ENGLISHMAN

It was so.   While men chide they will admire him,
And frowning, praise.   I could nigh prophesy
That the unwonted crosses he has borne
In his career of sharp vicissitude
Will tinct his story with a tender charm,
And grant the memory of his strenuous feats
As long a lease within the minds of men
As conquerors hold there.—Does the sheet give news
Of how the troops reached home ?

CITIZEN (looking again at the paper)

                Yes ; from your press
It quotes that they arrived at Plymouth Sound
Mid dreadful weather and much suffering.
It states they looked the very ghosts of men,
So heavily had hunger told on them,
And the fatigues and toils of the retreat.
Several were landed dead, and many died
As they were borne along.   At Portsmouth, too,
Sir David Baird, still helpless from his wound,
Was carried in a cot, sheet-pale and thin,
And Sir John Hope, lank as a skeleton.—
Thereto is added, with authority,
That a new expedition soon will fit,
And start again for Spain.

ENGLISHMAN

             I have heard as much.

CITIZEN

You'll do it next time, sir.   And so shall we !

Second Citizen
(regarding the church tower opposite)

You witnessed the High Service over there
They held this morning ?   (To the Englishman.)

Englishman

          Ay ; I did get in ;
Though not without hard striving, such the throng ;
But travellers roam to waste who shyly roam,
And I pushed like the rest.

Second Citizen

          Our young Archduchess
Maria Louisa was, they tell me, present ?

Englishman

O yes : the whole Imperial family,
And when the Bishop called all blessings down
Upon the Landwehr colours there displayed,
Enthusiasm touched the sky—she sharing it.

Second Citizen

Commendable in her, and spirited,
After the graceless insults to the Court
The Paris journals flaunt—not voluntarily,
But by his ordering.   Magician-like
He holds them in his fist, and at his squeeze
They bubble what he wills ! . . . Yes, she's a girl
Of patriotic build, and hates the French.
Quite lately she was overheard to say
She had met with most convincing auguries
That this year Bonaparte was starred to die.

ENGLISHMAN

Your arms must render its fulfilment sure.

SECOND CITIZEN

Right !   And we have the opportunity,
By upping to the war in suddenness,
And catching him unaware.   The pink and flower
Of all his veteran troops are now in Spain
Fully engaged with yours ; while those he holds
In Germany are scattered far and wide.

FIRST CITIZEN
(looking up again from his newspaper)

I see here that he vows and guarantees
Inviolate bounds to all our territories
If we but pledge to carry out forthwith
A prompt disarmament.   Since that's his price
Hell burn his guarantees !   Too long he has fooled
    us.
(To the Englishman) I drink, sir, to your land's con-
    sistency.
While we and all the kindred Europe States
Alternately have wooed and warred with him,
You have not bent to blowing hot and cold,
But held you sturdily inimical !

ENGLISHMAN (laughing)

Less Christian-like forgiveness mellows us
Than Continental souls !   (They drink.)

A band is heard in a distant street, with shouting.   Enter
third and fourth citizens, followed by others.

FIRST CITIZEN
More news afloat ?

Third and Fourth Citizens

Yea ; an announcement that the Archduke Charles
Is given the chief command.

First, Second, etc., Citizens

                 Huzza ! Right so !

A clinking of glasses, rising from seats, and general enthusiasm.

Second Citizen

If war had not so patly been declared,
Our howitzers and firelocks of themselves
Would have gone off to shame us ! This forenoon
Some of the Landwehr met me ; they are hot
For setting out, though but few months enrolled.

Englishman

That moves reflection somewhat. They are young
For measuring with the veteran files of France !

First Citizen

Napoléon's army swarms with tender youth,
His last conscription besomed into it
Thousands of merest boys. But he contrives
To mix them in the field with seasoned frames.

Second Citizen

The sadly-seen mistake this country made
Was that of grounding hostile arms at all.
We should have fought irreconcilably—
Have been consistent as the English are.
The French are our hereditary foes,
And this adventurer of the saucy sword,

This sacrilegious slighter of our shrines,
Stands author of our ills . . .
Our harvest fields and fruits he tramples on,
Accumulating ruin in our land.
Think of what mournings in the last sad war
'Twas his to instigate and answer for !
Time never can efface the glint of tears
In palaces, in shops, in fields, in cots,
From women widowed, sonless, fatherless,
That then oppressed our eyes. There is no salve
For such deep harrowings but to fight again ;
Th' enfranchisement of Europe hangs thereon,
And long she has lingered for the sign to crush
    him :
That signal we have given ; the time is come !

                     (Thumping on the tables.)

FIFTH CITIZEN (at another table, looking up from
        his paper and speaking across)

I see that Russia has declined to aid us,
And says she knows that Prussia likewise must ;
So that the mission of Prince Schwarzenberg
To Alexander's Court has closed in failure.

THIRD CITIZEN

Ay—through his being honest—fatal sin !—
Probing too plainly for the Emperor's ears
His ominous friendship with Napoléon.

ENGLISHMAN

Some say he was more than honest with the Tsar ;
Hinting that his becoming an ally
Makes him accomplice of the Corsican
In the unprincipled dark overthrow
Of his poor trusting childish Spanish friends—
Which gave the Tsar offence.

THIRD CITIZEN

              And our best bid—
The last, most delicate dish—a tastelessness.

FIRST CITIZEN

What was Prince Schwarzenberg's best bid, I pray ?

THIRD CITIZEN

The offer of the heir of Austria's hand
For Alexander's sister the Grand-Duchess.

ENGLISHMAN

He could not have accepted, if or no :
She is inscribed as wife for Bonaparte.

FIRST CITIZEN

I doubt that text !

ENGLISHMAN

           Time's context soon will show.

SECOND CITIZEN

The Russian Cabinet can not for long
Resist the ardour of the Russian ranks
To march with us the moment we achieve
Our first loud victory !

    A band is heard playing afar, and shouting. People are
seen hurrying past in the direction of the sounds. Enter sixth
citizen.

SIXTH CITIZEN

             The Archduke Charles
Is passing along the Ringstrass' just by now,
His regiment at his heels !

The younger sitters jump up with animation, and go out, the elder mostly remaining.

SECOND CITIZEN

Realm never faced
The grin of a more fierce necessity
For horrid war, than ours at this tense time !

The sounds of band-playing and huzzaing wane away. Citizens return.

FIRST CITIZEN

More news, my friends, of swiftly swelling zeal ?

RE-ENTERED CITIZENS

Ere passing down the Ring, the Archduke paused
And gave the soldiers speech, enkindling them
As sunrise a confronting throng of panes
That glaze a many-windowed east façade :
Hot volunteers vamp in from vill and plain—
More than we need in furthest sacrifice !

FIRST, SECOND, ETC., CITIZENS

Huzza ! Right so ! Good ! Forwards ! God
be praised !

They stand up, and a clinking of glasses follows, till they subside to quietude and a reperusal of newspapers. Nightfall succeeds. Dancing-rooms are lit up in an opposite street, and dancing begins. The figures are seen gracefully moving round to the throbbing strains of a string-band, which plays a new waltzing movement with a war-like name, soon to spread over Europe. The dancers sing patriotic words as they whirl.

The night closes over.

ACT FOURTH

SCENE I

A ROAD OUT OF VIENNA

It is a morning in early May. Rain descends in torrents, accompanied by peals of thunder. The tepid downpour has caused the trees to assume as by magic a clothing of limp green leafage, and has turned the ruts of the uneven highway into little canals.

A drenched travelling-chariot is passing, with a meagre escort. In the interior are seated four women: the ARCHDUCHESS MARIA LOUISA, in age about eighteen; her stepmother the EMPRESS OF AUSTRIA, third wife of FRANCIS, only four years older than the ARCHDUCHESS; and two ladies of the Austrian Court. Behind come attendant carriages bearing servants and luggage.

The inmates remain for the most part silent, and appear to be in a gloomy frame of mind. From time to time they glance at the moist spring scenes which pass without in a perspective distorted by the rain-drops that slide down the panes, and by the blurring effect of the travellers' breathings. Of the four the one who keeps in the best spirits is the ARCHDUCHESS, a fair, blue-eyed, full-figured, round-lipped maiden.

MARIA LOUISA

Whether the rain comes in or not I must open the window. Please allow me.

(She straightway opens it.)

EMPRESS (groaning)

Yes—open or shut it—I don't care. I am too ill to care for anything! (The carriage jolts into a hole.)

316

O woe ! To think that I am driven away from my
husband's home in such a miserable conveyance,
along such a road, and in such weather as this.
(Peal of thunder.)   There are his guns !

MARIA LOUISA

No, my dear one. It cannot be his guns. They
told us when we started that he was only half-way
from Ratisbon hither, so that he must be nearly a
hundred miles off as yet ; and a large army cannot
move fast.

EMPRESS

He should never have been let come nearer than
Ratisbon ! The victory at Echmühl was fatal for
us. O Echmühl, Echmühl ! I believe he will overtake us before we get to Buda.

FIRST LADY-IN-WAITING

If so, your Majesty, shall we be chained as
prisoners and marched to Paris ?

EMPRESS

Undoubtedly. But I shouldn't much care. It
would not be worse than this. . . . I feel sodden
all through me, and frowzy, and broken !

(She closes her eyes as if to doze.)

MARIA LOUISA

It is dreadful to see her suffer so ! (Shutting the
window.) If the roads were not so bad I should not
mind. I almost wish we had stayed ; though when
he arrives the cannonade will be terrible.

First Lady-in-Waiting

I wonder if he will get into Vienna. Will his men knock down all the houses, madam ?

Maria Louisa

If he do get in, I am sure his triumph will not be for long. My uncle the Archduke Charles is at his heels ! I have been told many important prophecies about Bonaparte's end, which is fast nearing, it is asserted. It is he, they say, who is referred to in the Apocalypse. He is doomed to die this year at Cologne, in an inn called " The Red Crab." I don't attach too much importance to all these predictions, but O, how glad I should be to see them come true !

Second Lady-in-Waiting

So should we all, madam. What would become of his divorce-scheme then ?

Maria Louisa

Perhaps there is nothing in that report. One can hardly believe such gossip.

Second Lady-in-Waiting

But they say, your Imperial Highness, that he certainly has decided to sacrifice the Empress Joséphine, and that at the meeting last October with the Emperor Alexander at Erfurt, it was even settled that he should marry as his second wife the Grand-Duchess Anne.

Maria Louisa

I am sure that the Empress her mother will never allow one of the house of Romanoff to marry with a bourgeois Corsican. I wouldn't if I were she !

FIRST LADY-IN-WAITING

Perhaps, your Highness, they are not so particular in Russia, where they are rather new themselves, as we in Austria, with your ancient dynasty, are in such matters.

MARIA LOUISA

Perhaps not. Though the Empress-mother is a pompous old thing, as I have been told by Prince Schwarzenberg, who was negotiating there last winter. My father says it would be a dreadful misfortune for our country if they were to marry. Though if we are to be exiled I don't see how anything of that sort can matter much. . . . I hope my father is safe !

An officer of the escort rides up to the carriage window, which is opened.

EMPRESS (unclosing her eyes)

Any more misfortunes ?

OFFICER

A rumour is a-wind, your Majesty,
That the French host, the Emperor in its midst,
Lannes, Masséna, and Bessières in its van,
Advancing hither along the Ratisbon road,
Has seized the castle and town of Ebersberg,
And burnt all down, with frightful massacre,
Vast heaps of dead and wounded being consumed,
So that the streets stink strong with frizzled flesh.—
The enemy, ere this, has crossed the Traun,
Hurling brave Hiller's army back on us,
And marches on Amstetten—thirty miles
Less distant from Vienna than before !

EMPRESS

The Lord show mercy to us ! But O why
Did not the Archdukes intercept the foe ?

OFFICER

His Highness Archduke Charles, your Majesty,
After his sore repulse Bohemia-wards,
Could not proceed with strength and speed enough
To close in junction with the Archduke John
And Archduke Louis, as was their intent.
So Marshal Lannes swings swiftly on Vienna,
With Oudinot's and Demont's force of foot ;
Then Masséna and all his mounted men,
And then Napoléon, Guards, and Cuirassiers,
And the main body of the Imperial might.

EMPRESS

Alas for poor Vienna !

OFFICER

Even so !
Your Majesty has fled it none too soon.

The window is shut, and the procession disappears behind
the sheets of rain.

SCENE II

THE ISLAND OF LOBAU, WITH WAGRAM BEYOND

The north horizon at the back of the bird's-eye prospect is
the high ground stretching from the Bisamberg on the left to
the plateau of Wagram on the right. In front of these eleva-

tions spreads the wide plain of the Marchfeld, open, treeless, and with scarcely a house upon it.[1]

In the foreground the Danube crosses the scene with a graceful slowness, looping itself round the numerous wooded islands therein. The largest of these, immediately under the eye, is the Lobau, which stands like a knot in the gnarled grain represented by the running river.

On this island can be discerned, closely packed, an enormous dark multitude of foot, horse, and artillery in French uniforms, the numbers reaching to a hundred and seventy thousand.

Lifting our eyes to discover what may be opposed to them we perceive on the Wagram plateau aforesaid, and right and left in front of it, extended lines of Austrians, whitish and glittering, to the number of a hundred and forty thousand.

The July afternoon turns to evening, the evening to twilight. A species of simmer which pervades the living spectacle raises expectation till the very air itself seems strained with suspense. A huge event of some kind is awaiting birth.

DUMB SHOW

The first change under the cloak of night is that the tightly packed regiments on the island are got under arms. The soldiery are like a thicket of reeds in which every reed should be a man.

A large bridge connects the island with the further shore, as well as some smaller bridges. Opposite are high redoubts and ravelins that the Austrians have constructed for opposing the passage across, which the French ostentatiously set themselves to attempt by the large bridge, amid heavy cannonading.

But the movement is a feint, though this is not perceived by the Austrians as yet. The real movement is on the right hand of the foreground, behind a spur of the isle, and out of sight of the enemy; where several large rafts and flat boats, each capable of carrying three hundred men, are floated out from a screened creek.

Chosen battalions enter upon these, which immediately begin to cross with their burden. Simultaneously from other screened nooks secretly prepared floating bridges, in sections, are moved forth, joined together, and defended by those who crossed on the rafts.

At two o'clock in the morning the thousands of cooped soldiers begin to cross the bridges, producing a scene which, on such a scale, was never before witnessed in the history of war. A great discharge from the batteries accompanies this manœuvre, arousing the Austrians to a like cannonade.

---

[1] At this date.

The night has been obscure for summer-time, and there is no moon. The storm now breaks in a tempestuous downpour, with lightning and thunder. The tumult of nature mingles so fantastically with the tumult of projectiles that flaming bombs and forked flashes cut the air in company, and the noise from the mortars alternates with the noise from the clouds.

From bridge to bridge and back again a gloomy-eyed figure stalks, as it has stalked the whole night long, with the restlessness of a wild animal. Plastered with mud, and dribbling with rain-water, it bears no resemblance to anything dignified or official. The figure is that of NAPOLÉON, urging his multitudes over.

By daylight the great mass of the men is across the water. At six the rain ceases, the mist uncovers the face of the sun, which bristles on the helmets and bayonets of the French. A hum of amazement rises from the Austrian hosts, who turn staring faces southward and perceive what has happened, and the columns of their enemies standing to arms on the same side of the stream with themselves, and preparing to turn their left wing.

NAPOLÉON rides along the front of his forces, which now spread out upon the plain, and are ranged in order of battle.

Dumb Show ends, and the point of view changes.

SCENE III

THE FIELD OF WAGRAM

The battlefield is now viewed reversely, from the windows of a mansion at Wolkersdorf, to the rear of the Austrian position. The aspect of the windows is nearly south, and the prospect includes the plain of the Marchfeld, with the isled Danube and Lobau in the extreme distance. Ten miles to the south-west, rightwards, the faint summit of the tower of St. Stephen's, Vienna, appears. On the middle-left stands the compact plateau of Wagram, so regularly shaped as to seem as if constructed by art. On the extreme left the July sun has lately risen.

Inside the room are discovered the EMPEROR FRANCIS and some household officers in attendance ; with the War-Minister and Secretaries at a table at the back. Through open doors can be seen in an outer apartment adjutants, equerries, aides, and other military men. An officer in waiting enters.

OFFICER

Hooded by night the French have shifted, sire,
And much revised their stations of the eve
By thwart and wheeling moves upon our left,
And on our centre—projects unforeseen
Till near accomplished.

FRANCIS

           But I am advised
By oral message that the Archduke Charles,
Since the sharp strife last night, has mended, too,
His earlier dispositions, stiffened files,
Sped iron orders to the Archduke John,
To bring in swiftest marches all his might,
And pounce with heavy impact on the French
From nigh their rear.

OFFICER

           'Tis good, sire; such a swoop
Will raise an obstacle to their retreat
And refuge in the fastness of the isle;
And show this victory-gorged adventurer
That striking with a river in his rear
Is not the safest tactic to be played
Against an Austrian front equipt like ours!

The EMPEROR FRANCIS and others scrutinize through their glasses the positions and movements of the Austrian divisions, which appear on the plain as pale masses, emitting flashes from arms and helmets under the July rays, and reaching from the Tower of Neusiedel on the left, past Wagram, into the village of Stammersdorf on the right. Beyond their lines are spread out the darker-hued French, almost parallel to the Austrians.

FRANCIS

Those moving masses toward the right I deem
The forces of Klenau and Kollowrath,
Sent to support Prince John of Lichtenstein
In his attack that way ?

An interval.

　　　　　　　　　　Now that they've gained
The right there, why is not the attack begun ?

OFFICER

They are beginning on the left wing, sire.

The EMPEROR *resumes his glass and beholds bodies of men descending from the hills by Neusiedel, and crossing the Russbach river towards the French—a movement which has been going on for some time.*

Meanwhile the French stride stoutly on our midst !

FRANCIS (turning thither)

Where we are weakest !　It surpasses me
To understand why was our centre thinned
To pillar up our right already strong,
Where nought is doing, while our left assault
Stands ill-supported ?

Time passes in silence.

　　　　　　　　　　Yes ; it is so.　See,
The enemy strikes Rossenberg in flank,
Compelling him to fall behind the Russbach !

The EMPEROR *gets excited, and his face perspires.　At length he cannot watch through his glass, and walks up and down.*

Penned useless here my nerves annoy my sight !
Inform me what you note.—I should opine
The Wagram height behind impregnable ?

Another silence, broken by the distant roar of the guns.

OFFICER (at his glass)

Klenau and Kollowrath are pounding on !
To turn the enemy's left with our strong right
Is, after all, a plan that works out well.
Hiller and Lichtenstein conjoin therein.

FRANCIS

I hear from thence appalling cannonades.

OFFICER

'Tis theirs, your Majesty.   Now we shall see
If the French read that there the danger lies.

FRANCIS

I only pray that Bonaparte refrain
From spying danger there till all too late !

OFFICER (involuntarily, after a pause)

Ah, Heaven !

FRANCIS (turning sharply)

Well, well ?   What changes figure now ?

OFFICER

They pierce our centre, sire !   We are, despite,
Not centrally so weak as I supposed.
Well done, Bellegarde !

FRANCIS (glancing to the centre)

And what has he well done ?

OFFICER

The French in fierce fume broke through Aderklaa ;
But Bellegarde, pricking along the plain behind,
Has charged and driven them back disorderedly.
The Archduke Charles bounds thither, as I shape,
In person to support him !

> The EMPEROR returns to his spyglass ; and they and others watch in silence, sometimes the right of their front, sometimes the centre.

FRANCIS

It is so !
That right attack of ours spells victory,
And Austria's grand salvation ! . . . (Time passes.)
Turn your glass,
And closely scan Napoléon and his aides
Hand-galloping towards his centre-left
To strengthen it against the brave Bellegarde.
Does your eye reach him ?—That white horse, alone
In front of those that move so rapidly.

OFFICER

It does, sire ; though my glass can conjure not
So cunningly as yours. . . . That horse must be
The famed Euphrates—him the Persian king
Sent Bonaparte as gift.

> A silence. NAPOLÉON reaches a carriage that is moving across. It bears MASSÉNA, who, having received a recent wound, is unable to ride.

FRANCIS

See, the white horse and horseman pause beside
A coach for some strange reason rolling there. . . .
That white-horsed rider—yes !—is Bonaparte,
By the aides hovering round. . . .

New war-wiles have been worded ; we shall spell
Their purport soon enough !   (An interval.)
                        The French take heart
To stand to our battalions steadfastly,
And hold their ground, having the Emperor near !

Time passes.   An aide-de-camp enters.

AIDE

The Archduke Charles is pierced in the shoulder, sire;
He strove too far in beating back the French
At Aderklaa, and was nearly ta'en.
The wound's not serious.—On our right we win,
And deem the battle ours.

Enter another aide-de-camp.

SECOND AIDE

Your Majesty,

We have borne them back through Aspern village-
   street
And Essling is recovered.   What counts more,
Their bridges to the rear we have nearly grasped,
And panic-struck they crowd the few left free,
Choking the track, with cries of " All is lost ! "

FRANCIS

Then is the land delivered.   God be praised !

[Exeunt aides.

   An interval, during which the EMPEROR and his companions
again remain anxiously at their glasses.

There is a curious feature I discern
To have come upon the battle.   On our right
We gain ground rapidly ; towards the left
We lose it ; and the unjudged consequence
Is that the armies' whole commingling mass
Moves like a monstrous wheel.   I like it not !

Enter another aide-de-camp.

THIRD AIDE

Our left wing, sire, recedes before Davout,
Whom nothing can withstand !   Two corps he threw
Across the Russbach up to Neusiedel,
While he himself assailed the place in front.
Of the divisions one pressed on and on,
Till lodged atop.   They would have been hurled
    back——

FRANCIS

But how goes it with us in sum ?   pray say !

THIRD AIDE

We have been battered off the eastern side
Of Wagram plateau.

FRANCIS

              Where's the Archduke John ?
Why comes he not ?   One man of his here now
Were worth a host anon.   And yet he tarries !

                            [Exit third aide.

    Time passes, while they reconnoitre the field with strained
eyes.

Our centre-right, it seems, round Neusiedel,
Is being repulsed !   May the kind Heaven forbid
That good Hess' Homberg should be yielding there !

    The Minister in attendance comes forward, and the EMPEROR
consults him ; then walking up and down in silence. Another
aide-de-camp enters.

FOURTH AIDE

Sire, Neusiedel has just been wrenched from us,
And the French right is on the Wagram crest ;
Nordmann has fallen, and Veczay : Homberg, I
    learn,

Warteachben, Muger—almost all our best—
Bleed more or less profusely !

*A gloomy silence. Exit fourth aide. Ten minutes pass.
Enter an officer in waiting.*

FRANCIS

What guns are those that groan from Wagram
    height ?

OFFICER

Alas, Davout's !   I have climbed the roof-top, sire,
And there discerned the truth.

Cannonade continues. A long interval of suspense. The
EMPEROR *returns to his glass.*

FRANCIS

                A part of it !
There seems to be a grim, concerted lunge
By the whole strength of France upon our right,
Centre, and left wing simultaneously !

OFFICER

Most viciously upon the centre, sire,
If I mistook not, hard by Sussenbrunn ;
The assault is led by Bonaparte in person,
Who shows himself with marvellous recklessness,
Yet like a phantom-fiend receives no hurt.

FRANCIS (still gazing)

Ha ! Now the Archduke Charles has seen the
    intent,
And taken steps against it.   Sussenbrunn
Must be the threatened thing. (Silence.) What an
    advance !—
Straight hitherward.   Our centre girdles them.—
Surely they'll not persist ?   Who heads that charge ?

OFFICER

They say Macdonald, sire.

FRANCIS

                   Meagrest remains
Will there be soon of those in that advance !
We are burning them to bones by our hot fire.
They are almost circumscribed : if fully so
The battle's ours ! What's that behind them, eh ?

OFFICER

Their last reserves, that they may feed the front,
And sterilize our hope !

FRANCIS

                Yes, their reserve—
Dragoons and cuirassiers—charge in support.
You see their metal gleaming as they come.
Well, it is neck or nothing for them now !

OFFICER

It's nothing, sire.   Their charge of cavalry
Has desperately failed.

FRANCIS

               Their foot press on,
However, with a battery in front
Which deals the foulest damage done us yet.

             (Time passes.)

They *are* effecting lodgment, after all.
Who would have reckoned on't—our men so firm !

        Re-enter first aide-de-camp.

FIRST AIDE

The Archduke Charles retreats, your Majesty ;
And the issue wears a dirty look just now.

FRANCIS (gloomily)

Yes : I have seen the signs for some good while.
But he retreats with blows, and orderly.

Time passes, till the sun has rounded far towards the west.
The features of the battle now materially change. The French
have regained Aspern and Essling ; the Austrian army is
crumpled back from the Danube and from the heights of
Wagram, which, as viewed from Wolkersdorf, face the afternoon
shine, the French established thereon glittering in the rays.

FRANCIS (choking a sigh)

The turn has passed. We are worsted, but not
     whelmed ! . . .
The French advance is laboured, and but slow.
—This might have been another-coloured day
If but the Archduke John had joined up promptly ;
Yet still he lags !

ANOTHER OFFICER (lately entered)

           He's just now coming, sire.
His columns glimmer in the Frenchmen's rear,
Past Siebenbrunn's and Loebensdorf's smoked hills.

FRANCIS (impatiently)

Ay—coming *now* ! Why could he not be *come* !

(They watch intently.)

We can see nothing of that side from here.

Enter a general officer, who speaks to the Minister at the
back of the room.

Minister (coming forward)

Your Majesty, I now must needs suggest,
Pursuant to conclusions reached this morn,
That since the front and flower of all our force
Is seen receding to the Bisamberg,
These walls no longer yield safe shade for you,
Or facile outlook.   Scouts returning say
Either Davout, or Bonaparte himself,
With the mid-columns of his forward corps,
Will pant up hitherward in fierce pursuit,
And may intrude beneath this very roof.
Not yet, I think ; it may not be to-night ;
But we should stand prepared.

Francis
                                        If we must go
We'll go with a good grace, unfeignedly !
Who knows to-morrow may not see regained
What we have lost to-day ?

             Re-enter fourth aide-de-camp.

Fourth Aide (breathlessly)

                              The Archduke John,
Discerning our main musters in retreat,
Abandons an advance that throws on him
The enemy's whole brunt if he bear on.

Francis

Alas for his devotion !   Let us go.
Such weight of sadness as we shoulder now
Will wring us down to sleep in stall or stye,
If even that be found ! . . . Think ! Bonaparte,
By reckless riskings of his life and limb,

Has turned the steelyard of our strength to-day,
Whilst I have idled here ! . . . May brighter times
Attend the cause of Europe far in Spain,
And British blood flow not, as ours, in vain !

> [Exeunt the EMPEROR FRANCIS, ministers,
> officers, and attendants.

The night comes, and the scene is obscured.

SCENE IV

THE FIELD OF TALAVERA

It is the same month and weather as in the preceding scene.
Talavera town, on the river Tagus, is at the extreme right
of the foreground ; a mountain range on the extreme left.
The allied army under SIR ARTHUR WELLESLEY stretches
between—the English on the left, the Spanish on the right—
part holding a hill to the left-centre of the scene, divided
from the mountains by a valley, and part holding a redoubt
to the right-centre. This army of more than fifty thousand
all told, of which twenty-two thousand only are English, has
its back to the spectator.

Beyond, in a wood of olive, oak, and cork, are the fifty to
sixty thousand French, facing the spectator and the allies.
Their right includes a strong battery upon a hill which fronts
the one on the English left.

Behind all, the heights of Salinas close the prospect, the
small river Alberche flowing at their foot from left to right
into the Tagus, which advances in foreshortened perspective
to the town at the right front corner of the scene as aforesaid.

DUMB SHOW

The hot and dusty July afternoon having turned to twilight,
shady masses of men start into motion from the French
position, come towards the foreground, silently ascend the
hill on the left of the English, and assail the latter in a violent
outburst of fire and lead. They nearly gain possession of the
hill ascended.

CHORUS OF RUMOURS (aerial music)

Talavera tongues it as ten o' the night-time :
Now come Ruffin's slaughterers surging upward,
Backed by bold Vilatte's. From the vale Lapisse, too,
    Darkly outswells there.—

Down the vague veiled incline the English fling them,
Bended bayonets prodding the enemy backward :
So the first fierce charge of the ardent Frenchmen
    England repels there !

Having fallen back into the darkness the French presently
reascend in yet larger masses. The high square knapsack
which every English foot-soldier carries, and his shako, and its
tuft, outline themselves against the dim light as the ranks
stand awaiting the shock.

CHORUS OF RUMOURS

Pushing spread they !—shout as they reach the
    summit !—
Strength and stir new-primed in their plump battalions :
Puffs of flame blown forth on the lines opposing
    Higher and higher.

There those hold them mute, though at speaking
    distance—
Mute, while clicking flints, and the crash of volleys
Whelm the weighted gloom with immense distraction
    Pending their fire.

Fronting heads, helms, brows can each ranksman read
    there,
Epaulettes, hot cheeks and the shining eyeball,
(Called for a trice from night by the fleeting pan-flash)
    Pressing them nigher !

The French again fall back in disorder into the hollow, and
LAPISSE draws off on the right. As the sinking sound of the
muskets tells what has happened the English raise a shout.

CHORUS OF PITIES

Thus the dim nocturnal ado of conflict
Closes with the roar of receding gun-fire.
Harness loosened then, and their day-long strenuous
      Temper unbending,

Worn-out lines lie down where they late stood
            staunchly—
Cloaks around them rolled—by the bivouac embers :
There at dawn to stake in the dynasts' death-game
      All, till the ending !

SCENE V

THE SAME

DUMB SHOW (continued)

The morning breaks. There is another murderous attempt to dislodge the English from the hill, the assault being pressed with a determination that excites the admiration of the English themselves.

The French are seen descending into the valley, crossing it, and climbing it on the English side under the fire of HILL's whole division, all to no purpose. In their retreat they leave behind them on the slopes nearly two thousand lying.

The day advances to noon, and the air trembles in the intense heat. The combat flags, and is suspended.

SPIRIT OF THE PITIES

What do I see but thirsty, throbbing bands
From these inimic hosts defiling down
In homely need towards the prattling stream
That parts their enmities, and drinking there !
They get to grasping hands across the rill,
Sealing their sameness as earth's sojourners.—
What more could plead the wryness of the times
Than such unstudied piteous pantomimes !

Spirit Ironic

It is only that Life's queer mechanics chance to work out in this grotesque shape just now. The groping tentativeness of an Immanent Will (as grey old Years describes it) cannot be asked to learn logic at this time of day! The spectacle of Its instruments, set to riddle one another through, and then to drink together in peace and concord, is where the humour comes in, and makes the play worth seeing!

Spirit Sinister

Come, Sprite, don't carry your ironies too far, or you may wake up the Unconscious Itself, and tempt It to let all the gory clock-work of the show run down to spite me!

The drums roll, and the men of the two nations part from their comradeship at the Alberche brook, the dark masses of the French army assembling anew. Sir Arthur Wellesley has seated himself on a mound that commands a full view of the contested hill, and remains there motionless a long time. When the French form for battle he is seen to have come to a conclusion. He mounts, gives his orders, and the aides ride off.

The French advance steadily through the sultry atmosphere, the skirmishers in front, and the columns after, moving, yet seemingly motionless. Their eighty cannon peal out and their shots mow every space in the line of them. Up the great valley and the terraces of the hill whose fame is at that moment being woven, comes Vilatte, boring his way with foot and horse, and Ruffin's men following behind.

According to the order given, the Twenty-third Light Dragoons and the German Hussars advance at a chosen moment against the head of these columns. On the way they disappear.

Spirit of the Pities

Why this bedevilment? What can have chanced?

Spirit of Rumour

It so befalls that as their chargers near
The inimical wall of flesh with its iron frise,

A treacherous chasm uptrips them : zealous men
And docile horses roll to dismal death
And horrid mutilation.

SPIRIT OF THE PITIES

Those who live
Even now advance !   I'll see no more.   Relate.

SPIRIT OF RUMOUR

Yes, those pant on.   Then further Frenchmen cross,
And Polish Lancers, and Westphalian Horse,
Who ring around these luckless Islanders,
And sweep them down like reeds by the river-brink
In scouring floods ; till scarce a man remains.

Meanwhile on the British right SEBASTIANI'S corps has
precipitated itself in column against GENERAL CAMPBELL'S
division, the division of LAPISSE against the centre, and at
the same time the hill on the English left is again assaulted.
The English and their allies are pressed sorely here, the bellow-
ing battery tearing lanes through their masses.

SPIRIT OF RUMOUR (continuing)

The French reserves of foot and horse now on,
Smiting the Islanders in breast and brain
Till their mid-lines are shattered. . . . Now there ticks
The moment of the crisis ; now the next,
Which brings the turning stroke.

SIR ARTHUR WELLESLEY sends down the Forty-eighth
regiment under COLONEL DONELLAN to support the wasting
troops.   It advances amid those retreating, opening to let
them pass.

SPIRIT OF RUMOUR (continuing)

Then pales, enerved,
The hitherto unflinching enemy !
Lapisse is pierced to death ; the flagging French
Decline into the hollows whence they came.

The too exhausted English and reduced
Lack strength to follow.—Now the western sun,
Conning with unmoved visage quick and dead,
Gilds horsemen slackening, and footmen stilled,
Till all around breathes drowsed hostility.
     Last, the swealed herbage lifts a leering light,
And flames traverse the field ; and hurt and slain,
Opposed, opposers, in a common plight
Are scorched together on the dusk champaign.

     The fire dies down, and darkness enwraps the scene.

SCENE VI

BRIGHTON. THE ROYAL PAVILION

It is the birthday dinner-party of the PRINCE OF WALES. In the floridly decorated banqueting-room stretch tables spread with gold and silver plate, and having artificial fountains in their midst.

Seated at the tables are the PRINCE himself as host—rosy, well curled, and affable—the DUKES OF YORK, CLARENCE, KENT, SUSSEX, CUMBERLAND, and CAMBRIDGE, with many noblemen, including LORDS HEADFORT, YARMOUTH, BERKELEY, EGREMONT, CHICHESTER, DUDLEY, SAY AND SELE, SOUTH-AMPTON, HEATHFIELD, ERSKINE, KEITH, C. SOMERSET, G. CAVENDISH, R. SEYMOUR, and others ; SIR C. POLE, SIR E. G. DE CRESPIGNY, MR. SHERIDAN ; Generals, Colonels, and Admirals, and the REV. MR. SCOTT.

The PRINCE'S band plays in the adjoining room. The banquet is drawing to its close, and a boisterous conversation is in progress.

Enter COLONEL BLOOMFIELD with a dispatch for the PRINCE, who looks it over amid great excitement in the company. In a few moments silence is called.

PRINCE OF WALES

I have the joy, my lords and gentlemen,
To rouse you with the just imported tidings

From General Wellesley through Lord Castlereagh
Of a vast victory (noisy cheers) over the French in
    Spain.
The place—called Talavera de la Reyna
(If I pronounce it rightly)—long unsung,
Wears now the crest and blazonry of fame ! (Cheers.)
The heads and chief contents of the dispatch
I read you as succinctly as I can. (Cheers.)

SHERIDAN (singing sotto voce)

" Now foreign foemen die and fly,
Dammy, we'll drink little England dry ! "

    The PRINCE reads the parts of the dispatch that describe
the battle, amid intermittent cheers.

PRINCE OF WALES (continuing)

Such is the substance of the news received,
Which, after Wagram, strikes us genially
As sudden sunrise through befogged night shades !

SHERIDAN (privately)

  Begad, that's good, sir ! You are a poet born,
while the rest of us are but made, and bad at that.

    The health of the army in Spain is drunk with acclamations.

PRINCE OF WALES (continuing)

In this achievement we, alas ! have lost
Too many ! Yet such blanks must ever be.—
Mackenzie, Langworth, Beckett of the Guards,
Have fallen of ours ; while of the enemy
Generals Lapisse and Morlot are laid low.—
Drink to their memories !

They drink in silence.

                    Other news, my friends,
Received to-day is of like hopeful kind.

The Great War-Expedition to the Scheldt (cheers)
Which lately sailed, has found a favouring wind,
And by this hour has touched its destined shores.
The enterprise will soon be hot aglow,
The invaders making first the Cadsand coast,
And then descending swift on Walcheren Isle.
But items of the next step are withheld
Till later days, from obvious policy.   (Cheers.)

Faint throbbing sounds, like the notes of violoncellos and contrabassos reach the ear from some building not far off as the speaker pauses.

In worthy emulation of us here
The county holds to-night a birthday ball,
Which flames with all the fashion of the town.
I have been asked to patronize their revel,
And sup with them, and likewise you, my guests.
We have good reason, with such news to bear !
Thither we haste and join our loyal friends,
And stir them with this live intelligence
Of our staunch regiments on the Spanish plains.

(Applause.)

With them we'll now knit hands and beat the
    ground,
And bring in dawn as we whirl round and round !
There are some fair ones in their set to-night,
And such we need here in our bachelor-plight.

(Applause.)

The PRINCE, his brothers, and a large proportion of the other Pavilion guests, swagger out in the direction of the Castle assembly-rooms adjoining, and the deserted banqueting-hall grows dark. In a few moments the back of the scene opens, revealing the assembly-rooms behind.

SCENE VII

THE SAME. THE ASSEMBLY ROOMS

The rooms are lighted with candles in brass chandeliers, and a dance is in full movement to the strains of a string-band. A signal is given, shortly after the clock has struck eleven, by MR. FORTH, Master of Ceremonies.

FORTH

His Royal Highness comes, though somewhat late,
But never too late for welcome ! (Applause.) Dancers,
     stand,
That we may do fit homage to the Prince
Who soon may shine our country's gracious king.

After a brief stillness a commotion is heard at the door, the band strikes up the National air, and the PRINCE enters, accompanied by the rest of the visitors from the Pavilion. The guests who have been temporarily absent now crowd in, till there is hardly space to stand.

PRINCE OF WALES
(wiping his face and whispering to Sheridan)

What shall I say to fit their feelings here ?
Damn me, that other speech has stumped me quite !

SHERIDAN (whispering)

If heat be evidence of loy——

PRINCE OF WALES

If what ?

SHERIDAN

If heat be evidence of loyalty,
Et cætera—something quaint like that might please
    'em.

PRINCE OF WALES (to the company)

If heat be evidence of loyalty,
This room affords it truly without question ;
If heat be not, then its accompaniment
Most surely 'tis to-night.   The news I bring,
Good ladies, friends, and gentlemen, perchance
You have divined already ?   That our arms—
Engaged to thwart Napoléon's tyranny
Over the jaunty, jocund land of Spain
Even to the highest apex of our strength—
Are rayed with victory !   (Cheers.)   Lengthy was the
    strife.
And fierce, and hot ;   and sore the suffering ;
But proudly we endured it ;   and shall hear,
No doubt, the tale of its far consequence
Ere many days.   I'll read the details sent.   (Cheers.)

He reads again from the dispatch amid more cheering, the
ball-room guests crowding round.   When he has done he
answers questions ;   then continuing :

Meanwhile our interest is, if possible,
As keenly waked elsewhere.   Into the Scheldt
Some forty thousand bayonets and swords,
And twoscore ships o' the line, with frigates, sloops,
And gunboats sixty more, make headway now,
Bleaching the waters with their bellying sails ;
Or maybe they already anchor there,
And that the level ooze of Walcheren shore
Rings with the voices of that landing host
In every twang of British dialect,
Clamorous to loosen fettered Europe's chain !
                                        (Cheers.)

A Noble Lord (aside to Sheridan)

Prinny's outpouring tastes suspiciously like your brew, Sheridan. I'll be damned if it is his own concoction. How d'ye sell it a gallon?

Sheridan

I don't deal that way nowadays. I give the recipe, and charge a duty on the gauging. It is more artistic, and saves trouble.

The company proceed to the supper-rooms, and the ball-room sinks into solitude.

Spirit of the Pities

So they pass on. Let be!—But what is this—
A moan?—all frailly floating from the east
To usward, even from the forenamed isle? . . .
Would I had not broke nescience, to inspect
A world so ill-contrived!

Spirit of the Years

          But since thou hast
We'll hasten to the isle; and thou'lt behold—
Such as it is—the scene its coasts enfold.

SCENE VIII

WALCHEREN

A marshy island at the mouth of the Scheldt, lit by the low sunshine of an evening in late summer. The horizontal rays from the west lie in yellow sheaves across the vapours that the day's heat has drawn from the sweating soil. Sour grasses grow in places, and strange fishy smells, now warm, now cold,

pass along. Brass-hued and opalescent bubbles, compounded
of many gases, rise where passing feet have trodden the damper
spots. At night the place is the haunt of the Jack-lantern.

DUMB SHOW

A vast army is encamped here, and in the open spaces
are infantry on parade—skeletoned men, some flushed, some
shivering, who are kept moving because it is dangerous to stay
still. Every now and then one falls down, and is carried away
to a hospital with no roof, where he is laid, bedless, on the
ground.

In the distance soldiers are digging graves for the funerals
which are to take place after dark, delayed till then that the
sight of so many may not drive the living melancholy-mad.
Faint noises are heard in the air.

Shade of the Earth

What storm is this of souls dissolved in sighs,
And what the dingy gloom it signifies?

Spirit of the Pities

We catch a lamentation shaped thuswise :

Chorus of Pities (aerial music)

" *We who withstood the blasting blaze of war*
When marshalled by the gallant Moore awhile,
Beheld the grazing death-bolt with a smile,
Closed combat edge to edge and bore to bore,
       Now rot upon this Isle !

" *The ever wan morass, the dune, the blear*
Sandweed, and tepid pool, and putrid smell,
Emaciate purpose to a fractious fear,
Beckon the body to its last low cell—
       A chink no chart will tell.

" *O ancient Delta, where the fen-lights flit !*
Ignoble sediment of loftier lands,

Thy humour clings about our hearts and hands
And solves us to its softness, till we sit
     As we were part of it.

" *Such force as fever leaves is maddened now,*
With tidings trickling in from day to day
Of others' differing fortunes, wording how
They yield their lives to baulk a tyrant's sway—
     Yield them not vainly, they !

" *In champaigns green and purple, far and near,*
In town and thorpe where quiet spire-cocks turn,
Through vales, by rocks, beside the brooding burn
Echoes the aggressor's arrogant career ;
     And we pent pithless here !

" *Here, where each creeping day the creeping file*
Draws past with shouldered comrades score on score,
Bearing them to their lightless last asile,
Where weary wave-wails from the clammy shore
     Will reach their ears no more.

" *We might have fought, and had we died, died well,*
Even if in dynasts' discords not our own ;
Our death-spot some sad haunter might have shown,
Some tongue have asked our sires or sons to tell
     The tale of how we fell ;

" *But such bechanced not.   Like the mist we fade,*
No lustrous lines engrave in story we,
Our country's chiefs, for their own fames afraid,
Will leave our names and fates by this pale sea
     To perish silently ! "

SPIRIT OF THE YEARS

Why must ye echo as mechanic mimes
These mortal minions' bootless cadences,
Played on the stops of their anatomy

As is the mewling music on the strings
Of yonder ship-masts by the unweeting wind,
Or the frail tune upon this withering sedge
That holds its papery blades against the gale ?
—Men pass to dark corruption, at the best,
Ere I can count five score : these why not now ?—
The Immanent Shaper builds Its beings so
Whether ye sigh their sighs with them or no !

The night fog enwraps the isle and the dying English army.

ACT FIFTH

SCENE I

PARIS. A BALLROOM IN THE HOUSE OF CAMBACÉRÈS

    The many-candled saloon at' the ARCH-CHANCELLOR's is visible through a draped opening, and a crowd of masked dancers in fantastic costumes revolve, sway, and intermingle to the music that proceeds from an alcove at the further end of the same apartment. The front of the scene is a withdrawing-room of smaller size, now vacant, save for the presence of one sombre figure, that of NAPOLÉON, seated, and apparently watching the moving masquerade.

SPIRIT OF THE PITIES

Napoléon even now unbraces not
From stress of state affairs, which hold him grave
Through revels that might win the King of Spleen
To toe a measure !   I would speak with him.

SPIRIT OF THE YEARS

Speak if thou wilt whose speech nor mars nor mends !

SPIRIT OF THE PITIES (into Napoléon's ear)

Why thus and thus Napoléon ?   Can it be
That Wagram with its glories, shocks, and shames,
Still leaves athirst the palate of thy pride ?

NAPOLÉON (answering as in soliloquy)

The trustless, timorous lease of human life
Warns me to hedge in my diplomacy.
The sooner, then, the safer ! Ay, this eve,
This very night, will I take steps to rid
My morrows of the weird contingencies
That vision round and make one hollow-eyed. . . .
The unexpected, lurid death of Lannes—
Rigid as iron, reaped down like a straw—
Tiptoed Assassination haunting round
In unthought thoroughfares, the near success
Of Staps the madman, argue to forbid
The riskful blood of my previsioned line
And potence for dynastic empery
To linger vialled in my veins alone.
Perhaps within this very house and hour,
Under an innocent mask of Love or Hope,
Some enemy queues my ways to coffin me. . . .
　　When at the first clash of the late campaign,
A bold belief in Austria's star prevailed,
There pulsed quick pants of expectation round
Among the cowering kings, that too well told
What would have fared had I been overthrown !
So ; I must send down shoots to future time
Who'll plant my standard and my story there ;
And a way opens.—Better I had not
Bespoke a wife from Alexander's house.
Not there now lies my look. But done is done !

　　The dance ends and masks enter, BERTHIER *among them.*
NAPOLÉON *beckons to him, and he comes forward.*

God send you find amid this motley crew
Frivolities enough, friend Berthier—eh ?
My thoughts have worn oppressive shades despite
　　such !
What scandals of me do they bandy here ?
These close disguises render women bold—
Their shames being of the light, not of the thing—
And your sagacity has garnered much,

I make no doubt, of ill and good report,
That marked our absence from the capital ?

BERTHIER

Methinks, your Majesty, the enormous tale
Of your campaign, like Aaron's serpent-rod,
Has swallowed up the smaller of its kind.
Some speak, 'tis true, in counterpoise thereto,
Of English deeds by Talavera town,
Though blurred by their exploit at Walcheren,
And all its crazy, crass futilities.

NAPOLÉON

Yet was the exploit well featured in design,
Large in idea, and imaginative ;
I had not deemed the blinkered English folk
So capable of view.   Their fate contrived
To place an idiot at the helm of it,
Who marred its working, else it had been hard
If things had not gone seriously for us.
—But see, a lady saunters hitherward
Whose gait proclaims her Madame Metternich,
One that I fain would speak with.

NAPOLÉON rises and crosses the room towards a lady-masker
who has just appeared in the opening. BERTHIER draws off,
and the EMPEROR, unceremoniously taking the lady's arm,
brings her forward to a chair, and sits down beside her as
dancing is resumed.

MADAME METTERNICH
                                    In a flash
I recognized you, sire ; as who would not
The bearer of such deep-delved charactery ?

NAPOLÉON

The devil, madame, take your piercing eyes !
It's hard I cannot prosper in a game
That every coxcomb plays successfully.

—So here you are still, though your loving lord
Disports him at Vienna ?

MADAME METTERNICH

                Paris, true,
Still holds me ; though in quiet, save to-night,
When I have been expressly prayed come hither,
Or I had not left home.

NAPOLÉON

                I sped that prayer !—
I have a wish to put a case to you,
Wherein a woman's judgment, such as yours,
May be of signal service.   (He lapses into reverie.)

MADAME METTERNICH

                Well ?   The case—

NAPOLÉON

Is marriage—mine.

MADAME METTERNICH

             It is beyond me, sire !

NAPOLÉON

You glean that I have decided to dissolve
(Pursuant to monitions murmured long)
My union with the present Empress—formed
Without the Church's due authority ?

MADAME METTERNICH

Vaguely.   And that light tentatives have winged
Betwixt your Majesty and Russia's court,
To moot that one of their Grand-Duchesses
Should be your Empress-wife.   Nought else I know.

NAPOLÉON

There have been such approachings; more, worse
    luck.
Last week Champagny wrote to Alexander
Asking him for his sister—yes or no.

MADAME METTERNICH

What " worse luck " lies in that, your Majesty,
If severance from the Empress Joséphine
Be fixed unalterably ?

NAPOLÉON

            This worse luck lies there :
If your Archduchess, Marie Louise the fair,
Would straight accept my hand, I'd offer it,
And throw the other over.   Faith, the Tsar
Has shown such backwardness in answering me,
Time meanwhile trotting, that I have ample ground
For such withdrawal.—Madame, now, again,
Will your Archduchess marry me or no ?
That is, will her good sire assent thereto ?

MADAME METTERNICH

Your sudden questions quite confound my sense !
It is impossible to answer them.

NAPOLÉON

Well, madame, now I'll put it to you thus :
Were you in the Archduchess Marie's place
Would you accept my hand—and heart therewith ?

MADAME METTERNICH

I should refuse you—most assuredly ! [1]

   [1] So Madame Metternich to her husband in reporting this interview.
But who shall say !

NAPOLÉON (laughing roughly)

Ha-ha ! That's frank. And devilish cruel too !
—Well, write to your husband. Ask him what he
   thinks,
And let me know.

MADAME METTERNICH

                    Indeed, sire, why should I ?
There goes the Ambassador, Prince Schwarzenberg,
Successor to my spouse. He's now the groove
And proper conduit of diplomacy
Through whom to broach this matter to his Court.

NAPOLÉON

Do you, then, broach it through him, madame,
   pray ;
Now, here, to-night.

MADAME METTERNICH

                    I will, informally,
To humour you, on this recognizance,
That you leave not the business in my hands,
But clothe your project in official guise
Through him to-morrow ; so safeguarding me
From foolish seeming, as the babbler forth
Of a fantastic and unheard of dream.

NAPOLÉON

I'll send Eugène to him, as you suggest.
Meanwhile prepare him. Make your stand-point
   this :
Children are needful to my dynasty,
And if one woman cannot mould them for me,
Why, then, another must.

                        [Exit NAPOLÉON abruptly.
   Dancing continues. Madame METTERNICH sits on, musing.
Enter SCHWARZENBERG.

MADAME METTERNICH

The Emperor has just left me.   We have tapped
This theme and that ; his Empress and—his next.
Ay, so !   Now, guess you anything ?

SCHWARZENBERG

                    Of her ?
No more than that the stock of Romanoff
Will not supply the spruce commodity.

MADAME METTERNICH

And that the would-be customer turns toe
To our shop in Vienna.

SCHWARZENBERG

             Marvellous ;
And comprehensible but as the dream
Of Delaborde, of which I have lately heard.
It will not work !—What think you, madame, on't ?

MADAME METTERNICH

That it will work, and is as good as wrought !—
I break it to you thus, at his request.
In brief time Prince Eugène will wait on you,
And make the formal offer in his name.

SCHWARZENBERG

Which I can but receive *ad referendum,*
And shall initially make clear as much,
Disclosing not a glimpse of my own mind !
Meanwhile you make good Metternich aware ?

Madame Metternich

I write this midnight, that amaze may pitch
To coolness ere your messenger arrives.

Schwarzenberg

This radiant revelation flicks a gleam
On many circling things !—the courtesies
Which graced his bearing towards our officers
Amid the tumults of the late campaign,
His wish for peace with England, his affront
At Alexander's tedious-timed reply . . .
Well, it will thrust a thorn in Russia's side,
If I err not, whatever else betide !   [Exeunt.

The maskers surge into the foreground of the scene, and
their motions become more and more fantastic. A strange
gloom begins and intensifies, until only the high lights of their
grinning figures are visible. These also, with the whole ball-
room, gradually darken, and the music softens to silence.

SCENE II

PARIS.   THE TUILERIES

The evening of the next day. A saloon of the Palace, with
folding-doors communicating with a dining-room. The doors
are flung open, revealing on the dining-table an untouched
dinner, Napoléon and Joséphine rising from it, and de
Bausset, chamberlain-in-waiting, pacing up and down. The
Emperor and Empress come forward into the saloon, the
latter pale and distressed, and patting her eyes with her
handkerchief.

The doors are closed behind them ; a page brings in coffee ;
Napoléon signals to him to leave. Joséphine goes to pour
out the coffee, but Napoléon pushes her aside and pours
it out himself, looking at her in a way which causes her to sink
cowering into a chair like a frightened animal.

JOSÉPHINE

I see my doom, my friend, upon your face !

NAPOLÉON

You see me bored by Cambacérès' ball.

JOSÉPHINE

It means divorce !—a thing more terrible
Than carrying elsewhere the dalliances
That formerly were mine. I kicked at that ;
But now agree, as I for long have done,
To any infidelities of act
May I be yours in name !

NAPOLÉON

     My mind must bend
To other things than our domestic pettings :
The Empire orbs above our happiness,
And 'tis the Empire dictates this divorce.
I reckon on your courage and calm sense
To breast with me the law's formalities,
And get it through before the year has flown.

JOSÉPHINE

But are you *really* going to part from me ?
O no, no, my dear husband ; no, in truth,
It cannot be my Love will serve me so !

NAPOLÉON

I mean but mere divorcement, as I said,
On simple grounds of sapient sovereignty.

JOSÉPHINE

But nothing have I done save good to you :—
Since the fond day we wedded into one
I never even have *thought* you jot of harm !
Many the happy junctures when you have said
I stood as guardian-angel over you,
As your Dame Fortune, too, and endless things
Of such-like pretty tenour—yes, you have !
Then how can you so gird against me now ?
You had not pricked me with it much of late,
And so I hoped and hoped the ugly spectre
Had been laid dead and still.

NAPOLÉON (impatiently)

                              I tell you, dear,
The thing's decreed, and even the princess chosen.

JOSÉPHINE

Ah—so—the princess chosen ! . . . I surmise
It is none else than the Grand-Duchess Anne :
Gossip was right—though I would not believe.
She's young ; but no great beauty !—Yes, I see
Her silly, soulless eyes and horrid hair ;
In which new gauderies you'll forget sad me !

NAPOLÉON

Upon my soul you are childish, Joséphine :
A woman of your years to pout it so !—
I say it's not the Tsar's Grand-Duchess Anne.

JOSÉPHINE

Some other Fair, then.   You whose name can nod
The flower of all the world's virginity
Into your bed, will well take care of that !
(Spitefully.)   She may not have a child, friend, after
    all.

NAPOLÉON (drily)

You hope she won't, I know !—But don't forget
Madame Walewska did, and had she shown
Such cleverness as yours, poor little fool,
Her withered husband might have been displaced,
And her boy made my heir.—Well, let that be.
The severing parchments will be signed by us
Upon the fifteenth, prompt.

JOSÉPHINE

                    What—I have to sign
My putting away upon the fifteenth next ?

NAPOLÉON

Ay—both of us.

JOSÉPHINE (falling on her knees)

                    So far advanced—so far !
Fixed ?—for the fifteenth ?   O I do implore you,
My very dear one, by our old, old love,
By my devotion, don't, don't cast me off
Now, after these long years !

NAPOLÉON

                    Heavens, how you jade me !
Must I repeat that I don't cast you off ;
We merely formally arrange divorce—
We live and love, but call ourselves divided.

A silence.

JOSÉPHINE (with sudden calm)

Very well.   Let it be.   I must submit !   (Rises.)

NAPOLÉON

And this much likewise you must promise me,
To act in the formalities thereof
As if you shaped them of your own free will.

JOSÉPHINE

How can I—when no freewill's left in me ?

NAPOLÉON

You are a willing party—do you hear ?

JOSÉPHINE (quivering)

I hardly—can—bear this !—It is—too much
For a poor weak and broken woman's strength !
But—but I yield !—I am so helpless now ;
I give up all—ay, kill me if you will,
I won't cry out !

NAPOLÉON

        And one thing further still,
You'll help me in my marriage overtures
To win the Duchess—Austrian Marie she,—
Concentring all your force to forward them.

JOSÉPHINE

It is the—last humiliating blow !—
I cannot—O, I will not !

NAPOLÉON (fiercely)

         But you *shall* !
And from your past experience you may know
That what I say I mean !

JOSÉPHINE (breaking into sobs)

O my dear husband—do not make me—don't !
If you but cared for me—the hundredth part
Of how—I care for you, you could not be
So cruel as to lay this torture on me.
It hurts me so !—it cuts me like a sword.
Don't make me, dear ! Don't, will you ! O, O, O !

(She sinks down in a hysterical fit.)

NAPOLÉON (calling)

Bausset !

Enter DE BAUSSET, Chamberlain-in-waiting.

Bausset, come in and shut the door.
Assist me here. The Empress has fallen ill.
Don't call for help. We two can carry her
By the small private staircase to her rooms.
Here—I will take her feet.

They lift JOSÉPHINE between them and carry her out. Her moans die away as they recede towards the stairs.

Enter two servants, who remove coffee-service, readjust chairs, etc.

FIRST SERVANT

So, poor old girl, she's wailed her *Miserere Mei,*
as Mother Church says. I knew she was to get the
sack ever since he came back.

SECOND SERVANT

Well, there will be a little civil huzzaing, a little
crowing and cackling among the Bonapartes at the
downfall of the Beauharnais family at last, mark me
there will ! They've had their little hour, as the
poets say, and now 'twill be somebody else's turn.
O it is droll ! Well, Father Time is a great philosopher, if you take him right. Who is to be the new
woman ?

FIRST SERVANT

She that contains in her own corporation the necessary particulars.

SECOND SERVANT

And what may they be ?

FIRST SERVANT

She must be young.

SECOND SERVANT

Good.   She must.   The country must see to that.

FIRST SERVANT

And she must be strong.

SECOND SERVANT

Good again.   She must be strong.   The doctors will see to that.

FIRST SERVANT

And she must be fruitful as the vine.

SECOND SERVANT

Ay, by God.   She must be fruitful as the vine. That, Heaven help him, he must see to himself, like the meanest multiplying man in Paris.

[Exeunt servants.

Re-enter NAPOLÉON with his stepdaughter, QUEEN HORTENSE.

NAPOLÉON

Your mother is too rash and reasonless—
Wailing and fainting over statesmanship
Which is no personal caprice of mine,
But policy most painful—forced on me
By the necessities of this country's charge.
Go to her ; see if she be saner now ;
Explain it to her once and once again,
And bring me word what impress you may make.

HORTENSE goes out.   CHAMPAGNY is shown in.

Champagny, I have something clear to say
Now, on our process after the divorce.
The question of the Russian Duchess Anne
Was quite inept for further toying with.
The years rush on, and I grow nothing younger.
So I've made up my mind—committed me
To Austria and the Hapsburgs—good or ill !
It was the best, most practicable plunge,
And I have plunged it.

CHAMPAGNY

         Austria, say you, sire ?
I reckoned that but as a scurrying dream !

NAPOLÉON

Well, so it was.   But such a pretty dream
That its own charm transfixed it to a notion,
That showed itself in time a sanity,
Which hardened in its turn to a resolve
As firm as any built by mortal mind.—
The Emperor's consent must needs be won ;
But I foresee no difficulty there.
The young Archduchess is a bright blond thing
By general story ; and considering, too,
That her good mother childed seventeen times,

It will be hard if she can fashion not
The modest one or two that I require.

Enter DE BAUSSET with dispatches.

DE BAUSSET

The courier, sire, from Petersburg is here,
And brings these letters for your Majesty.

[Exit DE BAUSSET.

NAPOLÉON (after silently reading)

Ha-ha !   It never rains unless it pours :
Now I can have the other readily.
The proverb hits me aptly : " Well they do
Who doff the old love ere they don the new ! "

(He glances again over the letter.)

Yes, Caulaincourt now writes he has every hope
Of quick success in settling the alliance !
The Tsar is willing—even is anxious for it,
His sister's youth the single obstacle.
The Empress-mother, hitherto against me,
Ambition-fired, verges on suave consent,
Likewise the whole Imperial family.
What irony is all this to me now !
Time lately was when I had leapt thereat.

CHAMPAGNY

You might, of course, sire, give th' Archduchess up,
Seeing she looms uncertainly as yet,
While this does so no longer.

NAPOLÉON

No—not I.

My sense of my own dignity forbids
My watching the slow clocks of Muscovy !

Why have they dallied with my tentatives
In pompous silence since the Erfurt day ?
—And Austria, too, affords a safer hope.
The young Archduchess is much less a child
Than is the other, who, Caulaincourt says,
Will be incapable of motherhood
For six months yet or more—a grave delay.

CHAMPAGNY

Your Majesty appears to have trimmed your sail
For Austria ; and no more is to be said !

NAPOLÉON

Except that there's the house of Saxony
If Austria fail.—Then, very well, Champagny,
Write you to Caulaincourt accordingly.

CHAMPAGNY

I will, your Majesty.

[Exit CHAMPAGNY.

Re-enter QUEEN HORTENSE.

NAPOLÉON

Ah, dear Hortense,
How is your mother now ?

HORTENSE

Calm ; quite calm, sire.
I pledge me you need have no further fret
From her entreating tears.   She bids me say
That now, as always, she submits herself
With chastened dignity to circumstance,
And will descend, at notice, from your throne—
As in days earlier she ascended it—
In questionless obedience to your will.

It was your hand that crowned her ; let it be
Likewise your hand that takes her crown away.
As for her children, we shall be but glad
To follow and withdraw ourselves with her,
The tenderest mother children ever knew,
From grandeurs that have brought no happiness !

NAPOLÉON (taking her hand)

But, Hortense, dear, it is not to be so !
You must stay with me, as I said before.
Your mother, too, must keep her royal state,
Since no repudiation stains this need.
Equal magnificence will orb her round
In aftertime as now.   A palace here,
A palace in the country, wealth to match,
A rank in order next my future wife's,
And conference with me as my truest friend.
Now we will seek her—Eugène, you, and I—
And make the project clear.

> [Exeunt NAPOLÉON and HORTENSE.
> The scene darkens and shuts.

SCENE III

VIENNA.   A PRIVATE APARTMENT IN THE IMPERIAL
PALACE

The EMPEROR FRANCIS discovered, paler than usual, and
somewhat flurried.

Enter METTERNICH the Prime Minister—a thin-lipped, long-
nosed man with inquisitive eyes.

FRANCIS

I have been expecting you some minutes here,
The thing that fronts us brooking brief delay.—
Well, what say you by now on this strange offer ?

METTERNICH

My views remain the same, your Majesty :
The policy of peace that I have upheld,
Both while in Paris and of late time here,
Points to this step as heralding sweet balm
And bandaged veins for our late crimsoned realm.

FRANCIS

Agreed.   As monarch I perceive therein
A happy doorway for my purposings.
It seems to guarantee the Hapsburg crown
A quittance of distractions such as those
That leave their shade on many a backward year !—
There is, forsooth, a suddenness about it,
And it would aid us had we clearly keyed
The cryptologues of which the world has heard
Between Napoléon and the Russian Court—
Begun there with the selfsame motiving.

METTERNICH

I would not, sire, one second ponder it.
It was an obvious first crude cast-about
In the important reckoning of means
For his great end, a strong monarchic line.
The more advanced the more it profits us ;
For sharper, then, the quashing of such views,
And wreck of that conjunction in the aims
Of France and Russia, marked so much of late
As jeopardizing quiet neighbours' thrones.

FRANCIS

If that be so, on the domestic side
There seems no bar.   Speaking as father solely,
I see secured to her the proudest fate
That woman can daydream.   And I could hope
That private bliss would not be wanting her !

METTERNICH

A hope well seated, sire.   The Emperor,
Imperious and determined in his rule,
Is easy-natured in domestic life,
As my long time in Paris amply proved.
Moreover, the accessories of his glory
Have been, and will be, admirably designed
To fire the fancy of a young Princess.

FRANCIS

Thus far you satisfy me. . . . So, to close,
Or not to close with him, is now the thing.

METTERNICH

Your Majesty commands the issue quite :
The Father of his people can alone
In such a case give answer—yes or no.
Vagueness and doubt have ruined Russia's chance ;
Let not, then, such be ours.

FRANCIS

                              You mean, if I,
You'd answer straight.   What would that answer
     be ?

METTERNICH

In state affairs, sire, as in private life,
Times will arise when even the faithfullest squire
Finds him unfit to jog his chieftain's choice,
On whom responsibility must lastly rest.
And such times are pre-eminently, sire,
Those wherein thought alone is not enough
To serve the head as guide.   As Emperor,
As father, both, to you, to you in sole
Must appertain the privilege to pronounce
Which track stern duty bids you tread herein.

FRANCIS

Affection is my duty, heart my guide.—
Without constraint or prompting I shall leave
The big decision in my daughter's hands.
Before my obligations to my people
Must stand her wish.   Go, find her, Metternich,
Take her the tidings.   She is free with you,
And will speak out.

             (Looking forth upon the terrace.)

                   She's here at hand, I see :
I'll call her in.   Then tell me what's her mind.

    He beckons from the window, and goes out in another
direction.

METTERNICH

So much for form's sake !   Can the river-flower
The current drags, direct its face up-stream ?
What she must do she will; nought else at all.

    Enter through one of the windows MARIA LOUISA in garden-
costume, fresh-coloured, girlish, and smiling.   METTERNICH
bends.

MARIA LOUISA

O how, dear Chancellor, you startled me !
Please pardon my so brusquely bursting in.
I saw you not.—Those five poor little birds
That haunt out there beneath the pediment,
Snugly defended from the north-east wind,
Have lately disappeared.   I sought a trace
Of scattered feathers, which I dread to find !

METTERNICH

They are gone, I ween, the way of tender flesh
At the assaults of winter, want, and foes.

MARIA LOUISA

It is too melancholy thinking, that !
Don't say it.—But I saw the Emperor here ?
Surely he beckoned to me ?

METTERNICH

                    Sure, he did,
Your gracious Highness ; and he has left me here
To break vast news that will make good his call.

MARIA LOUISA

Then do.   I'll listen.   News from near or far ?

                                        [She seats herself.

METTERNICH

From far—though of such distance-dwarfing might
That far may read as near eventually.
But, dear Archduchess, with your kindly leave
I'll speak straight out.   The Emperor of the French
Has sent to-day to make, through Schwarzenberg,
A formal offer of his heart and hand,
His honours, dignities, imperial throne,
To you, whom he admires above all those
The world can show elsewhere.

MARIA LOUISA (frightened)

                    My husband—he ?
What, an old man like him !

METTERNICH (cautiously)

                    He's scarcely old,
Dear lady.   True, deeds densely crowd in him ;
Turn months to years in calendaring his span ;
Yet by Time's common clockwork he's but young.

MARIA LOUISA

So wicked, too !

METTERNICH (nettled)

Well—that's a point of view.

MARIA LOUISA

But, Chancellor, think what things I have said
     of him !
Can women marry where they have taunted so ?

METTERNICH

Things ?   Nothing inexpungeable, I deem,
By time and true good humour.

MARIA LOUISA

                              O I have !
Horrible things.   Why—ay, a hundred times—
I have said I wished him dead !   At that strained
     hour
When the first voicings of the late war came,
Thrilling out how the French were smitten sore
And Bonaparte retreating, I clapped hands
And answered that I hoped he'd lose his head
As well as lose the battle !

METTERNICH

                          Words.   But words !
Born like the bubbles of a spring that come
Of zest for springing—aimless in their shape.

MARIA LOUISA

It seems indecent, mean, to wed a man
Whom one has held such fierce opinions of !

METTERNICH

My much beloved Archduchess, and revered,
Such things have been !   In Spain and Portugal
Like enmities have led to intermarriage.
In England, after warring thirty years
The Red and White Rose wedded.

MARIA LOUISA (after a silence)

Tell me, now,
What does my father wish ?

METTERNICH

His wish is yours.
Whatever your Imperial Highness feels
On this grave verdict of your destiny,
Home, title, future sphere, he bids you think
Not of himself, but of your own desire.

MARIA LOUISA (reflecting)

My wish is what my duty bids me wish.
Where a wide Empire's welfare is in poise,
That welfare must be pondered, not my will.
I ask of you, then, Chancellor Metternich,
Straightway to beg the Emperor my father
That he fulfil his duty to the realm,
And quite subordinate thereto all thought
Of how it personally impinge on me.

A slight noise as of something falling is heard in the room.
They glance momentarily, and see that a small enamel portrait
of MARIE ANTOINETTE, which was standing on a console-table,
has slipped down on its face.

SPIRIT OF THE YEARS

What mischief's this ?   The Will must have Its way.

Spirit Sinister

Perhaps Earth shivered at the lady's say ?

Shade of the Earth

I own thereto. When France and Austria wed
My echoes are men's groans, my dews are red ;
So I have reason for a passing dread !

Metternich

Right nobly phrased, Archduchess ; wisely too.
I will acquaint your sire the Emperor
With these your views. He waits them anxiously.

(Going.)

Maria Louisa

Let me go first. It much confuses me
To think—But I would fain let thinking be !

[She goes out trembling.
Enter FRANCIS by another door.

Metternich

I was about to seek your Majesty.
The good Archduchess luminously holds
That in this weighty question you regard
The Empire. Best for it is best for her.

Francis (moved)

My daughter's views thereon do not surprise me.
She is too staunch to pit a private whim
Against the fortunes of a commonwealth.
During your speech with her I have taken thought
To shape decision sagely. An assent
Would yield the Empire many years of peace,

And leave me scope to heal those still green sores
Which linger from our late unhappy moils.
Therefore, my daughter not being disinclined,
I know no basis for a negative.
Send, then, a courier prompt to Paris : say
The offer made for the Archduchess' hand
I do accept—with this defined reserve,
That no condition, treaty, bond, attach
To such alliance save the tie itself.
There are some sacrifices whose grave rites
No bargain must contaminate.   This is one—
This personal gift of a beloved child !

METTERNICH (leaving)

I'll see to it this hour, your Majesty,
And cast the words in keeping with your wish.
(To himself as he goes)
Decently done ! . . . He slipped out " sacrifice,"
And scarce could hide his heartache for his girl.
Well ached it !—But when these things have to be
It is as well to breast them stoically.

[Exit METTERNICH.

The clouds draw over.

SCENE IV

LONDON.   A CLUB IN ST. JAMES'S STREET

A winter midnight. Two members are conversing by the
fire, and others are seen lolling in the background, some of
them snoring.

FIRST MEMBER

I learn from a private letter that it was carried
out in the Emperor's Cabinet at the Tuileries—
just off the throne-room, where they all assembled

in the evening,—Boney and the wife of his bosom
(in pure white muslin from head to foot, they say),
the Kings and Queens of Holland, Westphalia, and
Naples, the Princess Pauline, and one or two more ;
the officials present being Cambacérès the Chancellor, and Count Regnaud. Quite a small party.
It was over in a few minutes—short and sweet,
like a donkey's gallop.

SECOND MEMBER

Anything but sweet for her. How did she stand
it ?

FIRST MEMBER

Serenely, I believe, while the Emperor was
making his speech renouncing her ; but when it
came to her turn to say she renounced him she
began sobbing mightily, and was so completely
choked up that she couldn't get out a word.

SECOND MEMBER

Poor old dame ! I pity her, by God ; though
she had a rattling good spell while it lasted.

FIRST MEMBER

They say he was a bit upset, too, at sight of her
tears. But I dare vow that was put on. Fancy
Boney caring a curse what a woman feels. She
had learnt her speech by heart, but that did not
help her : Regnaud had to finish it for her, the
ditch that overturned her being where she was
made to say that she no longer preserved any hope
of having children, and that she was pleased to
show her attachment by enabling him to obtain
them by another woman. She was led off fainting.

A turning of the tables, considering how madly jealous she used to make him by her flirtations !

Enter a third member.

SECOND MEMBER

How is the debate going ? Still braying the Government in a mortar ?

THIRD MEMBER

They are. Though one thing everybody admits : young Peel has made a wonderful first speech in seconding the address. There has been nothing like it since Pitt. He spoke rousingly of Austria's misfortunes—went on about Spain, of course, showing that we must still go on supporting her, winding up with a brilliant peroration about—what were the words—" the fiery glance of freedom which flashed incessantly from the indignant eyes of the British soldier ! "—Oh, well : it was all learnt beforehand, of course.

SECOND MEMBER

I wish I had gone down. But the wind soon blew the other way ?

THIRD MEMBER

Then Gower rapped out his amendment. That was good, too, by God.

SECOND MEMBER

Well, the war must go on. And that being the general conviction this censure and that censure are only so many blank cartridges.

THIRD MEMBER

Blank ? Damn me, were they ! Gower's was a palpable hit when he said that Parliament had placed unheard-of resources in the hands of Ministers last year, to make this year's results to the country worse than if they had been afforded no resources at all. Every single enterprise of theirs had been a beggarly failure.

SECOND MEMBER

Anybody could have said it, come to that.

THIRD MEMBER

Yes, because it is so true. However, when he began to lay on with such rhetoric as " the treasures of the nation lavished in wasteful thoughtlessness," —" thousands of our troops sacrificed wantonly in the pestilential swamps of Walcheren," and gave the details we know so well, Ministers wriggled a good one, though 'twas no news to 'em. Castlereagh kept on starting forward as if he were going to jump up and interrupt, taking the strictures entirely as a personal affront.

Enter a fourth member.

SEVERAL MEMBERS

Who's speaking now ?

FOURTH MEMBER

I don't know. I have heard of nobody later than Ward.

SECOND MEMBER

The fact is that, as Whitbread said to me to-day, the materials for condemnation are so

prodigious that we can scarce marshal them into
argument. We are just able to pour 'em out one
upon t'other.

THIRD MEMBER

Ward said, with the blandest air in the world :
" Censure ?   Do his Majesty's Ministers expect
censure ? Not a bit. They are going about asking
in tremulous tones if anybody has heard when
their impeachment is going to begin."

SEVERAL MEMBERS

Haw-haw-haw !

THIRD MEMBER

Then he made another point. After enumerat-
ing our frightful failures—Spain, Walcheren, and
the rest—he said : " But Ministers have not failed
in everything. No ; in one thing they have been
strikingly successful. They have been successful
in their attack upon Copenhagen—because it was
directed against an ally ! " Mighty fine, wasn't
it ?

SECOND MEMBER

How did Castlereagh stomach that ?

THIRD MEMBER

He replied then. Donning his air of injured
innocence he proved the honesty of his intentions
—no doubt truly enough. But when he came to
Walcheren nothing could be done. The case was
hopeless, and he knew it, and foundered. However,
at the division, when he saw what a majority was
going out on his side he was as frisky as a child.

Canning's speech was grave, with bits of shiny ornament stuck on—like the brass nails on a coffin, Sheridan says.

> Fifth and sixth members stagger in, arm-and-arm.

FIFTH MEMBER

The 'vision is—'jority of ninety-six againsht—Gov'ment—I mean—againsht us. Which is it—hey ?   (To his companion.)

SIXTH MEMBER

Damn majority of—damn ninety-six—against damn amendment !

> (They sink down on a sofa.)

SECOND MEMBER

Gad, I didn't expect the figure would have been quite so high !

THIRD MEMBER

The one conviction is that the war in the Peninsula is to go on, and as we are all agreed upon that, what the hell does it matter what their majority is ?

> Enter SHERIDAN. They all turn inquiringly.

SHERIDAN

Have ye heard the latest ?

SECOND MEMBER

Ninety-six against us.

SHERIDAN

O no—that's ancient history. I'd forgot it.

Third Member

A revolution, because Ministers are not impeached and hanged ?

Sheridan

That's in contemplation, when we've got their confessions. But what I meant was from over the water—it is a deuced sight more serious to us than a debate and division that are only like the Liturgy on a Sunday—known beforehand to all the congregation. Why, Bonaparte is going to marry Austria forthwith—the Emperor's daughter Maria Louisa.

Third Member

The Lord look down ! Our late respected crony Austria ! Why, in this very night's debate they have been talking about the laudable principles we have been acting upon in affording assistance to the Emperor Francis in his struggle against the violence and ambition of France !

Second Member

Boney safe on that side, what may not befall !

Third Member

We had better make it up with him, and shake hands all round.

Second Member

Shake heads seems most natural in the case. O House of Hapsburg, how hast thou fallen !

Enter Whitbread, Lord Hutchinson, Lord George Cavendish, George Ponsonby, Windham, Lord Grey,

BARING, ELLIOT, and other members, some drunk. The conversation becomes animated and noisy; several move off to the card-room, and the scene closes.

SCENE V

THE OLD WEST HIGHWAY OUT OF VIENNA

The spot is where the road passes under the slopes of the Wiener Wald, with its beautiful forest scenery.

DUMB SHOW

A procession of enormous length, composed of eighty carriages—many of them drawn by six horses and one by eight—and escorted by detachments of cuirassiers, yeomanry, and other cavalry, is quickening its speed along the highway from the city.

The six-horse carriages contain a multitude of Court officials, ladies of the Court, and other Austrian nobility. The eight-horse coach contains a rosy, blue-eyed girl of eighteen, with full red lips, round figure, and pale auburn hair. She is MARIA LOUISA, and her eyes are red from recent weeping. The COUNTESS DE LAZANSKY, Grand Mistress of the Household, in the carriage with her, and the other ladies of the Palace behind, have a pale, proud, yet resigned look, as if conscious that upon their sex had been laid the burden of paying for the peace with France. They have been played out of Vienna with French marches, and the trifling incident has helped on their sadness.

The observer's vision being still bent on the train of vehicles and cavalry, the point of sight is withdrawn high into the air, till the huge procession on the brown road looks no more than a file of ants crawling along a strip of garden-matting. The spacious terrestrial outlook now gained shows this to be the great road across Europe from Vienna to Munich, and from Munich westerly to France.

The puny concatenation of specks being exclusively watched, the surface of the earth seems to move along in an opposite direction, and in infinite variety of hill, dale, woodland, and champaign. Bridges are crossed, ascents are climbed, plains are galloped over, and towns are reached, among them Saint Polten, where night falls.

Morning shines, and the royal crawl is resumed, and continued through Linz, where the Danube is reapproached, and
the girl looks pleased to see her own dear Donau still. Presently
the tower of Braunau appears, where the animated dots pause
for formalities, this being the frontier; and MARIA LOUISA
becomes MARIE LOUISE and a Frenchwoman, in the charge
of French officials.

After many breaks and halts, during which heavy rains
spread their gauzes over the scene, the roofs and houses of
Munich disclose themselves, suggesting the tesseræ of an
irregular mosaic. A long stop is made here.

The tedious advance continues. Vine-circled Stuttgart, flat
Carlsruhe, the winding Rhine, storky Strassburg, pass in
panorama beneath us as the procession is followed. With
Nancy and Bar-le-Duc sliding along, the scenes begin to assume
a French character, and soon we perceive Châlons and ancient
Rheims. The last day of the journey has dawned. Our vision
flits ahead of the cortège to Courcelles, a little place which
must be passed through before Soissons is reached. Here the
point of sight descends to earth, and the Dumb Show ends.

SCENE VI

COURCELLES

It is now seen to be a quiet roadside village, with a humble
church in its midst, opposite to which stands an inn, the highway
passing between them. Rain is still falling heavily. Not a soul
is visible anywhere.

Enter from the west a plain, lonely carriage, travelling in a
direction to meet the file of coaches that we have watched.
It stops near the inn, and two men muffled in cloaks alight
by the door away from the hostel and towards the church,
as if they wished to avoid observation. Their faces are those
of NAPOLÉON and MURAT his brother-in-law. Crossing the
road through the mud and rain they stand in the church
porch, and watch the descending drifts.

NAPOLÉON (stamping an impatient tattoo)

One gets more chilly in a wet March, however
mild, than in a dry, however cold, the devil if he

don't ! What time do you make it now ? That
clock doesn't go.

MURAT (drily, looking at his watch)

Yes, it does ; and it is right. If clocks were to
go as fast as your wishes just now it would be
awkward for the rest of the world.

NAPOLÉON (chuckling good-humouredly)

How we have dished the Soissons folk, with
their pavilions, and purple and gold hangings for
bride and bridegroom to meet in, and stately
ceremonial to match, and their thousands looking
on ! Here we are where there's nobody. Ha, ha !

MURAT

But why should they be dished, sire ? The
pavilions and ceremonies were by your own orders.

NAPOLÉON

Well, as the time got nearer I couldn't stand the
idea of dawdling about there.

MURAT

The Soissons people will be in a deuce of a taking
at being made such fools of !

NAPOLÉON

So let 'em. I'll make it up with them somehow.—She can't be far off now, if we have timed
her rightly. (He peers out into the rain and listens.)

MURAT

I don't quite see how you are going to manage when she does come. Do we go before her towards Soissons when you have greeted her here, or follow in her rear ? Or what do we do ?

NAPOLÉON

Heavens, I know no more than you ! Trust to the moment and see what happens. (A silence.) Hark—here she comes ! Good little girl ! Up to time !

The distant squashing in the mud of a multitude of hoofs and wheels is succeeded by the appearance of outriders and carriages, horses and horsemen, splashed with sample clays of the districts traversed. The vehicles slow down to the inn. NAPOLÉON's face fires up, and, followed by MURAT, he rushes into the rain towards the coach that is drawn by eight horses, containing the blue-eyed girl. He holds off his hat at the carriage-window.

MARIE LOUISE (shrinking back inside)

Ah, Heaven ! Two highwaymen are upon us !

THE EQUERRY D'AUDENARDE (simultaneously)

The Emperor !

The steps of the coach are hastily lowered, NAPOLÉON, dripping, jumps in and embraces her. The startled ARCH-DUCHESS, with much blushing and confusion, recognizes him.

MARIE LOUISE (tremulously, as she recovers
herself)

You are so much—better looking than your portraits—that I hardly knew you ! I expected you at Soissons. We are not at Soissons yet ?

NAPOLÉON

No, my dearest spouse, but we are together!
(Calling out to the equerry.)   Drive through Soissons—
pass the pavilion of reception without stopping, and
don't halt till we reach Compiègne.

He sits down in the coach and is shut in, MURAT laughing
silently at the scene.   Exeunt carriages and riders towards
Soissons.

CHORUS OF IRONIC SPIRITS (aerial music)

First 'twas a finished coquette,
And now it's a raw ingénue.—
Blonde instead of brunette,
An old wife doffed for a new.
She'll bring him a baby,
As quickly as maybe,
And that's what he wants her to do,
Hoo-hoo!
And that's what he wants her to do!

SPIRIT OF THE YEARS

What lewdness lip those wry-formed phantoms there?

IRONIC SPIRITS

Nay, Showman Years!   With holy reverent air
We hymn the nuptials of the Imperial pair.

The rain thickens to a mist and obscures the scene.

SCENE VII

PETERSBURG.　THE PALACE OF THE EMPRESS-
MOTHER

    One of the private apartments is disclosed, in which the
Empress-mother and Alexander are seated.

EMPRESS-MOTHER

So one of Austrian blood his pomp selects
To be his bride and bulwark—not our own.
Thus are you coolly shelved !

ALEXANDER

               Me, mother dear ?
You, faith, if I may say it dutifully !
Had all been left to me, some time ere now
He would have wedded Kate.

EMPRESS-MOTHER

             How so, my son ?
Catharine was plighted, and it could not be.

ALEXANDER

Rather you swiftly pledged and married her,
To let Napoléon have no chance that way.
But Anne remained.

EMPRESS-MOTHER

          How Anne ?—so young a girl !
Sane Nature would have cried indecency
At such a troth.

ALEXANDER

       Time would have tinkered that,
And he was well-disposed to wait awhile ;
But the one test he had no temper for
Was the apparent slight of unresponse
Accorded his impatient overtures
By our suspensive poise of policy.

EMPRESS-MOTHER

A backward answer is our country's card—
The special style and mode of Muscovy.
We have grown great upon it, my dear son,
And may such practice rule our centuries through !
The necks of those who rate themselves our peers
Are cured of stiffness by its potency.

ALEXANDER

The principle in this case, anyhow,
Is shattered by the facts : since none can doubt
Your policy was counted an affront,
And drove my long ally to Austria's arms,
With what result to us must yet be seen !

EMPRESS-MOTHER

May Austria win much joy of the alliance !
Marrying Napoléon is a midnight leap
For any Court in Europe, credit me,
If ever such there were !   What he may carve
Upon the coming years, what murderous bolt
Hurl at the rocking Constitutions round,
On what dark planet he may land himself
In his career through space, no sage can say.
One thing we may assume as certainty—
That he will never rest in righteous rule.

ALEXANDER

Well—possibly ! . . . And maybe all is best
That he engrafts his lineage not on us.—
But, honestly, Napoléon none the less
Has been my friend, and I regret the dream
And fleeting fancy of a closer tie !

EMPRESS-MOTHER

Ay ; your regrets are sentimental ever.
That he'll be writ no son-in-law of mine
Is no regret to me ! But an affront
There is, no less, in his evasion on't,
Wherein the bourgeois quality of him
Veraciously peeps out. I would be sworn
He set his minions parleying with the twain—
Yourself and Francis—simultaneously,
Else no betrothal could have speeded so !

ALEXANDER

Despite the hazard of offence to one ?

EMPRESS-MOTHER

More than the hazard ; the necessity.

ALEXANDER

There's no offence to me.

EMPRESS-MOTHER

            There should be, then.
I am a Romanoff by marriage merely,
But I do feel a rare belittlement
And loud laconic brow-beating herein !

ALEXANDER

No, mother, no ! I am the Tsar—not you,
And I am only piqued in moderateness.
Marriage with France was near my heart—I own it—
What then ? It has been otherwise ordained.

[A silence.

EMPRESS-MOTHER

Here comes dear Anne. Speak not of it before her.

Enter the GRAND-DUCHESS, a girl of sixteen.

ANNE

Alas ! the news is that poor Prussia's queen,
Spirited Queen Louisa, once so fair,
Is slowly dying, mother ! Did you know ?

ALEXANDER (betraying emotion)

Ah !—such I dreaded from the earlier hints.
Poor soul—her heart was slain some time ago.

ANNE

What do you mean by that, my brother dear ?

EMPRESS-MOTHER

He means, my child, that he as usual spends
Much sentiment upon the foreign fair,
And hence leaves little for his folk at home.

ALEXANDER

I mean, Anne, that her country's overthrow
Let death into her heart. The Tilsit days
Taught me to know her well, and honour her.

She was a lovely woman even then ! . . .
Strangely, the present English Prince of Wales
Was wished to husband her.   Had wishes won,
They might have varied Europe's history.

ANNE

Napoléon, I have heard, admired her once ;
How he must grieve that soon she'll be no more !

EMPRESS-MOTHER

Napoléon and your brother loved her both.

            [Alexander shows embarrassment.

But whatsoever grief be Alexander's,
His will be none who feels but for himself.

ANNE

O mother, how can you mistake him so !
He worships her who is to be his wife,
The fair Archduchess Marie.

EMPRESS-MOTHER

                  Simple child,
As yet he has never seen her, or but barely.
That is a tactic suit, with love to match !

ALEXANDER (with vainly veiled tenderness)

High-souled Louisa ;—when shall I forget
Those Tilsit gatherings in the long-sunned
    June ! . . .
Napoléon's gallantries deceived her quite,
Who fondly felt her pleas for Magdeburg
Had won him to its cause ; the while, alas !
His cynic sense but posed in cruel play !

EMPRESS-MOTHER

Bitterly mourned she her civilities
When time unlocked the truth, that she had choked
Her indignation at his former slights
And slanderous sayings for a baseless hope,
And wrought no tittle for her country's gain.
I marvel why you mourn a frustrate tie
With one whose wiles could wring a woman so !

ALEXANDER (uneasily)

I marvel also, when I think of it !

EMPRESS-MOTHER

Don't listen to us longer, dearest Anne.

[Exit ANNE.

—You will uphold my judging by and by,
That as a suitor we are well quit of him,
And that blind Austria will rue the hour
Wherein she plucks for him her fairest flower !

The scene shuts.

SCENE VIII

PARIS.   THE GRAND GALLERY OF THE LOUVRE
AND THE SALON-CARRÉ ADJOINING

The view is up the middle of the Gallery, which is now a
spectacle of much magnificence.   Backed by the large paintings on the walls are double rows on each side of brightly
dressed ladies, the pick of Imperial society, to the number of
four thousand, one thousand in each row ; and behind these
standing up are two rows on each side of men of privilege and
fashion.   Officers of the Imperial Guard are dotted about as
marshals.

Temporary barriers form a wide passage up the midst,

leading to the Salon-Carré, which is seen through the opening
to be fitted up as a chapel, with a gorgeous altar, tall candles,
and cross.   In front of the altar is a platform with a canopy
over it.   On the platform are two gilt chairs and a prie-dieu.

The expectant assembly does not continuously remain in the
seats, but promenades and talks, the voices at times rising to
a din amid the strains of the orchestra, conducted by the
EMPEROR'S Director of Music.   Refreshments in profusion are
handed round, and the extemporized cathedral resolves itself
into a gigantic café of persons of distinction under the Empire.

SPIRIT SINISTER

*All day have they been waiting for their galanty-
show, and now the hour of performance is on the strike.
It may be seasonable to muse on the sixteenth Louis
and the bride's great-aunt, as the nearing procession
is, I see, appositely crossing the track of the tumbril
which was the last coach of that respected lady. . . .
It is now passing over the site of the scaffold on which
she lost her head. . . . Now it will soon be here.*

Suddenly the heralds enter the Gallery at the end towards
the Tuileries, the spectators ranging themselves in their places.
In a moment the wedding procession of the EMPEROR and
EMPRESS becomes visible.   The civil marriage having already
been performed, Napoléon and Marie Louise advance together
along the vacant pathway towards the Salon-Carré, followed
by the long suite of illustrious personages, and acclamations
burst from all parts of the Grand Gallery.

SPIRIT OF THE PITIES

*Whose are those forms that pair in pompous train
Behind the hand-in-hand half-wedded ones,
With faces speaking sense of an adventure
Which may close well, or not so ?*

RECORDING ANGEL (reciting)

*First there walks
The Emperor's brother Louis, Holland's King ;
Then Jérôme of Westphalia with his spouse ;*

The mother-queen, and Julie Queen of Spain,
The Prince Borghèse and the Princess Pauline,
Beauharnais the Vice-King of Italy,
And Murat King of Naples, with their Queens ;
Baden's Grand-Duke, Arch-Chancellor Cambacérès,
Berthier, Lebrun, and, not least, Talleyrand.
Then the Grand Marshal and the Chamberlain,
The Lords-in-Waiting, the Grand Equerry,
With waiting-ladies, women of the chamber,
And others called by office, rank, or fame.

SPIRIT OF RUMOUR

New, many, to Imperial dignities ;
Which, won by character and quality
In those who now enjoy them, will become
The birthright of their sons in aftertime.

SPIRIT OF THE YEARS

It fits thee not to augur, quick-eared Shade.
Ephemeral at the best all honours be,
These even more ephemeral than their kind,
So random-fashioned, swift, perturbable !

SPIRIT OF THE PITIES

Napoléon looks content—nay, shines with joy.

SPIRIT OF THE YEARS

Yet see it pass, as by a conjuror's wand.

    Thereupon Napoléon's face blackens as if the shadow of a winter night had fallen upon it. Resentful and threatening, he stops the procession and looks up and down the benches.

SPIRIT SINISTER

    This is sound artistry of the Immanent Will : it relieves the monotony of so much good-humour.

NAPOLÉON (to the Chapel-master)

Where are the Cardinals ?   And why not here ?

(He speaks so loud that he is heard throughout the Gallery.)

ABBÉ DE PRADT (trembling)

Many are present here, your Majesty ;
But some are feebled by infirmities
Too common to their age, and cannot come.

NAPOLÉON

Tell me no nonsense !   Half absent themselves
Because they *will* not come.   The factious fools !
Well, be it so.   But they shall flinch for it !

MARIE LOUISE looks frightened.   The procession moves on.

SPIRIT OF THE PITIES

I seem to see the thin and headless ghost
Of the yet earlier Austrian, here, too, queen,
Walking beside the bride, with frail attempts
To pluck her by the arm !

SPIRIT OF THE YEARS

                              Nay, think not so.
No trump unseals earth's sepulchres to-day :
We are the only phantoms now abroad
On this mud-moulded ball !   Through sixteen years
She has decayed in a back-garden yonder,
Dust all the showance time retains of her,
Senseless of hustlings in her former house,
Lost to all count of crowns and bridalry—
Even of her Austrian blood.   No : what thou seest
Springs of thy quavering fancy, stirred to dreams
By yon tart phantom's phrase.

MARIE LOUISE (sadly to Napoléon)

I know not why,

I love not this day's doings half so well
As our quaint meeting-time at Compiègne.
A clammy air creeps round me, as from vaults
Peopled with looming spectres, chilling me
And angering you withal !

NAPOLÉON

O, it is nought

To trouble you : merely, my cherished one,
Those devils of Italian Cardinals !—
Now I'll be bright as ever—you must, too.

MARIE LOUISE

I'll try.

Reaching the entrance to the Salon-Carré amid strains of
music the EMPEROR and EMPRESS are received and incensed by
the CARDINAL GRAND ALMONERS. They take their seats
under the canopy, and the train of notabilities seat themselves
further back, the persons-in-waiting stopping behind the
Imperial chairs.

The ceremony of the religious marriage now begins. The
choir intones a hymn, the EMPEROR and EMPRESS go to the
altar, remove their gloves, and make their vows.

SPIRIT IRONIC

*The English Church should return thanks for this
wedding, seeing how it will purge of coarseness the
picture-sheets of that artistic nation, which will hardly
be able to caricature the new wife as it did poor
plebeian Joséphine. Such starched and ironed mon-
archists cannot sneer at a woman of such a divinely
dry and crusted line as the Hapsburgs !*

Mass is next celebrated, after which the TE DEUM is chanted
in harmonies that whirl round the walls of the Salon-Carré

and quiver down the long Gallery. The procession then
re-forms and returns, amid the flutterings and applause of
the dense assembly. But Napoléon's face has not lost the
sombre expression which settled on it. The pair and their
train pass out by the west door, and the congregation disperses
in the other direction, the cloud-curtain closing over the scene
as they disappear.

ACT SIXTH

SCENE I

THE LINES OF TORRÈS VÉDRAS

A bird's-eye perspective is revealed of the peninsular tract of Portuguese territory lying between the shining pool of the Tagus on the east, and the white-frilled Atlantic lifting rhythmically on the west. As thus beheld the tract features itself somewhat like a late-Gothic shield, the upper edge from the dexter to the sinister chief being the lines of Torrès Védras, stretching across from the mouth of the Zezambre on the left to Alhandra on the right, and the south or base point being Fort S. Julian. The roofs of Lisbon appear at the sinister base, and in a corresponding spot on the opposite side Cape Roca.

It is perceived in a moment that the northern verge of this nearly coast-hemmed region is the only one through which access can be gained to it by land, and a close scrutiny of the boundary there reveals that means are being adopted to effectually prevent such access.

From east to west along it runs a chain of defences, dotted at intervals by dozens of circular and square redoubts, either made or in the making, two of the latter being of enormous size. Between these stretch unclimbable escarpments, stone walls, and other breastworks, and in front of all a double row of abattis, formed of the limbs of trees.

Within the outer line of defence is a second, constructed on the same principle, its course being bent to take advantage of natural features. This second rampart is finished, and appears to be impregnable.

The third defence is far off southward, girdling the very base point of the shield-shaped tract of country ; and is not more than a twelfth of the length of the others. It is a continuous entrenchment of ditches and ramparts, and its object —that of covering a forced embarkation—is rendered apparent by some rocking English transports off the shore hard by.

DUMB SHOW

Innumerable human figures are busying themselves like cheese-mites all along the northernmost frontage, under-cutting easy slopes into steep ones, digging ditches, piling stones, felling trees, dragging them, and interlacing them along the front as required.

On the second breastwork, which is completed, only a few figures move.

On the third breastwork, which is fully matured and equipped, minute red sentinels creep backwards and forwards noiselessly.

As time passes three reddish-grey streams of marching men loom out to the north, advancing southward along three roads towards three diverse points in the first defence. These form the English army, entering the lines for shelter. Looked down upon, their motion seems peristaltic and vermicular, like that of three caterpillars. The division on the left is under Picton, in the centre under Leith and Cole, and on the extreme right, by Alhandra, under Hill. Beside one of the roads two or three of the soldiers are dangling from a tree by the neck, probably for plundering.

The Dumb Show ends, and the point of view sinks to the earth.

SCENE II

THE SAME. OUTSIDE THE LINES

The winter day has gloomed to a stormful evening, and the road outside the first line of defence forms the foreground of the stage.

Enter in the dusk from the hills to the north of the entrench-ment, near Calandrix, a group of horsemen, which includes MASSÉNA, in command of the French forces, FOY, LOISON, and other officers of his staff.

They ride forward in the twilight and tempest, and recon-noitre, till they see against the sky the ramparts blocking the road they pursue. They halt silently. MASSÉNA, puzzled, endeavours with his glass to make out the obstacle.

MASSÉNA

Something stands here to peril our advance,
Or even prevent it !

Foy

    These are the English lines—
Their outer horns and tusks—whereof I spoke,
Constructed by Lord Wellington of late
To keep his foothold firm in Portugal.

Masséna

Thrusts he his burly, bossed disfigurements
So far to north as this ? I had pictured me
They lay much nearer Lisbon. Little strange
Lord Wellington rode placid at Busaco
With this behind his back ! Well, it is hard
But that we turn them somewhere, I assume ?
They scarce can close up every southward gap
Between the Tagus and the Atlantic Sea.

Foy

I hold they can, and do ; although, no doubt,
By searching we shall spy some raggedness
Which customed skill may force.

Masséna

      Plain 'tis, no less,
We may heap corpses vainly hereabout,
And crack good bones in waste. By human power
This passes mounting ! What say you's behind ?

Loison

Another line exactly like the first,
But more matured. Behind its back a third.

Masséna

How long have these prim ponderosities
Been rearing up their foreheads to the moon ?

LOISON

Some months in all.   I know not quite how long.
They are Lord Wellington's select device,
And, like him, heavy, slow, laborious, sure.

MASSÉNA

May he enjoy their sureness.   He deserves to.
I had no inkling of such barriers here.
A good road runs along their front, it seems,
Which offers us advantage. . . . What a night !

The tempest cries dismally about the earthworks above
them, as the reconnoitrers linger in the slight shelter the lower
ground affords. They are about to turn back.

Enter from the cross-road to the right JUNOT and some
more officers. They come up at a signal that the others are
those they lately parted from.

JUNOT

We have ridden along as far as Calandrix,
Favoured therein by this disordered night,
Which tongues its language to the disguise of ours ;
And find amid the vale an open route
That, well manœuvred, may be practicable.

MASSÉNA

I'll look now at it, while the weather aids.
If it may serve our end when all's prepared
So good.   If not, some other to the west.

Exeunt MASSÉNA, JUNOT, LOISON, FOY, and the rest by the
paved crossway to the right.

The wind continues to prevail as the spot is left desolate,
the darkness increases, rain descends more heavily, and the
scene is blotted out.

SCENE III

PARIS.   THE TUILERIES

The anteroom to the EMPRESS MARIE LOUISE's bed-chamber, in which are discovered NAPOLÉON in his dressing-gown, the DUCHESS OF MONTEBELLO, and other ladies-in-waiting, CORVISART the first physician, and the second physician BOURDIER.

The time is before dawn.   The EMPEROR walks up and down, throws himself on a sofa, or stands at the window.   A cry of anguish comes occasionally from within.

NAPOLÉON opens the door and speaks into the bed-chamber.

NAPOLÉON

How now, Dubois ?

VOICE OF DUBOIS THE ACCOUCHEUR (nervously)

Less well, sire, than I hoped ;
I fear no skill can save them both.

NAPOLÉON (agitated)

Good God !

Exit CORVISART into the bed-room.   Enter DUBOIS.

DUBOIS (with hesitation)

Which life is to be saved ?   The Empress, sire,
Lies in great jeopardy.   I have not known
In my long years of many-featured practice
An instance in a thousand fall out so.

NAPOLÉON

Then save the mother, pray !   Think but of her ;
It is her privilege, and my command.—

Don't lose your head, Dubois, at this tight time :
Your furthest skill can work but what it may.
Fancy that you are merely standing by
A shop-wife's couch, say, in the Rue Saint Denis ;
Show the aplomb and phlegm that you would show
Did such a bed receive your ministry.

[Exit Dubois.

Voice of Marie Louise (faintly within)

O pray, pray don't ! Those ugly things terrify
me ! Why should I be tortured even if I am but
a means to an end ! Let me die ! It was cruel
of him to bring this upon me !

Exit Napoléon impatiently to the bed-room.

Voice of Madame de Montesquiou (within)

Keep up your spirits, madame ! I have been
through it myself, and I assure you there is no
danger to you. It is going on all right, and I am
holding you.

Voice of Napoléon (within)

Heaven above ! Why did you not keep those
cursed sugar-tongs out of her sight ? How is she
going to get through it if you frighten her like this ?

Voice of Dubois (within)

If you will pardon me, your Majesty,
I must implore you not to interfere !
I'll not be scapegoat for the consequence
If, sire, you do ! Better for her sake far
Would you withdraw. The sight of your concern
But agitates and weakens her endurance.
I will inform you all, and call you back
If things should worsen here.

Re-enter Napoléon from the bed-chamber. He half shuts
the door, and remains close to it listening, pale and nervous.

BOURDIER

                I ask you, sire,
To harass yourself less with this event,
Which may amend anon : I much regret
The honoured mother of your Majesty,
And sister too, should both have left ere now,
Whose solace would have bridged these anxious
     hours.

NAPOLÉON (absently)

As we were not expecting it so soon
I begged they would sit up no longer here. . . .
She ought to get along ; she has help enough
With that half-dozen of them at hand within—
Skilled Madame Blaise the nurse, and two besides,
Madame de Montesquiou and Madame Ballant——

DUBOIS (speaking through the doorway)

Past is the question, sire, of which to save !
The child is dead ; the while her Majesty
Is getting through it well.

NAPOLÉON

               Praise Heaven for that !
I'll not grieve overmuch about the child. . . .
Never shall she go through this strain again
To lay down a dynastic line for me.

DUCHESS OF MONTEBELLO (aside to second lady)

    He only says that now. In cold blood it would
be far otherwise. That's how men are.

VOICE OF MADAME BLAISE (within)

Doctor, the child's alive !
        (The cry of an infant is heard.)

VOICE OF DUBOIS (calling from within)

Sire, both are saved.

NAPOLÉON rushes into the chamber, and is heard kissing MARIE LOUISE.

VOICE OF MADAME BLAISE (within)

A vigorous boy, your Imperial Majesty. The brandy and hot napkins brought him to.

DUCHESS OF MONTEBELLO

It is as I expected. A healthy young woman of her build had every chance of doing well, despite the doctors.

An interval.

NAPOLÉON (re-entering radiantly)

We have achieved a healthy heir, good dames,
And in the feat the Empress was most brave,
Although she suffered much—so much, indeed,
That I would sooner father no more sons
Than have so fair a fruit-tree undergo
Another wrenching of such magnitude.

He walks to the window, pulls aside the curtains, and looks out. It is a joyful spring morning. The Tuileries' gardens are thronged with an immense crowd, kept at a little distance off the Palace by a cord. The windows of the neighbouring houses are full of gazers, and the streets are thronged with halting carriages, their inmates awaiting the event.

SPIRIT OF THE YEARS (whispering to Napoléon)

At this high hour there broods a woman nigh,
Ay, here in Paris, with her child and thine,
Who might have played this part with truer eye
To thee and to thy contemplated line!

NAPOLÉON (soliloquizing)

Strange that just now there flashes on my soul
That little one I loved in Warsaw days,
Marie Walewska, and my boy by her !—
She was shown faithless by a foul intrigue
Till fate sealed up her opportunity. . . .
But what's one woman's fortune more or less
Beside the schemes of kings !—Ah, there's the
    news !

          A gun is heard from the Invalides.

CROWD (excitedly)

One !

   Another report of the gun, and another, succeed.

Two ! Three ! Four !

   The firing and counting proceed to twenty-one, when there
is great suspense. The gun fires again, and the excitement is
doubled.

Twenty-two ! A boy !

   The remainder of the counting up to a hundred-and-one is
drowned in huzzas. Bells begin ringing, and from the Champ
de Mars a balloon ascends, from which the tidings are scattered
in hand-bills as it floats away across France.
   Enter the PRESIDENT OF THE SENATE, CAMBACÉRÈS, BER-
THIER, LEBRUN, and other officers of state. NAPOLÉON turns
from the window.

CAMBACÉRÈS

Unstinted gratulations and goodwill
We bring to your Imperial Majesty,
While still resounds the superflux of joy
With which your people welcome this live star
Upon the horizon of our history !

President of Senate

All blessings at their goodliest will grace
The advent of this New Messiah, sire,
Of fairer prospects than the former one,
Whose coming at so apt an hour endues
The widening glory of your high exploits
With permanence, and flings the dimness far
That cloaked the future of our chronicle !

Napoléon

My thanks ; though, gentlemen, upon my soul
You might have drawn the line at the Messiah.
But I excuse you.—Yes, the boy has come ;
He took some coaxing, but he's here at last.—
And what news brings the morning from without ?
I know of none but this the Empress now
Trumps to the world from the adjoining room.

President of Senate

Nothing in Europe, sire, that can compare
In magnitude therewith to more effect
Than with an eagle some frail finch or wren.
To wit : the ban on English trade prevailing,
Subjects our merchant-houses to such strain
That many of the best see bankruptcy
Like a grim ghost ahead.　Next week, they say
In secret here, six of the largest close.

Napoléon

It shall not be !　Our burst of natal joy
Must not be sullied by so mean a thing :
Aid shall be rendered.　Much as we may suffer,
England must suffer more, and I am content.
What has come in from Spain and Portugal ?

BERTHIER

Vaguely-voiced rumours, sire, but nothing more,
Which travel countries quick as earthquake-thrills,
No mortal knowing how.

NAPOLÉON

Of Masséna ?

BERTHIER

Yea.   He retreats for prudence' sake, it seems,
Before Lord Wellington.   Dispatches soon
Must reach your Majesty, explaining all.

NAPOLÉON

Ever retreating !   Why declines he so
From all his olden prowess ?   Why, again,
Did he give battle at Busaco lately,
When Lisbon could be marched on without strain ?
Why has he dallied by the Tagus bank
And shunned the obvious course ?   I gave him Ney,
Soult, and Junot, and eighty thousand men,
And he does nothing.   Really it might seem
As though we meant to let this Wellington
Be even with us there !

BERTHIER

His mighty forts
At Torrès Védras hamper Masséna,
And quite preclude advance.

NAPOLÉON

O well—no matter :
Why should I linger on these haps of war
Now that I have a son !

Exeunt NAPOLÉON by one door and by another the PRESIDENT
OF THE SENATE, CAMBACÉRÈS, LEBRUN, BERTHIER, and officials.

CHORUS OF IRONIC SPIRITS (aerial music)

The Will Itself is slave to him,
And holds it blissful to obey !—
He said, " Go to ; it is my whim

" To bed a bride without delay,
Who shall unite my dull new name
With one that shone in Caesar's day.

" She must conceive—you hear my claim ?—
And bear a son—no daughter, mind—
Who shall hand on my form and fame

" To future times as I have designed ;
And at the birth throughout the land
Must cannon roar and alp-horns wind ! "

The Will grew conscious at command,
And ordered issue as he planned.

The interior of the Palace is veiled.

SCENE IV

SPAIN.   ALBUERA

The dawn of a mid-May day in the same spring shows the village of Albuera with the country around it, as viewed from the summit of a line of hills on which the English and their allies are ranged under Beresford. The landscape swept by the eye includes to the right foreground a hill loftier than any, and somewhat detached from the range. The green slopes behind and around this hill are untrodden—though in a few hours to be the sanguinary scene of the most murderous struggle of the whole war.

The village itself lies to the left foreground, with its stream flowing behind it from the distance on the right. A creeping

brook at the bottom of the heights held by the English joins
the stream by the village. Behind the stream some of the
French forces are visible. Away behind these stretches a
great wood several miles in area, out of which the Albuera
stream emerges, and behind the furthest verge of the wood
the morning sky lightens momently. The birds in the wood,
unaware that this day is to be different from every other day
they have known there, are heard singing their overtures with
their usual serenity.

DUMB SHOW

As objects grow more distinct it can be perceived that some
strategic dispositions of the night are being completed by the
French forces, which the evening before lay in the woodland
to the front of the English army. They have emerged during
the darkness, and large sections of them—infantry, cuirassiers,
and artillery—have crept round to BERESFORD'S right without
his suspecting the movement, where they lie hidden by the great
hill aforesaid, though not more than half-a-mile from his right
wing.

SPIRIT OF THE YEARS

A hot ado goes forward here to-day,
If I may read the Immanent Intent
　　From signs and tokens blent
With weird unrest along the firmament
Of causal coils in passionate display.
—Look narrowly, and what you witness say.

SPIRIT OF THE PITIES

I see red smears upon the sickly dawn,
And seeming drops of gore. On earth below
Are men—unnatured and mechanic-drawn—
Mixt nationalities in row and row,
　　Wheeling them to and fro
In moves dissociate from their souls' demand,
For dynasts' ends that few even understand!

SPIRIT OF THE YEARS

Speak more materially, and less in dream.

SPIRIT OF RUMOUR

I'll do it. . . . The stir of strife grows well defined
Around the hamlet and the church thereby :
Till, from the wood, the ponderous columns wind,
Guided by Godinot, with Werlé nigh.
They bear upon the vill. But the gruff guns
Of Dickson's Portuguese
Punch spectral vistas through the maze of these ! . . .
More Frenchmen press, and roaring antiphons
Of cannonry contuse the roofs and walls and trees.

SPIRIT OF THE PITIES

Wrecked are the ancient bridge, the green spring plot,
The blooming fruit-tree, the fair flower-knot !

SPIRIT OF RUMOUR

Yet the true mischief to the English might
Is meant to fall not there. Look to the right,
And read the shaping scheme by yon hill-side,
Where cannon, foot, and brisk dragoons you see,
With Werlé and Latour-Maubourg to guide,
Waiting to breast the hill-brow bloodily.

BERESFORD now becomes aware of this project on his flank, and sends orders to throw back his right to face the attack. The order is not obeyed. Almost at the same moment the French rush is made, the Spanish and Portuguese allies of the English are beaten back, and the hill is won. But two English divisions bear from the centre of their front, and plod desperately up the hill to retake it.

SPIRIT SINISTER

Now he among us who may wish to be
A skilled practitioner in slaughtery,
Should watch this hour's fruition yonder there,
And he will know, if knowing ever were,
How mortals may be freed their fleshly cells,

And quaint red doors set ope in sweating fells,
By methods swift and slow and foul and fair!

The English, who have plunged up the hill, are caught in a
heavy mist, that hides from them an advance in their rear of
the lancers and hussars of the enemy. The lines of the Buffs,
the Sixty-sixth, and those of the Forty-eighth, who were with
them, in a chaos of smoke, steel, sweat, curses, and blood,
are beheld melting down like wax from an erect position to
confused heaps. Their forms lie rigid, or twitch and turn,
as they are trampled over by the hoofs of the enemy's horse.
Those that have not fallen are taken.

SPIRIT OF THE PITIES

It works as you, uncanny Phantom, wist! . . .
Whose is that towering form
   That tears across the mist
To where the shocks are sorest?—his with arm
Outstretched, and grimy face, and bloodshot eye,
Like one who, having done his deeds, will die?

SPIRIT OF RUMOUR

He is one Beresford, who heads the fight
   For England here to-day.

SPIRIT OF THE PITIES

                He calls the sight
Despite himself!—parries yon lancer's thrust,
And with his own sword renders dust to dust!

The ghastly climax of the strife is reached; the combatants
are seen to be firing grape and canister at speaking distance,
and discharging musketry in each other's faces when so close
that their complexions may be recognized. Hot corpses, their
mouths blackened by cartridge-biting, and surrounded by
cast-away knapsacks, firelocks, hats, stocks, flint-boxes, and
priming-horns, together with red and blue rags of clothing,
gaiters, epaulettes, limbs, and viscera, accumulate on the slopes,
increasing from twos and threes to half-dozens, and from half-
dozens to heaps, which steam with their own warmth as the
spring rain falls gently upon them.

The critical instant has come, and the English break. But a comparatively fresh division, with fusileers, is brought into the turmoil by HARDINGE and COLE, and these make one last strain to save the day, and their names and lives. The fusileers mount the incline, and issuing from the smoke and mist startle the enemy by their arrival on a spot deemed won.

SEMICHORUS I OF THE PITIES (aerial music)

They come, beset by riddling hail ;
They sway like sedges in a gale ;
They fail, and win, and win, and fail. Albuera !

SEMICHORUS II

They gain the ground there, yard by yard,
Their brows and hair and lashes charred,
Their blackened teeth set firm and hard.

SEMICHORUS I

Their mad assailants rave and reel,
And face, as men who scorn to feel,
The close-lined, three-edged prongs of steel.

SEMICHORUS II

Till faintness follows closing-in,
When, faltering headlong down, they spin
Like leaves. But those pay well who win Albuera.

SEMICHORUS I

Out of six thousand souls that sware
To hold the mount, or pass elsewhere,
But eighteen hundred muster there.

SEMICHORUS II

Pale Colonels, Captains, ranksmen lie,
Facing the earth or facing sky ;—
They strove to live, they stretch to die.

SEMICHORUS I

Friends, foemen, mingle ; heap and heap.—
Hide their hacked bones, Earth !—deep, deep, deep,
Where harmless worms caress and creep.

CHORUS

Hide their hacked bones, Earth !—deep, deep, deep,
Where harmless worms caress and creep.—
What man can grieve ? what woman weep ?
Better than waking is to sleep.   Albuera !

The night comes on, and darkness covers the battle-field.

SCENE V

WINDSOR CASTLE.   A ROOM IN THE KING'S APARTMENTS

The walls of the room are padded, and also the articles of furniture, the stuffings being overlaid with satin and velvet, on which are worked in gold thread monograms and crowns. The windows are guarded, and the floor covered with thick cork, carpeted. The time is shortly after the last scene.

The KING is seated by a window, and two of Dr. WILLIS's attendants are in the room. His MAJESTY is now seventy-two ; his sight is very defective, but he does not look ill. He appears to be lost in melancholy thought, and talks to himself reproachfully, a hurried manner on occasion being the only irregular symptom that he betrays.

KING

In my lifetime I did not look after her enough —enough—enough ! And now she is lost to me, and I shall never see her more. Had I but known, had I but thought of it ! Gentlemen, when did I lose the Princess Amelia ?

FIRST ATTENDANT

The second of last November, your Majesty.

KING

And what is it now ?

FIRST ATTENDANT

Now, sir, it is the beginning of June.

KING

Ah, June, I remember ! . . . The June flowers
are not for me. I shall never see them ; nor will
she. So fond of them as she was. . . . Even if I
were living I would never go where there are
flowers any more ! No : I would go to the bleak,
barren places that she never would walk in, and
never knew, so that nothing might remind me of
her, and make my heart ache more than I can bear !
. . . Why, the beginning of June ?—that's when
they are coming to examine me ! (He grows excited.)

FIRST ATTENDANT (to second attendant, aside)

Dr. Reynolds ought not to have reminded him
of their visit. It only disquiets him and makes
him less fit to see them.

KING

How long have I been confined here ?

FIRST ATTENDANT

Since November, sir ; for your health's sake
entirely, as your Majesty knows.

KING

What, what ? So long ? Ah, yes. I must bear it. This is the fourth great black gulf in my poor life, is it not ? The fourth.

A signal at the door. The second attendant opens it and whispers.

Enter softly SIR HENRY HALFORD, DR. WILLIAM HEBERDEN, DR. ROBERT WILLIS, DR. MATTHEW BAILLIE, *the* KING'S APOTHECARY, *and one or two other gentlemen.*

KING (straining his eyes to discern them)

What ! Are they come ? What will they do to me ? How dare they ! I am Elector of Hanover ! (Finding Dr. Willis is among them he shrieks.) O, they are going to bleed me—yes, to bleed me ! (Piteously.) My friends, don't bleed me—pray don't ! It makes me so weak to take my blood. And the leeches do, too, when you put so many. You will not be so unkind, I am sure !

WILLIS (to Baillie)

It is extraordinary what a vast aversion he has to bleeding—that most salutary remedy, fearlessly practised. He submits to leeches as yet, but I won't say that he will for long without being strait-jacketed.

KING (catching some of the words)

You will strait-jacket me ? O no, no !

WILLIS

Leeches are not effective, really. Dr. Home, when I mentioned it to him yesterday, said he would bleed him till he fainted if he had charge of him !

KING

O will you do it, sir, against my will,
And put me, once your king, in needless pain ?
I do assure you truly, my good friends,
That I have done no harm ! In sunnier years
Ere I was throneless, withered to a shade,
Deprived of my divine authority—
When I was hale, and ruled the English land—
I ever did my utmost to promote
The welfare of my people, body and soul !
Right many a morn and night I have prayed and
     mused
How I could bring them to a better way.
So much of me you surely know, my friends,
And will not hurt me in my weakness here !

(He trembles.)

SPIRIT OF THE PITIES

The tears that lie about this plightful scene
Of heavy travail in a suffering soul,
Mocked with the forms and feints of royalty
While scarified by briery Circumstance,
Might drive Compassion past her patiency
To hold that some mean, monstrous ironist
Had built this mistimed fabric of the Spheres
To watch the throbbings of its captive lives,
(The which may Truth forfend), and not thy said
Unmaliced, unimpassioned, nescient Will !

SPIRIT OF THE YEARS

Mild one, be not too touched with human fate.
Such is the Drama : such the Mortal state :
No sigh of thine can null the Plan Predestinate !

HALFORD

We have come to do your Majesty no harm.
Here's Dr. Heberden, whom I am sure you like,

And this is Dr. Baillie.   We arrive
But to inquire and gather how you are,
Thereon to let the Privy Council know,
And give assurance for your people's good.

    A brass band is heard playing in a distant part of Windsor.

KING

Ah—what does that band play for here to-day ?
She has been dead and I so short a time ! . . .
Her little hands are hardly cold as yet ;
But they can show such cruel indecency
As to let trumpets play !

HALFORD

                They guess not, sir,
That you can hear them, or their chords would
    cease.
Their boisterous music fetches back to me
That, of our errands to your Majesty,
One was congratulation most sincere
Upon this glorious victory you have won.
The news is just in port ; the band booms out
To celebrate it, and to honour you.

KING

A victory ?   I ?   Pray where ?

HALFORD

                Indeed so, sir :
Hard by Albuera—far in harried Spain—
Yes, sir ; you have achieved a victory
Of dash unmatched and feats unparalleled !

KING

He says I have won a battle ?   But I thought
I was a poor afflicted captive here,
In darkness lingering out my lonely days,
Beset with terror of these myrmidons
That suck my blood like vampires !   Ay, ay, ay !—
No aims left to me but to quicken death
To quicklier please my son !—And yet he says
That I have won a battle !   O God, curse, damn !
When will the speech of the world accord with
        truth,
And men's tongues roll sincerely !

GENTLEMAN (aside)

                                Faith, 'twould seem
As if the madman were the sanest here !

The KING's face has flushed, and he becomes violent. The
attendants rush forward to him.

SPIRIT OF THE PITIES

Something within me aches to pray
To some Great Heart, to take away
This evil day, this evil day !

CHORUS IRONIC

Ha-ha !   That's good.   Thou'lt pray to It :—
But where do Its compassions sit ?
Yea, where abides the heart of It ?

Is it where sky-fires flame and flit,
Or solar craters spew and spit,
Or ultra-stellar night-webs knit ?

What is Its shape ?   Man's counterfeit ?
That turns in some far sphere unlit
The Wheel which drives the Infinite ?

SPIRIT OF THE PITIES

Mock on, mock on ! Yet I'll go pray
To some Great Heart, who haply may
Charm mortal miseries away !

The KING's paroxysm continues. The attendants hold him.

HALFORD

This is distressing. One can never tell
How he will take things now. I thought Albuera
A subject that would surely solace him.
These paroxysms—have they been bad this week ?
   (To attendants.)

FIRST ATTENDANT

Sir Henry, no. He has quite often named
The late Princess, as gently as a child
A little bird found starved.

WILLIS (aside to apothecary)

I must increase the opium to-night, and lower
him by a double set of leeches since he won't stand
the lancet quietly.

APOTHECARY

You should take twenty ounces, doctor, if a
drop—indeed, go on blooding till he's unconscious.
He is too robust by half. And the watering-pot
would do good again—not less than six feet above
his head. See how heated he is.

WILLIS

Curse that town band. It will have to be
stopped.

HEBERDEN

The same thing is going on all over England, no doubt, on account of this victory.

HALFORD

When he is in a more domineering mood he likes such allusions to his rank as king. . . . If he could resume his walks on the terrace he might improve slightly. But it is too soon yet. We must consider what we shall report to the Council. There is little hope of his being much better. What do you think, Willis ?

WILLIS

None. He is done for this time !

HALFORD

Well, we must soften it down a little, so as not to upset the Queen too much, poor woman, and distract the Council unnecessarily. Eldon will go pumping up bucketfuls, and the Archbishops are so easily shocked that a certain conventional reserve is almost forced upon us.

WILLIS (returning from the King)

He is already better. The paroxysm has nearly passed. Your opinion will be far more favourable before you leave.

The KING soon grows calm, and the expression of his face changes to one of dejection. The attendants leave his side : he bends his head, and covers his face with his hand, while his lips move as if in prayer. He then turns to them.

KING (meekly)

I am most truly sorry, gentlemen,
If I have used language that would seem to show
Discourtesy to you for your good help
In this unhappy malady of mine !
My nerves unstring, my friends ; my flesh grows
     weak :
" The good that I would do I leave undone,
The evil which I would not, that I do ! "
Shame, shame on me !

WILLIS (aside to the others)

    Now he will be as low as before he was in the
other extreme.

KING

A king should bear him kingly ; I, of all,
One of so long a line.   O shame on me ! . . .
—This battle that you speak of ?—Spain, of course ?
Ah—Albuera !   And many fallen—eh ?   Yes ?

HALFORD

Many hot hearts, sir, cold, I grieve to say.
There's Major-General Hoghton, Captain Bourke,
And Herbert of the Third, Lieutenant Fox,
And Captains Erck and Montague, and more.
With Majors-General Cole and Stewart wounded,
And Quartermaster-General Wallace too :
A total of three generals, colonels five,
Five majors, fifty captains ; and to these
Add ensigns and lieutenants sixscore odd,
Who went out, but returned not.   Heavily tithed
Were the attenuate battalions there
Who stood and bearded Death by the hour that day !

KING

O fearful price for victory !   Add thereto
All those I lost at Walcheren.—A crime
Lay there ! . . . I stood on Chatham's being sent :
It wears on me, till I am unfit to live !

WILLIS (aside to the others)

Don't let him get on that Walcheren business.
There will be another outbreak.   Heberden, please
ye talk to him.   He fancies you most.

HEBERDEN

I'll tell him some of the brilliant feats of the
battle.   (He goes and talks to the KING.)

WILLIS (to the rest)

Well, my inside begins to cry cupboard.   I had
breakfast early.   We have enough particulars now
to face the Queen's Council with, I should say, Sir
Henry ?

HALFORD

Yes.—I want to get back to town as soon as
possible to-day.   Mrs. Siddons has a party at her
house at Westbourne to-night, and all the world
is going to be there.

BAILLIE

Well, I am not.   But I have promised to take
some friends to Vauxhall, as it is a grand gala
and fireworks night.   Miss Farren is going to sing
" The Canary Bird."—The Regent's fête, by the
way, is postponed till the nineteenth, on account
of this relapse.   Pretty grumpy he was at having
to do it.   All the world will be *there*, sure !

WILLIS

And some from the Shades, too, of the fair
sex.—Well, here comes Heberden. He has pacified
his Majesty nicely. Now we can get away.

The physicians withdraw softly, and the scene is covered.

SCENE VI

LONDON. CARLTON HOUSE AND THE STREETS ADJOINING

It is a cloudless midsummer evening, and as the west fades
the stars beam down upon the city, the evening-star hanging
like a jonquil blossom. They are dimmed by the unwonted
radiance which spreads around and above Carlton House. As
viewed from aloft the glare rises through the skylights, floods
the forecourt towards Pall Mall, and kindles with a diaphanous
glow the huge tents in the gardens that overlook the Mall.
The hour has arrived of the Prince Regent's festivity.

A stream of carriages and sedan-chairs, moving slowly,
stretches from the building along Pall Mall into Piccadilly and
Bond Street, and crowds fill the pavements watching the
bejewelled and feathered occupants. In addition to the grand
entrance inside the Pall Mall colonnade there is a covert little
" chair-door " in Warwick Street for sedans only, by which
arrivals are perceived to be slipping in almost unobserved.

SPIRIT IRONIC

What domiciles are those, of singular expression,
Whence no guest comes to join the gemmed procession ;
That, west of Hyde, this, in the Park-side Lane,
Each front beclouded like a mask of pain ?

SPIRIT OF RUMOUR

Therein the princely host's two spouses dwell ;
A wife in each. Let me inspect and tell.

The walls of the two houses—one in Park Lane, the other at Kensington—become transparent.

I see within the first his latter wife—
That Caroline of Brunswick whose brave sire
Yielded his breath on Jena's reeking plain,
And of whose kindred other yet may fall
Ere long, if character indeed be fate.—
She idles feasting, and is full of jest
As each gay chariot rumbles to the rout.
" I rank like your Archbishops' wives," laughs she ;
" Denied my husband's honours.   Funny me ! "

Suddenly a Beau on his way to the Carlton House festival halts at her house, calls, and is shown in.

He brings her news that a fresh favourite rules
Her husband's ready heart ; likewise of those
Obscure and unmissed courtiers late deceased,
Who have in name been bidden to the feast
By blundering scribes.

The Princess is seen to jump up from table at some words from her visitor, and clap her hands.

                These tidings, juxtaposed,
Have fired her hot with curiosity,
And lit her quick invention with a plan.

Princess of Wales

Mine God, I'll go disguised—in some dead name
And enter by the leetle, sly, chair-door
Designed for those not welcomed openly.
There unobserved I'll note mine new supplanter !
'Tis indiscreet ?   Let indiscretion rule,
Since caution pensions me so scurvily !

Spirit Ironic

Good.   Now for the other sweet and slighted spouse.

SPIRIT OF RUMOUR

The second roof shades the Fitzherbert Fair ;
Reserved, perverse.   As coach and coach roll by
She mopes within her lattice ; lampless, lone,
As if she grieved at her ungracious fate,
And yet were loth to kill the sting of it
By frankly forfeiting the Prince and town.
" Bidden," says she, " but as one low of rank,
And go I will not so unworthily,
To sit with common dames ! "—A flippant friend
Writes then that a new planet sways to-night
The sense of her erratic lord ; whereon
The fair Fitzherbert muses hankeringly.

MRS. FITZHERBERT (soliloquizing)

The guest-card which I publicly refused
Might, as a fancy, privately be used ! . . .
Yes—one last look—a wordless, wan farewell
To this false life which glooms me like a knell,
And him, the cause ; from some hid nook survey
His new magnificence ;—then go for aye !

SPIRIT OF RUMOUR

She cloaks and veils, and in her private chair
Passes the Princess also stealing there—
Two honest wives, and yet a differing pair !

SPIRIT IRONIC

With dames of strange repute, who bear a ticket
For screened admission by the private wicket.

CHORUS OF IRONIC SPIRITS (aerial music)

A wife of the body, a wife of the mind,
A wife somewhat frowsy, a wife too refined :

Could the twain but grow one, and no other dames be,
No husband in Europe more steadfast than he !

SPIRIT OF THE YEARS

Cease fooling on weak waifs who love and wed
But as the unweeting Urger may bestead !—
See them withinside, douce and diamonded.

The walls of Carlton House open, and the spectator finds
himself confronting the revel.

SCENE VII

THE SAME. THE INTERIOR OF CARLTON HOUSE

A central hall is disclosed, radiant with constellations of
candles, lamps, and lanterns, and decorated with flowering
shrubs. An opening on the left reveals the Grand Council-
chamber prepared for dancing, the floor being chalked with
arabesques having in the centre " G. III. R.," with a crown,
arms, and supporters. Orange-trees and rose-bushes in bloom
stand against the walls. On the right hand extends a glittering vista of the supper-rooms and tables, now crowded with
guests. This display reaches as far as the conservatory westward, and branches into long tents on the lawn.

On a dais at the chief table, laid with gold and silver plate,
the Prince Regent sits like a lay figure, in a state chair of
crimson and gold, with six servants at his back. He swelters
in a gorgeous uniform of scarlet and gold lace which represents
him as a Field Marshal, and he is surrounded by a hundred-and-
forty of his particular friends.

Down the middle of this state-table runs a purling brook
crossed by quaint bridges, in which gold and silver fish frisk
about between banks of moss and flowers. The whole scene is
lit with wax candles in chandeliers, and in countless candelabra
on the tables.

The people at the upper tables include the Duchess of York,
looking tired from having just received as hostess most of the
ladies present, except those who have come informally, Louis
XVIII. of France, the Duchess of Angoulême, all the English
Royal Dukes, nearly all the ordinary Dukes and Duchesses ;

also the Lord Chancellor, the Speaker, the Chancellor of the Exchequer and other Ministers, the Lord Mayor and Lady Mayoress, all the more fashionable of the other Peers, Peeresses, and Members of Parliament, Generals, Admirals, and Mayors, with their wives. The ladies of position wear, almost to the extent of a uniform, a nodding head-dress of ostrich feathers with diamonds, and gowns of white satin embroidered in gold or silver, on which, owing to the heat, dribbles of wax from the chandeliers occasionally fall.

The Guards' bands play, and attendants rush about in blue and gold lace.

Spirit of the Pities

The Queen, the Regent's mother, sits not here ;
Wanting, too, are his sisters, I perceive ;
And it is well.   With the distempered King
Immured at Windsor, sore distraught or dying,
It borders nigh on an indecency
In their regard, that this loud feast is kept,
A thought not strange to many, as I read,
Even of those gathered here.

Spirit Ironic

My dear phantom and crony, the gloom upon their faces is due rather to their having borrowed those diamonds at eleven per cent than to their loyalty to a suffering monarch ! But let us test the feeling. I'll spread a report.

He calls up the Spirit of Rumour, who scatters whispers through the assemblage.

A Guest (to his neighbour)

Have you heard this report—that the King is dead ?

Another Guest

It has just reached me from the other side. Can it be true ?

Third Guest

I think it probable. He has been very ill all the week.

Prince Regent

Dead ?   Then my fête is spoilt, by God !

Sheridan

Long live the King !   (He holds up his glass and bows to the Regent.)

Marchioness of Hertford
(the new favourite, to the Regent)

The news is more natural than the moment of it ! It is too cruel to you that it should happen now !

Prince Regent

Damn me, though ; can it be true ?   (He provisionally throws a regal air into his countenance.)

Duchess of York (on the Regent's left)

I hardly can believe it.   This forenoon
He was reported mending.

Duchess of Angoulême (on the Regent's right)

On this side
They are asserting that the news is false—
That Buonaparté's child, the " King of Rome,"
Is dead, and not your royal father, sire.

Prince Regent

That's mighty fortunate !   Had it been true,
I should have been abused by all the world—

The Queen the keenest of the chorus too—
Though I have been postponing this pledged feast
Through days and weeks, in hopes the King would
    mend,
Till expectation fusted with delay.
But give a dog a bad name—or a Prince !
So, then, it is this new-come King of Rome
Who has passed or ever the world has welcomed
    him ! . . .
Call him a king—that pompous upstart's son—
Beside us scions of the ancient lines !

DUKE OF BEDFORD

I think that rumour untrue also, sir. I heard it
as I drove up from Woburn this evening, and it
was contradicted then.

PRINCE REGENT

Drove up this evening, did ye, Duke ? Why
did you cut it so close ?

DUKE OF BEDFORD

Well, it so happened that my sheep-shearing
dinner was fixed for this very day, and I couldn't
put it off. So I dined with them there at one
o'clock, discussed the sheep, rushed off, drove the
two-and-forty miles, jumped into my clothes at
my house here, and reached your Royal Highness's
door in no very bad time.

PRINCE REGENT

Capital, capital. But, 'pon my soul, 'twas a
close shave !

Soon the babbling and glittering company rise from supper,
and begin promenading through the rooms and tents, the

REGENT setting the example, and mixing up and talking unceremoniously with his guests of every degree. He and the group round him disappear into the remoter chambers; but many concentrate in the Grecian Hall, which forms the foreground of the scene, whence a glance can be obtained into the ball-room, now filled with dancers.

The band is playing the tune of the season, " The Regency Hornpipe," which is danced as a country-dance by some thirty couples; so that by the time the top couple have danced down the figure they are quite breathless. Two young lords talk desultorily as they survey the scene.

FIRST LORD

Are the rumours of the King of Rome's death confirmed ?

SECOND LORD

No. But they are probably true. He was a feeble brat from the first. I believe they had to baptize him on the day he was born. What can one expect after such presumption—calling him the New Messiah, and God knows what all. Ours is the only country which did not write fulsome poems about him. " Wise English ! " the Tsar Alexander said drily when he heard it.

FIRST LORD

Ay ! The affection between that Pompey and Caesar has begun to cool. Alexander's soreness at having his sister thrown over so cavalierly is not salved yet.

SECOND LORD

There is much besides. I'd lay a guinea there will be a war between Russia and France before another year has flown.

FIRST LORD

Prinny looks a little worried to-night.

SECOND LORD

Yes. The Queen don't like the fête being held, considering the King's condition. She and her friends say it should have been put off altogether. But the Princess of Wales is not troubled that way. Though she was not asked herself she went wildly off and bought her people new gowns to come in. Poor maladroit woman! . . .

Another new dance of the year is started, and another long line of couples begin to foot it.

That's a pretty thing they are doing now. What d'ye call it?

FIRST LORD

"Speed the Plough." It is just out. They are having it everywhere. The next is to be one of those foreign things in three-eight time they call Waltzes. I question if anybody is up to dancing 'em here yet.

"Speed the Plough" is danced to its conclusion, and the band strikes up "The Copenhagen Waltz."

SPIRIT IRONIC

Now for the wives. They both were tearing hither,
Unless reflection sped them back again;
But dignity that nothing else may bend
Succumbs to woman's curiosity,
So deem them here. Messengers, call them nigh!

The PRINCE REGENT, having gone the round of the other rooms, now appears at the ball-room door, and stands looking at the dancers. Suddenly he turns, and gazes about with a ruffled face. He sees a tall, red-faced man near him—LORD YARMOUTH, one of his friends (afterwards Marquis of Hertford).

PRINCE REGENT

Cursed hot here, Yarmouth. Hottest of all for me!

YARMOUTH

Yes, it is warm, sir.   Hence I do not dance.

PRINCE REGENT

H'm.   What I meant was of another order ;
I spoke it figuratively.

YARMOUTH

O indeed, sir ?

PRINCE REGENT

She's here.   I heard her voice.   I'll swear I did !

YARMOUTH

Who, sir ?

PRINCE REGENT

Why, the Princess of Wales.   Do you think I
could mistake those beastly German Ps and Bs
of hers ?—She asked to come, and was denied ;
but she's got here, I'll wager ye, through the chair-
door in Warwick Street, which I arranged for a
few ladies whom I wished to come privately.
(He looks about again, and moves till he is by a door which
affords a peep up the grand staircase.)   By God, Yarmouth,
I see *two* figures up there who shouldn't be here—
leaning over the balustrade of the gallery !

YARMOUTH

Two figures, sir.   Whose are they ?

PRINCE REGENT

She is one.   The Fitzherbert is t'other !   O I
am almost sure it is !   I would have welcomed her,

but she bridled and said she wouldn't sit down at my table as a plain " Mrs." to please anybody. As I had sworn that on this occasion people should sit strictly according to their rank, I wouldn't give way. Why the devil did she come like this ? 'Pon my soul, these women will be the death o' me !

YARMOUTH (looking cautiously up the stairs)

I can see nothing of her, sir, nor of the Princess either. There is a crowd of idlers up there leaning over the bannisters, and you may have mistaken some others for them.

PRINCE REGENT

O no. They have drawn back their heads. There have been such infernal mistakes made in sending out the cards that the biggest w—— in London might be here. She's watching Lady Hertford, that's what she's doing. For all their indifference, both of them are as jealous as two cats over one tom.

Somebody whispers that a lady has fainted upstairs.

That's Maria, I'll swear ! She's always doing it. Whenever I hear of some lady fainting about upon the furniture at my presence, and sending for a glass of water, I say to myself, There's Maria at it again, by God !

SPIRIT IRONIC

Now let him hear their voices once again.

The REGENT starts as he seems to hear from the stairs the tongues of the two ladies growing louder and nearer, the PRINCESS pouring reproaches into one ear, and MRS. FITZ-HERBERT into the other.

Prince Regent

'Od seize 'em, Yarmouth ; this will drive me mad !
If men of blood must mate with only one
Of those dear damned deluders called the Sex,
Why has Heaven teased us with the taste for
    change ?—
God, I begin to loathe the whole curst show !
How hot it is ! Get me a glass of brandy,
Or I shall swoon off too. Now let's go out,
And find some fresher air upon the lawn.
Here Yarmouth, Moira ; quick and come along.

    Exit the Prince Regent with Lords Moira and Yar-
mouth. The band strikes up " La Belle Catarina," and a new
figure is formed.

Spirit of the Years

Phantoms, ye strain your powers unduly here,
Making faint fancies as they were indeed
The Mighty Will's firm work.

Spirit Ironic

                  Nay, Father, nay ;
The wives prepared to hasten hitherward
Under the names of some gone down to death,
Who yet were bidden. Must they not be here ?

Spirit of the Years

There lie long leagues between a woman's word—
" She will, indeed she will ! "—and acting on't.
Whether those came or no, thy antics cease,
And let the revel wear it out in peace.

    Enter Spencer Perceval, the Prime Minister, a small,
pale, grave-looking man, and an Under-Secretary of State,
meeting.

UNDER-SECRETARY

Is the King of Rome really dead, and the
gorgeous gold cradle wasted ?

PERCEVAL

O no, he is alive and waxing strong :
That tale has been set travelling more than once.
But touching it, there booms upon our ear
A graver import, unimpeachable.

UNDER-SECRETARY

Your speech is dark.

PERCEVAL

        Well, a new war in Europe.
Before the year is out there may arise
A red campaign outscaling any seen.
Russia and France the parties to the strife—
Ay, to the death !

UNDER-SECRETARY

        By Heaven, sir, do you say so ?

Enter CASTLEREAGH, a tall, handsome man with a Roman
nose, who, seeing them, approaches.

PERCEVAL

Ha, Castlereagh. Till now I have missed you here.
This news is startling for us all, I say !

CASTLEREAGH

My mind is blank on it ! Since I left office
I know no more what villainy's afoot,
Or virtue either, than an anchoret
Who mortifies the flesh in some lone cave.

PERCEVAL

Well, happily that may not last for long.
But this grave pother that's just now agog
May reach such radius in its consequence
As to outspan our lives ! Yes, Bonaparte
And Alexander—late such bosom-friends—
Are closing to a mutual murder-bout
At which the lips of Europe will wax wan.
Bonaparte says the fault is not with him,
And so says Alexander. But we know
The Austrian knot began their severance,
And that the Polish question largens it.
Nothing but time is needed for the clash.
And if so be that Wellington but keep
His foot in the Peninsula awhile,
Between the pestle and the mortar-stone
Of Russia and of Spain, Napoléon's brayed.

SPIRIT OF RUMOUR (to the Spirit of the Years)

Permit me now to join them and confirm,
By what I bring from far, their forecasting ?

SPIRIT OF THE YEARS

I'll go. Thou knowest not greatly more than they.

The SPIRIT OF THE YEARS enters the apartment in the
shape of a pale, hollow-eyed gentleman wearing an embroidered
suit. At the same time re-enter the REGENT, LORDS MOIRA,
YARMOUTH, KEITH, LADY HERTFORD, SHERIDAN, the DUKE
OF BEDFORD, with many more notables. The band changes
into the popular dance, " Down with the French," and the
characters aforesaid look on at the dancers.

SPIRIT OF THE YEARS (to Perceval)

Yes, sir ; your text is true. In closest touch
With European courts and cabinets,
The imminence of dire and deadly war

Betwixt these east and western emperies
Is lipped by special pathways to mine ear.
You may not see the impact : ere it come
The tomb-worm may caress thee (Perceval shrinks); *but*
     believe
Before five more have joined the shotten years
Whose useless films infest the foggy Past,
Traced thick with teachings glimpsed unheedingly,
The rawest Dynast of the group concerned
Will, for the good or ill of mute mankind,
Down-topple to the dust like soldier Saul,
And Europe's mouldy-minded oligarchs
Be propped anew ; while garments roll in blood
To confused noise, with burning, and fuel of fire.
Nations shall lose their noblest in the strife,
And tremble at the tidings of an hour !

     (He passes into the crowd and vanishes.)

PRINCE REGENT (who has heard with parted lips)

    Who the devil is he ?

PERCEVAL

    One in the suite of the French princes, perhaps,
sir ?—though his tone was not monarchical. He
seems to be a foreigner.

CASTLEREAGH

    His manner was that of an old prophet, and his
features had a Jewish cast, which accounted for his
Hebraic style.

PRINCE REGENT

    He could not have known me, to speak so freely
in my presence !

Sheridan

I expected to see him write on the wall, like the gentleman with the Hand at Belshazzar's Feast.

Prince Regent (recovering)

He seemed to know a damn sight more about what's going on in Europe, sir (to Perceval), than your Government does, with all its secret information.

Perceval

He is recently over, I conjecture, your Royal Highness, and brings the latest impressions.

Prince Regent

By Gad, sir, I shall have a comfortable time of it in my regency, or reign, if what he foresees be true! But I was born for war; it is my destiny!

He draws himself up inside his uniform and stalks away. The group dissolves, the band continuing stridently, " Down with the French," as dawn glimmers in.

Soon the Regent's guests begin severally and in groups to take leave.

Spirit of the Pities

Behold To-morrow riddles the curtains through,
And labouring life without shoulders its cross anew!

Chorus of the Years (aerial music)

Why watch we here? Look all around
Where Europe spreads her crinkled ground,
From Osmanland to Hekla's mound,
> *Look all around!*

Hark at the cloud-combed Ural pines ;
See how each, wailful-wise, inclines ;
Mark the mist's labyrinthine lines ;

Behold the tumbling Biscay Bay ;
The Midland main in silent sway ;
As urged to move them, so move they.

No less through regal puppet-shows
The rapt Determinator throes,
That neither good nor evil knows !

Chorus of the Pities

Yet It may wake and understand
Ere Earth unshape, know all things, and
With knowledge use a painless hand,
                A painless hand !

Solitude reigns in the chambers, and the scene shuts up.

PART THIRD

PART THIRD

CHARACTERS

I. Phantom Intelligences

{ THE ANCIENT SPIRIT OF THE
   YEARS.
  CHORUS OF THE YEARS.

{ THE SPIRIT OF THE PITIES.
  CHORUS OF THE PITIES.

{ SPIRITS SINISTER AND IRONIC.
  CHORUSES OF SINISTER AND
   IRONIC SPIRITS.

{ THE SPIRIT OF RUMOUR.
  CHORUS OF RUMOURS.

THE SHADE OF THE EARTH.

SPIRIT MESSENGERS.

RECORDING ANGELS.

II. Persons

The names printed in italics are those of mute figures.

MEN

THE PRINCE REGENT.
The Royal Dukes.
THE DUKE OF RICHMOND.
The Duke of Beaufort.
LIVERPOOL, Prime Minister.
CASTLEREAGH, Foreign Secretary.
*Vansittart, Chancellor of the
   Exchequer.*
Palmerston, War Secretary.
PONSONBY.
BURDETT,   ⎫
WHITBREAD,   ⎬ Of the
Tierney, Romilly, ⎭ Opposition.
Other Members of Parliament.
TWO ATTACHÉS.
A DIPLOMATIST.
*Ambassadors, Ministers, Peers,
   and other persons of Quality
   and Office.*

———

WELLINGTON.
UXBRIDGE.

PICTON.
HILL.
CLINTON.
Colville.
COLE.
BERESFORD.
Pack and Kempt.
Byng.
Vivian.
*W. Ponsonby, Vandeleur, Colqu-
   houn-Grant, Maitland, Adam,
   and C. Halkett.*
*Graham, Le Marchant, Pakenham,
   and Sir Stapleton Cotton.*
SIR W. DE LANCEY.
FITZROY SOMERSET.
COLONELS FRASER, H. HALKETT,
   COLBORNE, *Cameron, Hep-
   burn,* LORD SALTOUN, *C.
   Campbell.*
SIR NEIL CAMPBELL.
Sir Alexander Gordon, BRIDGE-
   MAN, TYLER, *and other*
   AIDES.

CAPTAIN MERCER.
Other Generals, Colonels, and Military Officers.
Couriers.

A SERGEANT OF DRAGOONS.
Another SERGEANT.
A SERGEANT of the 15th Hussars.
A SENTINEL. *Bâtmen.*
AN OFFICER'S SERVANT.
Other non-Commissioned Officers and Privates of the British Army.
English Forces.

___

SIR W. GELL, Chamberlain to the Princess of Wales.
MR. LEGH, a Wessex Gentleman.
Another GENTLEMAN.
THE VICAR OF DURNOVER.
Signor Tramezzini and other Members of the Opera Company.
M. Rozier, a dancer.

LONDON CITIZENS.
A RUSTIC and a YEOMAN.
A MAIL-GUARD.
TOWNSPEOPLE, *Musicians, Villagers, etc.*

___

THE DUKE OF BRUNSWICK.
THE PRINCE OF ORANGE.
Count Alten.
Von Ompteda, Baring, Duplat, and other Officers of the King's-German Legion.
Perponcher, Best, Kielmansegge, Wincke, and other Hanoverian Officers.
Bylandt and other Officers of the Dutch-Belgian troops.
SOME HUSSARS.
King's - German, Hanoverian, Brunswick, and Dutch-Belgian Forces.

___

BARON VAN CAPELLEN, Belgian Secretary of State.
The Dukes of Arenberg and d'Ursel.
THE MAYOR OF BRUSSELS.
CITIZENS AND IDLERS of Brussels.

___

NAPOLÉON BONAPARTE.
JOSEPH BONAPARTE.
Jérôme Bonaparte.

THE KING OF ROME.
Eugène de Beauharnais.
Cambacérès, Arch-Chancellor to Napoléon.
TALLEYRAND.
CAULAINCOURT.
DE BAUSSET.

___

MURAT, King of Naples.
SOULT, Napoléon's Chief of Staff.
NEY.
DAVOUT.
MARMONT.
BERTHIER.
BERTRAND.
BESSIÈRES.
AUGEREAU, MACDONALD, LAURISTON, CAMBRONNE.
Oudinot, Friant, Reille, d'Erlon, Drouot, Victor, Poniatowski, Jourdan, and other Marshals, and General and Regimental Officers of Napoléon's Army.
RAPP, MORTIER, LARIBOISIÈRE.
Kellermann and Milhaud.
COLONELS FABVRIER, MARBOT, MALLET, HEYMÈS, and others.
French AIDES and COURIERS.
DE CANISY, Equerry to the King of Rome.
COMMANDANT LESSARD.
Another COMMANDANT.
BUSSY, an Orderly Officer.
SOLDIERS of the Imperial Guard and others.
STRAGGLERS ; A MAD SOLDIER.
French Forces.

___

HOREAU, BOURDOIS, and *Ivan,* physicians.
MÉNEVAL, Private Secretary to Napoléon.
DE MONTROND, an emissary of Napoléon's.
Other Secretaries to Napoléon.
CONSTANT, Napoléon's Valet.
ROUSTAN, Napoléon's Mameluke.
TWO POSTILLIONS.
A TRAVELLER.
CHAMBERLAINS and *Attendants.*
SERVANTS at the Tuileries.
FRENCH CITIZENS and *Townspeople.*

___

THE KING OF PRUSSIA.
BLÜCHER.
MÜFFLING, Wellington's Prussian Attaché.
GNEISENAU.
Zieten.
Bülow.
Kleist, Steinmetz, Thielemann, Falkenhausen.
Other Prussian General and Regimental Officers.
A Prussian PRISONER of the French.
Prussian Forces.

_____

FRANCIS, Emperor of Austria.
METTERNICH, Chancellor and Foreign Minister.
Hardenberg.
NEIPPERG.
Schwarzenberg, Field-Marshal.
Meerfeldt, Klenau, Hesse-Homburg, and other Austrian Generals.
Viennese Personages of rank and fashion.
Austrian Forces.

_____

THE EMPEROR ALEXANDER of Russia.
Nesselrode.
KUTÚZOF.
Bennigsen.
Barclay de Tolly, Dokhtórof, Bagration, Platoff, Tchichagoff, Miloradovitch, and other Russian Generals.
Rostopchin, Governor of Moscow.
SCHUVALOFF, a Commissioner.
A RUSSIAN OFFICER under Kutúzof.
Russian Forces.
Moscow Citizens.

_____

Alava, Wellington's Spanish Attaché.
Spanish and Portuguese Officers.
Spanish and Portuguese Forces.
Spanish Citizens.

_____

Minor Sovereigns and Princes of Europe.
LEIPZIG CITIZENS.

WOMEN

CAROLINE, PRINCESS OF WALES.
The Duchess of York.
THE DUCHESS OF RICHMOND.
The Duchess of Beaufort.
LADY H. DALRYMPLE.
Lady de Lancey.
LADY CHARLOTTE CAMPBELL.
Lady Anne Hamilton.
A YOUNG LADY AND HER MOTHER.
MRS. DALBIAC, a Colonel's wife.
MRS. PRESCOTT, a Captain's wife.
Other English Ladies of note and rank.
Madame Grassini and other Ladies of the Opera.
Madame Angiolini, a dancer.
VILLAGE WOMEN.
SOLDIERS' WIVES AND SWEETHEARTS.
A SOLDIER'S DAUGHTER.

_____

THE EMPRESS MARIE LOUISE.
The Empress of Austria.
MARIA CAROLINA of Naples.
Queen Hortense.
Lætitia, Madame Bonaparte.
The Princess Pauline.
THE DUCHESS OF MONTEBELLO.
THE COUNTESS OF MONTESQUIOU.
THE COUNTESS OF BRIGNOLE.
Other Ladies-in-Waiting on Marie Louise.

THE EX-EMPRESS JOSÉPHINE.
LADIES-IN-WAITING on Joséphine.
Another FRENCH LADY.
FRENCH MARKET-WOMEN.
A SPANISH LADY.
French and Spanish Women of pleasure.
Continental Citizens' Wives.
Camp-followers.

ACT FIRST

SCENE I

THE BANKS OF THE NIEMEN, NEAR KOWNO

The foreground is a hillock on a broken upland, seen in summer evening twilight. On the left, further back, are the dusky forests of Wilkowsky; on the right is the vague shine of a large river.

Emerging from the wood below the eminence appears a shadowy amorphous thing in motion, the central or Imperial column of NAPOLÉON's Grand Army for the invasion of Russia, comprising the corps of OUDINOT, NEY, and DAVOUT, with the Imperial Guard. This, with the right and left columns, makes up the host of nearly half a million, all starting on their march to Moscow. The EMPEROR is pausing on the hillock. The air is warm.

While the rearmost regiments are arriving, NAPOLÉON rides ahead with GENERAL HAXEL and one or two others to reconnoitre the river. NAPOLÉON's horse stumbles and throws him. He picks himself up before he can be helped.

SPIRIT OF THE YEARS (to Napoléon)

The portent is an ill one, Emperor ;
An ancient Roman would retire thereat !

NAPOLÉON

Whose voice was that, jarring upon my thought
So insolently ?

HAXEL AND OTHERS

Sire, we spoke no word.

NAPOLÉON

Then, whoso spake, such portents I defy !

[He remounts.

When the reconnoitrers again come back to the foreground
of the scene the huge array of columns is standing quite still,
in circles of companies, the captain of each in the middle with
a paper in his hand. He reads from it a proclamation. They
quiver emotionally, like leaves stirred by a wind. NAPOLÉON
and his staff reascend the hillock, and his own words as repeated
to the ranks reach his ears, while he himself delivers the same
address to those about him.

NAPOLÉON

Soldiers, wild war is on the board again ;
The lifetime-long alliance Russia swore
At Tilsit, for the English realm's undoing,
Is violate beyond refurbishment,
And she intractable and unashamed.
Russia is forced on by fatality :
She cries, her destiny must be outwrought,
Meaning at our expense.   Does she then dream
We are no more the men of Austerlitz,
With nothing left of our old featfulness ?
    She offers us the choice of sword or shame ;
We have made that choice unhesitatingly !
Then let us forthwith stride the Niemen flood,
Let us bear war into her great gaunt land,
And spread our glory there as otherwhere,
So that a stable peace shall stultify
The evil seed-bearing that Russian wiles
Have nourished upon Europe's choked affairs
These fifty years !

The midsummer night darkens.   They all make their
bivouacs and sleep.

SPIRIT OF THE PITIES

Something is tongued afar.

SPIRIT OF THE YEARS

The Russian counter-proclamation rolls,
But we alone have gift to catch it here.

DISTANT VOICE IN THE WIND

The hostile hatchings of Napoléon's brain
Against our Empire, long have harassed us
And mangled all our mild amenities.
So, since the hunger for embranglement
That gnaws this man, has left us optionless,
And haled us recklessly to horrid war,
We have promptly mustered our well-hardened hosts,
And, counting on our call to the Most High,
Have forthwith set our puissance face to face
Against Napoléon's.—Ranksmen! officers!
You fend your lives, your land, your liberty.
I am with you. Heaven frowns on the aggressor.

SPIRIT IRONIC

Ha! " Liberty " is quaint, and pleases me,
Sounding from such a soil!

Midsummer-day breaks, and the sun rises on the right, revealing the position clearly. The eminence overlooks for miles the river Niemen, now mirroring the morning rays. Across the river three temporary bridges have been thrown, and towards them the French masses streaming out of the forest descend in three columns.

They sing, shout, fling their shakos in the air and repeat words from the proclamation, their steel and brass flashing in the sun. They narrow their columns as they gain the three bridges, and begin to cross—horse, foot, and artillery.

NAPOLÉON has come from the tent in which he has passed the night to the high ground in front, where he stands, the sun yellowing his face, watching through his glass the committal of his army to the enterprise. DAVOUT, NEY, MURAT, OUDINOT, Generals HAXEL and ÉBLÉ, NARBONNE, and others surround him.

It turns to a day of drowsing heat, and the Emperor draws a deep breath as he shifts his weight from one puffed calf to

the other.   The light cavalry, the foot, the artillery having
passed, the heavy horse now crosses, their glitter outshining
the ripples on the stream.

A messenger enters.   NAPOLÉON reads papers that are
brought, and frowns.

NAPOLÉON

The English heads decline to recognize
The government of Joseph, King of Spain,
As that of " the now-ruling dynasty " ;
But only Ferdinand's !—I'll get to Moscow,
And send thence my rejoinder.   France shall wage
Another fifty years of wasting war
Before a Bourbon shall remount the throne
Of restless Spain ! . . .

(A flash lights his eyes.)

But this long journey now just set a-trip
Is my choice way to India ; and 'tis there
That I shall next bombard the British rule.
With Moscow taken, Russia prone and crushed,
To attain the Ganges is simplicity—
Auxiliaries from Tiflis backing me.
Once ripped by a French sword, the scaffolding
Of English merchant-mastership in Ind
Will fall a wreck. . . . Vast, it is true, must bulk
An Eastern scheme so planned ; but I could work
    it. . . .
Man has, worse fortune, but scant years for war ;
I am good for another five !

SPIRIT OF THE PITIES

Why doth he go ?—
I see returning in a chattering flock
Bleached skeletons, instead of this array
Invincibly equipped.

SPIRIT OF THE YEARS

I'll show you why.

The unnatural light before seen usurps that of the sun, bringing into view, like breezes made visible, the films or brain-tissues of the Immanent Will, that pervade all things, ramifying through the whole army, NAPOLÉON included, and moving them to Its inexplicable artistries.

NAPOLÉON (with sudden despondency)

That which has worked will work !—Since Lodi
    Bridge
The force I then felt move me moves me on
Whether I will or no ; and oftentimes
Against my better mind. . . . Why am I here ?
—By laws imposed on me inexorably !
History makes use of me to weave her web
To her long while aforetime-figured mesh
And contemplated charactery : no more.
Well, war's my trade ; and whencesoever springs
This one in hand, they'll label it with my name !

The natural light returns and the anatomy of the Will disappears. NAPOLÉON mounts his horse and descends in the rear of his host to the banks of the Niemen. His face puts on a saturnine humour, and he hums an air.

> Malbrough s'en va-t-en guerre,
> Mironton, mironton, mirontaine ;
> Malbrough s'en va-t-en guerre,
> Ne sait quand reviendra !

[Exeunt NAPOLÉON and staff.

SPIRIT SINISTER

It is kind of his Imperial Majesty to give me a lead.
    (Sings.)

> *Monsieur d'Malbrough est mort,*
> *Mironton, mironton, mirontaine ;*
> *Monsieur d'Malbrough est mort,*
> *Est mort et enterré !*

Anon the figure of NAPOLÉON, diminished to the aspect of a doll, reappears in front of his suite on the plain below. He rides across the swaying bridge. Since the morning the sky has grown overcast, and its blackness seems now to envelop the retreating array on the other side of the stream. The storm bursts, with thunder and lightning, the river turns leaden, and the scene is blotted out by the torrents of rain.

SCENE II

THE FORD OF SANTA MARTA, SALAMANCA

We are in Spain, on a July night of the same summer, the air being hot and heavy. In the darkness the ripple of the river Tormes can be heard over the ford, which is near the foreground of the scene on the right.

Against the gloomy north sky to the left, lightnings flash, revealing rugged heights in that quarter. From the heights comes to the ear the tramp of soldiery, broken and irregular, as by obstacles in their descent; as yet they are some distance off. On heights to the right hand, on the other side of the river, glimmer the bivouac fires of the French under MARMONT. The lightning quickens, with rolls of thunder, and a few large drops of rain fall.

A sentinel stands close to the ford, and beyond him is the ford-house, a shed open towards the roadway and the spectator. It is lit by a single lantern, and occupied by some half-dozen English dragoons with a sergeant and corporal, who form part of a mounted patrol, their horses being picketed at the entrance. They are seated on a bench, and appear to be waiting with some deep intent, speaking in murmurs only.

The thunderstorm increases till it drowns the noise of the ford and of the descending battalions, making them seem further off than before. The sentinel is about to retreat to the shed when he discerns two female figures in the gloom.

Enter MRS. DALBIAC and MRS. PRESCOTT, English officers' wives.

SENTINEL

Where there's war there's women, and where there's women there's trouble! (Aloud) Who goes there?

Mrs. Dalbiac

We must reveal who we are, I fear (to her companion). Friends ! (to sentinel).

Sentinel

Advance and give the countersign.

Mrs. Dalbiac

Oh, but we can't !

Sentinel

Consequent which, you must retreat. By Lord Wellington's strict regulations, women of loose character are to be excluded from the lines for moral reasons, namely, that they are often employed by the enemy as spies.

Mrs. Prescott

Dear good soldier, we are English ladies benighted, having mistaken our way back to Salamanca, and we want shelter from the storm.

Mrs. Dalbiac

If it is necessary I will say who we are.—I am Mrs. Dalbiac, wife of the Lieutenant-Colonel of the Fourth Light Dragoons, and this lady is the wife of Captain Prescott of the Seventh Fusileers. We went out to Christoval to look for our husbands, but found the army had moved.

Sentinel (incredulously)

" Wives ! "   Oh, not to-day !   I have heard such titles of courtesy afore ; but they never shake me.

" W " begins other female words than " wives ! "—
You'll have trouble, good dames, to get into
Salamanca to-night. You'll be challenged all the
way down, and shot without clergy if you can't give
the countersign.

Mrs. Prescott

Then surely you'll tell us what it is, good kind
man !

Sentinel

Well—have ye earned enough to pay for knowing ? Government wage is poor pickings for watching here in the rain. How much can ye stand ?

Mrs. Dalbiac

Half-a-dozen pesetas.

Sentinel

Very well, my dear. I was always tender-
hearted. Come along. (They advance and hand the
money.) The pass to-night is " Melchester Steeple."
That will take you into the town when the weather
clears. You won't have to cross the ford. You can
get temporary shelter in the shed there.

As the ladies move towards the shed the tramp of the
infantry draws near the ford, which the downfall has made to
purl more boisterously. The twain enter the shed, and the
dragoons look up inquiringly.

Mrs. Dalbiac (to dragoons)

The French are luckier than you are, men.
You'll have a wet advance across this ford, but they
have a dry retreat by the bridge at Alba.

SERGEANT OF PATROL (starting from a doze)

The moustachies a dry retreat ? Not they, my dear. A Spanish garrison is in the castle that commands the bridge at Alba.

MRS. DALBIAC

A peasant told us, if we understood rightly, that he saw the Spanish withdraw, and the enemy place a garrison there themselves.

The sergeant hastily calls up two troopers, who mount and ride off with the intelligence.

SERGEANT

You've done us a good turn, if it is true, darlin'. Not that Lord Wellington will believe it when he gets the news. . . . Why, if my eyes don't deceive me, ma'am, that's Colonel Dalbiac's lady !

MRS. DALBIAC

Yes, sergeant. I am over here with him, as you have heard, no doubt, and lodging in Salamanca. We lost our way, and got caught in the storm, and want shelter awhile.

SERGEANT

Certainly, ma'am. I'll give you an escort back as soon as the division has crossed and the weather clears.

MRS. PRESCOTT (anxiously)

Have you heard, sergeant, if there's to be a battle to-morrow ?

SERGEANT

Yes, ma'am. Everything shows it.

Mrs. Dalbiac (to Mrs. Prescott)

Our news would have passed us in. We have wasted six pesetas.

Mrs. Prescott (mournfully)

I don't mind that so much as that I have brought the children from Ireland. This coming battle frightens me !

Spirit of the Years

This is her prescient pang of widowhood.
Ere Salamanca clang to-morrow's close
She'll find her consort stiff among the slain !

The infantry regiments now reach the ford. The storm increases in strength, the stream flows more furiously ; yet the columns of foot enter it and begin crossing. The lightning is continuous ; the faint lantern in the ford-house is paled by the sheets of fire without, which flap round the bayonets of the crossing men and reflect upon the foaming torrent.

Chorus of Pities (aerial music)

The skies fling flame on this ancient land !
And drenched and drowned is the burnt blown sand
That spreads its mantle of yellow-grey
Round old Salmantica to-day ;
While marching men come, band on band,
Who read not as a reprimand
To mortal moils that, as 'twere planned
In mockery of their mimic fray,
     The skies fling flame.

Since sad Coruña's desperate stand
Horrors unsummed, with heavy hand,
Have smitten such as these ! But they
Still headily pursue their way,
Though flood and foe confront them, and
     The skies fling flame.

The whole of the English division gets across by degrees, and their invisible tramp is heard ascending the opposite heights as the lightnings dwindle and the spectacle disappears.

SCENE III

THE FIELD OF SALAMANCA

The battlefield — an undulating and sandy expanse — is lying under the sultry sun of a July afternoon. In the immediate left foreground rises boldly a detached dome-like hill known as the Lesser Arapeile, now held by English troops. Further back, and more to the right, rises another and larger hill of the kind—the Greater Arapeile ; this is crowned with French artillery in loud action, and the French marshal, MARMONT, Duke of RAGUSA, stands there. Further to the right, in the same plane, stretch the divisions of the French army. Still further to the right, in the distance, on the Ciudad Rodrigo highway, a cloud of dust denotes the English baggage-train seeking security in that direction. The city of Salamanca itself, and the river Tormes on which it stands, are behind the back of the spectator.

On the summit of the lesser hill, close at hand, WELLINGTON, glass at eye, watches the French division THOMIÈRE, which has become separated from the centre of the French army. Round and near him are aides and other officers, in animated conjecture on MARMONT's intent, which appears to be a move on the Ciudad Rodrigo road aforesaid, under the impression that the English are about to retreat that way.

The English commander descends from where he was standing to a nook under a wall, where a meal is roughly laid out. Some of his staff are already eating there. WELLINGTON takes a few mouthfuls without sitting down, walks back again, and looks through his glass at the battle as before. Balls from the French artillery fall around.

Enter his aide-de-camp, FITZROY SOMERSET.

FITZROY SOMERSET (hurriedly)

The French make movements of grave consequence— Extending to the left in mass, my lord.

WELLINGTON

I have just perceived as much ; but not the cause.

(He regards longer.)

Marmont's good genius is deserting him !

Shutting up his glass with a snap, WELLINGTON calls several aides and despatches them down the hill. He goes back behind the wall and takes some more mouthfuls.

By God, Fitzroy, if we shan't do it now !

(to SOMERSET).

Mon cher Alava, Marmont est perdu !

(to his SPANISH ATTACHÉ).

FITZROY SOMERSET

Thinking we mean no real attack on him,
He schemes to swoop on our retreating-line.

WELLINGTON

Ay ; and to cloak it by this cannonade.
With that in eye he has bundled leftwardly
Thomière's division ; mindless that thereby
His wing and centre's mutual maintenance
Dissolves into a yawning vacancy.
So be it. Good. His laxness is our luck !

As a result of the orders sent off by the aides, several British divisions advance across the French front on the Greater Arapeile and elsewhere. The French shower bullets into them ; but an English brigade under PACK assails the nearer French on the Arapeile, now beginning to cannonade the English in the hollows beneath.

Light breezes blow towards the French, and they get in their faces the dust-clouds and smoke from the masses of English in motion, and a powerful sun in their eyes.

MARMONT and his staff are sitting on the top of the Greater Arapeile only half a cannon-shot from WELLINGTON on the Lesser ; and, like WELLINGTON, he is gazing through his glass.

Spirit of Rumour

Appearing to behold the full-mapped mind
Of his opponent, Marmont arrows forth
Aide after aide towards the forest's hem,
To spirit on his troops out-trailing thence,
And prop the lone division Thomière,
For whose recall his voice has rung in vain.
Wellington mounts and seeks out Pakenham,
Who pushes to the arena from the right,
And, spurting to the left of Marmont's line,
Shakes Thomière with lunges leonine.

When the manœuvre's meaning hits his sense,
Marmont hies hotly to the imperilled place,
Where see him fall, sore smitten.— Bonnet rides
And dons the burden of the chief command,
Marking dismayed the Thomière column there
Shut up by Pakenham like bellows-folds
Against the English Fourth and Fifth hard by ;
And while thus crushed, Dragoon-Guards and Dragoons,
Under Le Marchant's hands (of Guernsey he),
Are launched upon them by Sir Stapleton,
And their scathed files are double-scathed anon.

Cotton falls wounded.   Pakenham's bayoneteers
Shape for the charge from column into rank ;
And Thomière finds death thereat point-blank !

Semichorus I of the Pities (aerial music)

In fogs of dust the cavalries hoof the ground ;
Their prancing squadrons shake the hills around :
Le Marchant's heavies bear with ominous bound
                    Against their opposites !

Semichorus II

A bullet crying along the cloven air
Gouges Le Marchant's groin and rankles there ;

In Death's white sleep he soon joins Thomière,
And all he has fought for, quits !

In the meantime the battle has become concentrated in the middle hollow, and WELLINGTON descends thither from the English Arapeile.

The fight grows fiercer. COLE and LEITH now fall wounded ; then BERESFORD, who directs the Portuguese, is struck down and borne away. On the French side fall BONNET who succeeded MARMONT in command, MANNE, CLAUSEL, and FEREY, the last hit mortally.

Now fortune sways in favour of the English, now in favour of the French. WELLINGTON sees that the crisis has come, and orders up his reserve. The fresh muscle and spirit turn the scale, and the French abandon the Greater Arapeile.

Their disordered main body retreats into the forest and disappears ; and just as darkness sets in, the English stand alone on the crest, the distant plain being lighted only by musket-flashes from the vanishing enemy. In the close foreground vague figures on horseback are audible in the gloom.

VOICE OF WELLINGTON

I thought they looked as they'd be scurrying soon !

VOICE OF AN AIDE

Foy bears into the wood in middling trim ;
Maucune strikes out for Alba-Castle bridge.

VOICE OF WELLINGTON

Speed the pursuit, then, towards the Huerta ford ;
Their only scantling of escape lies there ;
The river coops them semicircle-wise,
And we shall have them like a swathe of grass
Within a sickle's curve !

VOICE OF AIDE

Too late, my lord.
They are crossing by the aforesaid bridge at Alba.

VOICE OF WELLINGTON

Impossible.   The guns of Carlos rake it
Sheer from the castle walls.

VOICE OF AIDE

           Tidings have sped
Just now therefrom, to this undreamed effect :
That Carlos has withdrawn the garrison :
The French command the Alba bridge themselves !

VOICE OF WELLINGTON

Blast him, he's disobeyed his orders, then !
How happened this ?   How long has it been known ?

VOICE OF AIDE

Some ladies some few hours have rumoured it,
But unbelieved.

VOICE OF WELLINGTON

   Well, what's done can't be undone. . . .
By God, though, they've just saved themselves
     thereby
From capture to a man !

VOICE OF A GENERAL

          We've not struck ill,
Despite this slip, my lord. . . . And have you heard
That Colonel Dalbiac's wife rode in the charge
Behind her spouse to-day ?

VOICE OF WELLINGTON

        Did she though : did she !
Why that must be Susanna, whom I know—
A Wessex woman, blithe, and somewhat fair. . . .

Not but that great irregularities
Arise from such exploits.—And was it she
I noticed wandering to and fro below here,
Just as the French retired ?

Voice of another Officer

                    Ah no, my lord.
That was the wife of Prescott of the Seventh,
Hoping beneath the heel of hopelessness,
As these young women will !—Just about sunset
She found him lying dead and bloody there,
And in the dusk we bore them both away.[1]

Voice of Wellington

Well, I'm damned sorry for her.   Though I wish
The women-folk would keep them to the rear :
Much awkwardness attends their pottering round !

   The talking shapes disappear, and as the features of the field
grow undistinguishable the comparative quiet is broken by gay
notes from guitars and castanets in the direction of the city,
and other sounds of popular rejoicing at Wellington's victory.
People come dancing out from the town, and the merry-making
continues till midnight, when it ceases, and darkness and silence
prevail everywhere.

Semichorus I of the Years (aerial music)

What are Space and Time ?   A fancy !—
Lo, by Vision's necromancy
Muscovy will now unroll ;
Where for cork and olive-tree
Starveling firs and birches be.

---

[1] The writer has been unable to discover what became of this unhappy
lady and her orphaned infants.—(The foregoing note, which appeared in
the first edition of this drama, was the means of bringing from a
descendant of the lady referred to the information that she remarried,
and lived and died at Venice ; and that both her children grew up and did
well.—1909.)

SEMICHORUS II

Though such features lie afar
From events Peninsular,
These, amid their dust and thunder,
Form with those, as scarce asunder,
Parts of one compacted whole.

CHORUS

Marmont's Aide, then, like a swallow
Let us follow, follow, follow,
Over hill and over hollow,
Past the plains of Teute and Pole !

There is semblance of a sound in the darkness as of a rushing through the air.

SCENE IV

THE FIELD OF BORODINO

Borodino, seventy miles west of Moscow, is revealed in a bird's-eye view from a point above the position of the French Grand Army, advancing on the Russian capital.

We are looking east, towards Moscow and the army of Russia, which bars the way thither. The sun of latter summer, sinking behind our backs, floods the whole prospect, which is mostly wild, uncultivated land with patches of birch-trees. NAPOLÉON's army has just arrived on the scene, and is making its bivouac for the night, some of the later regiments not having yet come up. A dropping fire of musketry from skirmishers ahead keeps snapping through the air. The Emperor's tent stands in a ravine in the foreground amid the squares of the Old Guard. Aides and other officers are chatting outside. The point of view lowers.

Enter NAPOLÉON, who dismounts, speaks to some of his suite, and disappears inside his tent. An interval follows, during which the sun dips.

Enter COLONEL FABVRIER, aide-de-camp of MARMONT, just

arrived from Spain. An officer-in-waiting goes into NAPOLÉON'S
tent to announce FABVRIER, the Colonel meanwhile talking to
those outside.

AN AIDE

Important tidings thence, I make no doubt ?

FABVRIER

Marmont repulsed on Salamanca field,
And well-nigh slain, is the best tale I bring !

A silence. A coughing heard in NAPOLÉON'S tent.

Whose rheumy throat distracts the quiet so ?

AIDE

The Emperor's. He is thus the livelong day.

COLONEL FABVRIER is shown into the tent. An interval.
Then the husky accents of NAPOLÉON within, growing louder
and louder.

VOICE OF NAPOLÉON

If Marmont—so I gather from these lines—
Had let the English and the Spanish be,
They would have bent from Salamanca back,
Offering no battle, to our profiting !
We should have been delivered this disaster,
Whose bruit will harm us more than aught besides
That has befallen in Spain !

VOICE OF FABVRIER

                    I fear so, sire.

VOICE OF NAPOLÉON

He forced a conflict, to cull laurel crowns
Before King Joseph should arrive to share them !

VOICE OF FABVRIER

The army's ardour for your Majesty,
Its courage, its devotion to your cause,
Cover a myriad of the Marshal's sins.

VOICE OF NAPOLÉON

Why gave he battle without biddance, pray,
From the supreme commander ?   Here's the crime
Of insubordination, root of woes ! . . .
The time well chosen, and the battle won,
The English succours there had sidled off,
And their annoy in the Peninsula
Embarrassed us no more.   Behoves it me,
Some day, to face this Wellington myself !
Marmont too plainly is no match for him. . . . .
Thus he goes on : " To have preserved command
I would with joy have changed this early wound
For foulest mortal stroke at fall of day.
One baleful moment damnified the fruit
Of six weeks' wise strategics, whose result
Had loomed so certain ! "—(Satirically)   Well, we've
    but his word
As to their wisdom !   To define them thus
Would not have struck me but for his good prompt-
    ing ! . . .
No matter : On Moskowa's banks to-morrow
I'll mend his faults upon the Arapeile.
I'll see how I can treat this Russian horde
Which English gold has brought together here
From the four corners of the universe. . . .
Adieu.   You'd best go now and take some rest.

FABVRIER reappears from the tent and goes.   Enter DE
BAUSSET.

DE BAUSSET

The box that came—has it been taken in ?

An Officer

Yes, General. 'Tis laid behind a screen
In the outer tent. As yet his Majesty
Has not been told of it.

[DE BAUSSET goes into tent.

After an interval of murmured talk an exclamation bursts
from the EMPEROR. In a few minutes he appears at the tent
door, a valet following him bearing a picture. The EMPEROR's
face shows traces of emotion.

NAPOLÉON

Bring out a chair for me to poise it on.

Re-enter DE BAUSSET from the tent with a chair.

They all shall see it. Yes, my soldier-sons
Must gaze upon this son of mine own house
In art's presentment ! It will cheer their hearts.
That's a good light—just so.

He is assisted by DE BAUSSET to set up the picture in the
chair. It is a portrait of the young King of Rome playing at
cup-and-ball, the ball being represented as the globe. The
officers standing near are attracted round, and then the officers
and soldiers further back begin running up, till there is a great
crowd.

Let them walk past,
So that they see him all. The Old Guard first.

The Old Guard is summoned, and marches past surveying
the picture ; then other regiments.

SOLDIERS

The Emperor and the King of Rome for ever !

When they have marched past and withdrawn, and DE
BAUSSET has taken away the picture, NAPOLÉON prepares to
re-enter his tent. But his attention is attracted to the Russians.
He regards them through his glass.

Enter BESSIÈRES and RAPP.

NAPOLÉON

What slow, weird ambulation do I mark,
Rippling the Russian host ?

BESSIÈRES

                    A progress, sire,
Of all their clergy, vestmented, who bear
An image, said to work strange miracles.

NAPOLÉON watches. The Russian ecclesiastics pass through
the regiments, which are under arms, bearing the icon and other
religious insignia. The Russian soldiers kneel before it.

NAPOLÉON

Ay ! Not content to stand on their own strength,
They try to hire the enginry of Heaven.
I am no theologian, but I laugh
That men can be so grossly logicless,
When war, defensive or aggressive either,
Is in its essence Pagan, and opposed
To the whole gist of Christianity !

BESSIÈRES

'Tis to fanaticize their courage, sire.

NAPOLÉON

Better they'd wake up old Kutúzof.—Rapp,
What think you of to-morrow ?

RAPP

                    Victory ;
But, sire, a bloody one !

NAPOLÉON

So I foresee.

The scene darkens, and the fires of the bivouacs shine up ruddily, those of the French near at hand, those of the Russians in a long line across the mid-distance, and throwing a flapping glare into the heavens. As the night grows stiller the ballad-singing and laughter from the French mixes with a slow singing of psalms from their adversaries.

The two multitudes lie down to sleep, and all is quiet but for the sputtering of the green wood fires, which, now that the human tongues are still, seem to hold a conversation of their own.

SCENE V

THE SAME

The prospect lightens with dawn, and the sun rises red. The spacious field of battle is now distinct, its ruggedness being bisected by the great road from Smolensk to Moscow, which runs centrally from beneath the spectator to the furthest horizon. The field is also crossed by the stream Kalotcha, flowing from the right-centre foreground to the left-centre background, thus forming an X with the road aforesaid, inter-secting it in mid-distance at the village of Borodino.

Behind this village the Russians have taken their stand in close masses. Opposite stand the French, who have in their centre the Shevardino redoubt to the right of the Kalotcha. Here NAPOLÉON, in his usual blue-grey uniform, white waist-coat, and white leather breeches, chooses his position with BERTHIER and other officers of his suite.

DUMB SHOW

It is six o'clock, and the firing of a single cannon on the French side proclaims that the battle is beginning. There is a roll of drums, and the right-centre masses, glittering in the level shine, advance under NEY and DAVOUT and throw them-selves on the Russians, here defended by redoubts.

The French enter the redoubts, whereupon a slim, small man, GENERAL BAGRATION, brings across a division from the Russian right and expels them resolutely.

Semenovskoye is a commanding height opposite the right of the French, and held by the Russians. Cannon and columns, infantry and cavalry, assault it by tens of thousands, but cannot take it.

Aides gallop through the screeching shot and haze of smoke and dust between NAPOLÉON and his various marshals. The Emperor walks about, looks through his glass, goes to a camp-stool, on which he sits down, and drinks glasses of spirits and hot water to relieve his still violent cold, as may be discovered from his red eyes, raw nose, rheumatic manner when he moves, and thick voice in giving orders.

SPIRIT OF THE PITIES

So he fulfils the inhuman antickings
He thinks imposed upon him. . . . What says he?

SPIRIT OF RUMOUR

He says it is the sun of Austerlitz!

The Russians, so far from being driven out of their redoubts, issue from them towards the French. But they have to retreat, BAGRATION and his Chief of Staff being wounded. NAPOLÉON sips his grog hopefully, and orders a still stronger attack on the great redoubt in the centre.

It is carried out. The redoubt becomes the scene of a huge massacre. In other parts of the field also the action almost ceases to be a battle, and takes the form of wholesale butchery by the thousand, now advantaging one side, now the other.

SPIRIT OF THE YEARS

Thus do the mindless minions of the spell
In mechanized enchantment sway and show
A Will that wills above the will of each,
Yet but the will of all conjunctively;
A fabric of excitement, web of rage,
That permeates as one stuff the weltering whole.

SPIRIT OF THE PITIES

The ugly horror grossly regnant here
Wakes even the drowsed half-drunken Dictator
To all its vain uncouthness!

Spirit of Rumour

>   *Murat cries*
> *That on this much-anticipated day*
> *Napoléon's genius flags inoperative.*

The firing from the top of the redoubt has ceased. The French have got inside. The Russians retreat upon their rear, and fortify themselves on the heights there. Poniatowski furiously attacks them. But the French are worn out, and fall back to their station before the battle. So the combat dies resultlessly away. The sun sets, and the opposed and exhausted hosts sink to lethargic repose. Napoléon enters his tent in the midst of his lieutenants, and night descends.

Shade of the Earth

> *The fumes of nitre and the reek of gore*
> *Make my airs foul and fulsome unto me!*

Spirit Ironic

> *The natural nausea of a nurse, dear Dame.*

Spirit of Rumour

> *Strange : even within that tent no notes of joy*
> *Throb as at Austerlitz!* (signifying Napoléon's tent).

Spirit of the Pities

>   *But mark that roar—*
> *A mash of men's crazed cries entreating mates*
> *To run them through and end their agony;*
> *Boys calling on their mothers, veterans*
> *Blaspheming God and man.   Those shady shapes*
> *Are horses, maimed in myriads, tearing round*
> *In maddening pangs, the harnessings they wear*
> *Clanking discordant jingles as they tear!*

Spirit of the Years

It is enough.   Let now the scene be closed.

The night thickens.

SCENE VI

MOSCOW

The foreground is an open place amid the ancient irregular streets of the city, which disclose a jumble of architectural styles, the Asiatic prevailing over the European. A huge triangular white-walled fortress rises above the churches and coloured domes on a hill in the background, the central feature of which is a lofty tower with a gilded cupola, the Ivan Tower. Beneath the battlements of this fortress the Moskva River flows.

An unwonted rumbling of wheels proceeds from the cobble-stoned streets, accompanied by an incessant cracking of whips.

DUMB SHOW

Travelling carriages, teams, and waggons, laden with pictures, carpets, glass, silver, china, and fashionable attire, are rolling out of the city, followed by foot-passengers in streams, who carry their most precious possessions on their shoulders. Others bear their sick relatives, caring nothing for their goods, and mothers go laden with their infants. Others drive their cows, sheep, and goats, causing much obstruction. Some of the populace, however, appear apathetic and bewildered, and stand in groups asking questions.

A thin man with piercing eyes gallops about and gives stern orders.

Spirit of the Pities

Whose is the form seen ramping restlessly,
Geared as a general, keen-eyed as a kite,
Mid this mad current of close-filed confusion ;
High-ordering, smartening progress in the slow,

And goading those by their own thoughts o'er-goaded ;
Whose emissaries knock at every door
In rhythmal rote, and groan the great events
The hour is pregnant with ?

SPIRIT OF THE YEARS

Rostopchin he,
The city governor, whose name will ring
Far down the forward years uncannily !

SPIRIT OF RUMOUR

His arts are strange, and strangely do they move him :—
To store the stews with stuffs inflammable,
To bid that pumps be wrecked, captives enlarged
And primed with brands for burning, are the intents
His warnings to the citizens outshade !

When the bulk of the populace has passed out eastwardly the Russian army retreating from Borodino also passes through the city and into the country beyond without a halt. They mostly move in solemn silence, though many soldiers rush from their ranks and load themselves with spoil.

When they are got together again and have marched out, there goes by on his horse a strange scarred old man with a foxy look, a swollen neck and head, and a hunched figure. He is KUTÚZOF, surrounded by his lieutenants. Away in the distance by other streets and bridges with other divisions pass in like manner GENERALS BENNIGSEN, BARCLAY DE TOLLY, DOKHTÓROF, the mortally wounded BAGRATION in a carriage, and other generals, all in melancholy procession one way, like autumnal birds of passage. Then the rear-guard passes under MILORADOVITCH.

Next comes a procession of another kind.

A long string of carts with wounded men is seen, which trails out of the city behind the army. Their clothing is soiled with dried blood, and the bandages that enwrap them are caked with it.

The greater part of this migrant multitude takes the high road to Vladimir.

SCENE VII

THE SAME. OUTSIDE THE CITY

A hill forms the foreground, called the Hill of Salutation, near the Smolensk road.

Herefrom the city appears as a splendid panorama, with its river, its gardens, and its curiously grotesque architecture of domes and spires. It is the peacock of cities to Western eyes, its roofs twinkling in the rays of the September sun, amid which the ancient citadel of the Tsars—the Kremlin—forms a centre-piece.

There enter on the hill at a gallop NAPOLÉON, MURAT, EUGÈNE, NEY, DARU, and the rest of the Imperial staff. The French advance-guard is drawn up in order of battle at the foot of the hill, and the long columns of the Grand Army stretch far in the rear. The Emperor and his marshals halt, and gaze at Moscow.

NAPOLÉON

Ha! There she is at last. And it was time.

He looks round upon his army, its numbers attenuated to one-fourth of those who crossed the Niemen so joyfully.

Yes: it was time. . . . *Now* what says Alexander!

DARU

This is a foil to Salamanca, sire!

DAVOUT

What scores of bulbous church-tops gild the sky!
Souls must be rotten in this region, sire,
To need so much repairing!

NAPOLÉON

            Ay—no doubt. . . .
Prithee march briskly on, to check disorder,

                (to Murat).

Hold word with the authorities forthwith,

                (to Durasnel).

Tell them that they may swiftly swage their fears,
Safe in that mercy I by rule extend
To vanquished ones. I wait the city keys,
And will receive the Governor's submission
With courtesy due. Eugène will guard the gate
To Petersburg there leftward. You, Davout,
The gate to Smolensk in the centre here
Which we shall enter by.

VOICES OF ADVANCE-GUARD

            Moscow! Moscow!
This, this is Moscow city. Rest at last!

The words are caught up in the rear by veterans who have
entered the chief capitals of Europe except London, and are
echoed from rank to rank. There is a far-extended clapping
of hands, like the babble of waves, and companies of foot run
in disorder towards high ground to behold the spectacle,
waving their shakos on their bayonets.

The army now marches on, and NAPOLÉON and his suite
disappear citywards from the Hill of Salutation.

The day wanes ere the host has passed, and dusk begins to
prevail, when tidings reach the rear-guard that cause dismay.
They have been sent back lip by lip from the front.

SPIRIT IRONIC

An anticlimax to Napoléon's dream!

SPIRIT OF RUMOUR

They say no Governor attends with keys
To offer his submission gracefully.

The streets are solitudes, the houses sealed,
And stagnant silence reigns, save where intrudes
The rumbling of their own artillery wheels,
And their own foot-files' measured march along.
" Moscow deserted ?   What a monstrous thing ! "—
He shrugs his shoulders soon, contemptuously ;
" This, then, is how Muscovy fights ! " cries he.
    Meanwhile Murat has gained the Kremlin gates,
And finds them closed against him.   Battered these,
The fort reverberates vacant as the streets
But for some grinning wretches gaoled there.
Enchantment seems to sway from quay to keep,
And lock commotion in a century's sleep.

NAPOLÉON, reappearing in front of the city, follows MURAT
into it, and is again lost to view. He has entered the Kremlin.
    An interval. Something becomes visible on the summit of
the Ivan Tower.

CHORUS OF RUMOURS (aerial music)

Mark you thereon a small lone figure gazing
Upon his hard-gained goal ?   It is He !
The startled crows, their broad black pinions raising,
Forsake their haunts, and wheel disquietedly.

The scene slowly darkens.

Midnight hangs over the city. In the blackness to the
north of where the Kremlin stands appears what at first sight
seems a lurid, malignant star. It waxes larger. Almost simultaneously a north-east wind rises, and the light glows and
sinks with the gusts, proclaiming a fire, which soon grows
large enough to irradiate the fronts of adjacent buildings,
and to show that it is creeping on towards the Kremlin itself,
the walls of that fortress which face the flames emerging from
their previous shade.
    The fire can be seen breaking out also in numerous other
quarters. All the conflagrations increase, and become, as those
at first detached group themselves together, one huge furnace,
whence streamers of flame reach up to the sky, brighten the
landscape far around, and show the houses as if it were day.
The blaze gains the Kremlin, and licks its walls, but does not
kindle it. Explosions and hissings are constantly audible,

amid which can be fancied cries and yells of people caught
in the combustion.   Large pieces of canvas aflare sail away
on the gale like balloons.   Cocks crow, thinking it sunrise,
ere they are burnt to death.

SCENE VIII

THE SAME.   THE INTERIOR OF THE KREMLIN

A chamber containing a bed on which NAPOLÉON has been
lying.   It is not yet daybreak, and the flapping light of the
conflagration without shines in at the narrow windows.
    NAPOLÉON is discovered dressed, but in disorder and un-
shaven.   He is walking up and down the room in agitation.
There are present CAULAINCOURT, BESSIÈRES, and many of
the marshals of his guard, who stand in silent perplexity.

NAPOLÉON (sitting down on the bed)

No : I'll not go !   It is themselves who have done it.
My God, they are Scythians and barbarians still !

Enter MORTIER (just made Governor).

MORTIER

Sire, there's no means of fencing with the flames.
My creed is that these scurvy Muscovites,
Knowing our men's repute for recklessness,
Have fired the town, as if 'twere we had done it,
To burn our weary warriors and yourself
As by our own crazed act !

GENERAL LARIBOISIÈRE, an aged man, enters and approaches NAPOLÉON.

LARIBOISIÈRE

                    The wind howls higher !
Will you permit one so full-summed in years,
One so devoted, sire, to speak his mind ?

It is that your long lingering here entails
Much risk for you, your army, and ourselves,
In the embarrassment it throws on us
While taking steps to seek security,
By hindering venturous means.

Enter MURAT, PRINCE EUGÈNE, and the PRINCE OF NEUF-CHÂTEL.

MURAT

There is no choice
But leaving, sire.   Enormous bulks of powder
Lie housed beneath us ; and outside these panes
A park of our artillery stands unscreened.

NAPOLÉON (saturninely)

What I have won I disincline to cede !

VOICE OF A GUARD (without)

The Kremlin is aflame !

They look at each other.   Two officers of NAPOLÉON's guard
and an interpreter enter, with one of the Russian military
police as a prisoner.

FIRST OFFICER

We have caught this man
Firing the Kremlin : yea, in the very act !
It is extinguished temporarily,
We know not for how long.

NAPOLÉON

Inquire of him
What Satan set him on.   (They inquire.)

SECOND OFFICER

The governor,
He says ; the Count Rostopchin, sire.

Napoléon

So ! Even the ancient Kremlin is not sanct
From their infernal scheme ! Go, take him out ;
Make him a quick example to the rest.

*Exeunt guards with their prisoner to the court below,
whence a musket-volley resounds in a few minutes. Meanwhile
the flames pop and spit more loudly, and the window-panes of
the room they stand in crack and fall in fragments.*

Incendiarism afoot, and we unware
Of what foul tricks may follow, I will go.
Outwitted here, we'll march on Petersburg,
The devil if we won't !

The marshals murmur and shake their heads.

Bessières

　　　　　　　Your pardon, sire,
But we are all convinced that weather, time,
Provisions, roads, equipment, mettle, mood,
Serve not for such a perilous enterprise.

Napoléon remains in gloomy silence. Enter Berthier.

Napoléon (apathetically)

Well, Berthier. More misfortunes ?

Berthier

　　　　　　　　News is brought,
Sire, of the Russian army's whereabouts.
That fox Kutúzof, after marching east
As if he were conducting his whole force
To Vladimir, when at the Riazan Road
Down-doubled sharply south, and in a curve
Has wheeled round Moscow, making for Kalouga,
To strike into our base, and cut us off.

MURAT

Another reason against Petersburg !
Come what come may, we must defeat that army,
To keep a sure retreat through Smolensk on
To Lithuania.

NAPOLÉON (jumping up)

I must act !   We'll leave,
Or we shall let this Moscow be our tomb.
May Heaven curse the author of this war—
Ay, him, that Russian minister, self-sold
To England, who fomented it.—'Twas he
Dragged Alexander into it, and me !

The marshals are silent with looks of incredulity, and
Caulaincourt shrugs his shoulders.

Now no more words ; but hear.   Eugène and Ney
With their divisions fall straight back upon
The Petersburg and Zwenigarod Roads ;
Those of Davout upon the Smolensk route.
I will retire meanwhile to Petrowskoi.
Come, let us go.

NAPOLÉON and the marshals move to the door.   In leaving,
the Emperor pauses and looks back.

I fear that this event
Marks the beginning of a train of ills. . . .
Moscow was meant to be my rest,
My refuge, and—it vanishes away !

[Exeunt NAPOLÉON, marshals, etc.

The smoke grows denser and obscures the scene.

SCENE IX

THE ROAD FROM SMOLENSKO INTO LITHUANIA

The season is far advanced towards winter. The point of observation is high amongst the clouds, which, opening and shutting fitfully to the wind, reveal the earth as a confused expanse merely.

SPIRIT OF THE PITIES

Where are we ?   And why are we where we are ?

SHADE OF THE EARTH

Above a wild waste garden-plot of mine
Nigh bare in this late age, and now grown chill,
Lithuania called by some.   I gather not
Why we haunt here, where I can work no charm
Either upon the ground or over it.

SPIRIT OF THE YEARS

The wherefore will unfold.   The rolling brume
That parts, and joins, and parts again below us
In ragged restlessness, unscreens by fits
The quality of the scene.

SPIRIT OF THE PITIES

I notice now
Primeval woods, pine, birch—the skinny growths
That can sustain life well where earth affords
But sustenance elsewhere yclept starvation.

SPIRIT OF THE YEARS

And what see you on the far land-verge there,
Labouring from eastward towards our longitude ?

SPIRIT OF THE PITIES

An object like a dun-piled caterpillar,
Shuffling its length in painful heaves along,
Hitherward. . . . Yea, what is this Thing we see
Which, moving as a single monster might,
Is yet not one but many ?

SPIRIT OF THE YEARS

            Even the Army
Which was once called the Grand ; now in retreat
From Moscow's muteness, urged by That within it ;
Together with its train of followers—
Men, matrons, babes, in brabbling multitudes.

SPIRIT OF THE PITIES

And why such flight ?

SPIRIT OF THE YEARS

            Recorders, rise and say.

RECORDING ANGEL I (in minor plain-song)

The host has turned from Moscow where it lay,
And Israel-like, moved by some master-sway,
Is made to wander on and waste away !

ANGEL II

By track of Tarutino first it flits ;
Thence swerving, strikes at old Jaroslawitz ;
The which, accurst by slaughtering swords, it quits.

ANGEL I

Harassed, it treads the trail by which it came,
To Borodino, field of bloodshot fame,
Whence stare unburied horrors beyond name !

ANGEL II

And so and thus it nears Smolensko's walls,
And, stayed its hunger, starts anew its crawls,
Till floats down one white morsel, which appals.

What has floated down from the sky upon the Army is a flake of snow. Then come another and another, till natural features, hitherto varied with the tints of autumn, are confounded, and all is phantasmal grey and white.

The caterpillar shape still creeps laboriously nearer, but instead of increasing in size by the rules of perspective, it gets more attenuated, and there are left upon the ground behind it minute parts of itself, which are speedily flaked over, and remain as white pimples by the wayside.

SPIRIT OF THE YEARS

These atoms that drop off are snuffed-out souls
Who are enghosted by the caressing snow.

Pines rise mournfully on each side of the nearing object; ravens in flocks advance with it overhead, waiting to pick out the eyes of strays who fall. The snowstorm increases, descending in tufts which can hardly be shaken off. The sky seems to join itself to the land. The marching figures drop rapidly, and almost immediately become white grave-mounds.

Endowed with enlarged powers of audition as of vision, we are struck by the mournful taciturnity that prevails. Nature is mute. Save for the incessant flogging of the wind-broken and lacerated horses there are no sounds.

With growing nearness more is revealed. In the glades of the forest, parallel to the French columns, columns of Russians are seen to be moving. And when the French presently reach Krasnoye they are surrounded by packs of cloaked Cossacks, bearing lances like huge needles a dozen feet long. The fore-part of the French army gets through the town; the rear is assaulted by these and by infantry and artillery.

SPIRIT OF THE PITIES

The strange, one-eyed, white-shakoed, scarred old man,
Ruthlessly heading every onset made,
I seem to recognize.

SPIRIT OF THE YEARS

Kutúzof he :
The ceaselessly-attacked one, Michael Ney ;
A pair as stout as thou, Earth, ever hast twinned !
Kutúzof, ten years younger, would extirp
The invaders, and our drama finish here,
With Bonaparte a captive or a corpse.
But he is old ; death even has beckoned him ;
And thus the so near-seeming happens not.

NAPOLÉON himself can be discerned amid the rest, marching on foot through the snowflakes, in a fur coat and with a stout staff in his hand. Further back NEY is visible with the remains of the rear.

There is something behind the regular columns like an articulated tail, and as they draw on, it shows itself to be a disorderly rabble of followers of both sexes. So the whole miscellany arrives at the foreground, where it is checked by a large river across the track. The soldiers themselves, like the rabble, are in motley raiment, some wearing rugs for warmth, some quilts and curtains, some even petticoats and other women's clothing. Many are delirious from hunger and cold.

But they set about doing what is a necessity for the least hope of salvation, and throw a bridge across the stream.

The point of vision descends to earth, close to the scene of action.

SCENE X

THE BRIDGE OF THE BERESINA

The bridge is over the Beresina at Studzianka. On each side of the river are swampy meadows, now hard with frost, while further back are dense forests. Ice floats down the deep black stream in large cakes.

DUMB SHOW

The French sappers are working up to their shoulders in the water at the building of the bridge. Those so immersed work till, stiffened with ice to immobility, they die from the chill, when others succeed them.

Cavalry meanwhile attempt to swim their horses across, and some infantry try to wade through the stream.

Another bridge is begun hard by, the construction of which advances with greater speed ; and it becomes fit for the passage of carriages and artillery.

NAPOLÉON is seen to come across to the homeward bank, which is the foreground of the scene. A good portion of the army also, under DAVOUT, NEY, and OUDINOT, lands by degrees on this side. But VICTOR's corps is yet on the left or Moscow side of the stream, moving towards the bridge, and PARTON-NEAUX with the rear-guard, who has not yet crossed, is at Borissow, some way below, where there is an old permanent bridge partly broken.

Enter with speed from the distance the Russians under TCHAPLITZ. More under TCHICHAGOFF enter the scene down the river on the left or further bank, and cross by the old bridge of Borissow. But they are too far from the new crossing to intercept the French as yet.

PLATOFF with his Cossacks next appears on the stage which is to be such a tragic one. He comes from the forest and approaches the left bank likewise. So also does WITTGEN-STEIN, who strikes in between the uncrossed VICTOR and PAR-TONNEAUX. PLATOFF thereupon descends on the latter, who surrenders with the rear-guard ; and thus seven thousand more are cut off from the already emaciated Grand Army.

TCHAPLITZ, of TCHICHAGOFF's division, has meanwhile got round by the old bridge at Borissow to the French side of the new one, and attacks OUDINOT ; but he is repulsed with the strength of despair. The French lose a further five thousand in this.

We now look across the river at VICTOR and his division, not yet over, and still defending the new bridges. WITTGEN-STEIN descends upon him ; but he holds his ground.

The determined Russians set up a battery of twelve cannon, so as to command the two new bridges, with the confused crowd of soldiers, carriages, and baggage, pressing to cross. The battery discharges into the surging multitude. More Russians come up, and, forming a semicircle round the bridges and the mass of French, fire yet more hotly on them with round shot and canister. As it gets dark the flashes light up the strained faces of the fugitives. Under the discharge and the weight of traffic, the bridge for the artillery gives way, and the throngs upon it roll shrieking into the stream and are drowned.

SEMICHORUS I OF THE PITIES (aerial music)

*So loudly swell their shrieks as to be heard above the
roar of guns and the wailful wind,
Giving in one brief cry their last wild word on that
mock life through which they have harlequined!*

SEMICHORUS II

*To the other bridge the living heap betakes itself, the
weak pushed over by the strong;
They loop together by their clutch like snakes; in knots
they are submerged and borne along.*

CHORUS

*Then women are seen in the waterflow—limply bearing
their infants between wizened white arms stretching
above;
Yea, motherhood, sheerly sublime in her last despairing, and lighting her darkest declension with
limitless love.*

Meanwhile TCHICHAGOFF has come up with his twenty-seven
thousand men, and falls on OUDINOT, NEY, and "the Sacred
Squadron." Altogether we see forty or fifty thousand assailing
eighteen thousand half-naked, badly armed wretches, emaciated
with hunger and encumbered with several thousands of sick,
wounded, and stragglers.

VICTOR and his rear-guard, who have protected the bridges
all day, come over themselves at last. No sooner have they
done so than the final bridge is set on fire. Those who are upon
it burn or drown; those who are on the further side have
lost their last chance, and perish either in attempting to wade
the stream or at the hands of the Russians.

SEMICHORUS I OF THE PITIES (aerial music)

*What will be seen in the morning light?
What will be learnt when the spring breaks bright,
And the frost unlocks to the sun's soft sight?*

SEMICHORUS II

Death in a thousand motley forms ;
Charred corpses hooking each other's arms
In the sleep that defies all war's alarms !

CHORUS

Pale cysts of souls in every stage,
Still bent to embraces of love or rage,—
Souls passed to where History pens no page.

The flames of the burning bridge go out as it consumes to
the water's surface, and darkness mantles all, nothing continuing but the purl of the river and the clickings of floating ice.

SCENE XI

THE OPEN COUNTRY BETWEEN SMORGONI AND WILNA

The winter is more merciless, and snow continues to fall
upon a deserted expanse of unenclosed land in Lithuania.
Some scattered birch bushes merge in a forest in the background.

It is growing dark, though nothing distinguishes where the
sun sets. There is no sound except that of a shuffling of feet
in the direction of a bivouac. Here are gathered tattered men
like skeletons. Their noses and ears are frost-bitten, and pus is
oozing from their eyes.

These stricken shades in a limbo of gloom are among the
last survivors of the French army. Few of them carry arms.
One squad, ploughing through snow above their knees, and
with icicles dangling from their hair that clink like glass-
lustres as they walk, go into the birch wood, and are heard
chopping. They bring back boughs, with which they make a
screen on the windward side, and contrive to light a fire.
With their swords they cut rashers from a dead horse, and
grill them in the flames, using gunpowder for salt to eat them
with. Two others return from a search, with a dead rat and
some candle-ends. Their meal shared, some try to repair their

gaping shoes and to tie up their feet, that are chilblained to the bone.

A straggler enters, who whispers to one or two soldiers of the group. A shudder runs through them at his words.

FIRST SOLDIER (dazed)

What—gone, do you say ? Gone ?

STRAGGLER

Yes, I say gone !
He left us at Smorgoni hours ago.
The Sacred Squadron even he has left behind.
By this time he's at Warsaw or beyond,
Full pace for Paris.

SECOND SOLDIER (jumping up wildly)

Gone ? How did he go ?
No, surely ! He could not desert us so !

STRAGGLER

He started in a carriage, with Roustan
The Mameluke on the box : Caulaincourt, too,
Was inside with him. Monton and Duroc
Rode on a sledge behind.—The order bade
That we should not be told it for a while.

Other soldiers spring up as they realize the news, and stamp hither and thither, impotent with rage, grief, and despair, many in their physical weakness sobbing like children.

SPIRIT SINISTER

*Good. It is the selfish and unconscionable char-
acters who are so much regretted.*

STRAGGLER

He felt, or feigned, he ought to leave no longer
A land like Prussia 'twixt himself and home.

There was great need for him to go, he said,
To quiet France, and raise another army
That shall replace our bones.

SEVERAL (distractedly)

> Deserted us !
Deserted us !—O, after all our pangs
We shall see France no more !

Some become insane, and go dancing round. One of them
sings.

MAD SOLDIER'S SONG

I

Ha, for the snow and hoar !
Ho, for our fortune's made !
We can shape our bed without sheets to spread,
  And our graves without a spade.
  So foolish Life adieu,
  And ingrate Leader too.
  —Ah, but we loved you true !
Yet—he-he-he ! and ho-ho-ho !—
  We'll never return to you.

II

What can we wish for more ?
Thanks to the frost and flood
We are grinning crones—thin bags of bones
  Who once were flesh and blood.
  So foolish Life adieu,
  And ingrate Leader too.
  —Ah, but we loved you true !
Yet—he-he-he ! and ho-ho-ho !—
  We'll never return to you.

Exhausted, they again crouch round the fire. Officers and
privates press together for warmth. Other stragglers arrive,
and sit at the backs of the first. With the progress of the
night the stars come out in unusual brilliancy, Sirius and those
in Orion flashing like stilettos ; and the frost stiffens.

The fire sinks and goes out; but the Frenchmen do not move. The day dawns, and still they sit on.

In the background enter some light horse of the Russian army, followed by KUTÚZOF himself and a few of his staff. He presents a terrible appearance now—bravely serving though slowly dying, his face puffed with the intense cold, his one eye staring out as he sits in a heap in the saddle, his head sunk into his shoulders. The whole detachment pauses at the sight of the French asleep. They shout; but the bivouackers give no sign.

KUTÚZOF

Go, stir them up ! We slay not sleeping men.

The Russians advance and prod the French with their lances.

RUSSIAN OFFICER

Prince, here's a curious picture. They are dead.

KUTÚZOF (with indifference)

Oh, naturally. After the snow was down
I marked a sharpening of the air last night.
We shall be stumbling on such frost-baked meats
Most of the way to Wilna.

OFFICER (examining the bodies)

They all sit
As they were living still, but stiff as horns ;
And even the colour has not left their cheeks,
Whereon the tears remain in strings of ice.—
It was a marvel they were not consumed :
Their clothes are cindered by the fire in front,
While at their back the frost has caked them hard.

KUTÚZOF

'Tis well. So perish Russia's enemies !

Exeunt KUTÚZOF, his staff, and the detachment of horse in the direction of Wilna ; and with the advance of day the snow resumes its fall, slowly burying the dead bivouackers.

SCENE XII

PARIS. THE TUILERIES

An antechamber to the EMPRESS MARIE LOUISE's bedroom, at half-past eleven on a December night. The DUCHESS OF MONTEBELLO and another lady-in-waiting are discovered talking to the Empress.

MARIE LOUISE

I have felt unapt for anything to-night,
And I will now retire.

> She goes into her child's room adjoining.

DUCHESS OF MONTEBELLO

     For some long while
There has come no letter from the Emperor,
And Paris brims with ghastly rumourings
About the far campaign.   Not being beloved,
The town is over dull for her alone.

> Re-enter MARIE LOUISE.

MARIE LOUISE

The King of Rome is sleeping in his cot
Sweetly and safe.   Now, ladies, I am going.

She withdraws. Her tiring-women pass through into her chamber. They presently return and go out. A manservant enters, and bars the window-shutters with numerous bolts. Exit manservant. The Duchess retires. The other lady-in-waiting rises to go into her bedroom, which adjoins that of the Empress.

Men's voices are suddenly heard in the corridor without. The lady-in-waiting pauses with parted lips. The voices grow louder. The lady-in-waiting screams.

MARIE LOUISE hastily re-enters in a dressing-gown thrown over her night-clothes.

MARIE LOUISE

Great God, what altercation can that be ?
I had just verged on sleep when it aroused me !

A thumping is heard at the door.

VOICE OF NAPOLÉON (without)

Holà ! Pray let me in ! Unlock the door !

LADY-IN-WAITING

Heaven's mercy on us ! What man may it be
At such an hour as this ?

MARIE LOUISE

O it is he !

The lady-in-waiting unlocks the door. NAPOLÉON enters, scarcely recognizable, in a fur cloak and hood over his ears. He throws off the cloak and discloses himself to be in the shabbiest and muddiest attire. Marie Louise is agitated almost to fainting.

SPIRIT IRONIC

Is it with fright or joy ?

MARIE LOUISE

I scarce believe
What my sight tells me ! Home, and in such sad
    garb !   [NAPOLÉON embraces her.

NAPOLÉON

I have had great work in getting in, my dear !
They failed to recognize me at the gates,

Being sceptical at my poor hackney-coach
And poorer baggage. I had to show my face
In a fierce light ere they would let me pass,
And even then they doubted till I spoke.—
What think you, dear, of such a tramp-like spouse ?

(He warms his hands at the fire.)

Ha—it is much more comfortable here
Than on the Russian plains !

MARIE LOUISE (timidly)

You have suffered there ?—
Your face is hollow, and has lines in it ;
No marvel that they did not know you !

NAPOLÉON

Yes :
Disasters many and swift have swooped on me !—
Since crossing—ugh !—the Beresina River
I have been compelled to come incognito ;
Ay—as a fugitive and outlaw quite.

MARIE LOUISE

We'll thank Heaven, anyhow, that you are safe.
I had gone to bed, and everybody almost !
What, now, do you require ? Some food of course ?

The child in the adjoining chamber begins to cry, awakened
by the loud tones of NAPOLÉON.

NAPOLÉON

Ah—that's his little voice ! I'll in and see him.

MARIE LOUISE

I'll come with you.

Napoléon and the Empress pass into the other room. The lady-in-waiting calls up yawning servants and gives orders. The servants go to execute them.

Re-enter Napoléon and Marie Louise. The lady-in-waiting goes out.

Napoléon

I have said it, dear !
All the disasters summed in the bulletin
Shall be repaired.

Marie Louise

And are they terrible ?

Napoléon

Have you not read the last-sent bulletin,
Dear friend ?

Marie Louise

No recent bulletin has come.

Napoléon

Ah—I must have outstripped it on the way !

Marie Louise

And where is the Grand Army ?

Napoléon

Oh—that's gone.

Marie Louise

Gone ? But—gone where ?

Napoléon

Gone all to nothing, dear.

MARIE LOUISE (incredulously)

But some six hundred thousand I saw pass
Through Dresden Russia-wards ?

NAPOLÉON (flinging himself into a chair)

      Well, those men lie—
Or most of them—in layers of bleaching bones
'Twixt here and Moscow. . . . I have been subdued ;
But by the elements ; and them alone.
Not Russia, but God's sky has conquered me !

   (With an appalled look she sits beside him.)

From the sublime to the ridiculous
There's but a step !—I have been saying it
Throughout the leagues of my long journey home—
And that step has been passed in this affair ! . . .
Yes, briefly, it is quite ridiculous,
Whichever way you look at it.—Ha-ha !

MARIE LOUISE (simply)

But those six hundred thousand throbbing throats
That cheered me deaf at Dresden, marching east
So full of youth and spirits—all bleached bones—
Ridiculous ? Can it be so, dear, to—
Their mothers, say ?

NAPOLÉON (with a twitch of displeasure)

     You scarcely understand.
I meant the enterprise, and not its stuff. . . .
I had no wish to fight, nor Alexander,
But circumstance impaled us each on each ;
The Genius who outshapes my destinies
Did all the rest ! Had I but hit success,
Imperial splendour would have worn a crown
Unmatched in long-scrolled Time ! . . . Well, leave
  that now.—
What do they know about all this in Paris ?

MARIE LOUISE

I cannot say.   Black rumours fly and croak
Like ravens through the streets, but come to me
Thinned to the vague !—Occurrences in Spain
Breed much disquiet with these other things.
Marmont's defeat at Salamanca field
Ploughed deep into men's brows.   The cafés say
Your troops must clear from Spain.

NAPOLÉON

                   We'll see to that !
I'll find a way to do a better thing ;
Though I must have another army first—
Three hundred thousand quite.   Fishes as good
Swim in the sea as have come out of it.
But to begin, we must make sure of France,
Disclose ourselves to the good folk of Paris
In daily outings as a family group,
The type and model of domestic bliss
(Which, by the way, we are).   And I intend,
Also, to gild the dome of the Invalides
In best gold leaf, and on a novel pattern.

MARIE LOUISE

To gild the dome, dear ?   Why ?

NAPOLÉON

               To give them something
To think about.   They'll take to it like children,
And argue in the cafés right and left
On its artistic points.—So they'll forget
The woes of Moscow.

    A chamberlain-in-waiting announces supper.   MARIE LOUISE
and NAPOLÉON go out.   The room darkens and the scene
closes.

ACT SECOND

SCENE I

It is the eve of the longest day in the ensuing year; also the eve of the battle of Vitoria. The English army in the Peninsula, and their Spanish and Portuguese allies, are bivouacking on the western side of the Plain, about six miles from the town.

On some high ground on the left mid-distance may be discerned the MARQUIS OF WELLINGTON's tent, with GENERALS HILL, PICTON, PONSONBY, GRAHAM, and others of his staff, going in and out in consultation on the momentous event impending. Near the foreground are some hussars sitting round a fire, the evening being damp; their horses are picketed behind. In the immediate front of the scene are some troop-officers talking.

FIRST OFFICER

This grateful rest of four-and-twenty hours
Is priceless for our jaded soldiery;
And we have reconnoitred largely, too;
So the slow day will not have slipped in vain.

SECOND OFFICER
(looking towards the headquarter tent)

By this time they must nearly have dotted down
The methods of our master-stroke to-morrow:
I have no clear conception of its plan,
Even in its leading lines. What is decided?

494

FIRST OFFICER

There are outshaping three supreme attacks,
As I decipher.   Graham's on the left,
To compass which he crosses the Zadorra,
And turns the enemy's right.   On our right, Hill
Will start at once to storm the Puebla crests.
The Chief himself, with us here in the centre,
Will lead on by the bridges Tres-Puentes
Over the ridge there, and the Mendoza bridge
A little further up.—That's roughly it ;
But much and wide discretionary power
Is left the generals all.

The officers walk away, and the stillness increases, so that the conversation at the hussars' bivouac, a few yards further back, becomes noticeable.

SERGEANT YOUNG [1]

I wonder, I wonder how Stourcastle is looking this summer night, and all the old folks there !

SECOND HUSSAR

You was born there, I think I've heard ye say, Sergeant ?

SERGEANT YOUNG

I was.   And though I ought not to say it, as father and mother are living there still, 'tis a dull place at times.   Now Budmouth-Regis was exactly to my taste when we were there with the Court that summer, and the King and Queen a-wambling about among us like the most everyday old man and woman you ever see.   Yes, there was plenty going on, and only a pretty step from home.   Altogether we had a fine time !

[1] Thomas Young of Sturminster-Newton ; served twenty-one years in the Fifteenth (King's) Hussars; died 1853 ; fought at Vitoria, Toulouse, and Waterloo.

THIRD HUSSAR

You walked with a girl there for some weeks, Sergeant, if my memory serves ?

SERGEANT YOUNG

I did. And a pretty girl 'a was. But nothing came on't. A month afore we struck camp she married a tallow-chandler's dipper of Little Nicholas Lane. I was a good deal upset about it at the time. But one gets over things !

SECOND HUSSAR

'Twas a low taste in the hussy, come to that.— Howsomever, I agree about Budmouth. I never had pleasanter times than when we lay there. You had a song on it, Sergeant, in them days, if I don't mistake ?

SERGEANT YOUNG

I had ; and have still. 'Twas made up after we left by our bandmaster that used to conduct in front of Gloucester Lodge at the King's Mess every afternoon.

The Sergeant is silent for a minute, then suddenly bursts into melody.

SONG

BUDMOUTH DEARS

I

When we lay where Budmouth Beach is,
O, the girls were fresh as peaches,
With their tall and tossing figures and their eyes of
blue and brown !

And our hearts would ache with longing
As we paced from our sing-songing,
With a smart *Clink! Clink!* up the Esplanade and
down.

II

They distracted and delayed us
By the pleasant pranks they played us,
And what marvel, then, if troopers, even of regi-
ments of renown,
On whom flashed those eyes divine, O,
Should forget the countersign, O,
As we tore *Clink! Clink!* back to camp above the
town.

III

Do they miss us much, I wonder,
Now that war has swept us sunder,
And we roam from where the faces smile to where
the faces frown ?
And no more behold the features
Of the fair fantastic creatures,
And no more *Clink! Clink!* past the parlours of the
town ?

IV

Shall we once again there meet them ?
Falter fond attempts to greet them ?
Will the gay sling-jacket [1] glow again beside the
muslin gown ?—
Will they archly quiz and con us
With a sideway glance upon us,
While our spurs *Clink! Clink!* up the Esplanade
and down ?

[Applause from the other hussars.

More songs are sung, the night gets darker, the fires go out,
and the camp sleeps.

---

[1] Hussars, it may be remembered, used to wear a pelisse, dolman, or
" sling-jacket " (as the men called it), which hung loosely over the shoulder.
The writer is able to recall the picturesque effect of this uniform.

SCENE II

THE SAME, FROM THE PUEBLA HEIGHTS

It is now day; but a summer fog pervades the prospect. Behind the fog is heard the roll of bass and tenor drums and the clash of cymbals, with notes of the popular march " The Downfall of Paris."

By degrees the fog lifts, and the Plain is disclosed. From this·elevation, gazing north, the expanse looks like the palm of a monstrous right hand, a little hollowed, some half-dozen miles across, wherein the ball of the thumb is roughly represented by heights to the east, on which the French centre has gathered; the " Mount of Mars " and of the " Moon " (the opposite side of the palm) by the position of the English on the left or west of the plain; and the " Line of Life " by the Zadorra, an unfordable river running from the town down the plain, and dropping out of it through a pass in the Puebla Heights to the south, just beneath our point of observation —that is to say, towards the wrist of the supposed hand. The left of the English army under GRAHAM would occupy the " mounts " at the base of the fingers; while the bent finger-tips might represent the Cantabrian Hills beyond the plain to the north or back of the scene.

From the aforesaid stony crests of Puebla the white town and church towers of Vitoria can be descried on a slope to the right-rear of the field of battle. A warm rain succeeds the fog for a short while, bringing up the fragrant scents from the fields, vineyards, and gardens, now in the full leafage of June.

DUMB SHOW

All the English forces converge forward—that is, eastwardly —the centre over the west ridges, the right through the Pass to the south, the left down the Bilbao road on the north-west, the bands of the divers regiments striking up the same quick march, " The Downfall of Paris."

SPIRIT OF THE YEARS

You see the scene.   And yet you see it not.
What do you notice now ?

There immediately is shown visually the electric state of mind that animates WELLINGTON, GRAHAM, HILL, KEMPT, PICTON, COLVILLE, and other responsible ones on the British side ; and on the French KING JOSEPH stationary on the hill overlooking his own centre, and surrounded by a numerous staff that includes his adviser MARSHAL JOURDAN, with, far away in the field, GAZAN, D'ERLON, REILLE, and other marshals. This vision, resembling as a whole the interior of a beating brain lit by phosphorescence, in an instant fades again back to the normal.

Anon we see the English hussars with their flying pelisses galloping across the Zadorra on one of the Tres-Puentes in the midst of the field, as had been planned, the English lines in the foreground under HILL pushing the enemy up the slopes ; and far in the distance, to the left of Vitoria, whiffs of grey smoke followed by low rumbles show that the left of the English army under GRAHAM is pushing on there.

Bridge after bridge of the half-dozen over the Zadorra is crossed by the British ; and WELLINGTON, in the centre with PICTON, seeing the hill and village of Arinez in front of him (eastward) to be weakly held, carries the regiments of the seventh and third divisions in a quick run towards it. Supported by the hussars, they ultimately fight their way to the top, in a chaos of smoke, flame, dust, shouts, and booming echoes, loud-voiced PICTON, in an old blue coat and round hat, swearing as he goes.

Meanwhile the French who are opposed to the English right, in the foreground, have been turned by HILL ; the heights are all abandoned, and the columns fall back in a confused throng by the road to Vitoria, hard pressed by the British, who capture abandoned guns amid indescribable tumult, till the French make a stand in front of the town.

SPIRIT OF THE PITIES

What's toward in the distance ?—say !

SEMICHORUS I OF RUMOURS (aerial music)

Fitfully flash strange sights there ; yea,
Unwonted spectacles of sweat and scare
Behind the French, that make a stand
With eighty cannon, match in hand.—

Upon the highway from the town to rear
 An eddy of distraction reigns,
 Where lumbering treasure, baggage-trains,
Padding pedestrians, haze the atmosphere.

Semichorus II

Men, women, and their children fly,
 And when the English over-high
Direct their death-bolts, on this billowy throng
 Alight the too far-ranging balls,
 Wringing out piteous shrieks and calls
From the pale mob, in monotones loud and long.

Semichorus I

To leftward of the distant din
 Reille meantime has been driven in
By Graham's measured overmastering might.—
 Henceforward, masses of the foe
 Withdraw, and, firing as they go,
Pass rightwise from the cockpit out of sight.

Chorus

The sunset slants an ochreous shine
 Upon the English knapsacked line,
 Whose glistering bayonets incline
As bends the hot pursuit across the plain ;
 And tardily behind them goes
 Too many a mournful load of those
 Found wound-weak ; while with stealthy crawl,
 As silence wraps the rear of all,
Cloaked creatures of the starlight strip the slain.

SCENE III

THE SAME.   THE ROAD FROM THE TOWN

With the going down of the sun the English army finds itself in complete possession of the mass of waggons and carriages distantly beheld from the rear—laden with pictures, treasure, flour, vegetables, furniture, finery, parrots, monkeys, and women—most of the male sojourners in the town having taken to their heels and disappeared across the fields.

The road is choked with these vehicles, the women they carry including wives, mistresses, actresses, dancers, nuns, and prostitutes, which struggle through droves of oxen, sheep, goats, horses, asses, and mules—a Noah's-ark of living creatures in one vast procession.

There enters rapidly in front of this throng a carriage containing KING JOSEPH BONAPARTE and an attendant, followed by another vehicle with luggage.

JOSEPH (inside carriage)

The bare unblinking truth hereon is this :
The Englishry are a pursuing army,
And we a flying brothel !   See our men—
They leave their guns to save their mistresses !

The carriage is fired upon from outside the scene.   The KING leaps from the vehicle and mounts a horse.

Enter at full gallop from the left CAPTAIN WYNDHAM and a detachment of the Tenth Hussars in chase of the King's carriage ;   and from the right a troop of French dragoons, who engage with the hussars and hinder pursuit.   Exit KING JOSEPH on horseback ;   afterwards the hussars and dragoons go out fighting.

The British infantry enter irregularly, led by a sergeant of the Eighty-seventh, mockingly carrying MARSHAL JOURDAN'S bâton.   The crowd recedes.   The soldiers ransack the King's carriages, cut from their frames canvases by Murillo, Velasquez, and Zurbaran, and use them as package-wrappers, throwing the papers and archives into the road.

They next go to a waggon in the background, which contains

a large chest. Some of the soldiers burst it with a crash. It is
full of money, which rolls into the road. The soldiers begin
scrambling, but are restored to order ; and they march on.

Enter more companies of infantry, out of control of their
officers, who are running behind. They see the dollars, and
take up the scramble for them; next ransacking other waggons
and abstracting therefrom uniforms, ladies' raiment, jewels,
plate, wines, and spirits.

Some array them in the finery, and one soldier puts on a
diamond necklace ; others load themselves with the money
still lying about the road. It begins to rain, and a private
who has lost his kit cuts a hole in the middle of a deframed
old master, and, putting it over his head, wears it as a poncho.

Enter WELLINGTON and others, grimy and perspiring.

FIRST OFFICER

The men are plundering in all directions !

WELLINGTON

Let 'em.   They've striven long and gallantly.
—What documents do I see lying there ?

SECOND OFFICER (examining)

The archives of King Joseph's court, my lord ;
His correspondence, too, with Bonaparte.

WELLINGTON

We must examine it.   It may have use.

Another company of soldiers enters, dragging some equipages
that have lost their horses by the traces being cut. The carriages contain ladies, who shriek and weep at finding themselves
captives.

What women bring they there ?

THIRD OFFICER

Mixed sorts, my lord.
The wives of many young French officers,
The mistresses of more—in male attire.

Yon elegant hussar is one, to wit ;
She so disguised is of a Spanish house,—
One of the generals' loves.

WELLINGTON

Well, pack them off
To-morrow to Pamplona, as you can ;
We've neither list nor leisure for their charms.
By God, I never saw so many wh——s
In all my life before !

[Exeunt WELLINGTON, officers, and infantry.

A soldier enters with his arm round a lady in rich costume.

SOLDIER

We must be married, my dear.

LADY (not knowing his language)

Anything, sir, if you'll spare my life !

SOLDIER

There's neither parson nor clerk here.   But that
don't matter—hey ?

LADY

Anything, sir, if you'll spare my life !

SOLDIER

And if we've got to unmarry at cockcrow, why,
so be it—hey ?

LADY

Anything, sir, if you'll spare my life !

SOLDIER

A sensible 'ooman, whatever it is she says ; that
I can see by her pretty face. Come along then, my
dear. There'll be no bones broke, and we'll take
our lot with Christian resignation.

[*Exeunt soldier and lady.*

The crowd thins away as darkness closes in, and the growling
of artillery ceases, though the wheels of the flying enemy are
still heard in the distance. The fires kindled by the soldiers as
they make their bivouacs blaze up in the gloom, and throw
their glares a long way, revealing on the slopes of the hills
many suffering ones who have not yet been carried in. The
last victorious regiment comes up from the rear, fifing and
drumming ere it reaches its resting-place the last bars of " The
Downfall of Paris ":—

SCENE IV

A FÊTE AT VAUXHALL GARDENS

It is the Vitoria festival at Vauxhall. The orchestra of the
renowned gardens exhibits a blaze of lamps and candles arranged
in the shape of a temple, a great artificial sun glowing at the
top, and under it in illuminated characters the words " Vitoria "
and " Wellington." The band is playing the new air " The
Plains of Vitoria."

All round the colonnade of the rotunda are to be read in
like illumination the names of Peninsular victories, underneath
them figuring the names of British and Spanish generals who
led at those battles, surmounted by wreaths of laurel. The
avenues stretching away from the rotunda into the gardens
charm the eyes with their mild multitudinous lights, while
festoons of lamps hang from the trees elsewhere, and trans-
parencies representing scenes from the war.

The gardens and saloons are crowded, among those present
being the KING's sons—the DUKES OF YORK, CLARENCE, KENT,

and CAMBRIDGE—Ambassadors, peers, and peeresses, and other persons of quality, English and foreign.

In the immediate foreground on the left hand is an alcove, the interior of which is in comparative obscurity. Two foreign attachés enter it and sit down.

FIRST ATTACHÉ

Ah—now for the fireworks. They are under the direction of Colonel Congreve.

At the end of an alley, purposely kept dark, fireworks are discharged.

SECOND ATTACHÉ

Very good : very good.—This looks like the Duke of Sussex coming in, I think. Who the lady is with him I don't know.

Enter the DUKE OF SUSSEX in a Highland dress, attended by several officers in like attire. He walks about the gardens with LADY CHARLOTTE CAMPBELL.

FIRST ATTACHÉ

People have been paying a mighty price for tickets—as much as fifteen guineas has been offered, I hear. I had to walk up to the gates ; the number of coaches struggling outside prevented my driving near. It was as bad as the battle of Vitoria itself.

SECOND ATTACHÉ

So Wellington is made Field-Marshal for this achievement.

FIRST ATTACHÉ

Yes. By the by, you have heard of the effect of the battle upon the Conference at Reichenbach ? —that Austria is to join Russia and Prussia against

France ? So much for Napoléon's marriage ! I
wonder what he thinks of his respected father-in-
law now.

Second Attaché

Of course, an enormous subsidy is to be paid
to Francis by Great Britain for this face-about ?

First Attaché

Yes. As Bonaparte says, English guineas are
at the bottom of everything !—Ah, here comes
Caroline.

The PRINCESS OF WALES arrives, attended by LADY ANNE
HAMILTON and LADY GLENBERVIE. She is conducted forward
by the DUKE OF GLOUCESTER and COLONEL ST. LEDGER, and
wears a white satin train with a dark embroidered bodice,
and a green wreath with diamonds.

Repeated hurrahs greet her from the crowd. She bows
courteously.

Second Attaché

The people are staunch to her still ! . . . You
heard, sir, what Austrian Francis said when he
learnt of Vitoria ?—" A warm climate seems to
agree with my son-in-law no better than a cold one."

First Attaché

Ha-ha-ha !

Marvellous it is how this loud victory
Has couched the late blind Europe's Cabinets.
Would I could spell precisely what was phrased
'Twixt Bonaparte and Metternich at Dresden—
Their final word, I ween, till God knows when !—

Second Attaché

I own to feeling it a sorry thing
That Francis should take English money down
To throw off Bonaparte. 'Tis sordid, mean !
He is his daughter's husband after all.

FIRST ATTACHÉ

Ay ; yes ! . . . They say she knows not of it yet.

SECOND ATTACHÉ

Poor thing, I daresay it will harry her
When all's revealed.   But the inside on't is,
Since Castlereagh's return to power last year
Vienna, like Berlin and Petersburg,
Has harboured England's secret emissaries,
Primed, purse in hand, with the most lavish sums
To knit the league to drag Napoléon down. . . .
(More fireworks.) That's grand.—Here comes one Royal
    item more.

The DUCHESS OF YORK enters, attended by her ladies and
by the HON. B. CRAVEN and COLONEL BARCLAY.   She is
received with signals of respect.

FIRST ATTACHÉ

She calls not favour forth as Caroline can !

SECOND ATTACHÉ

To end my words :—Though happy for this realm,
Austria's desertion frankly is, by God,
Rank treachery !

FIRST ATTACHÉ

                Whatever it is, it means
Two hundred thousand swords for the Allies,
And enemies in batches for Napoléon
Leaping from unknown lairs.—Yes, something tells
    me
That this is the beginning of the end
For Emperor Bonaparte !

The PRINCESS OF WALES prepares to leave.   An English
diplomatist joins the attachés in the alcove.   The PRINCESS
and her ladies go out.

DIPLOMATIST

I saw you over here, and I came round. Cursed
hot and crowded, isn't it!

SECOND ATTACHÉ

What is the Princess leaving so soon for?

DIPLOMATIST

Oh, she has not been received in the Royal box
by the other members of the Royal Family, and
it has offended her, though she was told beforehand that she could not be. Poor devil! Nobody
invited her here. She came unasked, and she has
gone unserved.

FIRST ATTACHÉ

We shall have to go unserved likewise, I fancy.
The scramble at the buffets is terrible.

DIPLOMATIST

And the road from here to Marsh Gate is im-
passable. Some ladies have been sitting in their
coaches for hours outside the hedge there. We
shall not get home till noon to-morrow.

A VOICE (from the back)

Take care of your watches! Pickpockets!

FIRST ATTACHÉ

Good. That relieves the monotony a little.

Excitement in the throng. When it has subsided the band
strikes up a country dance, and stewards with white ribbons
and laurel leaves are seen bustling about.

SECOND ATTACHÉ

Let us go and look at the dancing. It is "Voulez-
vous danser "—no, it is not,—it is "Enrico"—two
ladies between two gentlemen.

> [They go from the alcove.

SPIRIT OF THE YEARS

From this phantasmagoria let us roam
To the chief wheel and capstan of the show,
Distant afar.   I pray you closely read
What I reveal—wherein each feature bulks
In measure with its value humanly.

The beholder finds himself, as it were, caught up on high,
and while the Vauxhall scene still dimly twinkles below, he
gazes southward towards Central Europe—the contorted and
attenuated écorché of the Continent appearing as in an earlier
scene, but now obscure under the summer stars.

Three cities loom out large : Vienna there,
Dresden, which holds Napoléon, over here,
And Leipzig, whither we shall shortly wing,
Out yonderwards.   'Twixt Dresden and Vienna
What thing do you discern?

SPIRIT OF THE PITIES

*   Something broad-faced,*
Flat-folded, parchment-pale, and in its shape
Rectangular; but moving like a cloud
The Dresden way.

SPIRIT OF THE YEARS

Yet gaze more closely on it.

SPIRIT OF THE PITIES

The object takes a letter's lineaments
Though swollen to mainsail measure,—magically,

I gather from your words ; and on its face
Are three vast seals, red—signifying blood
Must I suppose ?   It moves on Dresden town,
And dwarfs the city as it passes by.—
You say Napoléon's there ?

Spirit of the Years

*   The document,*
Sized to its big importance, as I told,
Bears in it formal declaration, signed,
Of war by Francis with his late-linked son,
The Emperor of France.   Now let us go
To Leipzig city, and await the blow.

A chaotic gloom ensues, accompanied by a rushing like that of a mighty wind.

ACT THIRD

SCENE I

The sitting-room of a private mansion. Evening. A large
stove-fire and candles burning. The October wind is heard
without, and the leaded panes of the old windows shake
mournfully.

SEMICHORUS I OF IRONIC SPIRITS (aerial music)

*We come ; and learn as Time's disordered deaf sands
    run*
That Castlereagh's diplomacy has wiled, waxed, won.
The beacons flash the fevered news to eyes keen bent
*That Austria's formal words of war are shaped, sealed,
    sent.*

SEMICHORUS II

*So ; Poland's three despoilers primed by Bull's gross
    pay*
*To stem Napoléon's might, he waits the weird wan
    day ;*
*His proffered peace declined with scorn, in fell force
    then*
*They front him, with yet ten-score thousand more
    massed men.*

At the back of the room CAULAINCOURT, DUKE OF VICENZA,
and JOUANNE, one of Napoléon's confidential secretaries, are

511

unpacking and laying out the Emperor's maps and papers.
In the foreground BERTHIER, MURAT, LAURISTON, and several
officers of Napoléon's suite, are holding a desultory conversation while they await his entry. Their countenances are
overcast.

MURAT

At least, the scheme of marching on Berlin
Is now abandoned.

LAURISTON

                    Not without high words :
He yielded, and gave order prompt for Leipzig,
But coldness and reserve have marked his mood
Towards us ever since.

BERTHIER

                    The march hereto
He has looked on as a retrogressive one,
And that, he ever holds, is courting woe.
To counsel it was doubtless full of risk,
And heaped us with responsibilities ;
—Yet 'twas your missive, sire, that settled it (to
      Murat).
How stirred he was !   " To Leipzig, or Berlin ? "
He kept repeating, as he drew and drew
Fantastic figures on the foolscap sheet,—
" The one spells ruin—t'other spells success,
And which is which ? "

MURAT (stiffly)

                    What better could I do ?
So far were the Allies from sheering off
As he supposed, that they had moved in march
Full fanfare hither !   I was duty-bound
To let him know.

LAURISTON

Assuming victory here,
If he should let the advantage slip him by
As on the Dresden day, he wrecks us all !
'Twas damnable—to ride back from the fight
Inside a coach, as though we had not won !

CAULAINCOURT (from the back)

The Emperor was ill : I have ground for knowing.

NAPOLÉON enters.

NAPOLÉON (buoyantly)

Comrades, the outlook promises us well !

MURAT (dryly)

Right glad are we you tongue such tidings, sire.
To us the stars have visaged differently ;
To wit : we muster outside Leipzig here
Levies one hundred and ninety thousand strong.
The enemy has mustered, *outside us,*
Three hundred and fifty thousand—if not more.

NAPOLÉON

All that is needful is to conquer them !
We are concentred here : they lie a-spread,
Which shrinks them to two-hundred-thousand
        power :—
Though that the urgency of victory
Is absolute, I admit.

MURAT

Yea ; otherwise
The issue will be worse than Moscow, sire !

MARMONT, DUKE OF RAGUSA (Wellington's adversary in Spain), is announced, and enters.

NAPOLÉON

Ah, Marmont ; bring you in particulars ?

MARMONT

Some sappers I have taken captive, sire,
Say the Allies will be at stroke with us
The morning next to-morrow's.—I am come,
Now, from the steeple-top of Liebenthal,
Where I beheld the enemy's fires bespot
The horizon round with raging eyes of flame :—
My vanward posts, too, have been driven in,
And I need succours—thrice ten thousand, say.

NAPOLÉON (coldly)

The enemy vexes not your vanward posts ;
You are mistaken.—Now, however, go ;
Cross Leipzig, and remain as the reserve.—
Well, gentlemen, my hope herein is this :
The first day to annihilate Schwarzenberg,
The second Blücher.   So shall we slip the toils
They are all madding to enmesh us in.

BERTHIER

Few are our infantry to fence with theirs !

NAPOLÉON (cheerfully)

We'll range them in two lines instead of three,
And so we shall look stronger by one-third.

BERTHIER (incredulously)

Can they be thus deceived, sire ?

NAPOLÉON

                Can they ?   Yes !
With all my practice I can err in numbers
At least one-quarter ; why not they one-third ?
Anyhow, 'tis worth trying at a pinch. . . .

        AUGEREAU is suddenly announced.

Good !   I've not seen him yet since he arrived.

        Enter AUGEREAU

Here you are then at last, old Augereau !
You have been looked for long.—But you are no
     more
The Augereau of Castiglione days ! (bitterly).

AUGEREAU

Nay, sire !   I still should be the Augereau
Of glorious Castiglione, could you give
The boys of Italy back again to me !

NAPOLÉON

Well, let it drop. . . . Only I notice round me
An atmosphere of scopeless apathy
Wherein I do not share.

AUGEREAU

              There are reasons, sire,
Good reasons, for despondence !   As I came
I learnt, past question, that Bavaria
Swerves on the very pivot of desertion.
This adds some threescore thousand to our foes.

NAPOLÉON (irritated)

That consummation long has threatened us ! . . .
Would that you showed the steeled fidelity
You used to show !   Except me, all are slack !

(To Murat) Why, even you yourself, my brother-in-
    law,
Have been inclining to abandon me !

MURAT (vehemently)

I, sire ?   It is not so !   I stand and swear
The grievous imputation is untrue.
You should know better than believe these things,
And well remember I have enemies
Who ever wait to slander me to you !

NAPOLÉON (more calmly)

Ah yes, yes.   That is so.—And yet—and yet
You have deigned to weigh the feasibility
Of treating me as Austria has done ! . . .
But I forgive you.   You are a worthy man ;
You feel real friendship for me.   You are brave.
Yet I was wrong to make a king of you.
If I had been content to draw the line
At vice-king, as with young Eugène, no more,
As he has laboured you'd have laboured too !
But as full monarch, you have foraged rather
For your own pot than mine !

> MURAT and the marshals are silent, and look at each other
> with troubled countenances. NAPOLÉON goes to the table at
> the back, and bends over the charts with CAULAINCOURT,
> dictating desultory notes to the secretaries.

SPIRIT IRONIC

                              A seer might say
This savours of a sad Last-Supper talk
'Twixt his disciples and this Christ of war !
> Enter an attendant.

ATTENDANT

The Saxon King and Queen and the Princess
Enter the city gates, your Majesty.

They seek the shelter of the civic walls
Against the risk of capture by the Allies.

NAPOLÉON

Ah, so ?   My friend Augustus, is he near ?
I will be prompt to meet him when he comes,
And safely quarter him.   (He returns to the map.)

An interval.   The clock strikes midnight.   The EMPEROR
rises abruptly, sighs, and comes forward.

I now retire,
Comrades.   Good-night, good-night.   Remember
well
All must prepare to grip with gory death
In the now voidless battle.   It will be
A great one and a critical ; one, in brief,
That will seal France's fate, and yours, and mine !

ALL (fervidly)

We'll do our utmost, by the Holy Heaven !

NAPOLÉON

Ah—what was that ?   (He pulls back the window-curtain.)

SEVERAL

It is our enemies,
Whose southern hosts are signalling to their north.

A white rocket is beheld high in the air.   It is followed by
a second, and a third.   There is a pause, during which NAPOLÉON
and the rest wait motionless.   In a minute or two, from the
opposite side of the city, three coloured rockets are sent up,
in evident answer to the three white ones.   NAPOLÉON muses,
and lets the curtain drop.

NAPOLÉON

Yes ; Schwarzenberg to Blücher. . . . It must be
To show that they are ready.   So are we !

He goes out without saying more.   The marshals and other
officers withdraw.

The room darkens, and ends the scene.

SCENE II

THE SAME.   THE CITY AND THE BATTLEFIELD

Leipzig is viewed in aerial perspective from a position above
the south suburbs, and reveals itself as standing in a plain,
with rivers and marshes on the west, north, and south of it,
and higher ground to the east and south-east.

At this date it is somewhat in the shape of the letter D,
the straight part of which is the river Pleisse.   Except as to
this side it is surrounded by armies—the inner horseshoe of
them being the French defending the city ; the outer horseshoe being the Allies about to attack it.

Far over the city—as it were at the top of the D—at Lin-
denthal, we see MARMONT stationed to meet BLÜCHER when
he arrives on that side.   To the right of him is NEY, and further
off to the right, on heights eastward, MACDONALD.   Then round
the curve towards the south in order, AUGEREAU, LAURISTON
(behind whom is NAPOLÉON himself and the reserve of Guards),
VICTOR (at Wachau), and PONIATOWSKI, near the Pleisse
River at the bottom of the D.   Near him are the cavalry of
KELLERMANN and MILHAUD, and in the same direction MURAT
with his, covering the great avenues of approach on the south.

Outside all these stands SCHWARZENBERG's army, of which,
opposed to MACDONALD and LAURISTON, are KLENAU's Austrians
and ZIETEN's Prussians, covered on the flank by Cossacks
under PLATOFF.   Opposed to VICTOR and PONIATOWSKI are
MEERFELDT and HESSE-HOMBURG's Austrians, WITTGENSTEIN's
Russians, KLEIST's Prussians, GUILAY's Austrians, with LICH-
TENSTEIN's and THIELMANN's light troops : thus reaching
round across the Elster into the morass on our near left—the
lower point of the D.

Semichorus I of Rumours (aerial music)

This is the combat of Napoléon's hope,
But not of his assurance!   Shrunk in power
He broods beneath October's clammy cope,
While hemming hordes wax denser every hour.

Semichorus II

He knows, he knows that though in equal fight
He stands as heretofore the matched of none,
A feeble skill is propped by numbers' might,
And now three hosts close round to crush out one!

DUMB SHOW

The Leipzig clocks imperturbably strike nine, and the battle which is to decide the fate of Europe, and perhaps the world, begins with three booms from the line of the Allies.   They are the signal for a general cannonade of devastating intensity.

So massive is the contest that we soon fail to individualize the combatants as beings, and can only observe them as amorphous drifts, clouds, and waves of conscious atoms, surging and rolling together ;   can only particularize them by race, tribe, and language.   Nationalities from the uttermost parts of Asia here meet those from the Atlantic edge of Europe for the first and last time.   By noon the sound becomes a loud droning, uninterrupted and breve-like, as from the pedal of an organ kept continuously down.

Chorus of Rumours

Now triple battle beats about the town,
And now contracts the huge elastic ring
Of fighting flesh, as those within go down,
Or spreads, as those without show faltering!

It becomes apparent that the French have a particular intention, the Allies only a general one.   That of the French is to break through the enemy's centre and surround his right. To this end Napoléon launches fresh columns, and simultaneously Oudinot supports Victor against Eugène of Würtemberg's right, while on the other side of him the cavalry of Milhaud and Kellermann prepares to charge.

NAPOLÉON's combination is successful, and drives back EUGÈNE. Meanwhile SCHWARZENBERG is stuck fast, useless, in the marshes between the Pleisse and the Elster.

By three o'clock the Allied centre, which has held out against the assaults of the French right and left, is broken through by the cavalry under MURAT, LATOUR-MAUBOURG, and KELLERMANN.

The bells of Leipzig ring.

CHORUS OF THE PITIES

Those chimings, ill-advised and premature !
Who knows if such vast valour will endure ?

The Austro-Russians are withdrawn from the marshes by SCHWARZENBERG. But the French cavalry also get entangled in the swamps, and simultaneously MARMONT is beaten at Möckern.

Meanwhile NEY, to the north of Leipzig, having heard the battle raging southward, leaves his position to assist in it. He has nearly arrived when he hears BLÜCHER attacking at the point he came from, and sends back some of his divisions.

BERTRAND has kept open the west road to Lindenau and the Rhine, the only French line of retreat.

Evening finds the battle a drawn one. With the nightfall three blank shots reverberate hollowly.

SEMICHORUS I OF RUMOURS

They sound to say that, for this moaning night,
As Nature sleeps, so too shall sleep the fight ;
Neither the victor.

SEMICHORUS II

　　　　　But, for France and him,
Half-won is losing !

CHORUS

　　　　　Yea, his hopes drop dim,
Since nothing less than victory to-day
Had saved a cause whose ruin is delay !

The night gets thicker and no more is seen.

SCENE III

THE SAME, FROM THE TOWER OF THE PLEISSENBURG

The tower commands a view of great part of the battlefield. Day has just dawned, and citizens, saucer-eyed from anxiety and sleeplessness, are discovered gazing.

FIRST CITIZEN

The wind waxed wild at midnight while I watched,
With flapping showers, and clouds that mopped the
    moon,
Till dawn began outheaving this huge day,
Pallidly—as if scared by its own child ;
This day that the Allies with bonded might
Have vowed to deal their felling finite blow.

SECOND CITIZEN

So must it be !   They have welded close the coop
Wherein our luckless Frenchmen are enjailed
With such compression that their front has shrunk
From five miles' farness to but half as far.—
Men say Napoléon made resolve last night
To marshal a retreat.   If so, his way
Is by the Bridge of Lindenau alone.

They look across in the cold east light at the long straight causeway from the Ranstädt Gate at the north-west corner of the town, and the Lindenau bridge over the Elster beyond.

FIRST CITIZEN

Last night I saw, like wolf-packs, hosts appear
Upon the Dresden road ; and then, anon,

The already stout arrays of Schwarzenberg
Grew stoutened more. I witnessed clearly, too,
Just before dark, the bands of Bernadotte
Come, hemming in the north more thoroughly.
The horizon glowered with a thousand fires
As the unyielding circle shut around.

As it grows lighter they scan and define the armies.

THIRD CITIZEN

Those lying there, 'twixt Connewitz and Dölitz,
Are the right wing of horse Murat commands.
Next, Poniatowski, Victor, and the rest.
Out here, Napoléon's centre at Probstheida,
Where he has bivouacked. Those round this way
Are his left wing with Ney, that face the north
Between Paunsdorf and Gohlis.—Thus, you see
They are skilfully sconced within the villages,
With cannon ranged in front. And every copse,
Dingle, and grove is packed with riflemen.

The heavy sky begins to clear with the full arrival of the
morning. The sun bursts out, and the previously dark and
gloomy masses glitter in the rays. It is now seven o'clock, and
with the shining of the sun the battle is resumed.

The army of Bohemia to the south and east, in three great
columns, marches concentrically upon NAPOLÉON'S new and
much-contracted line—the first column of thirty-five thousand
under BENNIGSEN ; the second, the central, forty-five thousand
under BARCLAY DE TOLLY ; the third, twenty-five thousand
under the PRINCE OF HESSE-HOMBURG.

An interval of suspense.

FIRST CITIZEN

Ah, see ! The French bend, falter, and fall back.

Another interval. Then a huge rumble of artillery resounds
from the north.

SEMICHORUS I OF RUMOURS (aerial music)

Now Blücher has arrived ; and now falls to !
Marmont withdraws before him.   Bernadotte
Touching Bennigsen, joins attack with him,
And Ney must needs recede.   This serves as sign
To Schwarzenberg to bear upon Probstheida—
Napoléon's keystone and dependence here.
But for long whiles he fails to win his will,
The chief himself being nigh—outmatching might with
    skill.

SEMICHORUS II

Ney meanwhile, stung still sharplier, still withdraws
Nearer the town and, met by new mischance,
Finds him forsaken by his Saxon wing—
Fair files of thrice twelve thousand footmanry.
But rallying those still true with signs and calls,
He warely closes up his remnant to the walls.

SEMICHORUS I

Around Probstheida still the conflict rolls
Under Napoléon's eye surpassingly.
Like sedge before the scythe the sections fall
And bayonets slant and reek.   Each cannon-blaze
Makes the air thick with human limbs ; while keen
Contests rage hand to hand.   Throats shout
    "advance,"
And forms walm, wallow, and slack suddenly.
Hot ordnance split and shiver and rebound,
And firelocks fouled and flintless overstrew the ground.

SEMICHORUS II

At length the Allies, daring tumultuously,
Find them inside Probstheida.   There is fixed
Napoléon's cardinal and centre hold.

But need to loose it grows his gloomy fear
As night begins to brown and treacherous mists appear.

Chorus

Then, on the three fronts of this reaching field,
A furious, far, and final cannonade
Burns from two thousand mouths and shakes the
    plain,
And hastens the sure end !   Towards the west
Bertrand keeps open the retreating-way,
Along which wambling waggons since the noon
Have crept in closening file.   Dusk falls full soon ;
The marching remnants drowse amid their talk,
And worn and harrowed horses slumber as they walk.

In the darkness of the distance spread cries from the maimed
animals and the wounded men.   Multitudes of the latter contrive to crawl into the city, until the streets are full of them.
Their voices are heard calling.

Second Citizen

They cry for water !   Let us now go down,
And do what mercy may.

                    [Exeunt citizens from the tower.

Spirit of the Pities

                    A fire is lit
Near to the Thonberg wind-wheel.   Can it be
Napoléon tarries yet ?   Let us go see.

The distant firelight becomes clearer and closer.

SCENE IV

THE SAME.   AT THE THONBERG WINDMILL

By the newly lighted fire NAPOLÉON is seen walking up and down, much agitated and worn. With him are MURAT, BERTHIER, AUGEREAU, VICTOR, and other marshals of corps that have been engaged in this part of the field—all perspiring, muddy, and fatigued.

NAPOLÉON

Baseness so gross I had not guessed of them !—
The thirty thousand false Bavarians
I looked on losing not unplacidly ;
But these troth-swearing sober Saxonry
I reckoned staunch, and standers by their king !
Thirty-five thousand gone !   It magnifies
A failure into a catastrophe. . . .
Murat, we must recede precipitately,
And not as hope had dreamed !   Begin it then
This very hour.—Berthier, write out the orders.—
Let me sit down.

A chair is brought out from the mill. NAPOLÉON sinks into it, and BERTHIER, stooping over the fire, begins writing to the Emperor's dictation, the marshals looking with gloomy faces at the flaming logs.

NAPOLÉON has hardly dictated a line when he stops short. BERTHIER turns round and finds that he has dropt asleep.

MURAT (sullenly)

        Far better not disturb him ;
He'll soon enough awake !

They wait, muttering to one another in tones expressing weary indifference to issues. NAPOLÉON sleeps heavily for a quarter of an hour, during which the moon rises over the field. At the end he starts up and stares around him with astonishment.

NAPOLÉON

Am I awake,
Or is this all a dream ?—Ah, no.   Too real ! . . .
And yet I have seen ere now a time like this.

The dictation is resumed.   While it is in progress there can
be heard between the words of NAPOLÉON the persistent cries
from the plain, rising and falling like those of a vast rookery
far away, intermingled with the trampling of hoofs and the
rumble of wheels.   The bivouac fires of the engirdling enemy
glow all around except for a small segment to the west—the
track of retreat, still kept open by BERTRAND, and already
taken by the baggage-waggons.

The orders for its adoption by the entire army being completed, NAPOLÉON bids adieu to his marshals, and rides with
BERTHIER and CAULAINCOURT into Leipzig.   Exeunt also the
others.

SEMICHORUS I OF PITIES

Now, as in the dream of one sick to death,
There comes a narrowing room
That pens him, body and limbs and breath,
To wait a hideous doom,

SEMICHORUS II

So to Napoléon in the hush
That holds the town and towers
Through this dire night, a creeping crush
Seems cincturing his powers.

The scene closes under a rimy mist, which makes a lurid
cloud of the firelights.

SCENE V

THE SAME. A STREET NEAR THE RANSTÄDT GATE

High old-fashioned houses form the street, along which, from the east of the city, is streaming a confusion of waggons, artillery, chariots, horsemen, foot-soldiers, camp-followers, and wounded, in hurried exit through the gate westward upon the highroad to Lindenau, Lützen, and the Rhine.

In front of an inn called the " Prussian Arms " are some attendants of NAPOLÉON waiting with horses.

FIRST OFFICER

He has just come from bidding the king and queen
A long good-bye. . . . Is it that they will pay
For his indulgence of their past ambition
By sharing now his ruin ?   Much the king
Did beg of him to leave them to their lot,
And shun the shame of capture needlessly.

> (He looks anxiously towards the door.)

I would he'd haste !   Each minute is of price.

SECOND OFFICER

The king will come to terms with the Allies.
They will not hurt him.   Though he has lost his all,
His case is not like ours !

The cheers of the approaching enemy grow louder.   NAPOLÉON comes out from the " Prussian Arms," haggard, unshaven, and in disordered attire.   He is about to mount, but, perceiving the blocked state of the street, he hesitates.

NAPOLÉON

          God, what a crowd !
I shall more fleetly gain the gate afoot.
There is a byway somewhere, I suppose ?

> A citizen approaches out of the inn.

Citizen

This alley, sire, will speed you to the gate ;
I shall be honoured much to point the way.

Napoléon

Then do, good friend. (To attendants) Bring on the
      horses there ;
If I arrive soonest I will wait for you.

> The citizen shows Napoléon the way into the alley.

Citizen

A garden's at the end, your Majesty,
Through which you pass.   Beyond there is a door
That opens to the Elster bank unbalked.

> Napoléon disappears into the alley. His attendants plunge amid the traffic with the horses, and thread their way down the street.
> Another citizen comes from the door of the inn and greets the first.

First Citizen

He's gone !

Second Citizen

I'll see if he succeed.

> He re-enters the inn and soon appears at an upper window.

First Citizen (from below)

You see him ?

Second Citizen (gazing)

He is already at the garden-end ;
Now he has passed out to the river-brim,
And plods along it towards the Ranstädt Gate. . . .

He finds no horse to meet him ! . . . And the throng
Thrusts him about, none recognizing him.
Ah—now the horses reach there ; and he mounts,
And hurries through the arch. . . . Again I see him—
Now he's upon the causeway in the marsh ;
Now rides across the bridge of Lindenau. . . .
And now, among the troops that choke the road
I lose all sight of him.

 A third citizen enters from the direction NAPOLÉON has
taken.

THIRD CITIZEN (breathlessly)

       I have seen him go !
And while he passed the gate I stood i' the crowd
So close I could have touched him ! Few discerned
In one so soiled the erst Arch-Emperor !—
In the lax mood of him who has lost all
He stood inert there, idly singing thin :
" Malbrough s'en va-t-en guerre ! " until his suite
Came up with horses.

SECOND CITIZEN (still gazing afar)

       Poniatowski's Poles
Wearily walk the level causeway now ;
Also, meseems, Macdonald's corps and Reynier's.
The frail-framed, new-built bridge has broken down :
They've but the old to cross by.

FIRST CITIZEN

         Feeble foresight !
They should have had a dozen.

SECOND CITIZEN

        All the corps—
Macdonald's, Poniatowski's, Reynier's—all—
Confusedly block the entrance to the bridge.

And—verily Blücher's troops are through the town,
And are debouching from the Ranstädt Gate
Upon the Frenchmen's rear !

A thunderous report stops his words, echoing through the
city from the direction in which he is gazing, and rattling
all the windows. A hoarse chorus of cries becomes audible
immediately after.

FIRST, THIRD, ETC., CITIZENS

Ach, Heaven !—what's that ?

SECOND CITIZEN

The bridge of Lindenau has been upblown !

SEMICHORUS I OF PITIES (aerial music)

There leaps to the sky an earthen wave,
And stones, and men, as though
Some rebel churchyard crew updrave
Their sepulchres from below.

SEMICHORUS II

To Heaven is blown Bridge Lindenau ;
Wrecked regiments reel therefrom ;
And rank and file in masses plough
The sullen Elster-Strom.

SEMICHORUS I

A gulf is Lindenau ; and dead
Are fifties, hundreds, tens ;
And every current ripples red
With marshals' blood and men's.

SEMICHORUS II

The smart Macdonald swims therein,
And barely wins the verge ;
Bold Poniatowski plunges in
Never to re-emerge !

First Citizen

Are not the French across as yet, God save them ?

Second Citizen (still gazing above)

Nor Reynier's corps, Macdonald's, Lauriston's,
Nor yet the Poles. . . . And Blücher's troops
    approach,
And all the French this side are prisoners.
—Now for our handling by the Prussian host ;
Scant courtesy for our King !

> Other citizens appear beside him at the window, and further
> conversation continues entirely above.

Chorus of Ironic Spirits

The Battle of the Nations now is closing,
    And all is lost to One, to many gained ;
The old dynastic routine reimposing,
    The new dynastic structure unsustained.

Now every neighbouring realm is France's warder,
    And smirking satisfaction will be feigned :
The which is seemlier ?—so-called ancient order,
    Or that the hot-breath'd war-horse ramp unreined ?

> The October night thickens and curtains the scene.

SCENE VI

THE PYRENEES.   NEAR THE RIVER NIVELLE

> Evening. The dining-room of Wellington's quarters.
> The table is laid for dinner. The battle of the Nivelle has just
> been fought.
> Enter Wellington, Hill, Beresford, Stewart, Hope,

CLINTON, COLBORNE, COLE, KEMPT (with a bound-up wound), and other officers.

WELLINGTON

It is strange that they did not hold their grand position more tenaciously against us to-day. By God, I don't quite see why we should have beaten them !

COLBORNE

My impression is that they had the stiffness taken out of them by something they had just heard of. Anyhow, startling news of some kind was received by those of the Eighty-eighth we took in the signal-redoubt after I summoned the Commandant.

WELLINGTON

Oh, what news ?

COLBORNE

I cannot say, my lord. I only know that the latest number of the *Imperial Gazette* was seen in the hands of some of them before the capture. They had been reading the contents, and were cast down.

WELLINGTON

That's interesting. I wonder what the news could have been ?

HILL

Something about Boney's army in Saxony would be most probable. Though I question if there's time yet for much to have been decided there.

BERESFORD

Well, I wouldn't say that. A hell of a lot of things may have happened there by this time.

COLBORNE

It was tantalizing, but they were just able to destroy the paper before we could prevent them.

WELLINGTON

Did you question them ?

COLBORNE

Oh yes. But they stayed sulking at being taken, and would tell us nothing, pretending that they knew nothing. Whether much were going on, they said, or little, between the army of the Emperor and the army of the Allies, it was none of their business to relate it ; so they kept a gloomy silence for the most part.

WELLINGTON

They will cheer up a bit and be more communicative when they have had some dinner.

COLE

They are dining here, my lord ?

WELLINGTON

I sent them an invitation an hour ago, which they have accepted. I could do no less, poor devils. They'll be here in a few minutes. See that they have plenty of Madeira to whet their whistles with. It will screw them up into a better key, and they'll not be so reserved.

The conversation on the day's battle becomes general. Enter as guests French officers of the Eighty-eighth regiment now prisoners on parole. They are welcomed by WELLINGTON and the staff, and all sit down to dinner.

For some time the meal proceeds almost in silence ; but wine
is passed freely, and both French and English officers become
talkative and merry.

WELLINGTON (to the French Commandant)

More cozy this, sir, than—I'll warrant me—
You found it in that damned redoubt to-day ?

COMMANDANT

The devil if 'tis not, monseigneur, sure !

WELLINGTON

So 'tis for us who were outside, by God !

COMMANDANT (gloomily)

No ; we were not at ease !   Alas, my lord,
'Twas more than flesh and blood could do, to fight
After such paralyzing tidings came.
More life may trickle out of men through thought
Than through a gaping wound.

WELLINGTON

                                 Your reference
Bears on the news from Saxony, I infer ?

SECOND FRENCH OFFICER

Yes : on the Emperor's ruinous defeat
At Leipzig city—brought to our startled heed
By one of the *Gazettes* just now arrived.

All the English officers stop speaking, and listen eagerly.

WELLINGTON

Where are the Emperor's headquarters now ?

COMMANDANT

My lord, there are no headquarters.

WELLINGTON

No headquarters ?

COMMANDANT

There are no French headquarters now, my lord,
For there is no French army ! France's fame
Is fouled. And how, then, could we fight to-day
With our hearts in our shoes !

WELLINGTON

Why, that bears out

What I but lately said ; it was not like
The brave men who have faced and foiled me here
So many a long year past, to give away
A stubborn station quite so readily.

BERESFORD

And what, messieurs, ensued at Leipzig then ?

SEVERAL FRENCH OFFICERS

Why, sirs, should we conceal it ? Thereupon
Part of our army took the Lützen road ;
But twenty thousand of our rear were ginned
Behind a blown-up bridge. Those in advance
Arrived at Lützen with the Emperor—
The scene of our once valiant victory !
In such sad sort retreat was hurried on,
Erfurt was gained with Blücher hot at heel.
To cross the Rhine seemed then our only hope ;
Alas, the Austrians and the Bavarians
Faced us in Hanau Forest, led by Wrede,
And dead-blocked our escape.

WELLINGTON

Ha.   Did they though !

SECOND FRENCH OFFICER

But if brave hearts were ever desperate,
Sir, we were desperate then !   We pierced them
    through,
Our loss unrecking.   So by Frankfurt's walls
We fared to Mainz, and there recrossed the Rhine.
A funeral procession, so we seemed,
Upon the long bridge that had rung so oft
To our victorious feet ! . . . What since has coursed
We know not, gentlemen.   But this we know,
That Germany echoes no French footfall now !

AN ENGLISH OFFICER

One sees not why it should.

SECOND FRENCH OFFICER

We'll leave it so.

Conversation on the Leipzig disaster continues till the
dinner ends.   The French prisoners courteously take their
leave and go out.

WELLINGTON

Very good set of fellows.   I could wish
They all were mine ! . . . Well, well ; there was no
    crime
In trying to ascertain these fat events :
They would have sounded soon from other tongues.

HILL

It looks like the first scene of act the last
For our and all men's foe !

WELLINGTON

             I count to meet
The Allies upon the cobble-stones of Paris
Before another half-year's suns have shone.
—But there's some work for us to do here yet :
The dawn must find us fording the Nivelle !

         Exeunt WELLINGTON *and officers.*

      The room darkens.

ACT FOURTH

SCENE I

THE UPPER RHINE

The view is from a vague altitude over the beautiful country traversed by the Upper Rhine, which stretches through it in bird's-eye perspective. At this date in Europe's history the stream forms the frontier between France and Germany.

It is the morning of New Year's Day, and the shine of the tardy sun reaches the fronts of the beetling castles, but scarcely descends far enough to touch the wavelets of the river winding leftwards across the many-leagued picture from Schaffhausen to Coblenz.

DUMB SHOW

At first nothing—not even the river itself—seems to move in the panorama. But anon certain strange dark patches in the landscape, flexuous and riband-shaped, are discerned to be moving slowly. Only one movable object on earth is large enough to be conspicuous herefrom, and that is an army. The moving shapes are armies.

The nearest, almost beneath us, is defiling across the river by a bridge of boats, near the junction of the Rhine and the Neckar, where the oval town of Mannheim, standing in the fork between the two rivers, has from here the look of a human head in a cleft stick. Martial music from many bands strikes up as the crossing is effected, and the undulating columns twinkle as if they were scaly serpents.

SPIRIT OF RUMOUR

It is the Russian host, invading France!

Many miles to the left, down-stream, near the little town of Caube, another army is seen to be simultaneously crossing the pale current, its arms and accoutrements twinkling in like manner.

SPIRIT OF RUMOUR

Thither the Prussian levies, too, advance !

Turning now to the right, far away by Basel (beyond which the Swiss mountains close the scene), a still larger train of war-geared humanity, two hundred thousand strong, is discernible. It has already crossed the water, which is much narrower here, and has advanced several miles westward, where its ductile mass of greyness and glitter is beheld parting into six columns, that march on in flexuous courses of varying direction.

SPIRIT OF RUMOUR

There glides carked Austria's invading force !—
Panting, too, Paris-wards with foot and horse,
Of one intention with the other twain,
And Wellington, from the south, in upper Spain.

All these dark and grey columns, converging westward by sure degrees, advance without opposition. They glide on as if by gravitation, in fluid figures, dictated by the conformation of the country, like water from a burst reservoir ; mostly snake-shaped, but occasionally with batrachian and saurian outlines. In spite of the immensity of this human mechanism on its surface, the winter landscape wears an impassive look, as if nothing were happening.

Evening closes in, and the Dumb Show is obscured.

SCENE II

PARIS. THE TUILERIES

It is Sunday just after mass, and the principal officers of the National Guard are assembled in the Salle des Maréchaux. They stand in an attitude of suspense, some with the print of sadness on their faces, some with that of perplexity.

The door leading from the Hall to the adjoining chapel is thrown open. There enter from the chapel with the last notes of the service the EMPEROR NAPOLÉON and the EMPRESS; and simultaneously from a door opposite MADAME DE MONTES-QUIOU, the governess, who carries in her arms the KING OF ROME, now a fair child between two and three. He is clothed in a miniature uniform of the Guards themselves.

MADAME DE MONTESQUIOU brings forward the child and sets him on his feet near his mother. NAPOLÉON, with a mournful smile, giving one hand to the boy and the other to MARIE LOUISE, *en famille*, leads them forward. The Guard bursts into cheers.

NAPOLÉON

Gentlemen of the National Guard and friends,
I have to leave you; and before I fare
To Heaven knows what of personal destiny,
I give into your loyal guardianship
Those dearest in the world to me; my wife,
The Empress, and my son the King of Rome.—
I go to shield your roofs and kin from foes
Who have dared to pierce the fences of your land;
And knowing that you house those dears of mine,
I start afar in all tranquillity,
Stayed by my trust in your fast faithfulness.

(Enthusiastic cheers from the Guard.)

OFFICERS (with emotion)

We proudly swear to justify the trust!
And never will we see another sit
Than you, or yours, on the great throne of France.

NAPOLÉON

I ratify the Empress' regency,
And re-confirm it on the last year's lines,
My brother Joseph stoutening her rule
As the Lieutenant-General of the State.—

Vex her with no divisions ; let regard
For property, for order, and for France
Be chief with all.   Know, gentlemen, the Allies
Are drunken with success.   Their late advantage
They have handled wholly for their own gross gain,
And made a pastime of my agony.
    That I go clogged with cares I sadly own ;
Yet I go primed with hope ; ay, in despite
Of a last sorrow that has sunk upon me,—
The grief of hearing, good and constant friends,
That my own sister's consort, Naples' king,
Blazons himself a backer of the Allies,
And marches with a Neapolitan force
Against our puissance under Prince Eugène.
    The varied operations to ensue
May bring the enemy largely Paris-wards ;
But suffer no alarm ; before long days
I will annihilate by flank and rear
Those who have risen to trample on our soil ;
And as I have done so many and proud a time,
Come back to you with ringing victory !—
Now, see : I personally present to you
My son and my successor ere I go.

He takes the child in his arms and carries him round to
the officers severally.   They are much affected and raise loud
cheers.

You stand by him and her ?   You swear as much ?

OFFICERS

We swear !

NAPOLÉON

This you repeat—you promise it ?

OFFICERS

We promise.   May the dynasty live for ever !

Their shouts, which spread to the Carrousel without, are echoed by the soldiers of the Guard assembled there. The EMPRESS is now in tears, and the EMPEROR supports her.

MARIE LOUISE

Such whole enthusiasm I have never known !—
Not even from the Landwehr of Vienna.

Amid repeated protestations and farewells NAPOLÉON, the EMPRESS, the KING OF ROME, MADAME DE MONTESQUIOU, etc., go out in one direction, and the officers of the National Guard in another.

The curtain falls for an interval.

When it rises again the apartment is in darkness, and its atmosphere chilly. The January night-wind howls without. Two servants enter hastily, and light candles and a fire. The hands of the clock are pointing to three.

The room is hardly in order when the EMPEROR enters, equipped for the intended journey ; and with him, his left arm being round her waist, walks MARIE LOUISE in a dressing-gown. On his right arm he carries the KING OF ROME and in his hand a bundle of papers. COUNT BERTRAND and a few members of the household follow.

Reaching the middle of the room, he kisses the child and embraces the EMPRESS, who is tearful, the child weeping likewise. NAPOLÉON takes the papers to the fire, thrusts them in, and watches them consume ; then burns other bundles brought by his attendants.

NAPOLÉON (gloomily)

Better to treat them thus ; since no one knows
What comes, or into whose hands he may fall !

MARIE LOUISE

I have an apprehension—unexplained—
That I shall never see you any more !

NAPOLÉON

Dismiss such fears. You may as well as not.
As things are doomed to be they will be, dear.

If shadows must come, let them come as though
The sun were due and you were trusting to it :
'Twill teach the world it wrongs in bringing them.

They embrace finally. Exeunt NAPOLÉON, etc. Afterwards MARIE LOUISE and the child.

SPIRIT OF THE YEARS

Her instinct forwardly is keen in cast,
And yet how limited.   True it may be
They never more will meet ; although—to use
The bounded prophecy I am dowered with—
The screen that will maintain their severance
Would pass her own believing ; proving it
No gaol-grille, no scath of scorching war,
But thin persuasion, pressing on her pulse
To breed aloofness and a mind averse ;
Until his image in her soul will shape
Dwarfed as a far Colossus on a plain,
Or figure-head that smalls upon the main.

The lights are extinguished and the hall is left in darkness.

SCENE III

THE SAME.   THE APARTMENTS OF THE EMPRESS

A March morning, verging on seven o'clock, throws its cheer-
less stare into the private drawing-room of MARIE LOUISE,
animating the gilt furniture to only a feeble shine. Two
chamberlains of the palace are there in waiting. They look
from the windows and yawn.

FIRST CHAMBERLAIN

Here's a watering for spring hopes ! Who
would have supposed when the Emperor left, and

appointed her Regent, that she and the Regency too would have to scurry after in so short a time !

SECOND CHAMBERLAIN

Was a course decided on last night ?

FIRST CHAMBERLAIN

Yes. The Privy Council sat till long past midnight, debating the burning question whether she and the child should remain or not. Some were one way, some the other. She settled the matter by saying she would go.

SECOND CHAMBERLAIN

I thought it might come to that. I heard the alarm beating all night to assemble the National Guard ; and I am told that some volunteers have marched out to support Marmont. But they are a mere handful : what can they do ?

A clatter of wheels and a champing and prancing of horses is heard outside the palace. MENÉVAL enters, and divers officers of the household ; then from her bedroom at the other end MARIE LOUISE, in a travelling dress and hat, leading the KING OF ROME, attired for travel likewise. She looks distracted and pale. Next come the DUCHESS OF MONTEBELLO, lady of honour, the COUNTESS DE LUÇAY, MADAME DE CASTIGLIONE, MADAME DE MONTESQUIOU, ladies of the palace, and others, all in travelling trim.

KING OF ROME (plaintively)

Why are we doing these strange things, mamma,
And what did we get up so early for ?

MARIE LOUISE

I cannot, dear, explain. So many events
Enlarge and make so many hours of one,
That it would be too hard to tell them now.

KING OF ROME

But you know why we are setting out like this ?
Is it because we fear our enemies ?

MARIE LOUISE

We are not sure that we are going yet.
It may be needful ; but don't ask me here.
Some time I'll tell you.

> She sits down irresolutely, and bestows recognitions on the
> assembled officials with a preoccupied air.

KING OF ROME (in a murmur)

                  I like being here best ;
And I don't want to go I know not where !

MARIE LOUISE

Run, dear, to Mamma 'Quiou and talk to her.
          (He goes across to MADAME DE MONTESQUIOU.)
I hear that women of the Royalist hope
           (to the DUCHESS OF MONTEBELLO)
Have bent them busy in their private rooms
With working white cockades these several days.—
Yes—I must go !

DUCHESS OF MONTEBELLO

            But why yet, Empress dear ?
We may soon gain good news ; some messenger
Hie from the Emperor or King Joseph hither ?

MARIE LOUISE

King Joseph I await. He's gone to eye
The outposts, with the Ministers of War,

To learn the scope and nearness of the Allies ;
He should almost be back.

A silence, till approaching feet are suddenly heard outside the door.

　　　　　　　　　　Ah, here he comes ;
Now we shall know !

Enter precipitately not Joseph but officers of the National Guard and others.

OFFICERS

　　　　　Long live the Empress-regent !
Do not quit Paris, pray, your Majesty.
Remain, remain.　We plight us to defend you !

MARIE LOUISE (agitated)

Gallant messieurs, I thank you heartily.
But by the Emperor's biddance I am bound.
He has vowed he'd liefer see me and my son
Blanched at the bottom of the smothering Seine
Than in the talons of the foes of France.—
To keep us sure from such, then, he ordained
Our swift withdrawal with the Ministers
Towards the Loire, if enemies advanced
In overmastering might.　They do advance ;
Marshals Marmont and Mortier are repulsed,
And that has come whose hazard he foresaw.
All is arranged ; the treasure is awheel,
And papers, seals, and cyphers packed therewith.

OFFICERS (dubiously)

Yet to leave Paris is to court disaster !

MARIE LOUISE (with petulance)

I shall do what I say ! . . . I don't know what—
What *shall* I do !

She bursts into tears and rushes into her bedroom, followed by the young KING *and some of her ladies. There is a painful silence, broken by sobbings and expostulations within. Re-enter one of the ladies.*

LADY

             She's sorely overthrown ;
She flings herself upon the bed distraught.
She says, " My God, let them make up their minds
To one or other of these harrowing ills,
And force me to't, and end my agony ! "

        An official enters at the main door.

OFFICIAL

I am sent here by the Minister of War
To her Imperial Majesty the Empress.

      Re-enter MARIE LOUISE *and the* KING OF ROME.

Your Majesty, my mission is to say
Imperious need dictates your instant flight.
A vanward regiment of the Prussian packs
Has gained the shadow of the city walls.

MENÉVAL

They are armed Europe's scouts !

    Enter CAMBACÉRÈS *the Arch-Chancellor,* COUNT BEAUHAR-
NAIS, CORVISART *the physician,* DE BAUSSET, DE CANISY *the equerry, and others.*

CAMBACÉRÈS

                Your Majesty,
There's not a trice to lose. The force well-nigh
Of all compacted Europe crowds on us,
And clamours at the walls !

BEAUHARNAIS

             If you stay longer,
You stay to fall into the Cossacks' hands.

The people, too, are waxing masterful :
They think the lingering of your Majesty
Makes Paris more a peril for themselves
Than a defence for you.   To fight is fruitless,
And wanton waste of life.   You have nought to do
But go ; and I, and all the Councillors,
Will follow you.

MARIE LOUISE

Then I was right to say
That I would go !   Now go I surely will,
And let none try to hinder me again !

[She prepares to leave.

KING OF ROME (crying)

I will not go !   I like to live here best !
Don't go to Rambouillet, mamma ; please don't.
It is a nasty place !   Let us stay here.
O Mamma 'Quiou, stay with me here ; pray stay !

MARIE LOUISE (to the Equerry)

Bring him down.

Exit MARIE LOUISE in tears, followed by ladies-in-waiting
and others.

DE CANISY

Come now, Monseigneur, come.

He catches up the boy in his arms and prepares to follow
the Empress.

KING OF ROME (kicking)

No, no, no !   I don't want to go away from my
house—I don't want to !   Now papa is away I
am the master !   (He clings to the door as the equerry is
bearing him through it.)

De Canisy

But you must go.

The child's fingers are pulled away. Exit DE CANISY *with
the* KING OF ROME, *who is heard screaming as he is carried
down the staircase.*

Madame de Montesquiou

I feel the child is right !
A premonition has enlightened him.
She ought to stay. But, ah, the die is cast !

*MADAME DE MONTESQUIOU and the remainder of the party
follow, and the room is left empty.*

Enter servants hastily.

First Servant

Sacred God, where are we to go to for grub and
good lying to-night ? What are ill-used men to do ?

Second Servant

I trudge like the rest. All the true philosophers
are gone, and the middling true are going. I made
up my mind like the truest that ever was as soon
as I heard the general alarm beat.

Third Servant

I stay here. No Allies are going to tickle our
skins. The storm which roots—Dost know what a
metaphor is, comrade ? I brim with them at this
historic time !

Second Servant

A weapon of war used by the Cossacks ?

Third Servant

Your imagination will be your ruin some day, my man ! It happens to be a weapon of wisdom used by me. My metaphor is one may'st have met with on the rare times when th'hast been in good society. Here it is : The storm which roots the pine spares the p—s—b—d. Now do ye see ?

First and Second Servants

Good ! Your teaching, friend, is as sound as true religion ! We'll not go. Hearken to what's doing outside. (Carriages are heard moving. Servants go to the window and look down.) Lord, there's the Duchess getting in. Now the Mistress of the Wardrobe ; now the Ladies of the Palace ; now the Prefects ; now the Doctors. What a time it takes ! There are near a dozen berlines, as I am a patriot ! Those other carriages bear treasure. How quiet the people are ! It is like a funeral procession. Not a tongue cheers her !

Third Servant

Now there will be a nice convenient time for a little good victuals and drink, and likewise pickings, before the Allies arrive, thank Mother Molly !

From a distant part of the city bands are heard playing military marches. Guns next resound. Another servant rushes in.

Fourth Servant

Montmartre is being stormed, and bombs are falling in the Chaussée d'Antin !

[Exit fourth servant.

Third Servant (pulling something from his pocket)

Then it is time for me to gird my armour on.

SECOND SERVANT

What hast there ?

Third servant holds up a crumpled white cockade and sticks it in his hair. The firing gets louder.

FIRST AND SECOND SERVANTS

Hast got another ?

THIRD SERVANT (pulling out more)

Ay—here they are ; at a price.

The others purchase cockades of third servant. A military march is again heard. Re-enter fourth servant.

FOURTH SERVANT

The city has capitulated ! The Allied sovereigns, so it is said, will enter in grand procession to-morrow : the Prussian cavalry first, then the Austrian foot, then the Russian and Prussian foot, then the Russian horse and artillery. And to cap all, the people of Paris are glad of the change. They have put a rope round the neck of the statue of Napoléon on the column of the Grand Army, and are amusing themselves with twitching it and crying " Strangle the tyrant ! "

SECOND SERVANT

Well, well ! There's rich colours in this kaleido-scopic world !

THIRD SERVANT

And there's comedy in all things—when they don't concern you. Another glorious time among

the many we've had since eighty-nine. We have
put our armour on none too soon. The Bourbons
for ever !

> [He leaves, followed by first and second servants.

FOURTH SERVANT

My faith, I think I'll turn Englishman in my
older years, where there's not these trying changes
in the Constitution !

> [Follows the others.

The Allies' military march waxes louder as the scene shuts.

SCENE IV

FONTAINEBLEAU. A ROOM IN THE PALACE

NAPOLÉON is discovered walking impatiently up and down,
and glancing at the clock every few minutes.

Enter NEY.

NAPOLÉON (without a greeting)

Well—the result ?   Ah, but your looks display
A leaden dawning to the light you bring !
What—not a regency ?   What—not the Empress
To hold it in trusteeship for my son ?

NEY

Sire, things like revolutions turn not back,
But go straight on.   Imperial governance
Is coffined for your family and yourself !
It is declared that military repose,
And France's well-doing, demand of you
Your abdication—unconditioned, sheer.

This verdict of the sovereigns cannot change,
And I have pushed on hot to let you know.

NAPOLÉON (with repression)

I   am   obliged   to   you.   You   have   told   me
    promptly !—
This was to be expected.   I had learnt
Of Marmont's late defection, and the Sixth's ;
The consequence I easily inferred.

NEY

The Paris folk are flaked with white cockades ;
Tricolors choke the kennels.   Rapturously
They clamour for the Bourbons and for peace.

NAPOLÉON (coldly)

I could give Paris peace as well as they !

NEY (dubiously)

Well, sire, you did not.   And I should assume
They have judged the future by the accustomed
    past.

NAPOLÉON (tartly)

I can draw inferences without assistance !

NEY (persisting)

They see the brooks of blood that have flowed
    forth ;
They feel their own bereavements ; so their mood
Asked no deep reasoning for its geniture.

NAPOLÉON

I have no remarks to make on that just now.
I'll think the matter over.   You shall know
By noon to-morrow my definitive.

NEY (turning to go)

I trust my saying what had to be said
Has not affronted you ?

NAPOLÉON (bitterly)

               No ; but your haste
In doing it has galled me, and has shown me
A heart that heaves no longer in my cause !
The skilled coquetting of the Government
Has nearly won you from old fellowship ! . . .
Well ; till to-morrow, marshal, then, Adieu.

                        [NEY goes.

Enter CAULAINCOURT and MACDONALD

Ney has got here before you ; and, I deem,
Has truly told me all ?

CAULAINCOURT

              We thought at first
We should have had success.   But fate said No ;
And abdication, making no reserves,
Is, sire, we are convinced, with all respect,
The only road, if you care not to risk
The Empress' loss of every dignity,
And magnified misfortunes thrown on France.

NAPOLÉON

I have heard it all ; and don't agree with you.
My assets are not quite so beggarly

That I must close in such a shameful bond !
What—do you rate as nought that I am yet
Full fifty thousand strong, with Augereau,
And Soult, and Suchet true, and many more ?
I still may know to play the Imperial game
As well as Alexander and his friends !
So — you will see. Where are my maps ? — eh,
    where ?
I'll trace campaigns to come ! Where's paper, ink,
To schedule all my generals and my means !

CAULAINCOURT

Sire, you have not the generals you suppose.

MACDONALD

And if you had, the mere anatomy
Of a real army, sire, that's left to you,
Must yield the war.   A bad example tells.

NAPOLÉON

Ah—from your manner it is worse, I see,
Than I cognize ! . . . O Marmont, Marmont,—
    yours,
Yours was the bad sad lead !—I treated him
As if he were a son !—defended him,
Made him a marshal out of sheer affection,
Built, as 'twere rock, on his fidelity !
" Forsake who may," I said, " I still have him."
Child that I was, I looked for faith in friends ! . . .
    Then be it as you will.   Ney's manner shows
That even he inclines to Bourbonry.—
I faint to leave France thus—curtailed, pared down
From her late spacious borders.   Of the whole
This is the keenest sword that pierces me. . . .
But all's too late : my course is closed, I see.

I'll do it—now.   Call in Bertrand and Ney ;
Let them be witness to my finishing !

In much agitation he goes to the writing-table and begins
drawing up a paper.   BERTRAND and NEY enter ;   and behind
them are seen through the doorway the faces of CONSTANT the
valet, ROUSTAN the Mameluke, and other servants.   All wait
in silence till the EMPEROR has done writing.   He turns in
his seat without looking up.

NAPOLÉON (reading)

" It having been declared by the Allies
That the prime obstacle to Europe's peace
Is France's empery by Napoléon,
This ruler, faithful to his oath of old,
Renounces for himself and for his heirs
The throne of France and that of Italy ;
Because no sacrifice, even of his life,
Is he averse to make for France's gain."
—And hereto do I sign.
                        (He turns to the table and signs.)
    The marshals, moved, rush forward and seize his hand.

                        Mark, marshals, here ;
It is a conquering foe I covenant with,
And not the traitors at the Tuileries
Who call themselves the Government of France !
Caulaincourt, go to Paris as before,
Ney and Macdonald too, and hand in this
To Alexander, and to him alone.

He gives the document, and bids them adieu almost without
speech.   The marshals and others go out.   NAPOLÉON continues sitting with his chin on his chest.

    An interval of silence.   There is then heard in the corridor
a sound of whetting.   Enter ROUSTAN the Mameluke, with a
whetstone in his belt and a sword in his hand.

ROUSTAN

After this fall, your Majesty, 'tis plain
You will not choose to live ; and knowing this
I bring to you my sword.

NAPOLÉON (with a nod)

I see you do,
Roustan.

ROUSTAN

Will you, sire, use it on yourself,
Or shall I pass it through you ?

NAPOLÉON (coldly)

Neither plan
Is quite expedient for the moment, man.

ROUSTAN

Neither ?

NAPOLÉON

There may be, in some suited time,
Some cleaner means of carrying out such work.

ROUSTAN

Sire, you refuse ?   Can you support vile life
A trice upon such terms ?   Why then, I pray,
Dispatch me with the weapon, or dismiss me.

(He holds the sword to NAPOLÉON, who shakes his head.)

I live no longer under such disgrace !

[Exit ROUSTAN haughtily.

NAPOLÉON vents a sardonic laugh, and throws himself on a
sofa, where he by and by falls asleep.
The door is softly opened.   ROUSTAN and CONSTANT
peep in.

CONSTANT

To-night would be as good a time to go as any.
He will sleep there for hours.   I have my few
francs safe, and I deserve them ; for I have stuck
to him honourably through fourteen trying years.

ROUSTAN

How many francs have you secured ?

CONSTANT

Well—more than you can count in one breath, or even two.

ROUSTAN

Where ?

CONSTANT

In a hollow tree in the Forest.　And as for *your* reward, you can easily get the keys of that cabinet, where there are more than enough francs to equal mine.　He will not have them, and you may as well take them as strangers.

ROUSTAN

It is not money that I want, but honour.　I leave, because I can no longer stay with self-respect.

CONSTANT

And I because there is no other such valet in the temperate zone, and it is for the good of society that I should not be wasted here.

ROUSTAN

Well, as you propose going this evening I will go with you, to lend a symmetry to the drama of our departure.　Would that I had served a more sensitive master !　He sleeps there quite indifferent to the dishonour of remaining alive !

NAPOLÉON shows signs of waking.　CONSTANT and ROUSTAN disappear.　NAPOLÉON slowly sits up.

NAPOLÉON

Here the scene lingers still !   Here linger I ! . . .
Things could not have gone on as they were going;
I am amazed they kept their course so long.
But long or short they have ended now—at last !

(Footsteps are heard passing through the court without.)

Hark at them leaving me !   So politic rats
Desert the ship that's doomed.   By morrow-dawn
I shall not have a man to shake my bed
Or say good-morning to !

SPIRIT OF THE YEARS

*   Herein behold*
How heavily grinds the Will upon his brain,
His halting hand, and his unlighted eye.

SPIRIT IRONIC

A picture this for kings and subjects too !

SPIRIT OF THE PITIES

Yet is it but Napoléon who has failed.
The pale pathetic peoples still plod on
Through hoodwinkings to light !

NAPOLÉON (rousing himself)

*   * This now must close.
Roustan misunderstood me, though his hint
Serves as a fillip to a flaccid brain. . . .
—How gild the sunset sky of majesty
Better than by the act esteemed of yore ?
Plutarchian heroes outstayed not their fame,
And what nor Brutus nor Themistocles
Nor Cato nor Mark Antony survived,
Why, why should I ?   Sage Cabanis, you primed
     me !

He unlocks a case, takes out a little bag containing a phial, pours from it a liquid into a glass, and drinks. He then lies down and falls asleep again.

Re-enter CONSTANT softly with a bunch of keys in his hand. On his way to the cabinet he turns and looks at NAPOLÉON. Seeing the glass and a strangeness in the EMPEROR, he abandons his object, rushes out, and is heard calling.

Enter MARET and BERTRAND.

BERTRAND (shaking the Emperor)

What is the matter, sire ? What's this you've
    done ?

NAPOLÉON (with difficulty)

Why did you interfere !—But it is well ;
Call Caulaincourt. I'd speak with him a trice
Before I pass.

> [MARET hurries out.

Enter IVAN the physician, and presently CAULAINCOURT.

Ivan, renew this dose ;
'Tis a slow workman, and requires a fellow ;
Age has impaired its early promptitude.

IVAN shakes his head and rushes away distracted. CAULAIN-COURT seizes NAPOLÉON's hand.

CAULAINCOURT

Why should you bring this cloud upon us now !

NAPOLÉON

Restrain your stricture. Let me die in peace.—
My wife and son I recommend to you ;
Give her this letter, and the packet there.
Defend my memory, and protect their lives.

> (They shake him. He vomits.)

CAULAINCOURT

He's saved—for good or ill—as may betide !

NAPOLÉON

God—here how difficult it is to die :
How easy on the passionate battle-plain !

> They open a window and carry him to it. He mends.

Fate has resolved what man could not resolve.
I must live on, and wait what Heaven may send !

> MACDONALD and other marshals re-enter. A letter is brought
> from MARIE LOUISE. NAPOLÉON reads it, and becomes more
> animated.

They are well ; and they will join me in my exile.
Yes : I will live ! The future who shall spell ?
My wife, my son, will be enough for me.—
And I will give my hours to chronicling
In stately words that stir futurity
The might of our unmatched accomplishments ;
And in the tale immortalize your names
By linking them with mine.

> He soon falls into a convalescent sleep. The marshals, etc.,
> go out.
> > The room is left in darkness.

SCENE V

BAYONNE. THE BRITISH CAMP

The foreground is an elevated stretch of land, dotted over
in rows with the tents of the Peninsular army. On a parade
immediately beyond the tents the infantry are drawn up,
awaiting something. Still further back, behind a brook, are
the French soldiery, also ranked in the same manner of repose-
ful expectation. In the middle-distance we see the town of

Bayonne, standing within its zigzag fortifications at the junction of the river Adour with the Nive.

On the other side of the Adour rises the citadel, a fortified angular structure standing detached. A large and brilliant tricolor flag is waving indolently from a staff on the summit. The Bay of Biscay, into which the Adour flows, is seen on the left horizon as a level line.

The stillness observed by the soldiery of both armies, and by everything else in the scene except the flag, is at last broken by the firing of a signal-gun from a battery in the town-wall. The eyes of the thousands present rivet themselves on the citadel. Its waving tricolor moves down the flagstaff and disappears.

The Regiments (unconsciously)

Ha-a-a-a !

In a few seconds there shoots up the same staff another flag—one intended to be white ; but having apparently been folded away a long time, it is mildewed and dingy.

From all the guns on the city fortifications a salute peals out. This is responded to by the English infantry and artillery with a feu-de-joie.

The Regiments

Hurrah-h-h-h !

The various battalions are then marched away in their respective directions and dismissed to their tents. The Bourbon standard is hoisted everywhere beside those of England, Spain, and Portugal.

The scene shuts.

SCENE VI

A HIGHWAY IN THE OUTSKIRTS OF AVIGNON

The Rhone, the old city walls, the Rocher des Doms and its edifices, appear at the back plane of the scene under the grey light of dawn. In the foreground several postillions and ostlers

with relays of horses are waiting by the roadside, gazing northward and listening for sounds. A few loungers have assembled.

FIRST POSTILLION

He ought to be nigh by this time. I should say
he'd be very glad to get to this here Isle of Elba,
wherever it may be, if words be true that he's
treated to such ghastly compliments on's way !

SECOND POSTILLION

Blast-me-blue, I don't care what happens to
him ! Look at Joachim Murat, him that's made
King of Naples ; a man who was only in the same
line of life as ourselves, born and bred in Cahors, out
in Perigord, a poor little whindling place not half as
good as our own. Why should he have been lifted
up to king's anointment, and we not even have had
a rise in wages ? That's what I say.

FIRST POSTILLION

But now, I don't find fault with that dispensation
in particular. It was one of our calling that the
Emperor so honoured, after all, when he might have
anointed a tinker, or a ragman, or a street woman's
pensioner even. Who knows but that we should
have been kings too, but for my crooked legs and
your running pole-wound ?

SECOND POSTILLION

We kings ? Kings of the underground country,
then, by this time, if we hadn't been too rotten-
fleshed to follow the drum. However, I'll think
over your defence, and I don't mind riding a stage
with him, for that matter, to save him from them

that mean mischief here. I've lost no sons by his
battles, like some others we know.

Enter a TRAVELLER *on horseback.*

Any tidings along the road, sir, of the Emperor
Napoléon that was ?

TRAVELLER

Tidings verily !   He and his escort are threatened
by the mob at every place they come to.   A courier
from the south whom I have met tells me that at an
inn a little way beyond here they have strung up his
effigy to the sign-post, smeared it with blood, and
placarded it " The Doom that awaits Thee ! "   He
is much delayed by such humorous insults.   I have
hastened along to escape the uproar.

SECOND POSTILLION

I don't know that you have escaped it.   The
mob has been waiting up all night for him here.

[Exit TRAVELLER *dubiously.*

MARKET-WOMAN (coming up)

I hope by the Virgin, as 'a called herself, that
there'll be no riots here !   Though I have not much
pity for a man who could treat his first wife as he
did, and that's my real feeling.   He might at least
have kept them both on, for half a husband is better
than none for poor women.   But I'd show mercy to
him, that's true, rather than have my stall upset,
and messes in the streets wi' folks' brains, and
stabbings, and I don't know what all !

FIRST POSTILLION

If we can do the horsing quietly out here, there
will be none of that.   He'll dash past the town with-

out stopping at the inn where they expect to waylay
him.—Hark, what's this coming ?

An approaching cortège is heard. Two couriers enter ; then
a carriage containing GENERAL DROUOT ; then a carriage with
NAPOLÉON and BERTRAND ; then others with the Commissioners of the Powers,—all on the way to Elba.

The carriages halt, and the change of horses is set about
instantly.   But before it is half completed BONAPARTE'S
arrival gets known, and throngs of men and women armed with
sticks and hammers rush out of Avignon and surround the
carriages.

POPULACE

Ogre of Corsica !   Odious tyrant !   Down with
Nicholas !

BERTRAND (looking out of carriage)

Silence, and doff your hats, you ill-mannered
devils !

POPULACE (scornfully)

Listen to him !   Is that the Corsican ?   No ;
where is he ?   Give him up ; give him up !   We'll
pitch him into the Rhone !

Some cling to the wheels of NAPOLÉON'S carriage, while
others, more distant, throw stones at it.   A stone breaks the
carriage window.

OLD WOMAN (shaking her fist)

Give me back my two sons, murderer !   Give me
back my children, whose flesh is rotting on the
Russian plains !

POPULACE

Ay ; give us back our kin — our fathers, our
brothers, our sons—victims to your curst ambition !

One of the mob seizes the carriage-door handle and tries
to unfasten it.   A valet of BONAPARTE'S seated on the box
draws his sword and threatens to cut the man's arm off.   The

doors of the Commissioners' coaches open, and SIR NEIL CAMPBELL, GENERAL KOLLER, and COUNT SCHUVALOFF—the English, Austrian, and Russian Commissioners—jump out and come forward.

CAMPBELL

Keep order, citizens ! Do you not know
That the ex-Emperor is wayfaring
To a lone isle, in the Allies' sworn care,
Who have given a pledge to Europe for his safety ?
His fangs being drawn, he gnashes powerless now
To do you further harm.

SCHUVALOFF

People of France,
Can you insult so miserable a being ?
He who gave laws to a cowed world stands now
At that world's beck, and asks its charity.
Cannot you see that merely to ignore him
Is the worst ignominy to tar him with,
By showing him he's no longer dangerous ?

OLD WOMAN

How do we know the villain mayn't come back ?
While there is life, my faith, there's mischief in him !

Enter an officer with the Town-guard.

OFFICER

Citizens, I am a zealot for the Bourbons,
As you well know.   But wanton breach of faith
I will not brook.   Retire !

The soldiers drive back the mob and open a passage forward. The Commissioners re-enter their carriages. NAPOLÉON puts his head out of his window for a moment.   He is haggard, shabbily dressed, yellow-faced, and wild-eyed.

NAPOLÉON

I thank you, captain ;
Also your soldiery : a thousand thanks !
(To Bertrand within) My God, these people of Avignon
    here
Are headstrong fools, like all Provençal folk.
—I won't go through the town !

BERTRAND

We'll round it, sire ;
And then, as soon as we get past the place,
You must disguise for the remainder miles.

NAPOLÉON

I'll mount the white cockade if they invite me !
What does it matter if I do or don't ?
In Europe all is past and over with me. . . .
Yes—all is lost in Europe for me now !

BERTRAND
I fear so, sire.

NAPOLÉON (after some moments)

But Asia waits a man,
And—who can tell ?

OFFICER OF GUARD (to postillions)

Ahead now at full speed,
And slacken not till you have slipped the town.

The postillions urge the horses to a gallop, and the carriages
are out of sight in a few seconds.

The scene shuts.

SCENE VII

MALMAISON. THE EMPRESS JOSÉPHINE'S
BEDCHAMBER

The walls are in white panels with gilt mouldings, and the
furniture is upholstered in white silk with needle-worked
flowers. The long windows and the bed are similarly draped,
and the toilet service is of gold. Through the panes appears
a broad flat lawn adorned with vases and figures on pedestals,
and entirely surrounded by trees—just now in their first fresh
green under the morning rays of Whitsunday. The notes of
an organ are audible from a chapel below, where the Pentecostal
Mass is proceeding.

JOSÉPHINE lies in the bed in an advanced stage of illness, the
ABBÉ BERTRAND standing beside her. Two ladies-in-waiting
are seated near. By the door into the ante-room, which is
ajar, HOREAU the physician-in-ordinary and BOURDOIS the
consulting physician are engaged in a low conversation.

HOREAU

Lamoureux says that leeches would have saved her
Had they been used in time, before I came.
In that case, then, why did he wait for me ?

BOURDOIS

Such Whys are now too late !   She is past all hope.
I doubt if aught had helped her.   Not disease,
But heart-break and repinings are the blasts
That wither her long bloom.   Soon we must tell
The Queen Hortense the worst, and the Viceroy.

HOREAU

Her death was made the easier task for grief
(As I regarded more than probable)

By her rash rising from a sore-sick bed
And donning thin and dainty May attire
To hail King Frederick-William and the Tsar
As banquet-guests, in the old regnant style.
A woman's innocent vanity !—but how dire.
She argued that amenities of State
Compelled the effort, since they had honoured her
By offering to come.　I stood against it,
Pleaded and reasoned, but to no account.
Poor woman, what she did or did not do
Was of small moment to the State by then !
The Emperor Alexander has been kind
Throughout his stay in Paris.　He came down
But yester-eve, of purpose to inquire.

BOURDOIS

Wellington is in Paris, too, I learn,
After his wasted battle at Toulouse.

HOREAU

Has his Peninsular army come with him ?

BOURDOIS

I hear they have shipped it to America,
Where England has another war on hand.
We have armies quite sufficient here already—
Plenty of cooks for Paris broth just now !
—Come, call we Queen Hortense and Prince Eugène.

[Exeunt physicians.

　The ABBÉ BERTRAND also goes out.　JOSÉPHINE murmurs
faintly.

FIRST LADY (going to the bedside)

I think I heard you speak, your Majesty ?

JOSÉPHINE

I asked what hour it was—if dawn or eve ?

FIRST LADY

Ten in the morning, Madame.   You forget
You asked the same but a brief while ago.

JOSÉPHINE

Did I ?   I thought it was so long ago ! . . .
I wished to go to Elba with him much,
But the Allies prevented me.   And why ?
I would not have disgraced him, or themselves !
I would have gone to him at Fontainebleau,
With my eight horses and my household train
In dignity, and quitted him no more. . . .
Although I am his wife no longer now,
I think I should have gone in spite of them,
Had I not feared perversions might be sown
Between him and the woman of his choice
For whom he sacrificed me.

SECOND LADY

                    It is more
Than she thought fit to do, your Majesty.

JOSÉPHINE

Perhaps she was influenced by her father's ire,
Or diplomatic reasons told against her.
And yet I was surprised she should allow
Aught secondary on earth to hold her from
A husband she has outwardly, at least,
Declared attachment to.

First Lady

Especially
With ever one at hand—his son and hers—
Reminding her of him.

Joséphine

Yes. . . . Glad am I
I saw that child of theirs, though only once.
But—there was not full truth—not quite, I fear—
In what I told the Emperor that day
He led him in to me at Bagatelle,
That 'twas the happiest moment of my life.
I ought not to have said it. No ! Forsooth
My feeling had too, too much gall in it
To let truth shape like that !—I also said
That when my arms were round him I forgot
That I was not his mother. So spoke I,
But O me,—I remembered it too well !—
He was a lovely child ; in his fond prate
His father's voice was eloquent. One might say
I am well punished for my sins against him !

Second Lady

You have harmed no creature, Madame ; much less
    him !

Joséphine

O but you don't quite know ! . . . My coquetries
In our first married years nigh racked him through.
I cannot think how I could wax so wicked ! . . .
He begged me come to him in Italy,
But I liked flirting in fair Paris best,
And would not go. The independent spouse
At that time was myself ; but afterwards
I grew to be the captive, he the free.
Always 'tis so : the man wins finally !

My faults I've ransomed to the bottom sou
If ever a woman did ! . . . I'll write to him—
I must—again, so that he understands.
Yes, I'll write now.   Get me a pen and paper.

FIRST LADY (to Second Lady)

'Tis futile !   She is too far gone to write ;
But we must humour her.

They fetch writing materials. On returning to the bed they
find her motionless. Enter EUGÈNE and QUEEN HORTENSE.
Seeing the state their mother is in, they fall down on their
knees by her bed. JOSÉPHINE recognizes them and smiles.
Anon she is able to speak again.

JOSÉPHINE (faintly)

                        I am dying, dears ;
And do not mind it—notwithstanding that
I feel I die regretted.   You both love me !—
And as for France, I ever have desired
Her welfare, as you know—have wrought all things
A woman's scope could reach to forward it. . . .
And to you now who watch my ebbing here,
Declare I that Napoléon's first-chose wife
Has never caused her land a needless tear.
Tell him—these things I have said—bear him my
       love—
Tell him—I could not write !

An interval. She spasmodically flings her arms over her
son and daughter, lets them fall, and becomes unconscious.
They fetch a looking-glass, and find that her breathing has
ceased. The clock of the Château strikes noon.

The scene is veiled.

SCENE VIII

LONDON. THE OPERA-HOUSE

The house is lighted up with a blaze of wax candles, and a State performance is about to begin in honour of the Allied sovereigns now on a visit to England to celebrate the Peace. Peace-devices adorn the theatre. A band can be heard in the street playing " The White Cockade."

An extended Royal box has been formed by removing the partitions of adjoining boxes. It is empty as yet, but the other parts of the house are crowded to excess, and somewhat disorderly, the interior doors having been broken down by besiegers, and many people having obtained admission without payment. The prevalent costume of the ladies is white satin and diamonds, with a few in lilac.

The curtain rises on the first act of the opera of " Aristodemo," MADAME GRASSINI and SIGNOR TRAMEZZINI being the leading voices. Scarcely a note of the performance can be heard amid the exclamations of persons half suffocated by the pressure.

At the end of the first act there follows a divertissement. The curtain having fallen, a silence of expectation succeeds. It is a little past ten o'clock.

Enter the Royal box the PRINCE REGENT, accompanied by the EMPEROR ALEXANDER OF RUSSIA, demonstrative in manner now as always, the KING OF PRUSSIA, with his mien of reserve, and many minor ROYAL PERSONAGES of Europe. There are moderate acclamations. At their back and in neighbouring boxes LORD LIVERPOOL, LORD CASTLEREAGH, officers in the suite of the sovereigns, interpreters, and others take their places.

The curtain rises again, and the performers are discovered drawn up in line on the stage. They sing " God save the King." The sovereigns stand up, bow, and resume their seats amid more applause.

A VOICE (from the gallery)

Prinny, where's your wife ?   (Confusion.)

EMPEROR OF RUSSIA (to Regent)

To which of us is the inquiry addressed, Prince ?

PRINCE REGENT

To you, sire, depend upon't—by way of compliment.

The second act of the Opera proceeds.

EMPEROR OF RUSSIA

Any later news from Elba, sir ?

PRINCE REGENT

Nothing more than rumours, which, 'pon my
honour, I can hardly credit.   One is that Bonaparte's valet has written to say that the ex-Emperor
is becoming imbecile, and is an object of ridicule to
the inhabitants of the island.

KING OF PRUSSIA

A blessed result, sir, if true.   If he is not imbecile
he is worse—planning how to involve Europe in
another war.   It was a short-sighted policy to offer
him a home so near as to ensure its becoming a hot-
bed of intrigue and conspiracy in no long time !

PRINCE REGENT

The ex-Empress, Marie-Louise, hasn't joined him
after all, I learn.   Has she remained at Schönbrunn
since leaving France, sires ?

EMPEROR OF RUSSIA

Yes, sir ; with her son.   She must never go back
to France.   Metternich and her father will know

better than let her do that. Poor young thing, I
am sorry for her all the same. She would have
joined Napoléon if she had been left to herself.—
And I was sorry for the other wife, too. I called at
Malmaison a few days before she died. A charming
woman ! *She* would have gone to Elba or to the
devil with him. Twenty thousand people crowded
down from Paris to see her lying in state last week.

PRINCE REGENT

Pity she didn't have a child by him, by God.

KING OF PRUSSIA

I don't think the other one's child is going to
trouble us much. But I wish Bonaparte himself
had been sent further away.

PRINCE REGENT

Some of our Government wanted to pack him off
to St. Helena—an island somewhere in the Atlantic,
or Pacific, or Great South Sea. But they were over-
ruled. 'Twould have been a surer game.

EMPEROR OF RUSSIA

One hears strange stories of his sayings and
doings. Some of my people were telling me to-day
that he says it is to Austria that he really owes his
fall, and that he ought to have destroyed her when
he had her in his power.

PRINCE REGENT

Dammy, sire, don't ye think he owes his fall to
his ambition to humble England by the rupture of
the Peace of Amiens, and trying to invade us, and
wasting his strength against us in the Peninsula ?

Emperor of Russia

I incline to think, with the greatest deference, that it was Moscow that broke him.

King of Prussia

The rejection of my conditions in the terms of peace at Prague, sires, was the turning-point towards his downfall.

Enter a box on the opposite side of the house the Princess of Wales, *attended by* Lady Charlotte Campbell, Sir W. Gell, *and others. Louder applause now rings through the theatre, drowning the sweet voice of the* Grassini *in " Aristodemo."*

Lady Charlotte Campbell

It is meant for your Royal Highness !

Princess of Wales

I don't think so, my dear. Punch's wife is nobody when Punch himself is present.

Lady Charlotte Campbell

I feel convinced that it is by their looking this way.

Sir W. Gell

Surely, ma'am, you will acknowledge their affection ?   Otherwise we may be hissed.

Princess of Wales

I know my business better than to take that morsel out of my husband's mouth. There—you see he enjoys it !   I cannot assume that it is meant for me unless they call my name.

The PRINCE REGENT rises and bows, the TSAR and the KING OF PRUSSIA doing the same.

LADY CHARLOTTE CAMPBELL

He and the others are bowing to you, ma'am!

PRINCESS OF WALES

Mine God, then; I will bow too! (She rises and bends to them.)

PRINCE REGENT

She thinks we rose on her account.—A damn fool! (Aside.)

EMPEROR OF RUSSIA

What—didn't we? I certainly rose in homage to her.

PRINCE REGENT

No, sire. We were supposed to rise to the repeated applause of the people.

EMPEROR OF RUSSIA

H'm. Your customs, sir, are a little puzzling. . . . (To the King of Prussia.) A fine-looking woman! I must call upon the Princess of Wales to-morrow.

KING OF PRUSSIA

I shall, at any rate, send her my respects by my chamberlain.

PRINCE REGENT (stepping back to Lord Liverpool)

By God, Liverpool, we must do something to stop 'em! They don't know what a laughing-stock they'll make of me if they go to her. Tell 'em they had better not.

LIVERPOOL

I can hardly tell them now, sir, while we are celebrating the Peace and Wellington's victories.

PRINCE REGENT

Oh, damn the peace, and damn the war, and damn Boney, and damn Wellington's victories !— the question is, how am I to get over this infernal woman !—Well, well,—I must write, or send Tyr- whitt to-morrow morning, begging them to abandon the idea of visiting her for politic reasons.

The Opera proceeds to the end, and is followed by a hymn and chorus laudatory of peace. Next a new ballet by MONSIEUR VESTRIS, in which M. ROZIER and MADAME ANGIOLINI dance a pas-de-deux. Then the Sovereigns leave the theatre amid more applause.

The pit and gallery now call for the PRINCESS OF WALES unmistakably. She stands up and is warmly acclaimed, return- ing three stately curtseys.

A VOICE

Shall we burn down Carlton House, my dear, and him in it ?

PRINCESS OF WALES

No, my good folks ! Be quiet. Go home to your beds, and let me do the same.

After some difficulty she gets out of the house. The people thin away. As the candle-snuffers extinguish the lights a shouting is heard without.

VOICES OF CROWD

Long life to the Princess of Wales ! Three cheers for a woman wronged !

The Opera-house becomes lost in darkness.

ACT FIFTH

SCENE I

ELBA. THE QUAY, PORTO FERRAJO

Night descends upon a beautiful blue cove, enclosed on three sides by mountains. The port lies towards the western (right-hand) horn of the concave, behind it being the buildings of the town; their long white walls and rows of windows rise tier above tier on the steep incline at the back, and are intersected by narrow alleys and flights of steps that lead up to forts on the summit.

Upon a rock between two of these forts stands the Palace of the Mulini, NAPOLÉON's residence in Ferrajo. Its windows command the whole town and port.

CHORUS OF IRONIC SPIRITS (aerial music)

The Congress of Vienna sits,
And war becomes a war of wits,
Where every Power perpends withal
Its dues as large, its friends' as small;
Till Priests of Peace prepare once more
To fight as they have fought before!

In Paris there is discontent;
Medals are wrought that represent
One now unnamed. Men whisper, " He
Who once has been, again will be ! "

DUMB SHOW

Under cover of the dusk there assembles in the bay a small flotilla comprising a brig called *l'Inconstant* and several lesser vessels.

Spirit of Rumour

The guardian on behalf of the Allies
Absents himself from Elba.   Slow surmise
Too vague to pen, too actual to ignore,
Have strained him hour by hour, and more and more.
He takes the sea to Florence, to declare
His doubts to Austria's ministrator there.

Spirit Ironic

When he returns, Napoléon will be—where ?

Boats put off from these ships to the quay, where are now discovered to have silently gathered a body of grenadiers of the Old Guard.   The faces of Drouot and Cambronne are revealed by the occasional fleck of a lantern to be in command of them.   They are quietly taken aboard the brig, and a number of men of different arms to the other vessels.

Chorus of Rumours (aerial music)

Napoléon is going,
And nought will prevent him ;
He snatches the moment
Occasion has lent him !

And what is he going for,
Worn with war's labours ?
—To reconquer Europe
With seven hundred sabres.

About eight o'clock we observe that the windows of the Palace of the Mulini are lighted and open, and that two women sit at them : the Emperor's mother and the Princess Pauline. They wave adieux to some one below, and in a short time a little open low-wheeled carriage, drawn by the Princess Pauline's two ponies, descends from the house to the port. The crowd exclaims " The Emperor ! " Napoléon appears in his grey great-coat, and is much fatter than when he left France.   Bertrand sits beside him.

He quickly alights and enters the waiting boat.   It is a tense moment.   As the boat rows off the sailors sing the Marseillaise, and the gathered inhabitants join in. When the boat reaches the brig its sailors join in also, and shout " Paris or death ! " Yet the singing has a melancholy cadence. A gun fires as a signal of departure. The night is warm and balmy for the season. Not a breeze is there to stir a sail, and the ships are motionless.

CHORUS OF RUMOURS

Haste is salvation ;
And still he stays waiting :
The calm plays the tyrant,
His venture belating !

Should the corvette return
With the anxious Scotch colonel,
Escape would be frustrate,
Retention eternal.

Four aching hours are spent thus. NAPOLÉON remains silent on deck, looking at the town lights, whose reflections bore like augers into the waters of the bay. The sails hang flaccidly. Then a feeble breeze, then a strong south wind, begins to belly the sails ; and the vessels move.

CHORUS OF RUMOURS

The south wind, the south wind,
The south wind will save him,
Embaying the frigate
Whose speed would enslave him ;
Restoring the Empire
That Fortune once gave him !

The moon rises, and the ships silently disappear over the horizon as it mounts higher into the sky.

SCENE II

VIENNA. THE IMPERIAL PALACE

The fore-part of the scene is the interior of a dimly lit gallery
with an openwork screen or grille on one side of it that commands a bird's-eye view of the grand saloon below. At present the screen is curtained. Sounds of music and applause in
the saloon ascend into the gallery, and an irradiation from the
same quarter shines up through chinks in the curtains of the
grille.

Enter the gallery MARIE LOUISE and the COUNTESS OF
BRIGNOLE, followed by the COUNT NEIPPERG, a handsome
man of forty-two with a bandage over one eye.

COUNTESS OF BRIGNOLE

Listen, your Majesty. You gather all
As well as if you moved amid them there,
And are advantaged with free scope to flit
The moment the scene palls.

MARIE LOUISE

                              Ah, my dear friend,
To put it so is flower-sweet of you ;
But a fallen Empress, doomed to furtive peeps
At scenes her open presence would unhinge,
Reads not much interest in them ! Yet, in truth,
'Twas gracious of my father to arrange
This glimpse-hole for my curiosity.
—But I must write a letter ere I look ;
You can amuse yourself with watching them.—
Count, bring me pen and paper. I am told
Madame de Montesquiou has been distressed
By some alarm ; I write to ask its shape.

NEIPPERG spreads writing materials on a table, and MARIE
LOUISE sits. While she writes he stays near her. MADAME DE
BRIGNOLE goes to the screen and parts the curtains.

The light of a thousand candles blazes up into her eyes from
below. The great hall is decorated in white and silver, enriched
by evergreens and flowers. At the end a stage is arranged,
and Tableaux Vivants are in progress thereon, representing
the history of the House of Austria, in which figure the most
charming women of the Court.

There are present as spectators nearly all the notables who
have assembled for the Congress, including the EMPEROR OF
AUSTRIA himself, his gay wife, who quite eclipses him, the
EMPEROR ALEXANDER, the KING OF PRUSSIA—still in the
mourning he has never abandoned since the death of QUEEN
LOUISA,—the KING OF BAVARIA and his son, METTERNICH,
TALLEYRAND, WELLINGTON, NESSELRODE, HARDENBERG ; and
minor princes, ministers, and officials of all nations.

COUNTESS OF BRIGNOLE (suddenly from the grille)

Something has happened—so it seems, Madame !
The Tableau gains no heed from them, and all
Turn murmuring together.

MARIE LOUISE
What may it be ?

She rises with languid curiosity, and COUNT NEIPPERG
adroitly takes her hand and leads her forward. All three
look down through the grille.

NEIPPERG

Some strange news, certainly, your Majesty,
Is being discussed.—I'll run down and inquire.

MARIE LOUISE (playfully)

Nay—stay you here. We shall learn soon enough.

NEIPPERG

Look at their faces now. Count Metternich
Stares at Prince Talleyrand—no muscle moving.

The King of Prussia blinks bewilderedly
Upon Lord Wellington.

MARIE LOUISE (concerned)

                  Yes ; so it seems. . . .
They are thunderstruck. See, though the music
    beats,
The ladies of the Tableau leave their place,
And mingle with the rest, and quite forget
That they are in masquerade.   The sovereigns show
By far the gravest mien. . . . I wonder, now,
If it has aught to do with me or mine ?
Disasters mostly have to do with me !

COUNTESS OF BRIGNOLE

Those rude diplomatists from England there,
At your Imperial father's consternation,
And Russia's, and the King of Prussia's gloom,
Shake shoulders with hid laughter !   That they call
The English sense of humour, I infer,—
To see a jest in other people's troubles !

MARIE LOUISE (hiding her presages)

They ever take things thus phlegmatically :
The safe sea scantles Continental scares
In their regard.   I wish it did in mine !
But Wellington laughs not, as I discern.

NEIPPERG

Perhaps, though fun for the other English here,
It means new work for him.   Ah—notice now
The music makes no more pretence to play !
Sovereigns and ministers have moved apart,
And talk, and leave the ladies quite aloof—
Even the Grand Duchesses and Empress, all—
Such mighty cogitations trance their minds !

MARIE LOUISE (with more anxiety)

Poor ladies ; yea, they draw into the rear,
And whisper ominous words among themselves !
Count Neipperg—I must ask you now—go glean
What evil lowers.   I am riddled through
With strange surmises and more strange alarms !

The COUNTESS OF MONTESQUIOU enters.

Ah—we shall learn it now.   Well—what, madame ?

COUNTESS OF MONTESQUIOU (breathlessly)

Your Majesty, the Emperor Napoléon
Has vanished out of Elba !   Whither flown,
And how, and why, nobody says or knows.

MARIE LOUISE (sinking into a chair)

My divination pencilled on my brain
Something not unlike that !   The rigid mien
That mastered Wellington suggested it. . . .
Complicity will be ascribed to me,
Unwitting though I stand ! . . .   (A pause.)
                      He'll not succeed !
And my fair plans for Parma will be marred,
And my son's future fouled !—I must go hence,
And instantly declare to Metternich
That I know nought of this ; and in his hands
Place me unquestioningly, with dumb assent.
To serve the Allies. . . . Methinks that I was born
Under an evil-coloured star, whose ray
Darts death at joys !—Take me away, Count.—You
    (to the two ladies)
Can stay and see the end.

                  [Exeunt MARIE LOUISE and NEIPPERG.

    MESDAMES DE MONTESQUIOU and DE BRIGNOLE go to the
grille and watch and listen.

VOICE OF ALEXANDER (below)

I told you, Prince, that it would never last !

VOICE OF TALLEYRAND

Well, sire, you should have sent him to the Azores,
Or the Antilles, or best, Saint-Helena.

VOICE OF THE KING OF PRUSSIA

Instead, we send him but two days from France,
Give him an island as his own domain,
A military guard of large resource,
And millions for his purse !

ANOTHER VOICE

                  The immediate cause
Must be a negligence in watching him.
The British Colonel Campbell should have seen
That apertures for flight were wired and barred
To such a cunning bird !

ANOTHER VOICE

                  By all report
He took the course direct to Naples Bay.

VOICES (of new arrivals)

He has made his way to France—so all tongues tell—
And landed there, at Cannes !   (Excitement.)

COUNTESS OF BRIGNOLE

                  Do now but note
How cordial intercourse resolves itself
To sparks of sharp debate !   The lesser guests

Are fain to steal unnoticed from a scene
Wherein they feel themselves as surplusage
Beside the official minds.—I catch a sign
The King of Prussia makes the English Duke ;
They leave the room together.

COUNTESS OF MONTESQUIOU

                              Yes ; wit wanes,
And all are going—Prince de Talleyrand,
The Emperor Alexander, Metternich,
The Emperor Francis. . . . So much for the Congress !
Only a few blank nobodies remain,
And they seem terror-stricken. . . . Blackly ends
Such fair festivities.   The red god War
Stalks Europe's plains anew !

    The curtain of the grille is dropped.   MESDAMES DE MONTES-
QUIOU and DE BRIGNOLE leave the gallery.   The light is extinguished there and the scene disappears.

SCENE III

LA MURE, NEAR GRENOBLE

    A lonely road between a lake and some hills, two or three
miles outside the village of la Mure, is discovered. A battalion
of the Fifth French royalist regiment of the line, under COM-
MANDANT LESSARD, is drawn up in the middle of the road with
a company of sappers and miners, comprising altogether about
eight hundred men.
    Enter to them from the south a small detachment of lancers
with an aide-de-camp at their head. They ride up to within
speaking distance.

LESSARD

They are from Bonaparte.   Present your arms !

AIDE (calling)

We'd parley on Napoléon's behalf,
And fain would ask you join him.

LESSARD

All parole
With rebel bands the Government forbids.
Come five steps further, and we fire !

AIDE

To France,
And to posterity through fineless time,
Must you then answer for so foul a blow
Against the common weal !

NAPOLÉON'S aide-de-camp and the lancers turn about and
ride back out of sight. The royalist troops wait. Presently
there reappears from the same direction a small column of
soldiery, representing the whole of NAPOLÉON's little army
shipped from Elba. It is divided into an advance-guard under
COLONEL MALLET, and two bodies behind, a troop of Polish
lancers under COLONEL JERMANWSKI on the right side of the
road, and some officers without troops on the left, under MAJOR
PACCONI.

NAPOLÉON rides in the midst of the advance-guard, in the
old familiar " redingote grise," cocked hat, and tricolor cockade,
his well-known profile keen against the hills. He is attended
by GENERALS BERTRAND, DROUOT, and CAMBRONNE. When
they get within a gun-shot of the royalists the men are halted.
NAPOLÉON dismounts and steps forward.

NAPOLÉON

Direct the men
To lodge their weapons underneath the arm,
Points downward. I shall not require them here.

COLONEL MALLET

Sire, is it not a needless jeopardy
To meet them thus ? The sentiments of these

We do not know, and the first trigger pressed
May end you.

NAPOLÉON

I have thought it out, my friend,
And value not my life as in itself,
But as to France, severed from whose embrace
I am dead already.

He repeats the order, which is carried out. There is a
breathless silence, and people from the village gather round
with tragic expectations. NAPOLÉON walks on alone towards
the Fifth battalion, throwing open his great-coat and revealing
his uniform and the ribbon of the Legion of Honour. Raising
his hand to his hat he salutes.

LESSARD

Present arms !

The firelocks of the royalist battalion are levelled at
NAPOLÉON.

NAPOLÉON (still advancing)

Men of the Fifth,
See—here I am ! . . . Old friends, do you not know
    me ?
If there be one among you who would slay
His Chief of proud past years, let him come on
And do it now !   (A pause.)

LESSARD (to his next officer)

They are death-white at his words !
They'll fire not on this man.   And I am helpless.

SOLDIERS (suddenly)

Why yes ! We know you, father. Glad to see ye !
The Emperor for ever ! Ha ! Huzza !

They throw their arms upon the ground, and, rushing
forward, sink down and seize NAPOLÉON's knees and kiss his

hands. Those who cannot get near him wave their shakos
and acclaim him passionately. BERTRAND, DROUOT, and
CAMBRONNE come up.

NAPOLÉON (privately)

All is accomplished, Bertrand !   Ten days more,
And we are snug within the Tuileries.

The soldiers tear out their white cockades and trample
on them, and disinter from the bottom of their knapsacks
tricolors, which they set up.

NAPOLÉON's own men now arrive, and fraternize with and
embrace the soldiers of the Fifth. When the emotion has subsided NAPOLÉON forms the whole body into a square and
addresses them.

Soldiers, I come with these few faithful ones
To save you from the Bourbons,—treasons, tricks,
Ancient abuses, feudal tyranny—
From which I once of old delivered you.
The Bourbon throne is illegitimate
Because not founded on the nation's will,
But propped up for the profit of a few.
Comrades, is this not so ?

A GRENADIER

                    Yes, verily, sire.
You are the Angel of the Lord to us ;
We'll march with you to death or victory !

                                (Shouts.)

At this moment a howling dog crosses in front of them with
a white cockade tied to its tail. The soldiery of both sides
laugh loudly.

NAPOLÉON forms both bodies of troops into one column.
Peasantry run up with buckets of sour wine and a single glass ;
NAPOLÉON takes his turn with the rank and file in drinking
from it. He bids the whole column follow him to Grenoble
and Paris. Exeunt soldiers headed by NAPOLÉON.

The scene shuts.

SCENE IV

SCHÖNBRUNN

The gardens of the Palace. Fountains and statuary are seen around, and the Gloriette colonnade rising against the sky on a hill behind.

The ex-EMPRESS MARIE LOUISE is discovered walking up and down. Accompanying her is the KING OF ROME—now a blue-eyed, fair-haired child—in the charge of the COUNTESS OF MONTESQUIOU. Close by is COUNT NEIPPERG, and at a little distance MÉNEVAL, her attendant and NAPOLÉON's adherent.

The EMPEROR FRANCIS and METTERNICH enter at the other end of the parterre.

MARIE LOUISE (with a start)

Here are the Emperor and Prince Metternich.
Wrote you as I directed ?

NEIPPERG

     Promptly so.
I said your Majesty had had no part
In this mad move of your Imperial spouse,
And willed yourself a ward of the Allies ;
Adding, that you had vowed irrevocably
To enter France no more.

MARIE LOUISE

     Your worthy zeal
Has been a trifle swift. My meaning stretched
Not quite so far as that. . . . And yet—and yet
It matters little. Nothing matters much !

The EMPEROR and METTERNICH come forward. NEIPPERG retires.

FRANCIS

My daughter, you did not a whit too soon
Voice your repudiation.   Have you seen
What the Allies have papered Europe with ?

MARIE LOUISE

I have seen nothing.

FRANCIS

Please you read it, Prince.

METTERNICH (taking out a paper)

" The Powers assembled at the Congress here
Owe it to their own troths and dignities,
And to the furtherance of social order,
To make a solemn Declaration, thus :
By breaking the convention as to Elba,
Napoléon Bonaparte forthwith destroys
His only legal title to exist,
And as a consequence has hurled himself
Beyond the pale of civil intercourse.
Disturber of the tranquillity of the world,
There can be neither peace nor truce with him,
And public vengeance is his self-sought doom.—
Signed by the Plenipotentiaries."

MARIE LOUISE (pale)

                                        O God,
How terrible ! . . . What shall—— (she begins weeping).

KING OF ROME

                              Is it papa
They want to hurt like that, dear Mamma 'Quiou ?
Then 'twas no good my praying for him so ;

And I can see that I am not going to be
A King much longer !

COUNTESS OF MONTESQUIOU (retiring with the child)

                  Pray for him, Monseigneur,
Morning and evening just the same !   They plan
To take you off from me.   But don't forget—
Do as I say !

           KING OF ROME

           Yes, Mamma 'Quiou, I will !—
But why have I no pages now ?   And why
Does my mamma the Empress weep so much ?

      COUNTESS OF MONTESQUIOU

We'll talk elsewhere.

    [MONTESQUIOU and the KING OF ROME withdraw to back.

          FRANCIS

             At least, then, you agree
Not to attempt to follow Paris-wards
Your conscience-lacking husband, and create
More troubles in the State ?—Remember this,
I sacrifice my every man and horse
Ere he rule France again.

        MARIE LOUISE

             I am pledged already
To hold by the Allies ; let that suffice !

        METTERNICH

For the clear good of all, your Majesty,
And for your safety and the King of Rome's,

It most befits that your Imperial father
Should have sole charge of the young king hence-
        forth,
While these convulsions rage.   That this is so
You will see, I think, in view of being installed
As Parma's Duchess, and take steps therefor.

MARIE LOUISE (coldly)

I understand the terms to be as follows :
Parma is mine—my very own possession,—
And as a counterquit, the guardianship
Is ceded to my father of my son,
And I keep out of France.

METTERNICH

                    And likewise this :
All missives that your Majesty receives
Under Napoléon's hand, you tender straight
The Austrian Cabinet, the seals unbroke ;
With those received already.

FRANCIS

                    You discern
How vastly to the welfare of your son
This course must tend ? Duchess of Parma throned
You shine a wealthy woman, to endow
Your son with fortune and large landed fee.

MARIE LOUISE (bitterly)

I must have Parma : and those being the terms
Perforce accept !   I weary of the strain
Of statecraft and political embroil :
I long for private quiet ! . . . And now wish
To say no more at all.

     MÉNEVAL, who has heard her latter remarks, turns sadly
away.

FRANCIS

There's nought to say ;
All is in train to work straightforwardly.

[FRANCIS and METTERNICH depart.

MARIE LOUISE retires towards the child and the COUNTESS
OF MONTESQUIOU at the back of the parterre, where they are
joined by NEIPPERG.

Enter in front DE MONTROND, a secret emissary of NAPOLÉON,
disguised as a florist examining the gardens. MÉNEVAL recognizes him and comes forward.

MÉNEVAL

Why are you here, de Montrond ? All is hopeless !

DE MONTROND

Wherefore ? The offer of the Regency
I come empowered to make, and will conduct her
Safely to Strassburg with her little son,
If she shrink not to breech her as a man,
And tiptoe from a postern unperceived ?

MÉNEVAL

Though such quaint gear would mould her to a
    youth
Fair as Adonis on a hunting morn,
Yet she'll refuse ! A German prudery
Sits on her still ; more, kneaded by their arts
There's no will left to her. I conjured her
To hold aloof, sign nothing. But in vain.

DE MONTROND (looking towards Marie Louise)

I fain would put it to her privately !

MÉNEVAL

A thing impossible.   No word to her
Without a word to him you see with her,
Neipperg to wit.   She grows indifferent
To dreams as Regent ; visioning a future
Wherein her son and self are two of three,
But where the third is not Napoléon.

DE MONTROND (in sad surprise)

I may as well go hence then as I came,
And kneel to Heaven for one thing—that success
Attend Napoléon in the coming throes !

MÉNEVAL

I'll walk with you for safety to the gate,
Though I am as the Emperor's man suspect,
And any day may be dismissed.   If so
I go to Paris.
                              [Exeunt MÉNEVAL and DE MONTROND.

SPIRIT IRONIC

Had he but persevered, and biassed her
To slip the breeches on, and hie away,
Who knows but that the map of France had shaped
As it will never now !

    There enters from the other side of the gardens MARIA
CAROLINA, ex-Queen of Naples, grandmother of MARIE LOUISE.
The latter, dismissing MONTESQUIOU and the child, comes
forward.

MARIA CAROLINA

I have crossed from Hetzendorf to kill an hour ;
Why art so pensive, dear ?

MARIE LOUISE

　　　　　　　Ah, why ! My lines
Rule ruggedly. You doubtless have perused
This vicious cry against the Emperor ?
He's outlawed—to be caught alive or dead,
Like any noisome beast !

MARIA CAROLINA

　　　　　　Nought have I heard,
My child. But these vile tricks, to pluck you from
Your nuptial plightage and your rightful glory
Make me belch oaths !—You shall not join your
　　　husband
Do they assert ? My God, I know one thing,
Outlawed or no, I'd knot my sheets forthwith,
Were I but you, and steal to him in disguise,
Let come what would come ! Marriage is for life.

MARIE LOUISE

Mostly ; not always : not with Joséphine ;
And, maybe, not with me. But, that apart,
I could do nothing so outrageous now.
Too many things, dear grand-dame, you forget.
A puppet I, by force inflexible,
Was bid to wed Napoléon at a nod,—
The man acclaimed to me from cradle-days
As the incarnate of all evil things,
The Antichrist himself.—I kissed the cup,
Gulped down the inevitable, and married him ;
But none the less I saw myself therein
The lamb whose innocent flesh was dressed to grace
The altar of dynastic ritual !—
Hence Elba flung no duty-call to me,
Neither does Paris now.

MARIA CAROLINA

I do perceive
They have worked on you to much effect already !
Go, join your Count ; he waits you, dear.—Well,
    well ;
The way the wind blows needs no cock to tell !

Exeunt severally QUEEN MARIA CAROLINA *and* MARIE
LOUISE *with* NEIPPERG.

The sun sets over the gardens and the scene fades.

SCENE V

LONDON. THE OLD HOUSE OF COMMONS

The interior of the Chamber appears as in Scene III., Act I.,
Part I., except that the windows are not open and the trees
without are not yet green.

Among the Members discovered in their places are, of min-
isters and their supporters, LORD CASTLEREAGH the Foreign
Secretary, VANSITTART Chancellor of the Exchequer, BATHURST,
PALMERSTON the War Secretary, ROSE, PONSONBY, ARBUTH-
NOT, LUSHINGTON, GARROW the Attorney-General, SHEPHERD,
LONG, PLUNKETT, BANKES ; and among those of the Opposi-
tion SIR FRANCIS BURDETT, WHITBREAD, TIERNEY, ABER-
CROMBY, DUNDAS, BRAND, DUNCANNON, LAMBTON, HEATH-
COTE, SIR SAMUEL ROMILLY, G. WALPOLE, RIDLEY, OSBORNE,
and HORNER.

Much interest in the debate is apparent, and the galleries
are full. LORD CASTLEREAGH rises.

CASTLEREAGH

At never a moment in my stressed career,
Amid no memory-moving urgencies,
Have I, sir, felt so gravely set on me
The sudden, vast responsibility

That I feel now.   Few things conceivable
Could more momentous to the future be
Than what may spring from counsel here to-night
On means to meet the plot, unparalleled,
In full fierce play elsewhere.   Sir, this being so,
And seeing how the events of these last days
Menace the toil of twenty anxious years,
And peril all that period's patient aim,
No auguring mind can doubt that counterstrokes
Of steadiest purpose only, will effect
Deliverance from a world-calamity
As dark as any in the dens of Time.
    Now, what we notice front and foremost is
That this convulsion speaks not, pictures not
The heart of France.   It comes of artifice—
From the unique and sinister influence
Of a smart army-gamester—upon men
Who have shared his own excitements, spoils, and
        crimes.—
This man, who calls himself most impiously
The Emperor of France by Grace of God,
Has, in the scale of human character,
Dropt down so low, that he has set at nought
All pledges, stipulations, guarantees,
And stepped upon the only pedestal
On which he cares to stand—his lawless will.
Indeed, it is a fact scarce credible
That so mysteriously in his own breast
Did this adventurer lock the plot he planned,
That his companion Bertrand, chief in trust,
Was unapprised thereof until the hour
In which the order to embark was given !
    I think the House will readily discern
That the wise, wary trackway to be trod
By our own country in the crisis reached,
Must lie 'twixt two alternatives,—of war
In concert with the Continental Powers,
Or of an armed and cautionary course
Sufficing for the present pucker of things.

Whatever differences of view prevail
On the so serious and impending question—
Whether in point of prudent reckoning
'Twere better let the Power set up exist,
Or promptly at the outset deal with it—
Still, to all eyes it is imperative
That some mode of safeguardance be devised ;
And if I cannot range before the House,
At this stage, all the reachings of the case,
I will, if needful, on some future day
Poise these nice matters on their merits here.
　　Meanwhile I have to move :
That an address unto His Royal Highness
Be humbly offered for his gracious message,
And to assure him that his faithful Commons
Are fully roused to the dark hazardries
To which the life and equanimity
Of Europe are exposed by deeds in France,
In contravention of the plighted pacts
At Paris in the course of yester-year.
　　That, in a cause of such wide-waked concern,
It doth afford us real relief to know
That concert with His Majesty's Allies
Is being effected with no loss of time—
Such concert as will thoroughly provide
For Europe's full and long security.　(Cheers.)
　　That we, with zeal, will speed such help to him
So to augment his force by sea and land
As shall empower him to set afoot
Swift measures meet for its accomplishing.　(Cheers.)

BURDETT

It seems to me almost impossible,
Weighing the language of the noble lord,
To catch its counsel,—whether peace or war.　(Hear,
　　hear.)
If I translate his words to signify

The high expediency of watch and ward,
That we may not be taken unawares,
I own concurrence ; but if he propose
To plunge this realm into a sea of blood
To reinstate the Bourbon line in France,
I should but poorly do my duty here
Did I not lift my voice protestingly
Against so ruinous an enterprise !
   Sir, I am old enough to call to mind
The first fierce frenzies for the selfsame end,
The fruit of which was to endow this man,
The object of your apprehension now,
With such a might as could not be withstood
By all of banded Europe, till he roamed
And wrecked it wantonly on Russian plains.
Shall, then, another score of scourging years
Distract this land to make a Bourbon king ?
Wrongly has Bonaparte's late course been called
A rude incursion on the soil of France.—
Who ever knew a sole and single man
Invade a nation thirty million strong,
And gain in some few days full sovereignty
Against that nation's will !—The truth is this :
The nation longed for him, and has obtained
    him. . . .
   I have beheld the agonies of war
Through many a weary season ; seen enough
To make me hold that scarcely any goal
Is worth the reaching by so red a road.
No man can doubt that this Napoléon stands
As Emperor of France by Frenchmen's wills.
Let the French settle, then, their own affairs ;
I say we shall have nought to apprehend !—
   Much as I might advance in proof of this,
I'll dwell not thereon now.   I am satisfied
To give the general reasons which, in brief,
Balk my concurrence in the Address proposed.
                               (Cheers.)

PONSONBY

My words will be but few, for the Address
Constrains me to support it as it stands.
So far from being the primary step to war,
Its sense and substance is, in my regard,
To leave the House to guidance by events
On the grave question of hostilities.
    The statements of the noble lord, I hold,
Have not been candidly interpreted
By grafting on to them a headstrong will,
As does the honourable baronet,
To rob the French of Buonaparté's rule,
And force them back to Bourbon monarchism.
That our free land, at this abnormal time,
Should put her in a pose of wariness,
No unwarped mind can doubt.   Must war revive,
Let it be quickly waged ; and quickly, too,
Reach its effective end : though 'tis my hope,
My ardent hope, that peace may be preserved.

WHITBREAD

Were it that I could think, as does my friend,
That ambiguity of sentiment
Informed the utterance of the noble lord
(As oft does ambiguity of word),
I might with satisfied and sure resolve
Vote straight for the Address.   But eyeing well
The flimsy web there woven to entrap
The credence of my honourable friends,
I must with all my energy contest
The wisdom of a new and hot crusade
For fixing who shall fill the throne of France !
    Already are the seeds of mischief sown :
The Declaration at Vienna, signed
Against Napoléon, is, in my regard,
Abhorrent, and our country's character
Defaced by our subscription to its terms !

If words have any meaning it incites
To sheer assassination ; it proclaims
That any meeting Bonaparte may slay him ;
And, whatso language the Allies now hold,
In that outburst, at least, was war declared.
The noble lord to-night would second it,
Would seem to urge that we full arm, then wait
For just as long, no longer, than would serve
The preparations of the other Powers,
And then—pounce down on France !

CASTLEREAGH

                No, no !   Not so.

WHITBREAD

Good God, then, what are we to understand ?—
However, this denial is a gain,
And my misapprehension owes its birth
Entirely to that mystery of phrase
Which taints all rhetoric of the noble lord.
   Well, what is urged for new aggression now,
To vamp up and replace the Bourbon line ?
One of the wittiest men who ever sat here [1]
Said half our nation's debt had been incurred
In efforts to suppress the Bourbon power,
The other half in efforts to restore it, (laughter)
And I must deprecate a further plunge
For ends so futile !   Why, since Ministers
Craved peace with Bonaparte at Châtillon,
Should they refuse him peace and quiet now ?
   This brief amendment therefore I submit
To limit Ministers' aggressiveness
And make self-safety all their chartering :
" We at the same time earnestly implore
That the Prince Regent graciously induce
Strenuous endeavours in the cause of peace,
So long as it be done consistently
With the due honour of the English crown."
                       (Cheers.)

[1] Sheridan.

CASTLEREAGH

The arguments of Members opposite
Posit conditions which experience proves
But figments of a dream ;—that honesty,
Truth, and good faith in this same Bonaparte
May be assumed and can be acted on :
This of one who is loud to violate
Bonds the most sacred, treaties the most grave ! . . .
   It follows not that since this realm was won
To treat with Bonaparte at Châtillon,
It can treat now.   And as for assassination,
The sentiments outspoken here to-night
Are much more like to urge to desperate deeds
Against the persons of our good Allies,
Than are, against Napoléon, statements signed
By the Vienna plenipotentiaries !
   We are, in fine, but too well warranted
On moral grounds to strike at Bonaparte,
If we at any crisis reckon it
Expedient so to do.   The Government
Will act throughout in concert with the Allies,
And Ministers are well within their rights
To claim that their responsibility
Be not disturbed by hackneyed forms of speech
                                (" Oh, oh ")
Upon war's horrors, and the bliss of peace,—
Which none denies !   (Cheers.)

PONSONBY

           I ask the noble lord
If that his meaning and pronouncement be
Immediate war ?

CASTLEREAGH

I have not phrased it so.

Opposition Cries

The question is unanswered !

There are excited calls, and the House divides. The result is announced as thirty-seven for WHITBREAD's amendment, and against it two hundred and twenty.

The clock strikes twelve as the House adjourns.

SCENE VI

WESSEX. DURNOVER GREEN, CASTERBRIDGE

On a patch of green grass on Durnover Hill, in the purlieus of Casterbridge, a rough gallows has been erected, and an effigy of NAPOLÉON hung upon it. Under the effigy are faggots of brushwood.

It is the dusk of a spring evening, and a great crowd has gathered, comprising male and female inhabitants of the Durnover suburb, and villagers from distances of many miles. Also are present some of the county yeomanry in white leather breeches and scarlet, volunteers in scarlet with green facings, and the REVEREND MR. PALMER, vicar of the parish, leaning against the post of his garden door, and smoking a clay pipe of preternatural length. Also PRIVATE CANTLE from Egdon Heath, and SOLOMON LONGWAYS of Casterbridge. The Durnover band, which includes a clarionet, serpent, oboe, tambourine, cymbals, and drum, is playing " Lord Wellington's Hornpipe." The soldiers have been riddling the effigy with balls.

A rustic enters at a furious pace by the eastern road, in shirt sleeves, with his smock-frock on his arm.

RUSTIC (wiping his face)

Says I, please God I'll lose a quarter to zee he burned ! And I left Stourcastle at dree o'clock to a minute. And if I'd known that I should be too late to zee the beginning on't, I'd have lost a half to be a bit sooner.

Yeoman

Oh, you be soon enough good-now. He's just going to be lighted.

Rustic

But shall I zee en die ?   I wanted to zee if he'd die hard.

Yeoman

Why, you don't suppose that Boney himself is to be burned here ?

Rustic

What—not Boney that's to be burned ?

A Woman

Why, bless the poor man, no ! This is only a mommet they've made of him, that's got neither chine nor chitlings. His innerds be only a lock of straw from Bridle's barton.

Longways

He's made, neighbour, of a' old cast jacket and breeches from our barracks here. Likeways Grammer Pawle gave us Cap'n Megg's old Zunday shirt that she'd saved for tinder-box linnit ; and Keeper Tricksey of Mellstock emptied his powder-horn into a barm-bladder, to make his heart wi'.

Rustic (vehemently)

Then there's no honesty left in Wessex folk nowadays at all ! " Boney's going to be burned on Durnover Green to-night,"—that was what a pa'cel of chaps said to me out Stourcastle way, and

I thought, to be sure I did, that he'd been catched sailing from his islant and landed at Budmouth and brought to Casterbridge Jail, the natural retreat of malefactors!—False deceivers—making me lose a quarter who can ill afford it; and all for nothing!

Longways

'Tisn't a mo'sel o' good for thee to cry out against Wessex folk, when 'twas all thy own stunpoll ignorance.

The VICAR OF DURNOVER removes his pipe and spits perpendicularly.

Vicar

My dear misguided man, you don't imagine that we should be so inhuman in this Christian country as to burn a fellow-creature alive?

Rustic

Faith, I won't say I didn't! Durnover folk have never had the highest of Christian characters, come to that. And I didn't know but that even a pa'son might backslide to such things in these gory times—I won't say on a Zunday, but on a week-night like this—when we think what a blasphemious rascal he is, and that there's not a more charnel-minded villain towards womenfolk in the whole world.

The effigy has by this time been kindled, and they watch it burn, the flames making the faces of the crowd brass-bright, and lighting the grey tower of Durnover Church hard by.

Woman (singing)

Bayonets and firelocks!
   I wouldn't my mammy should know't,
But I've been kissed in a sentry-box,
   Wrapped up in a soldier's coat!

Private Cantle

Talk of backsliding to burn Boney, I can backslide to anything when my blood is up, or rise to anything, thank God for't! Why, I shouldn't mind fighting Boney single-handed, if so be I had the choice o' weapons, and fresh Rainbarrow flints in my flint-box, and could get at him downhill. Yes, I'm a dangerous hand with a pistol now and then! . . . Hark, what's that? (A horn is heard eastward on the London Road.) Ah, here comes the mail. Now we may learn something. Nothing boldens my nerves like news of slaughter!

Enter mail-coach and steaming horses. It halts for a minute while the wheel is skidded and the horses stale.

Several

What was the latest news from abroad, guard, when you left Piccadilly White-Horse-Cellar?

Guard

You have heard, I suppose, that he's given up to public vengeance, by Gover'ment orders? Anybody may take his life in any way, fair or foul, and no questions asked. But Marshal Ney, who was sent to fight him, flung his arms round his neck and joined him with all his men. Next, the telegraph from Plymouth sends news landed there by *The Sparrow*, that he has reached Paris, and King Louis has fled. But the air got hazy before the telegraph had finished, and the name of the place he had fled to couldn't be made out.

The Vicar of Durnover blows a cloud of smoke, and again spits perpendicularly.

Vicar

Well, I'm d—— Dear me—dear me! The Lord's will be done.

GUARD

And there are to be four armies sent against him—English, Proosian, Austrian, and Roosian : the first two under Wellington and Blücher. And just as we left London a show was opened of Boney on horseback as large as life, hung up with his head downwards. Admission one shilling ; children half-price. A truly patriot spectacle !—Not that yours here is bad for a simple country-place.

The coach drives on down the hill, and the crowd reflectively watches the burning.

WOMAN (singing)

I

My Love's gone a-fighting
    Where war-trumpets call,
The wrongs o' men righting
    Wi' carbine and ball,
And sabre for smiting,
    And charger, and all !

II

Of whom does he think there
    Where war-trumpets call ?
To whom does he drink there,
    Wi' carbine and ball
On battle's red brink there,
    And charger, and all ?

III

Her, whose voice he hears humming
    Where war-trumpets call,
" I wait, Love, thy coming
    Wi' carbine and ball,

And bandsmen a-drumming
Thee, charger and all ! "

The flames reach the powder in the effigy, which is blown to rags. The band marches off playing " When War's Alarms," the crowd disperses, the vicar stands musing and smoking at his garden door till the fire goes out and darkness curtains the scene.

ACT SIXTH

SCENE I

THE BELGIAN FRONTIER

The village of Beaumont stands in the centre foreground of a bird's-eye prospect across the Belgian frontier from the French side, being close to the frontier on the Belgian side. A vast forest recedes from it towards the river Sambre further back in the scene, which pursues a crinkled course between high banks from Maubeuge on the left to Charleroi on the right.

In the shadows that muffle all objects, innumerable bodies of infantry and cavalry are discerned bivouacking in and around the village. This mass of men forms the central column of NAPOLÉON's army.

The right column is seen at a distance on that hand, also near the frontier, on the road leading towards Charleroi; and the left column by Solre-sur-Sambre, where the frontier and the river nearly coincide.

The obscurity thins and the June dawn appears.

DUMB SHOW

The bivouacs of the central column become broken up, and a movement ensues rightwards on Charleroi. The twelve regiments of cavalry which are in advance move off first; in half an hour more bodies move, and more in the next half-hour, till by eight o'clock the whole central army is gliding on. It defiles in strands by narrow tracks through the forest. Riding impatiently on the outskirts of the columns is MARSHAL NEY, who has as yet received no command.

As the day develops, sights and sounds to the left and right reveal that the two outside columns have also started, and are creeping towards the frontier abreast with the centre. That the whole forms one great movement, co-ordinated by one mind, now becomes apparent. Preceded by scouts the three columns converge.

The advance through dense woods by narrow paths takes time. The head of the middle and main column forces back some outposts, and reaches Charleroi, driving out the Prussian general ZIETEN. It seizes the bridge over the Sambre and blows up the gates of the town.

The point of observation now descends close to the scene.

In the midst comes the EMPEROR with the Sappers of the Guard, the Marines, and the Young Guard. The clatter brings the scared inhabitants to their doors and windows. Cheers arise from some of them as NAPOLÉON passes up the steep street. Just beyond the town, in front of the Bellevue Inn, he dismounts. A chair is brought out, in which he sits and surveys the whole valley of the Sambre. The troops march past cheering him, and drums roll and bugles blow. Soon the EMPEROR is found to be asleep.

When the rattle of their passing ceases the silence wakes him. His listless eye falls upon a half-defaced poster on a wall opposite—the Declaration of the Allies.

NAPOLÉON (reading)

" . . . Bonaparte destroys the only legal title on which his existence depended. . . . He has deprived himself of the protection of the law, and has manifested to the Universe that there can be neither peace nor truce with him. The Powers consequently declare that Napoléon Bonaparte has placed himself without the pale of civil and social relations, and that as an enemy and disturber of the tranquillity of the world he has rendered himself liable to public vengeance."

His flesh quivers, and he turns with a start, as if fancying that some one may be about to stab him in the back. Then he rises, mounts, and rides on.

Meanwhile the right column crosses the Sambre without difficulty at Châtelet, a little lower down ; the left column at Marchienne a little higher up ; and the three limbs combine into one vast army.

As the curtain of the mist is falling, the point of vision soars again, and there is afforded a brief glimpse of what is doing far away on the other side. From all parts of Europe long and sinister black files are crawling hitherward in serpentine lines, like slowworms through grass. They are the advancing armies of the Allies. The Dumb Show ends.

SCENE II

A BALLROOM IN BRUSSELS [1]

It is a June midnight at the DUKE AND DUCHESS OF RICHMOND'S. A band of stringed instruments shows in the background. The room is crowded with a brilliant assemblage of more than two hundred of the distinguished people sojourning in the city on account of the war and other reasons, and of local personages of State and fashion. The ball has opened with " The White Cockade."

Among those discovered present either dancing or looking on are the DUKE and DUCHESS as host and hostess, their son and eldest daughter, the Duchess's brother, the DUKE OF WELLINGTON, the PRINCE OF ORANGE, the DUKE OF BRUNSWICK, BARON VAN CAPELLEN the Belgian Secretary of State, the DUKE OF ARENBERG, the MAYOR OF BRUSSELS, the DUKE AND DUCHESS OF BEAUFORT, GENERAL ALAVA, GENERAL OUDENARDE, LORD HILL, LORD AND LADY CONYNGHAM, SIR HENRY AND LADY SUSAN CLINTON, SIR H. AND LADY HAMILTON DALRYMPLE, SIR WILLIAM AND LADY DE LANCEY, LORD UXBRIDGE, SIR JOHN BYNG, LORD PORTARLINGTON, LORD EDWARD SOMERSET, LORD HAY, COLONEL ABERCROMBY, SIR HUSSEY VIVIAN, SIR A. GORDON, SIR W. PONSONBY, SIR DENIS PACK, SIR JAMES KEMPT, SIR THOMAS PICTON, GENERAL MAITLAND, COLONEL CAMERON, many other officers, English, Hanoverian, Dutch, and Belgian, ladies English and foreign, and Scotch reel-dancers from Highland regiments.

The " Hungarian Waltz " having also been danced, the hostess calls up the Highland soldiers to show the foreign guests what a Scotch reel is like. The men put their hands

---

[1] This famous ball has become so embedded in the history of the Hundred Days as to be an integral part of it. Yet in spite of the efforts that have been made to locate the room which saw the memorable gathering (by the present writer more than thirty years back, among other enthusiasts), a dispassionate judgment must deny that its site has as yet been proven. Even Sir W. Fraser is not convincing. The event happened less than a century ago, but the spot is almost as phantasmal in its elusive mystery as towered Camelot, the palace of Priam, or the hill of Calvary. [1907.]

on their hips and tread it out briskly. While they stand aside
and rest " The Hanoverian Dance " is called.

Enter LIEUTENANT WEBSTER, A.D.C. to the PRINCE OF
ORANGE. The Prince goes apart with him and receives a
dispatch. After reading it he speaks to WELLINGTON, and
the two, accompanied by the DUKE OF RICHMOND, retire into
an alcove with serious faces. WEBSTER, in passing back across
the ballroom, exchanges a hasty word with two or three of
the guests known to him, a young officer among them, and
goes out.

YOUNG OFFICER (to partner)

The French have passed the Sambre at Charleroi !

PARTNER

What—does it mean that Bonaparte indeed
Is bearing down upon us ?

YOUNG OFFICER

That is so.
The one who hurled the news in passing out
Is Aide to the Prince of Orange, bringing him
Dispatches from Rebecque, his chief of Staff,
Now at the front, not far from Braine le Comte ;
He says that Ney, leading the French van-guard,
Has burst on Quatre-Bras.

PARTNER

O horrid time !
Will you, then, have to go and face them there ?

YOUNG OFFICER

I shall, of course, sweet. Promptly too, no doubt.

(He gazes about the room.)

See—the news spreads ; the dance is paralyzed.

They are all whispering round.   (The band stops.)
   Here comes one more,
He's the attaché from the Prussian force
At our headquarters.

Enter GENERAL MÜFFLING. He looks prepossessed, and
goes straight to WELLINGTON and RICHMOND in the alcove,
who by this time have been joined by the DUKE OF BRUNSWICK.

SEVERAL GUESTS (at back of room)

                Yes, you see, it's true !
The army will prepare to march this dawn.

PICTON (to another general)

I am damn glad we are to be off. Pottering
about here pinned to petticoat tails—it does one
no good, but blasted harm !

ANOTHER GUEST

The ball cannot go on, can it ? Didn't the
Duke know the French were so near ? If he did,
how could he let us run risks so coolly ?

LADY HAMILTON DALRYMPLE (to partner)

A deep concern weights those responsible
Who gather in the alcove. Wellington
Affects a cheerfulness in outward port,
But cannot rout his real anxiety !

The DUCHESS OF RICHMOND goes to her husband.

DUCHESS

Ought I to stop the ball ? It hardly seems
right to let it continue if all be true.

RICHMOND

I have put that very question to Wellington, my dear. He says that we need not hurry off the guests. The men have to assemble some time before the officers, who can stay on here a little longer without inconvenience ; and he would prefer that they should, not to create a panic in the city, where the friends and spies of Napoléon are all agog for some such thing, which they would instantly communicate to him to take advantage of.

DUCHESS

Is it safe to stay on ? Should we not be thinking about getting the children away ?

RICHMOND

There's no hurry at all, even if Bonaparte were really sure to enter. But he's never going to set foot in Brussels—don't you imagine it for a moment.

DUCHESS (anxiously)

I hope not. But I wish we had never brought them here !

RICHMOND

It is too late, my dear, to wish that now. Don't be flurried ; make the people go on dancing.

The DUCHESS returns to her guests. The DUKE rejoins WELLINGTON, BRUNSWICK, MÜFFLING, and the PRINCE OF ORANGE in the alcove.

WELLINGTON

We need not be astride till five o'clock
If all the men are marshalled well ahead.

The Brussels citizens must not suppose
They stand in serious peril. . . . He, I think,
Directs his main attack mistakenly ;
It should have been through Mons, not Charleroi.

MÜFFLING

The Austrian armies, and the Russian too,
Will show nowhere in this.   The thing that's done,
Be it a historied feat or nine days' fizz,
Will be done long before they join us here.

WELLINGTON

Yes, faith ; and 'tis a pity.   But, by God,
Blücher, I think, and I can make a shift
To do the business without troubling 'em !
Though I've an infamous army, that's the truth,—
Weak, and but ill-equipped,—and what's as bad,
A damned unpractised staff !

MÜFFLING

We'll hope for luck.
For certain Blücher concentrates by now
Near Ligny, as he says in his dispatch.
Your Grace, I glean, will mass at Quatre-Bras ?

WELLINGTON

Ay, now we are sure this move on Charleroi
Is no mere feint.   Though I had meant Nivelles. . . .
Have ye a good map, Richmond, near at hand ?

RICHMOND

In the next room there's one.   (Exit RICHMOND.)

WELLINGTON calls up various general officers and aides from other parts of the room. PICTON, UXBRIDGE, HILL, CLINTON, VIVIAN, MAITLAND, PONSONBY, SOMERSET, and others join him in succession, receive orders, and go out severally.

PRINCE OF ORANGE

As my divisions seem to lie around
The probable point of impact, it behoves me
To start at once, Duke, for Genappe, I deem ?
Being in Brussels, all for this damned ball,
The dispositions out there have, so far,
Been made by young Saxe Weimar and Perponcher,
On their own judgment quite.   I go, your Grace ?

WELLINGTON

Yes, certainly.   'Tis now desirable.
Farewell !   Good luck, until we meet again,
The battle won !

[Exit PRINCE OF ORANGE, and, shortly after, MÜFFLING.

RICHMOND returns with a map, which he spreads out on the table. WELLINGTON scans it closely.

Napoléon has befooled me,
By God he has,—gained four-and-twenty hours'
Good march upon me !

RICHMOND

What do you mean to do ?

WELLINGTON

I have bidden the army concentrate in strength
At Quatre-Bras.   But we shan't stop him there ;
So I must fight him *here.*

(He marks Waterloo with his thumb-nail.)

Well, now I have sped
All necessary orders I may sup,
And then must say good-bye. (To Brunswick.) This
    very day
There will be fighting, Duke. You are fit to start ?

BRUNSWICK (coming forward)

I leave almost this moment.—Yes, your Grace—
And I sheath not my sword till I have avenged
My father's death. I have sworn it !

WELLINGTON

My good friend,
Something too solemn knells beneath your words.
Take cheerful views of the affair in hand,
And fall to't with *sang froid* !

BRUNSWICK

But I have sworn !
Adieu. The rendezvous is Quatre-Bras ?

WELLINGTON

Just so. The order is unchanged. Adieu ;
But only till a later hour to-day ;
I see it is one o'clock.

WELLINGTON and RICHMOND go out of the alcove and join
the hostess, BRUNSWICK's black figure being left there alone.
He bends over the map for a few seconds.

SPIRIT OF THE YEARS

O Brunswick, Duke of Deathwounds ! Even as he
For whom thou wear'st that filial weedery
Was waylaid by my tipstaff nine years since,

So thou this day shalt feel his fendless tap,
And join thy sire !

BRUNSWICK (starting up)

     I am stirred by inner words,
As 'twere my father's angel calling me,—
That prelude to our death my lineage know !

  He stands in a reverie for a moment ; then, bidding adieu
to the DUCHESS OF RICHMOND and her daughter, goes slowly
out of the ballroom by a side-door.

DUCHESS

The Duke of Brunswick bore him gravely here.
His sable shape has struck me all the eve
As one of those romantic presences
We hear of—seldom see.

WELLINGTON (phlegmatically)

     Romantic,—well,
It may be so.   Times often, ever since
The late Duke's death, his mood has tinged him thus.
He is of those brave men who danger see,
And seeing front it,—not of those, less brave
But counted more, who face it sightlessly.

YOUNG OFFICER (to partner)

The Generals slip away !   I, Love, must take
The cobbled highway soon.   Some hours ago
The French seized Charleroi ; so they loom nigh.

PARTNER (uneasily)

Which tells me that the hour you draw your sword
Looms nigh us likewise !

Young Officer

                          Some are saying here
We fight this very day.   Rumours all-shaped
Fly round like cockchafers !

Suddenly there echoes into the ballroom a long-drawn
metallic purl of sound, making all the company start :

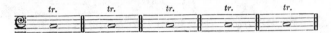

                          Ah—there it is,
Just as I thought !   They are beating the Générale.

The loud roll of side-drums is taken up by other drums
further and further away, till the hollow noise spreads all over
the city.   Dismay is written on the faces of the women.   The
Highland non-commissioned officers and privates march
smartly down the ballroom, and disappear.

Spirit of the Pities

Discerned you stepping out in front of them
That figure—of a pale drum-major kind,
Or fugleman—who wore a cold grimace ?

Spirit of the Years

He was my old friend Death, in rarest trim,
The occasion favouring his husbandry !

Spirit of the Pities

Are those who marched behind him, then, to fall ?

Spirit of the Years

Ay, all well-nigh, ere Time have houred three-score.

PARTNER

Surely this cruel call to instant war
Spares space for one dance more, that memory
May store when you are gone, while I—sad me !—
Wait, wait and weep. . . . Yes—one there is to be !

SPIRIT IRONIC

Methinks flirtation grows too tender here !

COUNTRY DANCE : " THE PRIME OF LIFE " [1]

The sense of looming tragedy carries emotion to its climax.
All the younger officers stand up with their partners, forming
several figures of fifteen or twenty couples each. The air is
ecstasizing, and both sexes abandon themselves to the movement.

Nearly half an hour passes before the figure is danced down.
Smothered kisses follow the conclusion. The silence is broken
from without by more long hollow rolling notes, so near that
they thrill the window-panes.

SEVERAL

'Tis the Assemble.   Now, then, we must go !

The officers bid farewell to their partners and begin leaving
in twos and threes. When they are gone the women mope
and murmur to each other by the wall, and listen to the tramp
of men and slamming of doors in the streets without.

LADY HAMILTON DALRYMPLE

The Duke has borne him gaily here to-night.
The youngest spirits scarcely capped his own.

DALRYMPLE

Maybe that, finding himself blade to blade
With Bonaparte at last, his blood gets quick.
French lancers of the Guard were seen at Frasnes
Last midnight ; so the clash is not far off.

[They leave.

---

[1] A favourite figure at this period.

DE LANCEY (to his wife)

I take you to our door, and say good-bye,
And go thence to the Duke's and wait for him.
In a few hours we shall be all in motion
Towards the scene of—what we cannot tell !
You, dear, will haste to Antwerp till it's past,
As we have arranged.

                                        [They leave.

WELLINGTON (to Richmond)

                    Now I must also go,
And snatch a little snooze ere harnessing.
The Prince and Brunswick have been gone some
    while.

    RICHMOND walks to the door with him. Exit WELLINGTON.
RICHMOND returns.

DUCHESS (to Richmond)

Some of these left renew the dance, you see.
I cannot stop them ; but with memory hot
Of those late gone, of where they are gone, and why,
It smacks of heartlessness !

RICHMOND

                    Let be ; let be ;
Youth comes not twice to fleet mortality !

    The dancing, however, is fitful and spiritless, few but
civilian partners being left for the ladies. Many of the latter
prefer to sit in reverie while waiting for their carriages.

SPIRIT OF THE PITIES

When those stout men-at-arms drew doorward there,
I saw a like grimacing shadow march
And pirouette before no few of them.
Some of themselves beheld it ; some were blind.

SPIRIT OF THE YEARS

Which were so ushered ?

SPIRIT OF THE PITIES

*   Brunswick, who saw and knew;*
One also moved before Sir Thomas Picton,
Who coolly conned and drily spoke to it ;
Another danced in front of Ponsonby,
Who failed of heeding his.—De Lancey, Hay,
Gordon, and Cameron, and many more
Were footmanned by like phantoms from the ball.

SPIRIT OF THE YEARS

Multiplied shimmerings of my Protean friend,
Who means to couch them shortly.   Thou wilt eye
Many fantastic moulds of him ere long,
Such as, bethink thee, thou hast eyed before.

SPIRIT OF THE PITIES

I have—too often !

The attenuated dance dies out, the remaining guests depart, the musicians leave the gallery and depart also. RICHMOND goes to a window and pulls back one of the curtains. Dawn is barely visible in the sky, and the lamps indistinctly reveal that long lines of British infantry have assembled in the street. In the irksomeness of waiting for their officers with marching-orders, they have lain down on the pavements, where many are soundly sleeping, their heads on their knapsacks and their arms by their side.

DUCHESS

Poor men. Sleep waylays them. How tired they
     seem !

RICHMOND

They'll be more tired before the day is done.
A march of eighteen miles beneath the heat,

And then to fight a battle ere they rest,
Is what foreshades.—Well, it is more than bed-time ;
But little sleep for us or any one
To-night in Brussels !

He draws the window-curtain and goes out with the
DUCHESS. Servants enter and extinguish candles. The scene
closes in darkness.

SCENE III

CHARLEROI. NAPOLÉON'S QUARTERS

The same midnight. NAPOLÉON is lying on a bed in his
clothes. In consultation with SOULT, his Chief of Staff, who is
sitting near, he dictates to his Secretary orders for the morrow.
They are addressed to KELLERMANN, DROUOT, LOBAU, GÉRARD,
and other of his marshals. SOULT goes out to dispatch them.

The Secretary resumes the reading of reports. Presently
MARSHAL NEY is announced. He is heard stumbling up the
stairs, and enters.

NAPOLÉON

Ah, Ney ; why come you back ?   Have you secured
The all-important Crossways ?—safely sconced
Yourself at Quatre-Bras ?

NEY

                Not, sire, as yet.
For, marching forwards, I heard gunnery boom,
And, fearing that the Prussians had engaged you,
I stood at pause.   Just then——

NAPOLÉON

                  My charge was this :
Make it impossible at any cost
That Wellington and Blücher should unite.

As it's from Brussels that the English come,
And from Namur the Prussians, Quatre-Bras
Lends it alone for their forgathering :
So, why exists it if not in your hands ?

NEY

My reason, sire, was rolling from my tongue.—
Hard on the boom of guns, dim files of foot
Which read to me like massing Englishry—
The vanguard of all Wellington's array—
I half-discerned.   So, in pure wariness,
I left the Bachelu columns there at Frasnes,
And hastened back to tell you.

NAPOLÉON

      Ney ; O Ney !
I fear you are not the man that once you were ;
Of yore so daring, such a faint-heart now !
I have ground to know the foot that flustered you
Were but a few stray groups of Netherlanders ;
For my good spies in Brussels send me cue
That up to now the English have not stirred,
But cloy themselves with nightly revel there.

NEY (bitterly)

Give me one rich last opportunity
Before you speak like that !

NAPOLÉON

    You soon will have one ! . . .
But now—no more of this.   I have other glooms
Upon my soul—the much-disquieting news
That Bourmont has deserted to our foes
With his whole staff.

NEY

    We can afford to let him.

NAPOLÉON

It is what such betokens, not their worth,
That whets it ! . . . Love, respect for me, have waned ;
But I will right that.   We've good chances still.
You must return foot-fleet to Quatre-Bras ;
There Kellermann's cuirassiers will promptly join you
To bear the English backward Brussels way.
I go on towards Fleurus and Ligny now.—
If Blücher's force retreat, and Wellington's
Lie somnolent in Brussels one day more,
I snare that city sans a single shot ! . . .
   Now, friend, downstairs you'll find some supper
      ready,
Which you must tuck in sharply, and then off.
The past day has not ill-advantaged us ;
We have stalked upon the two chiefs unawares,
And in such sites that they must fight apart.
Now for a two hours' rest.—Comrade, adieu
Until to-morrow !

NEY

Till to-morrow, sire !
[Exit NEY.

NAPOLÉON falls asleep, and the Secretary waits till dictation
shall be resumed. BUSSY, the orderly officer, comes to the
door.

BUSSY

Letters—arrived from Paris.   (Hands letters.)

SECRETARY

He shall have them
The moment he awakes.   These eighteen hours
He's been astride ; and is not what he was.—
Much news from Paris ?

BUSSY

     I can only say
What's not the news.   The courier has just told me
He'd nothing from the Empress at Vienna
To bring his Majesty.   She writes no more.

SECRETARY

And never will again !   In my regard
That bird's forsook its nest for good and all.

BUSSY

All that they hear in Paris from her court
Is through our spies there.   One of them reports
This rumour of her : that the Archduke John,
In taking leave to join our enemies here,
Said, " O, my poor Louise ; I am grieved for you,
And what I hope is, that he'll be run through,
Or shot, or break his neck, for your own good
No less than ours."

NAPOLÉON (waking)

    By " he " denoting me ?

BUSSY (starting)

Just so, your Majesty.

NAPOLÉON (peremptorily)

    What said the Empress ?

BUSSY

She gave no answer, sire, that rumour bears.

NAPOLÉON

Count Neipperg, whom they have made her
    chamberlain,
Interred his wife last spring—is it not so ?

BUSSY

He did, your Majesty.

NAPOLÉON

H'm. . . . You may go.

[Exit BUSSY.

*The Secretary reads letters aloud in succession. He comes
to the last ; begins it ; reaches a phrase, and stops abruptly.*

Mind not ! Read on. No doubt the usual threat,
Or prophecy, from some mad scribe ? Who signs it?

SECRETARY

The subscript is " The Duke of Enghien ! "

NAPOLÉON (starting up)

Bah, man ! A treacherous trick ! A hoax—no
    more !
Is that the last ?

SECRETARY

The last, your Majesty.

NAPOLÉON

Then now I'll sleep. In two hours have me called.

SECRETARY

I'll give the order, sire.

[The Secretary goes.

The candles are removed, except one, and NAPOLÉON endeavours to compose himself.

SPIRIT IRONIC

A little moral panorama would do him no harm, after that reminder of the Duke of Enghien.   Shall it be, young Compassion ?

SPIRIT OF THE PITIES

*What good—if that old Years tells us be true ?
But I say naught.   To ordain is not for me !*

Thereupon a vision passes before NAPOLÉON as he lies, comprising hundreds of thousands of skeletons and corpses in divers stages of decay.   They rise from his various battle-fields, the flesh dropping from them, and gaze reproachfully at him.   His intimate officers who have been slain he recognizes among the crowd.   In front is the DUKE OF ENGHIEN as showman.

NAPOLÉON (in his sleep)

Why, why should this reproach be dealt me now ?
Why hold me my own master, if I be
Ruled by the pitiless Planet of Destiny ?

He jumps up in a sweat and puts out the last candle ;   and the scene is curtained by darkness.

SCENE IV

A CHAMBER OVERLOOKING A MAIN STREET IN BRUSSELS

A June sunrise; the beams struggling through the window-curtains. A canopied bed in a recess on the left. The quick notes of " Brighton Camp, or the Girl I've left behind me," strike sharply into the room from fifes and drums without. A young lady in a dressing-gown, who has evidently been awaiting the sound, springs from the bed like a hare from its form, undraws the window-curtains and opens the window.

Columns of British soldiery are marching past from the Parc southward out of the city by the Namur Gate. The windows of other houses in the street rattle open, and become full of gazers.

A tap at the door. An older lady enters, and comes up to the first.

YOUNGER LADY (turning)

O mamma—I didn't hear you !

ELDER LADY

I was sound asleep till the thumping of the drums set me fantastically dreaming, and when I awoke I found they were real. Did they wake you too, my dear ?

YOUNGER LADY (reluctantly)

I didn't require waking. I hadn't slept since we came home.

ELDER LADY

That was from the excitement of the ball. There are dark rings round your eyes. (The fifes and drums are now opposite, and thrill the air in the room.) Ah—

that " Girl I've left behind me ! "—which so many thousands of women have throbbed an accompaniment to, and will again to-day if ever they did !

YOUNGER LADY (her voice faltering)

It is rather cruel to say that just now, mamma. There, I can't look at them after it ! (She turns and wipes her eyes.)

ELDER LADY

I wasn't thinking of ourselves—certainly not of you.—How they press on—with those great knapsacks and firelocks and, I am told, fifty-six rounds of ball-cartridge, and four days' provisions in those haversacks. How can they carry it all near twenty miles and fight with it on their shoulders ! . . . Don't cry, dear. I thought you would get sentimental last night over somebody. I ought to have brought you home sooner. How many dances did you have ? It was impossible for me to look after you in the excitement of the war-tidings.

YOUNGER LADY

Only three—four.

ELDER LADY

Which were they ?

YOUNGER LADY

" Enrico," the " Copenhagen Waltz " and the " Hanoverian," and the " Prime of Life."

ELDER LADY

It was very foolish to fall in love on the strength of four dances.

YOUNGER LADY (evasively)

Fall in love ? Who said I had fallen in love ?
What a funny idea !

ELDER LADY

Is it ? . . . Now here come the Highland Brigade
with their pipes and their " Hieland Laddie."
How the sweethearts cling to the men's arms.
(Reaching forward.) There are more regiments following. But look, that gentleman at the opposite
window knows us. I cannot remember his name.
(She bows and calls across.) Sir, which are these ?

GENTLEMAN OPPOSITE

The Ninety-second. Next come the Forty-ninth,
and next the Forty-second—Sir Denis Pack's brigade.

ELDER LADY

Thank you.—I think it is that gentleman we
talked to at the Duchess's, but I am not sure.
(A pause : another band.)

GENTLEMAN OPPOSITE

That's the Twenty-eighth. (They pass, with their
band and colours.) Now the Thirty-second are coming
up—part of Kempt's brigade. Endless, are they
not !

ELDER LADY

Yes, Sir. Has the Duke passed out yet ?

GENTLEMAN OPPOSITE

Not yet. Some cavalry will go by first, I think.
The foot coming up now are the Seventy-ninth.

(They pass.) . . . These next are the Ninety-fifth. (They pass.) . . . These are the First Foot-guards. (They pass, playing " British Grenadiers.") . . . The Fusi-leer-guards now. (They pass.) . . . Now the Cold-streamers. (They pass. He looks up towards the Parc.) Several Hanoverian regiments under Colonel Best are coming next. (They pass, with their bands and colours. An interval.)

ELDER LADY (to daughter)

Here are the hussars. How much more they carry to battle than at reviews. The hay in those great nets must encumber them. (She turns and sees that her daughter has become pale.) Ah, now I know! *He* has just gone by. You exchanged signals with him, you wicked girl! How do you know what his character is, or if he'll ever come back ?

The younger lady goes and flings herself on her face upon the bed, sobbing silently. Her mother glances at her, but leaves her alone. An interval. The prancing of a group of horsemen is heard on the cobble-stones without.

GENTLEMAN OPPOSITE (calling)

Here comes the Duke !

ELDER LADY (to younger)

You have left the window at the most important time ! The Duke of Wellington and his staff-officers are passing out.

YOUNGER LADY

I don't want to see him. I don't want to see anything any more !

Riding down the street comes WELLINGTON in a grey frock-coat and small cocked hat, frigid and undemonstrative; accompanied by four or five Generals of his suite, the Deputy Quarter-master-general DE LANCEY, LORD FITZROY SOMERSET, Aide-de-camp, and GENERAL MÜFFLING.

GENTLEMAN OPPOSITE

He is the Prussian officer attached to our headquarters, through whom Wellington communicates
with Blücher, who, they say, is threatened by the
French at Ligny at this moment.

The elder lady turns to her daughter, and going to the bed
bends over her, while the horses' tramp of WELLINGTON and
his staff clatters more faintly in the street, and the music
of the last retreating band dies away towards the Forest of
Soignes.

Finding that her daughter is hysterical with grief she quickly
draws the window-curtains to screen the room from the houses
opposite.   Scene ends.

SCENE V

THE FIELD OF LIGNY

The same day later.   A prospect of the battlefield of Ligny
southward from the roof of the windmill of Bussy, which stands
at the centre and highest point of the Prussian position, about
six miles south-east of Quatre-Bras.

The ground slopes downward along the whole front of the
scene to a valley through which wanders the Ligne, a muddy
stream bordered by sallows.   On both sides of the stream, in
the middle plane of the picture, stands the village of Ligny,
composed of thatched cottages, gardens, and farm-houses
with stone walls;   the main features, such as the church,
churchyard, and village - green being on the further side of
the Ligne.

On that side the land reascends in green wheatfields to an
elevation somewhat greater than that of the foreground,
reaching away to Fleurus in the right-hand distance.

In front, on the slopes between the spectator and the
village, is the First Corps of the Prussian army commanded
by ZIETEN, its First Brigade under STEINMETZ occupying the
most salient point.   The Corps under THIELMANN is ranged
to the left, and that of PIRCH to the rear, in reserve to ZIETEN.
In the centre-front, just under the mill, BLÜCHER on a fine
grey charger is intently watching, with his staff.

Something dark is seen to be advancing over the horizon by Fleurus, about three miles off. It is the van of NAPOLÉON's army, approaching to give battle.

At this moment hoofs are heard clattering along a road that passes behind the mill; and there come round to the front the DUKE OF WELLINGTON, his staff-officers, and a small escort of cavalry.

WELLINGTON and BLÜCHER greet each other at the foot of the windmill. They disappear inside, and can be heard ascending the ladders.

Enter on the roof WELLINGTON and BLÜCHER, followed by FITZROY SOMERSET, GNEISENAU, MÜFFLING, and others. Before renewing their conversation they peer through their glasses at the dark movements on the horizon. WELLINGTON's manner is deliberate, judicial, almost indifferent; BLÜCHER's eager and impetuous.

WELLINGTON

They muster not as yet in near such strength
At Quatre-Bras as here.

BLÜCHER

          'Tis from Fleurus
They come debouching. I, perforce, withdrew
My forward posts of cavalry at dawn
In face of their light cannon. . . . They'll be here,
I reckon, soon!

WELLINGTON (still with glass)

        I clearly see his staff,
And if my eyes don't lie, the Arch-one too. . . .
It is the whole Imperial army, Prince,
That we've before us. (A silence.) Well, we'll cope
   with them!
What would you have me do?

BLÜCHER is so absorbed in what he sees that he does not heed.

GNEISENAU

            Duke, this I'd say :
Events suggest to us that you come up
With all your force, behind the village here,
And act as our reserve.

MÜFFLING

            But Bonaparte,
Pray note, has redistributed his strength
In fashion that you fail to recognize.
I am against your scheme.

BLÜCHER (lowering his glass)

            Signs notify
Napoléon's plans are changed ! He purports now
To strike our left—between Sombreffe and Brye. . . .
If so, I have to readjust my ward.

WELLINGTON

One of his two divisions that we scan
Outspreading from Fleurus, seems bent on Ligny,
The other on Saint-Amand.

BLÜCHER

            Well, I shall see
In half an hour, your Grace.   If what I deem
Be what he means, Von Zieten's corps forthwith
Must stand to their positions : Pirch out here,
Henckel at Ligny, Steinmetz at La Haye.

WELLINGTON

So that, your Excellency, as I opine,
I go and sling my strength on their left wing—
Manœuvring to outflank 'em on that side.

BLÜCHER

True, true.   Our plan uncovers of itself ;
You bear down everything from Quatre-Bras
Along the road to Frasnes.

WELLINGTON

                I will, by God.
I'll bear straight on to Gosselies, if needs !

GNEISENAU

Your Excellencies, if I may be a judge,
Such movement will not tend to unity ;
It leans too largely on a peradventure,
Most speculative in its contingencies !

   A silence ; till the officers of the staff remark to each other
that concentration is best in any circumstances.   A general
discussion ensues.

BLÜCHER (concludingly)

We will expect you, Duke, to our support.

WELLINGTON

I must agree that, in the sum, it's best.
So be it then.   If not attacked myself
I'll come to you.—Now I return with speed
To Quatre-Bras.

BLÜCHER

            And I descend from here
To give close eye and thought to things below ;
No more can well be studied where we stand.

   Exeunt from roof WELLINGTON, BLÜCHER and the rest.
They reappear below, and WELLINGTON and his suite gallop
furiously away in the direction of Quatre-Bras.

               An interval.

DUMB SHOW (below)

Three reports of a cannon give the signal for the French attack. NAPOLÉON's army advances down the slopes of green corn opposite, bands and voices joining in songs of victory. The French come in three grand columns; VANDAMME's on the left (the spectator's right) against Saint-Amand, the most forward angle of the Prussian position. GÉRARD's in the centre bears down upon Ligny. GROUCHY's on the French right is further back. Far to the rear can be discerned NAPOLÉON, the Imperial Guard, and MILHAUD's cuirassiers halted in reserve.

This formidable advance is preceded by swarms of tirailleurs, who tread down the high wheat, exposing their own men in the rear.

Amid cannonading from both sides they draw nearer to the Prussians, though lanes are cut through them by the latter's guns. They drive the Prussians out of Ligny; who, however, rally in the houses, churchyard, and village green.

SPIRIT OF THE PITIES

I see an unnatural Monster, loosely jointed,
With an Apocalyptic Being's shape,
And limbs and eyes a hundred thousand strong,
And fifty thousand heads ; which coils itself
About the buildings there.

SPIRIT OF THE YEARS

             Thou dost indeed.
It is the Monster Devastation.   *Watch.*

Round the church they fight without quarter, shooting face to face, stabbing with unfixed bayonets, and braining with the butts of muskets. The village catches fire, and soon becomes a furnace. The crash of splitting timbers as doors are broken through, the curses of the fighters, rise into the air, with shouts of " En avant ! " from the further side of the stream, and " Vorwärts ! " from the nearer.

The battle extends to the west by Le Hameau and Saint-Amand la Haye ; and Ligny becomes invisible under a shroud of smoke.

VOICES (at the base of the mill)

This sun will go down gorily for us !
The English, sharply sighed for by Prince Blücher,

Cannot appear.   Wellington words across
That hosts have set on him at Quatre-Bras,
And leave him not one bayonet to spare !

The truth of this intelligence is apparent.   A low dull sound
heard lately from the direction of Quatre-Bras has increased to
a roaring cannonade.

The scene abruptly closes.

SCENE VI

THE FIELD OF QUATRE-BRAS

The same day.   The view is southward, and the straight
gaunt highway from Brussels (behind the spectator) to Charleroi
over the hills in front, bisects the picture from foreground to
distance.   Near in sight, where it is elevated and open, there
crosses it obliquely, at a point called Les Quatre-Bras, another
road which comes from Nivelle, five miles to the gazer's right
rear, and goes to Namur, twenty miles ahead to the left.   At
a distance of five or six miles in this latter direction it passes
near the previous scene, Ligny, whence the booming of guns
can be continuously heard.

Between the cross-roads in the centre of the scene and the
far horizon the ground dips into a hollow, on the other side
of which the same straight road to Charleroi is seen climbing
the crest, and over it till out of sight.   From a hill on the right
hand of the mid-distance a large wood, the wood of Bossu,
reaches up nearly to the crossways, which give their name to
the buildings thereat, consisting of a few farm-houses and an
inn.

About three-quarters of a mile off, nearly hidden by the
horizon towards Charleroi, there is also a farmstead, Gémion-
court ; another, Piraumont, stands on an eminence a mile
to the left of it, and somewhat in front of the Namur road.

DUMB SHOW

As this scene uncovers the battle is beheld to be raging at
its height, and to have reached a keenly tragic phase.   WELLING-
TON has returned from Ligny, and the main British and
Hanoverian position, held by the men who marched out of

Brussels in the morning, under officers who danced the previous night at the Duchess's, is along the Namur road to the left of the perspective, and round the cross-road itself. That of the French, under NEY, is on the crests further back, from which they are descending in imposing numbers. Some advanced columns are assailing the English left, while through the smoke-hazes of the middle of the field two lines of skirmishers are seen firing at each other—the southernmost dark blue, the northernmost dull red. Time lapses till it is past four o'clock.

SPIRIT OF RUMOUR

The cannonade of the French ordnance-lines
Has now redoubled. New and denser packs
Of foot, supported by fleet cavalry,
Straightly impinge upon the Brunswick bands
That hug the tangled tree-clumps of Bossu. . . .
Above some regiments of the assaulting French
A flag like midnight swims upon the air,
To say no quarter may be looked for there !

The Brunswick soldiery, much notched and torn by the French grape-shot, now lie in heaps. The DUKE OF BRUNSWICK himself, desperate to keep them steady, lights his pipe, and rides slowly up and down in front of his lines previous to the charge which follows.

SPIRIT OF RUMOUR

The French have heaved them on the Brunswickers,
And borne them back. Now comes the Duke's told time.
He gallops at the head of his hussars—
Those men of solemn and appalling guise,
Full-clothed in black, with nodding hearsy plumes,
A shining silver skull and cross of bones
Set upon each, to byspeak his slain sire. . . .
Concordantly, the expected bullet starts
And finds the living son.

BRUNSWICK reels to the ground. His troops, disheartened, lose their courage and give way.

The French front columns, and the cavalry supporting them, shout as they advance. The Allies are forced back upon the

English main position. WELLINGTON is in personal peril for a time, but he escapes it by a leap of his horse.

A curtain of smoke drops. An interval. The curtain reascends.

SPIRIT OF THE PITIES

Behold again the Dynasts' gory gear !
Since we regarded, what has progressed here ?

RECORDING ANGEL (in recitative)

Musters of English foot and their allies
Came palely panting by the Brussels way,
And, swiftly stationed, checked their counter-braves.
Ney, vexed by lack of like auxiliaries,
Bade then the columned cuirassiers to charge
In all their edged array of weaponcraft.
Yea ; thrust replied to thrust, and fire to fire ;
The English broke, till Picton prompt to prop them
Sprang with fresh foot-folk from the covering rye.
*   Next Piré's cavalry took up the charge. . . .*
And so the action sways.   The English left
Is turned at Piraumont ; whilst on their right
Perils infest the greenwood of Bossu ;
Wellington gazes round with dubious view ;
England's long fame in fight seems sepulchred,
And ominous roars swell loudlier Ligny-ward.

SPIRIT OF RUMOUR

New rage has wrenched the battle since thou'st writ ;
Hot-hasting succours of light cannonry
Lately come up, relieve the English stress ;
Kellermann's cuirassiers, both man and horse
All plated over with the brass of war,
Are rolling on the highway.   More brigades
Of British, soiled and sweltering, now are nigh,
Who plunge within the boscage of Bossu ;

Where in the hidden shades and sinuous creeps
Life-struggles can be heard, seen but in peeps.
Therewith the foe's accessions harass Ney,
Racked that no needful d'Erlon darks the way!

Inch by inch NEY has to draw off : WELLINGTON promptly
advances. At dusk NEY's army finds itself back at Frasnes,
where he meets D'ERLON coming up to his assistance, too late.

The weary English and their allies, who have been on foot
ever since one o'clock the previous morning, prepare to bivouac
in front of the cross-roads. Their fires flash up for a while ;
and by and by the dead silence of heavy sleep hangs over them.
WELLINGTON goes into his tent, and the night darkens.

A Prussian courier from Ligny enters, who is conducted
into the tent to WELLINGTON.

SPIRIT OF THE PITIES

What tidings can a courier bring that count
Here, where such mighty things are native born ?

RECORDING ANGEL (in recitative)

The fury of the tumult there begun
Scourged quivering Ligny through the afternoon :
Napoléon's great intent grew substantive,
And on the Prussian pith and pulse he bent
His foretimed blow. Blücher, to butt the shock,
Called up his last reserves, and heading on,
With blade high brandished by his aged arm,
Spurred forward his white steed. But they, outspent,
Failed far to follow. Darkness coped the sky,
And storm, and rain with thunder. Yet once more
He cheered them on to charge. His horse, the while,
Pierced by a bullet, fell on him it bore.
He, trampled, bruised, faint, and in disarray
Dragged to a new mount, and was led away.
His ragged lines withdraw from sight and sound,
And their assailants camp upon the ground.

The scene shuts with midnight.

SCENE VII

BRUSSELS.   THE PLACE ROYALE

The same night, dark and sultry. A crowd of citizens throng
the broad Place. They gaze continually down the Rue de
Namur, along which arrive minute by minute carts and waggons
laden with wounded men. Other wounded limp into the city
on foot. At much greater speed enter fugitive soldiers from
the miscellaneous contingents of WELLINGTON'S army at
Quatre-Bras, who gesticulate and explain to the crowd that all
is lost and that the French will soon be in Brussels.

Baggage-carts and carriages, with and without horses, stand
before an hotel, surrounded by a medley of English and other
foreign nobility and gentry with their valets and maids.
Bulletins from the battlefield are affixed on the corner of the
Place, and people peer at them by the dim oil lights.

A rattle of hoofs reaches the ears, entering the town by the
same Namur gate. The riders disclose themselves to be Belgian
hussars, also from the field.

SEVERAL HUSSARS

The French approach !   Wellington is beaten.
Bonaparte is at our heels.

Consternation reaches a crisis. Horses are hastily put-to
at the hotel : people crowd into the carriages and try to drive
off. They get jammed together and hemmed in by the throng.
Unable to move they quarrel and curse despairingly in sundry
tongues.

Enter the MAYOR OF BRUSSELS, the BARON CAPELLEN, the
DUC D'URSEL, and officials.

BARON CAPELLEN

Affix the new bulletin.   It is a more assuring
one, and may quiet them a little.

A new bulletin is nailed over the old one.

MAYOR

Good people, calm yourselves. No victory has been won by Bonaparte. The noise of guns heard all the afternoon became fainter towards the end, showing beyond doubt that the retreat was away from the city.

A CITIZEN

The French are said to be forty thousand strong at Les Quatre-Bras, and no forty thousand British marched out against them this morning !

ANOTHER CITIZEN

And it is whispered that the city archives and the treasure-chest have been sent to Antwerp !

MAYOR

Only as a precaution. No good can be gained by panic. Sixty or seventy thousand of the Allies, all told, face Napoléon by this hour. Meanwhile who is to attend to the wounded that are being brought in faster and faster ? Fellow-citizens, do your duty by these unfortunates, and believe me that when engaged in such an act of mercy no enemy will hurt you.

CITIZENS

What can we do ?

MAYOR

I invite all those who have such, to bring mattresses, sheets, and coverlets to the Hôtel de Ville, also old linen and lint from the houses of the curés.

Many set out on this errand. An interval. Enter a courier, who speaks to the MAYOR and the BARON CAPELLEN.

BARON CAPELLEN (to Mayor)

Better inform them immediately, to prevent a panic.

MAYOR (to Citizens)

I grieve to tell you that the Duke of Brunswick, whom you saw ride out this morning, was killed this afternoon at Les Quatre - Bras. A musket-ball passed through his bridle-hand and entered his belly. His body is now arriving. Carry yourselves gravely.

A lane is formed in the crowd in the direction of the Rue de Namur ; and they wait. Presently an extemporized funeral procession, with the body of the DUKE on a gun-carriage, and a small escort of Brunswickers with carbines reversed, comes slowly up the street, their silver death's-heads shining in the lamplight. The agitation of the citizens settles into a silent gloom as the mournful train passes.

MAYOR (to Baron Capellen)

I noticed the strange look of prepossession on his face at the ball last night, as if he knew what was going to be.

BARON CAPELLEN

The Duchess mentioned it to me. . . . He hated the French, if any man ever did, and so did his father before him ! Here comes the English Colonel Hamilton, straight from the field. He will give us trustworthy particulars.

Enter COLONEL HAMILTON by the Rue de Namur. He converses with the MAYOR and the BARON on the issue of the struggle.

MAYOR

Now I will go to the Hôtel de Ville, and get it ready for those wounded who can find no room in private houses.

[Exeunt MAYOR, CAPELLEN, D'URSEL, HAMILTON, etc. severally.

Many citizens descend in the direction of the Hôtel de Ville to assist. Those who remain silently watch the carts bringing in the wounded till a late hour. The doors of houses in the Place and elsewhere are kept open, and the rooms within lighted, in expectation of more arrivals from the field.

A courier gallops up, who is accosted by idlers.

COURIER (hastily)

The Prussians are defeated at Ligny by Napoléon in person. He will be here to-morrow.

[Exit courier.

FIRST IDLER

The devil! Then I am for welcoming him. No Antwerp for me!

OTHER IDLERS (sotto voce)

Vive l'Empereur!

A warm summer fog from the Lower Town covers the Parc and the Place Royale.

SCENE VIII

THE ROAD TO WATERLOO

The view is now from Quatre-Bras backward along the road by which the English arrived. Diminishing in a straight line from the foreground to the centre of the distance it passes over Mont Saint-Jean and through Waterloo to Brussels.

It is now tinged by a moving mass of English and Allied infantry, in retreat to a new position at Mont Saint-Jean. The sun shines brilliantly upon the foreground as yet, but towards Waterloo and the Forest of Soignes on the north horizon it is overcast with black clouds which are steadily advancing up the sky.

To mask the retreat the English outposts retain their position on the battlefield in the face of NEY's troops, and keep up a desultory firing : the cavalry for the same reason remain, being drawn up in lines beside the intersecting Namur road.

Enter WELLINGTON, UXBRIDGE (who is in charge of the cavalry), MÜFFLING, VIVIAN, and others. They look through their field-glasses towards Frasnes, NEY's position since his retreat of yesternight, and also towards NAPOLÉON's at Ligny.

WELLINGTON

The noonday sun, striking so strongly there,
Makes mirrors of their arms.   That they advance
Their growing radiance shows.   Those gleams by Marbais
Suggest fixed bayonets.

UXBRIDGE

                      Vivian's glass reveals
That they are cuirassiers.   Ney's troops, too, near
At last, methinks, along this other road.

WELLINGTON

One thing is sure : that here the whole French force
Schemes to unite and sharply follow us.
It formulates our fence.   The cavalry
Must linger here no longer ; but recede
To Mont Saint-Jean, as rearguard of the foot.
From the intelligence that Gordon brings
'Tis pretty clear old Blücher had to take
A damned good drubbing yesterday at Ligny,
And has been bent hard back !   So that, for us,
Bound to the plighted plan, there is no choice
But to do like. . . . No doubt they'll say at home
That we've been well thrashed too.   It can't be helped,

They must ! . . . (He looks round at the sky.) A heavy
     rainfall threatens us,
To make it all the worse !

The speaker and his staff ride off along the Brussels road in
the rear of the infantry, and UXBRIDGE begins the retreat of
the cavalry.

      CAPTAIN MERCER enters with a light battery.

MERCER (excitedly)

                   Look back, my lord ;
Is it not Bonaparte himself we see
Upon the road I have come by ?

UXBRIDGE (looking through glass)

                       Yes, by Heaven ;
His face as clear-cut as the edge of a cloud
The sun behind shows up ! His suite and all !
Fire—fire ! And aim you well.

    The battery hastily makes ready and fires.

                 No ! It won't do.
He brings on mounted ordnance of his Guard,
So we're in danger here. Then limber up,
And off as soon as may be.

The English artillery and cavalry retreat at full speed, just
as the weather bursts, with flashes of lightning and drops of
rain. They all clatter off along the Brussels road, UXBRIDGE
and his aides galloping beside the column ; till no British are
left at Quatre-Bras except the slain.

The focus of the scene follows the retreating English army,
the highway and its margins panoramically gliding past the
vision of the spectator. The phantoms chant monotonously
while the retreat goes on.

CHORUS OF RUMOURS (aerial music)

Day's nether hours advance ; storm supervenes
In heaviness unparalleled, that screens

With water-woven gauzes, vapour-bred,
The creeping clumps of half-obliterate red—
Severely harassed past each round and ridge
By the inimical lance.   They gain the bridge
And village of Genappe, in equal fence
With weather and the enemy's violence.
—Cannon upon the foul and flooded road,
Cavalry in the cornfields mire-bestrowed,
With frothy horses floundering to their knees,
Make wayfaring a moil of miseries !
Till Britishry and Bonapartists lose
Their clashing colours for the tawny hues
That twilight sets on all its stealing tinct imbues.

The rising ground of Mont Saint-Jean, in front of Waterloo, is gained by the English vanguard and main masses of foot, and by degrees they are joined by the cavalry and artillery. The French are but little later in taking up their position amid the cornfields around La Belle Alliance.

Fires begin to shine up from the English bivouacs. Camp kettles are slung, and the men pile arms and stand round the blaze to dry themselves. The French opposite lie down like dead men in the dripping green wheat and rye, without supper and without fire.

By and by the English army also lies down, the men huddling together on the ploughed mud in their wet blankets, while some sleep sitting round the dying fires.

CHORUS OF THE YEARS (aerial music)

The eyelids of eve fall together at last,
And the forms so foreign to field and tree
Lie down as though native, and slumber fast !

CHORUS OF THE PITIES

Sore are the thrills of misgiving we see
In the artless champaign at this harlequinade,
Distracting a vigil where calm should be !

The green seems opprest, and the Plain afraid
Of a Something to come, whereof these are the proofs,—
Neither earthquake, nor storm, nor eclipse's shade !

CHORUS OF THE YEARS

Yea, the coneys are scared by the thud of hoofs,
And their white scuts flash at their vanishing heels,
And swallows abandon the hamlet-roofs.

The mole's tunnelled chambers are crushed by wheels,
The lark's eggs scattered, their owners fled ;
And the hedgehog's household the sapper unseals.

The snail draws in at the terrible tread,
But in vain ; he is crushed by the felloe-rim ;
The worm asks what can be overhead,

And wriggles deep from a scene so grim,
And guesses him safe ; for he does not know
What a foul red rain will be soaking him !

Beaten about by the heel and toe
Are butterflies, sick of the day's long rheum,
To die of a worse than the weather-foe.

Trodden and bruised to a miry tomb
Are ears that have greened but will never be gold,
And flowers in the bud that will never bloom.

CHORUS OF THE PITIES

So the season's intent, ere its fruit unfold,
Is frustrate, and mangled, and made succumb,
Like a youth of promise struck stark and cold ! . . .

And what of these who to-night have come ?

CHORUS OF THE YEARS

The young sleep sound ; but the weather awakes
In the veterans, pains from the past that numb ;

Old stabs of Ind, old Peninsular aches,
Old Friedland chills, haunt their moist mud bed,
Cramps from Austerlitz ; till their slumber breaks.

Chorus of Sinister Spirits

And each soul shivers as sinks his head
On the loam he's to lease with the other dead
From to-morrow's mist-fall till Time be sped !

The fires of the English go out, and silence prevails, save for the soft hiss of the rain that falls impartially on both the sleeping armies.

ACT SEVENTH

SCENE I

THE FIELD OF WATERLOO

An aerial view of the battlefield at the time of sunrise is disclosed.

The sky is still overcast, and rain still falls. A green expanse, almost unbroken, of rye, wheat, and clover, in oblong and irregular patches undivided by fences, covers the undulating ground, which sinks into a shallow valley between the French and English positions. The road from Brussels to Charleroi runs like a spit through both positions, passing at the back of the English into the leafy forest of Soignes.

The latter are turning out from their bivouacs. They move stiffly from their wet rest, and hurry to and fro like ants in an ant-hill. The tens of thousands of moving specks are largely of a brick-red colour, but the foreign contingent is darker.

Breakfasts are cooked over smoky fires of green wood. Innumerable groups, many in their shirt-sleeves, clean their rusty firelocks, drawing or exploding the charges, scrape the mud from themselves, and pipeclay from their cross-belts the red dye washed off their jackets by the rain.

At six o'clock they parade, spread out, and take up their positions in the line of battle, the front of which extends in a wavy riband three miles long, with three projecting bunches at Hougomont, La Haye Sainte, and La Haye.

Looking across to the French positions we observe that after advancing in dark streams from where they have passed the night they, too, deploy and wheel into their fighting-places—figures with red epaulettes and hairy knapsacks, their arms glittering like a display of cutlery at a hill-side fair.

They assume three concentric lines of crescent shape, that converge on the English midst, with great blocks of the Imperial Guard at the back of them. The rattle of their drums, their fanfarades, and their bands playing " Veillons au salut de l'Empire " contrast with the quiet reigning on the English side.

A knot of figures, comprising WELLINGTON with a suite of general and other staff-officers, ride backwards and forwards in front of the English lines, where each regimental colour floats in the hands of the junior ensign. The DUKE himself, now a man of forty-six, is on his bay charger Copenhagen, in light pantaloons, a small plumeless cocked hat, and a blue cloak, which shows its white lining when blown back.

On the French side, too, a detached group creeps along the front in preliminary survey. BONAPARTE—also forty-six—in a grey overcoat, is mounted on his white arab Marengo, and accompanied by SOULT, NEY, JÉRÔME, DROUOT, and other marshals. The figures of aides move to and fro like shuttle-cocks between the group and distant points in the field. The sun has begun to gleam.

SPIRIT OF THE PITIES

Discriminate these, and what they are,
Who stand so stalwartly to war.

SPIRIT OF THE YEARS

Report, ye Rumourers of things afar.

SEMICHORUS I OF RUMOURS (chanting)

Sweep first the Frenchmen's leftward lines along,
And eye the peaceful panes of Hougomont—
That seemed to hold prescriptive right of peace
In fee from Time till Time itself should cease !—
Jarred now by Reille's fierce foot-divisions three,
Flanked on their left by Piré's cavalry.—
The fourfold corps of d'Erlon, spread at length,
Compose the right, east of the famed chaussée—
The shelterless Charleroi-and-Brussels way,—
And Jacquinot's alert light-steeded strength
Still further right, their sharpened swords display.
Thus stands the first line.

SEMICHORUS II

Next behind its back
Comes Count Lobau, left of the Brussels track ;
Then Domon's horse, the horse of Subervie ;
Kellermann's cuirassed troopers twinkle-tipt,
And, backing d'Erlon, Milhaud's horse, equipt
Likewise in burnished steelwork sunshine-dipt :
So ranks the second line refulgently.

SEMICHORUS I

The third and last embattlement reveals
D'Erlon's, Lobau's, and Reille's foot-cannoniers,
And horse-drawn ordnance too, on massy wheels,
To strike with cavalry where space appears.

SEMICHORUS II

The English front, to left, as flanking force,
Has Vandeleur's hussars, and Vivian's horse ;
Next them pace Picton's rows along the crest ;
The Hanoverian foot-folk ; Wincké ; Best ;
Bylandt's brigade, set forward fencelessly,
Pack's northern clansmen, Kempt's tough infantry,
With gaiter, epaulet, spat, and philibeg ;
While Halkett, Ompteda, and Kielmansegge
Prolong the musters, near whose forward edge
Baring invests the Farm of Holy Hedge.

SEMICHORUS I

Maitland and Byng in Cooke's division range,
And round dun Hougomont's old lichened sides
A dense array of watching Guardsmen hides
Amid the peaceful produce of the grange,
Whose new-kerned apples, hairy gooseberries green,
And mint, and thyme, the ranks intrude between.—
Last, westward of the road that finds Nivelles,
Duplat draws up, and Adam parallel.

SEMICHORUS II

The second British line—embattled horse—
Holds the reverse slopes, screened, in ordered course ;
Dörnberg's, and Arentsschildt's, and Colquhoun-
    Grant's,
And left of them, behind where Alten plants
His regiments, come the " Household " Cavalry ;
And nigh, in Picton's rear, the trumpets call
The " Union " brigade of Ponsonby.
Behind these the reserves.   In front of all,
Or interspaced, with slow-matched gunners manned,
Upthroated rows of threatful ordnance stand.

The clock of Nivelles convent church strikes eleven in the distance.   Shortly after, coils of starch-blue smoke burst into being along the French lines, and the English batteries respond promptly, in an ominous roar that can be heard at Antwerp.

A column from the French left, six thousand strong, advances on the plantation in front of the château of Hougomont. They are played upon by the English ordnance ; but they enter the wood, and dislodge some battalions there.   The French approach the buildings, but are stopped by a loop-holed wall with a mass of English guards behind it.   A deadly fire bursts from these through the loops and over the summit.

NAPOLÉON orders a battery of howitzers to play upon the building.   Flames soon burst from it ; but the foot-guards still hold the courtyard.

SCENE II

THE SAME.   THE FRENCH POSITION

On a hillock near the farm of Rossomme a small table from the farmhouse has been placed ; maps are spread thereon, and a chair is beside it.   NAPOLÉON, SOULT, and other marshals are standing round, their horses waiting at the base of the slope.

NAPOLÉON looks through his glass at Hougomont. His elevated face makes itself distinct in the morning light as a gloomy resentful countenance, blue-black where shaven, and stained with snuff, with powderings of the same on the breast of his uniform. His stumpy figure, being just now thrown back, accentuates his stoutness.

NAPOLÉON

Let Reille be warned that these his surly sets
On Hougomont château, can scarce defray
Their mounting bill of blood.   They do not touch
The core of my intent—to pierce and roll
The centre upon the right of those opposed.
Thereon will turn the outcome of the day,
In which our odds are ninety to their ten !

SOULT

Yes—prove there time and promptitude enough
To call back Grouchy here.   Of his approach
I see no sign.

NAPOLÉON (roughly)

Hours past he was bid come.
—But naught imports it !   We are enough without
    him.
You have been beaten by this Wellington,
And so you think him great.   But let me teach you
Wellington is no foe to reckon with.
His army, too, is poor.   This clash to-day
Is not more serious for our seasoned files
Than breakfasting.

SOULT

Such is my earnest hope.

NAPOLÉON

Observe that Wellington still labours on,
Stoutening his right behind Gomont château,
But leaves his left and centre as before—
Weaker, if anything.   He plays our game !

WELLINGTON can, in fact, be seen detaching from his main
line several companies of Guards to check the aims of the
French on Hougomont.

Let me re-word my tactics.   Ney leads off
By seizing Mont Saint-Jean.   Then d'Erlon stirs
And heaves up his division from the left.
The second corps will move abreast of him,
The sappers nearing to entrench themselves
Within the aforesaid farm.

Enter an aide-de-camp.

AIDE

From Marshal Ney,
Sire, I bring hasty word that all is poised
To strike the vital stroke, and only waits
Your Majesty's command.

NAPOLÉON

Which he shall have
When I have scanned the hills for Grouchy's helms.

NAPOLÉON turns his glass to an upland four or five miles off
on the right, known as St. Lambert's Chapel Hill.   Gazing
more and more intently, he takes rapid pinches of snuff in
excitement, NEY's columns meanwhile standing for the word
to advance, eighty guns being ranged in front of La Belle
Alliance in support of them.

I see a darkly crawling, slug-like shape
Embodying far out there,—troops seemingly—
Grouchy's van-guard.   What think you ?

Soult (also examining closely)

Verily troops;

And, maybe, Grouchy's.   But the air is hazed.

NAPOLÉON

If troops at all, they are Grouchy's.   Why misgive,
And force on ills you fear!

ANOTHER MARSHAL

It seems a wood.

Trees don bold outlines in their new-leafed pride.

ANOTHER MARSHAL

It is the creeping shadow from a cloud.

ANOTHER MARSHAL

It is a mass of stationary foot;
I can descry piled arms.

NAPOLÉON sends off the order for NEY's attack—the grand
assault on the English midst, including the farm of La Haye
Sainte.   It opens with a half-hour's thunderous discharge of
artillery, which ceases at length to let D'ERLON's infantry
pass.

Four huge columns of these, shouting defiantly, push for-
wards in face of the reciprocal fire from the cannon of the
English.   Their effrontery carries them so near the Anglo-
Allied lines that the latter waver.   But PICTON brings up
PACK's brigade, before which the French in turn recede, though
they make an attempt on La Haye Sainte, whence BARING's
Germans pour a resolute fire.

WELLINGTON, who is seen afar as one of a group standing
by a great elm, orders OMPTEDA to send assistance to BARING,
as may be gathered from the darting of aides to and fro between
the points, like house-flies dancing their quadrilles.

East of the great highway the right columns of D'ERLON's
corps have climbed the slopes.   BYLANDT's sorely exposed

Dutch are broken, and in their flight disorder the ranks of the
English Twenty-eighth, the Carabineers of the Ninety-fifth
being also dislodged from the sand-pit they occupied.

Napoléon

All prospers marvellously !   Gomont is hemmed ;
La Haye Sainte too ; their centre jeopardized ;
Travers and d'Erlon dominate the crest,
And further strength of foot is following close.
Their troops are raw ; the flower of England's force
That fought in Spain, America now holds.—
To-night we sleep in Brussels !

Sir Thomas Picton, seeing what is happening, orders
Kempt's brigade forward.   It volleys murderously Donzelot's
columns of d'Erlon's corps, and repulses them.   As they
recede Picton is beheld shouting an order to charge.

Spirit of Rumour

I catch a voice that cautions Picton now
Against his rashness.   " What the hell care I,—
Is my curst carcase worth a moment's mind ?—
Come on ! " he answers.   Onwardly he goes !

His tall, stern, saturnine figure with its bronzed complexion
is on nearer approach discerned heading the charge.   As he
advances to the slope between the cross-roads and the sand-
pit, riding very conspicuously, he falls dead, a bullet in his
forehead.   His aide, assisted by a soldier, drags the body
beneath a tree and hastens on.   Kempt takes his command.

Next Marcognet is repulsed by Pack's brigade.   d'Erlon's
infantry and Travers's cuirassiers are charged by the Union
Brigade of Scotch[1] Greys, Royal Dragoons, and Inniskillens,
and cut down everywhere, the brigade following them so
furiously that Lord Uxbridge tries in vain to recall it.   On
its coming near the French it is overwhelmed by Milhaud's
cuirassiers, scarcely a fifth of the brigade returning.

An aide enters to Napoléon from General Domon.

---

[1] The spelling of the date is used.

AIDE

The General, on a far reconnaissance,
Says, sire, there is no room for longer doubt
That those debouching on St. Lambert's Hill
Are Prussian files.

NAPOLÉON

Then where is General Grouchy?

Enter COLONEL MARBOT with a prisoner.

Aha—a Prussian, too!   How comes he here!

MARBOT

Sire, my hussars have captured him near Lasnes—
A subaltern of the Silesian Horse.
A note from Bülow to Lord Wellington,
Announcing that a Prussian corps is close,
Was found on him.   He speaks our language, sire.

NAPOLÉON (to prisoner)

What force looms yonder on St. Lambert's Hill?

PRISONER

General Count Bülow's van, your Majesty.

A dismayed scowl crosses NAPOLÉON's sallow face.

NAPOLÉON

Where, then, did your main army lie last night?

PRISONER

At Wavre.

NAPOLÉON

But clashed it with no Frenchmen there?

PRISONER

With none. We deemed they had marched on
    Plancenoit.

NAPOLÉON (shortly)

Take him away. (The prisoner is removed.) Has
    Grouchy's whereabouts
Been sought, to apprize him of this Prussian trend ?

SOULT

Certainly, sire. I sent a messenger.

NAPOLÉON (bitterly)

A messenger ! Had my poor Berthier been here
Six would have insufficed ! Now then : seek Ney ;
Bid him to sling the valour of his braves
Fiercely on England ere Count Bülow come ;
And advertize the succours on the hill
As Grouchy's. (Aside) This is my one battle-chance ;
The Allies have many such ! (To SOULT) If Bülow
    nears,
He cannot join in time to share the fight.
And if he could, 'tis but a corps the more. . . .
This morning we had ninety chances ours,
We have threescore still. If Grouchy but retrieve
His fault of absence, conquest comes with eve !

          The scene shifts.

SCENE III

SAINT LAMBERT'S CHAPEL HILL

A hill half-way between Wavre and the field of Waterloo, five miles to the north-east of the scene preceding. The hill is wooded, with some open land around. To the left of the scene, towards Waterloo, is a valley.

DUMB SHOW

Marching columns in Prussian uniforms, coming from the direction of Wavre, debouch upon the hill from the road through the wood.

They are the advance-guard and two brigades of BÜLOW's corps, that have been joined there by BLÜCHER. The latter has just risen from the bed to which he has been confined since the battle of Ligny, two days back. He still looks pale and shaken by the severe fall and trampling he endured near the end of the action.

On the summit the troops halt, and a discussion between BLÜCHER and his staff ensues.

The cannonade in the direction of Waterloo is growing more and more violent. BLÜCHER, after looking this way and that, decides to fall upon the French right at Plancenoit as soon as he can get there, which will not be yet.

Between this point and that the ground descends steeply to the valley on the spectator's left, where there is a mud-bottomed stream, the Lasne ; the slope ascends no less abruptly on the other side towards Plancenoit. It is across this defile alone that the Prussian army can proceed thither—a route of unusual difficulty for artillery ; where, moreover, the enemy is suspected of having placed a strong outpost during the night to intercept such an approach.

A figure goes forward—that of MAJOR FALKENHAUSEN, who is sent to reconnoitre, and they wait a tedious time, the firing at Waterloo growing more tremendous. FALKENHAUSEN comes back with the welcome news that no outpost is there.

There now remains only the difficulty of the defile itself ; and the attempt is made. BLÜCHER is descried riding hither and thither as the guns drag heavily down the slope into the muddy bottom of the valley. Here the wheels get stuck, and the men, already tired by marching since five in the morning, seem inclined to leave the guns where they are. But the thunder from Waterloo still goes on, BLÜCHER exhorts his men by words and eager gestures, and they do at length get the guns across, though with much loss of time.

The advance-guard now reaches some thick trees called the Wood of Paris. It is followed by the LOSTHIN and HILLER divisions of foot, and in due course by the remainder of the two brigades. Here they halt, and await the arrival of the main body of BÜLOW's corps, and the third corps under THIELEMANN.

The scene shifts.

SCENE IV

THE FIELD OF WATERLOO. THE ENGLISH POSITION

WELLINGTON, on Copenhagen, is again under the elm-tree behind La Haye Sainte. Both horse and rider are covered with mud-splashes, but the weather having grown finer the DUKE has taken off his cloak.

UXBRIDGE, FITZROY SOMERSET, CLINTON, ALTEN, COLVILLE, DE LANCEY, HERVEY, GORDON, and other of his staff officers and aides are near him; there being also present GENERALS MÜFFLING, HÜGEL, and ALAVA; also TYLER, PICTON's aide. The roar of battle continues.

WELLINGTON

I am grieved at losing Picton ; more than grieved.
He was as grim a devil as ever lived,
And roughish-mouthed withal. But never a man
More stout in fight, more stoical in blame !

TYLER

Before he left for this campaign he said,
" When you shall hear of *my* death, mark my words,
You'll hear of a bloody day ! " and, on my soul,
'Tis true.

Enter another aide-de-camp.

AIDE

Sir William Ponsonby, my lords, has fallen.
His horse got mud-stuck in a new-ploughed plot,
Lancers surrounded him and bore him down,
And six then ran him through. The occasion sprung
Mainly from the Brigade's too reckless rush,
Sheer to the French front lines.

WELLINGTON (gravely)

Ah—so it comes !
The Greys were bound to pay—'tis always so—
Full dearly for their dash so far afield.
Valour unballasted but lands its freight
On the enemy's shore.—What has become of Hill ?

AIDE

We have not seen him latterly, your Grace.

WELLINGTON

By God, I hope I haven't lost him, too ?

BRIDGMAN (just come up)

Lord Hill's bay charger, being shot dead, your
        Grace,
Rolled over him in falling. He is bruised,
But hopes to be in place again betimes.

WELLINGTON

Praise Fate for thinking better of that frown !

It is now nearing four o'clock. La Haye Sainte is devastated by the second attack of NEY. The farm has been enveloped by DONZELOT's division, its garrison, the King's German Legion, having fought till all ammunition was exhausted.

The gates are forced open, and in the retreat of the late defenders
to the main Allied line they are nearly all cut or shot down.

Spirit of the Pities

O Farm of sad vicissitudes and strange !
Farm of the Holy Hedge, yet fool of change !
Whence lit so sanct a name on thy now violate grange ?

Wellington (to Müffling, resolutely)

Despite their fierce advantage here, I swear
By every God that war can call upon
To hold our present place at any cost,
Until your force coöperate with our lines !
To that I stand ; although 'tis bruited now
That Bülow's corps has only reached Ohain.
I've sent Freemantle hence to seek them there,
And give them inkling we shall need them soon.

Müffling (looking at his watch)

I had hoped that Blücher would be here ere this.

The staff turn their glasses on the French position.

Uxbridge

What movement can it be they contemplate ?

Wellington

A shock of cavalry on the hottest scale,
It seems to me. . . . (To aide) Bid him to reinforce
The front line with some second-line brigades ;
Some, too, from the reserve.

The Brunswickers advance to support Maitland's Guards,
and the Mitchell and Adam Brigades establish themselves
above Hougomont, which is still in flames. ·
    Ney, in continuation of the plan of throwing his whole

force on the British centre before the advent of the Prussians,
now intensifies his onslaught with the cavalry.   Terrific discharges of artillery initiate it to clear the ground.   A heavy
round-shot dashes through the tree over the heads of WELLING-
TON and his generals, and boughs and leaves come flying down
on them.

WELLINGTON

Good practice that !   I vow they did not fire
So dexterously in Spain.   (He calls up an aide.)   Bid
    Ompteda
Direct the infantry to lie tight down
On the reverse ridge-slope, to screen themselves
While these close shots and shells are teasing us ;
When the charge comes they'll cease.

                        [The order is carried out.

    NEY'S cavalry attack now matures.   MILHAUD'S cuirassiers
in twenty-four squadrons advance down the opposite decline,
followed and supported by seven squadrons of lancers and
twelve squadrons of chasseurs under DESNÖETTES.   They disappear for a minute in the hollow between the armies.

UXBRIDGE

Ah—now we have got their long-brewed plot ex-
    plained !

WELLINGTON (nodding)

That this was rigged for some picked time to-day
I had inferred.   But that it would be risked
Sheer on our lines, while still they stand unswayed,
In conscious battle-trim, I reckoned not.
It looks a madman's cruel enterprise !

FITZROY SOMERSET

We have just heard that Ney embarked on it
Without an order, ere its aptness riped.

Wellington

It may be so : he's rash.   And yet I doubt.
I know Napoléon.   If the onset fail
It will be Ney's ; if it succeed he'll claim it!

A dull reverberation of the tread of innumerable hoofs
comes from behind the hill, and the foremost troops rise into
view.

Spirit of the Pities

Behold the gorgeous coming of those horse,
Accoutred in kaleidoscopic hues
That would persuade us war has beauty in it !—
Discern the troopers' mien ; each with the air
Of one who is himself a tragedy :
The cuirassiers, steeled, mirroring the day ;
Red lancers, green chasseurs : behind the blue
The red ; the red before the green :
A lingering-on, till late in Christendom,
Of the barbaric trick to terrorize
The foe by aspect !

WELLINGTON directs his glass to an officer in a rich uniform
with many decorations on his breast, who rides near the front
of the approaching squadrons.   The DUKE's face expresses
admiration.

Wellington

It's Marshal Ney himself who heads the charge.
The finest cavalry commander, he,
That wears a foreign plume ; ay, probably
The whole world through !

Spirit Ironic

                                 And when that matchless chief
Sentenced shall lie to ignominious death
But technically deserved, no finger he
Who speaks will lift to save him !

SPIRIT OF THE PITIES

> *To his shame.*
> *We must discount war's generous impulses*
> *I sadly see.*

SPIRIT OF THE YEARS

> *Be mute, and let spin on*
> *This whirlwind of the Will!*

As NEY's cavalry ascends to the English position the swish of the horses' knees through the standing corn can be heard, and the reverberation of hoofs increases in strength. The English gunners stand with their port-fires ready, which are seen glowing luridly in the daylight. There is comparative silence.

A VOICE

Now, captains, are you loaded?

CAPTAINS

> Yes, my lord.

VOICE

Point carefully, and wait till their whole height
Shows up above the ridge.

When the squadrons rise in full view, within sixty yards of the cannon-mouths, the batteries fire, with a concussion that shakes the hill itself. Their shot punch holes through the front ranks of the cuirassiers, and horses and riders fall in heaps. But they are not stopped, hardly checked, galloping up to the mouths of the guns, passing between the pieces, and plunging among the Allied infantry behind the ridge, who, with the advance of the horsemen, have sprung up from their prone position and formed into squares.

SPIRIT OF RUMOUR

> *Ney guides the fore-front of the carabineers*
> *Through charge and charge, with rapid recklessness.*
> *Horses, cuirasses, sabres, helmets, men,*

Impinge confusedly on the pointed prongs
Of the English kneeling there, whose dim red shapes
Behind their slanted steel seem trampled flat
And sworded to the sward.   The charge recedes,
And lo, the tough lines rank there as before,
Save that they are shrunken.

SPIRIT OF THE PITIES

Hero of heroes, too,
Ney, (not forgetting those who gird against him).—
Simple and single-souled lieutenant he. . . .
Why should men's many-valued motions take
So barbarous a groove !

   The cuirassiers and lancers surge round the English and
Allied squares like waves, striking furiously on them and well-
nigh breaking them.   They stand in dogged silence amid the
French cheers.

WELLINGTON (to the nearest square)

Hard pounding this, my men !   I truly trust
You'll pound the longest !

SQUARE

Hip-hip-hip-hurrah !

MÜFFLING (again referring to his watch)

However firmly they may stand, in faith,
Their firmness must have bounds to it, because
There are bounds to human strength ! . . . Your
    Grace, I ride
To leftward now, to spirit Zieten on.

WELLINGTON

Good.   It is time !   I think he will be late,
However, in the field.

        MÜFFLING goes.   Enter an aide, breathless.

AIDE

Your Grace, the Ninety-fifth are patience-spent
With standing under fire so passing long.
They writhe to charge—or anything but stand !

WELLINGTON

Not yet.   They shall have at 'em later on.
At present keep them firm.

[Exit aide.

The Allied squares stand like little red-brick castles, independent of each other, and motionless except at the dry hurried
command " Close up ! " repeated every now and then as they
are slowly thinned.   On the other hand, under their firing and
bayonets a disorder becomes apparent among the charging
horse, on whose cuirasses the bullets snap like stones on window-
panes.   At this the Allied cavalry waiting in the rear advance ;
and by degrees they deliver the squares from their enemies,
who are withdrawn to their own position to prepare for a still
more strenuous assault.

The point of view shifts.

SCENE V

THE SAME.   THE WOMEN'S CAMP NEAR MONT
SAINT-JEAN

On the sheltered side of a clump of trees at the back of
the English position camp-fires are smouldering.   Soldiers'
wives, mistresses, and children from a few months to five or
six years of age, sit on the ground round the fires or on armfuls
of straw from the adjoining farm.   Wounded soldiers lie near
the women.   The wind occasionally brings the smoke and smell
of the battle into the encampment, the noise being continuous.
Two waggons stand near ; also a surgeon's horse in charge of a
bâtman, laden with bone-saws, knives, probes, tweezers, and
other surgical instruments.   Behind lies a woman who has
just given birth to a child, which a second woman is holding.

Many of the other women are shredding lint, the elder children assisting. Some are dressing the slighter wounds of the soldiers who have come in here instead of going further. Along the road near is a continual procession of bearers of wounded men to the rear. The occupants of the camp take hardly any notice of the thundering of the cannon. A camp-follower is playing a fiddle near.

Another woman enters.

WOMAN

There's no sign of my husband any longer. His battalion is half-a-mile from where it was. He looked back as they wheeled off towards the fighting-line, as much as to say, " Nancy, if I don't see 'ee again, this is good-bye, my dear." Yes, poor man ! . . . Not but what 'a had a temper at times !

SECOND WOMAN

I'm out of all that. My husband—as I used to call him for form's sake—is quiet enough. He was wownded at Quarter-Brass the day before yester-day, and died the same night. But I didn't know it till I got here, and then says I, " Widder or no widder, I mean to see this out."

A sergeant staggers in with blood dropping from his face.

SERGEANT

Damned if I think you will see it out, mis'ess, for if I don't mistake there'll be a retreat of the whole army on Brussels soon. We can't stand much longer !—For the love of God, have ye got a cup of water, if nothing stronger ? (They hand a cup.)

THIRD WOMAN (entering and sinking down)

The Lord send that I may never see again what I've been seeing while looking for my poor galliant

Joe ! The surgeon asked me to lend a hand ; and 'twas worse than opening innerds at a pig-killing.

(She faints.)

FOURTH WOMAN (to a little girl)

Never mind her, my dear ; come and help me with this one. (She goes with the girl to a soldier in red with buff facings who lies some distance off.) Ah—'tis no good. He's gone.

GIRL

No, mother. His eyes are wide open, a-staring to get a sight of the battle !

FOURTH WOMAN

That's nothing. Lots of dead ones stare in that silly way. It depends upon where they were hit. I was all through the Peninsula ; that's how I know. (She covers the horny gaze of the man. Shouts and louder discharges are heard.)—Heaven's high tower, what's that ?

Enter an officer's servant.[1]

SERVANT

Waiting with the major's spare hoss—up to my knees in mud from the rain that had come down like baccy-pipe stems all the night and morning— I have just seen a charge never beholded since the days of the Amalekites ! The squares still stand, but Ney's cavalry have made another attack. Their swords are streaming with blood, and their horses' hoofs squash out our poor fellows' bowels as they lie. A ball has sunk in Sir Thomas Picton's forehead and killed him like Goliath the Philistine. I don't see what's to stop the French. Well, it's the

---

[1] Samuel Clark; born 1779, died 1857. Buried at West Stafford, Dorset.

Lord's doing and marvellous in our eyes. Hullo, who's he? (They look towards the road.) A fine hale old gentleman, isn't he? What business has a man of that sort here?

Enter, on the highway near, the DUKE OF RICHMOND in plain clothes, on horseback, accompanied by two youths, his sons. They draw rein on an eminence, and gaze towards the battlefield.

RICHMOND (to son)

Everything looks as bad as possible just now. I wonder where your brother is? However, we can't go any nearer. . . . We'd better perhaps return, or we shall be caught in the stream of retreat, and they will be uneasy at home. . . . Yes, the bât-horses are already being moved off, and there are more and more fugitives. A ghastly finish to your mother's ball, by Gad if it isn't!

They turn their horses towards Brussels. Enter, meeting them, MR. LEGH, a Wessex gentleman, also come out to view the battle.

LEGH

Can you tell me, sir, how the battle is going?

RICHMOND

Badly, badly, I fear, sir. There will be a retreat soon, seemingly.

LEGH

Indeed! Yes, a crowd of fugitives are coming over the hill even now. What will these poor women do?

RICHMOND

God knows! They will be ridden over, I suppose. Though it is extraordinary how they do

contrive to escape destruction while hanging so
close to the rear of an action ! They are moving,
however. Well, we will move too.

Exeunt DUKE OF RICHMOND, sons, and MR. LEGH.

The point of view shifts.

SCENE VI

THE SAME.   THE FRENCH POSITION

NEY's charge of cavalry against the opposite upland has
been three times renewed without success. He collects the
scattered squadrons to renew it a fourth time. The glittering
host again ascends the confronting slopes over the bodies of
those previously left there, and amid horses wandering about
without riders, or crying as they lie with entrails trailing or
limbs broken.

NAPOLÉON falls into a drowsy stupefaction as he looks on
near the farm of Rossomme, till he nods in momentary sleep.

NAPOLÉON (starting up)

A horrible dream has gripped me—horrible !
I saw before me Lannes—just as he looked
That day at Aspern : mutilated, bleeding !
" What—blood again ? " he said to me.   " Still
     blood ? "

He further arouses himself, takes snuff vehemently, and
looks through his glass.

What time is it ?—Ah, these assaults of Ney's !
They are a blunder ; they've been enterprised
An hour too early ! . . . There Lhéritier goes
Onward with his division next Milhaud ;
Now Kellermann must follow up with his.
So one mistake makes many. Yes ; ay ; yes !

SOULT

I fear that Ney has compromised us here
Just as at Jena ; even worse !

NAPOLÉON

No less
Must we support him now he is launched on it. . . .
The miracle is that he is still alive !

NEY and his mass of cavalry again pass the English batteries
and disappear amid the squares beyond.

Their cannon are abandoned ; and their squares
Again environed—see !   I would to God
Murat could but be here !   Yet I disdained
His proffered service. . . . All my star asks now
Is to break some half-dozen of those blocks
Of English yonder.   He was the man to do it.

NEY and D'ERLON'S squadrons are seen emerging from the
English squares in a disorganized state, the attack having failed
like the previous ones.

An aide-de-camp enters to NAPOLÉON.

AIDE

The Prussians have debouched on our right rear
From Paris-wood ; and Losthin's infantry
Appear by Plancenoit ; Hiller's to leftwards.
Two regiments of their horse protect their front,
And three light batteries.

A haggard shade crosses NAPOLÉON'S face.

NAPOLÉON

What then !   That's not a startling force as yet.
A counter-stroke by Domon's cavalry
Must shatter them.   Lobau must bring his foot

Up forward, heading for the Prussian front,
Unrecking losses by their cannonade.

                                 [Exit aide.

    The din of battle continues. DOMON's horse are soon seen
advancing towards and attacking the Prussian hussars in front
of the infantry; and he next attempts to silence the Prussian
batteries playing on him by leading up his troops and cutting
down the gunners. But he has to fall back upon the infantry
of LOBAU.

             Enter another aide-de-camp.

AIDE

These tidings I report, your Majesty :—
Von Ryssel's and von Hacké's Prussian foot
Have lately sallied from the Wood of Paris,
Bearing on us ; no vast array as yet ;
But twenty thousand loom not far behind
These vaward marchers !

NAPOLÉON

        Ah !   They swarm thus thickly ?
But be they hell's own legions we'll defy them !—
Lobau's men will stand firm.

    He looks in the direction of the English lines, where NEY's
cavalry-assaults still linger furiously on.

                     But who rides hither,
Spotting the sky with clods in his high haste ?

SOULT

It looks like Colonel Heymès—come from Ney.

NAPOLÉON (sullenly)

And his face shows what clef his music's in !

    Enter COLONEL HEYMÈS, blood-stained, muddy, and breath
less.

HEYMÈS

The Prince of Moscow, sire, the Marshal Ney,
Bids me implore that infantry be sent
Immediately, to further his attack.
They cannot be dispensed with, save we fail !

NAPOLÉON (furiously)

Infantry !   Where the sacred God thinks he
I can find infantry for him !   Forsooth,
Does he expect me to create them—eh ?
Why sends he such a message, seeing well
How we are straitened here !

HEYMÈS

                              Such was the prayer
Of my commission, sire.   And I may say
That I myself have seen his strokes must waste
Without such backing.

NAPOLÉON
                    Why ?

HEYMÈS

                              Our cavalry
Lie stretched in swathes, fronting the furnace-
      throats
Of the English cannon as a breastwork built
Of reeking corpses.   Marshal Ney's third horse
Is shot.   Besides the slain, Donop, Guyot,
Delort, Lhéritier, Piquet, Travers, more,
Are vilely wounded.   On the other hand
Wellington has sought refuge in a square,
Few of his generals are not killed or hit,
And all is tickle with him.   But I see,
Likewise, that I can claim no reinforcement,
And will return and say so.

                                   [Exit HEYMÈS.

NAPOLÉON (to Soult, sadly)

                              Ney does win me !
I fain would strengthen him.—Within an ace
Of breaking down the English as he is,
'Twould write upon the sunset " Victory ! "—
But whom may spare we from the right here now ?
No single man !

An interval.

                              Life's curse begins, I see,
With helplessness ! . . . All I can compass is
To send Durutte to fall on Papelote,
And yet more strongly occupy La Haye,
To cut off Bülow's right from bearing up
And checking Ney's attack.   Further than this
None but the Gods can scheme !

SOULT hastily begins writing orders to that effect.

The point of view shifts.

SCENE VII

THE SAME.   THE ENGLISH POSITION

The din of battle continues.   WELLINGTON, UXBRIDGE, HILL,
DE LANCEY, GORDON, and others discovered near the middle
of the line.

SPIRIT OF RUMOUR

*It is a moment when the steadiest pulse
Thuds pit-a-pat.   The crisis shapes and nears
For Wellington as for his counter-chief.*

SPIRIT OF THE PITIES

*The hour is shaking him, unshakeable
As he may seem !*

Spirit of the Years

> *Know'st not at this stale time*
> *That shaken and unshaken are alike*
> *But demonstrations from the Back of Things ?*
> *Must I again reveal It as It hauls*
> *The halyards of the world ?*

A transparency as in earlier scenes again pervades the spectacle, and the ubiquitous urging of the Immanent Will becomes visualized. The web connecting all the apparently separate shapes includes WELLINGTON in its tissue with the rest, and shows him, like them, as acting while discovering his intention to act. By the lurid light the faces of every row, square, group, and column of men, French and English, wear the expression of that of people in a dream.

Spirit of the Pities (tremulously)

> *Yea, sire ; I see.*
> *Disquiet me, pray, no more !*

The strange light passes, and the embattled hosts on the field seem to move independently as usual.

Wellington (to Uxbridge)

Manœuvring does not seem to animate
Napoléon's methods now.   Forward he comes,
And pounds away on us in the ancient style,
Till he is beaten back in the ancient style ;
And so the see-saw sways !

The din increases. WELLINGTON's aide-de-camp, Sir A. GORDON, a little in his rear, falls mortally wounded. The DUKE turns quickly.

> But where is Gordon ?
> Ah—hit is he !   That's bad, that's bad, by God.

[GORDON is removed.   An aide enters.

Aide

Your Grace, the Colonel Ompteda has fallen,
And La Haye Sainte is now a bath of blood.

Nothing more can be done there, save with help.
The Rifles suffer sharply !

> An aide is seen coming from KEMPT.

WELLINGTON
> What says he ?

DE LANCEY

He says that Kempt, being riddled through and
    thinned,
Sends him for reinforcements.

WELLINGTON (with heat)
> Reinforcements ?
And where am I to get him reinforcements
In Heaven's name !   I've no reinforcements here,
As he should know.

AIDE (hesitating)
> What's to be done, your Grace ?

WELLINGTON

Done ?   Those he has left him, be they many or
    few,
Fight till they fall, like others in the field !

> [Exit aide.

> The Quartermaster-General DE LANCEY, riding by WELLING-
> TON, is struck by a lobbing shot that hurls him over the head
> of his horse.   WELLINGTON and others go to him.

DE LANCEY (faintly)

I may as well be left to die in peace !

WELLINGTON

He may recover.   Take him to the rear,
And call the best attention up to him.

DE LANCEY is carried off.   The next moment a shell bursts
close to WELLINGTON.

HILL (approaching)

I strongly feel you stand too much exposed !

WELLINGTON

I know, I know.   It matters not one damn !
I may as well be shot as not perceive
What ills are raging here.

HILL

                              Conceding such,
And as you may be ended momently,
A truth there is no blinking, what commands
Have you to leave me, should fate shape it so ?

WELLINGTON

These simply : to hold out unto the last,
As long as one man stands on one lame leg
With one ball in his pouch !—then end as I.

He rides on slowly with the others.   NEY'S charges, though
fruitless so far, are still fierce.   His troops are now reduced to
one-half.   Regiments of the BACHELU division, and the JAMIN
brigade, are at last moved up to his assistance.   They are
partly swept down by the Allied batteries, and partly notched
away by the infantry, the smoke being now so thick that the
position of the battalions is revealed only by the flashing of
the priming-pans and muzzles, and by the furious oaths heard
behind the cloud.   WELLINGTON comes back.

Enter another aide-de-camp.

AIDE

We bow to the necessity of saying
That our brigade is lessened to one-third,
Your Grace.   And those who are left alive of it
Are so unmuscled by fatigue and thirst
That some relief, however temporary,
Becomes sore need.

WELLINGTON

Inform your general
That his proposal asks the impossible !
That he, I, every Englishman afield,
Must fall upon the spot we occupy,
Our wounds in front.

AIDE

It is enough, your Grace.
I answer for't that he, those under him,
And I withal, will bear us as you say.

[Exit aide.

The din of battle goes on.   WELLINGTON is grave but calm.
Like those around him, he is splashed to the top of his hat
with partly dried mire, mingled with red spots ;   his face is
grimed in the same way, little courses showing themselves
where the sweat has trickled down from his brow and temples.

CLINTON (to Hill)

A rest would do our chieftain no less good,
In faith, than that unfortunate brigade !
He is tried damnably ; and much more strained
Than I have ever seen him.

HILL

Endless risks
He's running likewise.   What the hell would happen
If he were shot, is more than I can say !

WELLINGTON (calling to some near)

At Talavera, Salamanca, boys,
And at Vitoria, we saw smoke together ;
And though the day seems wearing doubtfully,
Beaten we must not be !   What would they say
Of us at home, if so ?

A CRY (from the French)

Their centre breaks !
Vive l'Empereur !

It comes from the FOY and BACHELU divisions, which are
rushing forward.   HALKETT'S and DUPLAT'S brigades intercept.   DUPLAT falls, shot dead ; but the venturesome French
regiments, pierced with converging fires, and cleft with shells,
have to retreat.

HILL (rejoining Wellington)

The French artillery-fire
To the right still renders regiments restive there
That have to stand.   The long exposure galls them.

WELLINGTON

They must be stayed as our poor means afford.
I have to bend attention steadfastly
Upon the centre here.   The game just now
Goes all against us ; and if staunchness fail
But for one moment with these thinning foot,
Defeat succeeds !

The battle continues to sway hither and thither with concussions, wounds, smoke, the fumes of gunpowder, and the
steam from the hot bodies of grape-torn horses and men.   One
side of a Hanoverian square is blown away ; the three remaining sides form themselves into a triangle.   So many of his
aides are cut down that it is difficult for WELLINGTON to get
reports of what is happening afar.   It begins to be discovered
at the front that a regiment of hussars, and others without
ammunition, have deserted, and that some officers in the rear,

honestly concluding the battle to be lost, are riding quietly off to Brussels. Those who are left unwounded of WELLINGTON's staff show gloomy misgivings at such signs, despite their own firmness.

SPIRIT SINISTER

> *One needs must be a ghost*
> *To move here in the midst 'twixt host and host !*
> *Their balls right tunefully through my ichor blow*
> *As I were an organ-stop.   It's merry so ;*
> *What damage mortal flesh must undergo !*

A Prussian officer enters to MÜFFLING, who has again rejoined the DUKE's suite. MÜFFLING hastens forward to WELLINGTON.

MÜFFLING

Blücher has just begun to operate ;
But owing to Gneisenau's stolid stagnancy
The body of our army looms not yet !
As Zieten's corps still plod behind Smohain
Their coming must be late.   Blücher's attack
Strikes the remote right rear of the enemy,
Somewhere by Plancenoit.

WELLINGTON

> A timely blow ;
But would that Zieten sped !   Well, better late
Than never.   We'll still stand.

The point of observation shifts.

SCENE VIII

THE SAME. LATER

NEY's long attacks on the centre with cavalry having failed, those left of the squadrons and their infantry-supports fall back pell-mell in broken groups across the depression between the armies.

Meanwhile BÜLOW, having engaged LOBAU's Sixth Corps, carries Plancenoit.

The artillery-fire between the French and the English continues. An officer of the Third Foot-guards comes up to WELLINGTON and those of his suite that survive.

OFFICER

Our Colonel Canning—coming I know not whence—

WELLINGTON

I lately sent him with important words
To the remoter lines.

OFFICER

                    As he returned
A grape-shot struck him in the breast ; he fell,
At once a dead man. General Halkett, too,
Has had his cheek shot through, but still keeps going.

WELLINGTON

And how proceeds De Lancey ?

OFFICER

                         I am told
That he forbids the surgeons waste their time
On him, who well can wait till worse are eased.

WELLINGTON

A noble fellow.

NAPOLÉON can now be seen, across the valley, pushing forward a new scheme of some sort, urged to it obviously by the visible nearing of further Prussian corps. The EMPEROR is as critically situated as WELLINGTON, and his army is now formed in a right angle (" en potence "), the main front to the English, the lesser to as many of the Prussians as have yet arrived. His gestures show him to be giving instructions of desperate import to a general whom he has called up.

SPIRIT IRONIC

He bids La Bedoyère to speed away
Along the whole sweep of the surging line,
And there announce to the breath-shotten bands
Who toil for a chimæra trustfully,
With seventy pounds of luggage on their loins,
That the dim Prussian masses seen afar
Are Grouchy's three-and-thirty thousand, come
To clinch a victory.

SPIRIT OF THE PITIES

But Ney demurs !

SPIRIT IRONIC

Ney holds indignantly that such a feint
Is not war-worthy. Says Napoléon then,
Snuffing anew, with sour sardonic scowl,
That he is choiceless.

SPIRIT SINISTER

Excellent Emperor !
He tops all human greatness ; in that he
To lesser grounds of greatness adds the prime,
Of being without a conscience.

LA BEDOYÈRE and orderlies start on their mission. The false intelligence is seen to spread, by the excited motion of the columns, and the soldiers can be heard shouting as their spirits revive.

WELLINGTON is beginning to discern the features of the coming onset, when COLONEL FRASER rides up.

FRASER

We have just learnt from a deserting captain,
One of the carabineers who charged of late,
That an assault which dwarfs all instances—
The whole Imperial Guard in welded weight—
Is shortly to be made.

WELLINGTON

        For your smart speed
My thanks.   My observation is confirmed.
We'll hasten now along the battle-line (to Staff),
As swiftest means for giving orders out
Whereby to combat this.

The speaker, accompanied by HILL, UXBRIDGE, and others —all now looking as worn and besmirched as the men in the ranks—proceed along the lines, and dispose the brigades to meet the threatened shock. The infantry are brought out of the shelter they have recently sought, the cavalry stationed in the rear, and the batteries of artillery hitherto kept in reserve are moved to the front.

The last Act of the battle begins.

There is a preliminary attack by DONZELOT's columns, combined with swarms of sharpshooters, to the disadvantage of the English and their allies. WELLINGTON has scanned it closely. FITZROY SOMERSET, his military secretary, comes up.

WELLINGTON

What casualty has thrown its shade among
The regiments of Nassau, to shake them so ?

SOMERSET

The Prince of Orange has been badly struck—
A bullet through his shoulder—so they tell ;
And Kielmansegge has shown some signs of stress.

Kincaird's tried line wanes leaner and more lean—
Whittled to a weak skein of skirmishers ;
The Twenty-seventh lie dead.

WELLINGTON

Ah yes—I know !

While they watch developments a cannon-shot passes and
knocks SOMERSET's right arm to a mash. He is assisted to the
rear.

NEY and FRIANT now lead forward the last and most
desperate assault of the day, in charges of the Old and Middle
Guard, the attack by DONZELOT and ALLIX further east still
continuing as a support. It is about a quarter-past eight,
and the midsummer evening is fine after the wet night and
morning, the sun approaching its setting in a sky of gorgeous
colours.

The picked and toughened Guard, many of whom stood in
the ranks at Austerlitz and Wagram, have been drawn up in
three or four échelons, the foremost of which now advances
up the slopes to the Allies' position. The others follow at
intervals, the drummers beating the " pas de charge."

CHORUS OF RUMOURS (aerial music)

Twice thirty throats of couchant cannonry—
Ranked in a hollow curve, to close their blaze
Upon the advancing files—wait silently
    Like swarthy bulls at gaze.

The Guard approaches nearer and more near :
To touch-hole moves each match of smoky sheen :
The ordnance roars : the van-ranks disappear
    As if wiped off the scene.

The aged Friant falls as it resounds ;
Ney's charger drops—his fifth on this sore day—
Its rider from the quivering body bounds
    And forward foots his way.

The cloven columns tread the English height,
Grasp guns, repulse battalions rank by rank,
While horse and foot artillery heavily bite
    Into their front and flank.

It nulls the power of a flesh-built frame
To live within that zone of missiles.   Back
The Old Guard, staggering, climbs to whence it came.
The fallen define its track !

The second échelon of the Imperial Guard has come up to the assault. Its columns have borne upon HALKETT's right. HALKETT, desperate to keep his wavering men firm, himself seizes and waves the flag of the Thirty-third, in which act he falls wounded. But the men rally. Meanwhile the Fifty-second, covered by the Seventy-first, has advanced across the front, and charges the Imperial Guard on the flank.

The third échelon next arrives at the English lines and squares ; rushes through the very focus of their fire, and seeing nothing more in front, raises a shout.

IMPERIAL GUARD

The Emperor !   It's victory !

WELLINGTON

Stand up, Guards !
Form line upon the front face of the square !

Two thousand of MAITLAND's Guards, hidden in the hollow roadway, thereupon spring up, form as ordered, and reveal themselves as a fence of levelled firelocks four deep. The flints click in a multitude, the pans flash, and volley after volley is poured into the bear-skinned figures of the massed French, who kill COLONEL D'OYLEY in returning the fire.

WELLINGTON

Now drive the fellows in !   They will not stand.

ADAM's brigade, including the Fifty-second under COLONEL COLBORNE, attacks the French guard.

COLBORNE (shouting)

Forward !   Right shoulders forward, Fifty-second !

WELLINGTON

Ha, Colborne—you say well !   Hie on ; hie on !
You'll do it now !

COLBORNE converges on the French guard with the Fifty-
second, and the former splits into two as the climax comes.
ADAM, MAITLAND, and COLBORNE pursue their advantage.
The Imperial columns are broken, and their confusion is increased by grape-shot from BOLTON's battery.

Campbell, this order next :
Vivian's hussars are to support, and bear
Against the cavalry towards Belle Alliance.
Go—let him know.

SIR C. CAMPBELL departs with the order.   Soon VIVIAN's
and VANDELEUR's light horse are seen advancing, and in due
time the French cavalry are rolled back.

WELLINGTON goes in the direction of the hussars with
UXBRIDGE.   A cannon-shot hisses past.

UXBRIDGE (starting)

I have lost my leg, by God !

WELLINGTON

By God, and have you !   Ay—the wind o' the shot
Blew past the withers of my Copenhagen
Like the foul sweeping of a witch's broom.—
Aha—they are giving way !

While UXBRIDGE is being helped to the rear, WELLINGTON
makes a sign to SALTOUN, Colonel of the First Footguards.

SALTOUN (shouting)

Boys, now's your time ;
Forward and win !

FRENCH VOICES

The Guard gives way—we are beaten !

They recede down the hill, carrying confusion into
NAPOLÉON's centre just as the Prussians press forward at

a right angle from the other side of the field. NAPOLÉON is seen standing in the hollow beyond La Haye Sainte, alone, except for the presence of COUNT FLAHAULT, his aide-de-camp. His lips move with a sudden exclamation.

SPIRIT OF THE YEARS

He says " Now all is lost ! The clocks of the world Strike my last empery-hour."

Towards La Haye Sainte the French of DONZELOT and ALLIX, who are fighting KEMPT, PACK, KRUSE, and LAMBERT, seeing what has happened to the Old and Middle Guard, lose heart and recede likewise ; so that the whole French line rolls back like a tide. Simultaneously the Prussians are pressing forward at Papelote and La Haye. The retreat of the French grows into a panic.

FRENCH VOICES (despairingly)

We are betrayed !

WELLINGTON rides at a gallop to the most salient point of the English position, halts, and waves his hat as a signal to all the army. The sign is answered by a cheer along the length of the line.

WELLINGTON

No cheering yet, my lads ; but bear ahead
Before the inflamed face of the west out there
Dons darkness. So you'll round your victory !

The few aides that are left unhurt dart hither and thither with this message, and the whole English host and its allies advance in an ordered mass down the hill except some of the artillery, who cannot get their wheels over the bank of corpses in front. Trumpets, drums, and bugles resound with the advance.

The streams of French fugitives as they run are cut down and shot by their pursuers, whose clothes and contracted features are blackened by smoke and cartridge-biting, and soiled with loam and blood. Some French blow out their own brains as they fly. The sun drops below the horizon while the slaughter goes on.

SPIRIT OF THE PITIES

Is this the last Esdraelon of a moil
For mortal man's effacement?

SPIRIT IRONIC

                     Warfare mere,
Plied by the Managed for the Managers;
To wit: by frenzied folks who profit nought
For those who profit all!

SPIRIT OF THE PITIES

                    Between the jars
Of these who live, I hear uplift and move
The bones of those who placidly have lain
Within the sacred garths of yon grey fanes—
Nivelles, and Plancenoit, and Braine l'Alleud—
Beneath unmemoried mounds through deedless years.
Their dry jaws quake: " What Sabaoth is this,
That shakes us in our unobtrusive shrouds,
As though our tissues did not yet abhor
The fevered feats of life? "

SPIRIT IRONIC

                   Mere fancy's feints!
How know the coffined what comes after them,
Even though it whirl them to the Pleiades?—
Turn to the real.

SPIRIT OF RUMOUR

              That hatless, smoke-smirched shape
There in the vale, is still the living Ney,
His sabre broken in his hand, his clothes
Slitten with ploughing ball and bayonet,
One epaulette shorn away. He calls out " Follow! "

And a devoted handful follow him
Once more into the carnage.   Hear his voice.

NEY (calling afar)

My friends, see how a Marshal of France can die!

SPIRIT OF THE PITIES

Alas, not here in battle, something hints,
But elsewhere ! . . . Who's the sworded brother-chief
Swept past him in the tumult ?

SPIRIT OF RUMOUR

                                                      D'Erlon he.

Ney cries to him :

NEY

              Be sure of this, my friend,
If we don't perish here at English hands,
Nothing is left us but the halter-noose
The Bourbons will provide !

SPIRIT IRONIC

                              A caustic wit,
And apt, to those who deal in adumbrations !

The brave remnant of the Imperial Guard repulses for a
time the English cavalry under Vivian, in which MAJOR
HOWARD and LIEUTENANT GUNNING of the Tenth Hussars
are shot. But the war-weary French cannot cope with the
pursuing infantry, helped by grape-shot from the batteries.

NAPOLÉON endeavours to rally them. It is his last effort
as a warrior ; and the rally ends feebly.

NAPOLÉON

They are crushed ! So it has ever been since Creçy !

He is thrown violently off his horse, and bids his page
bring another, which he mounts, and is lost to sight.

Spirit of Rumour

He loses his last chance of dying well !

The three or four heroic battalions of the Old and Middle Guard fall back step by step, halting to reform in square when they get badly broken and shrunk. At last they are surrounded by the English Guards and other foot, who keep firing on them and smiting them to smaller and smaller numbers. General Cambronne is inside the square.

Colonel Hugh Halkett (shouting)

Surrender ! And preserve those heroes' lives !

Cambronne (with exasperation)

Mer-r-r-rde ! . . . You've to deal with desperates,
    man, to-day :
Life is a byword here !

Hollow laughter, as from people in hell, comes approvingly from the remains of the Old Guard. The English proceed with their massacre, the devoted band thins and thins, and a ball strikes Cambronne, who falls, and is trampled over.

Spirit of the Years

Observe that all wide sight and self-command
Desert these throngs now driven to demonry
By the Immanent Unrecking. Nought remains
But vindictiveness here amid the strong,
And there amid the weak an impotent rage.

Spirit of the Pities

Why prompts the Will so senseless-shaped a doing ?

Spirit of the Years

I have told thee that It works unwittingly,
As one possessed, not judging.

Semichorus I of Ironic Spirits (aerial music)

Of Its doings if It knew,
What It does It would not do !

Semichorus II

Since It knows not, what far sense
Speeds Its spinnings in the Immense ?

Semichorus I

None ; a fixed foresightless dream
Is Its whole philosopheme.

Semichorus II

Just so ; an unconscious planning,
Like a potter raptly panning !

Chorus

Are then, Love and Light Its aim—
Good Its glory, Bad Its blame ?
Nay ; to alter evermore
Things from what they were before.

Spirit of the Years

Your knowings of the Unknowable declared,
Let the last pictures of the Play be bared.

Enter, fighting, more English and Prussians against the French. Ney is caught by the throng and borne ahead. Rullière hides an eagle beneath his coat and follows Ney. Napoléon is involved none knows where in the crowd of fugitives.

Wellington and Blücher come severally to the view. They meet in the dusk and salute warmly. The Prussian bands strike up " God save the King " as the two shake hands.

From his gestures of assent it can be seen that WELLINGTON accepts BLÜCHER's offer to pursue.

The reds disappear from the sky, and the dusk grows deeper. The action of the battle degenerates to a hunt, and recedes further and further into the distance southward. When the tramplings and shouts of the combatants have dwindled, the lower sounds are noticeable that come from the wounded : hopeless appeals, cries for water, elaborate blasphemies, and impotent execrations of Heaven and earth. In the vast and dusky shambles black slouching shapes begin to move, the plunderers of the dead and dying.

The night grows clear and beautiful, and the moon shines musingly down. But instead of the sweet smell of green herbs and dewy rye as at her last beaming upon these fields, there is now the stench of gunpowder and a muddy stew of crushed crops and gore.

SPIRIT OF THE YEARS

So hath the Urging Immanence used to-day
Its inadvertent might to field this fray ;
And Europe's wormy dynasties rerobe
Themselves in their old gilt, to dazzle anew the globe !

The scene is curtained by a night-mist.[1]

SCENE IX

THE WOOD OF BOSSU

It is midnight. NAPOLÉON enters a glade of the wood, a solitary figure on a jaded horse. The shadows of the boughs travel over his listless form as he moves along. The horse chooses its own path, comes to a standstill, and feeds. The tramp of BERTRAND, SOULT, DROUOT, and LOBAU's horses, gone forward in hope to find a way of retreat, is heard receding over the hill.

---

[1] One of the many Waterloo men known to the writer in his youth, John Bentley of the Fusileer Guards, used to declare that he lay down on the ground in such weariness that when food was brought him he could not eat it, and slept till next morning on an empty stomach. He died at Chelsea Hospital, 187–, aged eighty-six.

NAPOLÉON (to himself, languidly)

Here should have been some troops of Gérard's
     corps,
Left to protect the passage of the convoys,
Yet they, too, fail. . . . I have nothing more to
     lose,
But life !

Flocks of fugitive soldiers pass along the adjoining road
without seeing him. NAPOLÉON's head droops lower and lower
as he sits listless in the saddle, and he falls into a fitful sleep.
The moon shines upon his face, which is drawn and waxen.

SPIRIT OF THE YEARS

" *Sic diis immortalibus placet*,"—
" *Thus is it pleasing to the immortal gods*,"
As earthlings used to say.   Thus, to this last,
The Will in thee has moved thee, Bonaparte,
As we say now.

NAPOLÉON (starting)

                         Whose frigid tones are those,
Breaking upon my lurid loneliness
So brusquely ? . . . Yet, 'tis true, I have ever
     known
That such a Will I passively obeyed !

                                        [He drowses again.

SPIRIT IRONIC

Nothing care I for these high-doctrined dreams,
And shape the case in quite a common way,
So I would ask, Ajaccian Bonaparte,
Has all this been worth while ?

NAPOLÉON

                   O hideous hour,
Why am I stung by spectral questionings ?
Did not my clouded soul incline to match
Those of the corpses yonder, thou should'st rue
Thy saying, Fiend, whoever thou may'st be ! . . .
   Why did the death-drops fail to bite me close
I took at Fontainebleau ? Had I then ceased,
This deep had been unplumbed ; had they but
     worked,
I had thrown threefold the glow of Hannibal
Down History's dusky lanes !—Is it too late ? . . .
Yes. Self-sought death would smoke but damply
     here !
   If but a Kremlin cannon-shot had met me
My greatness would have stood : I should have
     scored
A vast repute, scarce paralleled in time.
As it did not, the fates had served me best
If in the thick and thunder of to-day,
Like Nelson, Harold, Hector, Cyrus, Saul,
I had been shifted from this jail of flesh,
To wander as a greatened ghost elsewhere.
—Yes, a good death, to have died on yonder
     field ;
But never a ball came passing down my way !
   So, as it is, a miss-mark they will dub me ;
And yet—I found the crown of France in the
     mire,
And with the point of my prevailing sword
I picked it up ! But for all this and this
I shall be nothing. . . .
To shoulder Christ from out the topmost niche
In human fame, as once I fondly felt,
Was not for me. I came too late in time
To assume the prophet or the demi-god,
A part past playing now. My only course
To make good showance to posterity
Was to implant my line upon the throne.

And how shape that, if now extinction nears ?
Great men are meteors that consume themselves
To light the earth.   This is my burnt-out hour.

SPIRIT OF THE YEARS

Thou sayest well.   Thy full meridian-shine
Was in the glory of the Dresden days,
When well-nigh every monarch throned in Europe
Bent at thy footstool.

NAPOLÉON

      Saving always England's—
Rightly dost say " well-nigh."—Not England's,—
    she
Whose tough, enisled, self-centred, kindless craft
Has tracked me, springed me, thumbed me by the
    throat,
And made herself the means of mangling me !

SPIRIT IRONIC

Yea, the dull peoples and the Dynasts both,
Those counter-castes not oft adjustable,
Interests antagonistic, proud and poor,
Have for the nonce been bonded by a wish
To overthrow thee.

SPIRIT OF THE PITIES

      Peace.   His loaded heart
Bears weight enough for one bruised, blistered while !

SPIRIT OF THE YEARS

Worthless these kneadings of thy narrow thought,
Napoléon ; gone thy opportunity !
Such men as thou, who wade across the world
To make an epoch, bless, confuse, appal,

Are in the elemental ages' chart
Like meanest insects on obscurest leaves
But incidents and grooves of Earth's unfolding ;
Or as the brazen rod that stirs the fire
Because it must.

The moon sinks, and darkness blots out NAPOLÉON and the scene.

AFTER SCENE

THE OVERWORLD

Enter the Spirit and Chorus of the Years, the Spirit and Chorus of the Pities, the Shade of the Earth, the Spirits Sinister and Ironic with their Choruses, Rumours, Spirit-messengers and Recording Angels.

Europe has now sunk netherward to its far-off position as in the Fore Scene, and it is beheld again as a prone and emaciated figure of which the Alps form the vertebræ, and the branching mountain-chains the ribs, the Spanish Peninsula shaping the head of the écorché. The lowlands look like a grey-green garment half-thrown off, and the sea around like a disturbed bed on which the figure lies.

Spirit of the Years

Thus doth the Great Foresightless mechanize
In blank entrancement now as evermore
Its ceaseless artistries in Circumstance
Of curious stuff and braid, as just forthshown.
Yet but one flimsy riband of Its web
Have we here watched in weaving—web Enorm,
Whose furthest hem and selvage may extend
To where the roars and plashings of the flames
Of earth-invisible suns swell noisily,
And onwards into ghastly gulfs of sky,
Where hideous presences churn through the dark—
Monsters of magnitude without a shape,
Hanging amid deep wells of nothingness.

Yet seems this vast and singular confection
Wherein our scenery glints of scantest size,
Inutile all—so far as reasonings tell.

702

Spirit of the Pities

Thou arguest still the Inadvertent Mind.—
But, even so, shall blankness be for aye ?
Men gained cognition with the flux of time,
And wherefore not the Force informing them,
When far-ranged aions past all fathoming
Shall have swung by, and stand as backward years ?

Spirit of the Years

What wouldst have hoped and had the Will to be ?—
How wouldst have pœaned It, if what hadst dreamed
Thereof were truth, and all my showings dream ?

Spirit of the Pities

The Will that fed my hope was far from thine,
One I would thus have hymned eternally :—

Semichorus I of the Pities (aerial music)

To Thee whose eye all Nature owns,
Who hurlest Dynasts from their thrones,[1]
And liftest those of low estate
We sing, with Her men consecrate !

Semichorus II

Yea, Great and Good, Thee, Thee we hail,
Who shak'st the strong, Who shield'st the frail,
Who hadst not shaped such souls as we
If tendermercy lacked in Thee !

Semichorus I

Though times be when the mortal moan
Seems unascending to Thy throne,

---

[1] καθεῖλε ΔΥΝΑΣΤΑΣ ἀπὸ θρόνων.—Magnificat.

Though seers do not as yet explain
Why Suffering sobs to Thee in vain;

SEMICHORUS II

We hold that Thy unscanted scope
Affords a food for final Hope,
That mild-eyed Prescience ponders nigh
Life's loom, to lull it by-and-by.

SEMICHORUS I

Therefore we quire to highest height
The Wellwiller, the kindly Might
That balances the Vast for weal,
That purges as by wounds to heal.

SEMICHORUS II

The systemed suns the skies enscroll
Obey Thee in their rhythmic roll,
Ride radiantly at Thy command,
Are darkened by Thy Masterhand!

SEMICHORUS I

And these pale panting multitudes
Seen surging here, their moils, their moods,
All shall " fulfil their joy " in Thee,
In Thee abide eternally!

SEMICHORUS II

Exultant adoration give
The Alone, through Whom all living live,
The Alone, in Whom all dying die,
Whose means the End shall justify!   Amen.

SPIRIT OF THE PITIES

So did we evermore sublimely sing ;
So would we now, despite thy forthshowing !

SPIRIT OF THE YEARS

Something of difference animates your quiring,
O half-convinced Compassionates and fond,
From chords consistent with our spectacle !
You almost charm my long philosophy
Out of my strong-built thought, and bear me back
To when I thanksgave thus. . . . Ay, start not,
*   Shades ;*
In the Foregone I knew what dreaming was,
And could let raptures rule ! But not so now.
Yea, I psalmed thus and thus. . . . But not so now !

SEMICHORUS I OF THE YEARS (aerial music)

O Immanence, That reasonest not
In putting forth all things begot,
Thou build'st Thy house in space—for what ?

SEMICHORUS II

O Loveless, Hateless !—past the sense
Of kindly eyed benevolence,
To what tune danceth this Immense ?

SPIRIT IRONIC

For one I cannot answer. But I know
'Tis handsome of our Pities so to sing
The praises of the dreaming, dark, dumb Thing
That turns the handle of this idle Show !

As once a Greek asked[1] I would fain ask too,
Who knows if all the Spectacle be true,

[1] Aesch. *Aga.* Cho. 478.

Or an illusion of the gods (the Will,
To wit) some hocus-pocus to fulfil ?

SEMICHORUS I OF THE YEARS (aerial music)

Last as first the question rings
Of the Will's long travailings ;
Why the All-mover,
Why the All-prover
Ever urges on and measures out the droning tune of
Things.[1]

SEMICHORUS II

Heaving dumbly
As we deem,
Moulding numbly
As in dream,
Apprehending not how fare the sentient subjects of Its
scheme.

SEMICHORUS I OF THE PITIES

Nay ;—shall not Its blindness break ?
Yea, must not Its heart awake,
Promptly tending
To Its mending
In a genial germing purpose, and for loving-kindness'
sake ?

SEMICHORUS II

Should It never
Curb or cure
Aught whatever
Those endure
Whom It quickens, let them darkle to extinction swift
and sure.

[1] Hor. *Epis.* i. 12.

CHORUS

But—a stirring thrills the air
Like to sounds of joyance there
   That the rages
   Of the ages
Shall be cancelled, and deliverance offered from the
   darts that were,
Consciousness the Will informing, till It fashion all
   things fair !

September 25, 1907.

THE HISTORICAL BACKGROUND

THE emphasis of Part First falls primarily on the threat of a French invasion of England; Nelson's defeat of the French navy at Trafalgar, and his own death; Napoleon's victory at Austerlitz; and the passing of Pitt. Hardy symbolically begins with Napoleon's assumption of the iron crown of Lombardy at the Cathedral of Milan, thus becoming King of Italy; but, true to epic tradition, he has begun in the middle of things. A reader must remember that Napoleon had taken over not only northern Italy (the Cisalpine republic), but also Piedmont, as well as control of Switzerland and Holland, and that he exerted enormous influence over both Spanish and German policy. The British, convinced that the Treaty of Amiens (March 1802) had foundered, and alarmed by Napoleon's overt preparations for war, declared war against France in May 1803. The state of readiness of England's armed forces, however, left much to be desired; the Army was undermanned, and two Militia Acts (1802 and 1803) underscored the inadequacy of a system of hastily trained substitutes. The volunteers, armed with pikes, would have proved no better a match for French soldiers than the militia, were Napoleon to cross the Channel successfully.

Hardy assumes, as did most Englishmen of the first decade of the nineteenth century, that Napoleon's building of an invasion fleet and a large number of ships of the line in various ports along the Channel coast, his repeated threats to invade, and his obvious need to secure rear positions before undertaking new military projects in central Europe, meant that Napoleon would have invaded England if Admiral Villeneuve had been able to provide support cover. The evidence is not clear-cut, however, and modern historians now entertain seriously the possibility that Napoleon was bluffing, and using an invasion threat as a diversionary tactic, one that would distract both England and the nations of Europe from perceiving the direction of his next major move.

The facts, as distinct from speculation, that Hardy treated are, briefly, these. Pitt was unable to persuade King George III to give office to Fox, or to allow Pitt to form a coalition government with his political enemies (Fox, the followers of Addington, and Grenville). A long debate about the Patent Parish Bill, which assigned the responsibility for recruitment to the parishes, forms the subject-matter of I, i, iii; Pitt supported it, Sheridan and Fox opposed it; and Pitt's side won the battle against repeal. (Other parliamentary debates and allusions to headline events that Hardy did not have time to work into full-fledged scenes are summarized in II, v, iv.) Pitt's problems as a wartime leader were enormously complicated by the need to expend energies simply on keeping himself in power.

On the other hand, Napoleon's frequent changes of mind about the role of his troop-transports (e.g., whether they should be outfitted to meet light opposition while at sea) and technical mismanagement of the invasion plans served Pitt well, in that they provided needed time to rearm. Pitt was able to exploit the Tsar Alexander's fears of Napoleon's expansionist policy, which directly affected Egypt and Turkey, and in early 1805 signed an alliance with Russia. In August of the same year Austria, alarmed by what had been happening in Germany and Italy, joined the alliance. Unfortunately for Pitt's plans for an invasion of northern Europe that would threaten Napoleon from the east, while Austria moved from the south, Prussia refused to co-operate, and the despatch of 26,000 men to the Weser was obviously inadequate to counter any swift retaliatory blow by the French Emperor.

Yet, in the clear hindsight of history, Pitt's gamble contributed to the destruction of whatever plans Napoleon may have entertained for making good his threat to invade England. By July 1805, Napoleon had mobilized 2000 transports and 90,000 men near Boulogne. All he needed – or so he publicly proclaimed on several occasions – was clear control of the Channel for a relatively short period of time. Everything depended on Admiral Villeneuve's navy, which had the responsibility for smashing any English ships not diverted by a French feint in the direction of the West Indies. But Napoleon did not await the outcome of his orders to Villeneuve. When Austria entered the war against him, he set off immediately on a lightning march against the Third European Coalition, mobilizing near the Danube; before the end of August the invasion army had disappeared from Boulogne.

The decisive naval engagement of Napoleon's career took place two months after the intended invasion (to whatever extent the threat was real) had been cancelled. Horatio Nelson (1758–1805), like Napoleon a man given to speaking of himself as serving some higher purpose or Destiny, pursued Villeneuve across the Atlantic, only to find that the French admiral had fled the West Indies on hearing of his approach. Napoleon ordered Villeneuve to unite his forces in the Channel and sail for the Mediterranean; Naples, the ultimate French target, would have been attacked by sea. Depressed by fears of Nelson and by despair at never satisfying the Emperor, Villeneuve finally emerged from various Channel ports with thirty-four ships of the line, on 20 October 1805, and confronted Nelson's twenty-seven ships off Cape Trafalgar. Nelson's strategy, which split off one-third of the French fleet, and the determination of his brave sailors led to the destruction of eighteen French ships and 5860 dead and wounded Frenchmen (the British lost 690). Nelson's death from a sniper's bullet saddened England, though the manner of his dying became part of a nation's legends. Trafalgar ended the possibility that Napoleon might, at a later time, revive his invasion schemes, and ensured the freedom of English military commanders to bring over to the Continent as many troops as they needed. Villeneuve's suicide at an inn at Rennes is, in Hardy's account (I, v, vi), as anticlimactic as it was in real life.

It is understandable that Napoleon's victory at Austerlitz (2 December 1805) should have seemed, at the time, as more than adequate compensation for the defeat of the French armada. The most complete and brilliant victory of Napoleon's career, Austerlitz followed the surrender at Ulm of the Austrian army of 25,000 men commanded by General Karl von Mack, and cost Napoleon's enemies – the Austrians and the Russians – more than 26,000 men; the French lost approximately 9000. The Treaty of Pressburg that concluded hostilities between France and Bavaria, acting as allies, and Austria, was designed to be both crushing and humiliating. Napoleon refused to listen to Talleyrand's counsel of moderation, and not only broke up the Coalition and neutralized Austria, but destroyed the Holy Roman Empire (Emperor Francis II abdicated as Holy Roman Emperor) and the Kingdom of Naples. Napoleon's negotiation of an alliance with Prussia's chief minister, Count von Haugwitz, ended any immediate threat from Prussia. The Confederation of the Rhine, which Napoleon created, ended Germany's medieval political alignments, and made possible, later in the century, Bismarck's unification of the separate German states.

At the age of forty-six, physically worn-out, a dismayed Pitt heard the news of Austerlitz, and died a bitterly disappointed statesman (23 January 1806). As Tomline says (I, vi, viii), 'The name of his disease is – Austerlitz!' And, as Part First draws to its sombre close, the reader knows that Napoleon will achieve a number of stunning military victories before his star of destiny deserts him.

Part Second has three main lines of interest: the Spanish War, Napoleon's engagements elsewhere in Europe, and his efforts to get rid of Josephine so that he may marry a royal princess who will guarantee the production of an heir. The first, which receives most attention, presupposes some familiarity with the major outlines of Spanish history during the first decade of the century. Charles IV was married to Queen Maria Luisa, and she, dissatisfied by his embraces, patronised a young guardsman, Manuel de Godoy, and made him a chief minister in the government. Ferdinand, the royal couple's oldest child, hated both his parents and Godoy. Since Godoy's favourites had replaced the more liberal ministers who had served Charles III, and since Godoy himself failed to see the dangers of an alliance with France, the treaty of 1796 that intertwined the interests of both nations inevitably worked to Spain's disadvantage. Both the Directory and Napoleon pursued national, and then imperial, goals. It took Godoy a long time to realise that Spain was invariably the loser in this alliance, but the timing of his awakened sense of outraged honour (after Trafalgar, Jena and Auerstadt) proved spectacularly poor. Moreover, his cupidity made him easy prey for the French. Napoleon used a partition-scheme of Portugal as bait to secure the co-operation of Godoy and King Louis of Etruria while he poured French troops into the northern provinces of Spain and Catalonia, and, simultaneously, he promised aid to Charles's son, the prince of Asturias, who wanted to destroy the influence of Godoy at court. Thus, by March 1808, while exploiting Spanish court intrigues, Napoleon was able to divide the forces of his unsuspecting enemy. Godoy advised the court to flee to America, and a Spanish mob, seeking to lynch him, was only temporarily appeased by the abdication of Charles IV. The prince of Asturias became, however briefly, Ferdinand VII, and Godoy went off to prison. Surprisingly, Ferdinand then failed to take up arms against Napoleon, which was the obvious expectation of the

people he supposedly ruled over; instead, he pledged allegiance
to the Emperor of France. Not unexpectedly, Charles IV also
sought the Emperor's protection, and a reversal of the abdication. A series of betrayals and farcical denunciation-scenes
followed. In May 1808, Napoleon managed to secure a document from Charles IV that surrendered, in favour of Napoleon,
all claims to the Spanish throne. Not knowing that his father
had already signed away his rights, Ferdinand was tricked into
signing an abdication-paper. He was promptly shipped off to
prison at the château of Valencay, and not released until 1814.
(Talleyrand, as owner of the château, was a moderately embarrassed jailer.)

May 2, 1808 (a date famous in Spanish history as *Dos de Mayo*)
marked the occasion of a bloody riot by Spaniards who resented
the news that Prince Francesco, thirteen years old and the last of
Charles IV's sons, was to be conducted to Bayonne. Although
the French troops soon gained control of the streets and began a
series of brutal mass executions, a popular uprising had begun
in earnest. It is ironic that Napoleon's brother, Joseph, who
became king of Spain as a direct result of French power politics,
might have given the Spanish people an enlightened administration. Time was not on his side. The Spanish people, who bitterly
resented the presence of a large French army, did not support
his policies. War broke out, both the formal, historically
recognisable kind that involved large armies manœuvring
against each other and fighting by traditional rules, and the
newer, infinitely more savage and unforgiving kind known as
guerilla warfare. Hardy's scenes show how bloody a battle-
ground Spain soon became, particularly after Napoleon assumed
direct command of 200,000 troops, crushed or scattered all
opposition (by early December 1808), and re-entered Madrid.
One of the stirring memories of British valour that can never be
forgotten has, as theme, the courageous stand of General Sir
John Moore at Corunna, after an agonising retreat from Astorga
in which 6000 men had died; but Moore's death was tragic, and
the battle he fought could not be accounted a victory against the
French. At this point, however, Napoleon left Spain, ordering
Marshal Soult to carry on the pursuit of Moore's army, and he
never returned. As a consequence, the plans for the reconquest
of Portugal fell through. The place-names of the Spanish War
become more than words as Hardy reminds us of the price in
blood paid by both sides: Vimiero and Talavera (both French
defeats), Torrès Védras, and particularly Albuera, which led to

the killing or wounding of more than two-thirds of the 6500 British infantry who took part. English valour matched Spanish courage. Constantly growing in stature was an English general, Wellington, who knew when to expend his troops for best effect in battle as well as how to conserve them.

The insatiable energies of Napoleon were not directed exclusively towards the winning of this war, partly because he consistently underrated the importance of the Spanish people (whom he regarded as rabble), partly because fierce opposition elsewhere to his military adventures proved distracting. The remarkable scene between Fox and the would-be assassin Guillet de la Gevrillière (II, i, i) is based on fact, and provides one small measure of the numerous ways in which Napoleon's enemies sought to confound him. The Grand Army's smashing victory at Jena (14 October 1806), won by Marshal Davout with 26,000 men against the Duke of Brunswick, who led 60,000 men, momentarily ended Prussian resistance. After the defeat of the Russian army at Friedland, the Treaty of Tilsit was arranged between Napoleon and Alexander during an extraordinary, and unrecorded, three-hour conversation on a raft moored in the middle of the Niemen River (June 1807). It called for peace between Russia and France, and for jointly conducted economic warfare. The latter policy turned into a very serious threat to England. It led directly to the British navy's attack on Copenhagen and destruction of the Danish fleet (August 1807), a raid more intense than Nelson's in 1801, and one more damaging to England's international relations. The war of 1809 reached one climax at the Battle of Aspern and Essling, and concluded with the bloody engagement of Wagram. Napoleon won this six-week campaign against the Austrians at the cost of more than 100,000 men on both sides. Even so, Napoleon could enjoy no peace, though he rejoiced at the disaster that overtook an English expedition of 40,000 men to the island of Walcheren in Holland (1809); enemy action and malaria took their toll, and the English had to retreat, ignominiously, from the Continent. Spain was not the only battlefront in flames during these eventful years. If, as some historians believe, 1808 was the flood-tide of Napoleon's fortunes, the wasting of French resources and manpower in the haemorrhage of Spain, as well as on the fields of a dozen nations during the years leading up to the Russian invasion of 1812, had far more serious consequences than the French Emperor could realise at the time.

Perhaps, as Part Second implies, Napoleon's attention was

distracted by his negotiations with the House of Habsburg to secure the hand of Marie Louise. Though he had cause to reciprocate Josephine's affection (and did), he knew that he was capable of fathering children and believed that Josephine was barren. Rumours and threats of assassination, and the attempt to kill him made by the son of a clergyman in 1809, accelerated Napoleon's plans to produce an heir. Since his negotiations for the hand of Alexander's sister Anne had fallen through, preventing a French–Russian dynasty from materialising, he moved swiftly, using Metternich, the new foreign minister of Austria, as his intermediary. Napoleon, who had been excommunicated by the Pope (11 June 1809), neither asked for nor received the Vatican's permission to divorce Josephine, and a civil divorce was granted (16 December). Marriage to the beautiful nineteen-year-old Marie Louise followed some three months later; pregnancy of the new French Empress was announced in June. Hardy's portrayal of conversations at the French, Austrian and English courts as being completely cynical is amply justified by the historical record, for Napoleon was regarded by European aristocracy as a dangerous ogre who somehow, in some way, had to be placated. The sacrifice of one more pawn, this time of a princess who neither then nor later had a reputation for high intelligence, was approved by all concerned. It gave Austria a chance to rearm, and the rest of Europe a breathing-space in which the future of Napoleon's career might be contemplated and, if possible, controlled or cut short.

Part Third records the history of the Russian invasion, the conclusion of the war in Spain, Napoleon's abdication as the Allies enter Paris, and the final Hundred Days leading to Waterloo. This is the longest section, and has more acts and scenes than either Part First or Part Second.

Napoleon's reasons for invading Russia have been dismissed by more than one historian as too frivolous to justify the million casualties that proved the inevitable consequence. Hardy, at any rate, does not waste much time on the frame of mind which formulated the decision, although it is true that Napoleon did contemplate the possibility of marching beyond Russia to India (III, i, i) and destroying there the commercial empire of the British in Asia. Leading more than half a million men, of whom some 400,000 came from Poland, Germany, Italy, and nations other than France, he crossed the Niemen on 23 June 1812, determined to win a swift and smashing victory against an army and nation he despised. He met little resistance as he marched towards Smolensk. Nevertheless, Alexander's invocation of Holy Mother Russia, the characterisation of Napoleon as the Antichrist (formulated by Russian priests), and a double-barrelled Russian policy of scorched-earth and retreat, made Napoleon's advance ever more risky as it progressed. Smolensk fell, a smoking, ruined city, but the main army that Napoleon had hoped to destroy slipped quietly away during the night. Worse was to come for the French. Barclay de Tolly, the Russian commander, was replaced by the more able Field-Marshal Kutuzov, who had gained his battle wisdom in the Polish and Turkish wars. Kutuzov's strategy, basically a modification of Barclay's, finally proved decisive. Before the battle of Borodino, religious icons were shown to the troops on the Russian side; a portrait of the King of Rome (Napoleon's son) to the French troops. The battle turned out to be appallingly bloody, indecisive, and costly for all concerned. Napoleon, who lost one-third of his troops by the time he entered Moscow (mid-September), kept hoping, in vain and at the cost of precious time before winter weather set in, that Alexander would sue for peace. The burning of Moscow cannot be blamed on any individual or military order, or on either side; yet the destruction and looting which followed the conflagration prevented Napoleon from using the city for winter headquarters. In mid-October Napoleon began his long retreat. His troops were burdened by the spoils of war, and slowed down by thousands of camp-followers. Rather than attack Kutuzov, he decided to take the road that led north towards Mozhaisk, retracing his steps. This decision forced him to repass Borodino, with its carnage made even worse by the passing of seven weeks. His army had to fight off Russian guerillas, and sporadic military actions by an increasingly emboldened enemy. French troops died by the thousands, without hope, as the heavy snows fell from the leaden skies, beginning in early November, and as the temperature plummeted well below zero.

Scenes of horror accompanied the Emperor as he moved on to Smolensk, Minsk and the bridge of the Beresina. Beyond the Beresina, the Grand Army, down to less than five thousand men, may be said to have disintegrated. Napoleon's return to Paris, a nightmarish trip through northern Europe that lasted two weeks, was for most Frenchmen the first news that the invasion force, so imposing, so glorious barely six months earlier, no longer existed. Napoleon was able to stifle a ludicrous (but withal very serious) uprising by General Claude François de Malet, but he could not prevent the outbreak of the War of Liberation, in which combined Russian and Prussian armies ended the French occupation of Prussia (1813), or the rapidly accelerating momentum of new enemies in the field.

The Spanish War, uninfluenced by Napoleon's personal direction, moved towards its own climax. The retreat of General Masséna, in the spring of 1811, signified the inability of his 63,000 troops to complete the offensive against Portugal that had begun in August of the previous year. These, only a fraction of the 370,000 French troops in Spain, were all the fighting effectives he had; the rest were garrison troops, committed to small holding operations. By the time Napoleon replaced Masséna with Marshal Marmont, the war had definitely turned in favour of Wellington's determined drive. Ciudad Rodrigo, Badajoz, Salamanca, and then Madrid (from which King Joseph and his court had fled) were all French defeats. Wellington finally destroyed the army led by Marshal Jourdan at Vitoria (21 June 1813); captured his artillery, ammunition, art treasures, currency and supplies; and moved to the Pyrenées, near the River Nivelle, as his last stop before crossing the border into France.

When Bernardotte, the brother-in-law of Joseph, the nominal King of Spain, became the prince royal of Sweden, and later King Charles XIV, he entered into an alliance with England, and sent several thousand troops into Pomerania as part of the bargain (March 1813). Napoleon was unable to win all the concessions he needed from Pope Pius VII, even though he arrested and bullied the Pope without mercy. He could not effect a reconciliation with the Church that might ease his relations with devout French Catholics. Though he conjured almost from thin air a new army of 200,000 conscripts and volunteers, they were inexperienced; his magic touch was no longer self-assured; and his rejection of the Treaty of Reichenbach, proffered by the Allies (June 1813), proved a serious mistake. Austria, taking advantage of the opportunity to rearm, declared war in mid-August; Emperor Francis felt no family loyalty to his son-in-law. Napoleon, confronted by 500,000 Allied troops in central Europe, plagued by deteriorating health and an unwonted indecisiveness, moved towards the climactic Battle of Leipzig (October 1813). Here his army suffered 40,000 casualties, and as he retreated towards France he lost at least an equal number. The Coalition, working through protracted and often angry negotiating sessions, finally created the modern concept of Great Powers at about the same time that its troops destroyed the remnants of Napoleon's army (the end of March 1814). The surrender of Paris was followed shortly afterwards by Napoleon's abdication. Disheartened by the defection of his generals and by the disinheriting of the King of Rome as his successor, Napoleon took poison, but the suicide attempt was unsuccessful, and once he had recovered he claimed that Destiny had again intervened to save him. His exile to Elba made possible restoration of the French frontiers of 1792 and the return of the legitimate Bourbon line, particularly of Louis XVIII.

Hardy makes much of the poignance of Josephine's fall from Napoleon's favour, and of the heartlessness of Marie Louise after Napoleon's abdication. The personal relationships that had soured or withered into indifference concern him more than the manœuvrings of Metternich and Talleyrand at the Congress of Vienna (September 1814 to June 1815), which might have stressed the sense of some of the Spirits' mocking comments about dynastic pretensions. But it is obvious, particularly after III, IV, that he wished to hasten to the concluding moments of bravura in Napoleon's career, and these are treated in the sixth and seventh Acts. Napoleon escaped from Elba, landed in southern France on 1 March 1815, and began his march on Paris. At Grenoble he faced garrison troops, and won them over to his side. Marshal Ney, sent to capture him, swore fealty to him. The Bourbons fled in abject terror, and the parliament of Louis XVIII was dissolved. Those among the common people who had been disenchanted by Bourbon rule (and there were many) looked hopefully to Napoleon's resumption of power. Europe, once again faced by the prospect of continual uproar, united in determination to end Napoleon's threat once and for all. The four Allied powers declared war against him as a person, and the Congress of Vienna hastily concluded its deliberations. Napoleon moved on to the field of war without allies, but with approximately 125,000 troops (12 June 1815). Wellington, given command of the Allied forces in the Netherlands, and Blücher, in charge of the Prussians, outnumbered him with 220,000 men. Napoleon's swift march, intended to drive a wedge between the armies of Wellington and Blücher, led to Charleroi, which the French occupied on 15 June. The news was brought to Wellington at the Duchess of Richmond's glittering ball. The next day the French won additional victories at Ligny and Quatre Bras. Napoleon, slow to follow up his advantage, ordered Marshal

Grouchy to harry Blücher's troops and prevent them from joining with those of Wellington. On the evening of 17 June, he arrived at the outskirts of Mont St Jean, near the village of Waterloo, and prepared for the crucial battle of the eighteenth.

Military historians generally believe that the fighting was more of a near thing than popular imagination appreciates. Wellington himself was impressed by the pounding given his troops. But eventually Blücher's army, delayed by bad weather and muddy roads, came to his rescue, as Wellington had expected it to do. Grouchy, unable to interfere seriously with Blücher's march, and the victim of faulty intelligence and orders delayed in transit, could not attack Bülow as crushingly as Napoleon had planned. Napoleon's order to commit the Guard was a sign of desperation; he had always protected them before from suicidal missions; and when they fell back, repulsed and shattered, the French troops broke ranks. It was the end of Napoleon's high-risk gamble. Wellington and his infantry had won the day, and Blücher's troops pursued the demoralized remnants of Napoleon's army. Napoleon himself, seen last in the wood of Bossu soliloquising about the meaning of his life (III, vii, ix), was soon to flee to Rochefort, hoping to find a frigate that might take him to America. The port there being under blockade, he decided to appeal to English mercy, and surrendered himself to Captain Maitland of the H.M.S. *Bellerophon*. After being transferred at Plymouth to the *Northumberland*, he was landed, ten weeks later, on St Helena. There, on 5 May 1821, he died.

NOTES ON THE MAJOR
HISTORICAL PERSONAGES

THE following brief annotations of the more interesting (and usually more important) historical personages are designed to provide the reader of *The Dynasts* with additional information over and beyond that supplied in the various acts and scenes. It is immediately obvious that Hardy did not bother to *invent* many characters; but he assumed perhaps more information on the part of his reader than was warranted almost a full century after the events he described had taken place. The names are arranged in the same sequence as Hardy records them for each of the three parts of the epic-drama. Some names are brought in to swell a progress; that is, they never speak and their silent function is indicated by italics in the list of 'Characters'. A few of these are described biographically, but for the most part I have chosen to supply data only for those who contribute significantly to the action. Napoleon, present in all three parts, requires no annotation of this kind. The entries, in all cases, concentrate on the years 1805–15.

PART FIRST

GEORGE III (George William Frederick) (1738–1820). During this critical decade the King was only intermittently sane, and suffered from the enormous problems created by his wayward son, the Prince of Wales. He refused Pitt the chance to work with a coalition government because of intense dislike of Fox. From 1810 on his insanity became permanent, and the Prince Regent assumed power under stringent conditions formulated by a government made wary by his notorious habits.

PITT, WILLIAM (1759–1806). From May 1804 until his death Pitt served as First Lord of the Treasury and Chancellor of the

Exchequer. He visited the King at Weymouth to ask him to accept the appointment of Fox and Grenville as cabinet members; his mission was unsuccessful. After news of the capitulation of Ulm, Malmesbury saw that Pitt was greatly affected, and had a foreboding that he might die (I, IV, i). After Trafalgar, Pitt attended the Lord Mayor's banquet in good spirits; but the news of Austerlitz may have destroyed his health, and he died at Putney, saying, as Hardy records, 'Oh, my country! how I leave my country!'

FOX, CHARLES JAMES (1749–1806). Fox spent most of his life as a member of the Opposition. He worked for peace with France until shortly before his death. After Pitt's death, he was appointed Foreign Secretary; in this office he met the would-be assassin of Napoleon (II, I, i). The incident became a pretext for reopening peace negotiations with France, but he finally concluded that the French were 'playing a false game', and that there was no hope of peace.

SHERIDAN, RICHARD BRINSLEY (1751–1816). Sheridan served as an M.P. between 1780 and 1812. Although initially opposed to any interference in France, he opposed Napoleon's making war on other countries. Later, he urged that Wellesley be sent to represent England in Spain's fight against Napoleon. In March 1805 he introduced a motion to repeal the Additional Force Bill because he believed that it had not accomplished its purpose, and was becoming merely a taxation measure. This is the debate reproduced in I, I, iii.

WINDHAM, WILLIAM (1750–1810). Windham, an M.P. between 1784 and 1810, supported the royalist cause and the war with France from its earliest days. He was pleased when open hostilities resumed after the peace of 1802. He served as Secretary of War and the Colonies under Grenville. He supported Sheridan's motion not only because he believed that Pitt's bill had failed to achieve its object, but also because he thought that the parish officers, who had been turned into recruiters by the bill, were unfit for such duties.

WHITBREAD, SAMUEL (1758–1815). A strong supporter of Fox, he worked for peace even during the years of the Napoleonic Wars. (After Napoleon's return from Elba, he argued that Britain should not return to war.) He saw no evidence, at the time of the debate over the repeal of the Additional Force Bill (1805), that the recruits entering local regiments were either sympathetic towards or enthusiastic about those regiments, as Pitt had predicted at the time the measure had been originally introduced. Thus, according to Whitbread, it had to be accounted a failure.

TIERNEY, GEORGE (1761–1830). Tierney's reputation derived in part from a stubborn refusal to heed the request, made by Fox, that members of the Opposition stop attending Parliament. In the same year (1798) he had a duel with Pitt; no one was hurt. He served as Treasurer of the Navy under Addington (1802–4). He objected to the Additional Force Bill on constitutional grounds.

FULLER, JOHN (1756?–1834). In 1805, serving as an M.P. for Sussex, Fuller disapproved of Windham's speech because he 'seemed to be an enemy to the volunteer system' (Hansard), and called for more substantial measures.

HARRIS, JAMES, first Earl of Malmesbury (1746–1820). He was a diplomatist who served in Spain, Russia, the Hague and Prussia. His knowledge of foreign languages and lands made him an invaluable resource even after his retirement from public life (because of his increasing deafness). Pitt frequently came to him for advice on foreign policy and occasional help with a translation (see I, iv, vi).

PHIPPS, SIR HENRY, first Earl of Mulgrave, first Viscount Normandy, and third Baron Mulgrave (1755–1831). He began his career in the Army, supported Pitt's foreign policy, and acted as one of his military advisers. At the time of I, iv, vi, he was serving as the Secretary for Foreign Affairs under Pitt; later (1807–10) he was First Lord of the Admiralty.

STEWART, ROBERT, second Marquess of Londonderry, better known as Viscount Castlereagh (1769–1822). Because he shifted political allegiances more than once, he stirred up intense controversy; in the main, however, his policies were Tory. He broke the conspiracy of the United Irishmen (1798), and helped to implement the Union of Great Britain and Ireland without Catholic Emancipation, using suave diplomacy, bribes, and patriotic exhortation as separate occasions demanded. He supported Pitt during Addington's administration, particularly in foreign affairs, and was a friend and admirer of Lord Wellesley. He served as Secretary of War in 1805, 1806, and again in 1807. He prevented Napoleon from gaining control of the Baltic;

helped to save Portugal's navy from Napoleon; reorganised and strengthened the English army and militia; but failed ignobly in the Walcheren expedition, and fell from power. He became involved in intrigues against Canning, the Foreign Secretary, who also entered into conspiracies against him; they duelled in 1809. He became Foreign Secretary in 1812, then leader of the House of Commons after Perceval's assassination. He was instrumental in securing Russia and Sweden as allies against the French, although many felt that the price paid by Britain was too high. He negotiated the Peace of 1814 (the Treaty of Chaumont), and prevented the break-up of the Alliance. He represented Great Britain at the Congress of Vienna (1814–15), and eloquently defended the principle of a balance of power among the European nations. After Napoleon escaped from Elba, Stewart made passionate speeches in the House of Commons, mobilising English opposition.

ADDINGTON, HENRY, first Viscount Sidmouth (1757–1844). A friend of Pitt, he helped him to negotiate the Peace of Amiens (1802). Believing in the sincerity of Napoleon, he put the country prematurely on a peace footing. Later, when Napoleon's intentions became plainer, he attempted to arm volunteers. His policies were, in general, ineffective and scorned, and in 1804 he resigned as First Lord of the Treasury and Chancellor of the Exchequer.

ROSE, GEORGE (1744–1818). During Pitt's second administration, he served as Vice-President of the Board of Trade, and joint Paymaster-General with Lord Somerset. He visited Pitt eight days before the minister's death, and then gave an account of Pitt's final hours.

CANNING, GEORGE (1770–1827). A follower of Pitt, something of a satirist, and Treasurer of the Navy from May 1804 until Pitt's death, he favoured vigorous prosecution of the war against Napoleon.

GREY, CHARLES, second Earl Grey, Viscount Howick, and Baron Grey (1764–1845). A follower of Fox, he was unable to enter Pitt's cabinet. He opposed the government's policy on Spain (1805), and became First Lord of the Admiralty in 1806, compiling a successful record of administration.

ABBOT, CHARLES, first Baron Colchester (1757–1829). Speaker of House of Commons (from February 1802). He cast the deciding vote on Whitbread's famous motion that impugned the conduct of Lord Melville as Treasurer of the Navy.

TOMLINE, SIR GEORGE PRETYMAN (1750–1827). He was Pitt's tutor at Cambridge; the two men became close friends. At Pitt's request, he was made Bishop of Lincoln (1787). He was with Pitt at his death (I, vi, viii), and it was to the Bishop that Pitt dictated his final instructions. Pitt signed the document which left Tomline the literary executor of his estate.

FARQUHAR, SIR WALTER (1738–1819). An excellent doctor (he served as physician in ordinary to the Prince of Wales) and a highly respected person, he attended Pitt, his friend, during his last ten days in Bath; then accompanied him home and did everything he could for him until his death (I, vi, viii).

NELSON, HORATIO, Viscount Nelson (1758–1805). At the time of his death Nelson was the vice-admiral in command of the British fleet that was fighting the French off Cape Trafalgar. The shot that passed through his lungs and spine mortally wounded him, and he lived but three hours more. Lady Hamilton (referred to in I, v, iv) was the mother of his daughter Horatia. Nelson's body, preserved in spirits, was brought home to England on the *Victory*; lay in state at Greenwich; and was finally buried in St Paul's Cathedral.

COLLINGWOOD, CUTHBERT, Lord Collingwood (1750–1810). The vice-admiral under Nelson's command at Trafalgar, Collingwood took over command of the fleet after Nelson's death. His decision not to carry out Nelson's last order to the fleet (to anchor) was considered controversial later, because many of the prize ships either foundered or escaped in the storm that followed the battle.

HARDY, SIR THOMAS MASTERMAN (1769–1839). Hardy (a distant relation of T.H.) was captain of the *Victory*, and for many practical purposes acted as captain of the fleet during the battle of Trafalgar. He was walking with Nelson on the quarter-deck when the admiral was shot, and stayed with him as much as his duties would allow until Nelson died.

SCOTT, JOHN (d.1805). At Nelson's request, the Admiralty complied with Scott's request to allow him to serve as Nelson's public secretary. Scott was killed by a round shot shortly before Nelson was wounded (I, v, ii).

BEATTY, SIR WILLIAM (d.1842). The surgeon on the *Victory* during the battle of Trafalgar, he attended Nelson during his last hours (I, v, iv), and later published *An Authentic Narrative of the Death of Lord Nelson.* . . .

MAGRATH, SIR GEORGE. He served as Nelson's surgeon on the *Victory* (1803–4), and then was made surgeon to the Naval Hospital at Gibraltar (December 1804).

SCOTT, ALEXANDER JOHN (1768–1840). At Nelson's request, he officially served as the chaplain of the *Victory*, while unofficially he served as Nelson's private secretary and interpreter. He received Nelson's last wishes shortly before the admiral's death (I, v, iv).

BURKE, the Purser (d.1815). During Nelson's dying hours, he fanned Nelson with paper and then held Nelson's bed up with his shoulders, so that the admiral would be in a comfortable position.

POLLARD, a midshipman. According to Beatty's narrative, he killed one of the two men 'left alive in the mizzen-top of the *Redoubtable* at the time of his Lordship's being wounded'.

ADAIR, CAPTAIN WILLIAM C. (d.1805). A captain of the Royal Marines, he was Inspecting Officer of Recruits attached to the *Victory* (1804–5). During the battle of Trafalgar, he was hit by a musketball while encouraging his men.

RAM, LIEUTENANT WILLIAM ANDREW (d.1805). Transferred to the *Victory* (April 1805), he died on 21 October during the battle of Trafalgar.

WHIPPLE, THOMAS (d.1805). The captain's clerk on board the *Victory*, he was killed 'by the wind of a round shot', that is, there were no marks or wounds on his body.

SECKER, SERGEANT-MAJOR. Along with two other seamen, he took Nelson to the cockpit after the admiral had been wounded.

DARU, PIERRE ANTOINE NOËL BRUNO (1767–1829). French statesman and writer, he served as councillor of state and an intendant-general of the army that was in Austria (1795–1805), then later held the same position with the army that was in Prussia (1806–7).

LAURISTON, JACQUES ALEXANDRE BERNARD LAW (1768–1828). Napoleon sent him (1805) to Villeneuve, hoping that the general might prod the timid admiral into action. He wrote to Napoleon from Ferrol, telling him that the fleet was going to Brest (I, ii, ii). Lauriston also fought at Austerlitz, in Russia, and at Leipzig, where he was taken prisoner.

MONGE, GASPARD, COMTE DE PÉLUSE (1746–1818). French mathematician, physicist and public official, he is credited with having founded modern descriptive geometry.

BERTHIER, LOUIS ALEXANDRE (1753–1815). Napoleon made him Prince of Neuchâtel and Wagram; chief of staff; and in other ways signified his approval of Berthier's military gifts. But Berthier acclaimed the return of the Bourbons in 1814, and was torn by divided allegiances at the time of Napoleon's return from Elba. The circumstances of his death are unclear.

MURAT, JOACHIM (1767–1815). He married Napoleon's sister in 1800; commanded Napoleon's cavalry at Austerlitz, and took over the remnant of the French Army after Napoleon deserted it on the retreat from Russia. He was present at Leipzig. When Napoleon escaped from Elba, Murat joined him, and was captured and executed in October 1815. (Murat was disappointed when Joseph Bonaparte was made King of Spain, especially since he himself had played so large a role in conquering the country; but Napoleon gave him the crown of Naples instead. Napoleon later thought he had made a mistake in making him a king rather than a viceroy. See III, iii, i.)

SOULT, NICOLAS JEAN DE DIEU (1769–1851). Napoleon made him a marshal of France (1804). He fought at Ulm, Austerlitz, and in the Prussian and Russian campaigns (1806–7). Although he was repulsed at Corunna, he pursued the British troops and forced them to leave Spain. He served as commander-in-chief in Spain (1809–10). When Napoleon returned from Elba, Soult joined him and was made chief of staff. After Waterloo, he was banished, but recalled in 1819.

NEY, MICHEL (1769–1815). He was created a marshal of France in 1804. He fought at Ulm and Jena. During the Russian campaign he commanded the third corps, and fought so well at Smolensk and Borodino that he received the title of Prince of Moskwa. In the retreat from Russia he commanded the rear-guard. After fighting at Leipzig, he turned to Louis XVIII, who made him a peer. When Napoleon returned from Elba, Ney was sent against him, but he again changed sides, and commanded the Old Guard at Waterloo. The Chamber of Peers, after Napoleon's defeat, condemned him for treason, and he was shot.

LANNES, JEAN, Duke of Montebello (1769–1809). He was created a marshal of France (1804). He fought at Ulm (1805), and at one point during the battle led the Emperor's horse from dangerous Austrian gunfire. He was present at Austerlitz and Jena. Mortally wounded at Essling (1809), he was taken to Vienna to die.

MARMONT, AUGUSTE FRÉDÉRIC LOUIS (1774–1825). He was created Duke of Ragusa (1808) and a marshal of France (1809). He fought at Ulm (1805). In 1812 he commanded the French troops when they were defeated at Salamanca by Wellington's army. Marmont himself was wounded during the battle. He fought at Leipzig (1813), and helped negotiate a truce with the Russians (1814). The result of the truce was Napoleon's abdication; the Bonapartists for ever after considered him a traitor.

DUPONT DE L'ÉTANG, PIERRE (1765–1840). He was in charge of a division of 6000 men during the attack on Ulm, and successfully fought against Archduke Ferdinand's 25,000 men. He prevented their escaping into Bohemia.

OUDINOT, NICOLAS CHARLES (1767–1847). Marshal of France, and created Duke of Reggio by Napoleon, he commanded the national guard during the Hundred Days leading to Waterloo.

DAVOUT, LOUIS NICOLAS (1770–1823). Created a marshal of France (1804), he fought at Austerlitz (I, VI, iii), and accompanied Napoleon during the Russian campaign. After Napoleon's return from Elba, he was made war minister. He also enjoyed the titles Duke of Auerstädt (1808) and Prince of Eckmuhl (1811).

VANDAMME, DOMINIQUE RENÉ, Count of Unseburg (1770–1830). He fought at Austerlitz (1805); was defeated and taken prisoner at the battle of Kulm (1813); made a peer during the Hundred Days, and put in command of the 3rd army corps. He distinguished himself at Wavre in the battle of Waterloo.

VILLENEUVE, PIERRE CHARLES JEAN BAPTISTE SYLVESTRE DE (1763–1806). He commanded the Toulon squadron (1805) when his ships, accompanied by the Spanish fleet, lured the British fleet to the West Indies. His decision to stop at Cadiz instead of going on to Brest (as ordered) led to the failure of Napoleon's plan to invade England. Realising that he was about to be replaced, he finally decided to fight; after the battle of Trafalgar, he was taken prisoner. While returning to Paris, after learning how the Emperor planned to receive him, he stabbed himself to death (April 1806).

DECRÈS, DENIS (1761–1820). He served as a vice-admiral and the Minister of Marine and Colonies; carried on an extensive private correspondence with Napoleon (he wrote all his letters personally); and received the brunt of Napoleon's rage when he told the Emperor that Villeneuve's letter indicated that the admiral had failed to leave Cadiz (I, III, i).

CAPRARA, GIOVANNI BATTISTA (1733–1810). Italian cardinal and diplomatist. Negotiated the concordat at Paris (1801). Napoleon procured for him the archbishopric of Milan (1802). Caprara approved a relatively autonomous status for the French Church, and accepted other compromises that the Vatican disliked. He helped out in the negotiations leading to the coronation of Napoleon by Pope Pius VII (1804), and crowned Napoleon King of Italy (1805).

FRANCIS II (of the Holy Roman Empire); also FRANCIS I (of Austria); German, Franz (1768–1835). He joined the first coalition against France (1793), the second (1799) and the third (1805), but met military defeat every time. He formally abdicated the crown of the Holy Roman Empire in 1806. He declared war against France in 1809, but the battle of Wagram led to the Peace of Vienna. His daughter, Marie Louise, married Napoleon (1810). He fought with the French against Russia (1812), and joined the anti-Napoleon coalition in 1813. The Congress of Vienna (1814–15) finally gave him more territory than he had lost in all his wars with France.

FERDINAND, THE ARCHDUKE (1781–1850). Grand Duke of Würzburg and an Austrian field-marshal. At Ulm, though under General Mack's command, he disagreed with his superior's strategy, and escaped from Ulm – losing more than half his men in flight – before the city was surrendered by the Austrians.

JOHN OF LICHTENSTEIN, PRINCE (1760–1836). An Austrian field-marshal, he fought in the Napoleonic Wars (1799–1814). After Austerlitz, Napoleon appointed him one of the negotiators in the peace settlement.

SCHWARZENBERG, PRINCE KARL PHILIPP OF (1771–1820). An Austrian field-marshal, he disagreed with Mack's plan at Ulm (I, IV, iii). He helped to negotiate the marriage of Napoleon to Marie Louise (II, v, i), and later served as ambassador to France. Napoleon asked him to lead the Austrian forces in the invasion of Russia (1812). He led the Austrian forces against Napoleon (1813), and won battles at Dresden and Leipzig.

MACK, KARL (1752–1828). Appointed by Emperor Francis I of Austria to accompany the Archduke Ferdinand into Bavaria, and to serve as his chief of staff, Mack was fooled by rumours of a British invasion, and finally was unable to retreat in time. He presented his sword to Napoleon (October 1805), saying, 'Here is the unfortunate Mack!'

JELLACHICH, GENERAL. One of the Austrian generals at Ulm, he feared that he was cut off from the city, and left with his troops for the Tyrol. He was able to escape with most of his men (5000 out of 6000).

RIESC, GENERAL. One of the Austrian generals under Mack's command at Ulm, he was ordered to take Elchingen and gain information about the French lines of communication. Although he did so, he lost Elchingen back to the French.

WEIROTHER, GENERAL. A Russian general, he planned the attack on the French at Austerlitz which led to a crushing defeat for the Russians.

ALEXANDER I OF RUSSIA (1777–1825). He joined the coalition against Napoleon (1805), but was defeated at Austerlitz and again at Eylau and Friedland (1807). He was then forced to sign the Treaty of Tilsit. The alliance between Russia and France ended when Napoleon entered Russian territory in 1812. Alexander participated in the battles of Dresden and Leipzig (1813); after the downfall of Napoleon, he travelled to England. He played an important role in the Congress of Vienna, and urged the Allies to fight as soon as he learned of Napoleon's escape from Elba.

KUTUZOV, MIKHAIL ILARIONOVICH, PRINCE OF SMOLENSK (1745–1813). Thiers describes him as 'an elderly man, [who] had lost the sight of one eye in consequence of a wound on the head, very corpulent, indolent, dissolute, greedy, but intelligent'. He commanded the Russian Army during Napoleon's wars with that nation; lost at Austerlitz (1805), and again at Borodino

(1812); but two months later was able to defeat Davout and Ney at Smolensk. He relied on bad weather to help subdue the French (see III, I, xi).

LANGERON, ANDRAULT DE (1763–1831). A French general in the Russian Army, he fought at Austerlitz, then at Leipzig, and entered Paris with the Allies.

BUXHÖWDEN, COUNT FRIEDRICH WILHELM VON (1750–1811). A Russian general, he distinguished himself in both the Polish and Swedish campaigns, and commanded the Russian left wing at Austerlitz.

MILORADOVICH, COUNT MIKHAIL (1770–1825). This Russian general fought at Austerlitz, Borodino, and against Napoleon's army during the retreat from Moscow. He served as military governor of St Petersburg (1818–25), and was killed in the Decembrist revolt there.

CHARLOTTE SOPHIA (1744–1818). Queen of George III, married in London, and crowned September 1761.

STANHOPE, LADY HESTER LUCY (1776–1839). From August 1803 until his death (1806), she lived with her uncle, William Pitt. She was his most trusted female friend, corresponded with his wide circle of acquaintances, and arranged the treasury banquets for him. Before he died, Pitt gave her his blessing, and at his request a pension was granted her.

LAMB, LADY CAROLINE (1785–1828). She married William Lamb (afterwards second Viscount Melbourne) in 1805. She became infatuated with Lord Byron, though the decline of the affair led her to caricature him in her first novel, *Glenarvon*; later she became mentally ill.

DAMER, ANNE SEYMOUR (1749–1828). A sculptress, she gave Napoleon a bust of Fox during the Hundred Days. Nelson sat for his bust after the battle of the Nile; she did a second bust of him for the Duke of Clarence. 'Her work must be appraised as that of an amateur fine lady. It was whispered that she received assistance from "ghosts" ' (*DNB*). She was a Whig in politics.

JOSÉPHINE, THE EMPRESS, *née* Marie Joséphine Rose Tascher de la Pagerie (1763–1814). She married Vicomte de Beauharnais in 1779, and they had two children, Eugène and Hortense. Two years after her husband's death (1794), she married Napoleon Bonaparte, and was crowned Empress of the French (1804). She gathered a brilliant society around her in Paris, and helped to solidify the bases of her husband's power. Since the marriage was childless, Napoleon dissolved it (December 1809), but allowed her to retain the title of Empress. If she had been permitted to accompany Napoleon in his exile, she would have done so (III, IV, vii).

PART SECOND

THE PRINCE OF WALES, afterwards Prince Regent (1762–1832). A partisan of Fox, whom his father detested, he shared in the triumph of the Rockingham ministry and the disgrace of its main supporters after its fall. He carried on a scandalous affair with the Roman Catholic widow of Mr Fitzherbert, one which led to a faked suicide attempt and finally (in 1785) a secret marriage. He was briefly reconciled to his father before the short-lived insanity period of 1788, but his regency would have been limited, under conditions set by Pitt, if the King had not recovered the next year. His life was marked by gambling, and he ran up huge debts. He gave up his wife in order to marry Princess Caroline, of Brunswick, from whom he soon separated; he returned to Mrs Fitzherbert (1796), but then refused her at his table any precedence above that to which her own position entitled her, and broke publicly with her in 1811; he then turned to Lady Hertford. His history of debt obligations and settlements, the attempts by others to reconcile him with his father, and the recurring fits of insanity of George III that led realists to expect a final collapse, understandably upset the public, who increasingly admired the father and detested the excesses of the son. The Regency Bill of 1811 began his reign. In January 1812 the Catholic question was debated. His daughter, the Princess Charlotte, took her mother's side, but he refused to allow her to see her mother. The years before Waterloo were marred by court resentments and public riots in England, largely as a consequence of his character failings.

PERCEVAL, SPENCER (1762–1812). Under Addington, he almost single-handedly defended the ministry in the House of Commons from the assaults of Pitt, Fox, Windham and their followers. He became Attorney-General under Pitt, and resigned as soon as Pitt died. In 1807 he became Chancellor of the Exchequer, and succeeded the Duke of Portland as Prime Minister (1809). He was assassinated by the demented bankrupt John Bellingham in the Palace of Westminster, while he was walking to the House of Commons.

RUSSELL, JOHN, sixth Duke of Bedford (1766–1839). After resigning as Lord-Lieutenant of Ireland (1807), he did not participate much in politics. The sheep-shearing at Woburn, discussed in II, VI, vii, was a famous event of the day. (A picture was painted of the ceremony in 1811.) Bedford spent most of his time at Woburn, and was mainly interested in agriculture and land-improvement.

HASTINGS, FRANCIS RAWDON, first Marquess of Hastings and second Earl of Moira (1754–1826). He served as a member of the Privy Council in the Ministry of All the Talents, and firmly supported the Prince Regent, even during the investigations of the Princess of Wales. Indeed, he had to defend himself against charges that he had secretly tried to procure evidence against Caroline.

WELLESLEY, SIR ARTHUR, afterwards Duke of Wellington (1769–1852). He went to Corunna as a lieutenant-general (1808), but returned after the Convention of Cintra to England, where he found that his advice was not listened to by his superiors. In 1809, having been given chief command, he returned to Portugal and soon thereafter invaded Spain. He defeated the French at Talavera, Salamanca and Vitoria, and then drove the French troops across the Pyrenees. He served as ambassador to France (1814), and represented Great Britain at the Congress of Vienna. After Napoleon's escape from Elba, he was given command of the Army in the Netherlands, and defeated Napoleon at Waterloo.

MOORE, SIR JOHN (1761–1809). After serving in Sweden, Moore went to Spain in 1808 (see II, II, v). He became commander-in-chief of the English Army while he was in Portugal. In late December, he retreated into Portugal, and arrived at Corunna on 13 January 1809. During the battle of Corunna (16 January), grapeshot struck him from his horse, and he died that evening, expressing the hope that his country would think that he had done his duty, and would do him justice.

HOPE, SIR JOHN, fourth Earl of Hopetoun (1765–1823). He became a lieutenant-general in 1808, and was with Sir John Moore in Portugal and Spain. During the battle of Corunna, he commanded the British left. After Moore's death and the wounding of Baird, he took command of the army.

BAIRD, SIR DAVID (1757–1829). After a distinguished military career in India, the Cape of Good Hope, the Nile and Egypt, he was sent to reinforce General Moore's army in Spain (1808). He became involved in the retreat to Corunna (the last of his battles). He could not serve under Wellington in Spain; Wellington had been his rival in India during the 1790s, and was still his junior; and Baird returned to England.

BERESFORD, WILLIAM CARR (1768–1854). He fought at Albuera (May 1811), and claimed the victory; but historians agree that the orders of Colonel Hardinge won the battle for the English. He accompanied Wellington (who thought well of him) to the Pyrenees, as they broke French resistance in Spain. Since he was in command of the troops in Portugal in 1815, he was not present at Waterloo.

ANDERSON, COLONEL JOSEPH (1789–1877). He fought in the Peninsular campaigns (1809–12), and was wounded at Talavera.

GRAHAM, THOMAS, Baron Lynedoch (1748–1843). He served as Moore's aide-de-camp in Sweden and Spain, and accompanied the general during the retreat to, and the battle at, Corunna. He was with Moore when he died; later that night, Moore's body was carried to Graham's quarters, where it remained until the next morning, when it was buried.

COLBORNE, SIR JOHN (1778–1863). In 1808 he became a major, and served as Sir John Moore's military secretary in Sweden and Portugal. He was with Moore during the retreat to Corunna, and it was the general's dying wish that Colborne should be granted a lieutenant-colonelcy. He fought with Wellington in Spain thereafter. After Napoleon's escape from Elba, he went to Belgium; during the battle of Waterloo, he led a charge into the Old Guard troops which greatly contributed to the British victory.

HARDINGE, SIR HENRY, first Viscount Hardinge of Lahore (1785–1856). He participated in the retreat to Corunna, and the battle there. He was with Sir John Moore when he was wounded, and assisted him to his quarters (II, iii, iii). At the battle of Albuera, he is credited with the British victory (II, vi, iv).

PAGET, SIR EDWARD (1775–1849). Commanded the reserve at Corunna (1809), and later became a lieutenant-general on the staff of the peninsular army under Wellington, to whom he became second-in-command in 1811.

FRASER, ALEXANDER MACKENZIE (1756–1809). He commanded an infantry brigade when he marched with General Moore into Spain. He served with distinction during the retreat through Galicia and in the battle of Corunna. Promoted to lieutenant-general, he led an infantry division to Walcheren. This ill-fated expedition ruined his health.

HILL, ROWLAND, first Viscount Hill (1772–1842). He fought in Portugal under Wellesley (1808), then under the Hon. John Hope during Moore's campaign in Spain. He was with the last brigade to embark at Corunna. At Talavera, he succeeded the wounded Paget. His strategy proved successful in the final stages of the Spanish campaign (1811–13); he fought with skill during the confused battles of Quatre Bras, Ligny and Waterloo.

NAPIER, SIR GEORGE THOMAS (1784–1855). He served with Sir John Moore in several campaigns, and was one of his aides-de-camp at Corunna.

AN ARMY CHAPLAIN. Identified by the *DNB* as the Reverend J. H. Symons, of the Brigade of Guards.

WILLIS, FRANCIS (1718–1807). He attended King George III during his first attack of madness (1788), and was a well-known figure in the English court.

HALFORD, SIR HENRY (1766–1844). In 1793 he was made physician extraordinary to King George III, who liked him so much that he created him a baronet (1809).

HEBERDEN, WILLIAM (1767–1845). He was appointed physician extraordinary to the Queen (1795), and to George III (1805). He was then made physician in ordinary, which was a higher appointment, to the Queen (1806) and the King (1809). He frequently attended George III during his last illness.

BAILLIE, MATTHEW (1761–1823). He was an anatomist famous for his work, *The Morbid Anatomy of some of the most important Parts of the Human Body*, which discussed the thoracic and abdominal organs and the brain. He served as physician extraordinary to King George III.

TROTTER, JOHN BERNARD (1775–1818). When Fox was appointed Foreign Secretary (February 1806), Trotter became his private secretary, and remained with him until his death in September of the same year. His book, *Memoirs of the latter years of Fox*, appeared in 1811.

BONAPARTE, JOSEPH (1768–1844). The elder brother of Napoleon, he was made King of Naples in 1806. In 1808 his brother sent him to Spain, where he reigned until 1813. There he had to deal with the problems of inadequate troops and money, the hatred of his subjects, and the insubordination of his generals. Moreover, Napoleon refused to accept any of his suggestions. After the French defeat at Vitoria, Napoleon ordered his retreat to France, where he lived in seclusion.

BONAPARTE, LOUIS (1778–1846). A brother of Napoleon, Louis Bonaparte reluctantly married Hortense de Beauharnais (1802), and reigned as King of Holland (1806–10), until his defiance of the ruinous Continental System – which protected Dutch interests – led Napoleon to depose him. He died in Italy.

BONAPARTE, JÉRÔME (1784–1860). The youngest brother of Napoleon, he was made King of Westphalia (1807). He was with his brother at Waterloo (see III, VII, i).

CAMBACÉRÈS, JEAN JACQUES (1753–1824). As the friend and chief counsellor of Napoleon, he served as Arch-Chancellor of the Empire from 1804 until Napoleon's abdication. During the regency of Marie Louise, he was her chief adviser.

TALLEYRAND-PÉRIGORD, CHARLES MAURICE DE (1754–1838). He served as Minister of Foreign Affairs between 1797 and 1807. After Fox's conversation with a would-be assassin (II, I, i), Fox and Talleyrand carried on a correspondence aimed at establishing peace between England and France. He accompanied Napoleon in the campaigns of Prussia and Poland, and was present at Tilsit (II, I, viii).

CAULAINCOURT, ARMAND (AUGUSTIN-LOUIS), MARQUIS DE (1773–1827). The Emperor's loyal Master of Horse from 1804 on, he was at Napoleon's side during several great battles. In 1807 he became ambassador to Russia, but was recalled in 1811, and taunted by Napoleon as Russian in his sympathies. He asked to be sent to Spain; but he returned with the Emperor to Paris after the Russian defeat. He negotiated the armistice in Silesia (1813), and later became a foreign minister known as the 'man of peace'. He signed the treaty that sent Napoleon to Elba.

LEBRUN, CHARLES-FRANÇOIS, DUC DE PLAISANCE (1739–1824). Treasurer of the Empire (1804–14), he instituted the Cours de Comptes, which became an important French institution. He supervised the integration of Liguria into the French Empire (1805–6), and served as Governor-General of Holland (1811–13).

DUROC, GERAUD-CHRISTOPHE-MICHEL (1772–1813). Duke of Friuli, Grand Marshal of the Palace (1804), and aide-de-camp to the First Consul, he organised the Polish light horse of the Guard; accompanied Napoleon to Spain and Russia; commanded the Imperial Guard; and was killed at Markersdorf.

PRINCE OF NEUCHÂTEL: see BERTHIER, Part First.

GRAND DUKE OF BERG: see MURAT, Part First.

EUGÈNE DE BEAUHARNAIS (1781–1824). The son of Joséphine by her first marriage, he was adopted by Napoleon (1806), who liked him and might have made him his heir if he had not believed that an adopted godson would face great difficulties in keeping the throne after his death. Eugène did not aspire to become Napoleon's successor, however. He served with Napoleon in the Russian campaign, and in 1814 organised the defence of France until Napoleon abdicated.

CHAMPAGNY, JEAN BAPTISTE (1756–1834). A French statesman called out of retirement by Napoleon, he served as Ambassador to Austria (1801–4). At the time of II, v, ii, he was serving as the Minister of Foreign Affairs, and in that capacity he took care of the foreign correspondence concerning the proposed marriage. At a council meeting which preceded Napoleon's final choice of a bride, he pointed out the advantages of an Austrian marriage. After Napoleon's first abdication, he acted as the emissary of Marie Louise to Francis I of Austria.

DE BAUSSET, CHAMBERLAIN. Hardy seems to have combined two historical figures here: M. de Beausset, the chamberlain who was on service when Joséphine went into convulsions, and who helped his mistress to her rooms (II, v, ii); and M. de Bossuet, the prefect of the palace who delivered the portrait of the King of Rome to Napoleon at Borodino (III, I, iv).

MASSÉNA, ANDRÉ (1758–1817). He distinguished himself in Napoleon's campaigns against Austria (1800 and 1809), but failed to defeat the English in Spain, partly because of poor co-operation from other commanders. Napoleon made him Duke of Rivoli (1808) and Prince of Essling (1810); but he went over to Louis XVIII after the Emperor's fall (1814), was raised to the peerage, and remained neutral during the Hundred Days.

JUNOT, ANDOCHE (1771–1813). A marshal of France, he commanded the army in Portugal (1807), and after a series of successes was appointed governor of that country. Wellesley defeated him at Vimiero (1808). Junot later served as one of the generals under Masséna at Torrès Védras (II, vi, i). He was made a scapegoat for the disaster which later took place in Russia.

FOY, MAXIMILIEN SÉBASTIEN (1775–1825). A French general, he served in Portugal and Spain (1808–12). Masséna sent him to Paris (November 1810) to explain the situation of the Army after the lines had been established at Torrès Védras (II, vi, ii). He served under Ney at Waterloo.

LOISON, JEAN BAPTISTE MAURICE (1770–1816). A French general, he served under Junot in Portugal, and later under Masséna in Spain.

PRADT, ABBÉ DE (Dominique de Pradt) (1759–1837). A Roman Catholic prelate, he was Napoleon's personal chaplain.

CORVISART DES MARETS, JEAN NICOLAS (1755–1821). As Napoleon's physician, he was present at the birth of the King of Rome, and was charged by Napoleon to attend Dubois.

DUBOIS, ANTOINE (1756–1837). Dubois, a doctor, was nervous because of the importance of this particular birth (the King of Rome), and Napoleon tried to calm him by making light of the responsibility. Thiers states that the child 'was born without any of those accidents which had been feared'.

GUILLET DE LA GEVRILLIÈRE. This is a false name for the man who offered to assassinate Napoleon.

LOUIS XVIII OF FRANCE (1755–1824). The brother of Louis XVI lived in Germany, Russia, Poland and England during the years in which Napoleon ruled France. He took the title of Louis XVIII after the death of his nephew, Louis XVII.

FREDERICK-WILLIAM III, King of Prussia (1770–1840). Queen Louisa urged him to fight the French, but the defeats at Jena and Auerstädt led directly to the humiliating Treaty of Tilsit. During the negotiations, he asked that Magdeburg be left part of Prussia (II, i, viii), and as a last resort he sent for Queen Louisa. Their entreaties failed, and he lost much of Prussia as a result of the Treaty. Victories at Leipzig and Waterloo helped to re-establish Prussia's position in Europe. After Napoleon had been sent to Elba, he visited England, and received an honorary degree at Oxford. He sent Caroline his compliments, by means of his steward, while he was in that country (III, IV, viii).

LUDWIG, FRIEDRICH, Prince of Hohenlohe-Ingelfingen (1746–1818). A Prussian general, he commanded part of the troops at Jena, and was defeated by the French. He received conflicting information about the fate of the army under the Duke of Brunswick (II, I, iv), but finally learned the truth. Later, the King of Prussia made him commander-in-chief. He retired in 1808.

CARLOS IV, King of Spain (1748–1819). He ruled from 1788 to 1808, when Napoleon forced him to abdicate. He allowed his minister Godoy and the Queen to make decisions that should have remained in his hands. The crowd depicted in II, II, ii made him fear that a revolution similar to the one in France had come to Spain, and he was easily convinced that Godoy's power had to be taken away in order to restore tranquillity.

FERNANDO, Prince of Asturias, son to Carlos IV (1784–1833). He opposed his mother, the Queen, and Godoy, and resisted the planned flight from Spain. He had received much attention from Beauharnais, Napoleon's emissary, and was ready to welcome the French as the deliverers of Spain. After his father's forced abdication (1808), he served as King Ferdinand VII until Napoleon imprisoned him. He was returned to power, again by Napoleon, in 1814.

GODOY, MANUEL DE (1767–1851). He began his career as a member of the bodyguard of Carlos IV, but gained power after he became a royal favourite. He was granted the title of 'Prince of Peace' after negotiation of the Treaty of Basel (1795). The final day of his power is dramatised in II, II, ii. The Spanish people knew of his affairs with the Queen and Josefa Tudo, and hated him; they forced the King to strip him of his authority.

COUNT DE MONTIJO. Born into a noble family, possessing a great fortune, he was nevertheless persecuted by the court. He led the crowd that gathered several days before the march on the palace (II, II, ii), and helped to forge the alliance between tradesmen and peasants that destroyed Godoy's reign.

METTERNICH, PRINCE KLEMENS WENZEL NEPOMUK LOTHAR VON (1773–1859). He became Foreign Minister in Austria (1809), and was a key figure in arranging the marriage between Marie Louise and Napoleon. During the Congress of Vienna, and after

Napoleon's return from Elba, he helped obtain the Duchy of Parma for Marie Louise, and kept her (without much difficulty) from returning to Napoleon. He also kept Austria out of the war between Russia and France.

CAROLINE AMELIA ELIZABETH, of Brunswick-Wolfenbüttel (1768–1821), Queen of George IV. Caroline and George were married in April 1795, but their relationship was soon troubled and they separated a year later. Her husband became Prince Regent in 1811, and, without the King to intercede for her, her position became hopeless. Her behaviour was at times indiscreet, but the circumstances which drove her to it were understandable and sympathised with by many Englishmen.

DUCHESS OF YORK. Eldest daughter of Frederick-William II, King of Prussia, and a popular figure in English society during this decade.

MARCHIONESS OF HERTFORD, ISABELLA ANNE INGAM SHEPHERD SEYMOUR (d.1836). A lady of great wealth and personal charm, the Marchioness, after her return from Ireland, became a major force in the life of the Prince of Wales. Because of her influence, Mrs Fitzherbert was not invited to take her usual place at the Prince's table when he gave the party at Carlton House (II, VI, vii).

FITZHERBERT, MARIA ANNE (1756–1837). Mrs Fitzherbert married the Prince of Wales on 21 December 1785. Although the Catholic Church considered the marriage legal, the British government did not. She was well received by the royal family, and lived with the Prince for several years; but the relationship ended when, at a party given at Carlton House for the French royal family, she was told that she had to sit according to her own rank, as mere Mrs Fitzherbert (see II, VI, vii).

HORTENSE DE BEAUHARNAIS, Queen of Holland (1783–1837). The daughter of Joséphine by her first marriage, she married Louis Napoleon (1802). The sentiments reported in II, v, ii are her own rather than her mother's.

DUCHESS OF MONTEBELLO. Napoleon chose her to serve as Marie Louise's first lady of honour. She was the widow of Marshal Lannes, who had been killed in battle in 1809.

MADAME DE MONTESQUIOU. The King of Rome was given into her charge as soon as he was born; she was known as the 'gouvernante of the children of France'.

DUCHESS OF ANGOULÊME, MARIE THÉRÈSE CHARLOTTE (1778–1851). The daughter of Louis XVI and Marie Antoinette, she remained an ardent royalist all her life.

LOUISA, Queen of Prussia (1776–1810). Her beauty, courage and kindness endeared her to the people. In July 1807 she travelled to Tilsit and dined with Napoleon (II, i, viii), but all her entreaties for a softening of the Emperor's harsh stand on Prussian concessions came to nothing.

MARIA LUISA, Queen of Spain (1751–1819). She was the dissolute, strong-willed wife of Carlos IV and the mistress of Godoy (and others). She planned with Godoy the retreat from Spain discussed in II, ii, ii. She agreed to have Godoy stripped of his offices because she was more interested in saving his life than his power.

MARIA LUISA DE BOURBON. Godoy married the niece of Charles III of Spain in order to advance himself at court; the marriage was not happy. She was in Godoy's palace when the mob entered (II, ii, ii), but was respectfully conducted to the palace of the King before the mob devastated Godoy's palace. Hardy may have changed her name to Thereza to avoid the reader's confusing her with the Queen of Spain, Maria Luisa. It is also possible that he confused her with her sister, Maria Theresa de Bourbon, who was involved in Godoy's marriage schemes for Ferdinand.

DOÑA JOSEFA TUDO. She was the mistress of Godoy for several years, and had children by him. He gave her wealth and power, and even had her made Countess of Castillo Fiél. She was seen coming out of Godoy's palace (II, ii, ii), and entering a carriage.

MARIA LUDOVICA OF ESTE (M. Louisa Beatrix). She married Francis I of Austria (January 1808), as his third wife.

MARIA LUISA (Marie Louise) (1791–1847). Historians disagree as to whether she was delighted or depressed by the prospect of becoming Napoleon's wife. (See II, v, iii.) She became the Emperor's second wife (1810), and their son, the King of Rome, was born in 1811. After Napoleon abdicated, she returned to Austria. She might have gone to Elba with her husband, but to do so would have meant becoming separated from her son. During the Congress of Vienna, she fought for the Duchy of Parma as an inheritance for her son; but to obtain it, she had to surrender to her father the guardianship of her son. She later married Count Neipperg (1821). (See III, v, ii and iv.)

MADAME METTERNICH. Eleonore von Kaunitz, granddaughter of Count Wenzel von Kaunitz, Austrian Chancellor under Maria Theresa and her successors, married Metternich in 1795.

THE EMPRESS-MOTHER OF RUSSIA (Sophia Dorothea of Wurtemburg; Russian name: Maria Fyodorovna). Hardy follows Thiers' version in II, v, vii, for although Thiers does not record a scene with the Empress-Mother, Alexander, and Anne, he states that the Empress-Mother married the Grand Duchess Catherine to the Duke of Oldenburg to avoid a possible marriage with Napoleon. It is not clear whether the Empress-Mother or Alexander hung back from accepting the proposal to the Grand Duchess Anne; although Alexander claimed it was his mother, he could hardly have told Napoleon that he himself did not approve.

GRAND DUCHESS ANNE (Anna) OF RUSSIA. The youngest sister of Alexander, Anne was only fifteen at the time of Napoleon's proposal. The French Emperor decided against marrying her not only because of Russia's delay in accepting the proposal, but also because of the problems that the Empress-Mother's insistence on Orthodox priests in France for her daughter, and the waiting until Anne was old enough to have children, would cause.

PART THIRD

LENNOX, CHARLES, fourth Duke of Richmond and Lennox (1764–1819). He fought a notorious duel with the Duke of York (1789), and later served as Lord-Lieutenant of Ireland (1807), with Colonel Wellesley as his chief secretary. The night before Quatre Bras (15 June 1815), he gave his famous ball. He was present at the battle of Waterloo.

SOMERSET, HENRY, seventh Duke of Beaufort (1792–1853). He served as aide-de-camp to the Duke of Wellington in the Peninsular Campaign (1812–14).

JENKINSON, ROBERT BANKS, second Earl of Liverpool (1770–1828). He served as secretary of state for foreign affairs (1809), secretary of state for war and the colonies (1809–1812), and Prime Minister in a Tory government (1812–1827). He vigorously supported Wellington, and later acted as a powerful moral force at the Congress of Vienna. His government chose St Helena as a suitable place of exile for Napoleon.

VANSITTART, NICHOLAS, first Baron Bexley (1766–1851). An able Chancellor of the Exchequer (1812), he was responsible for maintaining war taxes to pay the army and foreign subsidies. He used Rothschild to collect bullion secretly for war expenses on the Continent. Napoleon's escape from Elba led to a renewal of war taxes as well as the issuance of further loans.

TEMPLE, HENRY JOHN, third Viscount Palmerston in the peerage of Ireland (1784–1865). Secretary at War without a seat in the cabinet (1809), he stood between the spending authorities – the Secretary at War and the Commander-in-Chief – and the public; thus, he sought to achieve maximum efficiency for the Army at a reasonable cost.

PONSONBY, SIR FREDERIC CAVENDISH (1783–1837). He distinguished himself by heroic behaviour at Talavera, and led the 12th Light Dragoons in the Spanish War, fighting at Llerena, Salamanca, Vitoria and Waterloo.

BURDETT, SIR FRANCIS (1770–1844). He defended free speech, and opposed government abuses. He sat as a parliamentary reformer for thirty years.

ROMILLY, SIR SAMUEL (1757–1818). He was strongly influenced by Rousseau, the Encyclopedists of France, and Beccaria of Italy; he was active in the cause of legal reforms, and an impressive orator.

PAGET, SIR HENRY WILLIAM, first Marquess of Anglesey and second Earl of Uxbridge of the second creation (1768–1854). He was in command of cavalry in Spain under Sir John Moore, and of cavalry and horse artillery at Waterloo (he lost a leg in the latter battle).

PICTON, SIR THOMAS (1758–1815). He was indispensable to Wellington during the Spanish War. He harried Masséna's troops, then Marmont's. He was present at Vitoria (1813) and Toulouse (1814), and in command of the 5th Division and the reserve at Quatre Bras and Waterloo. There, after defeating Ney's infantry and repulsing the charges of French cavalry, he lost his life.

CLINTON, SIR HENRY THE YOUNGER (1771–1829). He served as adjutant-general with Sir John Moore in Spain, and defended Moore's posthumous reputation. He distinguished himself at Salamanca. Wellington asked for his services after Napoleon's escape from Elba, and he commanded the 3rd Division, taking severe bombardments from the French artillery and resisting cavalry charges.

COLVILLE, SIR CHARLES (1770–1843). He commanded a brigade, and later a division, in Spain (1810–1814), and a division in Belgium (1815).

COLE, SIR GALBRAITH LOWRY (1772–1842). He commanded the 4th Division in the Peninsular War (1809–1814), and was with Wellington as they pursued the French across the Pyrenees.

PACK, SIR DENIS (1772?–1823). He fought at Vimiero, Walcheren, Busaco, Almeida, Ciudad Rodrigo and Salamanca. He was wounded eight times during the Peninsular Campaign. He commanded a brigade of Picton's division at Quatre Bras and Waterloo.

KEMPT, SIR JAMES (1764–1854). Active in Spain, he earned Wellington's praise. He commanded the 8th Brigade under Picton at Quatre Bras and Waterloo. When Picton died, he assumed command.

BYNG, SIR JOHN (1772–1860). He had a distinguished career in Spain; repulsed Soult at the pass of Roncesvalles; and commanded a brigade under General Cooke at Waterloo.

VIVIAN, SIR RICHARD HUSSEY, first Baron Vivian (1775–1842). He fought with Sir John Moore in the retreat to Corunna. Wellington praised his services. In the final moments of Waterloo, his troops helped to turn the tide against Napoleon.

PONSONBY, SIR WILLIAM (1772–1815). He first distinguished himself at Llerena and Salamanca. At Waterloo he led the Union Brigade of heavy cavalry (Royals, Scots Greys and Iniskillings) in a famous charge on d'Erlon's shattered corps. He was killed by French lancers.

VANDELEUR, SIR JOHN ORMSBY (1763–1849). He rendered gallant service at Ciudad Rodrigo, Salamanca and Vitoria. He commanded the 4th Cavalry Brigade at Waterloo. After Lord Uxbridge was wounded, he commanded the British cavalry.

MAITLAND, SIR PEREGRINE (1777–1854). He served in Spain, and at Quatre Bras and Waterloo commanded the 1st Brigade of Guards.

ADAM, SIR FREDERICK (1781–1853). He was active in eastern Spain; as a major-general at Waterloo, he commanded a brigade in Lord Hill's division, and prevented the Old Guard from re-forming at a critical moment in the battle.

HALKETT, SIR COLIN (1774–1856). He accompanied Moore in his retreat, was on the Walcheren expedition, and fought at Albuera and Salamanca. He commanded the British brigade in the 3rd Division, and received four severe wounds in the battles of Quatre Bras and Waterloo. Wellington called him 'a very gallant and deserving officer'.

LE MARCHANT, JOHN GASPARD (1766–1812). He led an important brigade charge at Salamanca, and routed a French infantry division. He was killed towards the end of the battle.

PAKENHAM, SIR EDWARD MICHAEL (1778–1815). He commanded the 3rd Division at Salamanca, and broke the French centre. Wellington considered him one of his best generals. He was killed in the battle of New Orleans (1815).

COTTON, SIR STAPLETON, Viscount Combermere (1773–1865). He commanded a cavalry division in the Spanish War (1808–12), and served in the Pyrenees campaign (1813–14). He commanded the Allied cavalry in France, 1815–16.

DE LANCEY, SIR WILLIAM HOWE (1781?–1815). He was active in Spain; at Waterloo, holding the rank of deputy-quartermaster and general of the army in Belgium, a ricocheting cannon-ball struck him while he was talking to Wellington. He died a week later.

SOMERSET, LORD FITZROY JAMES HENRY, first Baron Raglan (1788–1855). He was an aide-de-camp to Wellington in Portugal and Spain, then became his military secretary (1811). He was present at all of Wellington's battles. He served as Wellington's secretary in Paris, after Napoleon's first abdication. Standing next to Wellington at Waterloo, he was struck by a bullet, and later had to have his arm amputated. Wellington praised him highly.

FRASER, ALEXANDER GEORGE, sixteenth Baron Saltoun (1785–1853). He shared the miseries of Sir John Moore's retreat, fought at Corunna, and participated in the Walcheren expedition. He was active in the final stages of the Spanish War. He defended the orchard of Hougoumont, where he lost two-thirds of his men. He led the famous charge on Napoleon's Old Guard. Wellington admired his talents.

HALKETT, HUGH, Baron von Halkett (1783–1863). He participated in the Corunna retreat and the Walcheren expedition. He commanded a battalion at Albuera, Salamanca and the Burgos retreat. Near Hougoumont he took General Cambronne (commander of the Imperial Guard) prisoner. Halkett dismissed as 'damned humbug' the traditional saying, 'La garde meurt, et ne se rend pas.' Hardy is probably closer to the truth (III, vii, viii).

CAMERON, SIR ALEXANDER (1781–1850). He proved resourceful in several emergencies during the Spanish War. He commanded a battalion at Salamanca, and, in 1815, served gallantly under Picton at Quatre Bras, before he led his own battalion at Waterloo. There he was wounded in the throat.

HEPBURN, FRANCIS, or FRANCIS KER (1779–1835). He served in Spain, and commanded a battalion at Quatre Bras and Waterloo. He occupied Hougoumont and held it, an important (though officially unrecognised) service to Wellington's strategy.

LORD SALTOUN: see FRASER, ALEXANDER GEORGE, Part Second.

CAMPBELL, SIR COLIN (1776–1847). A senior aide-de-camp to Sir Arthur Wellesley (1808), he served as assistant quartermaster-general at the headquarters of the army in the Peninsula. He served later as commandant at Wellington's headquarters (1815), and was present at Waterloo.

CAMPBELL, SIR NEIL (1776–1827). He fought in Portugal and Spain (1810–12), then with the Russians (1814); and he accompanied Napoleon to Elba as the official British commissioner. During one of his visits to Italy, Napoleon escaped, and began his Hundred Days. Campbell fought at Waterloo.

GORDON, SIR ALEXANDER (1786–1815). He fought at Corunna, and served as aide-de-camp to Lord Wellington in both Spain and Belgium. While he was rallying a battalion of Brunswickers near La Haye Sainte (18 June 1815), his thigh was shattered, and he died a few hours later.

GELL, SIR WILLIAM (1777–1836). A classical archaeologist and traveller, he accompanied Princess (later Queen) Caroline, as one of her chamberlains, when she left England for Italy. He defended her at her trial before the House of Lords (October 1820).

BRUNSWICK, DUKE FRIEDRICH WILHELM OF (1771–1815). Fourth son of Karl Wilhelm Ferdinand, Duke of Brunswick. Commanded 'Black Brunswickers' (1809) and lived in England (1809–13). Killed at Quatre Bras (1815).

THE PRINCE OF ORANGE, later William I of the Netherlands (1772–1843). Prince William, the son of Prince William V of Orange, the last stadtholder of the Netherlands, entered the Prussian – and later the Austrian – service after the French occupation of the Netherlands. He returned to the Netherlands (1813), and the Congress of Vienna gave him the title 'King of the Netherlands' (1815), which in turn gave him sovereignty over Belgium and the Grand Duchy of Luxembourg as well as the Netherlands.

ALTEN, COUNT KARL AUGUST VON (1764–1840). A Hanoverian soldier, he enlisted in the British Army and became a major-general. He served with the German Legion in wars against Napoleon, and campaigned in Spain under Sir John Moore and the Duke of Wellington. He was wounded at Waterloo.

THE KING OF ROME, NAPOLEON II (1811–32). The son of Napoleon I and Marie Louise, he was known as the King of Rome from 1811 to 1814. Napoleon's abdication (1814) was in favour of his son; but Napoleon II never ruled. After 1814, he was called the Prince of Parma (1814–18), though from 1815 on he lived as a virtual prisoner in Vienna. From 1818 until his death of tuberculosis, he bore the title Duke of Reichstadt.

BERTRAND, COMTE HENRI GRATIEN (1773–1844). A loyal follower of Napoleon, the French general served in all the Emperor's campaigns. When Napoleon was sent to Elba, Bertrand accompanied him; after Waterloo, he went with him to St Helena.

BESSIÈRES, JEAN BAPTISTE, Duc d'Istrie (1766–1813). A marshal of France, he fought with Napoleon in all the campaigns. He often differed with Napoleon (III, I, viii). The night before the battle at Lützen, he was killed by a stray bullet.

AUGEREAU, PIERRE FRANÇOIS CHARLES, Duc de Castiglione (1757–1816). A marshal of France, he fought in all of Napoleon's campaigns. The conversation with Napoleon dramatised in III, iii, i, is fairly close to Thiers' account. Augereau defected in 1815.

MACDONALD, ALEXANDRE (1765–1840). A French marshal of Scottish descent, he was created Duke of Taranto and distinguished himself at Wagram (1809), in the Peninsular War, and the Russian campaign. He was sent to negotiate Napoleon's abdication in 1814, and remained loyal to Louis XVIII during the Hundred Days.

CAMBRONNE, COMTE PIERRE JACQUES ÉTIENNE (1770–1842). He commanded the Old Guard at Waterloo (see entry for Hugh Halkett). After his return from England, he was exonerated by a court martial (1816).

FRIANT, COMTE LOUIS (1758–1829). A French general who fought with Napoleon in several campaigns, he commanded a division of the guard at Waterloo.

REILLE, HONORÉ CHARLES MICHEL JOSEPH, GENERAL COUNT (1775–1860). Fought with distinction at Wagram, Fleurus, Quatre Bras and Waterloo.

D'ERLON, COMTE JEAN BAPTISTE DROUET (1765–1844). A French general who fought with distinction at Jena and Waterloo.

DROUOT, COMTE ANTOINE (1774–1847). A French general, he was an aide-de-camp to Napoleon (1813), and accompanied him to Elba (1814). He went with Napoleon when the Emperor left the field of Waterloo, was arrested during the second Restoration, and was named as a beneficiary in Napoleon's will.

VICTOR, CLAUDE (or Claude Victor Perrin), Duc de Bellune (1766–1841). A marshal of France, he commanded the army in Spain (1808–9). He also served in Russia, Germany and France. During the Hundred Days he sided with the Bourbons.

PONIATOWSKI, PRINCE JÓZEF ANTONI (1763–1813). The nephew of King Stanislas-Augustus, this Polish prince served as a commander in Napoleon's army, and was created a marshal of France after fighting at Moscow, Smolensk and Leipzig. He drowned trying to swim the Elster (Leipzig), in an effort to follow Macdonald, who succeeded in making the crossing.

JOURDAN, COMTE JEAN BAPTISTE (1762–1833). He was created a marshal of France (1804); accompanied Joseph Bonaparte to Spain as his chief of staff; and was relieved by Soult (1809).

RAPP, COMTE JEAN (1772–1821). A French general, he served as aide-de-camp to Napoleon, and was wounded at Austerlitz. He helped to organise the Polish light horse; fought in the Russian campaign (III, I, iv); and supported him after his return from Elba.

MORTIER, ÉDOUARD ADOLPHE CASIMIR JOSEPH, Duc de Trévise (1768–1835). He was created a marshal of France (1804), and a duke (1808). When Napoleon left Moscow (III, I, viii), he stayed behind with 10,000 men, and before he evacuated the city, blew up the Kremlin.

LARIBOISIÈRE, GENERAL BASTON, COUNT DE. Commander-in-chief, grand artillery, he was raised to count (1808). Lauriston relieved him in Spain. He commanded the artillery of the Grand Army in Russia, and finally died of exhaustion (December 1812).

KELLERMANN, GENERAL FRANÇOIS-ÉTIENNE (1770–1835). He became a count, later marquis, and then Duke of Valmy. The son of a marshal (one who served as an aide to Napoleon), he fought in Spain before his final battles at Quatre Bras and Waterloo.

MILHAUD, GENERAL. Commander of a division of dragoons, he later commanded the 4th Cavalry Corps (cuirassiers) at Ligny, and charged at Waterloo.

FABVRIER, BARON CHARLES NICOLAS (1782–1855). At the time of III, I, iv, he was a colonel in the French Army, and had been sent to Borodino with news of the battle of Salamanca for the Emperor. He fought the next day, and later became a general in the French Army.

MARBOT, BARON JEAN BAPTISTE ANTOINE MARCELIN DE (1782–1854). Thiers records the capture of the Prussian sub-officer of the hussars, but not the name of the man who delivered him to Napoleon (III, VII, ii). Marbot was a French officer during the Napoleonic Wars.

MALLET, LT-COL. He was wounded at Krasny and Dresden; commanded the Second Chasseurs (1814); and was killed at Montmirail.

HEYMÈS, COLONEL. Ney had attacked sooner than he was ordered to do so, and sent his aide-de-camp, Colonel Heymès, to ask Napoleon for the support of the infantry. Napoleon's answer, at first irritated (III, VII, vi), was soon softened into a more encouraging message to Ney.

DE CANISY, equerry to Napoleon and later to the King of Rome, was in charge of the Emperor's baggage, wagons, cooks, horses, etc.

LESSARD, COMMANDANT. He commanded the 5th Battalion near La Mure when they met Napoleon (1815). He resisted Napoleon (III, v, iii) until it became evident that his men would not fight. Abandoned by them, he presented his sword to Napoleon. He was told to meet Napoleon at Grenoble.

BUSSY, COLONEL DE BELLY DE. Mayor of Beaurieux, he served as an aide-de-camp to Napoleon.

MÉNEVAL, BARON DE. He served as secretary to Napoleon, and later to Marie Louise (after the first abdication).

CONSTANT, or LOUIS-CONSTANT VÉRY. Napoleon's valet.

BLÜCHER, GEBHARD LEBERECHT (1742–1819). The Prussian field-marshal was the first to enter Leipzig (III, III, ii). He commanded the Prussian Army (1813–15), and, as III, VI, V, shows, he conferred with Wellington before the battles of Ligny and Quatre Bras. Although wounded personally, and defeated, at Ligny, he aided greatly in the victory of Waterloo, and afterwards, with his cavalry, pursued the fleeing French.

MÜFFLING, BARON KARL VON (1775–1851). A Prussian field-marshal, he served as attaché at Wellington's headquarters (1815), and for this reason appears with the English rather than with the Prussians in Hardy's scenes.

GNEISENAU, COUNT AUGUST NEITHARDT VON (1760–1831). A Prussian field-marshal, he helped to reorganise the Prussian Army after the Treaty of Tilsit. He fought at Leipzig. He was an important member of Blücher's staff at Ligny and Waterloo (III, VI, v).

ZIETEN, COUNT HANS ERNST KARL VON (1770–1848). He was a Prussian field-marshal who commanded a brigade (1813–14), and fought at Ligny and Waterloo.

BÜLOW, BARON FRIEDRICH WILHELM VON (1755–1816). A Prussian general, he fought at Leipzig, and served under Blücher at Waterloo.

STEINMETZ, KARL FRIEDRICH VON (1796–1877). A Prussian general who fought against Napoleon (1813–15).

HARDENBERG, PRINCE KARL A. VON (1750–1822). A moderate constitutional statesman and social reformer of Prussia, he found refuge in Vienna. He was convinced that the best way, indeed the only way, to preserve power in Europe was to preserve the ancient balance of power. He was able to maintain (though barely) the sovereignty of Prussia (1807–12).

NEIPPERG, COUNT ADAM ADALBERT VON (1775–1829). An Austrian general and diplomat, he was the chief confidant and friend of Marie Louise after her return to Austria. With his assistance, she was able to acquire the Duchy of Parma for her son's patrimony. He did much to influence her decision to remain in Austria after Napoleon's return. After the death of Napoleon, they married each other.

MEERVELDT, GENERAL. Austrian plenipotentiary at Leoben, and in the negotiating of the treaty of Campo Formio. He was captured by Napoleon, and sent back, at the battle of Leipzig, to ask for an armistice.

NESSELRODE, KARL ROBERT, COUNT (1780–1862). Of German descent, this Russian statesman had a significant role at the Congress of Vienna (1815), and guided Russian policy for some four decades.

BENNIGSEN, COUNT LEVIN AUGUST THEOPHIL (1745–1826). This Hanoverian general fought for the Russians against Napoleon (1806–14), particularly at Pultusk (near Warsaw), Eylau, Borodino and Leipzig. He was one of the leaders in the conspiracy to murder Tsar Paul I of Russia in 1801.

BARCLAY DE TOLLY, PRINCE MIKHAIL ANDREAS (1761–1818). A Russian field-marshal of Scottish descent, he fought at Pultusk, Eylau and everywhere he prudently could against Napoleon (1812). His retreat before Napoleon's army made him unpopular at court and with the public, and, after the defeat of Smolensk, he was replaced by Kutusov. He commanded the Russian contingent against Napoleon (1813).

BAGRATION, PRINCE PYOTR IVANOVICH (1765–1812). He fought against Murat at Hollabrunn; was present at Austerlitz, Eylau and Friedland; and was killed at Borodino (1812).

ROSTOPCHIN, COUNT FYODOR VASILIEVICH (1765–1826). A Russian politician, general and writer, he served as the governor of Moscow (1812), and is believed by some to have ordered the burning of the city.

LADY ANNE HAMILTON (1766–1846). Lady-in-waiting to, and close friend of, Queen Caroline, the wife of George IV.

MRS DALBIAC, SUSANNA ISABELLA, eldest daughter of a Yorkshire lieutenant-colonel. Sir William Francis Patrick Napier, the historian of the Peninsular War, warmly praised her courage. She was present at the battle of Salamanca, in which her husband participated.

MARIA CAROLINA OF NAPLES; also Bonaparte (Marie-Annonciade-), Caroline. She was Napoleon's youngest sister, and married General Joachim Murat (1800). Ambitious (as much so as her husband), she became Grand Duchess of Cleves and Berg, then Queen of Naples (1808–14), where she encouraged artists and writers. The birth of the King of Rome ended her hopes that her own son might succeed Napoleon; she and Murat intrigued against the French Emperor (1814–15); once Napoleon fell, Metternich (who loved her) tried to save Murat's throne, but Murat behaved so rashly that he was executed (1815), and Caroline escaped to Austria.

QUEEN HORTENSE. Queen of Holland, sister of Eugène Beauharnais, and adopted daughter of Napoleon.

BONAPARTE, LETIZIA (or Laetitia) RAMOLINO (1750–1836). She received the title of 'Madame Mère' when Napoleon, her son, became the French Emperor. She was admired for her simple virtues. After Waterloo, she found refuge in Rome.

BONAPARTE, MARIE PAULINA (also: Marie Pauline; originally Carlotta; after 1806, Duchess of Guastalla) (1780–1825). She was Napoleon's favourite sister, and married General Leclerc. After his death (1802), Napoleon arranged her marriage to Prince Camillo Borghese (1803), a member of the highest Roman nobility. She disliked Marie Louise, which made relations with her brother difficult; but after Waterloo she proved more loyal to him than any other sister or brother.

DRAMATISED VERSIONS OF
THE DYNASTS

HARDY protested early, and more than once, that he had no desire to see a dramatised production of *The Dynasts*. He was reacting against what he regarded as an unfair emphasis, in the first reviews, on the literary form of his epic-drama. Many critics pointed out what Hardy willingly conceded – that the work presented enormous obstacles to any stage-producer – and then proceeded to treat such limitations as an artistic defect (which Hardy, of course, would not grant).

Nevertheless, Hardy was to see within fifteen years four productions of selected scenes, and other productions followed his death. (For much of the information in the following paragraphs, I am deeply indebted to Desmond Hawkins, *Hardy, Novelist and Poet*, published by David & Charles, Newton Abbot and London: 1976. Long active in the BBC, Hawkins compiled a list of such dramatisations.)

The first production, entitled *Ye Merrie Maie Fayre*, was the briefest. The Reverend Roland Hill took three scenes, their settings Wessex, and combined them to provide a benefit performance for Dorchester church schools (1908).

The second began its run at the Kingsway Theatre, London, on 25 November 1914, and continued for seventy-two performances, closing on 30 January 1915. It was prepared by Hardy, at the request of Harley Granville-Barker, and Hardy not only cut, rearranged and wrote additional linking bits of dialogue, but added a Prologue and Epilogue. Hardy's selection of thirty scenes minimised the importance of the Immanent Will; stressed the English elements; and ran for three hours. Hardy was not proud of this version, and wrote on the flyleaf of the manuscript (now in the Dorset County Museum) that the abridgement was not to be 'published or reproduced at any time'. Nevertheless, some members of the audience were deeply moved by the wartime production. Rebecca West, after noting some reservations, concluded that she had gone to 'one of the greatest plays that have been on the English stage . . . unquestionably great and marvellously beautiful'.

The third production, like the first, was a local affair, but relatively ambitious. *Wessex Scenes from The Dynasts* was put on by the Hardy Players (22 June 1916, in Weymouth, and 6 and 7 December 1916, in Dorchester) for charities run by the Red Cross. Several London critics came to see it, and liked it. This version, like the one staged by Harley Granville-Barker, was specially prepared by Hardy. Perhaps most noteworthy, he added a romance between a young woman and a soldier. In the *Life* Hardy remarked that this version embraced 'scenes of a local character only, from which could be gathered in echoes of drum and trumpet and alarming rumours, the great events going on elsewhere'.

The fourth was acted on 10–14 February 1920, at Oxford. Sponsored by members of the Oxford Union Society, and played by members of the Oxford University Dramatic Society, this production used the text of the London version. Hardy travelled to Oxford to receive an honorary degree of D.C.L., and to see the play performed. Charles Morgan's account of Hardy's visit to Oxford, printed in the *Life*, suggests very strongly that Hardy's interest in attending the play preceded, and may have led to, the decision of the authorities at Oxford to award the degree. Hardy much preferred the Oxford production to the London one.

After Hardy's death radio broadcasts found *The Dynasts* playable material. In 1933 a BBC dramatisation of Part First, prepared by Alan Wade, who also produced it, attracted widespread notice. Barbara Burnham's version was used in 1940. A version by Muriel Pratt and Dallas Bower, produced by Val Gielgud, followed in 1943. Then came two full-scale productions. The first version, prepared by Henry Reed and produced by E. A. Harding and Douglas Cleverdon, was played in June 1951, during two separate weeks, as a series of six (approximately) ninety-minute episodes, for a total scheduled listening-time of nine hours and twenty minutes. Its length allowed for inclusion of the Fore Scene, of stage directions, and even of dumb shows. The Spirits, according to reviewers, were real presences, and the whole undertaking was well received.

So, too, was the second six-part dramatisation, which used a text prepared by Charles Lefeaux (who also produced). This was played in 1967.

'The Death of Nelson,' a vigorous twenty-minute dramatisation of selected Trafalgar scenes, was enacted by 'ten stout hearts and true' during the interval of a performance of the documentary-type play *The God-cursed Sun*, by Geoffrey Reeves and Albert Hunt, at Blandford, Dorset, in 1968. For those fortunate enough to see it, the interlude proved one of the highlights of the Thomas Hardy Festival that year.

NOTE ON THE TEXT

SYDNEY COCKERELL, in the process of carrying out Hardy's wishes for the distribution of manuscripts among a number of public collections, presented to the British Museum, in October 1911, a three-volume, fair-copy manuscript of *The Dynasts*. Originally bound in brown paper covers, the manuscript is today held in a B.M. binding of three-quarter leather.

In 1938 William R. Rutland lamented that 'no early drafts or notes' had been made available to scholars, and added, 'For some such manuscripts certainly exist.' As a matter of record, the Dorset County Museum, which houses the Memorial Library, owns six sheaves. The original form of III, I–IV, is written on the first four sheaves, and is labelled 'rough draft' (in Hardy's hand-writing); III, VI–VII, is written on the fifth and sixth sheaves. Extensive revisions mark these acts, which were written out after Part First and Part Second in the B.M. copy. As several scholars have pointed out, the discrepancies between the fair copy in the B.M. and the printed text of 1903–8 are numerous, but, so far as substance is concerned, relatively unimportant. The fullest and most critically discerning comparison between the six sheaves and the B.M. manuscript, as well as between the B.M. manuscript and the printed text of 1903–8, may be found in Walter Wright's *The Shaping of The Dynasts: A Study in Thomas Hardy* (1967), Chapter 5, 'The Text from Rough Draft to Book'.

The first issue of Part First was brought out by Macmillan & Co., Ltd. (1903). The occasion was of some importance in Hardy's career, as he was coming back to Macmillan after fifteen years with other publishers. Macmillan was to be his publisher for the rest of his life, and in 1944 purchased from the Estate of Florence Emily Hardy the literary copyrights for most of his work.

The second impression, revised, appeared in 1904. Although Richard L. Purdy notes, in his invaluable bibliographical study of Hardy editions, that 'The reason for it is not apparent, since Macmillan reported a stock of 1151 copies on 30 June of that year,' Hardy's interest in a new impression must have derived largely from a desire to minimise the impact on sales of a series of reviews, appearing during the first half of 1904, that made much of the crabbed language of Part First. For example, Max Beerbohm, in the *Saturday Review* (30 January), argued that Hardy's poetry revealed itself 'more surely and firmly through the medium of prose than through the medium of rhyme and metre'; the *Spectator* (20 February) claimed that the Spirits never spoke 'without expressing a banal thought in the worst verse', the metrics lacked music, and the rhythms were 'weak and impoverished'; the *Athenaeum* (23 January) said flatly that Hardy was 'unpoetic'; the *Literary World* (12 February) complained of 'the poverty of the blank verse', and expressed the opinion that Hardy had used, instead of poetry, 'matter almost prosier than prose'. To meet these objections, Hardy – after a brief period of dejection – reworked many of the specific words and phrases that had been objected to into a simpler or more colloquial language. (For half-a-dozen examples, see Purdy, p. 124.) A full study of these changes would tell us a great deal about Hardy's ability to learn from criticism, for there can be no question that Hardy was seeking to have the epic-drama judged as poetry. Indeed, he regretted that he had sent Part First to press before he had completed the next two parts, and said more than once to friends that a faulty judgement of the whole by critics and reviewers had been the unfortunate consequence. We may rejoice that Hardy did not live up to his threat, made in a letter to Edmund Gosse dated 17 January 1904, to discontinue the writing of his epic-drama. By 22 March when he wrote to Edward Clodd, he had made up his mind to go on with his work.

Part First did not sell well, nor did Part Second after its publication in February 1906. A second impression of Part Second was not called for until 1909. Not until the publication of the final Part, in February 1908, did the commercial picture brighten. The reviews were more discerning of what the total work signified in what was (even then) presumed to be the sunset-glow of his career. From 1908 on there was never any serious questioning of Hardy's right to devote so much time to the Napoleonic years. The reading public concurred. In 1910 a second edition of Part Third was printed, and late in the same year a one-volume edition of all three parts.

I am indebted to Chester Garrison's study, *The Vast Venture: Hardy's Epic-Drama The Dynasts* (1973), for the information that *The Dynasts* has gone through twenty-nine printings since 1910. 'From 1915 to 1931 it was, in one edition or another, reprinted almost yearly; from 1931 to the present it was re-issued about once every four years. According to my rough calculations,' Garrison writes, 'about seventy-three thousand copies have been sold' (p. 20). Macmillan has published nine printings from the 1910 plates, viz.: 1910, 1915, 1918, 1919, 1920, 1921, 1923, 1926 and 1931; six Thin Paper printings; seven two-volume Pocket Edition printings, and one Special Signed and Limited Edition. Moreover, as Macmillan informed Garrison, there have been three one-volume (pre-1910 plates) printings by Macmillan in New York, five printings in set editions (Wessex, Autograph, Anniversary, Mellstock, and Wessex reprinted), and a selection of scenes edited by J. H. Fowler, published in London in 1928. A Papermac edition – a Macmillan paperback imprint now defunct – was published in 1965; it contained an intro-duction by John Wain.

Of the set editions, only two need concern us. The Wessex Edition, publication of the individual titles of which extended from 1912 to 1931, has been described by Purdy as 'in every sense the definitive edition of Hardy's work and the last authority in question of text' (p. 286). The first two parts of *The Dynasts* were issued in one volume, Vol. II of the Verse; the third part was combined with *Time's Laughingstocks*, and numbered as Vol. III of the Verse. Both volumes (II and III) appeared in 1913. Hardy's revisions for the novels and prefaces were far more extensive than for the verse.

The Mellstock Edition (1919–20) was an édition de luxe, printed in 500 copies. The plates for the three volumes (XXXI–XXXIII) in which *The Dynasts* appeared in 1920 were com-pletely reset. Proofs were submitted to Hardy for the last set of revisions that he was to make on his epic-drama. In June 1919 Hardy sent to Macmillan five pages of corrections for the entire Mellstock Edition, and the appropriate changes were made. Unfortunately, not all the changes made for the Mellstock Edition were incorporated into reprintings of the Wessex Edition, or into reprintings of other versions of the text, after 1920. A line-by-line comparison of the Wessex and Mellstock Editions of *The Dynasts*, made by this editor, indicates that Hardy, as he made his final changes for the Mellstock Edition, now believed that his poem had reached the precise form, and the authoritative stage of text, that he had been seeking for more than a decade. However, a number of corrections are listed, in Hardy's handwriting, in the copies of the Wessex Edition in the Dorset County Museum, Dorchester. An examination of the lists by James Gibson has revealed some corrections which were not made in the Mellstock Edition. No correspondence survives, but as these additional corrections were made in subsequent Macmillan editions it is to be assumed that they were made at Hardy's request. They have therefore been incorporated in the New Wessex Edition. Apart from the renumbering of the pages consecutively and the grouping of the contents at the beginning, the New Wessex Edition is an exact photographic reproduction of Hardy's personally revised text of the Mellstock Edition, and represents best the great work as Hardy wished us to read it.

Wessex Edition	*Mellstock Edition*
Part First	
p. viii, 1. 5:	p. vi, 1. 5:
... Those Continental writers who had dealt imaginatively with Napoléon's career ...	... so many Continental writers who had dealt with Napoléon's career ...
p. 3:	p. 3:
Count Munster.	*Count Münster.*
p. 4:	p. 4:
The Emperor Alexander [comes after The Emperor Francis]	[*The Emperor Alexander* is moved down from the list of Austrian characters to the list of Russian characters.]
p. 12, 1. 11:	p. 12, 1. 11:
SEMICHORUS I. OF RUMOURS	SEMICHORUS I OF RUMOURS
p. 34, 1. 23:	p. 23, 1. 28:
forthwith.	forthwith!
p. 45, 1. 17:	p. 46, 1. 4:
a local thing called Christianity	a local cult called Christianity
p. 58, l. 4:	p. 59, l. 20:
Immediately after, NAPOLÉON ...	Immediately after NAPOLÉON ...
p. 61, l. 27:	p. 63, l. 26:
COUNT MUNSTER	COUNT MÜNSTER
p. 79, l. 22:	p. 82, l. 31:
Foreseeing ...	'Foreseeing ...
p. 84, l. 29:	p. 84, l. 30:
—We've had alarms	—We'd lately news

Wessex Edition	*Mellstock Edition*
p. 104, l. 13:	p. 111, l. 17:
Remember, too, what I have already told	Remember, too, what I have already told:
p. 128, ll. 3–4:	p. 133, ll. 27–8:
One far above forethinking; purposive,	One far above forethinking; pró-cessive,
Yet superconscious; a Clairvoyancy	Rapt, superconscious; a Clairvoyancy
p. 169, l. 35:	p. 179, l. 2:
And where that moment stood the stable-cock.	And where that moment beaked the stable-cock.
p. 172, l. 27:	p. 182, l. 2:
Yea, from the Vague we shape, like these,	Yea, from the Void we fetch, like these,

Part Second

p. xvi, l. 12:	p. vi, l. 23:
[Act Fifth: Scene V.] The old West Highway out of Vienna	[Act Fifth: Scene V.] The Old West Highway out of Vienna
p. 190, l. 26:	p. 17, l. 11:
Flanders-fed	Flanders-flung
p. 204, l. 2:	p. 31, l. 17:
Custrin	Cüstrin
p. 230, l. 2:	p. 58, l. 4:
And fond you with fair regularity;—	And fond you with a fair-shown frequency;—
p. 240, l. 25:	p. 69, l. 15:
The purposive, unmotived, dominant Thing	The pró-cessive, unmotived, dominant Thing [changed further in subsequent editions —see page 759]
p. 255, l. 4:	p. 84, l. 21:
By why this craze . . .	But why this craze . . .
p. 262, ll. 4–5:	p. 92, ll. 16–17:
An interval. More English troops pass on horses, mostly shoeless and foundered.	An interval. More English troops pass, on horses mostly shoeless and foundered.
p. 267, l. 32:	p. 98, l. 24:
Is Soult the Duke Dalmatia yet at hand?	Is Soult, the Duke Dalmatia, yet at hand?
p. 304, l. 32:	p. 138, l. 2:
Knells of night is vext Talavera tonguing:	Talavera tongues it as ten o' the night-time:
p. 363, ll. 7–8:	p. 199, l. 8:
. . . somewhat like a vair-shaped shield . . .	. . . somewhat like a late-Gothic shield . . .

Wessex Edition   *Mellstock Edition*

Part Third

Wessex Edition	Mellstock Edition
	p. 1:
And I heard sounds of insult, shame, and wrong	[Hardy omits the quotation, which is drawn from Tennyson's 'A Dream of Fair Women,' fourth stanza.]
And trumpets blown for wars	
p. 92, l. 7:	p. 95, l. 16:
... when they have had some dinner	... when they have had some dinner.
p. 167, last line:	p. 175, last line:
[The footnote is undated.]	[The footnote is followed by the year 1907, enclosed within brackets.]
p. 168, l. 11:	p. 176, l. 18:
The one who spoke to me in passing out	The one who hurled the news in passing out
p. 180, l. 5:	p. 188, l. 23:
Give me another opportunity	Give me one rich last opportunity
p. 183, ll. 19–20:	p. 192, ll. 14–15:
corpses in various stages of decay.	corpses in divers stages of decay.
p. 239, l. 11:	p. 251, l. 12:
It is about a quarter-past seven.	It is about a quarter-past eight.
. . .	. . .
p. 254, l. 27:	p. 267, l. 28:
As once a Greek asked [no footnote]	As once a Greek asked . . . [Footnote:]
	[1] Aesch. *Aga*. Cho. 461.
p. 256, l. 10:	p. 269, l. 10:
THE END OF 'THE DYNASTS'	*September* 25, 1907.
September 25, 1907	THE END

Additional corrections made in editions after 1922 and incorporated in the New Wessex Edition.

Part Second

p. 54, l. 12	Rumourers, tell *for* Rumours tell
p. 69, l. 13	mutative *for* pró-cessive
p. 110, l. 14	hasteful *for* quickly
p. 223, l. 17	Hoghton *for* Houghton

Part Third

p. 216, l. 3	things afar *for* things near and far
p. 267, l. 2	despite *for* despise

BIBLIOGRAPHY

(a) *Full-length treatments*

Bailey, J. O. *Thomas Hardy and the Cosmic Mind. A New Reading of The Dynasts* (Chapel Hill, N.C.: University of North Carolina Press, 1956)

Chakravarty, Amiya. *The Dynasts and the Post-War Age in Poetry* (London: Oxford University Press, 1938)

Garrison, Chester A. *The Vast Venture: Hardy's Epic-Drama The Dynasts* (Salzburg Studies in English Literature, ed. James Hogg, No. 18, 1973)

Dean, Susan. *Hardy's Poetic Vision in The Dynasts: The Diorama of a Dream* (Princeton, N.J.: Princeton University Press, 1977)

Orel, Harold. *Thomas Hardy's Epic-Drama: A Study of The Dynasts* (Lawrence, Kansas: University of Kansas Press, 1963)

Wright, Walter F. *The Shaping of The Dynasts. A Study in Thomas Hardy* (Lincoln, Nebraska: University of Nebraska Press, 1967)

(b) *Shorter studies*

Bailey, J. O. *The Poetry of Thomas Hardy: A Handbook and Commentary* (Chapel Hill, North Carolina: University of North Carolina Press, 1970), pp. 638–46

Brooks, Jean. *Thomas Hardy: The Poetic Structure* (Ithaca, N.Y.: Cornell University Press, 1971), pp. 276–301

Cassidy, John A. 'The Original Source of Hardy's *Dynasts*', *PMLA*, LXIX (December 1954), 1085–1110

Church, Richard. 'Thomas Hardy as Revealed in *The Dynasts*', *Études anglaises*, VII (January 1954), 70–9

Clifford, Emma. 'The "Trumpet-Major Notebook" and *The Dynasts*', *Review of English Studies* (New Series), VIII (May 1957), 149–61

763

Clifford, Emma. '*War and Peace* and *The Dynasts*', *Modern Philosophy*, LIV (August 1956), 33–44

Dickinson, Thomas H. 'Thomas Hardy's *The Dynasts*', *North American Review*, CXCV (April 1912), 526–42

Dobrée, Bonamy. '*The Dynasts*', *Southern Review*, VI (Summer 1940), 109–24

Fairchild, Hoxie N. 'The Immediate Source of *The Dynasts*', *PMLA*, LXVII (March 1952), 43–64

Fairley, Barker. 'Notes on the Form of *The Dynasts*', *PMLA*, XXXIV (September 1919), 401–15

Howe, Irving. *Thomas Hardy* (New York: Macmillan Co., 1967), pp. 147–59

Orel, Harold. 'Hardy and the Theatre', in *The Genius of Thomas Hardy*, ed. Margaret Drabble (London: Weidenfeld & Nicolson, 1976), pp. 94–108

Pinion, Frank B. *A Hardy Companion. A Guide to the Works of Thomas Hardy and Their Background* (London: Macmillan & Co. Ltd, 1968), pp. 101–15

Rutland, William R. *Thomas Hardy, A Study of His Writings and Their Background* (Oxford: Blackwell, 1938; reprinted New York: Russell & Russell, Inc., 1962), pp. 258–352

Sherman, George W. 'The Influence of London on *The Dynasts*', *PMLA*, LXIII (September 1948), 1017–28

Valakis, Apollo. 'The *Moira* of Aeschylus and the Immanent Will of Thomas Hardy,' *Classical Journal*, XXI (March 1926), 431–42